· Bartholomew ·

COMPACT WORLD ATLAS

To Dad

Happy Birthday

Love from Shirley.

• Bartholomew •

COMPACT WORLD ATLAS

Bartholomew

A Division of HarperCollins*Publishers*

Bartholomew
A Division of HarperCollins Publishers
Duncan Street, Edinburgh EH9 1TA

© Bartholomew 1993

First published by Bartholomew 1991
Revised 1992, 1993

ISBN 0 7028 2374 0

Printed in Hong Kong

F/B6689

CONTENTS

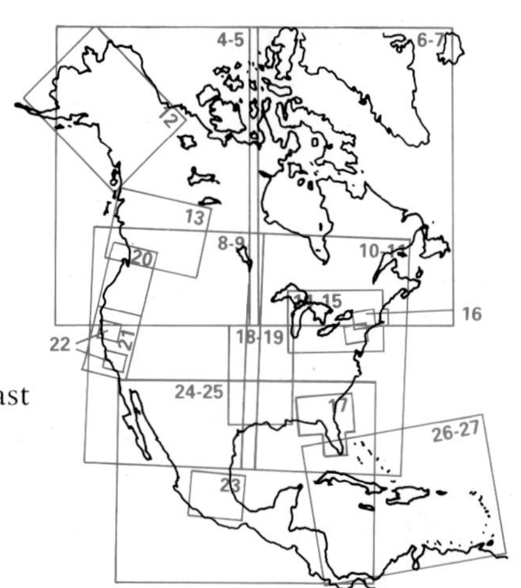

4-5
6-7
12
13
8-9
20
10-11
14-15
16
22
21
18-19
24-25
17
26-27
23

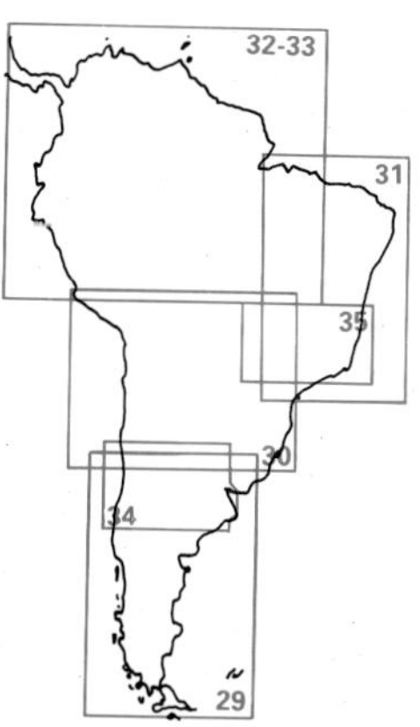

32-33
31
35
30
34
29

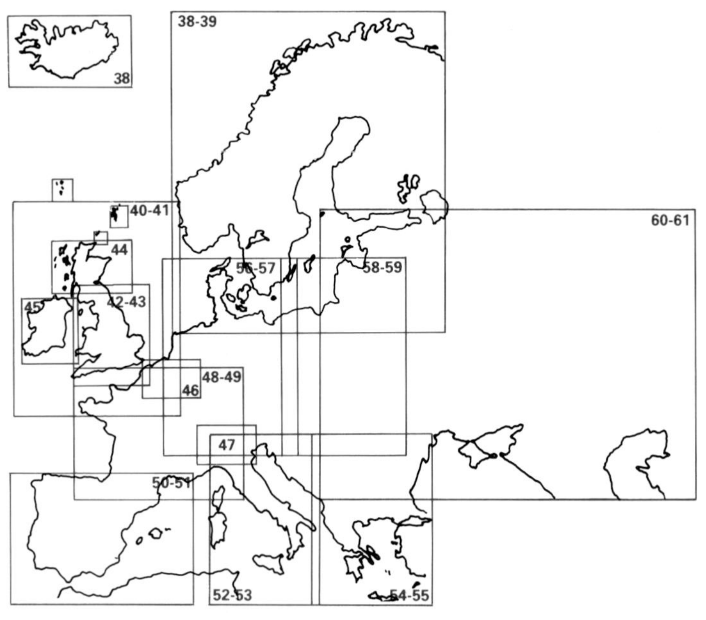
38
38-39
40-41
44
42-43
45
56-57
58-59
60-61
46
48-49
47
50-51
52-53
54-55

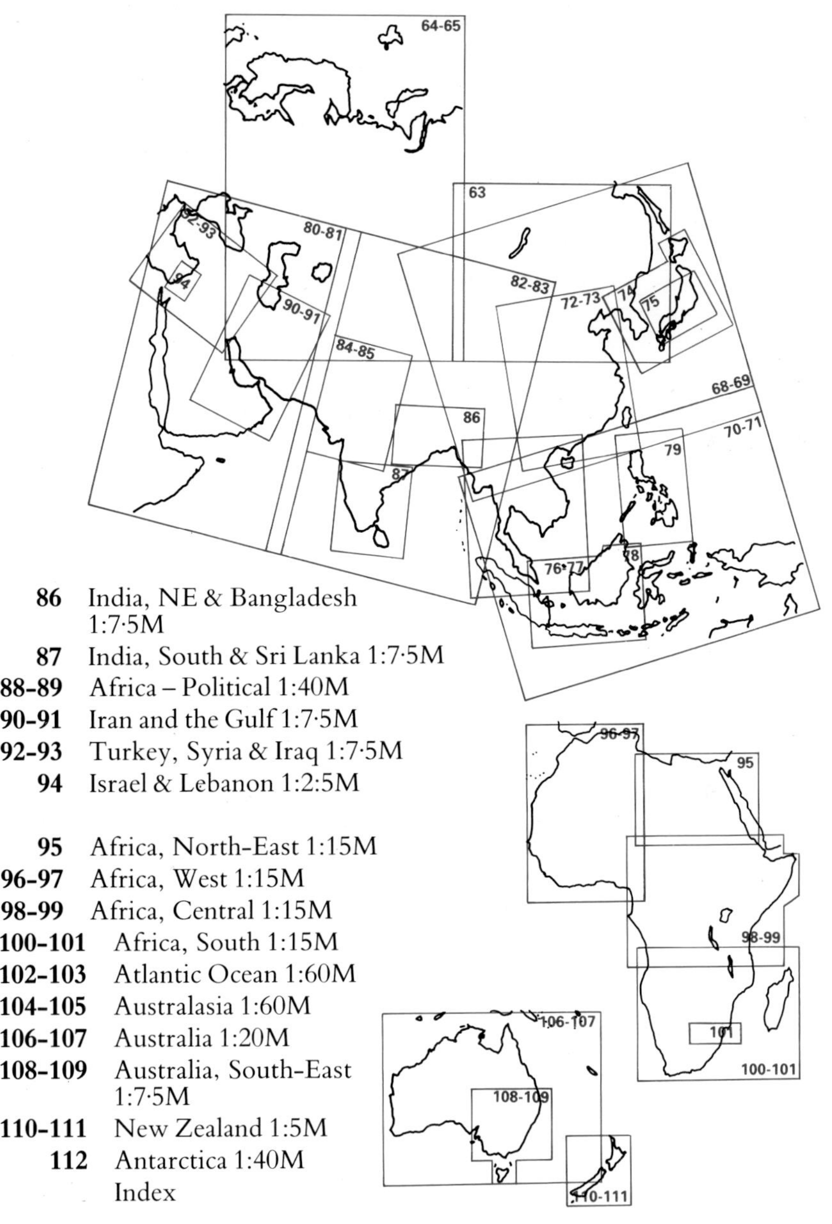
64-65
63
80-81
92-93
94
90-91
84-85
82-83
72-73
74
75
68-69
86
70-71
79
87
76-77
78
96-97
95
98-99
101
100-101
106-107
108-109
110-111

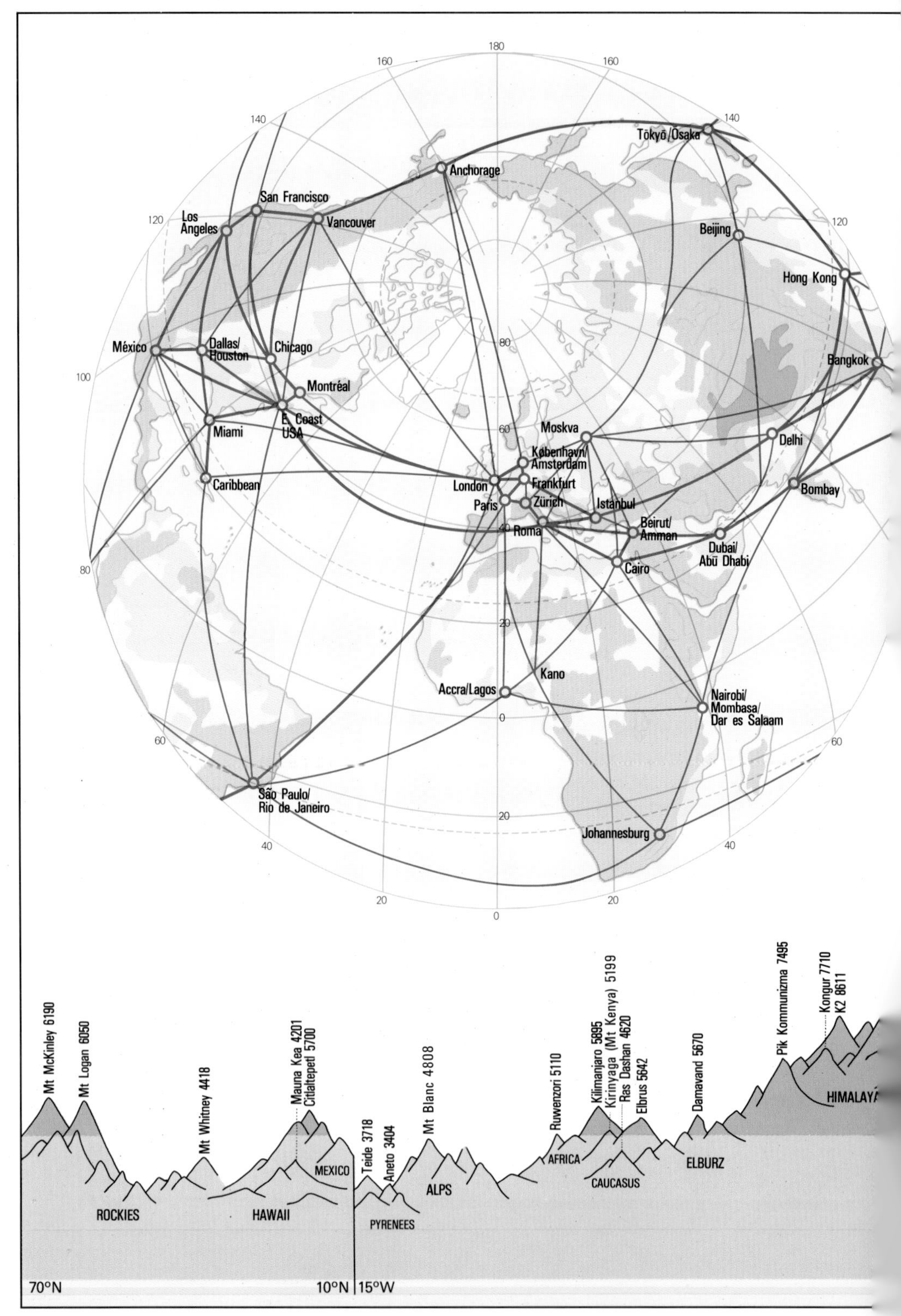
Anchorage
Tōkyō/Ōsaka
San Francisco
Los Angeles
Vancouver
Beijing
Hong Kong
México
Dallas/ Houston
Chicago
Bangkok
Montréal
E. Coast USA
Miami
Moskva
Delhi
København/ Amsterdam
Caribbean
London
Frankfurt
Bombay
Paris
Zürich
Istanbul
Roma
Beirut/ Amman
Dubai/ Abū Dhabi
Cairo
Kano
Accra/Lagos
Nairobi/ Mombasa/ Dar es Salaam
São Paulo/ Rio de Janeiro
Johannesburg
Mt McKinley 6190
Mt Logan 6050
Mt Whitney 4418
Mauna Kea 4201
Citlaltepetl 5700
Teide 3718
Aneto 3404
Mt Blanc 4808
Ruwenzori 5110
Kilimanjaro 5895
Kirinyaga (Mt Kenya) 5199
Ras Dashan 4620
Elbrus 5642
Damavand 5670
Pik Kommunizma 7495
Kongur 7710
K2 8611
ROCKIES
HAWAII
MEXICO
PYRENEES
ALPS
AFRICA
CAUCASUS
ELBURZ
HIMALAYA
70°N
10°N
15°W

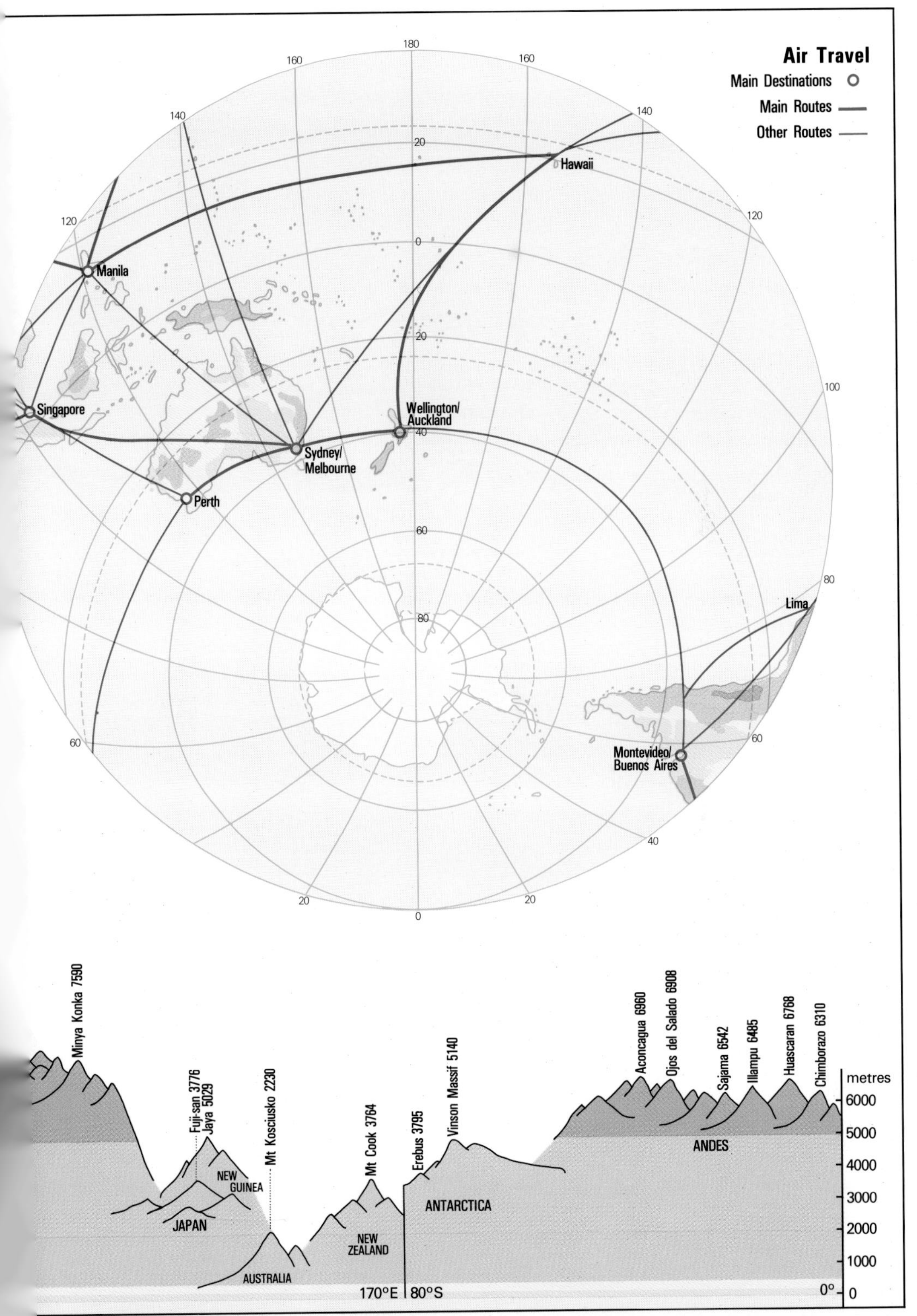

1:150M

Air Travel

Main Destinations ⚬
Main Routes ━━━
Other Routes ──

Hawaii

Manila

Singapore

Wellington/
Auckland

Sydney/
Melbourne

Perth

Lima

Montevideo/
Buenos Aires

Minya Konka 7590

Fuji-san 3776
Jaya 5029

NEW
GUINEA

Mt Kosciusko 2230

JAPAN

AUSTRALIA

Mt Cook 3764

NEW
ZEALAND

Erebus 3795

Vinson Massif 5140

ANTARCTICA

Aconcagua 6960

Ojos del Salado 6908

Sajama 6542

Illampu 6485

Huascaran 6768

Chimborazo 6310

ANDES

metres

6000
5000
4000
3000
2000
1000
0

170°E 80°S

0°

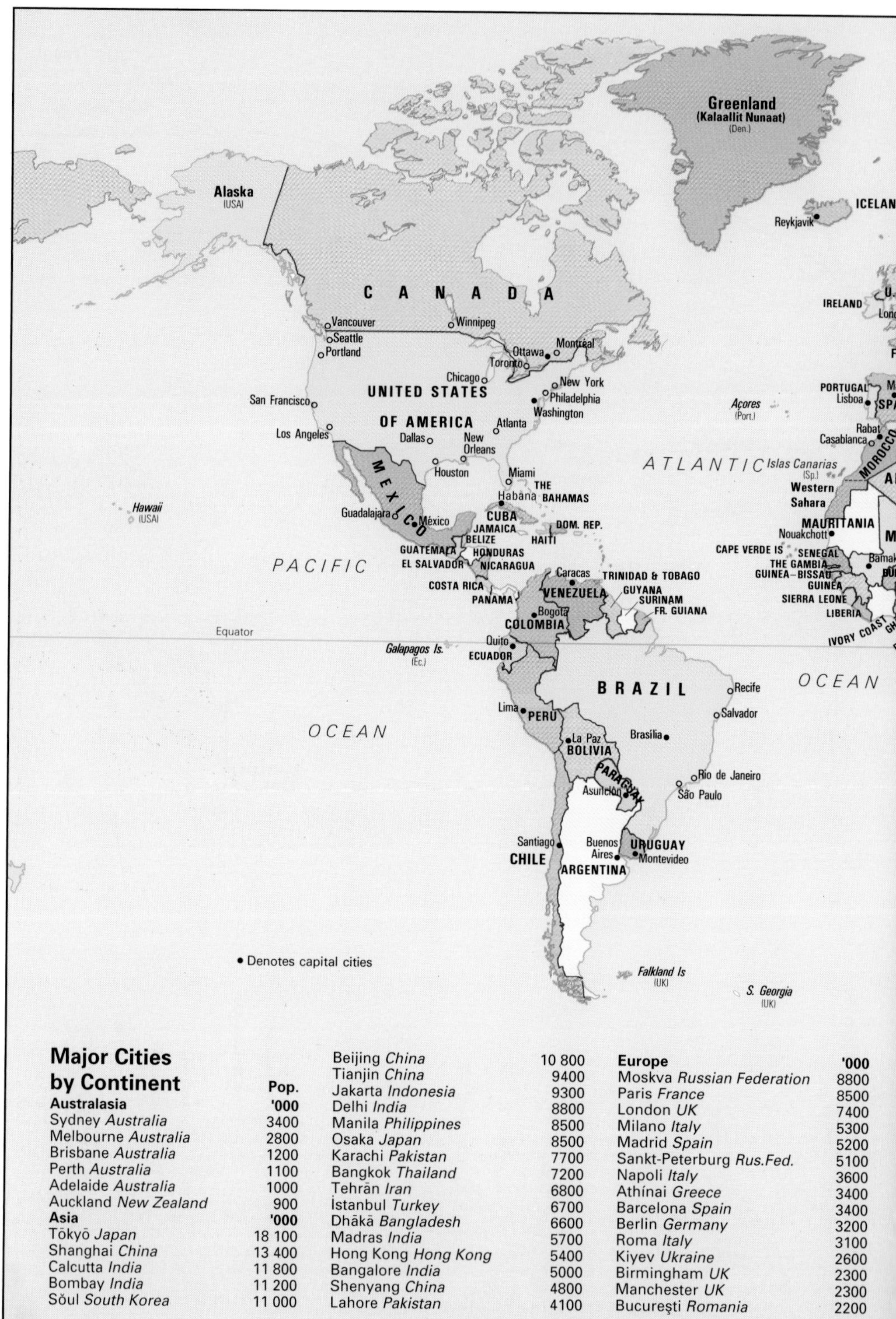

Greenland
(Kalaallit Nunaat)
(Den.)

ICELAND
Reykjavik

Alaska
(USA)

C A N A D A

IRELAND   U.K.
London

PORTUGAL   Madrid
Lisboa   SPAIN

Vancouver   Winnipeg
Seattle
Portland   Ottawa   Montréal
Toronto
Chicago   New York
San Francisco   Philadelphia
UNITED STATES   Washington
OF AMERICA   Atlanta
Los Angeles   Dallas   New
Orleans

FRA

Paris

Açores
(Port.)

Rabat
Casablanca

MOROCCO

ATLANTIC   Islas Canarias   ALG
(Sp.)

Hawaii
(USA)

Houston   Miami
THE
Habana   BAHAMAS
Guadalajara   México   CUBA
JAMAICA   DOM. REP.
BELIZE   HAITI
GUATEMALA   HONDURAS
EL SALVADOR   NICARAGUA
COSTA RICA   PANAMA

Western
Sahara

MAURITANIA   MA

Nouakchott
CAPE VERDE IS   SENEGAL
THE GAMBIA   Bamako
GUINEA-BISSAU   BURKI
GUINEA
SIERRA LEONE   LIBERIA

IVORY COAST   GHA
TO
BEN

MEXICO

PACIFIC

Caracas   TRINIDAD & TOBAGO
VENEZUELA   GUYANA
SURINAM
Bogotá   FR. GUIANA
COLOMBIA

Equator

Galapagos Is.
(Ec.)

Quito
ECUADOR

BRAZIL   Recife   OCEAN

OCEAN

Lima   PERÚ

La Paz
BOLIVIA

Brasília

Salvador

Rio de Janeiro
São Paulo

Asunción

PARAGUAY

Santiago   Buenos   URUGUAY
Aires   Montevideo
CHILE   ARGENTINA

● Denotes capital cities

Falkland Is
(UK)   S. Georgia
(UK)

Major Cities		Beijing *China*	10 800	**Europe**	**'000**
by Continent	**Pop.**	Tianjin *China*	9400	Moskva *Russian Federation*	8800
		Jakarta *Indonesia*	9300	Paris *France*	8500
Australasia	**'000**	Delhi *India*	8800	London *UK*	7400
Sydney *Australia*	3400	Manila *Philippines*	8500	Milano *Italy*	5300
Melbourne *Australia*	2800	Osaka *Japan*	8500	Madrid *Spain*	5200
Brisbane *Australia*	1200	Karachi *Pakistan*	7700	Sankt-Peterburg *Rus.Fed.*	5100
Perth *Australia*	1100	Bangkok *Thailand*	7200	Napoli *Italy*	3600
Adelaide *Australia*	1000	Tehrān *Iran*	6800	Athínai *Greece*	3400
Auckland *New Zealand*	900	İstanbul *Turkey*	6700	Barcelona *Spain*	3400
Asia	**'000**	Dhākā *Bangladesh*	6600	Berlin *Germany*	3200
Tōkyō *Japan*	18 100	Madras *India*	5700	Roma *Italy*	3100
Shanghai *China*	13 400	Hong Kong *Hong Kong*	5400	Kiyev *Ukraine*	2600
Calcutta *India*	11 800	Bangalore *India*	5000	Birmingham *UK*	2300
Bombay *India*	11 200	Shenyang *China*	4800	Manchester *UK*	2300
Sŏul *South Korea*	11 000	Lahore *Pakistan*	4100	Bucureşti *Romania*	2200

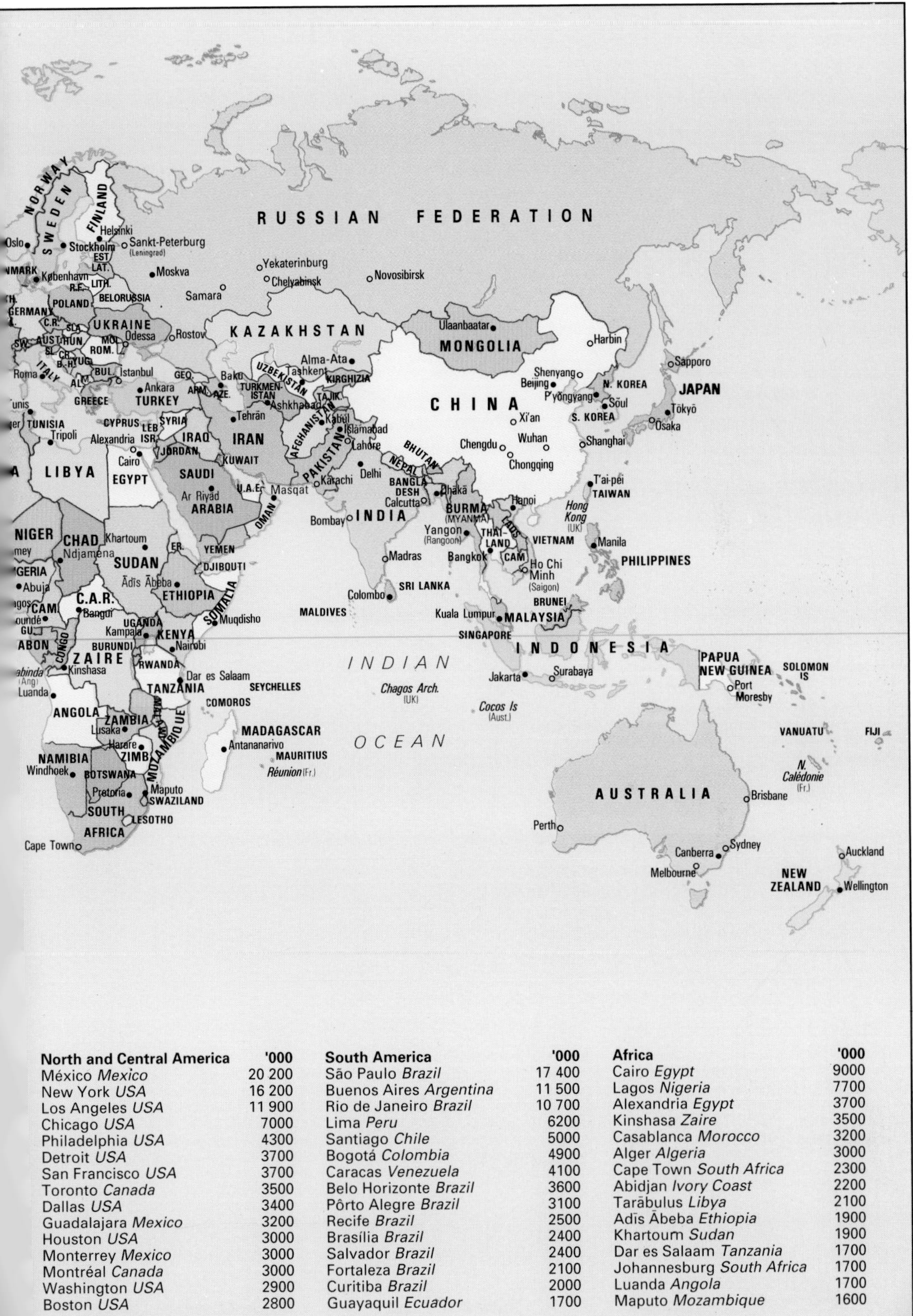

North and Central America	'000	South America	'000	Africa	'000
México *Mexico*	20 200	São Paulo *Brazil*	17 400	Cairo *Egypt*	9000
New York *USA*	16 200	Buenos Aires *Argentina*	11 500	Lagos *Nigeria*	7700
Los Angeles *USA*	11 900	Rio de Janeiro *Brazil*	10 700	Alexandria *Egypt*	3700
Chicago *USA*	7000	Lima *Peru*	6200	Kinshasa *Zaire*	3500
Philadelphia *USA*	4300	Santiago *Chile*	5000	Casablanca *Morocco*	3200
Detroit *USA*	3700	Bogotá *Colombia*	4900	Alger *Algeria*	3000
San Francisco *USA*	3700	Caracas *Venezuela*	4100	Cape Town *South Africa*	2300
Toronto *Canada*	3500	Belo Horizonte *Brazil*	3600	Abidjan *Ivory Coast*	2200
Dallas *USA*	3400	Pôrto Alegre *Brazil*	3100	Tarābulus *Libya*	2100
Guadalajara *Mexico*	3200	Recife *Brazil*	2500	Adis Ābeba *Ethiopia*	1900
Houston *USA*	3000	Brasília *Brazil*	2400	Khartoum *Sudan*	1900
Monterrey *Mexico*	3000	Salvador *Brazil*	2400	Dar es Salaam *Tanzania*	1700
Montréal *Canada*	3000	Fortaleza *Brazil*	2100	Johannesburg *South Africa*	1700
Washington *USA*	2900	Curitiba *Brazil*	2000	Luanda *Angola*	1700
Boston *USA*	2800	Guayaquil *Ecuador*	1700	Maputo *Mozambique*	1600

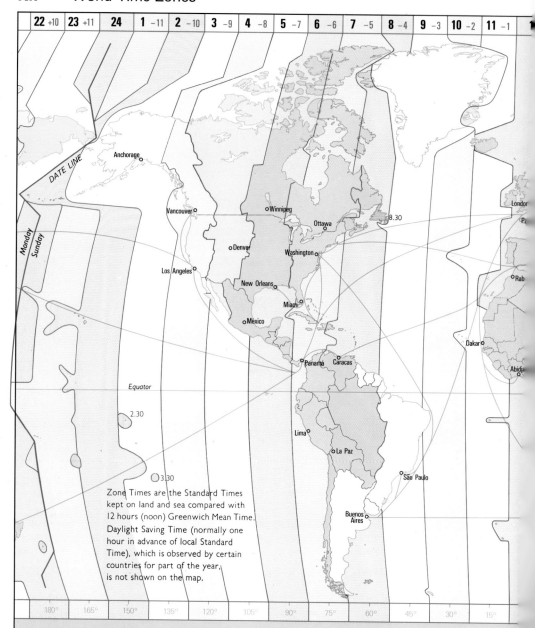

| 22 +10 | 23 +11 | 24 | 1 −11 | 2 −10 | 3 −9 | 4 −8 | 5 −7 | 6 −6 | 7 −5 | 8 −4 | 9 −3 | 10 −2 | 11 −1 |

DATE LINE

Monday
Sunday

Anchorage

Vancouver

Winnipeg

Ottawa

8.30

London

Pa

Denver

Washington

Los Angeles

New Orleans

Rab

Miami

México

Dakar

Panamá   Caracas

Abidja

Equator

2.30

Lima

La Paz

3.30

São Paulo

Zone Times are the Standard Times
kept on land and sea compared with
12 hours (noon) Greenwich Mean Time.
Daylight Saving Time (normally one
hour in advance of local Standard
Time), which is observed by certain
countries for part of the year,
is not shown on the map.

Buenos
Aires

180° 165° 150° 135° 120° 105° 90° 75° 60° 45° 30° 15°

Journey Times

Sail (via Cape)
164 days

Steam (via Cape)
43 days

Steam (via Suez)
30 days

Supertanker
(via Cape)
28 days

Singapore ←

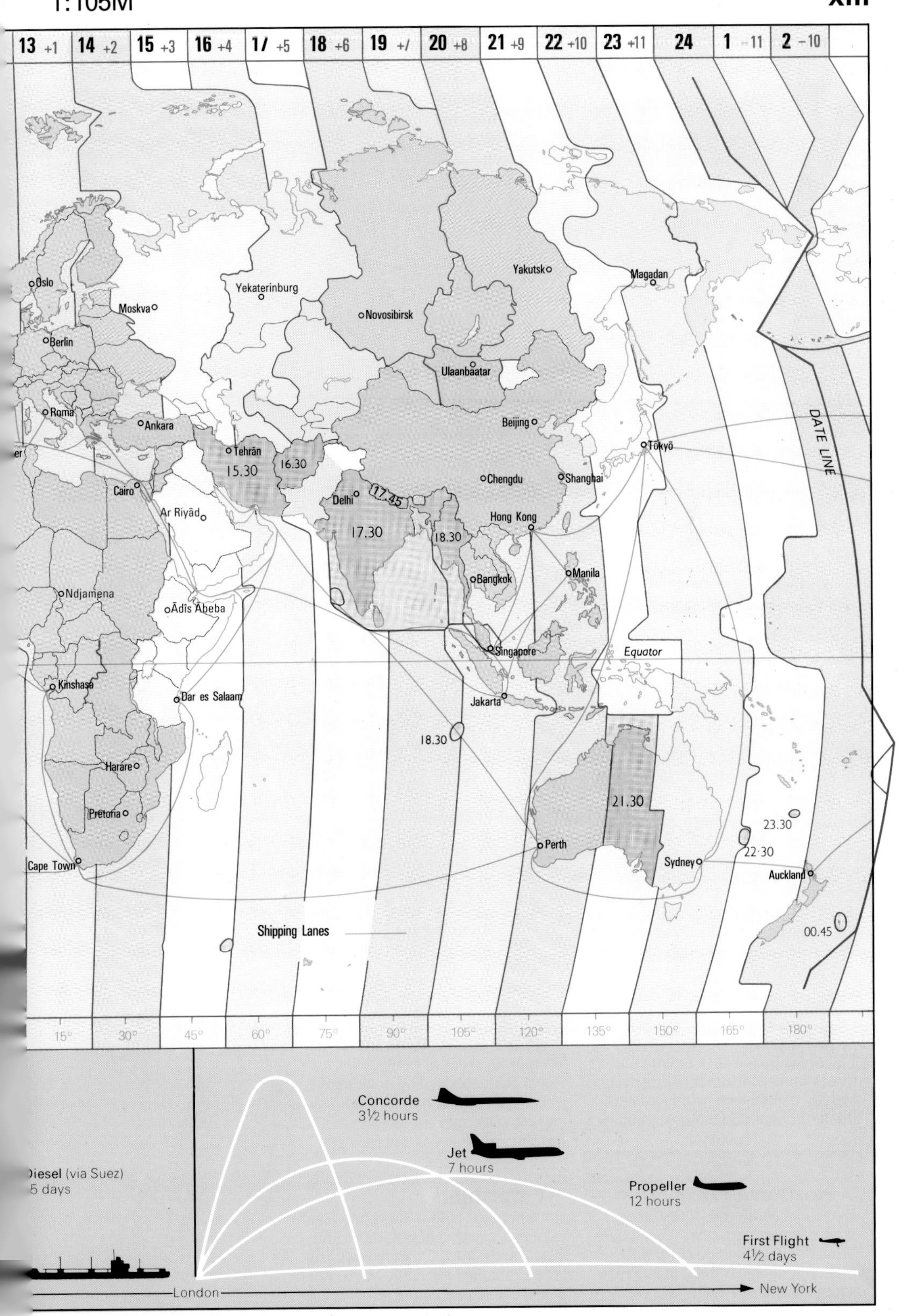

1:105M

| 13 +1 | 14 +2 | 15 +3 | 16 +4 | 17 +5 | 18 +6 | 19 +7 | 20 +8 | 21 +9 | 22 +10 | 23 +11 | 24 | 1 −11 | 2 −10 |

Oslo
Moskva
Berlin
Yekaterinburg
Novosibirsk
Yakutsk
Magadan
Roma
Ankara
Ulaanbaatar
Tehrān
15.30
16.30
Beijing
Tōkyō
Cairo
Chengdu
Shanghai
Ar Riyād
Delhi
17.45
Hong Kong
17.30
18.30
Bangkok
Manila
Ndjamena
Ādīs Ābeba
Singapore
Equator
Kinshasa
Dar es Salaam
Jakarta
18.30
Harare
Pretoria
21.30
23.30
Cape Town
Perth
Sydney
22·30
Auckland
00.45

DATE LINE

Shipping Lanes

15° 30° 45° 60° 75° 90° 105° 120° 135° 150° 165° 180°

Concorde
3½ hours

Jet
7 hours

Propeller
12 hours

First Flight
4½ days

Diesel (via Suez)
5 days

London ⟶ New York

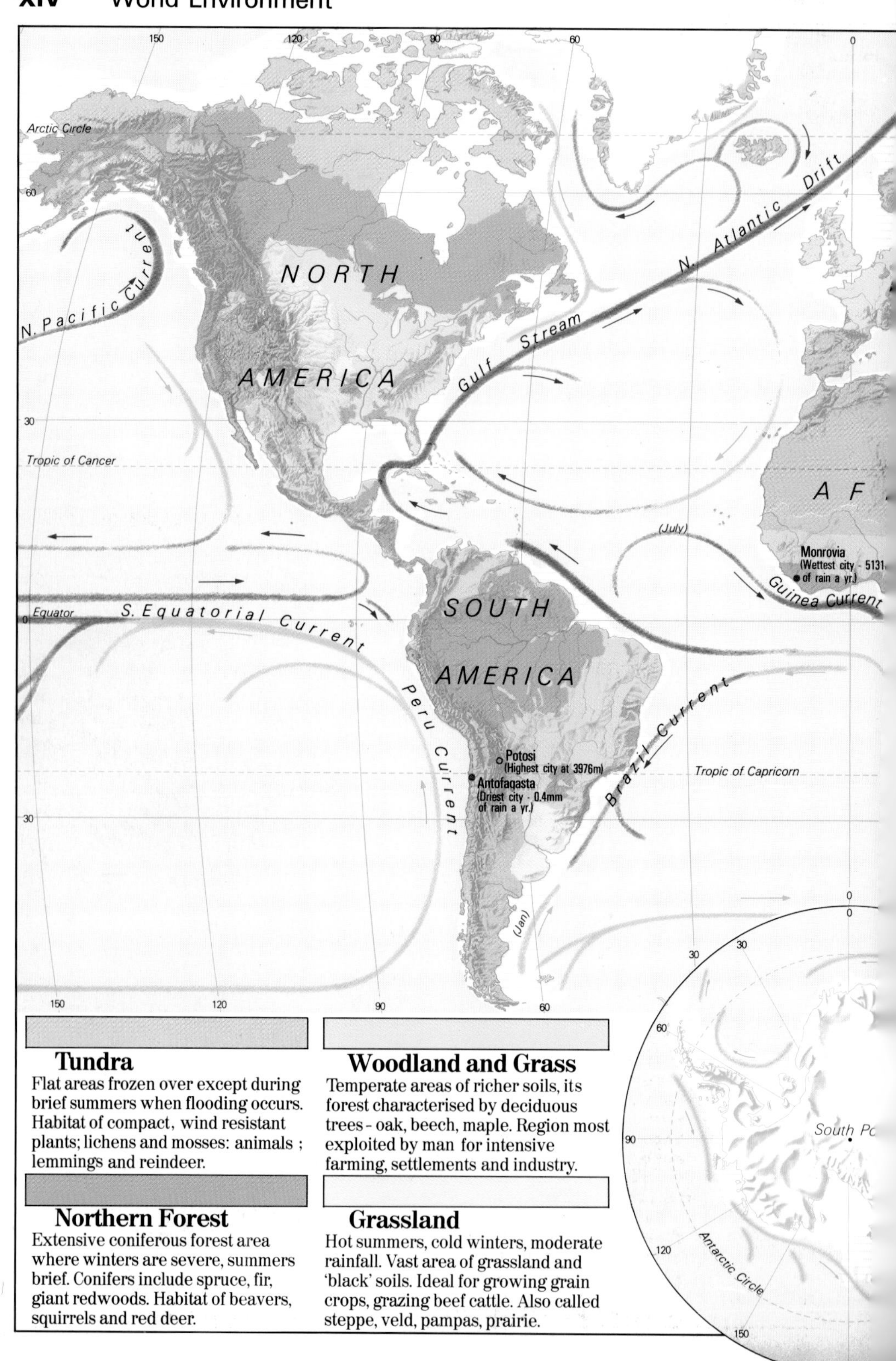

150 120 90 60 0

Arctic Circle

60

N. Pacific Current

NORTH

AMERICA

N. Atlantic Drift

N. Atlantic

Gulf Stream

30

Tropic of Cancer

A F

(July)

Monrovia
(Wettest city - 5131
• of rain a yr.)

Guinea Current

Equator   S. Equatorial Current

SOUTH

AMERICA

Peru Current

Brazil Current

Potosi
(Highest city at 3976m)
• Antofagasta
(Driest city - 0.4mm
of rain a yr.)

Tropic of Capricorn

30

(Jan)

150 120 90 60

0
0

30 30

60

South Po

90

Antarctic Circle

120

150

180

Tundra
Flat areas frozen over except during
brief summers when flooding occurs.
Habitat of compact, wind resistant
plants; lichens and mosses: animals ;
lemmings and reindeer.

Woodland and Grass
Temperate areas of richer soils, its
forest characterised by deciduous
trees - oak, beech, maple. Region most
exploited by man for intensive
farming, settlements and industry.

Northern Forest
Extensive coniferous forest area
where winters are severe, summers
brief. Conifers include spruce, fir,
giant redwoods. Habitat of beavers,
squirrels and red deer.

Grassland
Hot summers, cold winters, moderate
rainfall. Vast area of grassland and
'black' soils. Ideal for growing grain
crops, grazing beef cattle. Also called
steppe, veld, pampas, prairie.

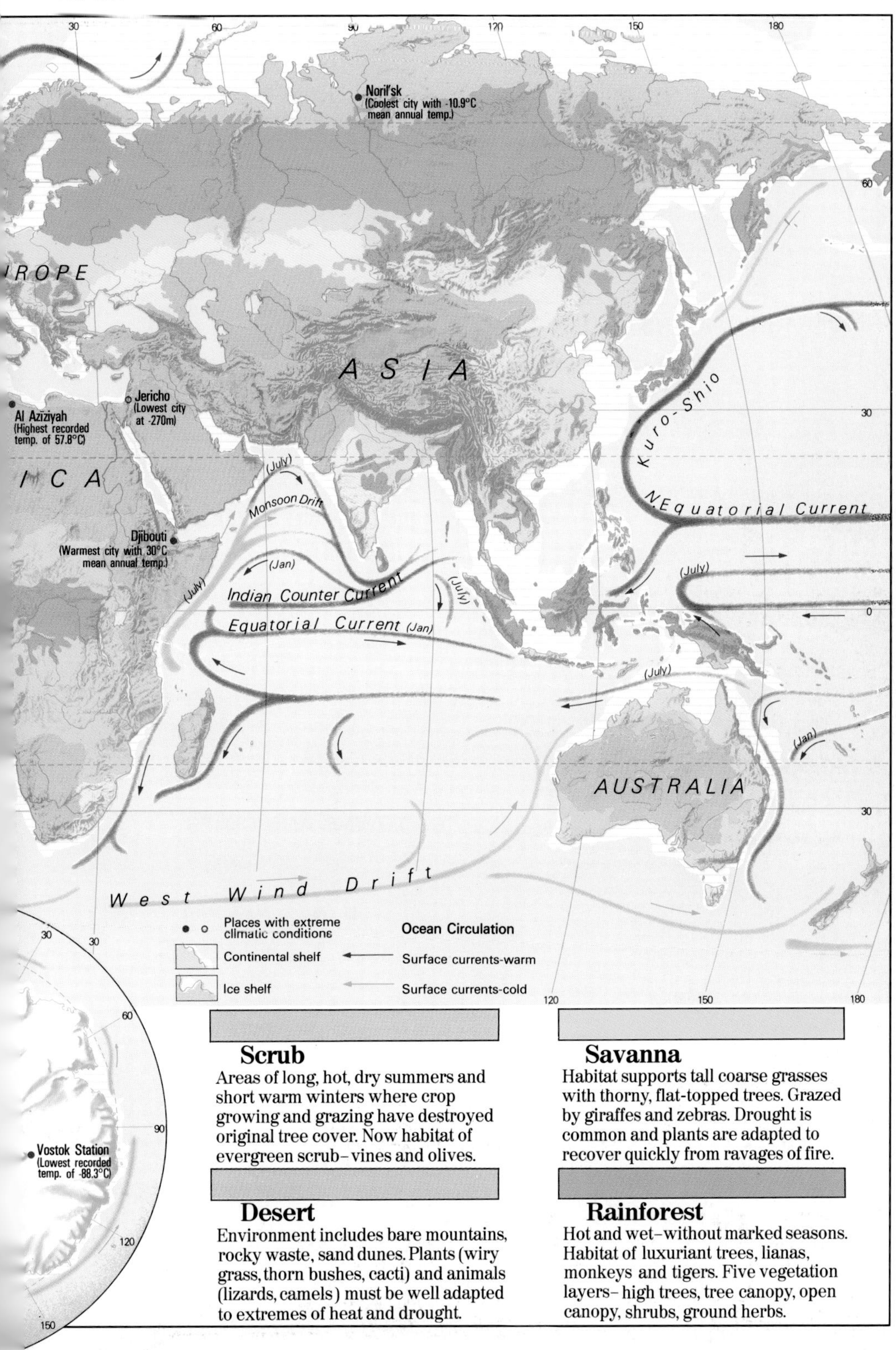

Noril'sk
(Coolest city with -10.9°C
mean annual temp.)

IROPE

A S I A

Al Aziziyah
(Highest recorded
temp. of 57.8°C)

Jericho
(Lowest city
at -270m)

ICA

Djibouti
(Warmest city with 30°C
mean annual temp.)

Kuro-Shio

N Equatorial Current

(July)

Monsoon Drift

(July)

(Jan)

Indian Counter Current

(July)

Equatorial Current (Jan)

(July)

AUSTRALIA

(Jan)

West Wind Drift

Vostok Station
(Lowest recorded
temp. of -88.3°C)

Places with extreme
climatic conditions

Continental shelf

Ice shelf

Ocean Circulation

Surface currents–warm

Surface currents–cold

Scrub
Areas of long, hot, dry summers and
short warm winters where crop
growing and grazing have destroyed
original tree cover. Now habitat of
evergreen scrub–vines and olives.

Savanna
Habitat supports tall coarse grasses
with thorny, flat-topped trees. Grazed
by giraffes and zebras. Drought is
common and plants are adapted to
recover quickly from ravages of fire.

Desert
Environment includes bare mountains,
rocky waste, sand dunes. Plants (wiry
grass, thorn bushes, cacti) and animals
(lizards, camels) must be well adapted
to extremes of heat and drought.

Rainforest
Hot and wet–without marked seasons.
Habitat of luxuriant trees, lianas,
monkeys and tigers. Five vegetation
layers– high trees, tree canopy, open
canopy, shrubs, ground herbs.

BOUNDARIES

	International
	International under Dispute
	Cease Fire Line
	Autonomous or State/ Administrative
	Maritime (National)
	International Date Line

COMMUNICATIONS

	Motorway/ Under Construction
	Major/ Other Road
	Under Construction
	Track
	Road Tunnel
	Car Ferry
	Main / Other Railway
	Under Construction
	Rail Ferry
	Rail Tunnel
	Canal
	International/ Other Airport

LANDSCAPE FEATURES

	Glacier, Ice Cap
	Marsh, Swamp
	Sand Desert, Dunes
	Freshwater
	Saltwater
	Seasonal
	Salt Pan

OTHER FEATURES

	River / Seasonal
	Pass, Gorge
	Dam, Barrage
	Waterfall, Rapid
	Aqueduct
	Reef
.217 ▲4231	Spot Height, Depth/ Summit, Peak
	Well
Δ ▲	Oil /Gas Field
Gas / Oil	Oil/ Natural Gas Pipeline
Gemsbok Nat. Pk	National Park
∴UR	Historic Site

LETTERING STYLES

CANADA	Independent Nation
FLORIDA	State, Province or Autonomous Region
Gibraltar (U.K.)	Sovereignty of Dependent Territory
Lothian	Administrative Area
LANGUEDOC	Historic Region
Loire **Vosges**	Physical Feature or Physical Region

TOWNS AND CITIES

Square symbols denote capital cities

■	●	**New York**	Major City
■	●	**Montréal**	City
□	○	Ottawa	Small City
■	•	**Québec**	Large Town
□	○	St John's	Town
□	○	Yorkton	Small Town
□	○	Jasper	Village
			Built-up-area

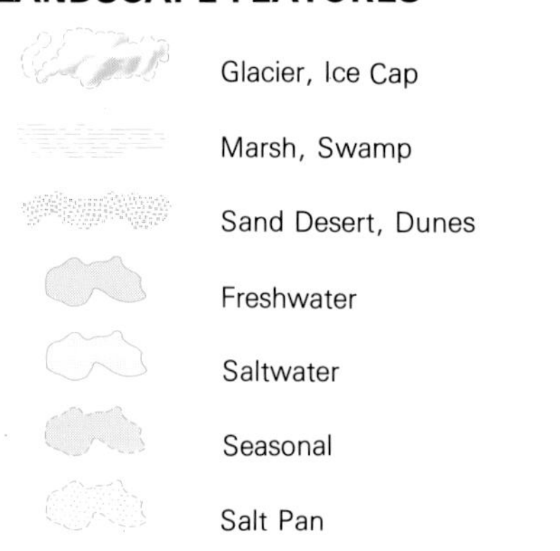

Depth   Sea Level   Height

0

8000m 6000m 4000m 2000m 200m

200m 500m 1000m 2000m 3000m 4000m 5000m 6000m

1:40M

| 400 | 800 | 1200 | 1600 km |

| 400 | 800 mls |

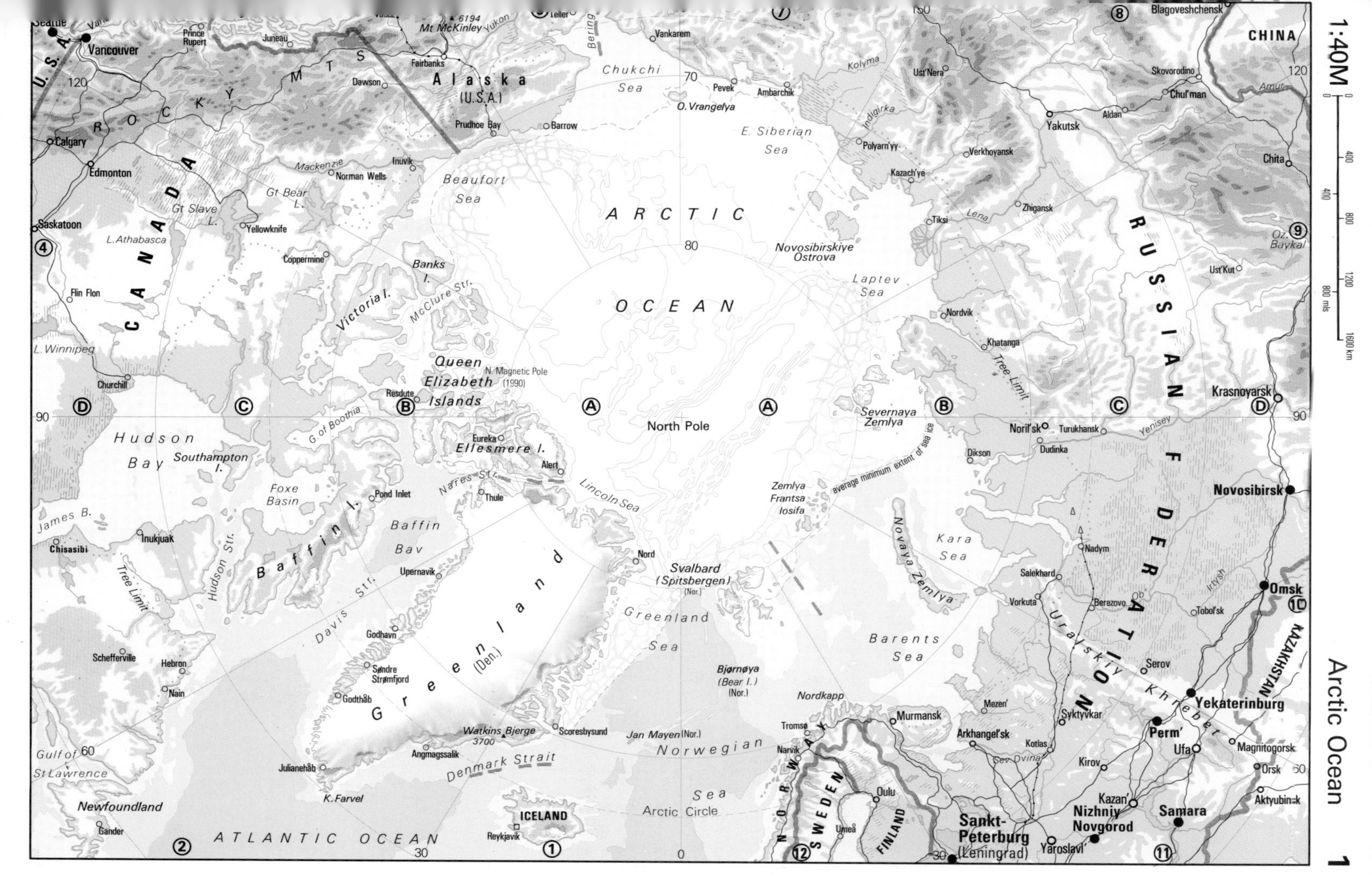

CHINA

Blagoveshchensk

Skovorodino

Chita

Oz. Baykal ⑨

Krasnoyarsk

Ust'Kut

Chul'man

Aldan

⑧

Yakutsk

Verkhoyansk

Zhigansk

Lena

Ust' Nera

Tiksi

Norilsk

Khatanga

Tree Limit

Dudinka

North⦵sk

Turukhansk

Dikson

Novosibirsk

Tobol'sk

Omsk ⑩

KAZAKHSTAN

Yekaterinburg

Ishim

Ufa

Orsk

Aktyubinsk

Magnitogorsk

Samara

⑪

RUSSIAN   FEDERATION

Nadym

Berezovo

Salekhard

Vorkuta

Ural'skiy   Khr.

Serov

Perm'

Kirov

Kotlas

Syktyvkar

Kazan

Nizhniy

Novgorod

Yaroslavl'

Mezen'

Arkhangel'sk

Sankt-

Peterburg

(Leningrad)

FINLAND

Oulu

Umeå

SWEDEN

Murmansk

Nordkapp

NORWAY

Tromsø

Narvik

Jan Mayen (Nor.)

Arctic Circle

Kara

Sea

Barents

Sea

Novaya Zemlya

Zemlya

Frantsa

Iosifa

Severnaya

Zemlya

average max. of sea ice

average minimum of sea ice

Svalbard

(Spitsbergen)

(Nor.)

Bjørnøya

(Bear I.)

(Nor.)

Norwegian

Sea

Greenland

Sea

Laptev

Sea

Novosibirskiye

Ostrova

A

ARCTIC

OCEAN

North Pole

B

E. Siberian

Sea

Kolyma

Kazach'ye

Polyarnyy

A

80

70

O. Vrangelya

Pevek

Ambarchik

Anadyr'

Uelen

Chukchi

Sea

Bering

Str.

Barrow

Beaufort

Sea

Prudhoe Bay

Fairbanks

Alaska

(U.S.A.)

Mt. McKinley

6194

Yukon

Dawson

Inuvik

Norman Wells

Gt. Bear

L.

Mackenzie

Coppermine

Gt. Slave L.

Yellowknife

Banks

I.

Victoria

I.

M'Clure Str.

G. of Boothia

Resolute

N. Magnetic Pole

(1990)

B

Queen

Elizabeth

Islands

Eureka

Ellesmere I.

Alert

Nord

Lincoln Sea

Nares Str.

Thule

Smith S.

Upernavik

Baffin

Bay

Pond Inlet

Foxe

Basin

Baffin

I.

Davis Str.

Denmark Strait

Watkins Bjerge

3700

Scoresbysund

Angmagssalik

ATLANTIC OCEAN

30

ICELAND

①

Reykjavik

GREENLAND

(Den.)

Søndre

Strømfjord

Godhavn

Godthåb

Julianehåb

K. Farvel

Holsteinsborg

C

D

Vancouver

Calgary

Edmonton

Saskatoon

R O C K Y   M T S

C A N A D A

L. Athabasca

Fin Flon

L. Winnipeg

Churchill

Hudson

Bay

Southampton

I.

James B.

Chisasibi

Schefferville

Tree Limit

Hebron

Nain

Newfoundland

Gander

St. Lawrence

Gulf of

60

②

Prince

Rupert

Juneau

Seattle

USA

120

90

90

0

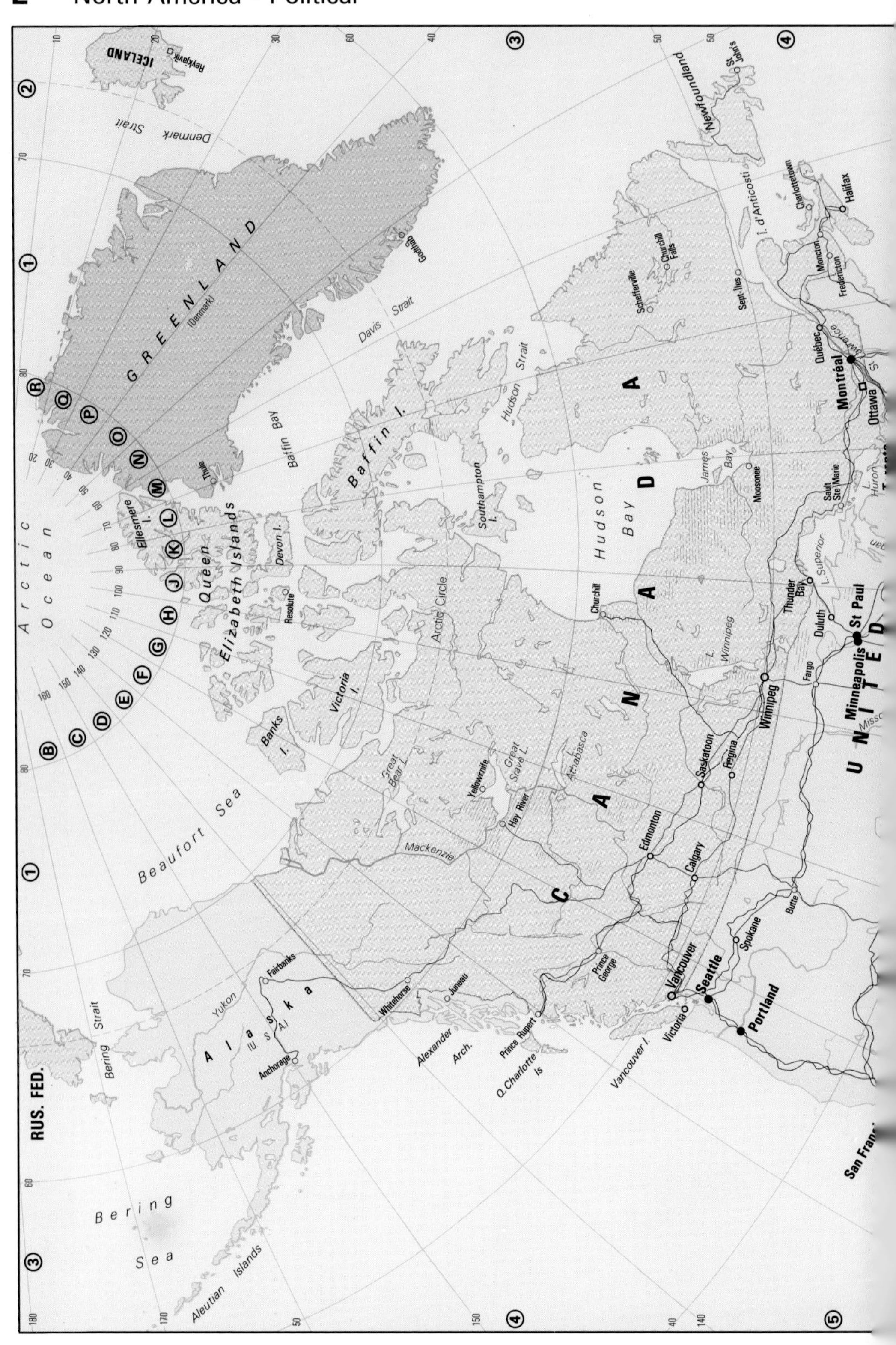
ICELAND
Reykjavik
Denmark Strait
GREENLAND
(Denmark)
Godthåb
Thule
Arctic Ocean
Ellesmere I.
Queen Elizabeth Islands
Devon I.
Resolute
Baffin Bay
Baffin I.
Davis Strait
Hudson Strait
Southampton I.
Hudson Bay
James Bay
Banks I.
Victoria I.
Arctic Circle
Beaufort Sea
Great Bear L.
Great Slave L.
Yellowknife
Hay River
Athabasca
Mackenzie
CANADA
Churchill
L. Winnipeg
Winnipeg
Saskatoon
Regina
Edmonton
Calgary
Prince George
Vancouver
Victoria
Vancouver I.
Q. Charlotte Is
Prince Rupert
Alexander Arch.
Juneau
Whitehorse
Fairbanks
Anchorage
Yukon
Alaska
(U.S.A.)
Bering Strait
Bering Sea
Aleutian Islands
RUS. FED.
Newfoundland
St John's
I. d'Anticosti
Schefferville
Churchill Falls
Sept-Îles
Moosonee
Charlottetown
Halifax
Moncton
Fredericton
Québec
Montréal
Ottawa
St Lawrence
Sault Ste Marie
L. Huron
L. Superior
Thunder Bay
Duluth
St Paul
Minneapolis
Fargo
UNITED
Butte
Spokane
Seattle
Portland
San Fran

1:35M

0 250 500 750 1000 1250 km
0 250 500 750 mls

30 20

ATLANTIC OCEAN

Bermuda (U.K.)

Boston
New York
Philadelphia
Washington
Norfolk
Cleveland
Baltimore
Detroit
L. Erie
Indianapolis
Nashville
Atlanta
Memphis
Birmingham
St Louis
Kansas City
Mississippi
New Orleans
Houston
Dallas
Fort Worth
San Antonio
Rio Grande
Monterrey
Torreón
Denver
Albuquerque
El Paso
Chihuahua
Colorado
Phoenix
Tucson
G. de California
Guadalupe (Mex.)
Los Angeles
San Diego
Ohio
Charleston
Jacksonville
Tampa
Miami

UNITED STATES OF AMERICA

THE BAHAMAS
Nassau

CUBA
Habana

Gulf of Mexico

Mérida
Tampico
Veracruz
México
Acapulco
Mazatlán
Guadalajara

M E X I C O

Tropic of Cancer

120 130

Guantánamo
HAITI
Port-au-Prince
Kingston
JAMAICA
DOMINICAN REP.
Sto. Domingo
Pto. Rico (U.S.A.)

DOMINICA
ST LUCIA
ST VINCENT
GRENADA
BAR-BADOS
TRINIDAD & TOBAGO

CARIBBEAN SEA

Netherlands Antilles

Caracas
Maracaibo
VENEZUELA

Sta. Marta
Barranquilla
Medellín
Bogotá
COLOMBIA

Quito
ECUADOR

PERU

BRAZIL
Negro

BELIZE
Belmopan
GUATEMALA
Guatemala
S.Salvador
EL SALVADOR
HONDURAS
Tegucigalpa
NICARAGUA
Managua
COSTA RICA
S.José
Panamá
PANAMA

I. del Coco (C.R.)
Malpelo (Col.)

Clipperton (Fr.)

Is. Revilla Gigedo (Mex.)

Galápagos Is. (Ecu.)
Equator

PACIFIC OCEAN

70 80 90 100 110

M
L
K
J
H
G

5 6 7 8

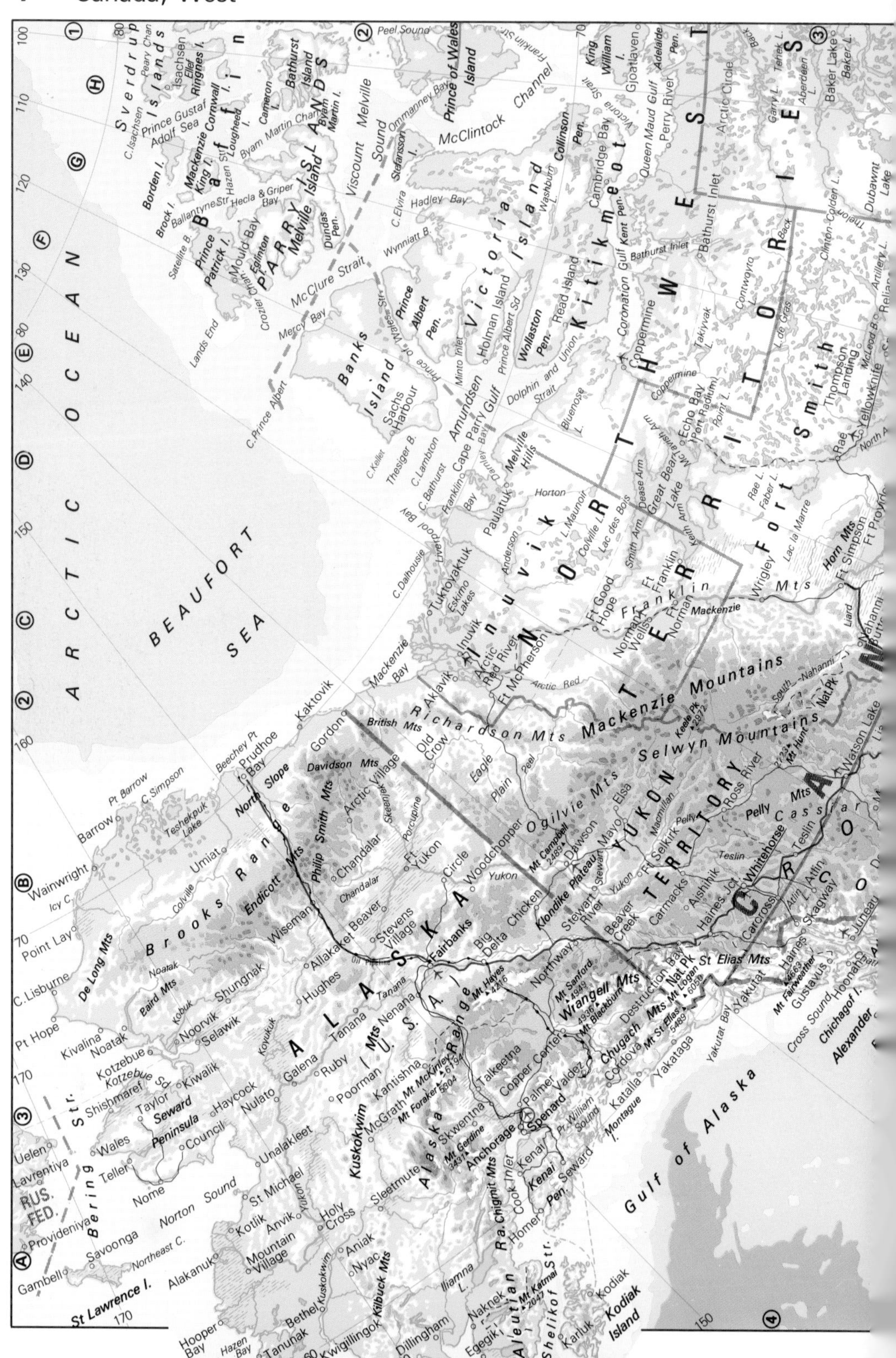
ARCTIC OCEAN
BEAUFORT SEA
Gulf of Alaska
ALASKA
U.S.A.
YUKON TERRITORY
NORTHWEST TERRITORIES
Banks Island
Victoria Island
Melville Island
PARRY ISLANDS
Sverdrup Islands
Brooks Range
Mackenzie Mountains
Selwyn Mountains
Richardson Mts
Ogilvie Mts
Alaska Range
Wrangell Mts
St Elias Mts
Bering Str.
Seward Peninsula
Kenai Pen.
Kodiak Island
St Lawrence I.
RUS. FED.
Great Bear Lake
Fairbanks
Anchorage
Whitehorse
Dawson
Inuvik
Nome
Barrow

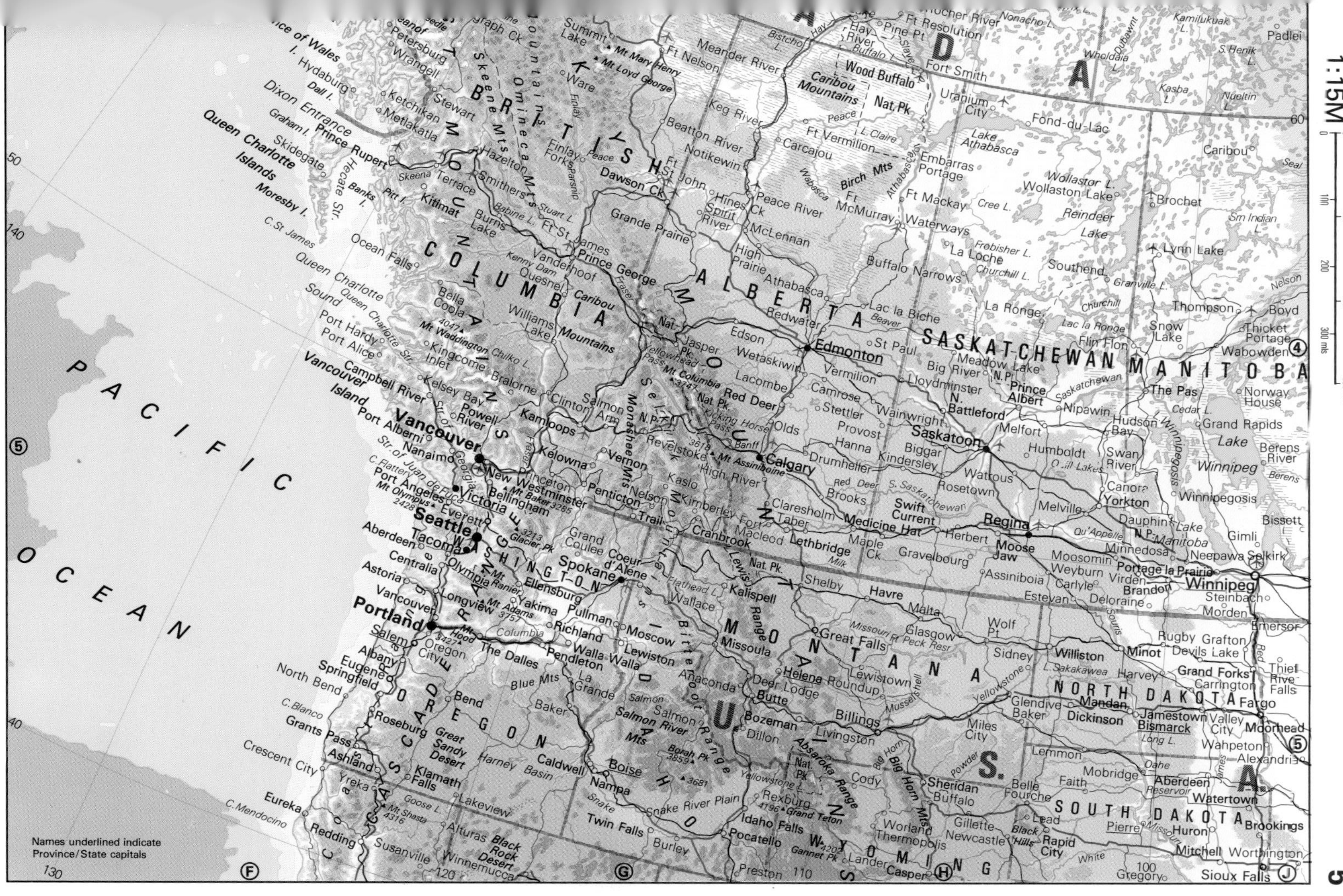
PACIFIC OCEAN
BRITISH COLUMBIA
ALBERTA
SASKATCHEWAN
MANITOBA
WASHINGTON
OREGON
IDAHO
MONTANA
WYOMING
NORTH DAKOTA
SOUTH DAKOTA
Vancouver
Victoria
Seattle
Portland
Edmonton
Calgary
Regina
Saskatoon
Winnipeg
Spokane
Queen Charlotte Islands
Vancouver Island
Names underlined indicate Province/State capitals

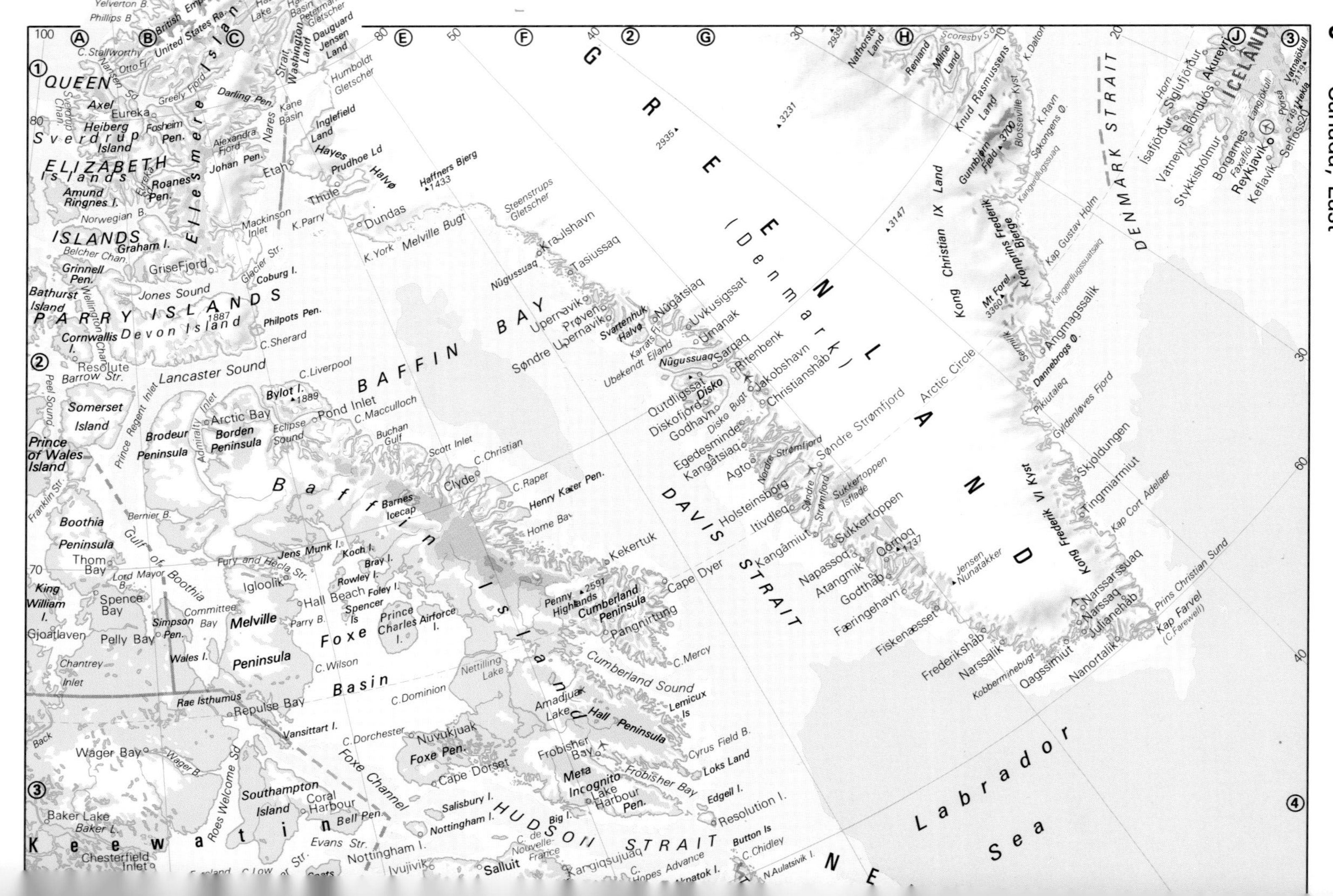
GREENLAND
(Denmark)
ICELAND
DENMARK STRAIT
DAVIS STRAIT
Labrador Sea
BAFFIN BAY
Baffin Island
Foxe Basin
Foxe Channel
HUDSON STRAIT
QUEEN ELIZABETH ISLANDS
PARRY ISLANDS
Sverdrup Is
Ellesmere Island
Devon Island
Lancaster Sound
Jones Sound
Gulf of Boothia
Boothia Peninsula
Melville Peninsula
Southampton Island
Cumberland Sound
Frobisher Bay
Arctic Circle
Kong Christian IX Land
Kong Frederik VI Kyst
Knud Rasmussens Land
Reykjavík
Akureyri
Godthåb
Thule
Resolute
Igloolik
Keewatin

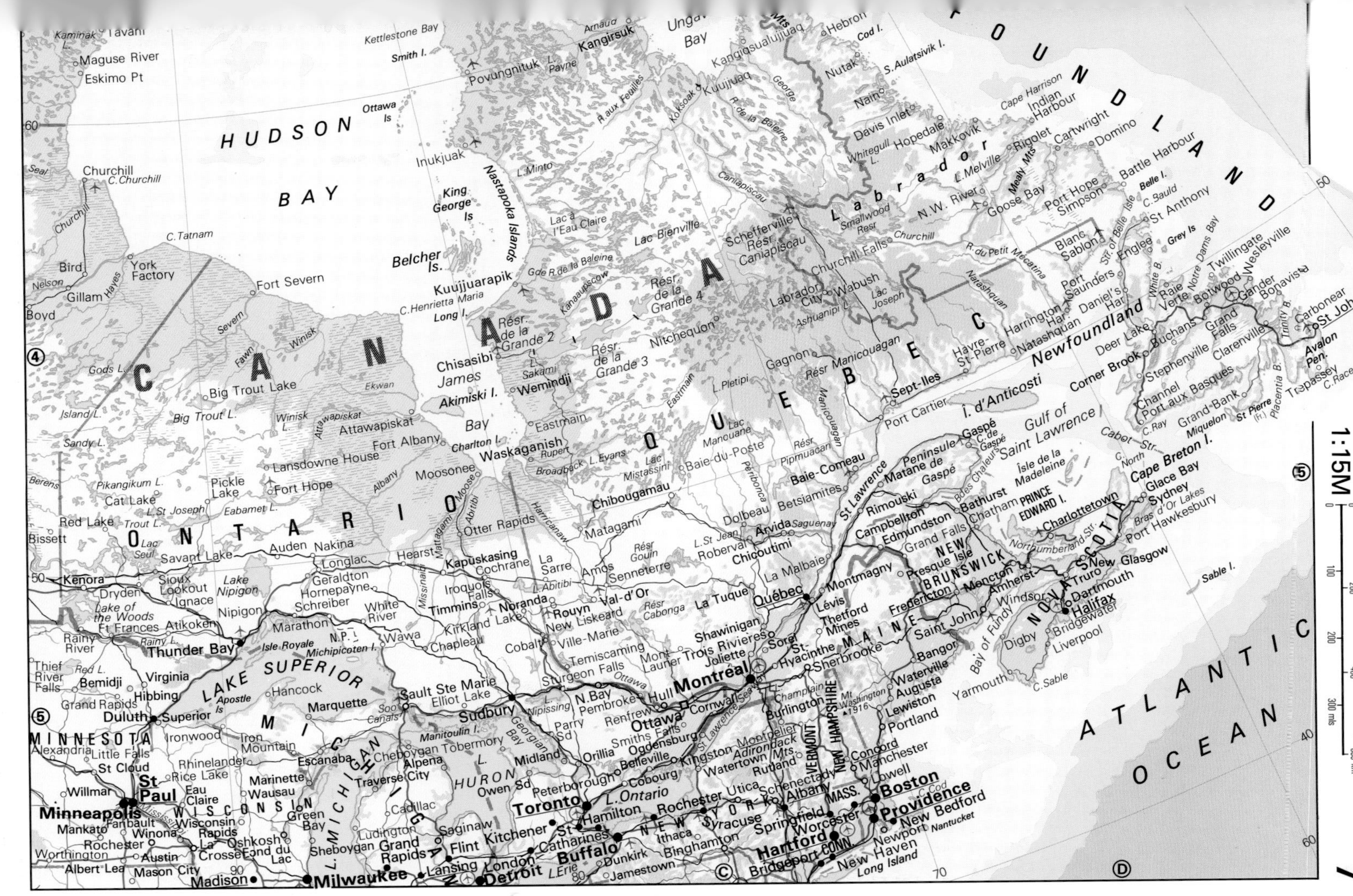

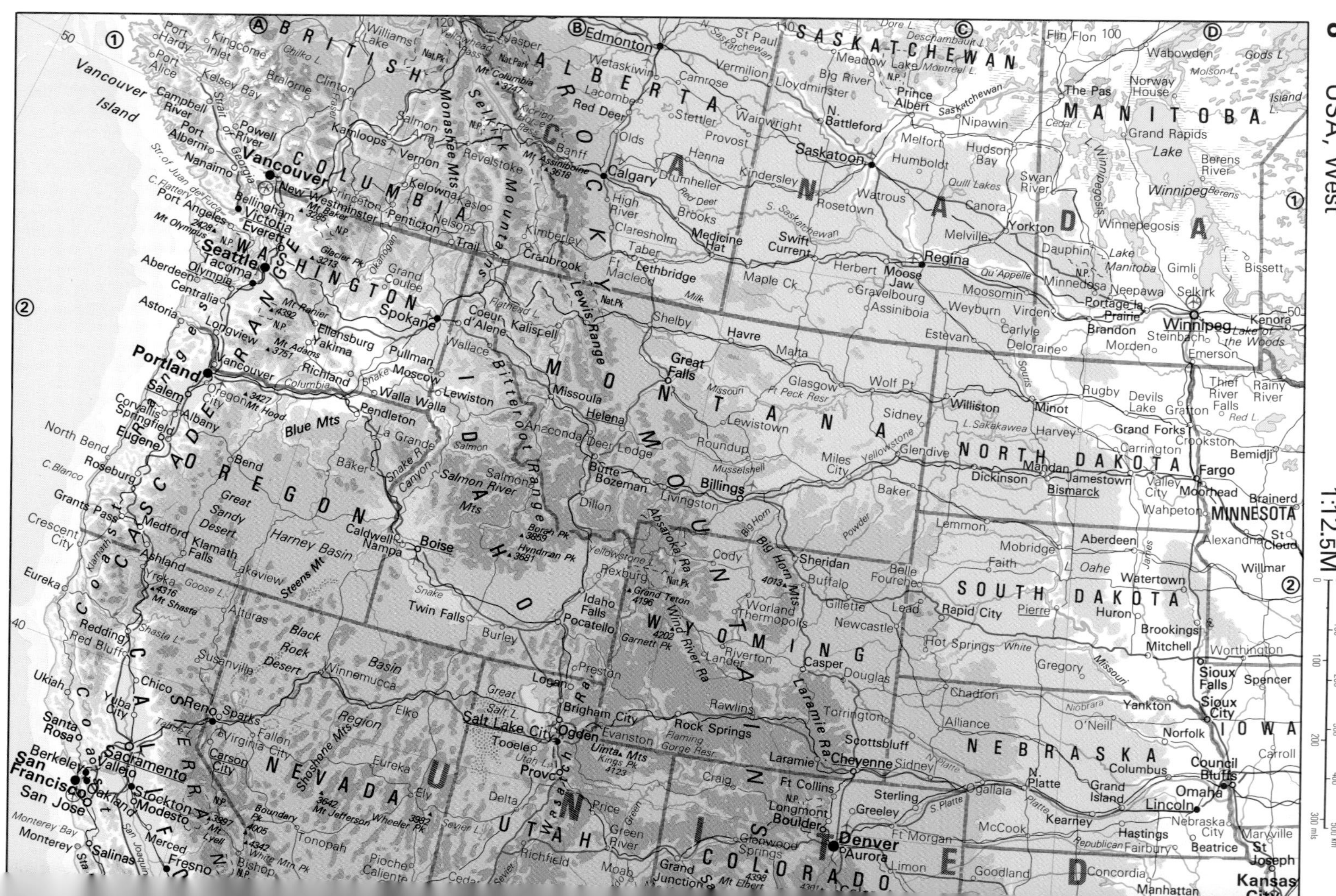

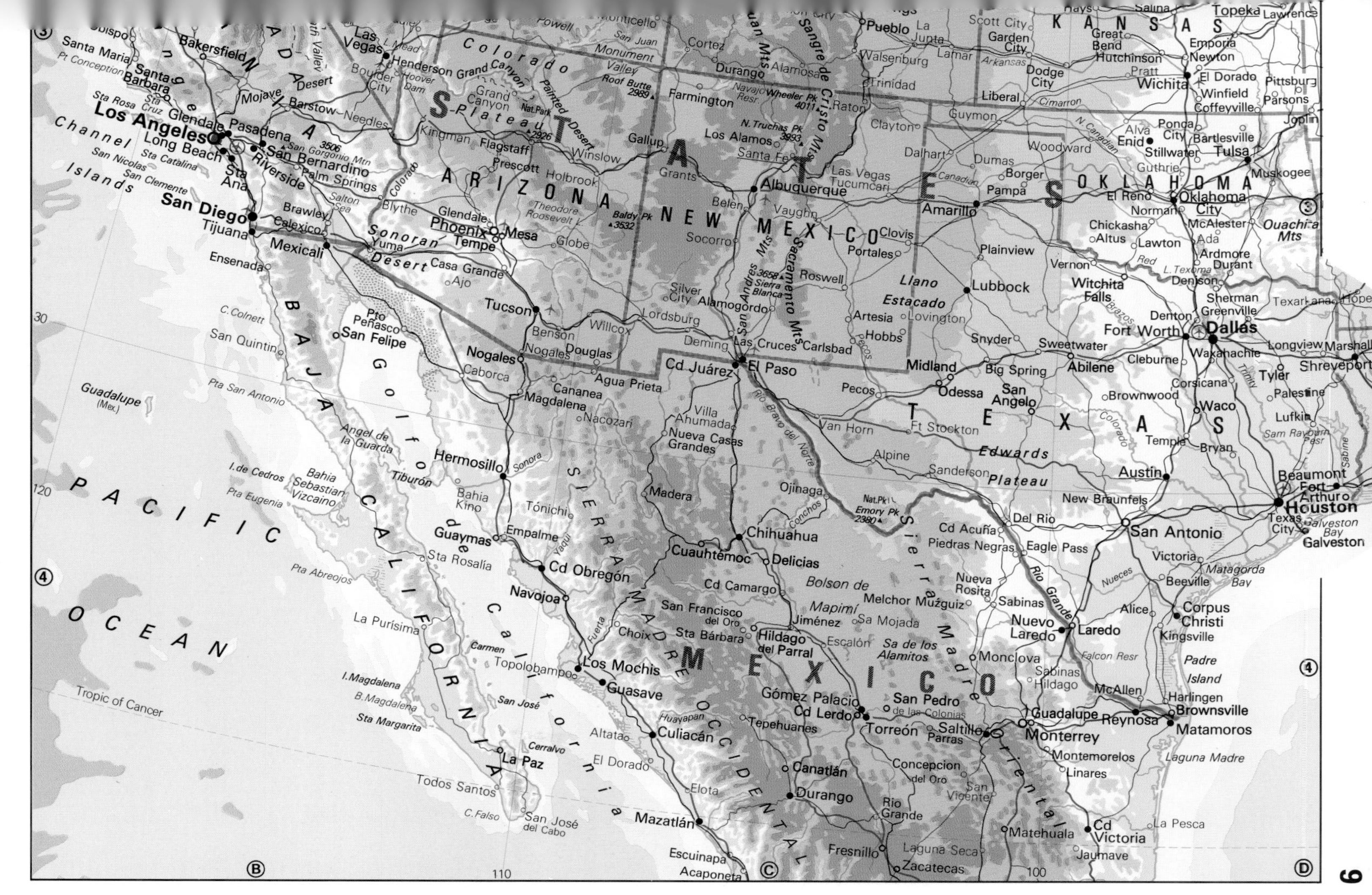
KANSAS
OKLAHOMA
TEXAS
NEW MEXICO
ARIZONA
NEVADA
UTAH
MEXICO
BAJA CALIFORNIA
PACIFIC OCEAN
Golfo de California
SIERRA MADRE OCCIDENTAL
Sierra Madre Oriental
Colorado Plateau
Sangre de Cristo Mts
Sacramento Mts
San Andres Mts
Llano Estacado
Edwards Plateau
Sonoran Desert
Painted Desert
Bolson de Mapimí
Channel Islands
Tropic of Cancer
Topeka
Lawrence
Emporia
Newton
Wichita
El Dorado
Winfield
Coffeyville
Pittsburg
Parsons
Joplin
Hutchinson
Great Bend
Pratt
Salina
Dodge City
Garden City
Scott City
Liberal
Tulsa
Muskogee
Bartlesville
Ponca City
Stillwater
Enid
Alva
Guthrie
Oklahoma City
Norman
El Reno
McAlester
Ada
Ardmore
Durant
Chickasha
Lawton
Altus
Woodward
Guymon
Ouachita Mts
Texarkana
Hope
Marshall
Shreveport
Longview
Tyler
Palestine
Lufkin
Sam Rayburn Resr
Sabine
Beaumont
Port Arthur
Houston
Galveston
Galveston Bay
Texas City
Sherman
Denison
Greenville
Dallas
Fort Worth
Denton
Waxahachie
Corsicana
Waco
Cleburne
Brownwood
Temple
Bryan
Austin
New Braunfels
San Antonio
Victoria
Beeville
Matagorda Bay
Corpus Christi
Kingsville
Padre Island
Harlingen
Brownsville
Matamoros
Laguna Madre
La Pesca
Alice
Nueces
Laredo
Nuevo Laredo
Falcon Resr
McAllen
Reynosa
Monterrey
Guadalupe
Sabinas Hidalgo
Montemorelos
Linares
Cd Victoria
Jaumave
Matehuala
Saltillo
Monclova
Sabinas
Nueva Rosita
Piedras Negras
Cd Acuña
Eagle Pass
Del Rio
Rio Grande
Wichita Falls
Vernon
Abilene
Sweetwater
Snyder
Big Spring
San Angelo
Midland
Odessa
Ft Stockton
Pecos
Van Horn
Alpine
Sanderson
Lubbock
Plainview
Amarillo
Borger
Pampa
Dumas
Dalhart
Clovis
Portales
Hobbs
Lovington
Artesia
Roswell
Carlsbad
El Paso
Cd Juárez
Las Cruces
Alamogordo
Deming
Silver City
Lordsburg
Albuquerque
Santa Fe
Los Alamos
Las Vegas
Tucumcari
Raton
Clayton
Belen
Vaughn
Socorro
Grants
Gallup
Farmington
Durango
Alamosa
Cortez
Trinidad
Walsenburg
Pueblo
La Junta
Lamar
Wheeler Pk 4011
N. Truchas Pk 3993
Sierra Blanca 3658
Baldy Pk 3532
Roof Butte 2989
Navajo Resr
Monument Valley
San Juan
Winslow
Holbrook
Flagstaff
Prescott
Grand Canyon
Nat. Park
Theodore Roosevelt L.
Globe
Mesa
Phoenix
Tempe
Glendale
Casa Grande
Ajo
Tucson
Benson
Willcox
Douglas
Nogales
Kingman
Yuma
Blythe
Henderson
Las Vegas
Boulder City
Hoover Dam
L. Mead
Needles
Barstow
Mojave Desert
Bakersfield
Mojave
Santa Barbara
Santa Maria
Pt Conception
Los Angeles
Glendale
Pasadena
Long Beach
Sta Ana
Riverside
San Bernardino
San Gorgonio Mtn 3506
Palm Springs
Salton Sea
Brawley
Calexico
Mexicali
San Diego
Tijuana
Ensenada
Sta Rosa
Sta Cruz
Sta Catalina
San Nicolas
San Clemente
Chihuahua
Delicias
Ojinaga
Cuauhtémoc
Cd Camargo
San Francisco del Oro
Sta Bárbara
Hildago del Parral
Jiménez
Gómez Palacio
Torreón
Cd Lerdo
San Pedro de las Colonias
Parras
Concepcion del Oro
San Vicente
Durango
Fresnillo
Zacatecas
Rio Grande
Canatlán
Tepehuanes
Madera
Nueva Casas Grandes
Villa Ahumada
Agua Prieta
Cananea
Nacozari
Magdalena
Caborca
Hermosillo
Bahia Kino
Guaymas
Empalme
Cd Obregón
Navojoa
Los Mochis
Guasave
Culiacán
Mazatlán
Escuinapa
Acaponeta
Topolobampo
Sta Rosalía
La Paz
Cerralvo
San José
Carmen
San José del Cabo
Todos Santos
C. Falso
Pto Peñasco
San Felipe
San Quintín
C. Colnett
Pta San Antonio
La Purísima
Pta Abreojos
Bahia Sebastian Vizcaino
I. de Cedros
Pta Eugenia
Tiburón
Angel de la Guarda
I. Magdalena
B. Magdalena
Sta Margarita
Guadalupe (Mex.)
Emory Pk 2380
Nat. Pk
Rio Bravo del Norte
Conchos
Sonora
Yaqui
Fuerte
Huayapan
Brazos
Colorado
Pecos
Red
L. Texoma
Canadian
N. Canadian
Cimarron
Arkansas
Trinity
Sa Mojada
Escalón
Melchor Múzquiz
Sa de los Alamitos
Tónichi
Choix
El Dorado
Altata
Elota
Laguna Seca
30
120
110
100
B
C
D
3
4

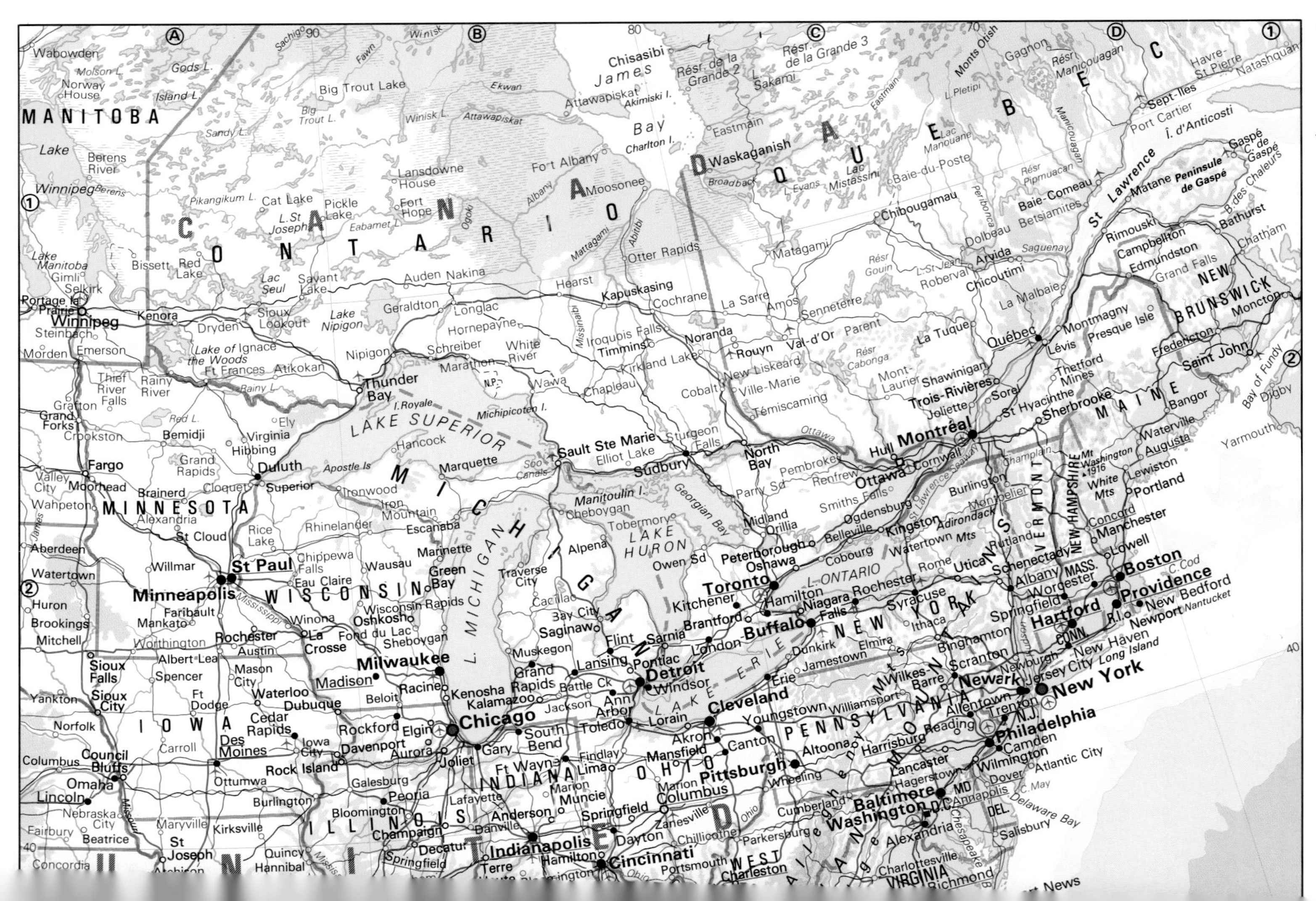
MANITOBA
ONTARIO
QUEBEC
NEW BRUNSWICK
MAINE
VERMONT
NEW HAMPSHIRE
MASS.
CONN.
R.I.
NEW YORK
PENNSYLVANIA
N.J.
DEL.
MD
OHIO
INDIANA
ILLINOIS
MICHIGAN
WISCONSIN
MINNESOTA
IOWA
WEST
VIRGINIA
James Bay
LAKE SUPERIOR
L. MICHIGAN
LAKE HURON
Georgian Bay
L. ONTARIO
LAKE ERIE
Lake Winnipeg
Lake Manitoba
Lake Nipigon
Lake of the Woods
St Lawrence
Bay of Fundy
Long Island
C. Cod
Péninsule de Gaspé
Î. d'Anticosti
Manitoulin I.
Winnipeg
Thunder Bay
Duluth
St Paul
Minneapolis
Milwaukee
Chicago
Detroit
Toronto
Cleveland
Buffalo
Pittsburgh
Ottawa
Montréal
Québec
Boston
Providence
Hartford
New York
Philadelphia
Baltimore
Washington D.C.
Cincinnati
Indianapolis
Columbus
Sault Ste Marie
Sudbury
Fargo
Omaha
Lincoln
Des Moines
Madison
Lansing
Toledo
Portland
Bangor
Saint John
Fredericton
Sept-Îles

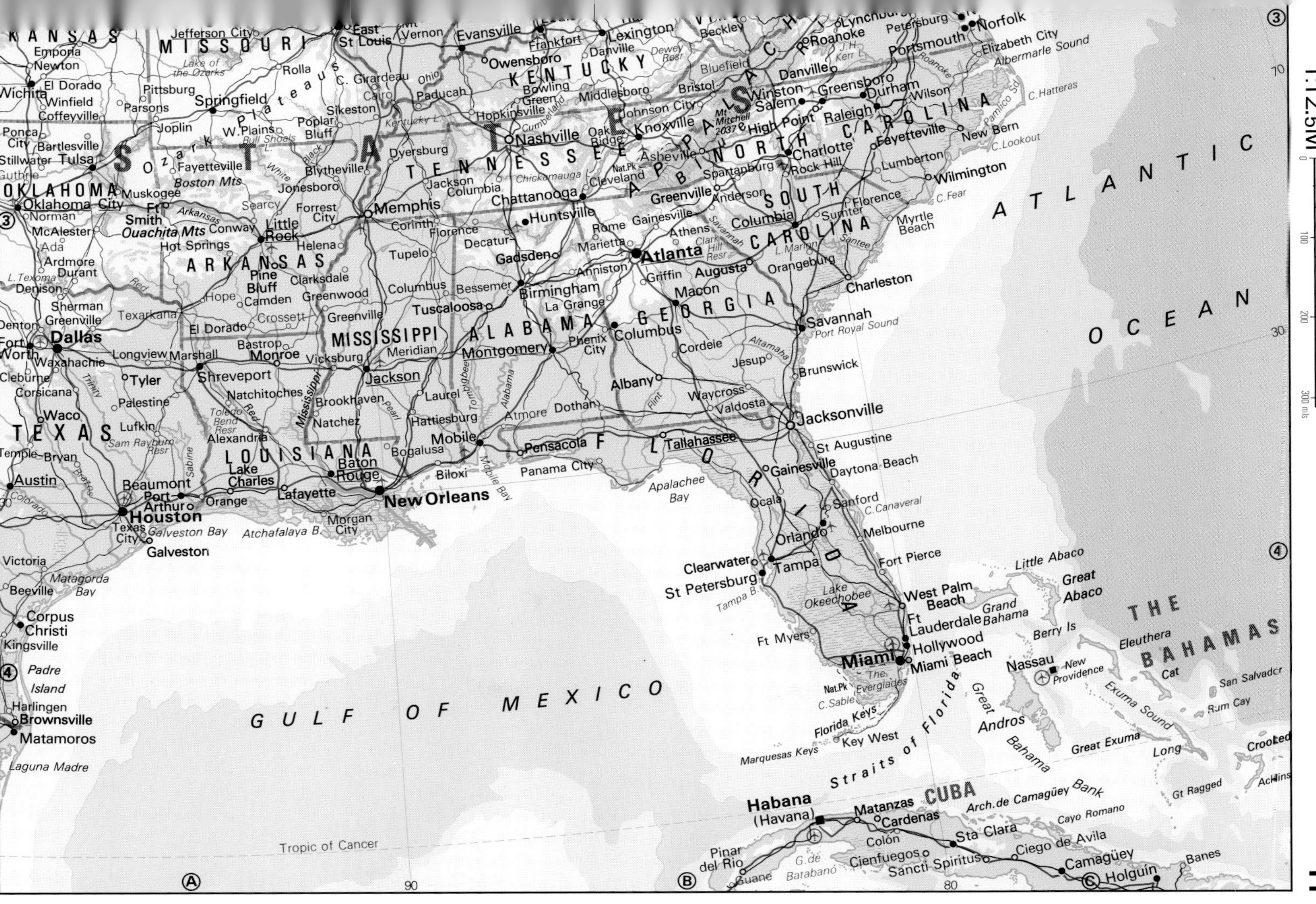

0	100	200	300	400	500 km
0	100		200		300 mls

THE BAHAMAS

Crooked
Acklins
San Salvador
Rum Cay
Cat
Eleuthera
Exuma Sound
Great Exuma
Long
Gt Ragged
Banes

Little Abaco
Great Abaco
Berry Is
New Providence
Nassau
Andros
Great Bahama
Bahama
Bank
Arch. de Camagüey
Cayo Romano
Camagüey
Holguín

Grand Bahama

ATLANTIC OCEAN

Norfolk
Portsmouth
Elizabeth City
Albemarle Sound
C. Hatteras
Petersburg
Lynchburg
Roanoke
C. Lookout
New Bern
Danville
Durham
Wilmington
Raleigh
Greensboro
Winston-Salem
High Point
Fayetteville
Lumberton
Myrtle Beach

NORTH CAROLINA
SOUTH CAROLINA

Charleston
Florence
Columbia
Orangeburg
Sumter
Rock Hill
Charlotte
Greenville
Spartanburg
Anderson

Savannah
Port Royal Sound
Brunswick
Jacksonville
St Augustine
Daytona Beach
Sanford
Melbourne
Fort Pierce

West Palm Beach
Ft. Lauderdale
Hollywood
Miami
Miami Beach

FLORIDA

Orlando
Tampa
Clearwater
St. Petersburg
Ft Myers
Lake Okeechobee
Nat Pk. Everglades
Florida Keys
Key West
Marquesas Keys

Straits of Florida

CUBA

Habana (Havana)
Matanzas
Cárdenas
Colón
Cienfuegos
Santa Clara
Sancti Spíritus
Ciego de Avila
Sta Clara
Pinar del Río
Gulf of Batabanó

GULF OF MEXICO

Tropic of Cancer

KENTUCKY
TENNESSEE
Atlanta
GEORGIA
ALABAMA
MISSISSIPPI
LOUISIANA
TEXAS
ARKANSAS
OKLAHOMA
MISSOURI
KANSAS

Memphis
Nashville
Knoxville
Chattanooga
Huntsville
Birmingham
Montgomery
Mobile
Biloxi
New Orleans
Baton Rouge
Lafayette
Lake Charles
Houston
Galveston
Beaumont
Port Arthur
Dallas
Fort Worth
Austin
Corpus Christi
Brownsville
Matamoros

St. Louis
Springfield
Tulsa
Oklahoma City
Little Rock
Shreveport
Jackson
Pensacola
Panama City
Tallahassee
Columbus
Macon
Augusta

1:10M

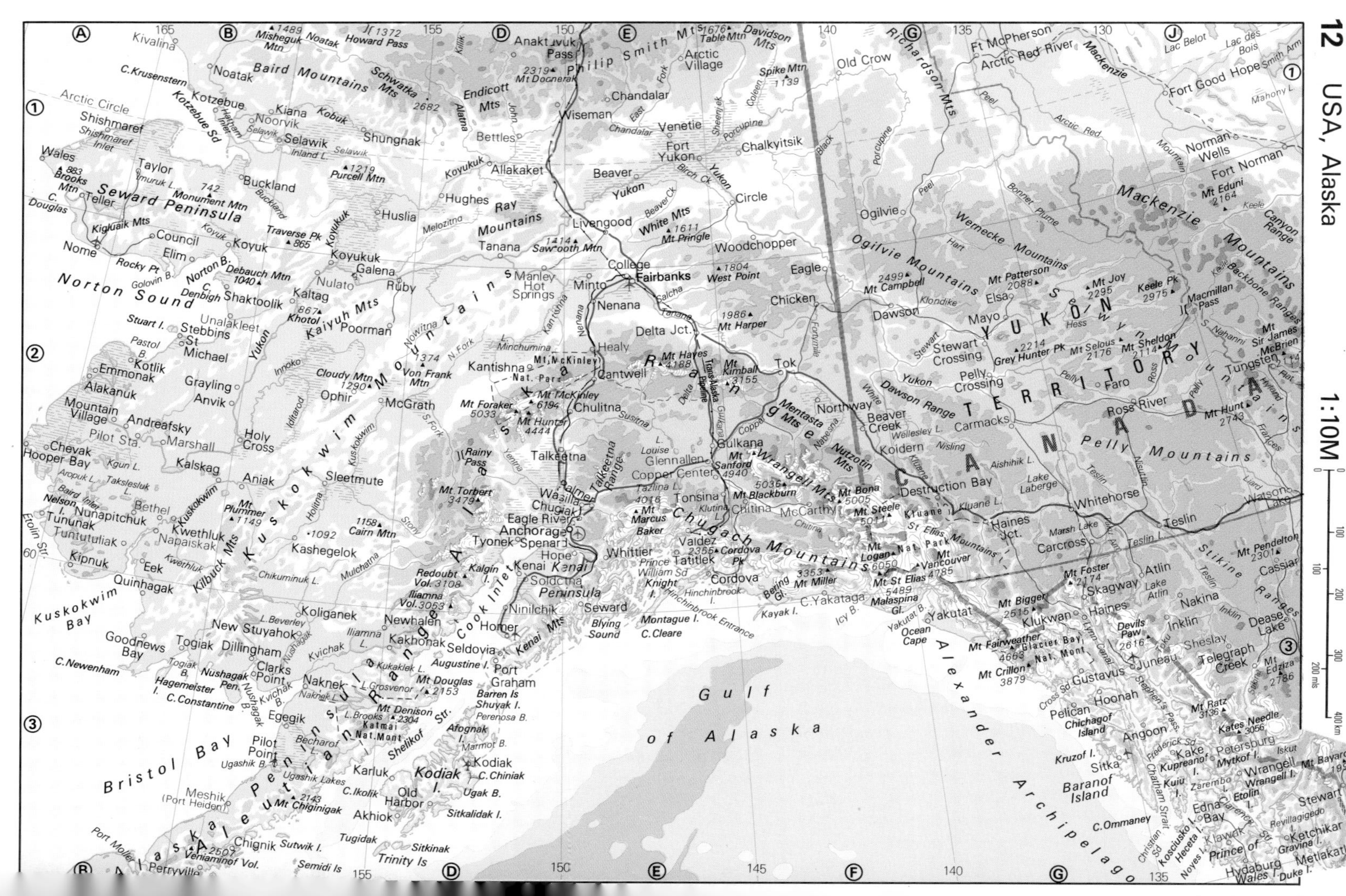

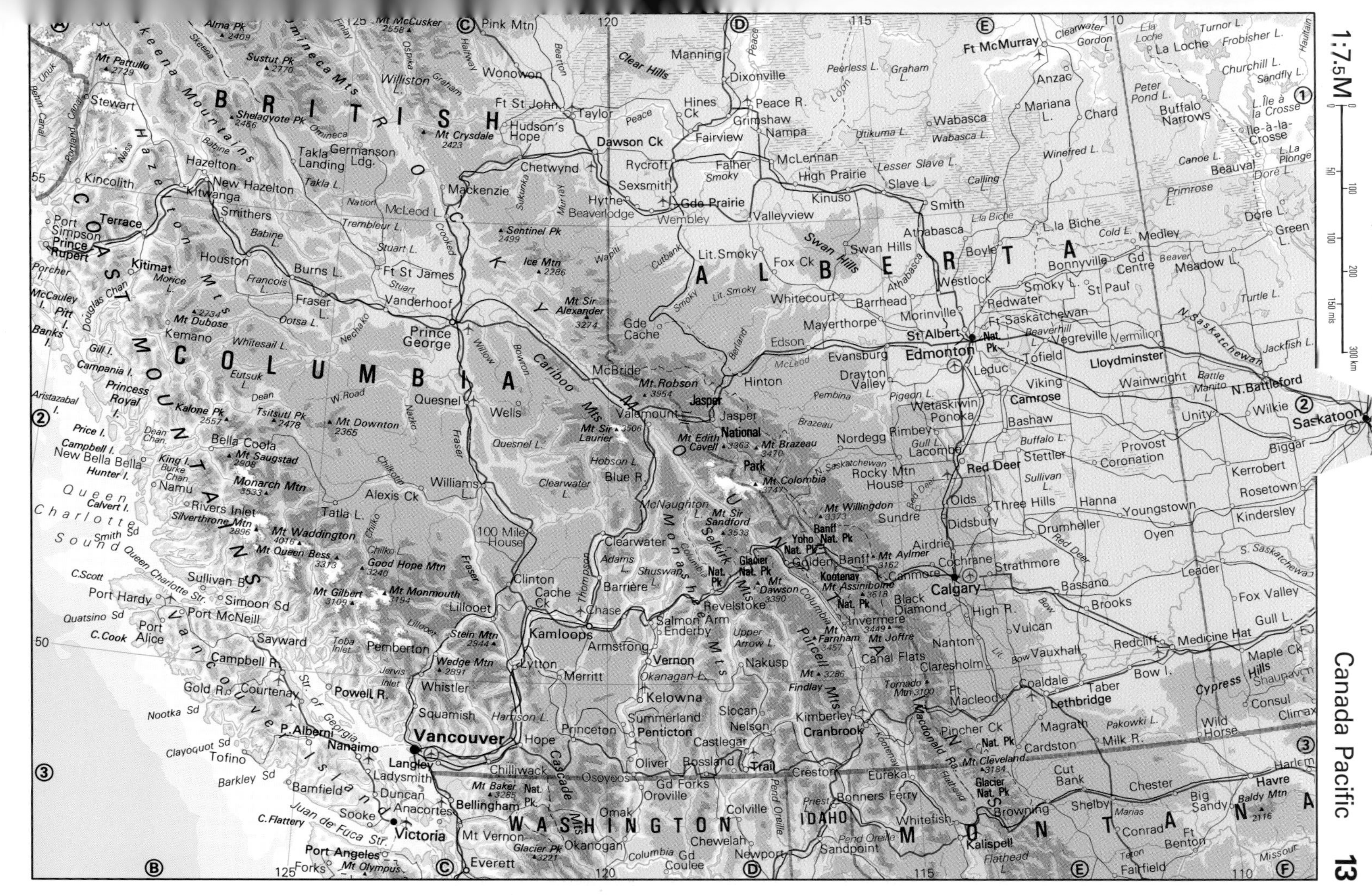
BRITISH COLUMBIA
ALBERTA
IDAHO
WASHINGTON
MONTANA
ROCKY MOUNTAINS
COAST MOUNTAINS
Cariboo Mts
Monashee Mts
Selkirk Mts
Purcell Mts
Cascade Mts
Hazelton Mts
Skeena Mountains
Omineca Mts
Clear Hills
Swan Hills
Cypress Hills
Vancouver
Victoria
Edmonton
Calgary
Saskatoon
Kamloops
Prince George
Prince Rupert
Kelowna
Vernon
Penticton
Lethbridge
Medicine Hat
Red Deer
Ft McMurray
Jasper
Banff
Nanaimo
Lloydminster
N.Battleford
Dawson Ck
Cranbrook
Trail
Vancouver Island
Queen Charlotte Sound
Str. of Georgia
Juan de Fuca Str.

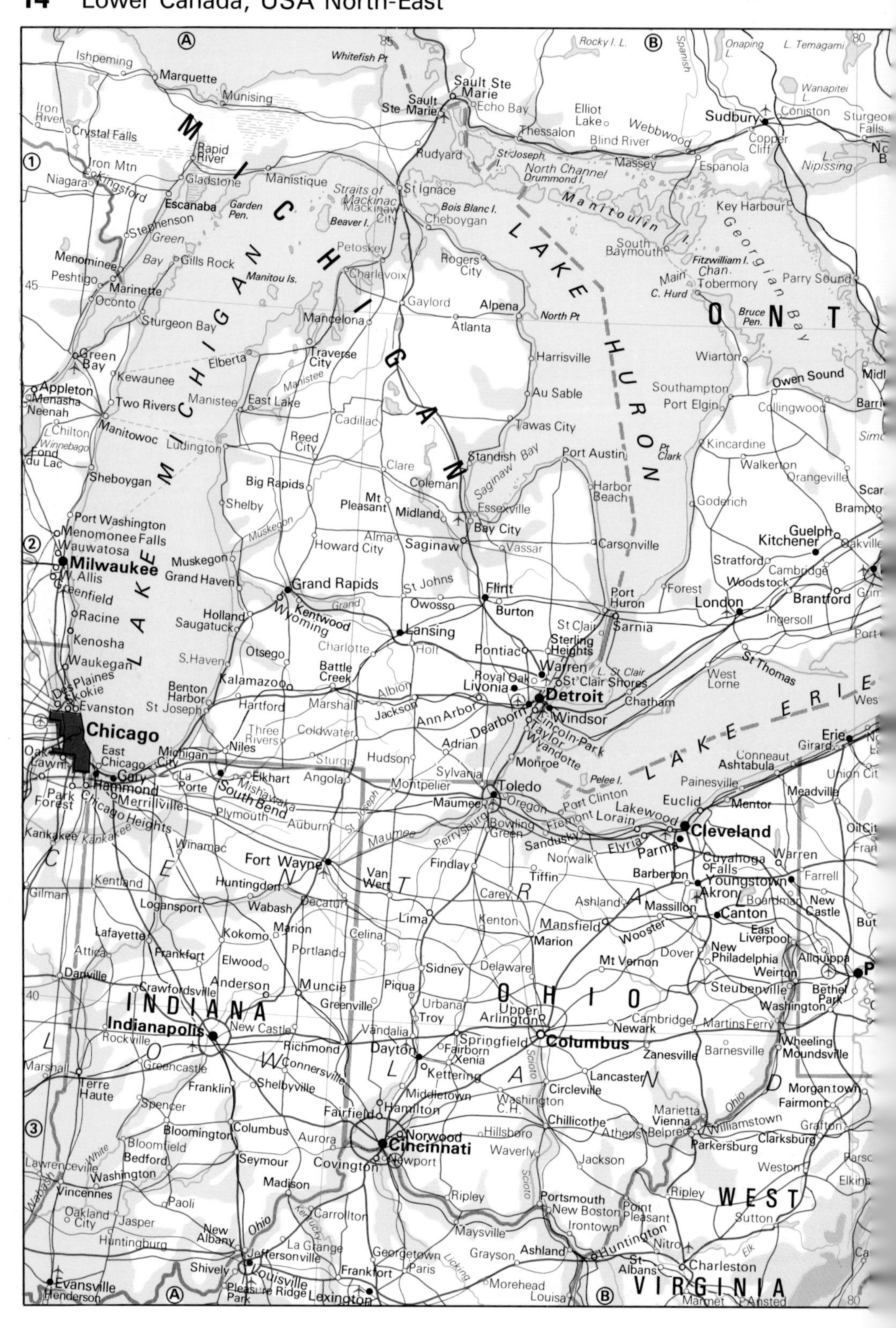
Ⓐ
Ⓑ
85
80
Rocky I. L.
Spanish
Onaping L.
L. Temagami
Wanapitei L.
Whitefish Pt
Ishpeming
Marquette
Munising
Sault Ste Marie
Sault Ste Marie
Echo Bay
Elliot Lake
Webbwood
Sudbury
Coniston
Sturgeon Falls
Iron River
Crystal Falls
Thessalon
Blind River
Copper Cliff
Rapid River
Rudyard
St Joseph I.
Massey
Espanola
L. Nipissing
Iron Mtn
Niagara
Kingsford
Manistique
Straits of Mackinac
St Ignace
North Channel
Drummond I.
Escanaba
Garden Pen.
Mackinaw City
Bois Blanc I.
Cheboygan
Manitoulin I.
Key Harbour
Beaver I.
Stephenson
Green Bay
Petoskey
South Baymouth
Georgian Bay
Menominee
Gills Rock
Rogers City
Fitzwilliam I.
Peshtigo
Marinette
Manitou Is.
Charlevoix
Main Chan.
Tobermory
Parry Sound
45
Oconto
Gaylord
Alpena
C. Hurd
Mancelona
Atlanta
North Pt
Bruce Pen.
Sturgeon Bay
ONT
Green Bay
Traverse City
Harrisville
Wiarton
Elberta
Kewaunee
Manistee
Au Sable
Southampton
Owen Sound
Appleton
Menasha
Neenah
Two Rivers
Manistee
East Lake
Port Elgin
Collingwood
Cadillac
Tawas City
L. Chilton
Manitowoc
L. Winnebago
Ludington
Reed City
Kincardine
Fond du Lac
Clare
Standish
Saginaw Bay
Port Austin
Pt Clark
Walkerton
Sheboygan
Big Rapids
Coleman
Harbor Beach
Orangeville
Mt Pleasant
Midland
Shelby
Essexville
Goderich
Port Washington
Bay City
Menomonee Falls
Alma
Muskegon
Howard City
Saginaw
Vassar
Carsonville
Kitchener
Guelph
Wauwatosa
Muskegon
Stratford
Cambridge
Milwaukee
Grand Haven
W. Allis
Greenfield
Grand Rapids
St Johns
Flint
Port Huron
Forest
Woodstock
Brantford
Owosso
London
Racine
Holland
Kentwood
Wyoming
Grand
Burton
Saugatuck
Lansing
St Clair
Sarnia
Ingersoll
Kenosha
Charlotte
Holt
Sterling Heights
Pontiac
Otsego
S.Haven
Waukegan
Battle Creek
Warren
St Thomas
Royal Oak
St Clair Shores
West Lorne
Kalamazoo
Des Plaines
Skokie
Benton Harbor
Albion
Livonia
Detroit
Chatham
Evanston
St Joseph
Hartford
Marshall
Jackson
Ann Arbor
Windsor
Dearborn
Lincoln Park
Taylor
Wyandotte
LAKE ERIE
Chicago
Three Rivers
Coldwater
Adrian
Erie
Girard
Oak Lawn
East Chicago
Michigan City
Niles
Sturgis
Hudson
Monroe
Conneaut
Ashtabula
Gary
Hammond
La Porte
Elkhart
Angola
Sylvania
Pelee I.
Painesville
Union City
Park Forest
South Bend
Mishawaka
Montpelier
Toledo
Meadville
Merrillville
Maumee
Oregon
Port Clinton
Euclid
Mentor
Chicago Heights
Plymouth
Auburn
St Joseph
Perrysburg
Bowling Green
Fremont
Lakewood
Lorain
Cleveland
Kankakee
Kankakee
Maumee
Sandusky
Elyria
Parma
Oil City
Winamac
Fort Wayne
Findlay
Norwalk
Cuyahoga Falls
Warren
Kentland
Huntingdon
Van Wert
Tiffin
Barberton
Youngstown
Farrell
Gilman
Logansport
Wabash
Decatur
Carey
Ashland
Akron
Massillon
Canton
Boardman
New Castle
Lima
Kenton
Mansfield
Wooster
East Liverpool
Lafayette
Kokomo
Marion
Celina
Marion
Attica
Frankfort
Portland
Dover
New Philadelphia
Aliquippa
Danville
Elwood
Sidney
Delaware
Mt Vernon
Weirton
Crawfordsville
Anderson
Muncie
Piqua
Steubenville
Bethel Park
40
INDIANA
Greenville
Urbana
OHIO
Washington
Troy
Upper Arlington
Cambridge
Newark
Martins Ferry
Indianapolis
New Castle
Vandalia
Springfield
Columbus
Wheeling
Moundsville
Rockville
Richmond
Dayton
Fairborn
Xenia
Zanesville
Barnesville
Marshall
Greencastle
Connersville
Kettering
Lancaster
Terre Haute
Franklin
Shelbyville
Middletown
Circleville
Morgantown
Washington C.H.
Spencer
Fairfield
Hamilton
Marietta
Fairmont
Vienna
Ohio
Chillicothe
Williamstown
Grafton
Bloomington
Columbus
Aurora
Norwood
Hillsboro
Athens
Belpre
Parkersburg
Clarksburg
Bloomfield
Cincinnati
Waverly
Bedford
Seymour
Covington
Newport
Jackson
Lawrenceville
Washington
White
Weston
Madison
Vincennes
Wabash
Paoli
Ripley
Portsmouth
Ripley
WEST
Carrollton
Point Pleasant
Oakland City
Jasper
New Boston
Elkins
Kentucky
Ironton
Sutton
New Albany
Ohio
Maysville
Huntingburg
Huntington
La Grange
Ashland
Nitro
Elk
Jeffersonville
Georgetown
Licking
Grayson
Shively
Louisville
Frankfort
Paris
St Albans
Charleston
Evansville
Pleasure Ridge Park
Morehead
VIRGINIA
Henderson
Lexington
Louisa
Marmet
Ansted

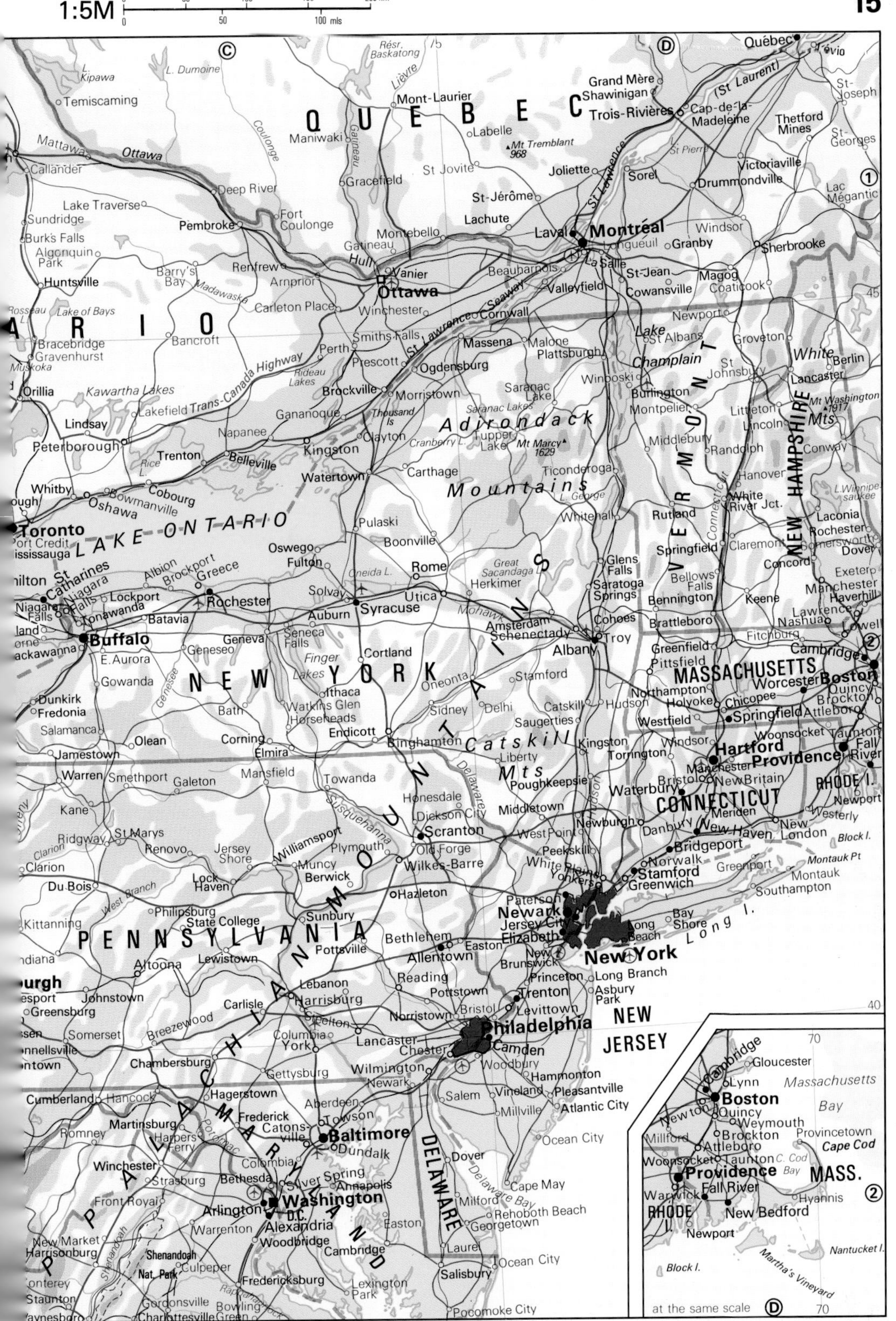

1:5M

0   50   100   150   200 km
0   50   100 mils

© Québec vio

Q U E B E C

Grand Mère
Shawinigan
Trois-Rivières

Mont-Laurier
Labelle
St Jovite
Mt Tremblant
968

Maniwaki

Cap-de-la-Madeleine
Thetford Mines
St-Joseph
St-Georges

Joliette
St-Jérôme
Lachute
St Pierre
Drummondville
Victoriaville

Deep River
Fort
Coulonge
Montebello
Gatineau
Hull
Vanier
Laval
Longueuil
Montréal
Granby
Sherbrooke
Lac Mégantic

Pembroke
Renfrew
Arnprior
Beauharnois
La Salle
St-Jean
Magog
Coaticook

Ottawa
Carleton Place
Winchester
Valleyfield
Cowansville
Newport

Bancroft
Smiths Falls
Perth
Cornwall
Lake
St Albans
Berlin
White
Mt Washington
1917

Brockville
Morristown
Prescott
Massena
Malone
Plattsburgh
Burlington
Champlain
Groveton
Lancaster

Gananoque
Clayton
Ogdensburg
Saranac
Lake
Winooski
St Johnsbury
Littleton
Lincoln
Conway

Kingston
Thousand
Is
Cranberry L
Tupper
Lake
Montpelier
Middlebury
Randolph
Laconia
Dover

Watertown
Carthage
Mt Marcy
1629
Ticonderoga
Rutland
Hanover
White
River Jct
Concord
Exeter

L A K E   O N T A R I O
Pulaski
Boonville
Whitehall
L George
Glens
Falls
Springfield
Claremont
Manchester
Haverhill

Oswego
Fulton
Rome
Great
Sacandaga
Lake
Saratoga
Springs
Bennington
Keene
Nashua
Lawrence
Lowell

Rochester
Greece
Oneida L
Herkimer
Amsterdam
Schenectady
Cohoes
Troy
Albany
Brattleboro
Fitchburg
Cambridge

N E W   Y O R K
Syracuse
Utica
Mohawk
Greenfield
Pittsfield
M A S S A C H U S E T T S
Worcester
Boston
Quincy
Brockton

Auburn
Cortland
Oneonta
Stamford
Northampton
Holyoke
Chicopee
Springfield
Attleboro
Fall River

Ithaca
Watkins Glen
Horseheads
Endicott
Sidney
Delhi
Catskill
Hudson
Westfield
Windsor
Hartford
Providence

Corning
Elmira
Binghamton
C a t s k i l l
M t s
Kingston
Torrington
New Britain
R H O D E I.
Westerly

Honesdale
Dickson City
Middletown
Poughkeepsie
Liberty
Waterbury
Meriden
C O N N E C T I C U T
Newport

Scranton
Old Forge
West Point
Newburgh
Danbury
New Haven
London
Block I.

Wilkes-Barre
Hazleton
Peekskill
White Plains
Norwalk
Bridgeport
Montauk Pt
Montauk

P E N N S Y L V A N I A
Sunbury
Bethlehem
Paterson
Newark
Jersey City
Yonkers
Stamford
Greenwich
Greenport
Southampton

Pottsville
Allentown
Easton
New
Brunswick
Elizabeth
New York
Long I.
Bay
Shore

Reading
Princeton
Long Branch
Asbury
Park

Harrisburg
Pottstown
Trenton

Lebanon
Norristown
Bristol
Levittown
N E W

Lancaster
Chester
Philadelphia
Camden
J E R S E Y

York
Woodbury
Hammonton

Wilmington
Salem
Vineland
Pleasantville
Atlantic City

Baltimore
Dundalk
D E L A W A R E
Ocean City

Columbia
Annapolis
Dover
Cape May

Silver
Spring
Milford
Rehoboth Beach

Washington
D.C.
Easton
Georgetown

Alexandria
Cambridge

Laurel
Ocean City

Salisbury

Pocomoke City

A P P A L A C H I A N   M O U N T A I N S

Inset (at the same scale):

Massachusetts
Bay

Gloucester
Boston
Quincy
Weymouth

Newton
Brockton
Provincetown
Cape Cod

Woonsocket
Attleboro
Taunton
C. Cod
Bay
M A S S.

Providence
Fall River
Hyannis

R H O D E
I.
New Bedford

Warwick

Newport
Nantucket I.

Block I.
Martha's Vineyard

O N T A R I O
Lake Traverse
Temiscaming
L. Kipawa
L. Dumoine
Mattawa
Ottawa

Callander
Sundridge
Algonquin
Park
Huntsville

Bracebridge
Gravenhurst
Muskoka
Orillia
Kawartha Lakes

Lindsay
Peterborough

Whitby
Oshawa
Bowmanville
Cobourg

Toronto
Mississauga
Hamilton
St Catharines
Niagara
Falls
Buffalo

Lockport
Tonawanda
Batavia
Geneva
Rochester

Dunkirk
Fredonia
E. Aurora
Geneseo
Seneca
Falls

Salamanca
Olean
Bath

Jamestown
Warren
Smethport
Galeton
Mansfield
Towanda

Kane
Williamsport
Muncy
Berwick

Ridgway
St Marys
Jersey
Shore

Du Bois
Renovo
Lock
Haven
Plymouth

Clarion
Philipsburg
State College

Kittanning
Altoona
Lewistown

Johnstown
Breezewood
Bedford
Carlisle

Greensburg
Somerset
Chambersburg
Gettysburg

Cumberland
Hancock
Hagerstown
Aberdeen

Martinsburg
Romney
Frederick
Catonsville
Towson

Winchester
Harpers
Ferry
Columbia
Bethesda

Strasburg
Front Royal
Arlington
Woodbridge

New Market
Warrenton
Culpeper

Harrisonburg
Shenandoah
Nat. Park
Fredericksburg

Monterey
Staunton
Gordonsville
Bowling
Green
Lexington
Park

Waynesboro
Charlottesville

0 25 50 75 100 km
0 25 50 mis

MASSACHUSETTS
NEW YORK
CONNECTICUT
RHODE ISLAND
NEW JERSEY
PENN.
NEW JERSEY
MARYLAND

Catskill Mountains
ATLANTIC OCEAN
Long Island Sound
Long Island
Great South Bay
Buzzards Bay
Martha's Vineyard
Rhode Island Sound
Block Island Sd
Block Island
Nomans Land
Vineyard Haven
Nomans Land
Delaware Bay
Chesapeake Bay
Blue Mt
South Mt
Blue Mt

Cobleskill, Richmondville, Schoharie, Middleburgh, Albany, Troy, Rensselaer, Cohoes, Watervliet, Adams, Williamstown, N. Adams, Readsboro, Hinsdale, Winchester, Greenville, Haverhill, Methuen, Newburyport, Ipswich, Nashua, Dracut, Lawrence, Salem, Lynn, Marblehead, Beverly, Gloucester
Stamford, Schenectady, Nassau, Cheshire, Shelburne, Greenfield, Northfield, Winchendon, Fitchburg, Clinton, Lowell
Grand Gorge, Prattsville, Coxsackie, Pittsfield, Mt Greylock 1064, S. Deerfield, Millers Falls, Athol, Gardner, Leominster, Waltham, Cambridge, *Massachusetts*, Boston
Shandaken, Saugerties, Chatham, Lenox, Dalton, Northampton, Amherst, Barre, Worcester, Marlboro, Newton, Framingham, Quincy Bay, Brookline, Quincy, Weymouth
Slide Mtn 1281, Ashokan Res, Catskill, Hudson, Stockbridge, Gt Barrington, Otis, Easthampton, Chicopee, Oxford, Milford, Southbridge, Norwood, Stoughton, Brockton
Kingston, Mt Everett 793, Canaan, Westfield, Springfield, Monson, Webster, Franklin, Mansfield, Attleboro, Bridgewater, Plymouth
Liberty, Ellenville, New Paltz, Millbrook, Rhinebeck, Winsted, Thompsonville, Windsor Locks, Stafford Springs, Putnam, Woonsocket, Taunton, Middleboro, Wareham
Monticello, Otisville, Walden, Highland, Poughkeepsie, Torrington, Hartford, Rockville, Storrs, Moosup, Central Falls, Cranston, Warwick, Warren, Fall River, Providence, Pawtucket
Port Jervis, Middletown, Beacon, Carmel, New Milford, Bristol, New Britain, Manchester, Willimantic, Jewett City, Jamestown, Newport, Bristol, New Bedford, Falmouth
Milford, Warwick, Hamburg, Haverstraw, Suffern, Waterbury, Southington, Colchester, Norwich, Uncasville, Wakefield, Westerly
Sussex, Franklin, Newton, Pompton Lakes, Butler, Paterson, Clifton, Passaic, White Plains, Yonkers, Bridgeport, Milford, New Haven, New London, Old Lyme, Clinton, Old Saybrook, Mystic, Fishers I., Gardiners I., Montauk Pt, Montauk
Dover, Morristown, E. Orange, Newark, Jersey City, Elizabeth, New York, Queens, Brooklyn, Staten I., Bronx, Huntington, Kings Park, Bay Shore, Sayville, Center Moriches, Southampton, East Hampton, Riverhead, Mattituck, Greenport, Sag Harbor
Bernardsville, Somerville, Long Beach

Milton, Bloomsburg, Danville, Catawissa, Hazleton, Newton, Butler, Port Chester
Lewisburg, Sunbury, Mt Carmel, Shamokin, Frackville, Mahanoy City, Tamaqua, Stroudsburg, Bangor, Hackettstown, Dover, Morristown, Paterson, Clifton, New York, Queens
Milroy, Middleburg, Herndon, Minersville, Pottsville, Palmerton, Belvidere, Washington, Bernardsville, Newark, Jersey City, Elizabeth, Bronx
Burnham, McClure, Lykens, Tremont, Pine Grove, Schuylkill Haven, Whitehall, Easton, Phillipsburg, Clinton, Somerville, Perth Amboy, Long Beach
Lewistown, Mifflintown, Millersburg, Hamburg, Allentown, Bethlehem, Emmaus, New Brunswick, Raritan Bay, Atlantic Highlands
Newport, Duncannon, Dauphin, Lebanon, Womelsdorf, Quakertown, Flemington, Princeton, South River, Red Bank, Long Branch
Harrisburg, Palmyra, Hershey, Shillington, Reading, Boyertown, Souderton, Lansdale, Doylestown, Morrisville, Trenton, Hightstown, Freehold, Asbury Park
Newville, Carlisle, Steelton, Middletown, Lititz, Ephrata, Pottstown, Warminster, Norristown, Levittown, Bordentown, Lakewood, Manasquan, Point Pleasant
Mt Holly Springs, Dillsburg, Elizabethtown, Columbia, Lancaster, Phoenixville, Philadelphia, Burlington, Lakehurst, Bretton Woods
Shippensburg, Manchester, York, Red Lion, Coatesville, Parkesburg, Downingtown, W. Chester, Chester, Camden, Mt Holly, Chatsworth, Toms River, Seaside Park
Gettysburg, Hanover, Glen Rock, Stewartstown, Kennett Square, Wilmington, Newark, Glassboro, Woodbury, Atco, Barnegat Bay, Barnegat
Waynesboro, Littlestown, Rising Sun, Penns Grove, Woodstown, Hammonton, Surf City
Emmitsburg, Westminster, Havre de Grace, Bel Air, Elkton, Salem, Elmer, Vineland, Egg Harbor City, Beach Haven
Frederick, Reisterstown, Towson, Cockeysville, Aberdeen, Edgewood, Middletown, Bridgeton, Millville, Mays Landing, Little Egg Harbor, Great Bay, Tuckerton
Mt Airy, Ellicott City, Baltimore, Dundalk, Cecilton, Smyrna, Port Norris, Woodbine, Pleasantville, Somers Point, Atlantic City
Damascus, Columbia, Catonsville, Chestertown, Dover, Ocean City, Great Egg Harbor
Leesburg, Gaithersburg, Rockville, Laurel, Glen Burnie, Centreville, Frederica, Stone Harbor
Wheaton, Silver Spring, Bowie, Queenstown, Annapolis, Greensboro, Wildwood, Cape May
Bethesda, Arlington, Fairfax, Alexandria, Washington D.C., Mayo, Queen Anne, Harrington, Denton, St Michaels, Greenwood, Milford, C. May Pt, Cape May Pt, C. Henlopen, *Cape May*

ATLANTIC OCEAN

1:5M

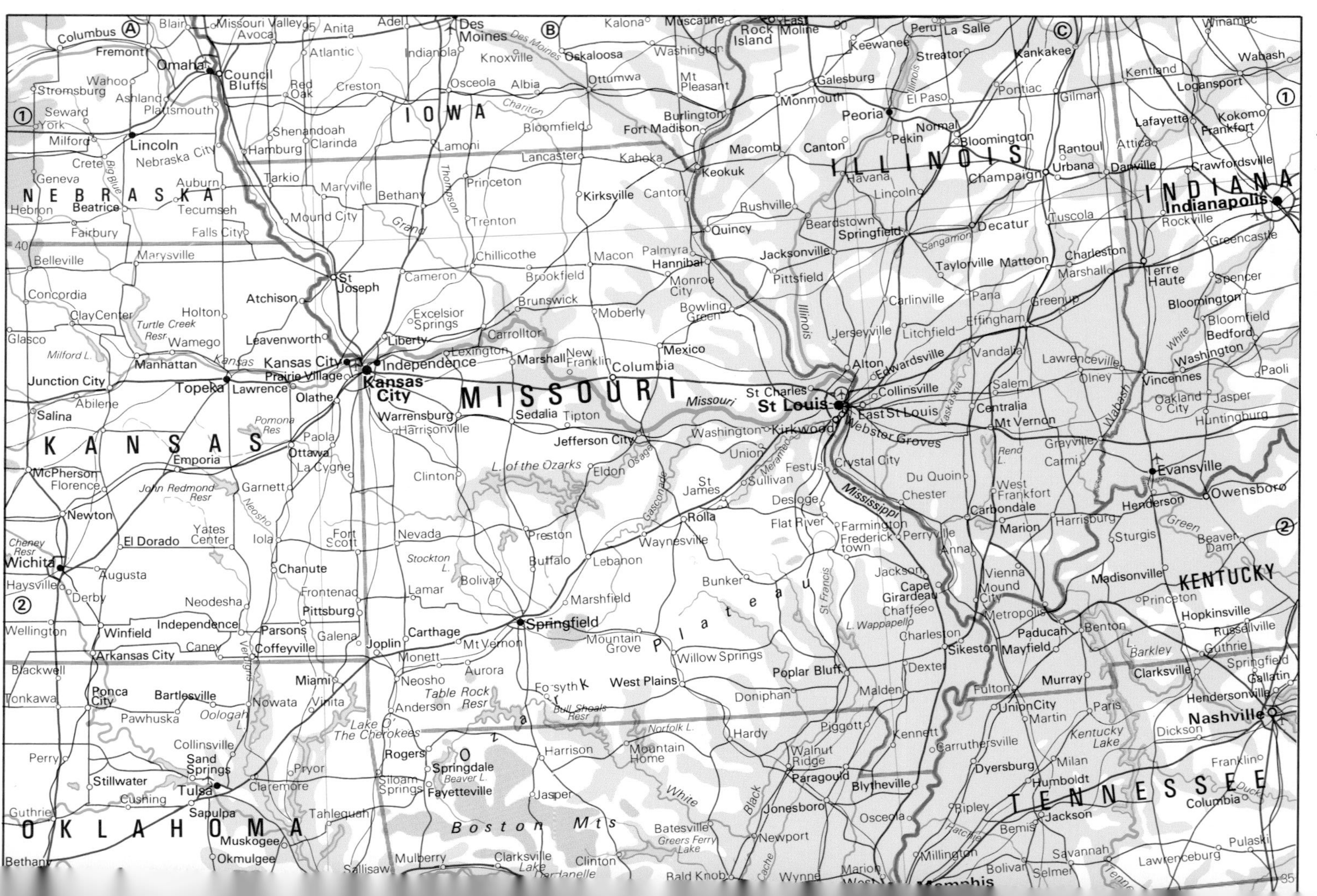
NEBRASKA
IOWA
ILLINOIS
INDIANA
KANSAS
MISSOURI
KENTUCKY
TENNESSEE
OKLAHOMA
Omaha
Council Bluffs
Lincoln
Des Moines
Peoria
Springfield
Decatur
Champaign
Indianapolis
St Joseph
Kansas City
Independence
Topeka
Wichita
Columbia
Jefferson City
St Louis
Evansville
Owensboro
Paducah
Nashville
Joplin
Tulsa
Muskogee
Missouri
Mississippi
Illinois
Wabash
L. of the Ozarks
Table Rock Resr
Lake O' The Cherokees
Kentucky Lake
Ozark Plateau
Boston Mts

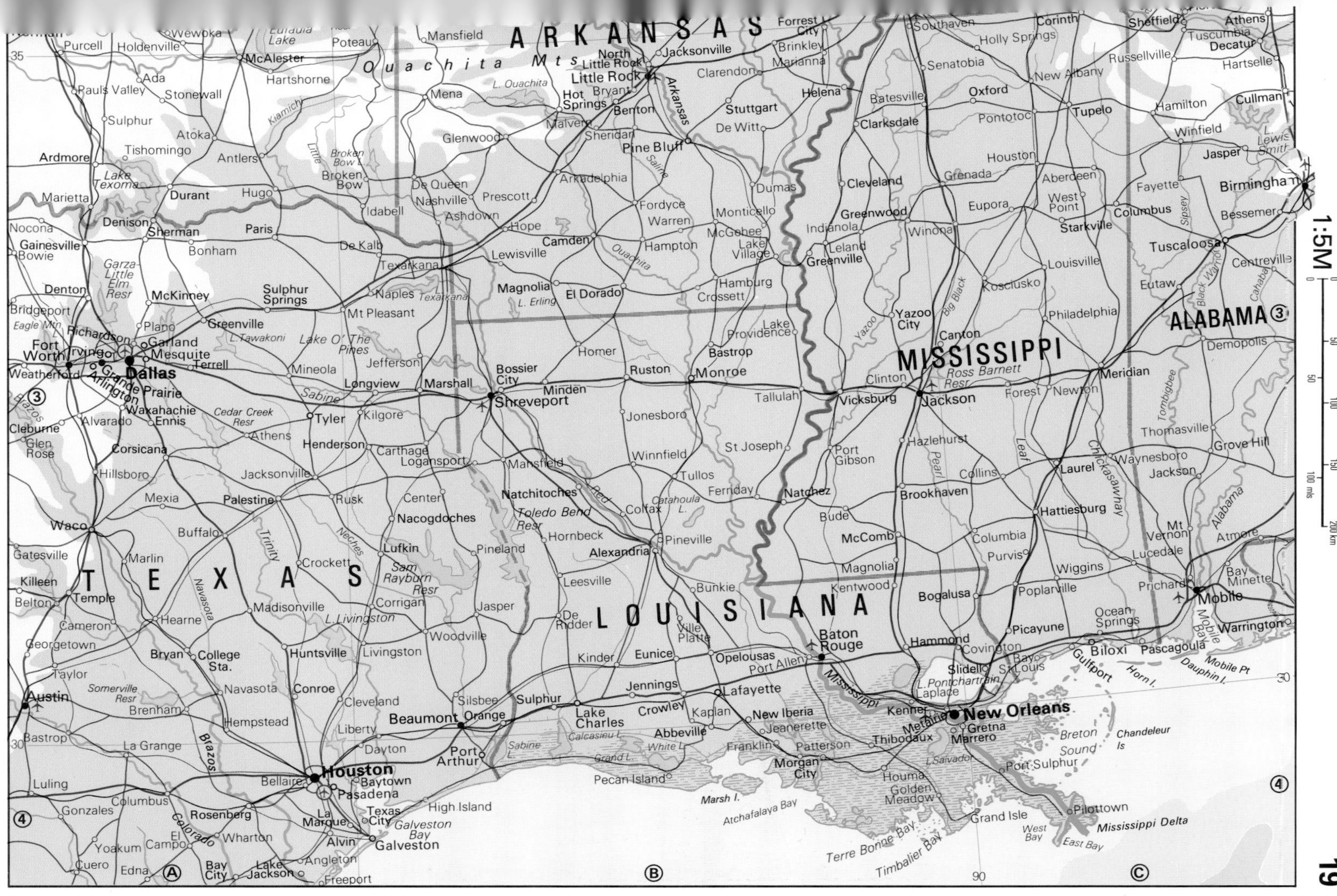

1:5M

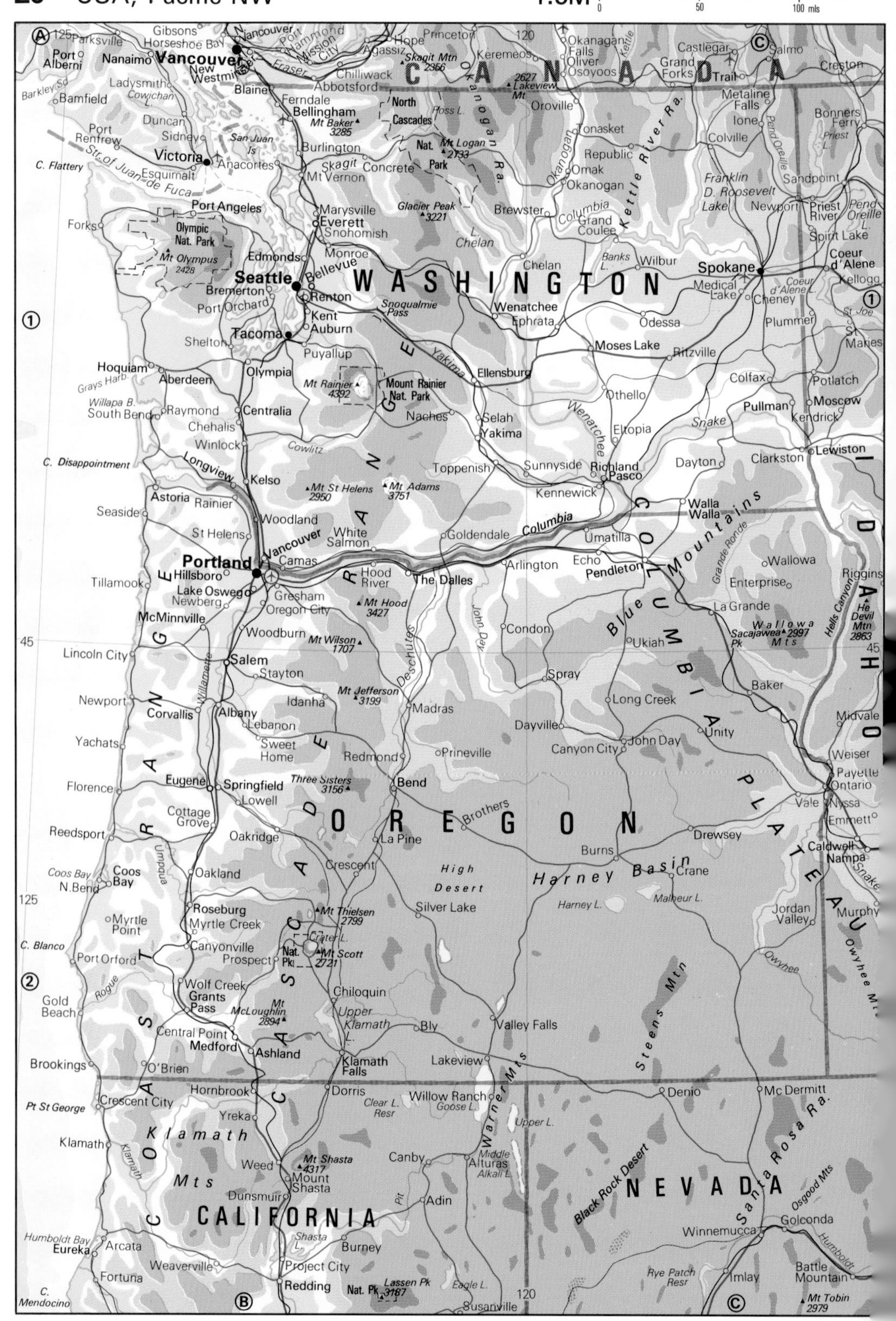

Ⓐ

Parksville 125
Gibsons
Horseshoe Bay
Vancouver
Nanaimo
Vancouver
New
Westmin
Ladysmith
Cowichan
Duncan
Sidney
San Juan
Is
Victoria
Anacortes
C. Flattery
Str. of Juan de Fuca
Port Angeles
Forks
Olympic
Nat. Park
Mt Olympus
2428
Edmonds
Seattle
Bellevue
Bremerton
Port Orchard
Renton
Kent
Auburn
Hoquiam
Shelton
Olympia
Aberdeen
Grays Harb
Willapa B.
South Bend
Raymond
Chehalis
Centralia
Winlock
C. Disappointment
Longview
Kelso
Astoria Rainier
Seaside
St Helens
Woodland
Tillamook
Portland
Hillsboro
Lake Oswego
Newberg
McMinnville
Lincoln City
Salem
Newport
Corvallis
Albany
Yachats
Lebanon
Sweet
Home
Florence
Eugene
Springfield
Lowell
Cottage
Grove
Reedsport
Oakridge
Coos Bay
Coos
N.Bend
Bay
Oakland
Myrtle
Point
Roseburg
Myrtle Creek
C. Blanco
Port Orford
Canyonville
Prospect
Gold
Beach
Wolf Creek
Grants
Pass
Central Point
Medford
Ashland
Brookings
O'Brien
Hornbrook
Pt St George
Crescent City
Yreka
Klamath
Weed
C.
Mendocino
Humboldt Bay
Eureka
Arcata
Fortuna
Weaverville

Barkley Sd
Bamfield
Port
Renfrew
Port
Alberti

Horseshoe Bay
Vancouver
Hammond
Mission
City
Hope Princeton 120
Agassiz
Chilliwack
Blaine
Ferndale
Bellingham
Abbotsford
North
Cascades
Ross L.
Mt Baker
3285
Burlington
Marysville
Everett
Snohomish
Mt Vernon
Concrete
Skagit
Glacier Peak
3221
Monroe
Snoqualmie
Pass
Tacoma
Puyallup
Mt Rainier
4392
Mount Rainier
Nat. Park
Naches
Ellensburg
Mt St Helens
2950
Mt Adams
3751
White
Salmon
Vancouver
Camas
Gresham
Oregon City
Woodburn
Mt Wilson
1707
Mt Hood
3427
Hood
River
The Dalles
Stayton
Idanha
Mt Jefferson
3199
Madras
Prineville
Three Sisters
3156
Bend
Redmond
La Pine
Crescent
High
Desert
Silver Lake
Chiloquin
Mt Thielsen
2799
Crater L.
Nat. Pk
Mt Scott
2721
Upper
Klamath
L.
Mt
McLoughlin
2894
Klamath
Falls
Dorris
Clear L.
Resr
Canby
Mt Shasta
4317
Mount
Shasta
Dunsmuir
Burney
CALIFORNIA
Shasta
L.
Project City
Redding
Lassen Pk
Nat. Pk 3167

Lakeview
Willow Ranch
Goose L.
Upper L.
Middle
Alturas
Alkali L.
Adin
Pit
Eagle L.
Susanville

Princeton 120
Keremeos
Okanagan
Oliver
Osoyoos
Oroville
Mt Logan
2733
Nat.
Park
Brewster
Okanogan
Omak
Chelan
Chelan
Wenatchee
Ephrata
Odessa
Moses Lake
Ritzville
Othello
Eltopia
Toppenish
Sunnyside
Kennewick
Goldendale
Columbia
Arlington
Echo
Pendleton
Condon
Ukiah
Spray
Long Creek
Dayville
Canyon City
John Day
Burns
Drewsey
Crane
Harney Basin
Harney L.
Malheur L.
Jordan
Valley
Denio
Mc Dermitt

Castlegar Salmo
Ⓒ
Grand
Forks
Trail
Creston
Metaline
Falls
Bonners
Ferry
Colville
Priest
L.
Sandpoint
Franklin
D. Roosevelt
Lake
Newport
Priest
River
Spirit L.
Coeur
d'Alene
Spokane
Medical
Lake
Cheney
Plummer
Coeur
d'Alene
Kellogg
St Joe
Maies
Colfax
Potlatch
Moscow
Kendrick
Pullman
Clarkston
Lewiston
Dayton
Walla
Walla
Umatilla
Wallowa
Enterprise
La Grande
Sacajawea
Pk
2997
Baker
Unity
Weiser
Payette
Ontario
Vale
Nyssa
Emmett
Caldwell
Nampa
Murphy
Winnemucca
Golconda
Battle
Mountain
Mt Tobin
2979

WASHINGTON

C A N A D A

2627
Lakeview
Mt
2366

Skagit Mtn
2366

CASCADE RANGE

C O L U M B I A

Yakima

Wenatchee

Snake

Grande Ronde

He
Devil
Mtn
2863
Hells Canyon

Blue Mountains

Wallowa
Mts

COLUMBIA PLATEAU

John Day

Deschutes

Brothers

Steens Mtn

Black Rock Desert

Warner Mts

Santa Rosa Ra.

Owyhee Mts

Owyhee

Humboldt

Rye Patch
Resr

Imlay

N E V A D A

O R E G O N

COAST RANGE

Willamette

Umpqua

Rogue

Klamath

Klamath
Mts

I D A H O

45

125

Ⓐ
①

②

Ⓑ

Ⓒ
①

45

120

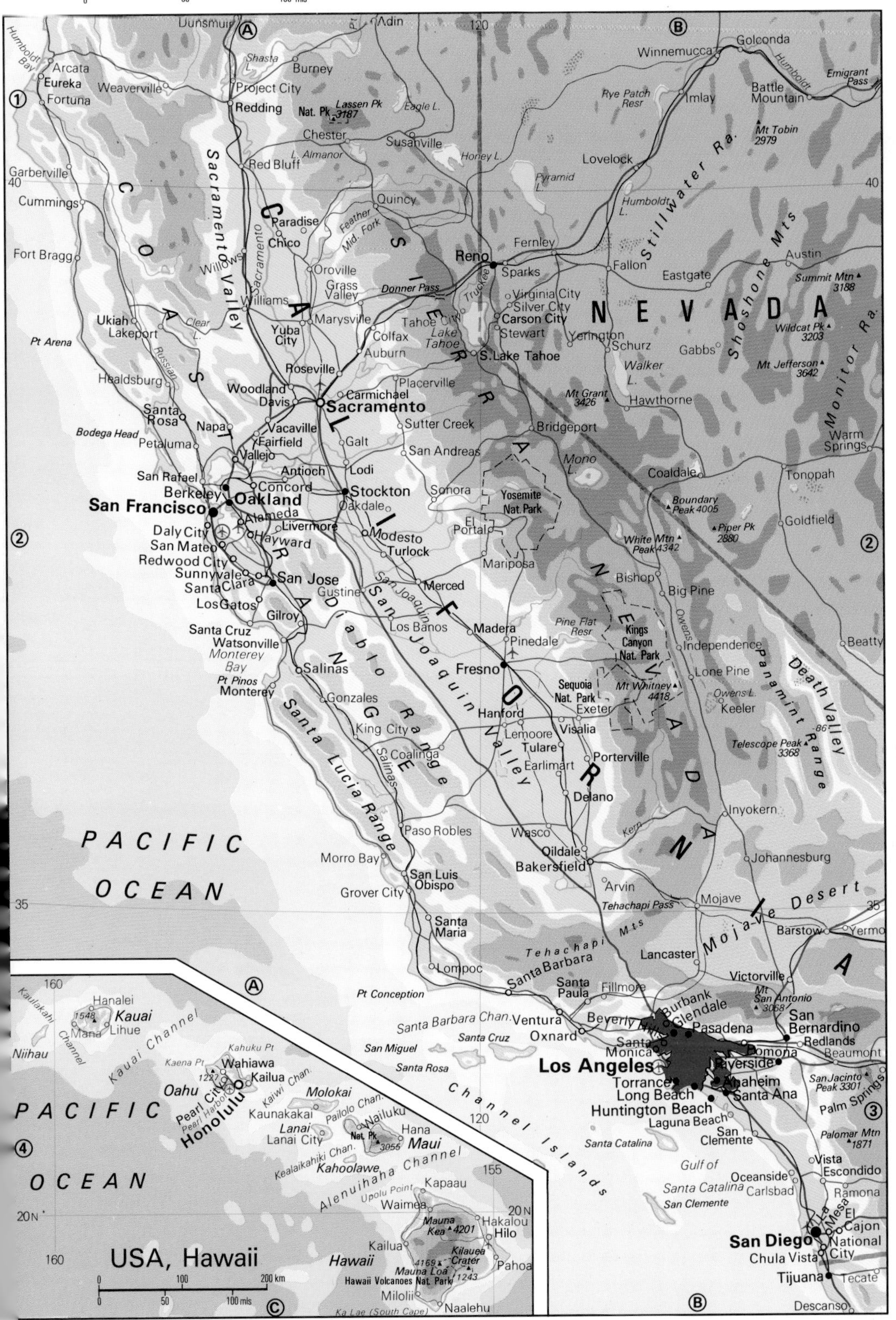
Dunsmuir
Adin
Humboldt Bay
Arcata
Eureka
Fortuna
Weaverville
Shasta L.
Burney
Project City
Redding
Nat. Pk
Lassen Pk 3187
Eagle L.
Chester
Susanville
L. Almanor
Red Bluff
Honey L.
Winnemucca
Golconda
Humboldt
Emigrant Pass
Rye Patch Resr
Imlay
Battle Mountain
Mt Tobin 2979
Lovelock
Pyramid L.
Stillwater Ra.
Humboldt L.
Shoshone Mts
Garberville
Cummings
Sacramento Valley
Sacramento
Quincy
Feather Mid. Fork
Paradise
Chico
Fort Bragg
Willows
Oroville
Grass Valley
Donner Pass
Truckee
Reno
Sparks
Fernley
Fallon
Eastgate
Austin
Summit Mtn 3188
Virginia City
Silver City
Carson City
Stewart
NEVADA
Wildcat Pk 3203
Williams
Marysville
Yuba City
Colfax
Tahoe City
Lake Tahoe
Yerington
Schurz
Gabbs
Monitor Ra.
Mt Jefferson 3642
Ukiah
Lakeport
Clear L.
Pt Arena
Russian
Auburn
S. Lake Tahoe
Walker L.
Healdsburg
Roseville
Placerville
Woodland
Davis
Carmichael
Sacramento
Mt Grant 3426
Hawthorne
Santa Rosa
Bodega Head
Napa
Vacaville
Fairfield
Sutter Creek
Bridgeport
Warm Springs
Petaluma
Vallejo
Galt
San Andreas
Mono L.
San Rafael
Antioch
Lodi
Coaldale
Tonopah
Berkeley
Concord
Oakland
Stockton
Sonora
Yosemite Nat. Park
Boundary Peak 4005
San Francisco
Alameda
Oakdale
Daly City
Livermore
Modesto
El Portal
Piper Pk 2880
Goldfield
San Mateo
Hayward
Turlock
White Mtn Peak 4342
Redwood City
Mariposa
Sunnyvale
Santa Clara
San Jose
Merced
Bishop
Big Pine
Los Gatos
Gustine
San Joaquin
Gilroy
Los Banos
Madera
Pine Flat Resr
Kings Canyon Nat. Park
Owens
Santa Cruz
Watsonville
Monterey Bay
Pinedale
Independence
Beatty
Fresno
Lone Pine
Pt Pinos
Monterey
Salinas
Diablo Range
San Joaquin Valley
Sequoia Nat. Park
Mt Whitney 4418
Owens L.
Keeler
Panamint Range
Death Valley
Gonzales
Hanford
Exeter
Santa Lucia Range
King City
Lemoore
Visalia
Tulare
Telescope Peak 3368
Salinas
Coalinga
Earlimart
Porterville
Delano
Inyokern
PACIFIC OCEAN
Paso Robles
Wasco
Kern
Morro Bay
Oildale
Bakersfield
Johannesburg
San Luis Obispo
Arvin
Grover City
Tehachapi Pass
Mojave
Mojave Desert
Santa Maria
Tehachapi Mts
Barstow
Yermo
Lancaster
Lompoc
Santa Barbara
Victorville
Pt Conception
Santa Paula
Fillmore
Mt San Antonio 3068
Santa Barbara Chan.
Ventura
Burbank
Glendale
Pasadena
San Bernardino
San Miguel
Santa Cruz
Oxnard
Beverly Hills
Santa Monica
Redlands
Pomona
Beaumont
Santa Rosa
Los Angeles
Riverside
San Jacinto Peak 3301
Channel Islands
Torrance
Anaheim
Long Beach
Santa Ana
Palm Springs
Huntington Beach
Laguna Beach
San Clemente
Palomar Mtn 1871
Santa Catalina
Gulf of Santa Catalina
Oceanside
Vista
Escondido
Carlsbad
San Clemente
Ramona
La Mesa
El Cajon
San Diego
National City
Chula Vista
Tijuana
Tecate
Descanso
CALIFORNIA
SIERRA NEVADA
COAST RANGES
Kaulakahi Channel
Hanalei
1548
Kauai
Mana
Lihue
Niihau
Kauai Channel
Kahuku Pt
Kaena Pt
Wahiawa
1227
Kailua
Oahu
Kaiwi Chan.
Molokai
Pearl City
Pearl Harbor
Honolulu
Kaunakakai
Pailolo Chan.
Wailuku
Lanai
Lanai City
Nat. Pk
3055
Hana
Maui
Kealaikahiki Chan.
Kahoolawe
Alenuihaha Channel
PACIFIC OCEAN
Upolu Point
Kapaau
Waimea
Mauna Kea 4201
Hakalou
Hilo
Kailua
Kilauea Crater
Hawaii
4169
Mauna Loa
1243
Pahoa
Hawaii Volcanoes Nat. Park
Milolii
Naalehu
Ka Lae (South Cape)
USA, Hawaii
0 100 200 km
0 50 100 mls

1:2.5M

0 25 50 75 100 km
0 25 50 mls

Lytton (A) Calistoga
Healdsburg L.Berryessa Woodland Folsom Placerville
Forestville St Helena Winters Davis Diamond Springs Camino (C)
Santa Rosa Yountville Vacaville Sacramento Carmichael Markleeville Coleville
Sebastopol Sonoma Napa Elmira Plymouth Highland Pk 3333 Topaz
Petaluma Fairfield Dixon Elk Grove Sutter Ck West Pt Bear Valley Devils Gate 2301
Galt Jackson Mokelumne Dardanelle Bridgeport Resr
Clements Mokelumne Hill Arnold Sonora Pass 2933 Bridgeport
Novato Vallejo Isleton Lodi San Andreas Pinecrest
San Rafael Pittsburg Antioch Angels Camp Murphys Mather Excelsior Mtn 3790
Mill Valley Richmond Concord Oakley Bellota Sonora L.Eleanor Tioga Pass Mt Dana 3978
Berkeley Mt Diablo Brentwood Stockton Melones Resr Groveland Tuolumne Mdws Mt Lyell 3991
San Francisco Oakland Byron Farmington Resr Oakdale Don Pedro Resr Coulterville El Portal Mt Ritter 4010
Alameda San Leandro Tracy Ripon Modesto Riverbank Modesto Resr Wawona Fish Camp
Daly City Hayward Manteca Ceres Turlock L.McClure Mariposa Mammoth Pool Resr
S.San Francisco Fremont Patterson Turlock Snelling Yosemite Bass Lake Kaiser Pk 3146
San Mateo Pleasanton Newman Merced Merced Planada Lakeshore Huntington L.
Redwood City Mountain View Coyote Gustine Atwater Merced Mariposa Raymond Chowchilla Pinedale Huntington L.
Palo Alto Sunnyvale San Jose Vol Los Banos Berenda Madera Friant Piedra
Santa Clara Los Gatos Dos Palos Firebaugh Herndon Clovis Minkler
Pescadero Boulder Creek Morgan Hill Gilroy S.Luis Resr Mendota Kerman Sanger Badger
Davenport Soquel Hollister Tres Pinos Helm Selma Reedley
Santa Cruz Watsonville San Juan Bautista Alisal Fresno Kingsburg Dinuba
Monterey Bay Castroville Salinas Pinnacles N.M. Kingsburg (C)
Pacific Grove Seaside Monterey Gonzales (B)
Carmel Carmel Valley

(B) Los Alamos Big Pine Mtn 2081 Gorman (C) (D) Helendale
Sta Ynez Lompoc Buellton Los Olivos San Rafael Mts Lake Hughes Rosamond L. Lancaster
Pt Arguello Solvang L.Cachuma Piru Cr Mirage L. Adelanto Victorville
Pt Conception Gaviota Goleta Santa Ynez Mts Ojai Fillmore Castaic Acton Wrightwood Hesperia
Santa Barbara Santa Paula Newhall San Gabriel Mts Mt San Antonio 3068 San Bernardino
Ventura Moorpark San Fernando Mt Wilson 1740 Pasadena Upland Highland
San Miguel Santa Barbara Channel Oxnard Camarillo Burbank Glendale Monrovia Pomona Ontario Colton Redlands
Santa Rosa Santa Cruz Anacapa Is Los Angeles Hollywood Beverly Hills Inglewood Whittier Riverside
Santa Cruz Chan. Santa Monica Torrance Lakewood Fullerton Anaheim Corona Perris
C h a n n e l Santa Monica Bay Redondo Beach Long Beach Garden Grove Orange Santa Ana Santiago Pk 1736 Elsinore
I s l a n d s Huntington Beach Newport Beach Costa Mesa
Santa Barbara Laguna Beach San Onofre Fall-brook
San Nicolas San Pedro Channel San Clemente Vista
Santa Catalina Avalon Oceanside
Outer Santa Barbara Channel Gulf of Santa Catalina Carlsbad
P A C I F I C Encinitas
Del Mar
San Clemente La Jolla
O C E A N San Diego

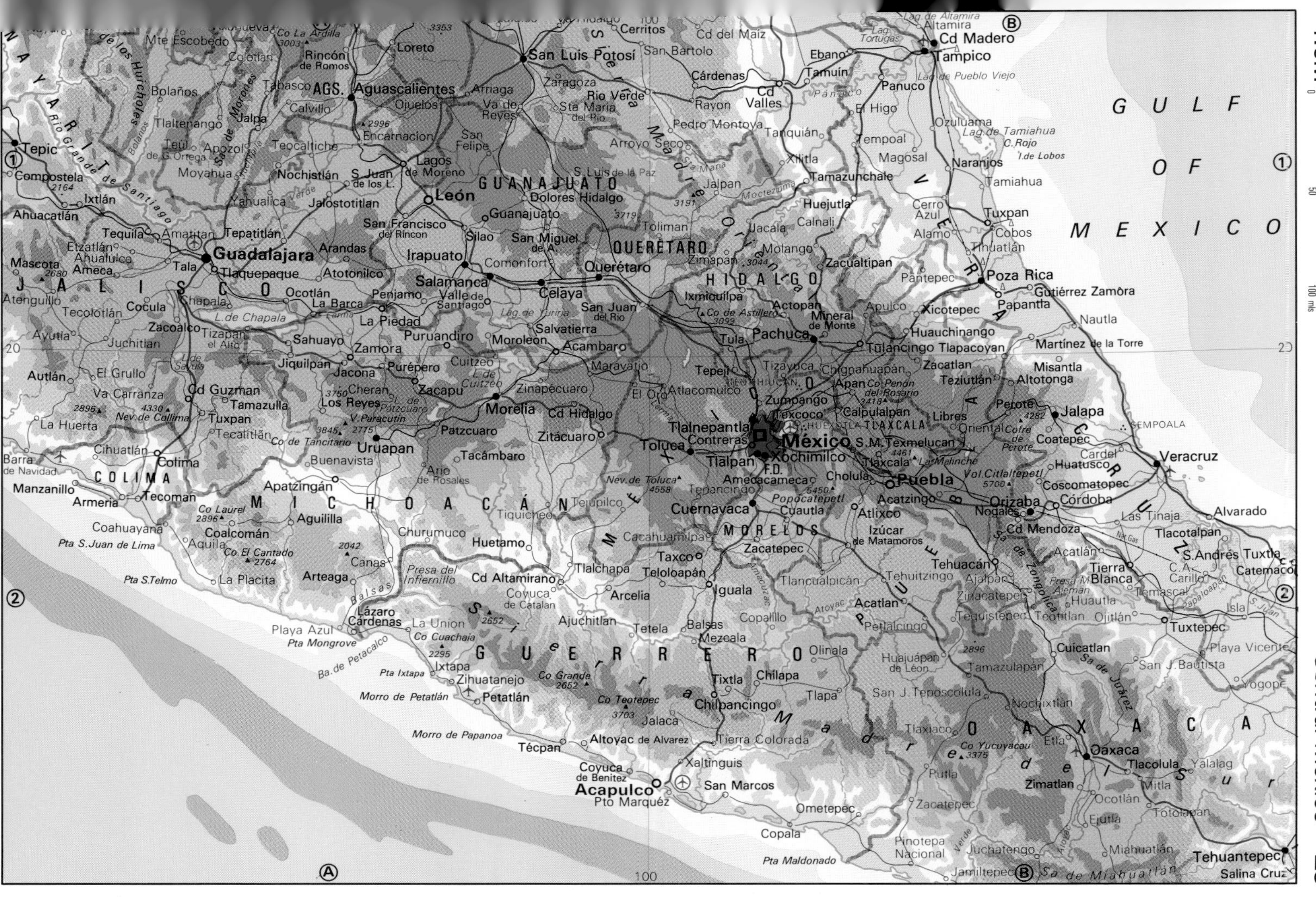

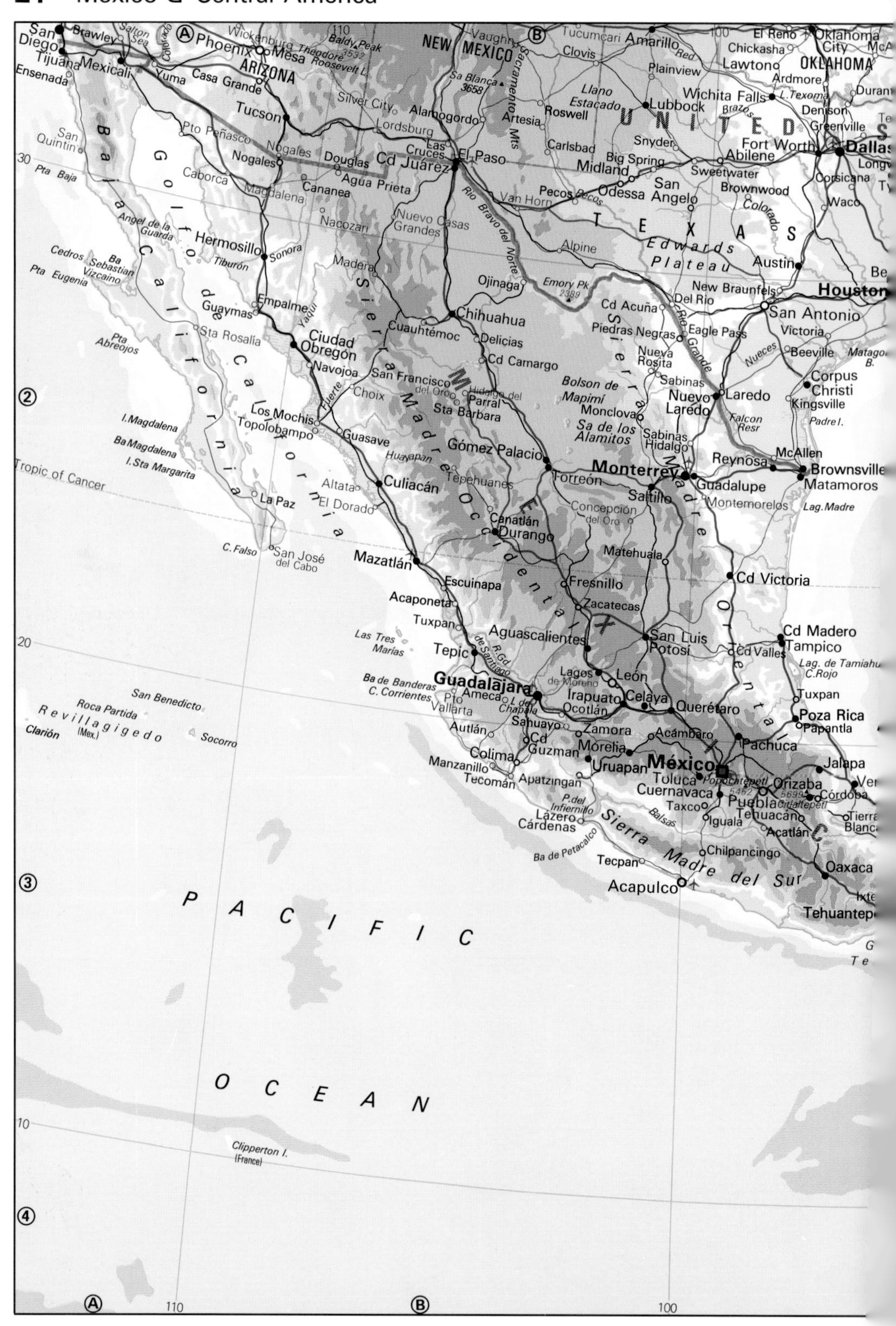
San Diego
Tijuana
Ensenada
Mexicali
Brawley
Yuma
Phoenix
Mesa
ARIZONA
Casa Grande
Tucson
Nogales
Douglas
Agua Prieta
Cananea
Nacozari
Caborca
Magdalena
Pto Peñasco
San Quintín
Pta Baja
Hermosillo
Sonora
Guaymas
Empalme
Ciudad Obregón
Navojoa
Los Mochis
Topolobampo
Guasave
Culiacán
Altata
El Dorado
Mazatlán
La Paz
San José del Cabo
C. Falso
Sta Rosalía
Cedros
Pta Eugenia
Ba Sebastian Vizcaino
Pta Abreojos
I. Magdalena
Ba Magdalena
I. Sta Margarita
Tropic of Cancer
Golfo de California
Baja California
NEW MEXICO
Silver City
Alamogordo
Artesia
Roswell
Lordsburg
Las Cruces
El Paso
Cd Juárez
Nuevo Casas Grandes
Madera
Chihuahua
Cuauhtémoc
Delicias
Cd Camargo
Ojinaga
Parral
Sta Barbara
Hidalgo del Parral
San Francisco del Oro
Sierra Madre Occidental
Sierra Madre Oriental
Sierra Madre del Sur
MEXICO
Gómez Palacio
Torreón
Durango
Canatlán
Tepehuanes
Escuinapa
Acaponeta
Tuxpan
Tepic
Las Tres Marías
Fresnillo
Zacatecas
Aguascalientes
San Luis Potosí
Matehuala
Saltillo
Monterrey
Guadalupe
Montemorelos
Monclova
Bolson de Mapimí
Sa de los Alamitos
Sabinas Hidalgo
Nuevo Laredo
Laredo
Reynosa
McAllen
Brownsville
Matamoros
Lag. Madre
Cd Victoria
Cd Madero
Tampico
Cd Valles
Tuxpan
Poza Rica
Papantla
Jalapa
Orizaba
Córdoba
Guadalajara
Ameca
Pto Vallarta
Autlán
Colima
Manzanillo
Tecomán
Cd Guzman
Sahuayo
Zamora
Morelia
Uruapan
Apatzingan
Lagos de Moreno
León
Irapuato
Celaya
Querétaro
Acámbaro
Pachuca
México
Toluca
Cuernavaca
Taxco
Puebla
Tehuacán
Iguala
Chilpancingo
Acapulco
Tecpan
Lázaro Cárdenas
Oaxaca
Acatlán
Revillagigedo (Mex.)
Roca Partida
San Benedicto
Socorro
Clarión
Clipperton I. (France)
PACIFIC OCEAN
UNITED STATES
TEXAS
OKLAHOMA
Amarillo
Tucumcari
Clovis
Plainview
Lubbock
Llano Estacado
Wichita Falls
Lawton
Chickasha
Oklahoma City
Ardmore
Denison
Greenville
Dallas
Fort Worth
Abilene
Sweetwater
Snyder
Big Spring
Midland
Odessa
San Angelo
Carlsbad
Pecos
Van Horn
Alpine
Brownwood
Corsicana
Waco
Austin
Houston
San Antonio
New Braunfels
Del Rio
Edwards Plateau
Cd Acuña
Piedras Negras
Eagle Pass
Nueva Rosita
Sabinas
Victoria
Beeville
Corpus Christi
Kingsville
Padre I.
Falcon Resr
Rio Bravo del Norte
Rio Grande
110
100
30
20
10

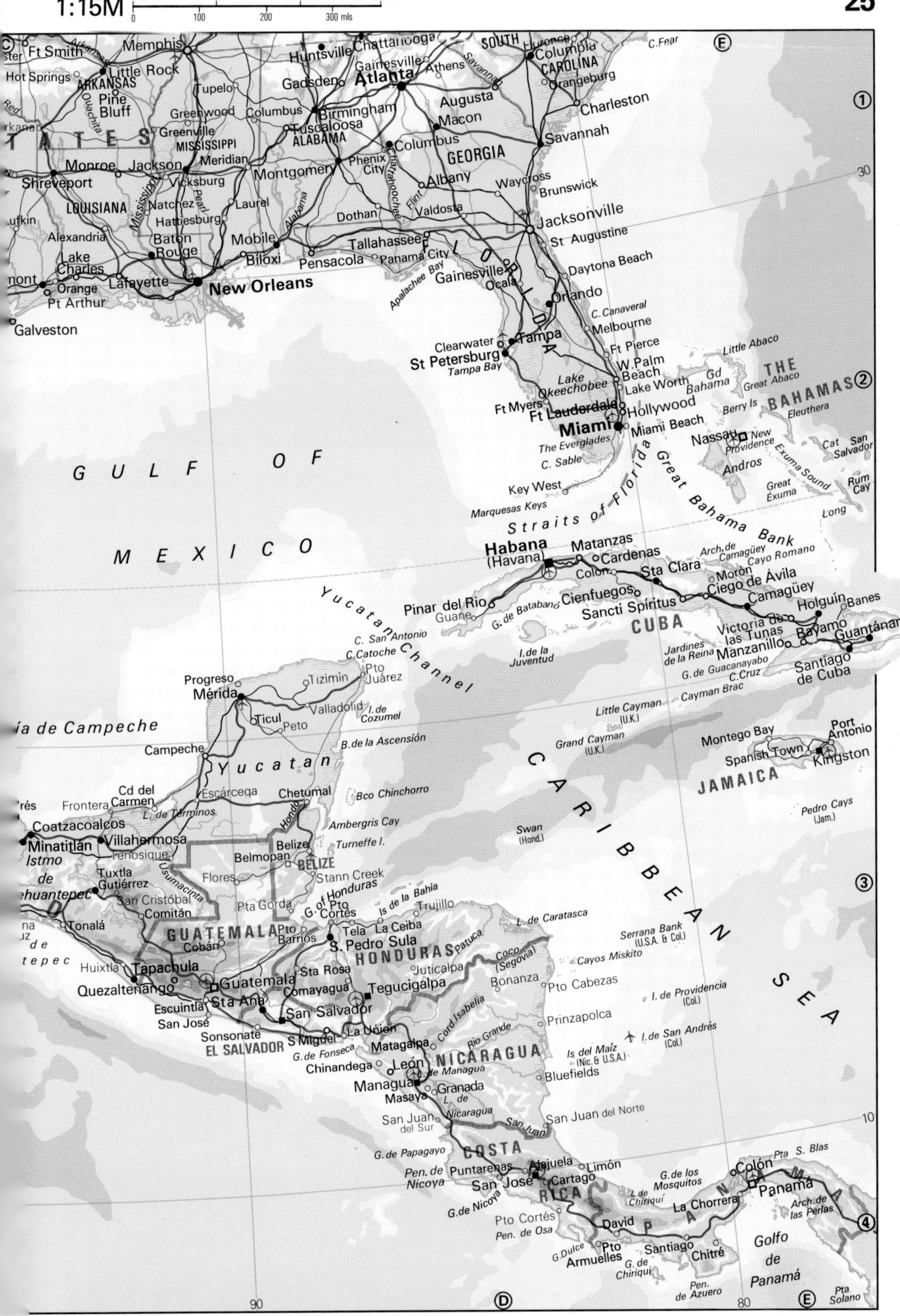

1:15M

200   400   600 km
100   200   300 mls

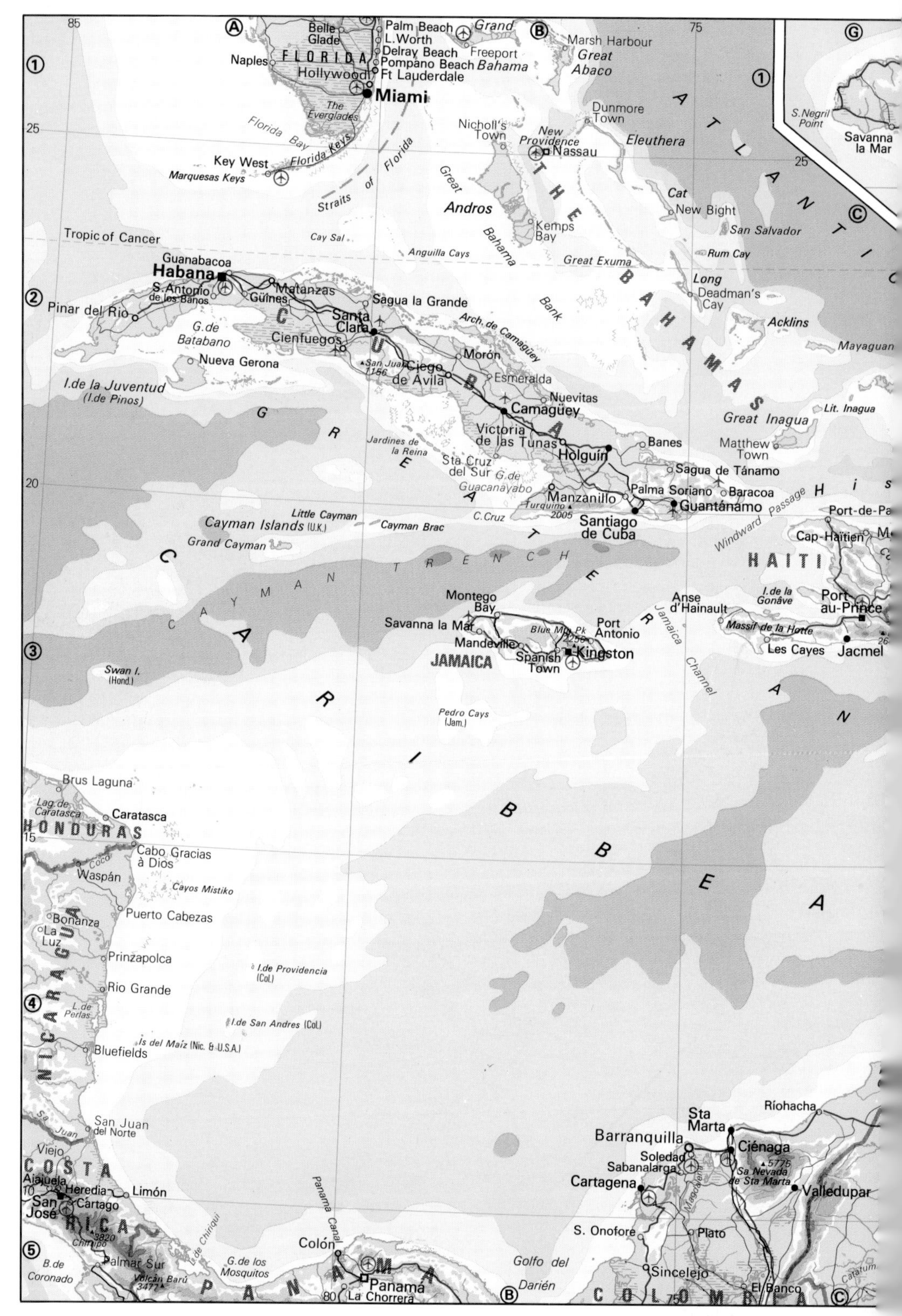

26 Caribbean

A · **B** · **G**

FLORIDA
Naples
Belle Glade
Palm Beach
L. Worth
Delray Beach
Pompano Beach
Ft Lauderdale
Hollywood
Miami
The Everglades
Florida Bay

Grand Bahama
Freeport
Marsh Harbour
Great Abaco

S. Negril Point
Savanna la Mar

Key West
Marquesas Keys
Florida Keys
Straits of Florida

Nicholl's Town
New Providence
Nassau
Dunmore Town
Eleuthera

Tropic of Cancer
Cay Sal
Anguilla Cays

Andros
Great Bahama Bank
Kemps Bay

Cat
New Bight
San Salvador

THE BAHAMAS

Guanabacoa
Habana
S. Antonio de los Baños
Güines
Matanzas
Sagua la Grande
Arch. de Camagüey

Rum Cay
Long
Deadman's Cay
Acklins
Mayaguan

Pinar del Río
G. de Batabano
Santa Clara
Cienfuegos

Nueva Gerona
San Juan 1156
Ciego de Avila
Morón
Esmeralda
Nuevitas

C U B A

I. de la Juventud
(I. de Pinos)

Camagüey
Victoria de las Tunas
Banes
Great Inagua
Lit. Inagua

Jardines de la Reina
Sta Cruz del Sur
G. de Guacanayabo
Holguín
Matthew Town

Little Cayman
Cayman Islands (U.K.)
Cayman Brac
Grand Cayman

C. Cruz
Turquino 2005
Manzanillo
Palma Soriano
Santiago de Cuba
Sagua de Tánamo
Baracoa
Guantánamo

Windward Passage
Port-de-Pa
Cap-Haïtien
HAITI

CAYMAN TRENCH

Montego Bay
Savanna la Mar
Mandeville
JAMAICA
Spanish Town
Kingston
Blue Mtn Pk 2256
Port Antonio

Jamaica Channel
I. de la Gonâve
Massif de la Hotte
Les Cayes
Port-au-Prince
Jacmel
26

C A R I B B E A N

Swan I. (Hond.)

Pedro Cays (Jam.)

Brus Laguna
Lag. de Caratasca
Caratasca

HONDURAS
Cabo Gracias à Dios
Cayos Mistiko
Waspán
Puerto Cabezas

I. de Providencia (Col.)

Bonanza
La Luz
Prinzapolca
Rio Grande

NICARAGUA
I. de Perlas

I. de San Andres (Col.)

Is del Maíz (Nic. & U.S.A.)
Bluefields

San Juan del Norte

Río Hacha
Sta Marta
Barranquilla
Ciénaga
Soledad
Sabanalarga
Sa Nevada de Sta Marta 5775
Valledupar

Viejo
COSTA RICA
Alajuela
Heredia
Cartago
San José
Chirripó
B. de Coronado
Palmar Sur
Volcán Barú 3471

Limón

Cartagena
S. Onofore
Plato
El Banco
Sincelejo

Panamá Canal
Colón
PANAMA
Panamá
La Chorrera
Golfo del Darién
COLOMBIA

ATLANTIC OCEAN

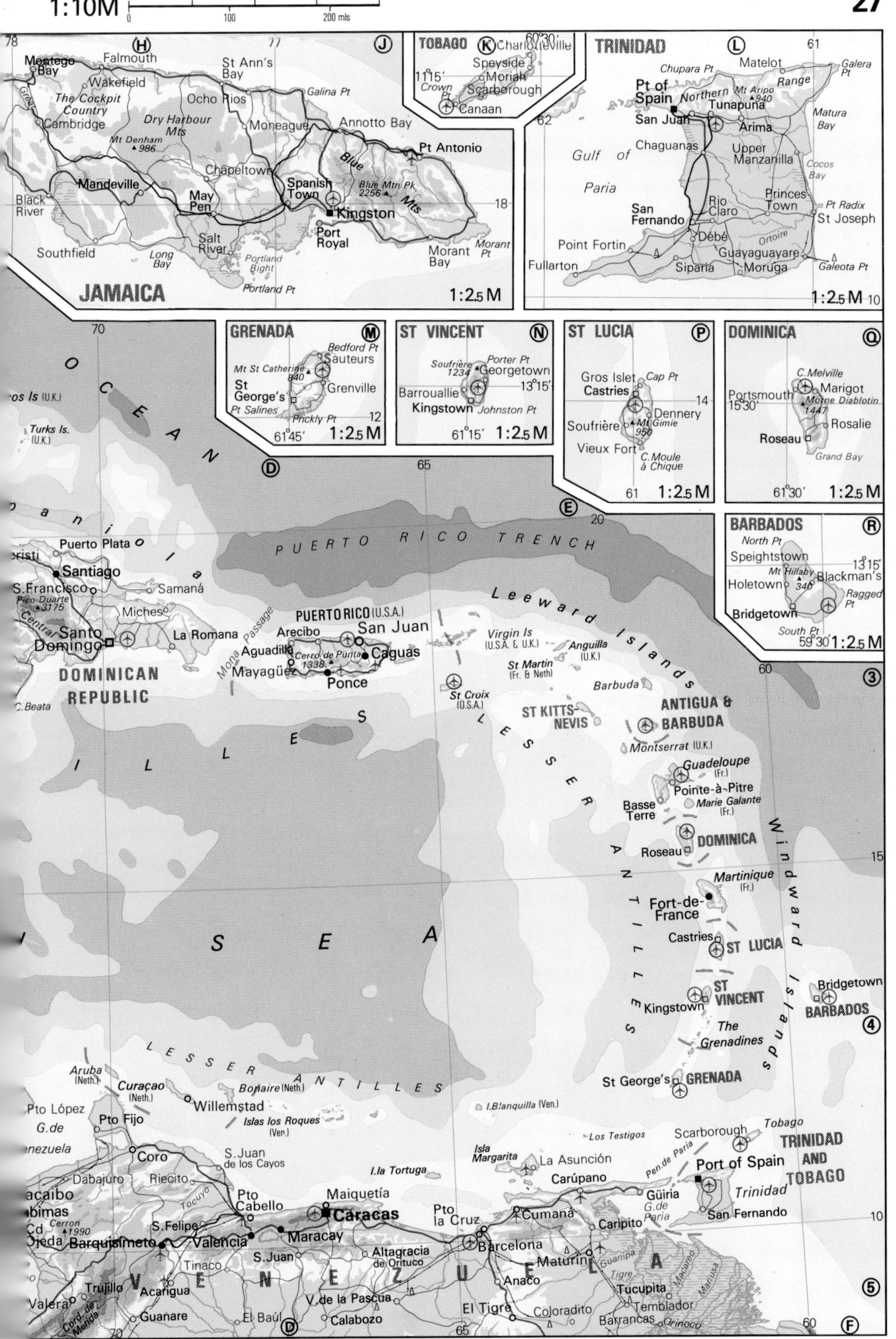

1:10M

100   200   300   400 km
0
100   200 mls

JAMAICA

78   (H)   77   18   77

Montego Bay   Falmouth   St Ann's Bay   Galina Pt
Wakefield   Ocho Rios
The Cockpit Country   Dry Harbour Mts
Cambridge   Moneague   Annotto Bay
Mt Denham ▲ 986   Chapelton   Pt Antonio
Mandeville   Blue Mtn Pk 2256 ▲   Blue Mts
May Pen   Spanish Town
Black River   Salt River   ■ Kingston   Morant Pt
Southfield   Long Bay   Port Royal
Portland Bight   Morant Bay
Portland Pt

1:2.5 M

TOBAGO   **TRINIDAD**

(J)   **TOBAGO**   (K)   Charlotteville   60°30'   (L)   61
Speyside   Matelot   Galera Pt
Moriah   Chupara Pt   Mt Aripo ▲ 940   Range
1°15'   Scarborough   Pt of Spain   Northern   Tunapuna   Matura Bay
Crown   Canaan   San Juan   Arima
62   Chaguanas   Upper Manzanilla   Cocos Bay
Gulf of Paria   Rio Claro   Princes Town   Pt Radix St Joseph
San Fernando   Débé   Ortoire
Point Fortin   Guayaguayare
Fullarton   Siparia   Moruga   Galeota Pt

1:2.5 M   10

GRENADA   (M)   **ST VINCENT**   (N)   **ST LUCIA**   (P)   **DOMINICA**   (Q)

70   Bedford Pt   Porter Pt   Cap Pt
Mt St Catherine 840   Sauteurs   Soufrière 1234   Georgetown   Gros Islet   14   C.Melville   Marigot
St George's   Grenville   13°15'   Castries   Portsmouth   Morne Diablotin   Rosalie
Pt Salines   Barrouallie   Dennery   15°30'   1447
Prickly Pt   12   Kingstown   Johnston Pt   Soufrière   Mt Gimie   Roseau
Turks Is (U.K.)   61°45'   1:2.5 M   61°15'   1:2.5 M   Vieux Fort   950   Grand Bay   61°30'   1:2.5 M
(D)   65   (E)   20   C.Moule à Chique   61   1:2.5 M

BARBADOS   (R)

North Pt   13°15'
Speightstown   Mt Hillaby ▲ 340   Blackman's
Holetown   Ragged Pt
Bridgetown   59°30'   1:2.5 M
South Pt

(3)

O C E A N

Turks Is (U.K.)

Puerto Plata   Samaná
S.Francisco   Michés
Santiago   La Romana
Pico Duarte ▲ 3175   Santo Domingo
Central   **DOMINICAN REPUBLIC**
C. Beata

Mona Passage

PUERTO RICO (U.S.A.)
Arecibo   San Juan
Aguadilla   Caguas
Mayagüez   Cerro de Punta 1338   Ponce

P U E R T O   R I C O   T R E N C H

Virgin Is (U.S.A. & U.K.)   Anguilla (U.K.)
St Martin (Fr. & Neth.)
St Croix (U.S.A.)   Barbuda

L e e w a r d   I s l a n d s

ST KITTS-NEVIS   **ANTIGUA & BARBUDA**
Montserrat (U.K.)
Guadeloupe (Fr.)
Pointe-à-Pitre   Marie Galante (Fr.)
Basse Terre
Roseau   **DOMINICA**
Martinique (Fr.)   15
Fort-de-France
Castries   **ST LUCIA**
Kingstown   **ST VINCENT**   Bridgetown   60
The Grenadines   **BARBADOS**
St George's   **GRENADA**   4

L E S S E R   A N T I L L E S

C A R I B B E A N   S E A

W i n d w a r d   I s l a n d s

Aruba (Neth.)   L E S S E R   A N T I L L E S
Curaçao (Neth.)   Bonaire (Neth.)
Willemstad   I.Blanquilla (Ven.)
Islas los Roques (Ven.)
Los Testigos   Scarborough   **TRINIDAD AND TOBAGO**
Pto López   Pto Fijo   I.la Tortuga   Isla Margarita   La Asunción   Tobago
G.de   Coro   Carúpano   Port of Spain
Venezuela   S.Juan de los Cayos   Maiquetía   Güiria   Trinidad
Dabajuro   Riecito   Pto Cabello   Pto la Cruz   G.de Paria   San Fernando
racaibo   Cerro ▲ 1990   ● **Caracas**   Cumaná   Caripito
abimas   S.Felipe   Maracay   Barcelona   Maturín   10
cd   Valencia   S.Juan   Altagracia de Orituco   Anaco   Tigre
jeda   Barquisimeto   Tinaco   Coloradito   Tucupita   60
Valera   Acarigua   V. de la Pascua   El Tigre   Barrancas   (F)
Trujillo   V E N E Z U E L A   Anaco   Orinoco
Guanare   El Baúl   Calabozo   5
Cord de Mérida   (D)   65

1°15'

1:40M

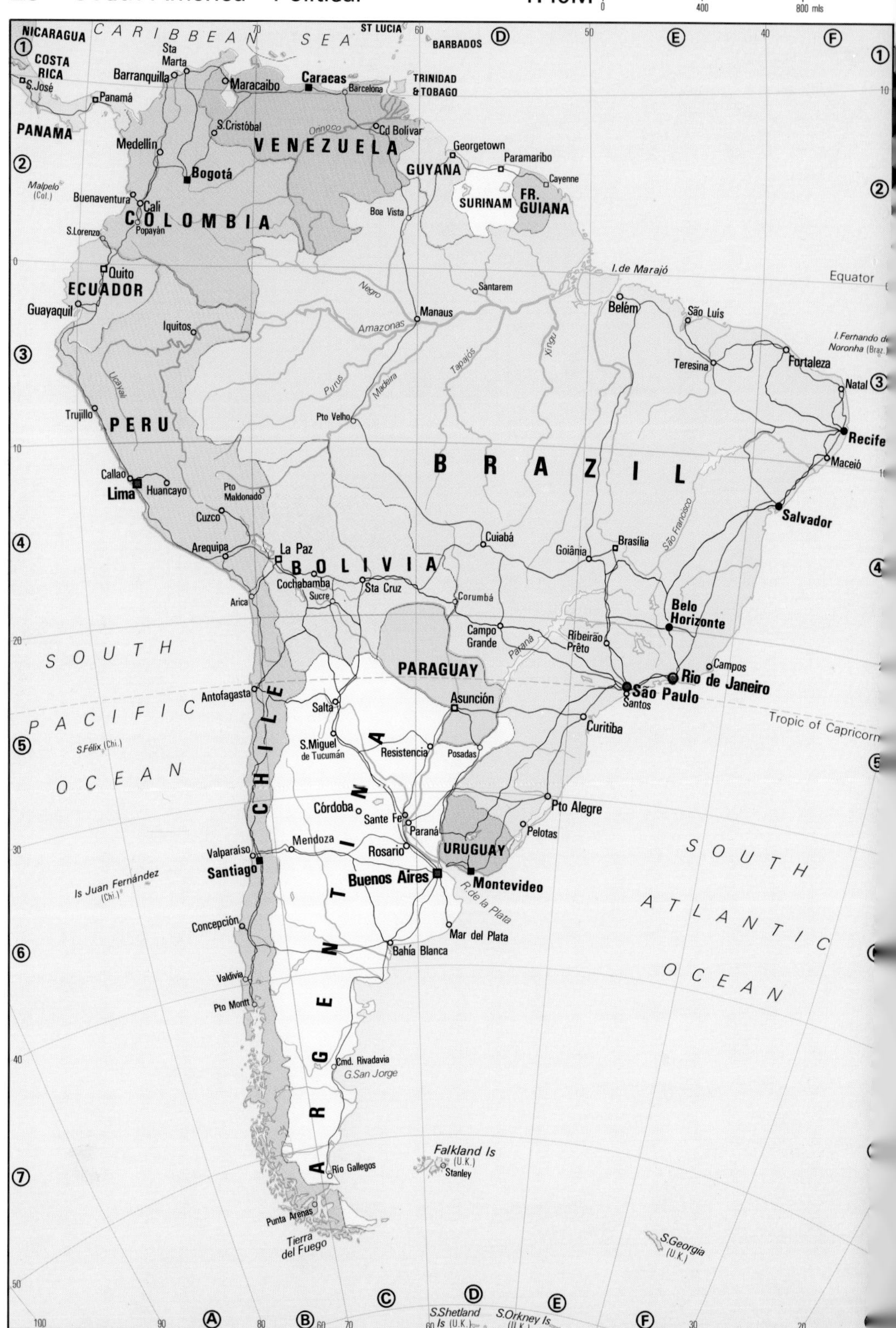
0 400 800 1200 1600 km
0 400 800 mls
CARIBBEAN SEA
NICARAGUA
COSTA RICA
S.José
Panamá
PANAMA
Barranquilla
Sta Marta
Maracaibo
Caracas
Barcelona
ST LUCIA
BARBADOS
TRINIDAD & TOBAGO
S.Cristóbal
Cd Bolívar
Orinoco
VENEZUELA
Medellín
Bogotá
Georgetown
Paramaribo
Cayenne
GUYANA
SURINAM
FR. GUIANA
Malpelo (Col.)
Buenaventura
Cali
Popayán
COLOMBIA
Boa Vista
S.Lorenzo
Quito
ECUADOR
Guayaquil
I.de Marajó
Equator
Santarem
Negro
Manaus
Amazonas
Belém
São Luís
Iquitos
I.Fernando de Noronha (Braz.)
Teresina
Fortaleza
Natal
Xingu
Tapajós
Purus
Madeira
Ucayali
Trujillo
PERU
Pto Velho
Recife
Maceió
BRAZIL
Callao
Lima
Huancayo
Pto Maldonado
Cuzco
Salvador
São Francisco
Cuiabá
Goiânia
Brasília
Arequipa
La Paz
BOLIVIA
Cochabamba
Sucre
Sta Cruz
Corumbá
Arica
Belo Horizonte
Campo Grande
Paraná
Ribeirão Prêto
SOUTH PACIFIC OCEAN
PARAGUAY
Campos
Rio de Janeiro
São Paulo
Santos
Antofagasta
Salta
Asunción
Tropic of Capricorn
Curitiba
S.Félix (Chi.)
S.Miguel de Tucumán
Resistencia
Posadas
CHILE
ARGENTINA
Pto Alegre
Córdoba
Sante Fe
Paraná
Pelotas
Valparaíso
Mendoza
Rosario
URUGUAY
Santiago
Buenos Aires
Montevideo
Is Juan Fernández (Chi.)
R de la Plata
SOUTH ATLANTIC OCEAN
Concepción
Mar del Plata
Bahía Blanca
Valdivia
Pto Montt
Cmd. Rivadavia
G.San Jorge
Falkland Is (U.K.)
Stanley
Río Gallegos
Punta Arenas
Tierra del Fuego
S.Georgia (U.K.)
S.Shetland Is (U.K.)
S.Orkney Is (U.K.)
A B C D E F
1 2 3 4 5 6 7
100 90 80 70 60 50 40 30 20 10

1:15M

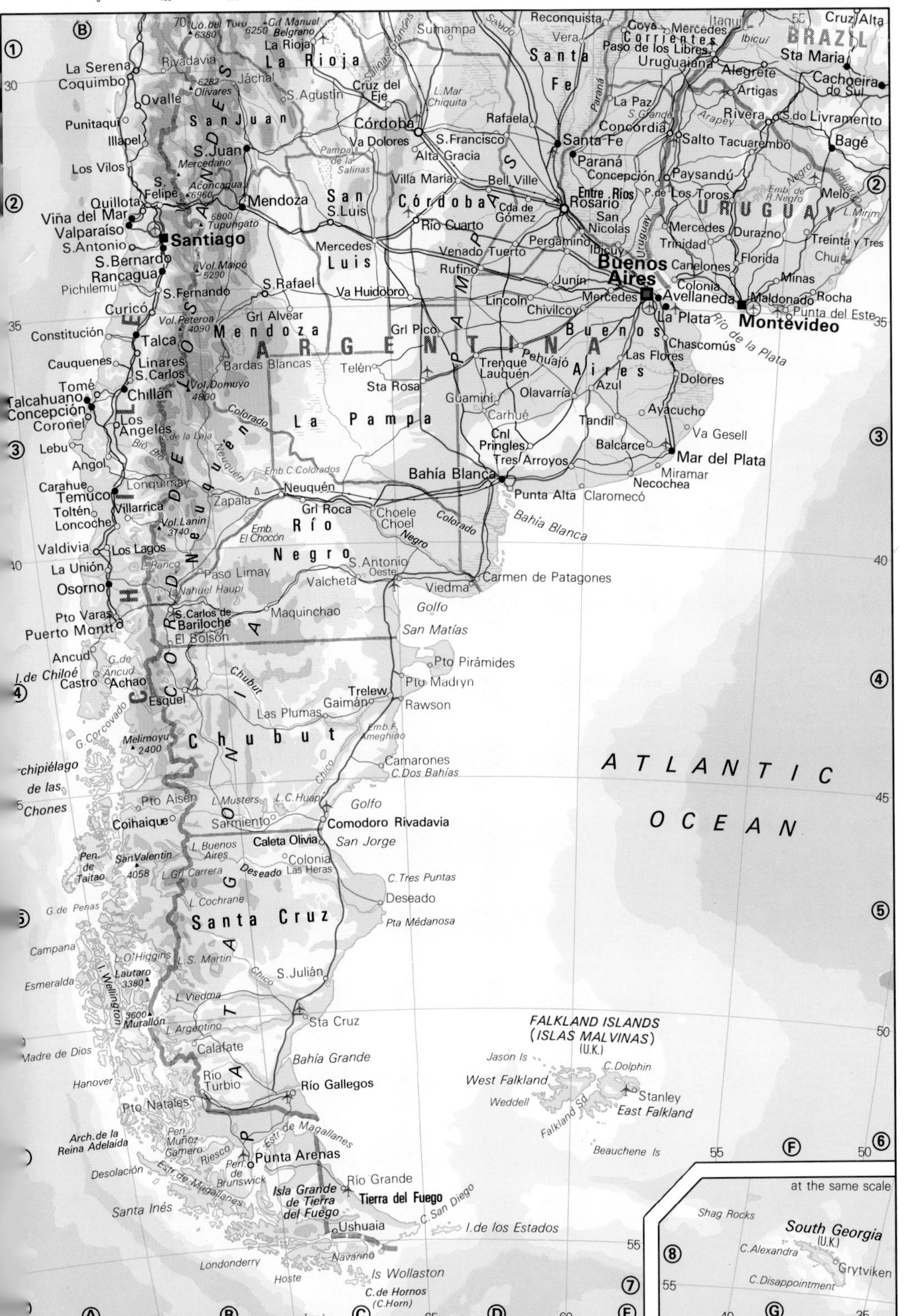

ATLANTIC

OCEAN

ARGENTINA

URUGUAY

BRAZIL

La Pampa

Mendoza

San Luis

Córdoba

Santa Fe

Entre Ríos

Buenos Aires

Río Negro

Chubut

Santa Cruz

PATAGONIA

Buenos Aires
Avellaneda
La Plata
Montevideo

Santiago

FALKLAND ISLANDS
(ISLAS MALVINAS)
(U.K.)

West Falkland
East Falkland
Stanley

South Georgia
(U.K.)
at the same scale
Grytviken

1:15M

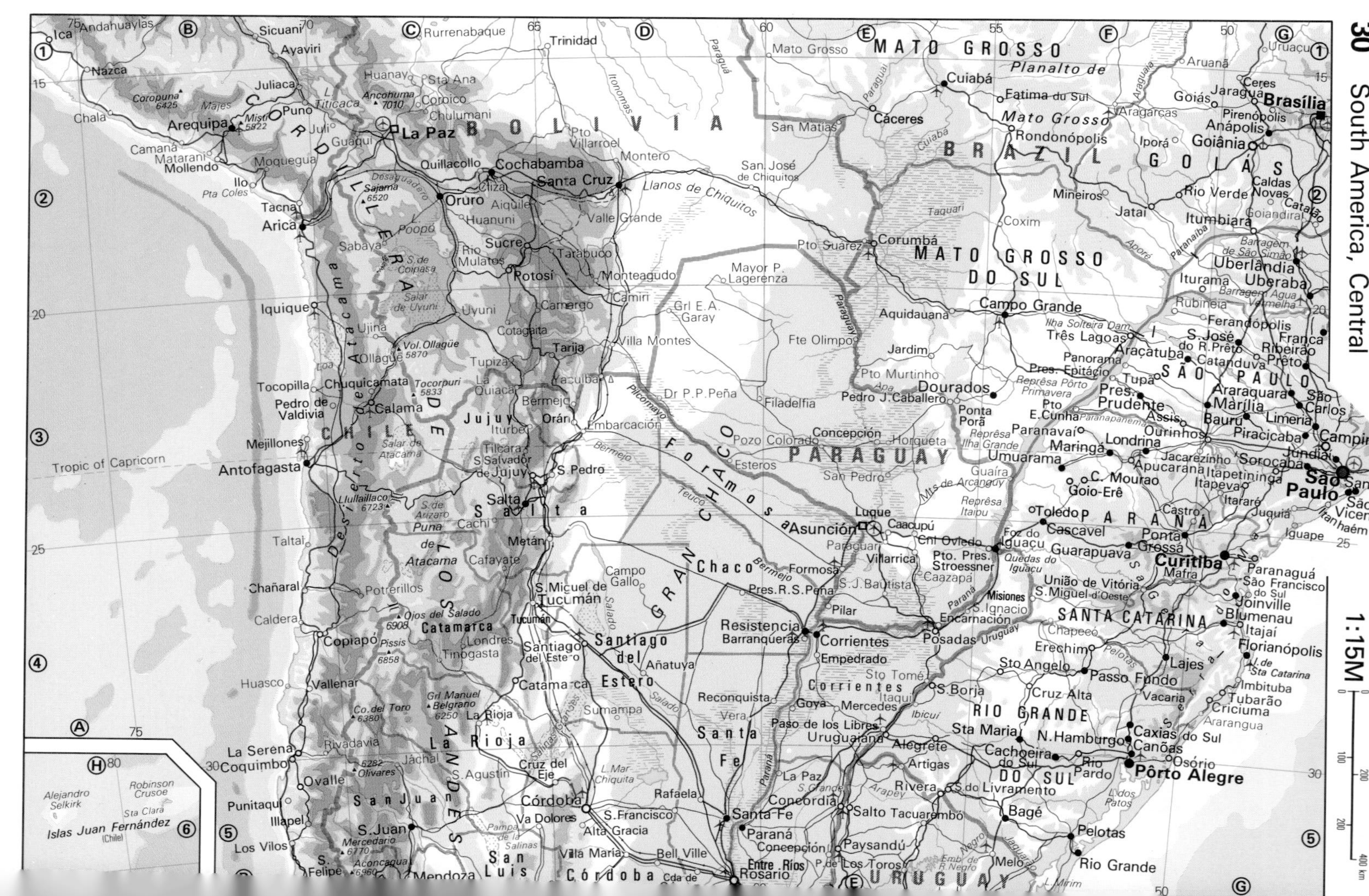

200 400 600 km
100 200 300 mls

Equator

PARÁ **MARANHÃO** **CEARÁ** **PIAUÍ** **PARAÍBA** **PERNAMBUCO** **ALAGOAS** **SERGIPE** **RIO GRANDE DO NORTE**

B R A Z I L

TOCANTINS **BAHIA** **GOIÁS** **MINAS GERAIS** **SÃO PAULO** **ESPÍRITO SANTO**

I. de Marajó
B. de Marajó
C. Maguarinho
Salinópolis
Bragança
Sapanema
Belém
Abaetetuba
Pinheiro
Alcântara
São Luís
Rosário
Parnaíba
Camocim
Acaraú
Itapipoca
Caucaia
Sobral
Sta Quitéria
Fortaleza (Ceará)
Rocas
I. Fernando de Noronha
Cametá
Monção
Chapadinha
Bacabal
Coroatá
Codó
Caxias
Piripiri
Campo Maior
Nova Russas
Canindé
Aracati
Areia Branca
Macau
Pta do Calcanhar
Tucuruí
Marabá
Imperatriz
Grajaú
Pto Franco
Teresina
Castelo
Crateús
Mombaça
Morada N
Quixadá
Acopiara
Patu
Caicó
Mossoró
Natal
Araguaína
Carolina
Balsas
Floriano
Oeiras
Picos
J. do Norte
Crato
Iguatu
Tauá
Sousa
Patos
Cabedelo
João Pessoa
C. do Araguaia
S.Raimundo Nonato
Paulistana
Salgueiro
Ouricuri
Sa Talhada
Caruaru
Limoeiro
Campina Grande
Olinda
Recife (Pernambuco)
São Félix
Petrolina
Juàzeiro
Garanhuns
Palmeira dos Ind.
Palmares
Barreiros
Goiânia
Brasília
Barragem de Sobradinho
Barra
Jacobina
Sen. do Bonfim
Propriá
ALAGOAS
Maceió
Penedo
Arapiraca
Barreiras
Ibotirama
R. de Jacuípe
Serrinha
Lagarto
Estância
Aracajú
Bom Jesus da Lapa
Iaçu
Feira de S.
Alagoinhas
Castro Alves
Cachoeira
Salvador (Bahia)
B. de T. os Santos
Caetité
Valença
Jequié
Ipiaú
Itabuna
Ilhéus
ATLANTIC OCEAN
Ceres
Formosa
Aruanã
Goiás
Jaraguá
Pirenópolis
Anápolis
Goiânia
São Francisco
Januária
Porteirinha
Vitória da Conquista
Itapetinga
Canavieiras
Belmonte
Pôrto Seguro
Montes Claros
Araçuaí
Sa do Chifre
Itamaraju
Caldas Novas
Rio Verde
Paracatu
Pirapora
Salinas
Teófilo Otôni
Nanuque
Iataí
Itumbiara
Goiandira
João Pinheiro
Corinto
Diamantina
Gov. Valadares
São Mateus
Catalão
Patos de Minas
Curvelo
Araguari
Itabira
Cnl Fabriciano
Linhares
Colatina
ESPÍRITO SANTO
Uberlândia
Uberaba
Araxá
Sete Lagoas
Belo Horizonte
Caratinga
Manhuaçu
Cariacíca
Vitória
Iturama
Divinópolis
Con. Lafaiete
Ponte Nova
Vila Velha
Rubinéia
Fernandópolis
Franca
S.João del Rei
Carangola
Cachoeiro de Itapemirim
S.José do R. Prêto
Barretos
Passos
Lavras
Barbacena
Juiz de Fora
S.João da Barra
Catanduva
Ribeirão Prêto
Pôços de Caldas
Pres. Prudente
Araraquara
S.Carlos
Campos
Assis
Marília
Limeira
Volta Redonda
Nova Friburgo
Petrópolis
Bauru
Piracicaba
Barra Mansa
Magé
Jacarezinho
Jundiaí
Campinas
Niterói
Itapeva
Sorocaba
São Paulo
Rio de Janeiro
Itapetininga
Santos
São Vicente
Juquiá
Itanhaém
Iguape
Castro
Ponta Grossa
Itararé
Guarapuava
Curitiba
Paranaguá
Mafra
São Francisco do Sul

Tropic of Capricorn

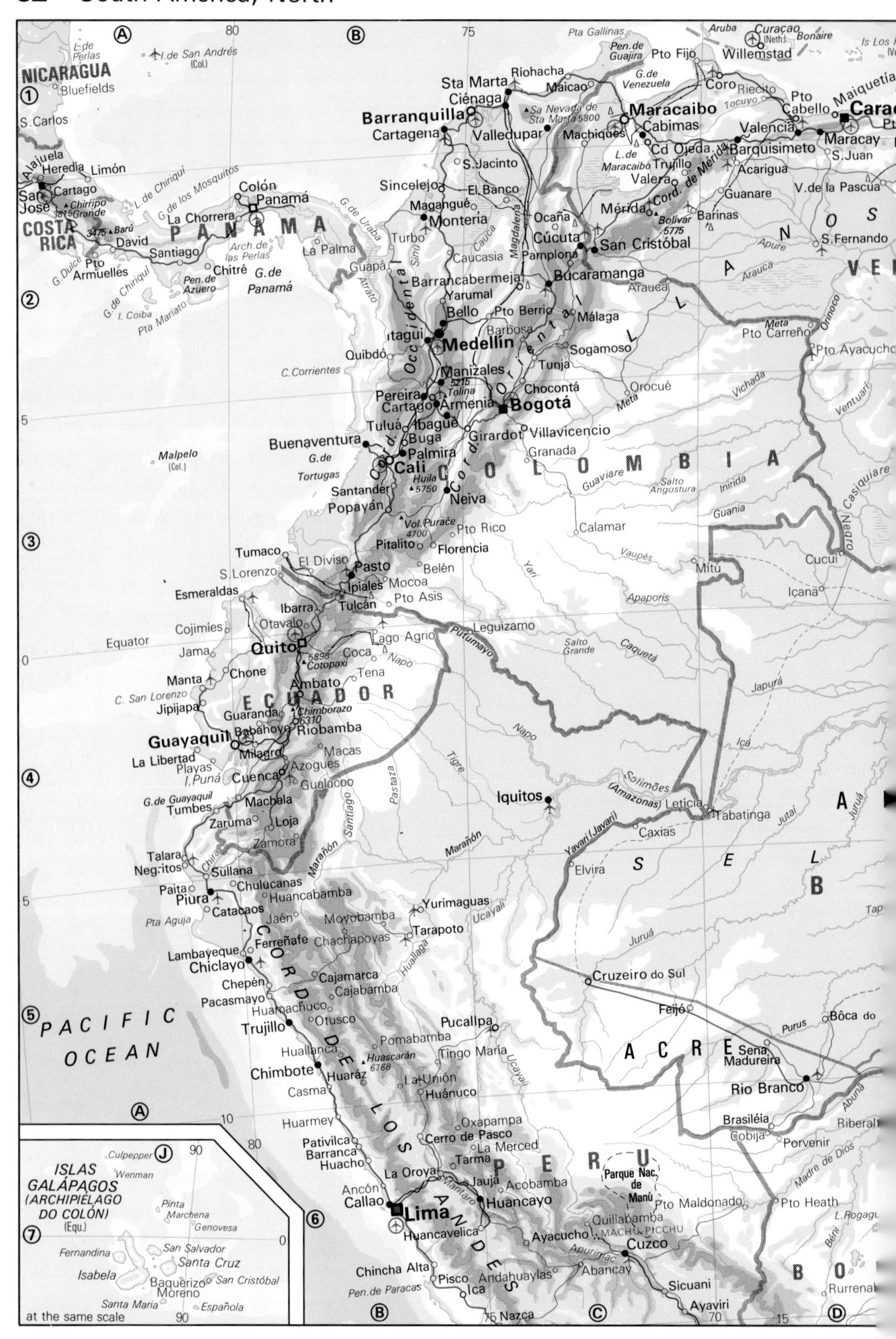

PACIFIC OCEAN

NICARAGUA
Bluefields
S. Carlos

COSTA RICA

PANAMA

COLOMBIA

ECUADOR

PERU

VENEZUELA

BOLIVIA

A C R E

S E L B A

ISLAS GALÁPAGOS (ARCHIPIÉLAGO DO COLÓN) (Equ.)
at the same scale

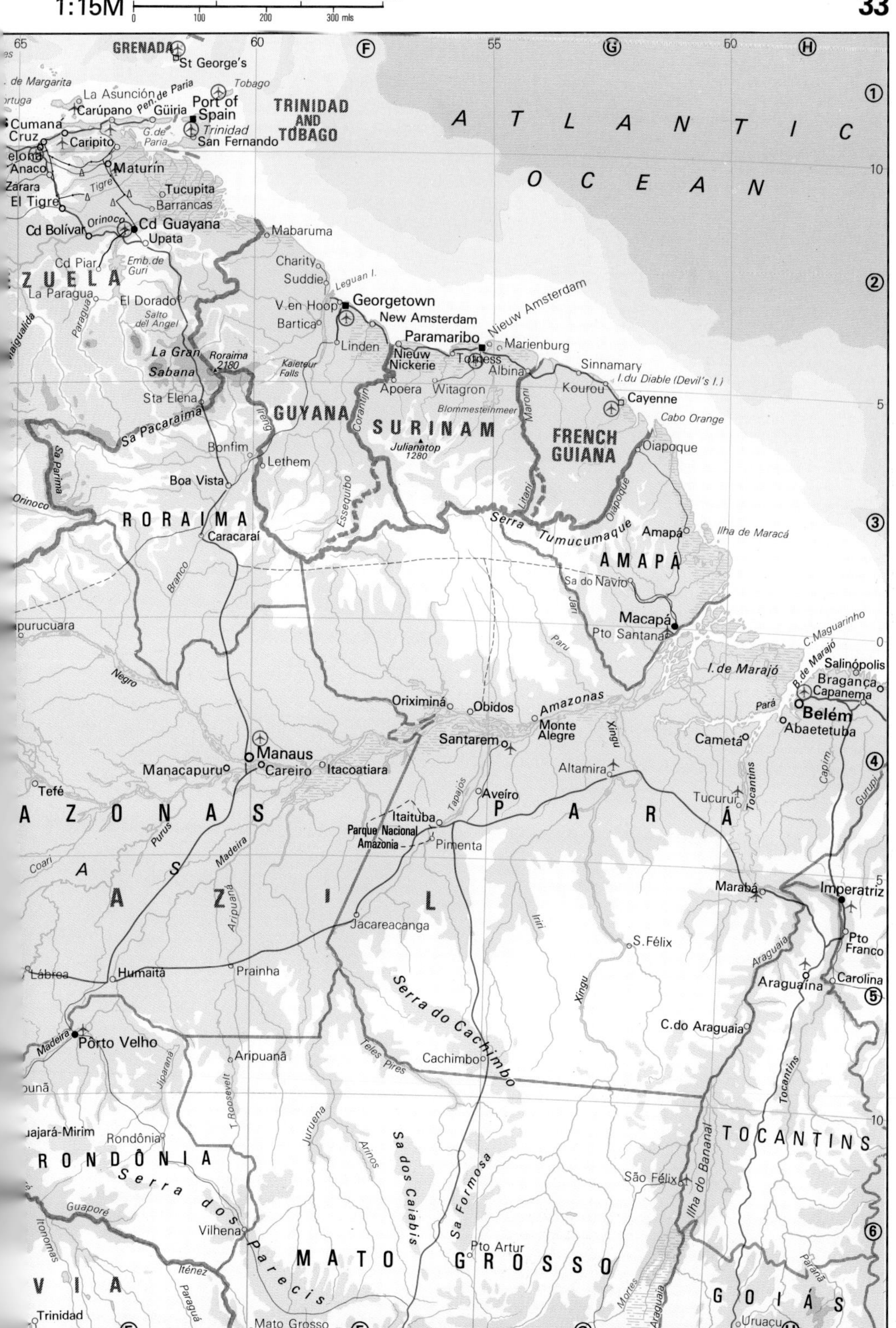

200   400   600 km
100   200   300 mls

GRENADA
St George's
. de Margarita
La Asunción
Carúpano Güiria
Cumana Cruz
Caripito
Anaco
Zarara Maturín
El Tigre
Cd Bolívar
Cd Piar
La Paragua
El Dorado
Sta Elena
Bonfim
Boa Vista

ATLANTIC

OCEAN

Tobago
Port of
Spain
Trinidad
San Fernando
TRINIDAD AND TOBAGO

Mabaruma
Charity
Suddie
V.en Hoop
Bartica
Linden
Georgetown
New Amsterdam
Nieuw
Nickerie
Paramaribo
Marienburg
Nieuw Amsterdam
Totness
Albina
Apoera Witagron
Sinnamary
I.du Diable (Devil's I.)
Kourou
Cayenne
Cabo Orange
Oiapoque

GUYANA
SURINAM
FRENCH GUIANA

Roraima
2180
La Gran
Sabana
Kaieteur
Falls
Julianatop
1280
Blommesteinmeer
Serra Tumucumaque

RORAIMA
Caracaraí
Lethem

Amapá
Ilha de Maracá
AMAPÁ
Sa do Navio
Jari
Pto Santana
Macapá

C. Maguarinho
B. de Marajó
I. de Marajó
Salinópolis
Bragança
Capanema
Belém
Abaetetuba

Oriximiná
Óbidos
Monte
Alegre
Santarem
Amazonas
Xingu
Cametá
Pará
Tefé
Manacapuru
Manaus
Careiro
Itacoatiara
Altamira
Tucuruí
Itaituba
Aveiro
Parque Nacional
Amazônia
Pimenta
Marabá
Imperatriz
Pto
Franco
Jacareacanga
S.Félix
Carolina
Lábrea Humaitá Prainha
Araguaína
Madeira
Pôrto Velho
Aripuanã
Cachimbo
C. do Araguaia
Serra do Cachimbo
Xingu
São Félix
Ilha do Bananal

RONDÔNIA
Serra dos Parecis
Vilhena
MATO **GROSSO**
Pto Artur
São Félix
Aruanã
Uruaçu
TOCANTINS
GOIÁS

Trinidad
Mato Grosso

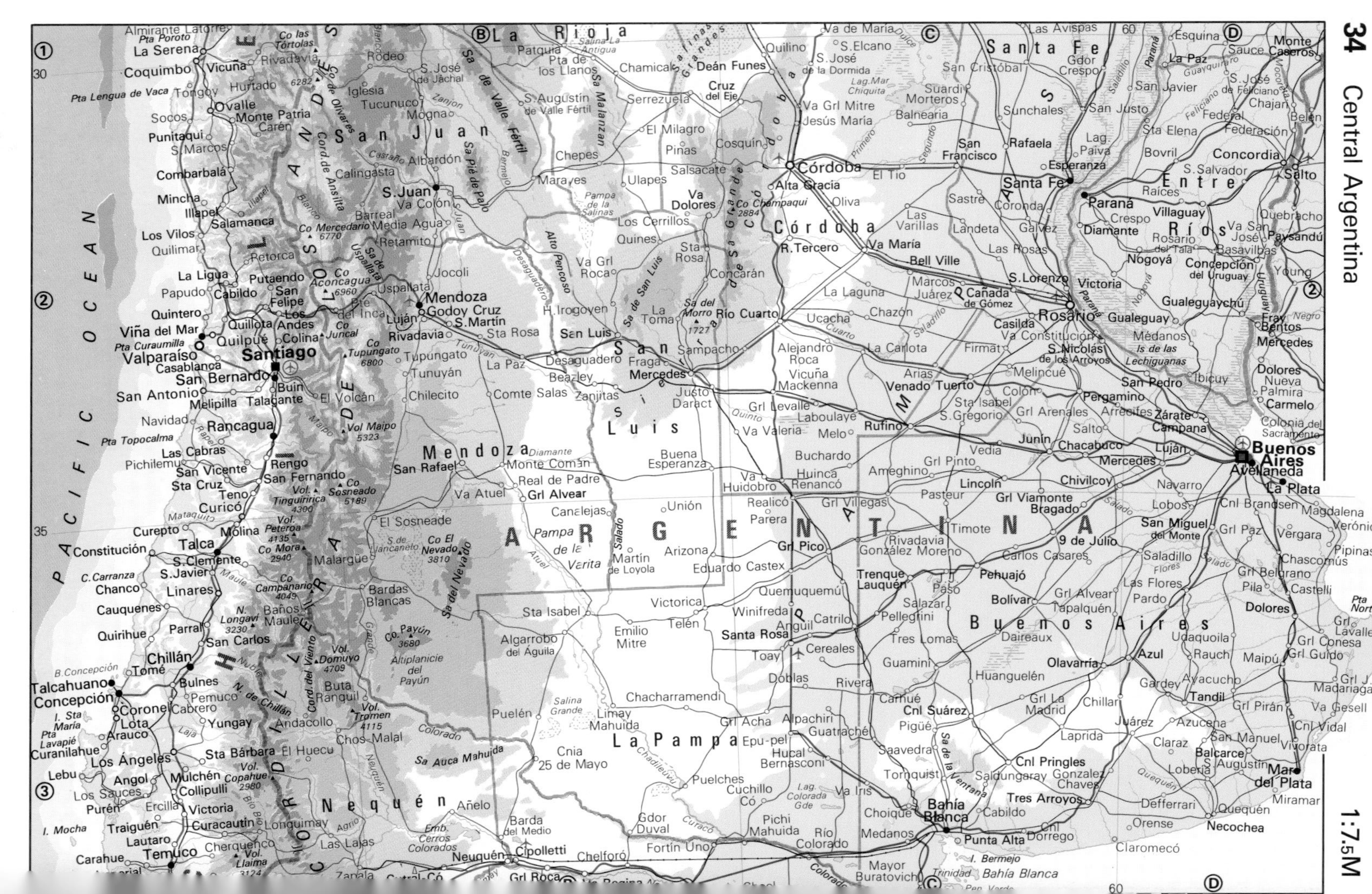
PACIFIC OCEAN
ARGENTINA
CORDILLERA
LOS ANDES
La Rioja
San Juan
Mendoza
San Luis
Córdoba
Santa Fe
Entre Ríos
Buenos Aires
La Pampa
Nequén
Buenos Aires
Santiago
Rosario
Córdoba
Mendoza
La Plata
Valparaíso
Concepción
Mar del Plata
Bahía Blanca
Santa Rosa
San Luis
Paraná
Santa Fe
Río Cuarto
Tandil
Neuquén
Temuco
Talca
Chillán
Rancagua

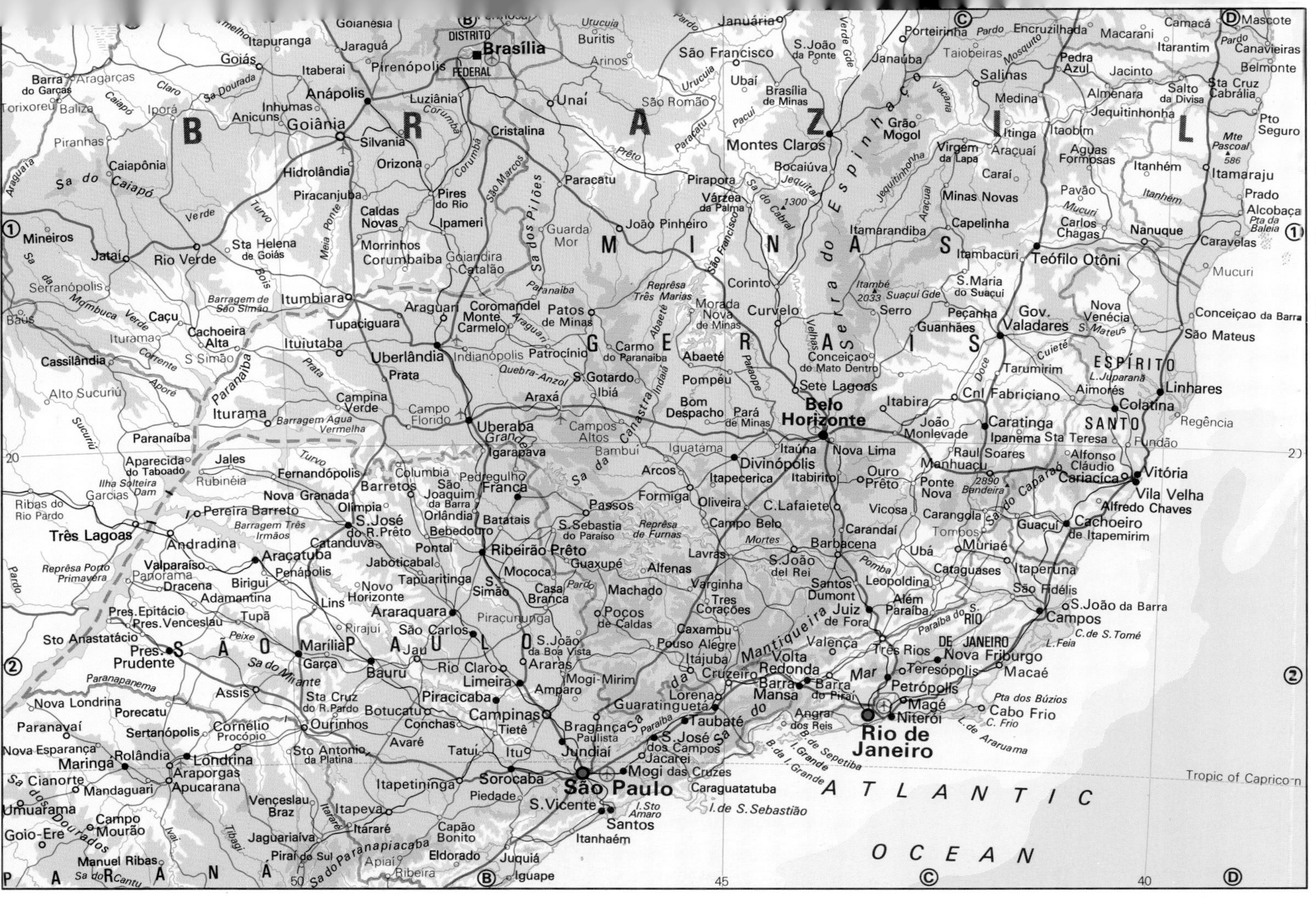
B R A Z I L
M I N A S G E R A I S
S Ã O P A U L O
ESPÍRITO SANTO
RIO DE JANEIRO
DISTRITO FEDERAL
P A R A N Á
A T L A N T I C O C E A N
Tropic of Capricorn
Brasília
Belo Horizonte
Rio de Janeiro
São Paulo
Vitória
Vila Velha
Goiânia
Anápolis
Uberlândia
Uberaba
Ribeirão Prêto
Campinas
Santos
Juiz de Fora
Montes Claros
Gov. Valadares
Teófilo Otôni
Linhares
Colatina
Campos
Niterói
Petrópolis
Londrina
Maringá
Bauru
Marília
Pres. Prudente
Três Lagoas
Sorocaba
Taubaté
S. José dos Campos
Volta Redonda
Araraquara
Franca
Divinópolis
Caratinga
Araxá
Patos de Minas
Catalão
Rio Verde
Jataí
Itumbiara
Piracicaba
Limeira
Jundiaí
São Carlos
Rio Claro
S. José do R. Prêto
Araçatuba
Barretos
Poços de Caldas
Varginha
Lavras
Barbacena
Cabo Frio
Macaé
Nova Friburgo
Teresópolis
Itabira
Sete Lagoas
Curvelo
Pirapora
Paracatu
Unaí
Januária
Cachoeiro de Itapemirim
Nanuque
Caravelas
Conceiçao da Barra
São Mateus
Mte Pascoal 586
Itambé 2033
2890 Bandeira
Sa do Espinhaço
Sa da Canastra
Sa da Mantiqueira
Sa do Mar
Sa dos Pilões
Paranaíba
Grande
São Francisco
Paranapanema
Doce
Jequitinhonha
Paraíba do Sul
Represa Três Marias
Represa de Furnas
Ilha Solteira Dam
I. de S. Sebastião
B. de Sepetiba
I. Grande
C. de S. Tomé
C. Frio
Pta dos Búzios
L. de Araruama
A B C D
1 2
20
40
45
50

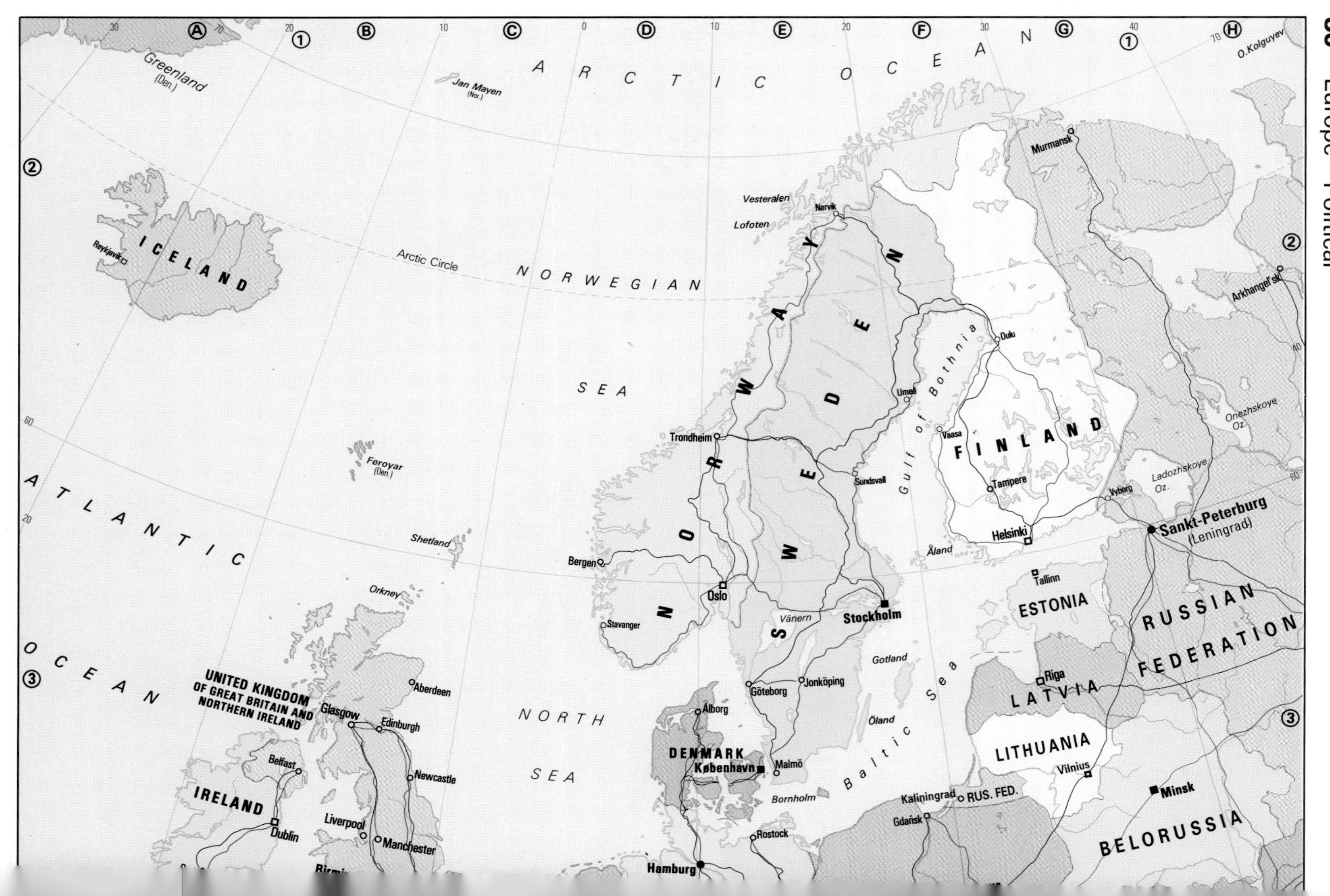
ARCTIC OCEAN
NORWEGIAN SEA
NORTH SEA
ATLANTIC OCEAN
Gulf of Bothnia
Baltic Sea
Arctic Circle
Greenland (Den.)
Jan Mayen (Nor.)
O.Kolguyev
ICELAND
Reykjavik
Føroyar (Den.)
Shetland
Orkney
NORWAY
Vesteralen
Lofoten
Narvik
Trondheim
Bergen
Oslo
Stavanger
SWEDEN
Umeå
Sundsvall
Stockholm
Vänern
Göteborg
Jönköping
Gotland
Öland
Malmö
Bornholm
FINLAND
Oulu
Vaasa
Tampere
Helsinki
Åland
Murmansk
Arkhangel'sk
Onezhskoye Oz.
Ladozhskoye Oz.
Vyborg
Sankt-Peterburg
(Leningrad)
RUSSIAN FEDERATION
Tallinn
ESTONIA
Riga
LATVIA
LITHUANIA
Vilnius
Minsk
BELORUSSIA
Kaliningrad
RUS. FED.
Gdańsk
Rostock
Hamburg
DENMARK
København
Ålborg
UNITED KINGDOM
OF GREAT BRITAIN AND
NORTHERN IRELAND
Aberdeen
Glasgow
Edinburgh
Newcastle
Liverpool
Manchester
Belfast
IRELAND
Dublin

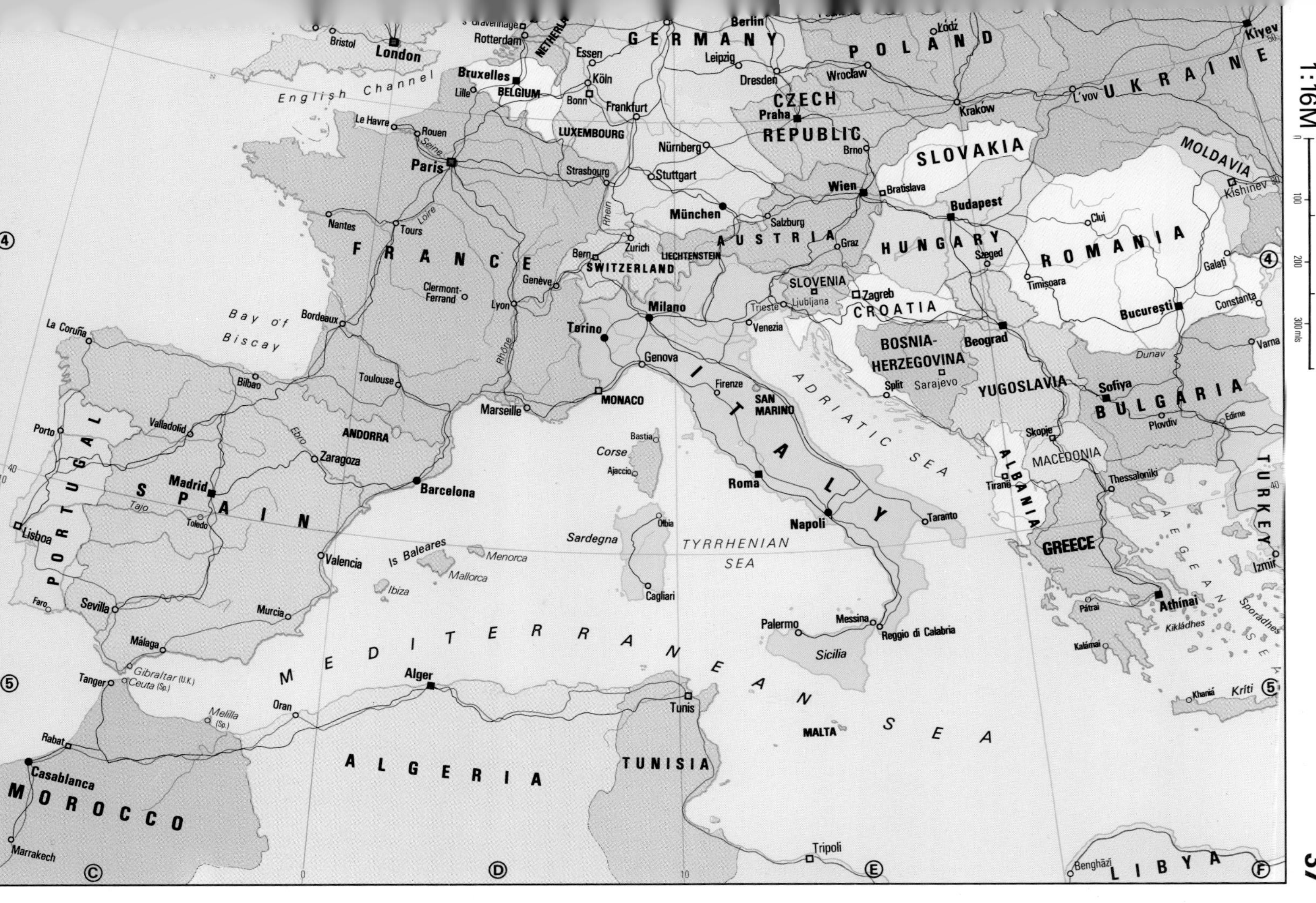

1:16M

200 400 600km
100 200 300 mls

UKRAINE
Kiyev
MOLDAVIA
Kishinev
Galați
Vama
Constanța
TURKEY
İzmit
Edirne
İzmir
Sporádhes

POLAND
L'vov
Łódź
Kraków

ROMANIA
Cluj
Timişoara
Bucureşti
Dunav
BULGARIA
Sofiya
Plovdiv
Edirne
Thessaloníki
AEGEAN SEA
Kaládhes
Athínai
Khaniá
Kríti

SLOVAKIA
Bratislava
Budapest
Szeged
HUNGARY
Beograd
YUGOSLAVIA
MACEDONIA
Skopje
Tiranë
ALBANIA
GREECE
Pátrai
Kalámai

GERMANY
Berlin
Dresden
Leipzig
Praha
CZECH REPUBLIC
Brno
Wrocław
Wien
Graz
AUSTRIA
CROATIA
Zagreb
SLOVENIA
Ljubljana
Trieste
BOSNIA-HERZEGOVINA
Sarajevo
Split
ADRIATIC SEA
Taranto
Reggio di Calabria
Messina
Sicilia
Palermo
MALTA
Tripoli
LIBYA
Benghazi

Essen
Köln
Bonn
Frankfurt
Nürnberg
Stuttgart
München
Salzburg
Venezia
Firenze
SAN MARINO
Roma
Napoli
TYRRHENIAN SEA
Tunis
TUNISIA

NETHERLANDS
Rotterdam
Bruxelles
BELGIUM
Lille
LUXEMBOURG
Strasbourg
Bern
Zürich
SWITZERLAND
LIECHTENSTEIN
Milano
Genova
MONACO
Torino
Corse
Bastia
Ajaccio
Sardegna
Olbia
Cagliari
MEDITERRANEAN SEA

London
Bristol
English Channel
Le Havre
Rouen
Paris
Seine
Loire
Tours
Nantes
FRANCE
Lyon
Rhône
Marseille
ANDORRA
Barcelona
Menorca
Baleares Is
Mallorca
Ibiza
Alger
ALGERIA
Oran

Bay of Biscay
Bordeaux
Toulouse
Zaragoza
Ebro
Valencia
Murcia
Melilla
MOROCCO

La Coruña
Porto
PORTUGAL
Lisboa
Madrid
SPAIN
Toledo
Tajo
Sevilla
Málaga
Gibraltar (U.K.)
Ceuta (Sp.)
Tanger
Rabat
Casablanca
Marrakech
Valladolid
Bilbao
Faro

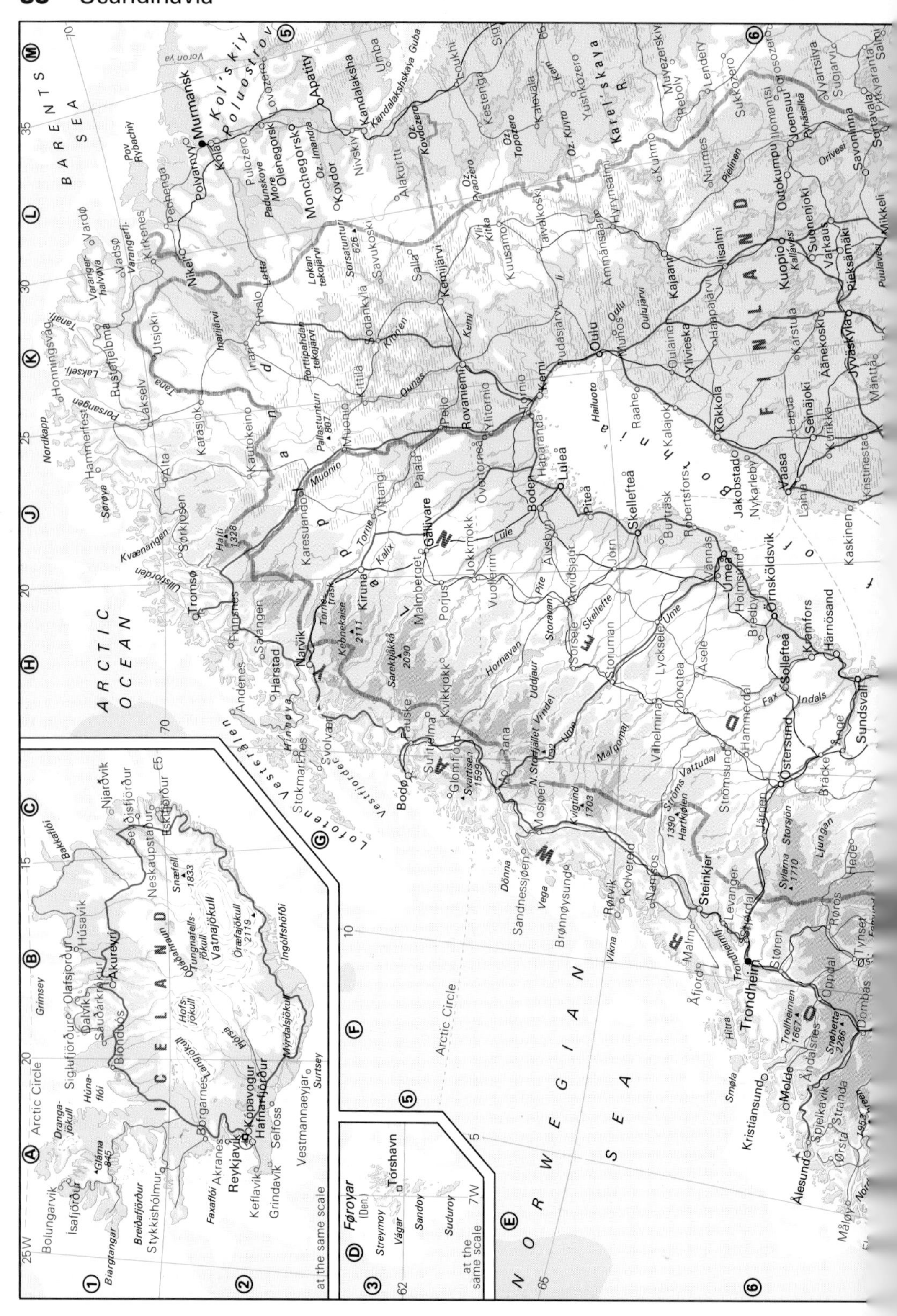

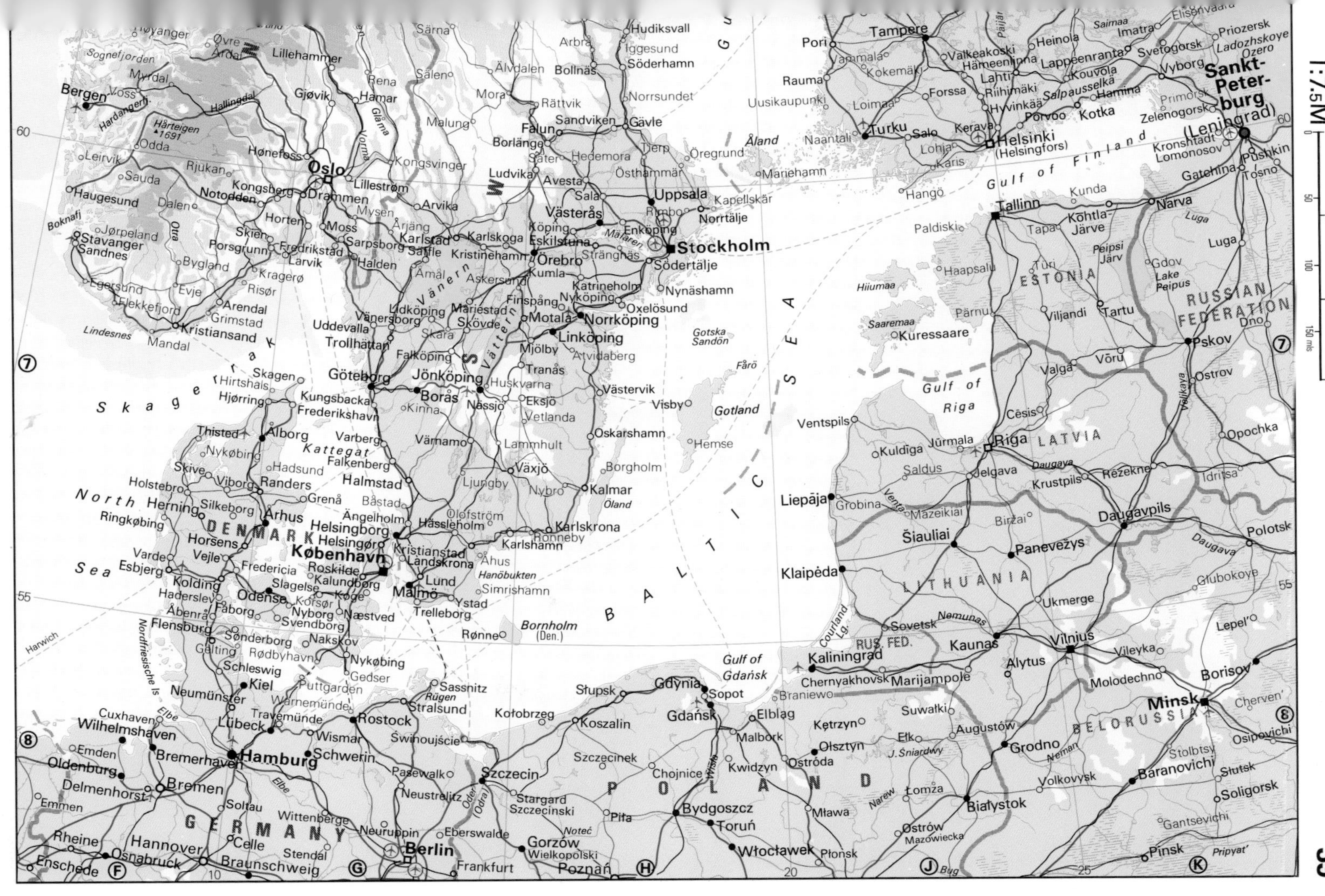
Sankt-Peterburg
(Leningrad)
RUSSIAN FEDERATION
ESTONIA
LATVIA
LITHUANIA
BELORUSSIA
POLAND
GERMANY
DENMARK
B A L T I C S E A
Gulf of Finland
Gulf of Riga
Gulf of Gdańsk
Skagerrak
Kattegat
North Sea
Helsinki
(Helsingfors)
Tallinn
Riga
Vilnius
Minsk
Stockholm
Oslo
København
Berlin
Tampere
Turku
Pori
Rauma
Lahti
Kotka
Vyborg
Narva
Tartu
Pskov
Pärnu
Daugavpils
Šiauliai
Kaunas
Klaipėda
Liepāja
Ventspils
Kaliningrad
Gdańsk
Gdynia
Sopot
Szczecin
Bydgoszcz
Toruń
Białystok
Grodno
Uppsala
Västerås
Örebro
Norrköping
Linköping
Jönköping
Göteborg
Borås
Malmö
Lund
Helsingborg
Kalmar
Karlskrona
Visby
Gotland
Öland
Bornholm
Rønne
Gävle
Falun
Karlstad
Bergen
Stavanger
Kristiansand
Drammen
Århus
Ålborg
Odense
Esbjerg
Kiel
Lübeck
Hamburg
Bremen
Rostock
Hannover
Braunschweig
Wilhelmshaven
Oldenburg
Osnabrück
Åland
Saaremaa
Hiiumaa
Lake Peipus
Daugava
Neman
Wisła
Oder (Odra)
Elbe
Pripyat'
Bug

1:5M

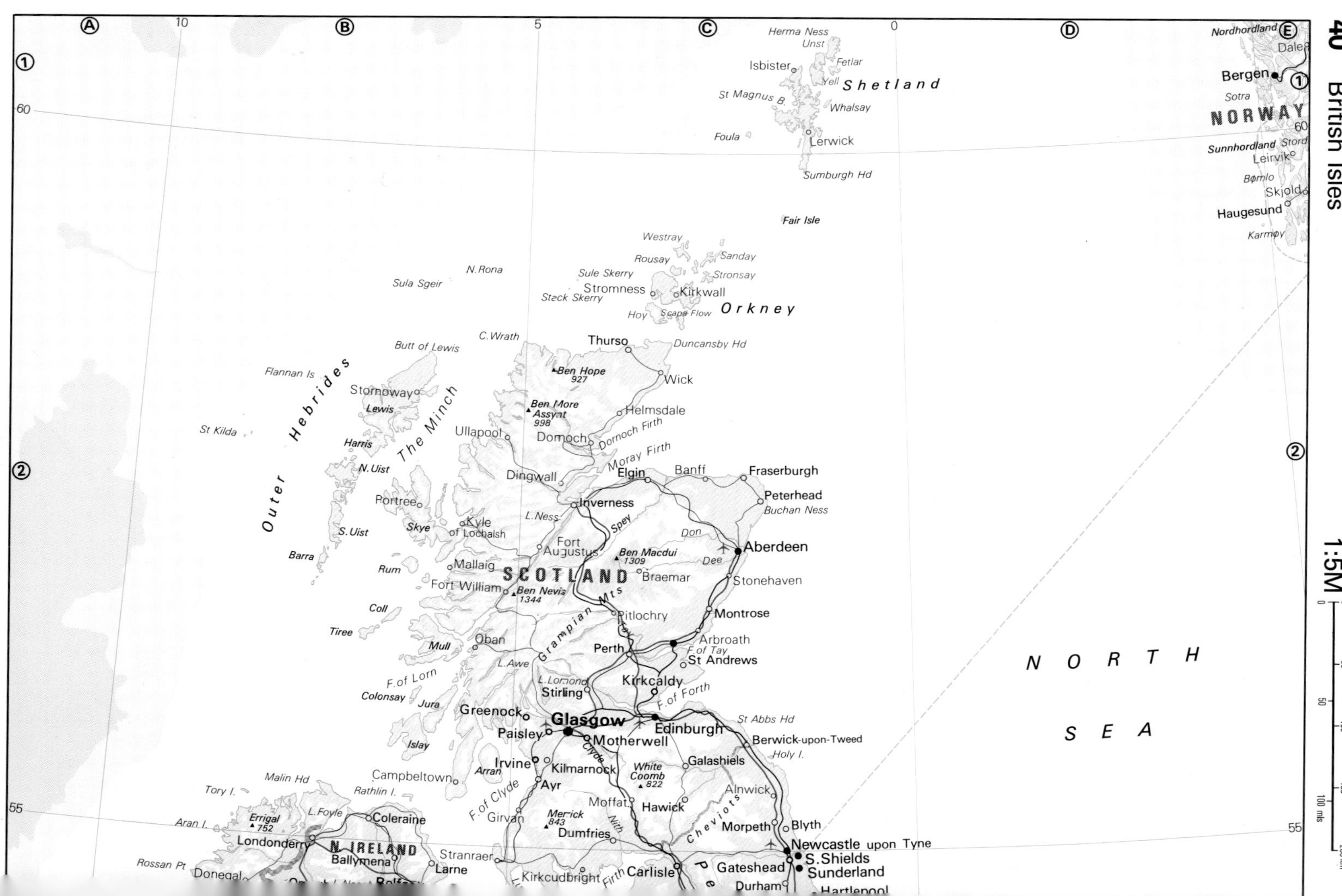
0 50 100 150 200 km
0 50 100 mls
NORTH SEA
NORWAY
Nordhordland
Dale
Bergen
Sotra
Sunnhordland
Stord
Leirvik
Bømlo
Skjold
Haugesund
Karmøy
Herma Ness
Unst
Isbister
Fetlar
Yell
Shetland
St Magnus B.
Whalsay
Foula
Lerwick
Sumburgh Hd
Fair Isle
Westray
Rousay
Sanday
Stronsay
Sule Skerry
Stromness
Kirkwall
Steck Skerry
Hoy
Scapa Flow
Orkney
N. Rona
Sula Sgeir
C. Wrath
Butt of Lewis
Thurso
Duncansby Hd
Ben Hope 927
Wick
Flannan Is
Stornoway
Lewis
Outer Hebrides
The Minch
Ben More Assynt 998
Helmsdale
St Kilda
Harris
Ullapool
Dornoch
Dornoch Firth
Moray Firth
N. Uist
Dingwall
Elgin
Banff
Fraserburgh
Peterhead
Buchan Ness
Portree
Inverness
L. Ness
Spey
Skye
Kyle of Lochalsh
S. Uist
Don
Fort Augustus
Ben Macdui 1309
Aberdeen
Barra
Dee
Rum
Mallaig
SCOTLAND
Braemar
Stonehaven
Fort William
Ben Nevis 1344
Grampian Mts
Coll
Pitlochry
Montrose
Tiree
Oban
Arbroath
Mull
Perth
F. of Tay
St Andrews
L. Awe
F. of Lorn
L. Lomond
Kirkcaldy
Colonsay
Jura
Stirling
F. of Forth
Greenock
Glasgow
Edinburgh
St Abbs Hd
Paisley
Motherwell
Berwick-upon-Tweed
Islay
Clyde
Holy I.
Irvine
Kilmarnock
White Coomb 822
Galashiels
Arran
Campbeltown
Ayr
Malin Hd
Rathlin I.
F. of Clyde
Alnwick
Tory I.
Moffat
Hawick
Cheviots
Errigal 752
L. Foyle
Coleraine
Girvan
Merrick 843
Morpeth
Blyth
Aran I.
Dumfries
Nith
Londonderry
N. IRELAND
Newcastle upon Tyne
Ballymena
Stranraer
S. Shields
Rossan Pt
Larne
Gateshead
Sunderland
Donegal
Kirkcudbright
Firth
Carlisle
Durham
Hartlepool
60
55
10
5
0

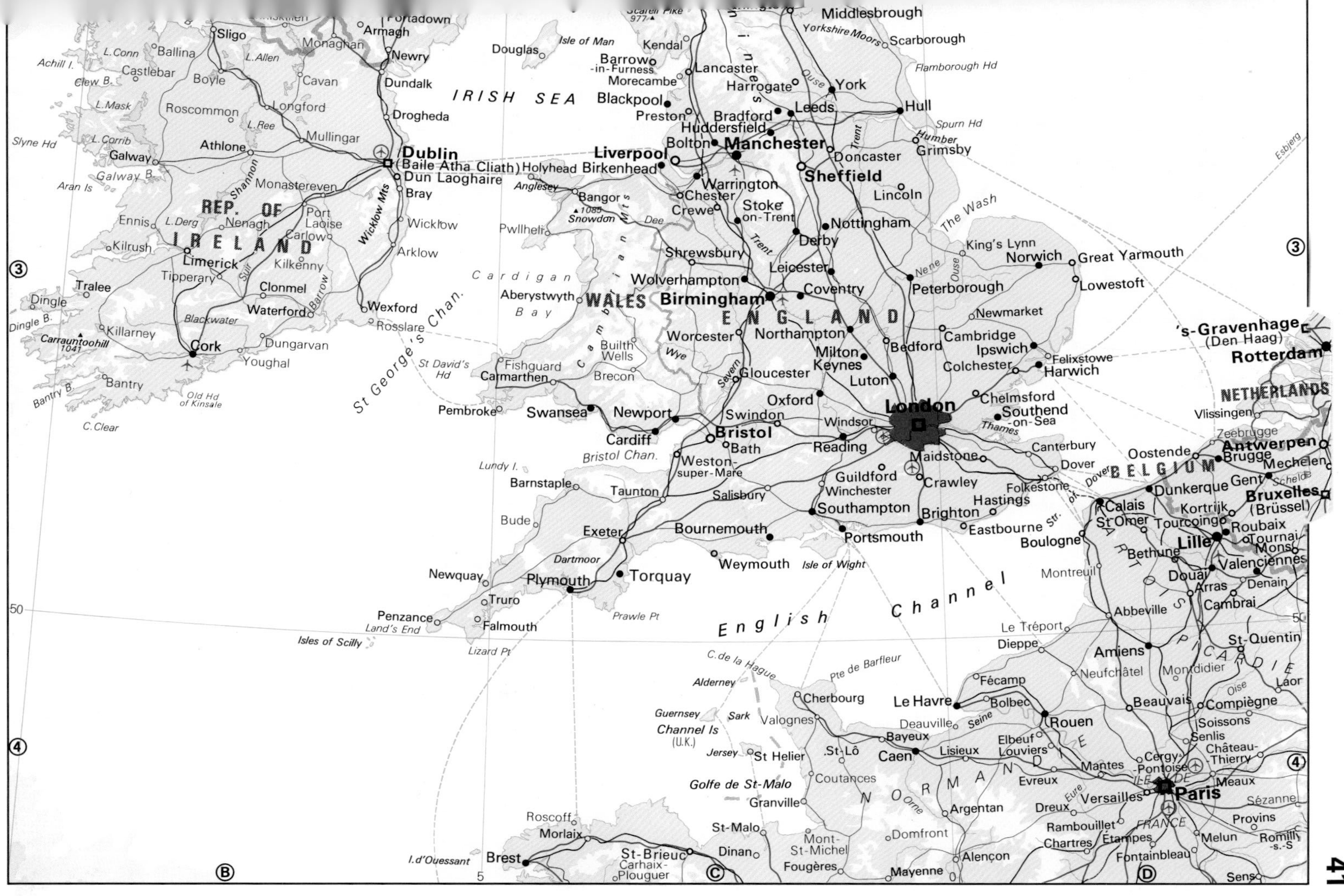
IRISH SEA
REP. OF IRELAND
Sligo
Ballina
Castlebar
Boyle
Roscommon
Longford
Mullingar
Athlone
Galway
Galway B.
Aran Is
Slyne Hd
Achill I.
Clew B.
L.Conn
L.Mask
L.Corrib
L.Allen
L.Ree
L.Derg
Shannon
Ennis
Kilrush
Limerick
Nenagh
Tipperary
Monastereven
Port Laoise
Carlow
Kilkenny
Clonmel
Waterford
Tralee
Dingle
Dingle B.
Killarney
Carrauntoohill 1041
Cork
Blackwater
Dungarvan
Youghal
Bantry
Bantry B.
Old Hd of Kinsale
C.Clear
Monaghan
Armagh
Portadown
Newry
Cavan
Dundalk
Drogheda
Dublin
(Baile Atha Cliath)
Dun Laoghaire
Bray
Wicklow Mts
Wicklow
Arklow
Wexford
Rosslare
Barrow
Suir
St George's Chan.
Isle of Man
Douglas
Holyhead
Anglesey
Bangor
1085 Snowdon
Pwllheli
Cardigan Bay
Aberystwyth
WALES
Cambrian Mts
Builth Wells
Brecon
Fishguard
Carmarthen
St David's Hd
Pembroke
Swansea
Newport
Cardiff
Bristol Chan.
Lundy I.
Barnstaple
Bude
Newquay
Truro
Falmouth
Penzance
Land's End
Isles of Scilly
Lizard Pt
Plymouth
Dartmoor
Torquay
Prawle Pt
Exeter
Taunton
Weston-super-Mare
Bristol
Bath
Salisbury
Bournemouth
Weymouth
Isle of Wight
Southampton
Winchester
Portsmouth
Guildford
Crawley
Brighton
Hastings
Eastbourne
Maidstone
Canterbury
Dover
Folkestone
Str. of Dover
ENGLAND
London
Thames
Southend-on-Sea
Chelmsford
Colchester
Harwich
Felixstowe
Ipswich
Cambridge
Newmarket
Norwich
Great Yarmouth
Lowestoft
King's Lynn
The Wash
Peterborough
Nene
Ouse
Bedford
Luton
Milton Keynes
Northampton
Oxford
Swindon
Reading
Windsor
Gloucester
Severn
Wye
Worcester
Birmingham
Wolverhampton
Coventry
Leicester
Shrewsbury
Derby
Nottingham
Trent
Stoke-on-Trent
Crewe
Chester
Dee
Warrington
Liverpool
Birkenhead
Manchester
Sheffield
Bolton
Huddersfield
Bradford
Leeds
Harrogate
York
Doncaster
Lincoln
Grimsby
Humber
Spurn Hd
Hull
Flamborough Hd
Scarborough
Yorkshire Moors
Middlesbrough
Lancaster
Barrow-in-Furness
Morecambe
Kendal
Blackpool
Preston
Scafell Pike 977
Esbjerg
'Gravenhage
(Den Haag)
Rotterdam
NETHERLANDS
Vlissingen
Zeebrugge
Antwerpen
Brugge
Mechelen
Schelde
Gent
Bruxelles
(Brüssel)
BELGIUM
Oostende
Dunkerque
Kortrijk
Tourcoing
Roubaix
Tournai
Mons
Lille
Calais
St Omer
Boulogne
Bethune
Douai
Valenciennes
Denain
Arras
Cambrai
ARTOIS
Montreuil
Abbeville
Le Tréport
Dieppe
Amiens
St-Quentin
Laon
PICARDIE
Neufchâtel
Montdidier
Oise
Beauvais
Compiègne
Soissons
Senlis
Château-Thierry
Fécamp
Le Havre
Bolbec
Rouen
Seine
Deauville
Elbeuf
Louviers
Lisieux
Bayeux
Caen
St-Lô
Coutances
Cherbourg
Pte de Barfleur
C.de la Hague
Alderney
Guernsey
Sark
Channel Is
(U.K.)
Jersey
St Helier
Valognes
Golfe de St-Malo
Granville
St-Malo
Dinan
Mont-St-Michel
Fougères
Domfront
Orne
NORMANDIE
Argentan
Alençon
Mayenne
Evreux
Mantes
Dreux
Eure
Cergy-Pontoise
ILE DE FRANCE
Paris
Versailles
Meaux
Sézanne
Provins
Rambouillet
Chartres
Étampes
Melun
Fontainebleau
Romilly-s.-S
Sens
Roscoff
Morlaix
Brest
I.d'Ouessant
St-Brieuc
Carhaix-Plouguer
English Channel
50
5
B
C
D
3
4

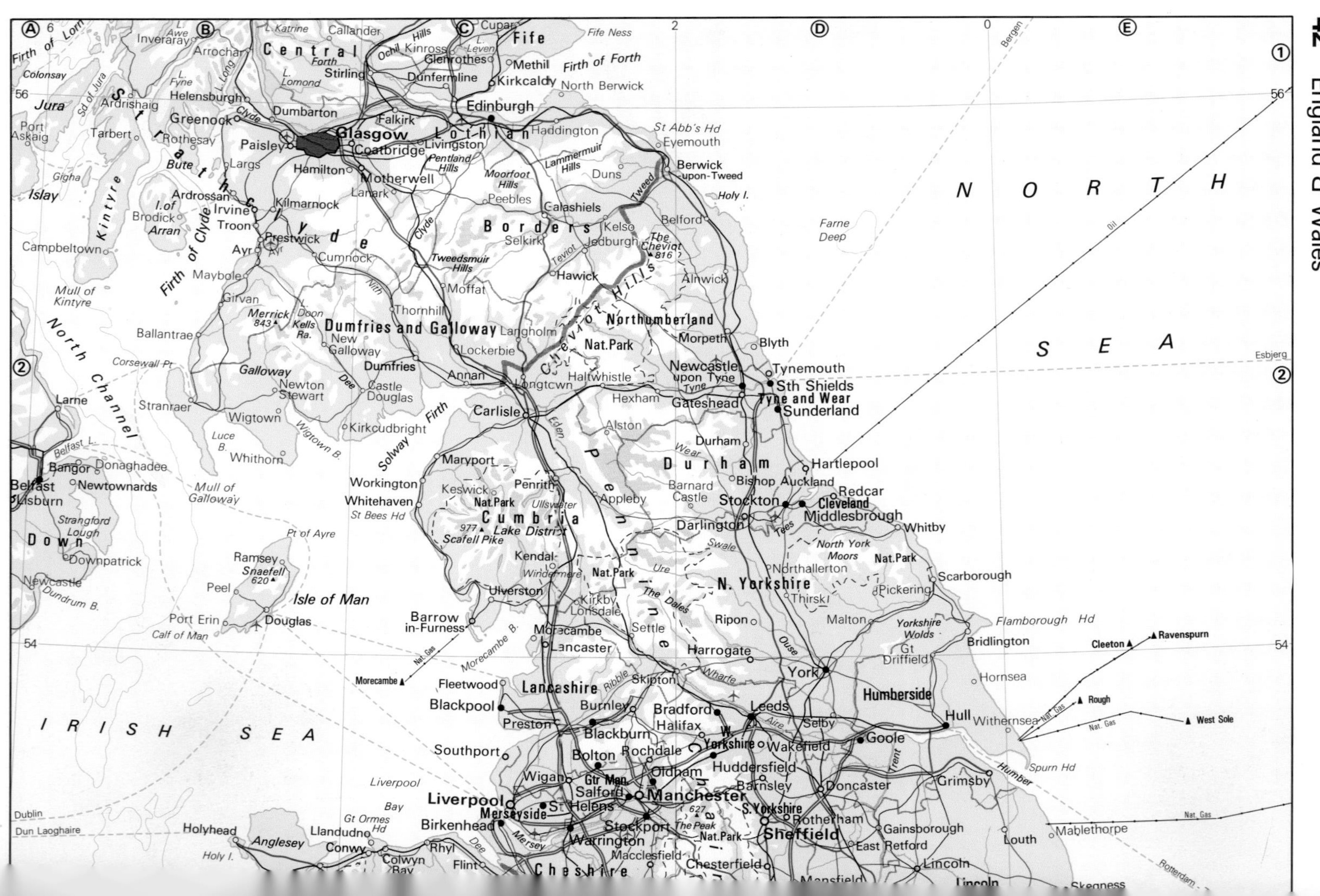
NORTH SEA
IRISH SEA
North Channel
Firth of Clyde
Firth of Forth
Solway Firth
Morecambe B.
Liverpool Bay
Isle of Man
Fife
Central
Lothian
Strathclyde
Borders
Dumfries and Galloway
Northumberland
Tyne and Wear
Durham
Cleveland
Cumbria
N. Yorkshire
Humberside
Lancashire
W. Yorkshire
S. Yorkshire
Gtr Man
Merseyside
Cheshire
Down
Edinburgh
Glasgow
Paisley
Greenock
Dumbarton
Stirling
Kirkcaldy
Berwick upon-Tweed
Carlisle
Newcastle upon Tyne
Gateshead
Sth Shields
Sunderland
Durham
Hartlepool
Stockton
Middlesbrough
Darlington
York
Leeds
Bradford
Hull
Grimsby
Doncaster
Sheffield
Manchester
Liverpool
Birkenhead
Blackpool
Preston
Lancaster
Barrow in-Furness
Douglas
Belfast
Larne
Cheviot Hills
Pennines
Lake District
Scafell Pike
North York Moors
Yorkshire Wolds
Flamborough Hd
Spurn Hd
Cleeton
Ravenspurn
Rough
West Sole
Morecambe
Nat. Gas
Oil
Esbjerg
Bergen
Rotterdam
Dublin
Dun Laoghaire

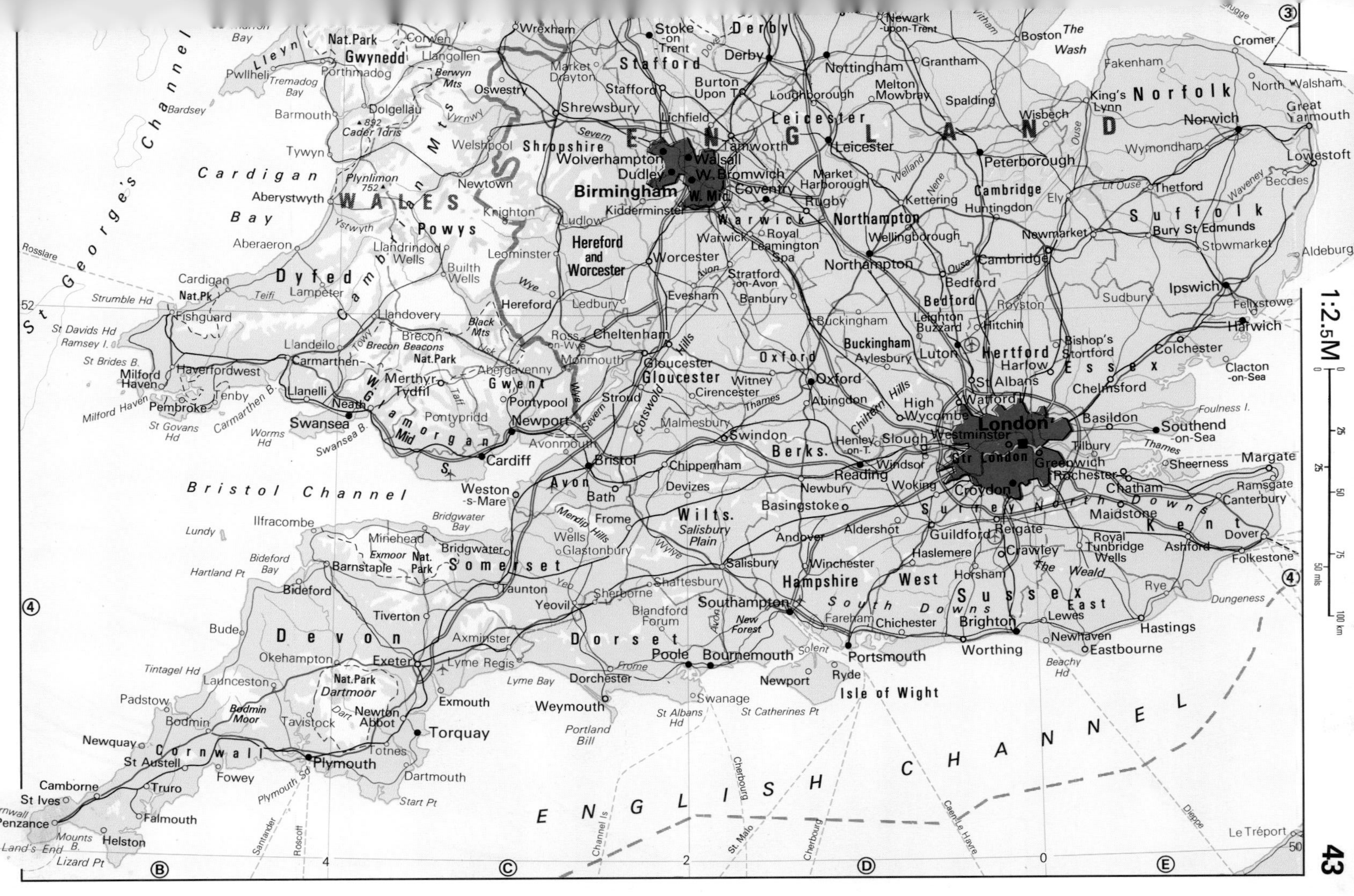

1:2.5M

25 50 75 100 km
25 50 mls

Shetland

Herma Ness · Unst · Fetlar · The Faither · Isbister · Hillswick · Papa Stour · Foula · St Magnus Bay · Brae · Whalsay · Scalloway · Lerwick · Bressay · Noss · Gruness · Fair Isle · Fitful Hd · Sumburgh Hd

Hanstholm-Bergen · Aberdeen · Stromness

at the same scale

Orkney

Papa Westray · N Ronaldsay · Sanday · Stronsay · Westray · Rousay · Eday · Shapinsay · Birsay · Kirkwall · Burray · S Ronaldsay · Duncansby Hd · Mainland · Scapa Flow · Lerwick · Stromness · Pentland Firth · John o' Groats · Dunnet Hd · Thurso

Hoy

NORTH SEA

Long Forties · Buchan Deep · Beatrice

Fraserburgh · Peterhead · Buchan Ness · Kinnairds Hd · Aberdeen · Girdle Ness · Stonehaven · Montrose · Arbroath

Berwick-upon-Tweed · St Abb's Hd · Eyemouth · Duns

GRAMPIAN

Banff · Lossiemouth · Elgin · Forres · Nairn · Keith · Huntly · Inverurie · Ythan · Deveron · Dufftown · Grantown-on-Spey · Ballater · Dee · Banchory · Braemar · Lochnagar 1155 · Ben Macdui 1310 · Cairngorms · A. Esk · Brechin · Forfar · N. Esk · Don · Spey · Findhorn

TAYSIDE

Blairgowrie · Pitlochry · Blair Atholl · Aberfeldy · Perth · Dundee · Arbroath · Sidlaw Hills

St Andrews · Fife Ness · Cupar · Leven · Kirkcaldy · Glenrothes · Methil · Firth of Forth · North Berwick · Haddington · Lammermuir Hills

FIFE
Fife

Dunfermline · Kinross · L. Leven · Edinburgh · Livingston · Bathgate · Falkirk · Central · Stirling · Glasgow · Paisley · Greenock · Helensburgh · Dumbarton · Motherwell · Hamilton · Coatbridge · Clyde · Loch Lomond · Rothesay

HIGHLAND

C. Wrath · Durness · Eddrachillis Bay · Loch Hope 927 · Ben Hope · Ben Loyal · Tongue · Eriboll · Ben More Assynt 998 · Lochinver · Enard Bay · Ullapool · Ben Kilbreck 961 · Lairg · Ben Klibreck · L. Shin · Brora · Helmsdale · Lybster · Wick · Pentland Firth · John o' Groats · Dunnet Hd · Thurso · S. Ronaldsay · Burray

Dunbeath · Latheron · Dingwall · Tain · Dornoch · Dornoch Firth · Tarbat Ness · Cromarty · Cromarty Firth · Moray Firth · Inverness · Ben Wyvis 1045 · Ben Dearg 1087 · Loch Broom · Gairloch · Greenstone Pt · Gruinard B. · Poolewe · L. Maree · L. Torridon · Beauly · Farrar · Glen Ness · Loch Ness · Ben Attow 1031 · Kyle of Lochalsh · Raasay · Portree · L. Snizort · Breadford · L. Bracadale · Cuillin Hills · Isle of Skye · Canna · Rum · Eigg · Muck

MONADHLIATH MTS
Monadhliath Mts · Aviemore · Kingussie · Loch Laggan

SCOTLAND
Scotland

Fort Augustus · L. Lochy · Fort William · Ben Nevis 1344 · Loch Linnhe · Ballachulish · Glencoe · L. Etive · Oban · L. Awe · Firth of Lorn · Mull · Tobermory · Ardnamurchan Pt · Coll · Tiree · Staffa · Iona · Colonsay · Jura · Sd of Jura · Port Askaig · Tarbert · Ardrishaig · Inveraray · L. Fyne · Arrochar · Crianlarich · L. Katrine · Callander · Killin · Ben Lawers · L. Tay · L. Earn · Crieff · Loch Rannoch · L. Ericht · L. Tummel · Garry

Mallaig · Arisaig · Morar · L. Morar · L. Nevis · L. Hourn · Knoydart · L. Sunart · Morvern · Uva · Lismore

Western Isles

Butt of Lewis · Flannan Is · Broad B. · Stornoway · Lewis · Scarp · Taransay · Harris · Tarbert · Loch Roag · Sd of Harris · Pabbay · N. Uist · Monach Is · Lochmaddy · Benbecula · South Uist · Eriskay · Barra · Sd of Barra · Castlebay · Barra Hd · Little Minch · North Minch · Minch

Sd of Raasay

NORTH SEA

1:2.5M

0 25 50 75 100 km
0 25 50 mls

Provinces and Counties

ULSTER

Donegal — Londonderry — Antrim — Tyrone — NORTHERN IRELAND — Fermanagh — Monaghan — Armagh — Down — Cavan — Louth

CONNAUGHT

Sligo — Mayo — Roscommon — Leitrim — Galway

LEINSTER

Longford — Westmeath — Meath — Offaly — Kildare — Dublin — Laois — Wicklow — Carlow — Kilkenny — Wexford

MUNSTER

Clare — Limerick — Tipperary — Kerry — Cork — Waterford

REPUBLIC OF IRELAND

Selected places

Malin Hd — Carndonagh — Portrush — Ballycastle — Coleraine — Ballymoney — Limavady — Buncrana — Londonderry — Strabane — Magherafelt — Antrim — Ballymena — Larne — Belfast — Newtownards — Bangor — Comber — Lisburn — Lurgan — Portadown — Armagh — Newry — Banbridge — Downpatrick — Newcastle — Warrenpoint — Dundalk — Drogheda

Errigal 752 — Gweebarra B. — Glenties — Killybegs — Donegal — Blue Stack 676 — Newton Stewart — Omagh — Enniskillen — Clones — Cootehill — Carrickmacross — Monaghan

Rossan Pt — Bundoran — Ballyshannon — Fintona — Melvin — Sligo — Leitrim — Boyle — Carrick on Shannon — Cavan — Kells — An Uaimh — Trim — Balbriggan — Swords

Benwee Hd — Erris Hd — Belmullet — Ballycastle — Ballina — Swinford — Ballaghaderreen — Castlebar — Westport — Claremorris — Castlerea — Roscommon — Longford — Mullingar — Athlone — Royal Canal

Achill — Clew Bay — Clare — Inishturk — Inishbofin — Inishshark — Mts of Connemara — Clifden — Slyne Hd — Bertraghboy B. — Galway — Athenry — Loughrea — Ballinasloe — Banagher — Birr — Portarlington — Naas — Kippure 754 — Bray — Greystones — Dún Laoghaire — Dublin (Baile Atha Cliath)

Inishmore — Aran Is — Inishmaan — Ballyvaghan — Gort — Ennistimon — Liscannor B. — Mutton — Milltown Malbay — Scarriff — Ennis — Killaloe — Nenagh — Roscrea — Templemore — Thurles — Portlaoise — Athy — Carlow — Tullow — Arklow — Wicklow — Gorey — Cahore Pt

Kilkee — Kilrush — Loop Hd — Mouth of the Shannon — Foynes — Rathkeale — Newcastle W. — Limerick — Tipperary — Kilkenny — Thomastown — Enniscorthy — Wexford — Rosslare — Fishguard

Listowel — Abbeyfeale — Rath Luirc — Cashel — Cahir — Carrick-on-Suir — Clonmel — New Ross — Waterford — Tramore — Carnsore Pt

Dingle — Tralee — Castleisland — Newmarket — Mitchelstown — Fermoy — Comeragh Mts — Waterford — Dungarvan — Hook Hd

Gt. Blasket — Dingle B. — 1041 — MacGillycuddys Reeks — Killarney — Boggeragh Mts — Mallow — Blackwater — Youghal — Mine Hd — Youghal Harb.

Valencia — Cahersiveen — Sneem — Kenmare — Macroom — Lee — Passage West — Cork — Cobh

Dursey — Kenmare River — Caha Mts — Bantry — Dunmanway — Bandon — Kinsale — Clonakilty

Bantry Bay — Skibbereen — Baltimore — Old Head of Kinsale — Mizen Hd — Roaringwater B. — C. Clear — Fastnet Rock — Kinsale

Tory I. — Sheep Haven — L. Swilly — Irishowen — Bloody Foreland — Aran I. — Donegal — Donegal Mts — Donegal Bay — Inishmurray — Sligo Bay — Ox Mts — Mts of Mayo — Nephin 807 — L. Conn — L. Mask — Lough Corrib — Suck — Shannon — Sl. Bloom — Lough Derg — Slievenamon — L. Ree — L. Ennell — L. Derravaragh — Sheelin — Oughter — Upper L. Erne — L. Allen — Boderg — Bowna — L. Neagh — Sperrin Mts — Antrim Hills — Mourne Mts — Carlingford L. — Dundalk Bay — Dunary Hd

L. Foyle — Fair Hd — Rathlin I. — Mull of Oa — Mull of Kintyre — Campbeltown — Kintyre — North Channel — Belfast L. — Strangford Lough

Kilkieran B. — Galway B. — Hags Hd — Lough Derg — Shannon — Nore — Barrow — Slaney — Liffey — Boyne — Erne — Blackwater — Lee — Moy

St George's Channel — Cherbourg-Le Havre

1:2.5M

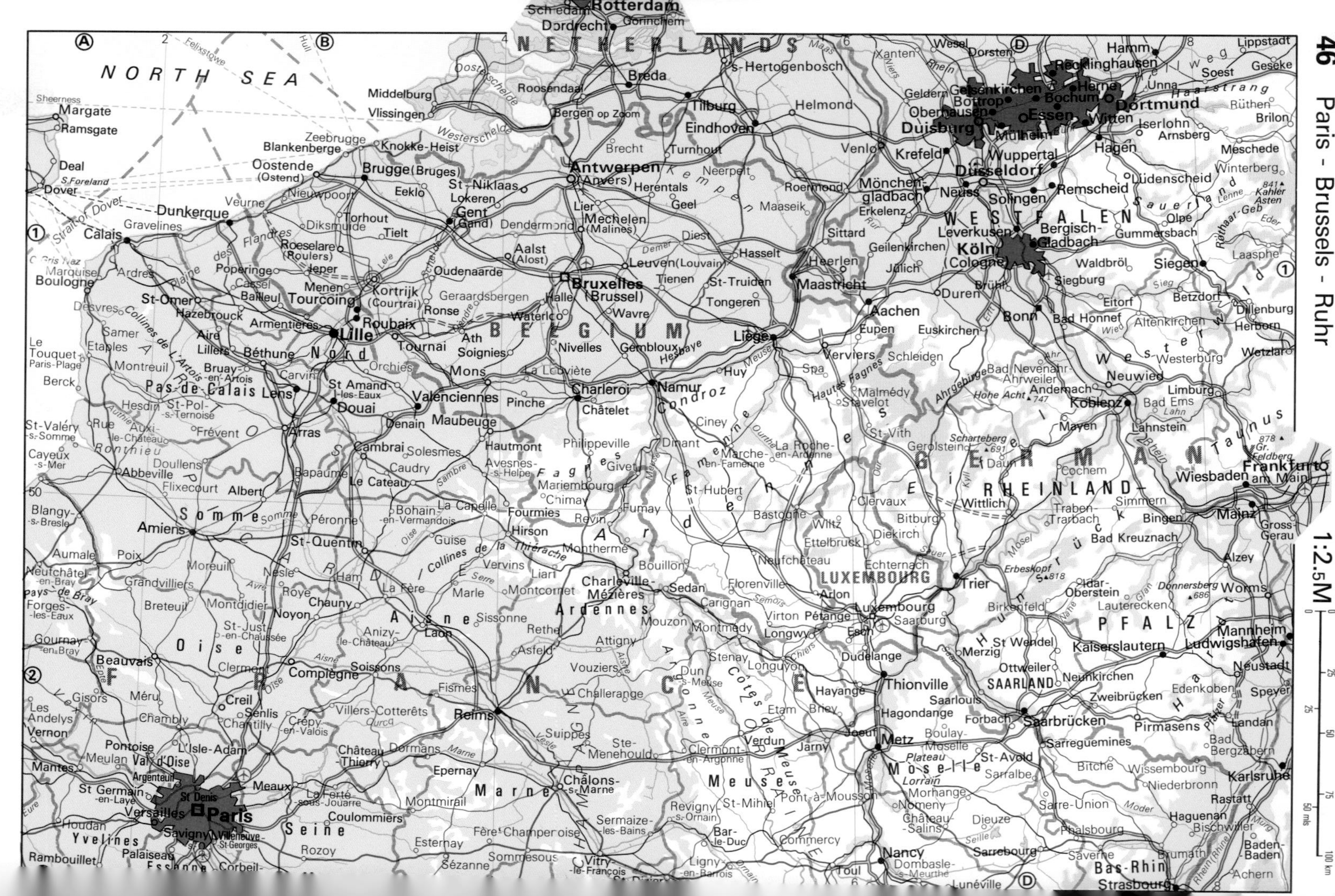

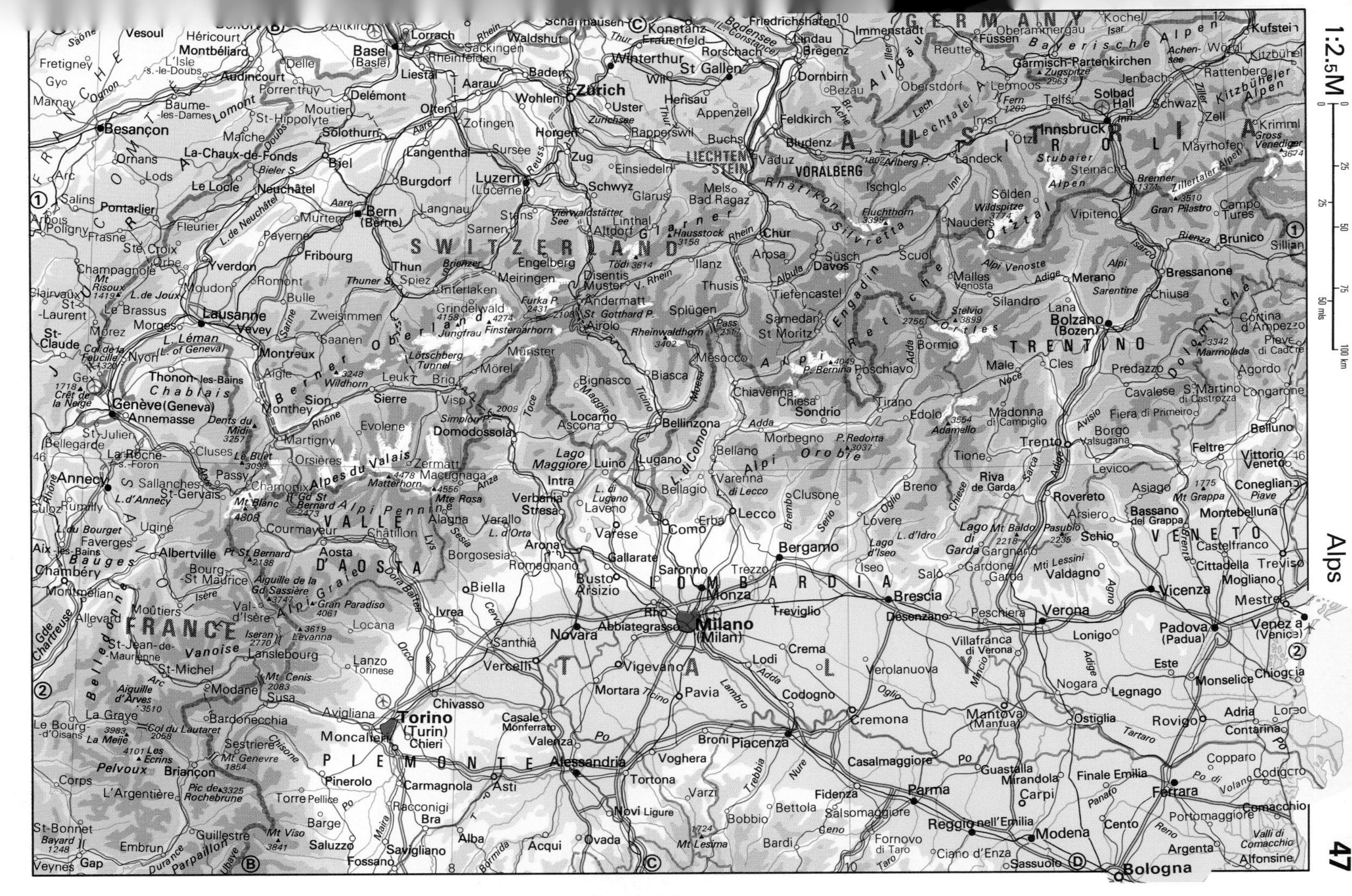
0 25 50 75 100 km
0 25 50 mls
GERMANY
AUSTRIA
SWITZERLAND
LIECHTENSTEIN
VORALBERG
TRENTINO
VENETO
LOMBARDIA
PIEMONTE
VALLE D'AOSTA
FRANCE
ITALY
Besançon
Basel (Basle)
Zürich
Bern (Berne)
Luzern (Lucerne)
Lausanne
Genève (Geneva)
Innsbruck
Bolzano (Bozen)
Trento
Milano (Milan)
Torino (Turin)
Bergamo
Brescia
Verona
Vicenza
Padova (Padua)
Venezia (Venice)
Bologna
Modena
Parma
Piacenza
Alessandria
Novara
Annecy
Chambéry

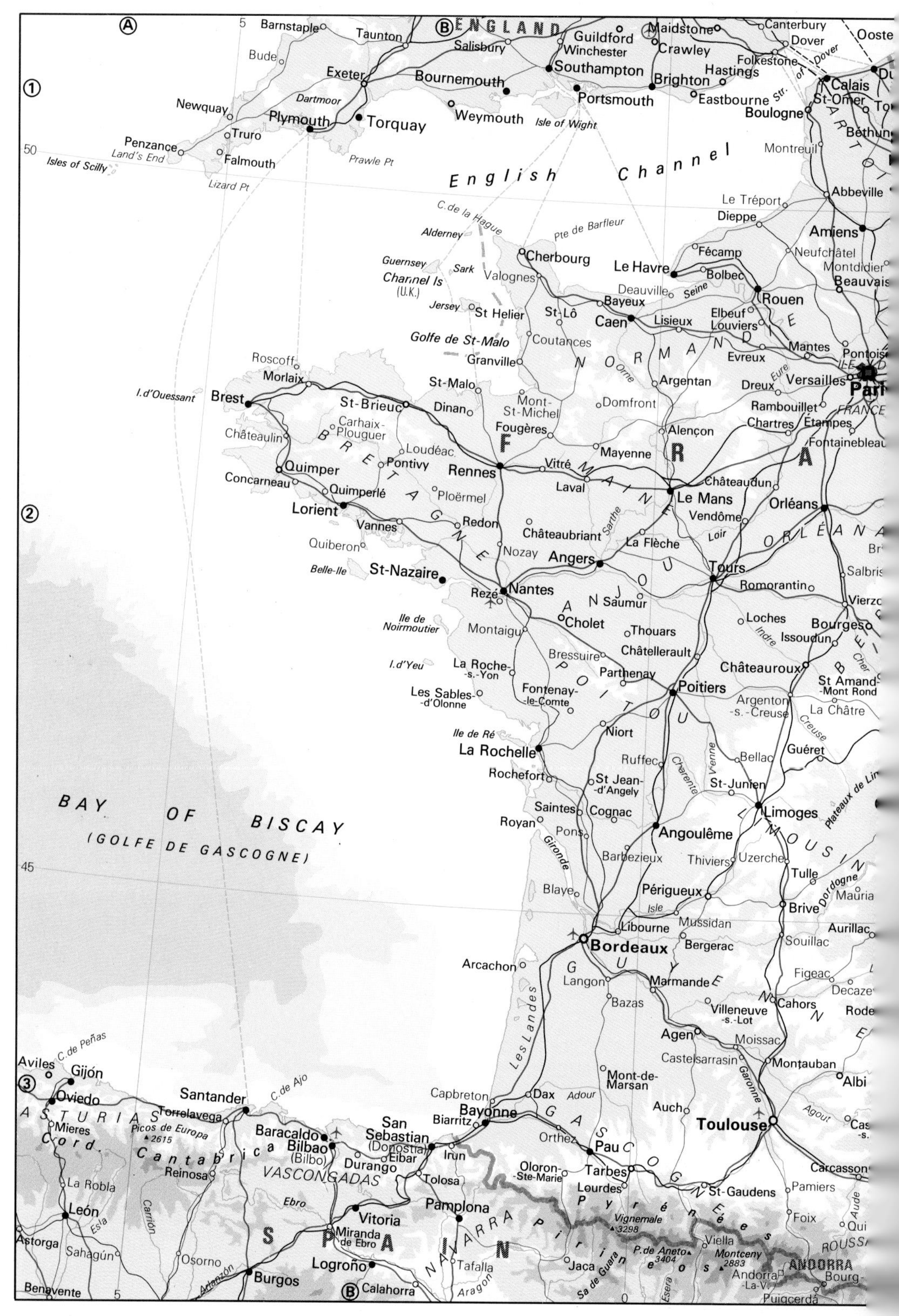
ENGLAND
English Channel
BAY OF BISCAY
(GOLFE DE GASCOGNE)
Channel Is
(U.K.)
Golfe de St-Malo
FRANCE
NORMANDIE
BRETAGNE
MAINE
ANJOU
POITOU
LIMOUSIN
GUYENNE
GASCOGNE
ORLÉANAIS
SPAIN
Pyrénées
Cantabrica
ASTURIAS
VASCONGADAS
NAVARRA
ANDORRA
Paris
Bordeaux
Toulouse
Nantes
Rennes
Brest
Le Havre
Rouen
Caen
Cherbourg
Le Mans
Tours
Orléans
Angers
Poitiers
Limoges
La Rochelle
Bilbao
Burgos
Pamplona
Plymouth
Southampton
Portsmouth
Brighton
Calais
Boulogne
Amiens
Dover
Isle of Wight
Bay of Biscay

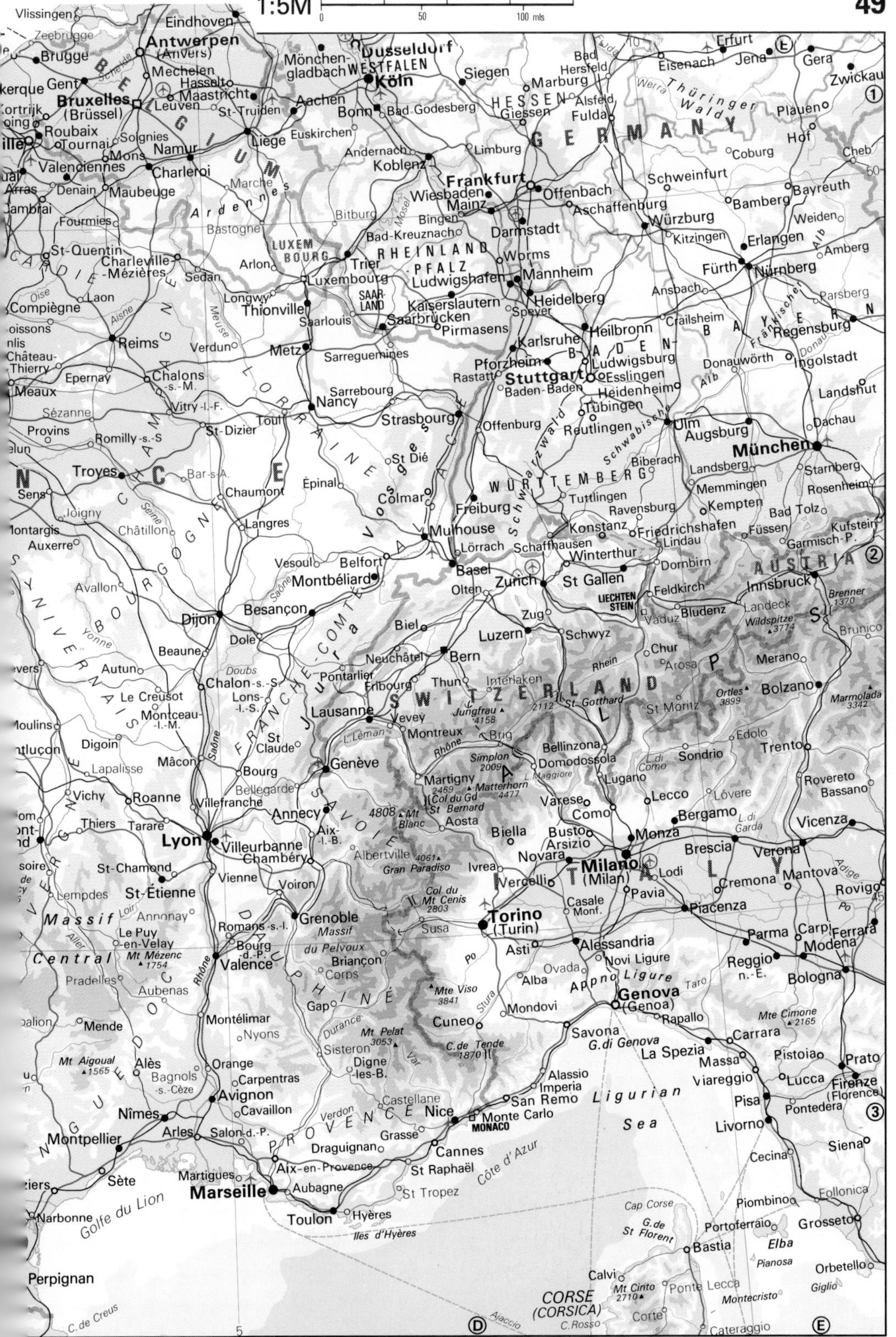
1:5M
0 50 100 150 200 km
0 50 100 mls
Vlissingen
Eindhoven
Zeebrugge
Antwerpen
(Anvers)
Brugge
Mechelen
Gent
Hasselt
Maastricht
Bruxelles
(Brüssel)
Leuven
St-Truiden
Roubaix
Tournai
Soignies
Mons
Namur
Liège
Valenciennes
Charleroi
Arras
Denain
Maubeuge
Cambrai
Fourmies
St-Quentin
Charleville-
-Mézières
Sedan
Compiègne
Laon
Reims
Château-
Thierry
Epernay
Chalons
-s.-M.
Meaux
Sézanne
Vitry-l.-F.
Provins
Romilly-s.-S
St-Dizier
Troyes
Sens
Joigny
Montargis
Auxerre
Châtillon
Chaumont
Langres
Avallon
Dijon
Beaune
Dole
Autun
Chalon-s.-S.
Le Creusot
Montceau-
-l.-M.
Lons-
-l.-S.
Moulins
Digoin
Mâcon
Lapalisse
Vichy
Roanne
Bourg
Villefranche
Thiers
Tarare
Lyon
Villeurbanne
St-Chamond
St-Étienne
Vienne
Lempdes
Massif
Central
Annonay
Le Puy
-en-Velay
Mt Mézenc
1754
Pradelles
Aubenas
Mende
Mt Aigoual
1565
Alès
Bagnols
-s.-Cèze
Nîmes
Montpellier
Sète
Narbonne
Golfe du Lion
Perpignan
C. de Creus
Mönchen-
gladbach
Düsseldorf
WESTFALEN
Köln
Aachen
Bonn
Bad Godesberg
Euskirchen
Siegen
Marburg
HESSEN
Giessen
Alsfeld
Fulda
Bad
Hersfeld
Eisenach
Erfurt
Jena
Gera
Zwickau
Thüringer
Wald
Plauen
Hof
Coburg
Cheb
GERMANY
Andernach
Koblenz
Limburg
Frankfurt
Offenbach
Wiesbaden
Mainz
Bingen
Aschaffenburg
Darmstadt
Schweinfurt
Bamberg
Bayreuth
Würzburg
Kitzingen
Weiden
Erlangen
Amberg
Fürth
Nürnberg
Marche
Ardennes
Bastogne
Bitburg
Bad-Kreuznach
LUXEMBOURG
Arlon
Trier
RHEINLAND
-PFALZ
Worms
Ludwigshafen
Mannheim
Luxembourg
Heidelberg
Ansbach
Parsberg
Longwy
Thionville
SAAR-
LAND
Kaiserslautern
Saarlouis
Saarbrücken
Speyer
Pirmasens
Heilbronn
Crailsheim
Regensburg
Verdun
Metz
Sarreguemines
Karlsruhe
BADEN
Ludwigsburg
Pforzheim
Rastatt
Stuttgart
Esslingen
Baden-Baden
Donauwörth
Ingolstadt
Nancy
Sarrebourg
Heidenheim
Landshut
Tübingen
Toul
Strasbourg
Offenburg
Reutlingen
Ulm
Augsburg
Dachau
München
St Dié
Biberach
Landsberg
Starnberg
Épinal
Colmar
WÜRTTEMBERG
Memmingen
Rosenheim
Freiburg
Tuttlingen
Ravensburg
Kempten
Bad Tolz
Konstanz
Friedrichshafen
Füssen
Kufstein
Mulhouse
Lörrach
Schaffhausen
Lindau
Garmisch-P.
Vesoul
Belfort
Winterthur
Dornbirn
AUSTRIA
Montbéliard
Basel
Zurich
St Gallen
Innsbruck
Olten
Feldkirch
LIECHTENSTEIN
Vaduz
Bludenz
Landeck
Brenner
1370
Besançon
Zug
Wildspitze
3774
Brunico
Biel
Luzern
Schwyz
Neuchâtel
Bern
Chur
Arosa
Merano
Pontarlier
Thun
Interlaken
Fribourg
SWITZERLAND
Ortles
3899
Bolzano
St Gotthard
2112
St Moritz
Marmolada
3342
Lausanne
Vevey
Jungfrau
4158
Montreux
Brig
L. Léman
Edolo
St
Claude
Bellinzona
Sondrio
Trento
Simplon
2009
Domodossola
Genève
Martigny
L. Maggiore
L. di Como
Lugano
Rovereto
Bellegarde
2469
Matterhorn
4477
Col du Gd
St Bernard
Bassano
Varese
Lecco
Lovere
Annecy
4808
Mt
Blanc
Aosta
Como
Bergamo
L. di
Garda
Vicenza
Aix-
-l.-B.
Biella
Busto
Arsizio
Monza
Brescia
Verona
Chambéry
Albertville
4061
Gran Paradiso
Ivrea
Novara
Milano
(Milan)
Lodi
Mantova
Vercelli
Cremona
Rovigo
Voiron
Col du
Mt Cenis
2803
Casale
Monf.
Pavia
Piacenza
Grenoble
Torino
(Turin)
Romans-s.-I.
Massif
du Pelvoux
Susa
Parma
Carpi
Ferrara
Bourg
-d.-P.
Valence
Asti
Alessandria
Modena
Briançon
Corps
Novi Ligure
Reggio
n.-E.
Ovada
Alba
Bologna
Mte Viso
3841
Appno Ligure
Gap
Cuneo
Mondovi
Genova
(Genoa)
Montélimar
Rapallo
Mte Cimone
2165
Nyons
Mt Pelat
3053
Savona
Carrara
Sisteron
G. di Genova
La Spezia
Digne
-les-B.
C. de Tende
1870
Massa
Pistoia
Prato
Orange
Alassio
Viareggio
Lucca
Firenze
(Florence)
Carpentras
Imperia
Avignon
Castellane
San Remo
Ligurian
Sea
Pisa
Pontedera
Cavaillon
Nice
Monte Carlo
MONACO
Livorno
Arles
Salon-d.-P.
Grasse
Draguignan
Cannes
Siena
PROVENCE
Aix-en-Provence
St Raphaël
Côte d'Azur
Cecina
Martigues
Marseille
Aubagne
St Tropez
Piombino
Follonica
Cap Corse
Toulon
Hyères
Iles d'Hyères
G. de
St Florent
Portoferraio
Grosseto
Bastia
Elba
Pianosa
Orbetello
Calvi
Giglio
Mt Cinto
2710
Ponte Lecca
Montecristo
CORSE
(CORSICA)
Corte
Ajaccio
C. Rosso
Cateraggio
D
E
1
2
3

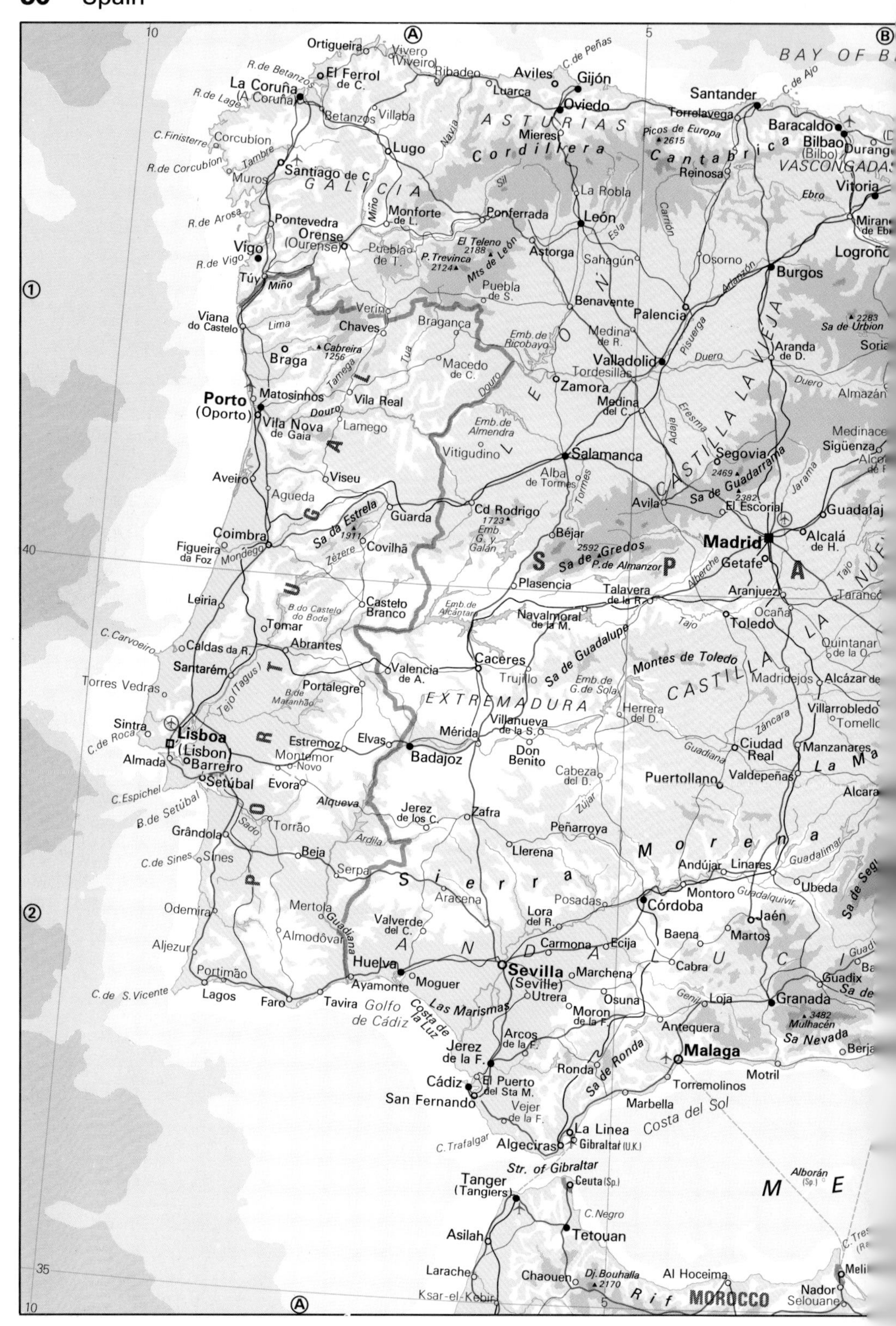
BAY OF B
Ortigueira
Vivero (Viveiro)
Ribadeo
El Ferrol de C.
R. de Betanzos
La Coruña (A Coruña)
R. de Lage
Betanzos
Villaba
Luarca
Aviles
C. de Peñas
Gijón
Oviedo
Santander
C. de Ajo
Torrelavega
Baracaldo
Bilbao (Bilbao)
Durango
VASCONGADAS
Vitoria
ASTURIAS
Mieres
Cordillera Cantabrica
Picos de Europa 2615
Reinosa
C. Finisterre
Corcubion
R. de Corcubion
Tambre
Santiago de C.
Muros
GALICIA
Lugo
Navia
Sil
La Robla
Ebro
R. de Arosa
Pontevedra
Miño
Monforte de L.
Ponferrada
León
Esla
Carrión
Orense (Ourense)
Vigo
R. de Vigo
Puebla de T.
El Teleno 2188
P. Trevinca 2124
Mts de León
Astorga
Sahagún
Osorno
Burgos
Logroño
Miranda de Ebro
Túy
Miño
Puebla de S.
Benavente
Arlanzón
Pisuerga
Palencia
Verín
Chaves
Bragança
Viana do Castelo
Lima
Cabreira 1256
Braga
Tua
Emb. de Ricobayo
Medina de R.
LEÓN
Valladolid
Tordesillas
Duero
Aranda de D.
2283 Sa de Urbion
Soria
Macedo de C.
Tamega
Zamora
Douro
Medina del C.
Almazán
Porto (Oporto)
Matosinhos
Vila Real
Vila Nova de Gaia
Douro
Lamego
Emb. de Almendra
Eresma
Adaja
CASTILLA LA VIEJA
Medinaceli
Sigüenza
Vitigudino
Salamanca
Segovia
2469
Sa de Guadarrama
2382
Jarama
Aveiro
Viseu
Alba de Tormes
Tormes
Agueda
Avila
El Escorial
Guadalajara
Guarda
Cd Rodrigo
1723
Sa da Estrela
1911
Emb. G. y Galán
Coimbra
Covilhã
Béjar
Madrid
Alcalá de H.
40
Figueira da Foz
Mondego
Zêzere
2592 Sa de Gredos
P. de Almanzor
Alberche
Getafe
SPAIN
PORTUGAL
Plasencia
Talavera de la R.
Aranjuez
Tajo
Tarancón
Leiria
Castelo Branco
B. do Castelo do Bode
Emb. de Alcántara
Navalmoral de la M.
Ocaña
Toledo
C. Carvoeiro
Tomar
Caldas da R.
Abrantes
Quintanar de la O.
Santarém
Tejo (Tagus)
Valencia de A.
Caceres
Trujillo
Sa de Guadalupe
Montes de Toledo
Madridejos
Alcázar de
Torres Vedras
Portalegre
B. de Matanhão
Emb. de G. de Sola
CASTILLA LA NUEVA
EXTREMADURA
Herrera del D.
Villarrobledo
Tomelloso
Sintra
C. de Roca
Lisboa (Lisbon)
Almada
Barreiro
Estremoz
Elvas
Mérida
Villanueva de la S.
Don Benito
Záncara
Guadiana
Ciudad Real
Manzanares
La Mancha
Montemor o-Novo
Badajoz
Cabeza del D.
Puertollano
Valdepeñas
Setúbal
Evora
C. Espichel
B. de Setúbal
Alqueva
Zújar
Alcaraz
Sado
Torrão
Jerez de los C.
Zafra
Grândola
Peñarroya
Ardila
C. de Sines
Sines
Beja
Llerena
Sierra Morena
Andújar
Linares
Guadalimar
Serpa
Ubeda
Sa de Segura
Aracena
Posadas
Montoro
Guadalquivir
Odemira
Mertola
Córdoba
Lora del R.
Jaén
Valverde del C.
Guadiana
Baena
Martos
Aljezur
Almodôvar
Carmona
Ecija
ANDALUCIA
Guadix
Huelva
Sevilla (Seville)
Marchena
Cabra
Portimão
Ayamonte
Moguer
Sa de
C. de S. Vicente
Lagos
Faro
Tavira
Golfo de Cádiz
Costa de la Luz
Las Marismas
Utrera
Osuna
Genil
Loja
Granada
Moron de la F.
3482 Mulhacén
Arcos de la F.
Antequera
Sa Nevada
Jerez de la F.
Sa de Ronda
Malaga
Berja
Ronda
Motril
Cádiz
El Puerto del Sta M.
Torremolinos
San Fernando
Vejer de la F.
Marbella
Costa del Sol
C. Trafalgar
Algeciras
La Linea
Gibraltar (U.K.)
Str. of Gibraltar
Alborán (Sp.)
Tanger (Tangiers)
Ceuta (Sp.)
ME
C. Negro
Asilah
Tetouan
C. Tres
35
Larache
Chaouen
Dj. Bouhalla 2170
Al Hoceima
Melilla
Nador
Selouane
Ksar-el-Kebir
Rif
MOROCCO
10
5

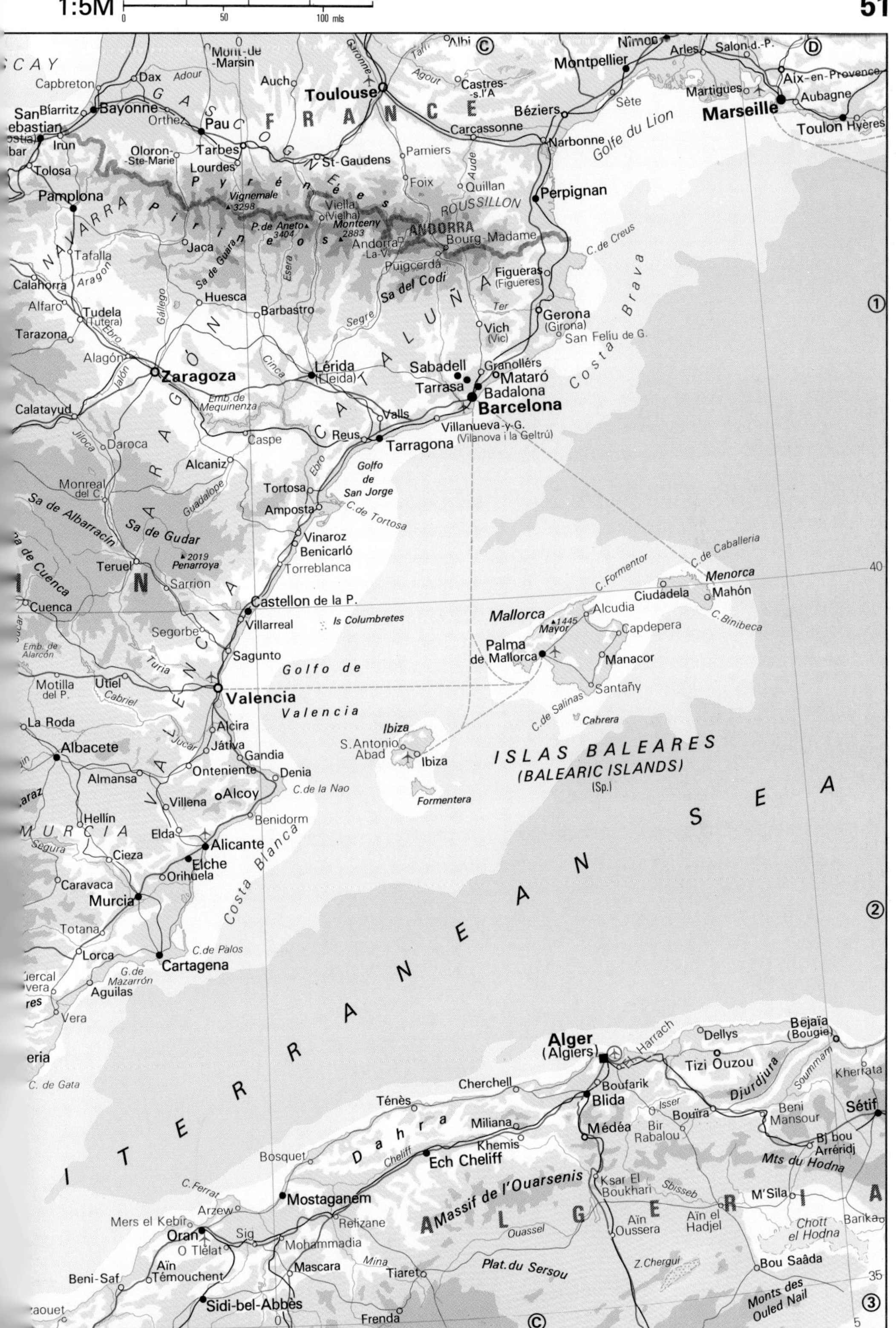

50   100   150   200 km
0   50   100 mls

CAY

Capbreton   Mont-de-Marsin
Biarritz   Dax   Adour   Auch
San Sebastian   Bayonne   Toulouse   Albi   C   Nîmes   Arles   Saloni d.P.   D
Irún   Orthez   Pau   FRANCE   Montpellier   Martigues   Aix-en-Provence
Tolosa   Oloron-Ste-Marie   Tarbes   St-Gaudens   Béziers   Sète   Aubagne
Pamplona   Lourdes   Pyrénées   Pamiers   Carcassonne   Narbonne   Golfe du Lion   Marseille   Toulon Hyères
Tafalla   Jaca   Vignemale   Foix   Quillan   Perpignan
Calahorra   Aragón   3298   Viella   Monteny   ANDORRA   Bourg-Madame
Alfaro   Huesca   P. de Aneto   2883   Andorra   Puigcerdá   C. de Creus
Tudela   3404   -La-V.   Figueras   Costa
Tarazona   Barbastro   Sa del Codí   (Figueres)   Brava
Alagón   CATALUÑA   Ter   Gerona   San Feliu de G.
Zaragoza   Segre   Vich   (Girona)
Calatayud   Lérida   Sabadell   (Vic)
Daroca   (Lleida)   Tarrasa   Mataró   40
Jiloca   Emb. de   Granollérs   Badalona
Mequinenza   Valls   Barcelona
Sa de Albarracín   Alcañiz   Caspe   Reus   Villanueva-y-G.   Costa
Monreal   Guadalope   (Vilanova i la Geltrú)   C. de Caballeria
del C.   Tarragona   C. de Formentor   Menorca
Sa de Gudar   Ebro   Golfo   Ciudadela   Mahón
Teruel   de   Vinaroz   San Jorge   C. Binibeca
2019   Benicarló   C. de Tortosa   Mallorca
Peñarroya   Sarrión   Torreblanca   Alcudia   Capdepera
Emb. de   Castellón de la P.   Is Columbretes   Mayor   1445
Alarcón   Segorbe   Villarreal   Palma   Manacor
Cuenca   Sagunto   de Mallorca
Motilla   Turia   Golfo de   Santañy
del P.   Utiel   VALENCIA   C. de Salinas   Cabrera
La Roda   Alcira   Valencia   Ibiza   ISLAS BALEARES
Albacete   Játiva   Gandia   S.Antonio   (BALEARIC ISLANDS)
Almansa   Ontenient   Denia   Abad   Ibiza   (Sp.)
Villena   Alcoy   C. de la Nao   Formentera
Hellín   Elda   Benidorm
MURCIA   Alicante   Costa
Cieza   Elche   Blanca   MEDITERRANEAN   SEA
Caravaca   Orihuela
Murcia
Totana   Lorca   C. de Palos
Cartagena   Alger   Harrach   Dellys   Bejaïa
Aguilas   G. de   (Algiers)   Tizi Ouzou   (Bougie)
Vera   Mazarrón   Boufarik   Kherrata
C. de Gata   Cherchell   Blida   Bouïra   Djurdjura   Sétif
Ténès   Miliana   Médéa   Bir   Beni
Bosquet   Cheliff   Khemis   Rabalou   Mansour
Dahra   Ech Cheliff   Isser   Bj bou
C. Ferrat   Mostaganem   Massif de l'Ouarsenis   Ksar El   Arréridj   M'Sila
Mers el Kebir   Arzew   A   Boukhari   Sbisseb
Oran   Relizane   L   Quassel   Aïn   Aïn el   Chott
O Tlelat   Sig   Ouarsera   Hadjel   el Hodna   Barika
Beni-Saf   Aïn   Mohammadia   Mina   Plat. du Sersou   Z. Chergui   Bou Saâda
Témouchent   Mascara   Tiareti   Monts des
Sidi-bel-Abbès   Frenda   Ouled Nail   35
C

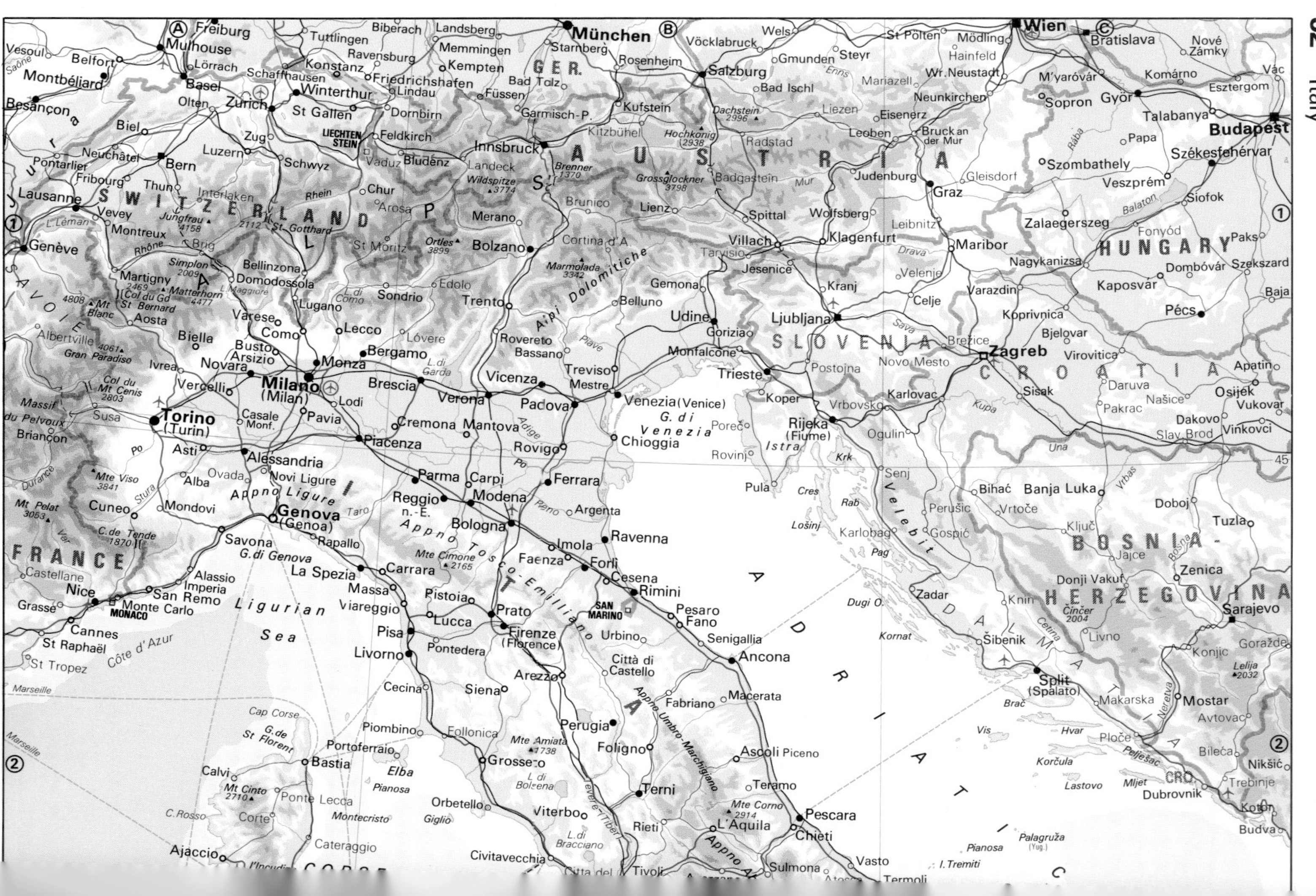
AUSTRIA
SWITZERLAND
HUNGARY
SLOVENIA
CROATIA
BOSNIA - HERZEGOVINA
FRANCE
ITALIA
ADRIATIC
Ligurian Sea
LIECHTENSTEIN
SAN MARINO
MONACO
Wien
Budapest
München
Zagreb
Ljubljana
Sarajevo
Milano (Milan)
Torino (Turin)
Genova (Genoa)
Venezia (Venice)
Firenze (Florence)
Bologna
Verona
Padova
Trieste
Bolzano
Innsbruck
Salzburg
Graz
Zürich
Bern
Genève
Lausanne
Basel
Nice
Split (Spalato)
Rijeka (Fiume)
Ancona
Perugia
Pescara
Pisa
Livorno
La Spezia
Parma
Modena
Ravenna
Rimini
Bastia
Ajaccio
Elba
Mte Viso 3841
Gran Paradiso 4061
Matterhorn 4477
Jungfrau 4158
Grossglockner 3798
Ortles 3899
Marmolada 3342

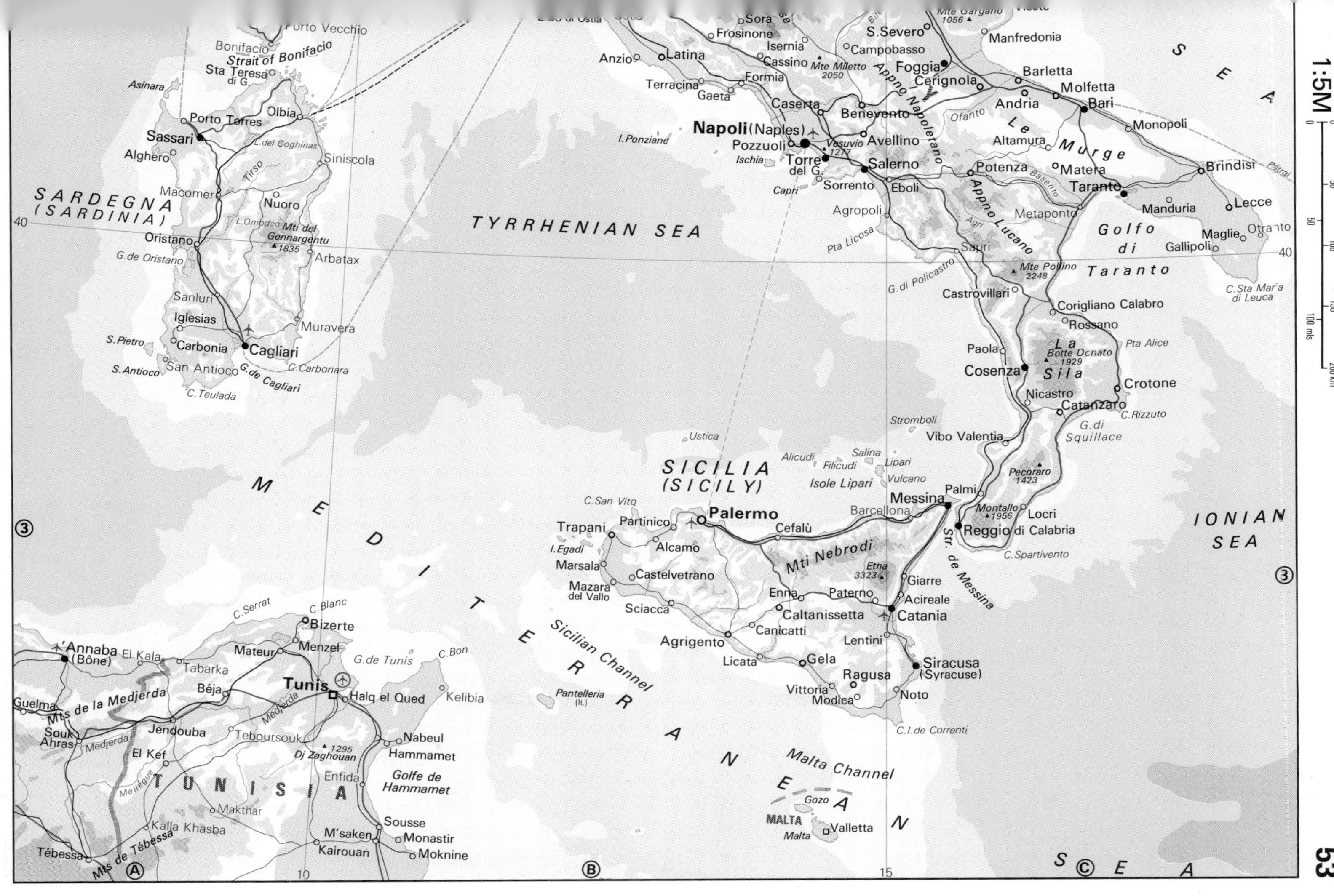

50 100 150 200 km
0 50 100 mls

Map labels

Seas:
IONIAN SEA
TYRRHENIAN SEA
MEDITERRANEAN SEA
Sicilian Channel
Malta Channel

SICILIA (SICILY)
SARDEGNA (SARDINIA)
TUNISIA

Lecce
Brindisi
Otranto
C. Sta Maria di Leuca
Maglie
Gallipoli
Monopoli
Manduria
Bari
Molfetta
Le Murge
Matera
Taranto
Golfo di Taranto
Altamura
Metaponto
Andria
Barletta
Manfredonia
Mte Gargano 1056
Foggia
Cerignola
S. Severo
Campobasso
Isernia
Benevento
Avellino
Caserta
Cassino Mte Miletto 2050
Sora
Frosinone
Latina
Anzio
Terracina
Gaeta
Formia
Napoli (Naples)
Vesuvio 1277
Pozzuoli
Ischia
Torre del Greco
Sorrento
Salerno
Eboli
Agropoli
Capri
I. Ponziane
Pta Licosa
G. di Policastro
Sapri
Appno Lucano
Potenza
Mte Pollino 2248
Basento
Agri
Castrovillari
Paola
Cosenza
Corigliano Calabro
Rossano
La Sila
Botte Donato 1928
Pta Alice
Crotone
C. Rizzuto
Catanzaro
G. di Squillace
Nicastro
Vibo Valentia
Pecoraro 1423
Montalto 1955
Palmi
Reggio di Calabria
Str. de Messina
C. Spartivento
Stromboli
Lipari
Vulcano
Salina
Filicudi
Alicudi
Isole Lipari
Ustica
C. San Vito
Trapani
I. Egadi
Marsala
Mazara del Vallo
Pantelleria (It.)
Partinico
Alcamo
Castelvetrano
Sciacca
Palermo
Cefalù
Mti Nebrodi
Barcellona
Messina
Giarre
Acireale
Catania
Etna 3323
Paternò
Lentini
Enna
Caltanissetta
Canicattì
Caltagirone
Gela
Licata
Agrigento
Vittoria
Modica
Ragusa
Noto
Siracusa (Syracuse)
C. I. de Correnti
C. I. de Correnti
MALTA
Gozo
Valletta
Malta

Porto Vecchio
Bonifacio
Strait of Bonifacio
Sta Teresa di G.
Olbia
Siniscola
Porto Torres
Asinara
Sassari
Alghero
Macomer
Nuoro
Mti del Gennargentu 1835
Arbatax
Oristano
G. di Oristano
Sanluri
Iglesias
Carbonia
S. Pietro
S. Antioco
C. Teulada
Cagliari
G. de Cagliari
C. Carbonara
Muravera

C. Bon
Kelibia
Nabeul
Hammamet
Golfe de Hammamet
Monastir
Moknine
Sousse
M'saken
Kairouan
C. Bianc
C. Cerrat
Bizerte
Menzel
Haïq el Oued
G. de Tunis
Tunis
Mateur
Teboursouk
Enfida
Dj Zaghouan 1295
Makthar
Kalâa Khasba
Tabarka
Béja
Jendouba
El Kef
TUNISIA
Annaba (Bône)
El Kala
Guelma
Souk Ahras
Tébessa
Mts de Tébessa

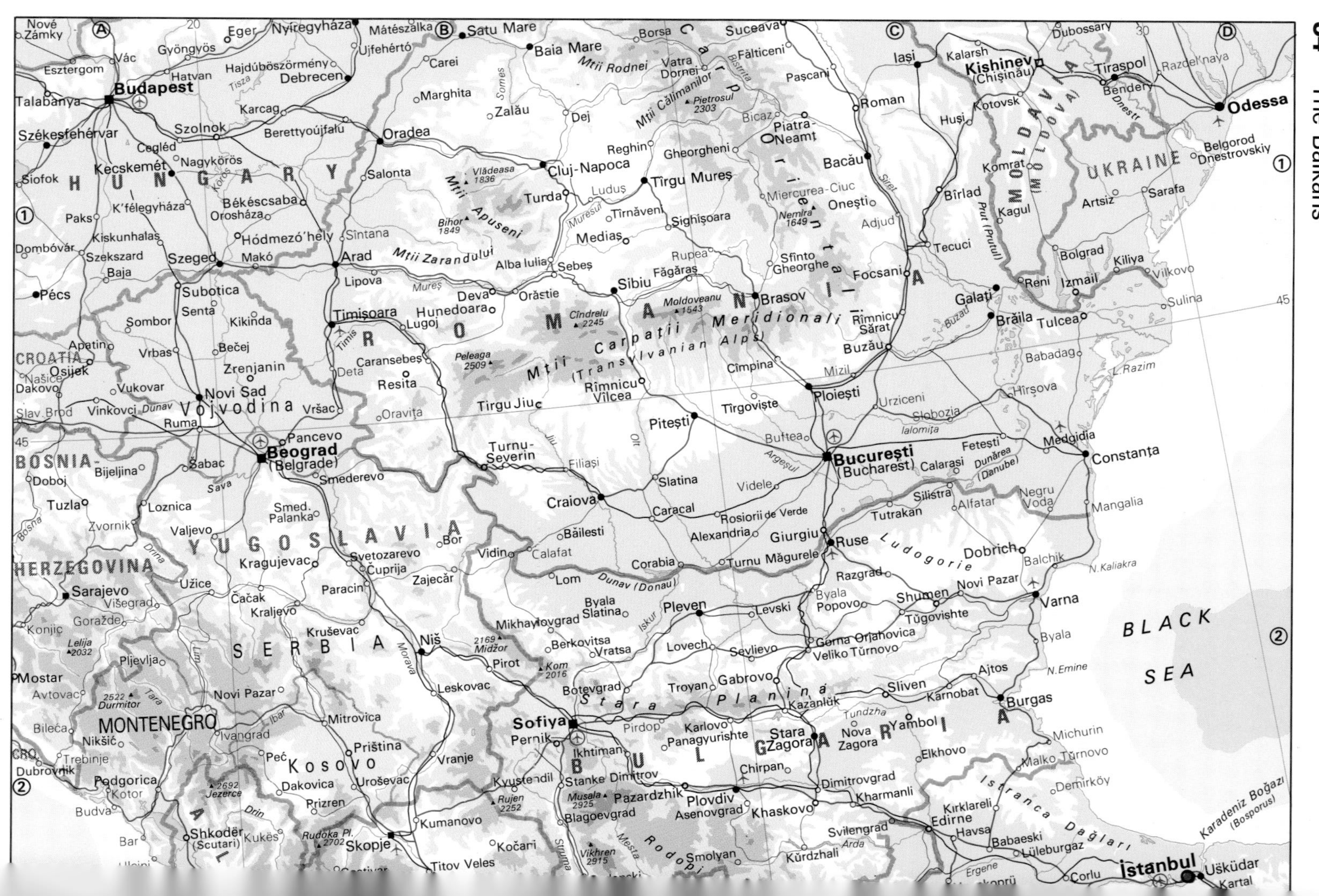
BLACK SEA
UKRAINE
MOLDAVA (MOLDOVA)
ROMANIA
BULGARIA
HUNGARY
YUGOSLAVIA
SERBIA
KOSOVO
Vojvodina
MONTENEGRO
BOSNIA-HERZEGOVINA
CROATIA
Carpatii Meridionali
Mtii Carpatii (Transylvanian Alps)
Stara Planina
Rodopi
Istranca Dağlari
Ludogorie
Mtii Apuseni
Mtii Rodnei
Mtii Zarandului
Odessa
Kishinev (Chişinău)
Tiraspol
Bucureşti (Bucharest)
Constanţa
Galaţi
Brăila
Tulcea
Iaşi
Ploieşti
Brasov
Sibiu
Cluj-Napoca
Timişoara
Oradea
Craiova
Piteşti
Sofiya
Plovdiv
Varna
Burgas
Ruse
Pleven
Stara Zagora
Istanbul
Üsküdar
Edirne
Budapest
Szeged
Debrecen
Kecskemét
Pécs
Beograd (Belgrade)
Novi Sad
Niš
Skopje
Sarajevo
Podgorica
Shkodër (Scutari)
Dunav (Donau)
Dunărea (Danube)
Prut (Prutul)
Dnestr
Siret
Mureş
Olt
Tisza
Sava
Morava
Drina
Karadeniz Boğazi (Bosporus)

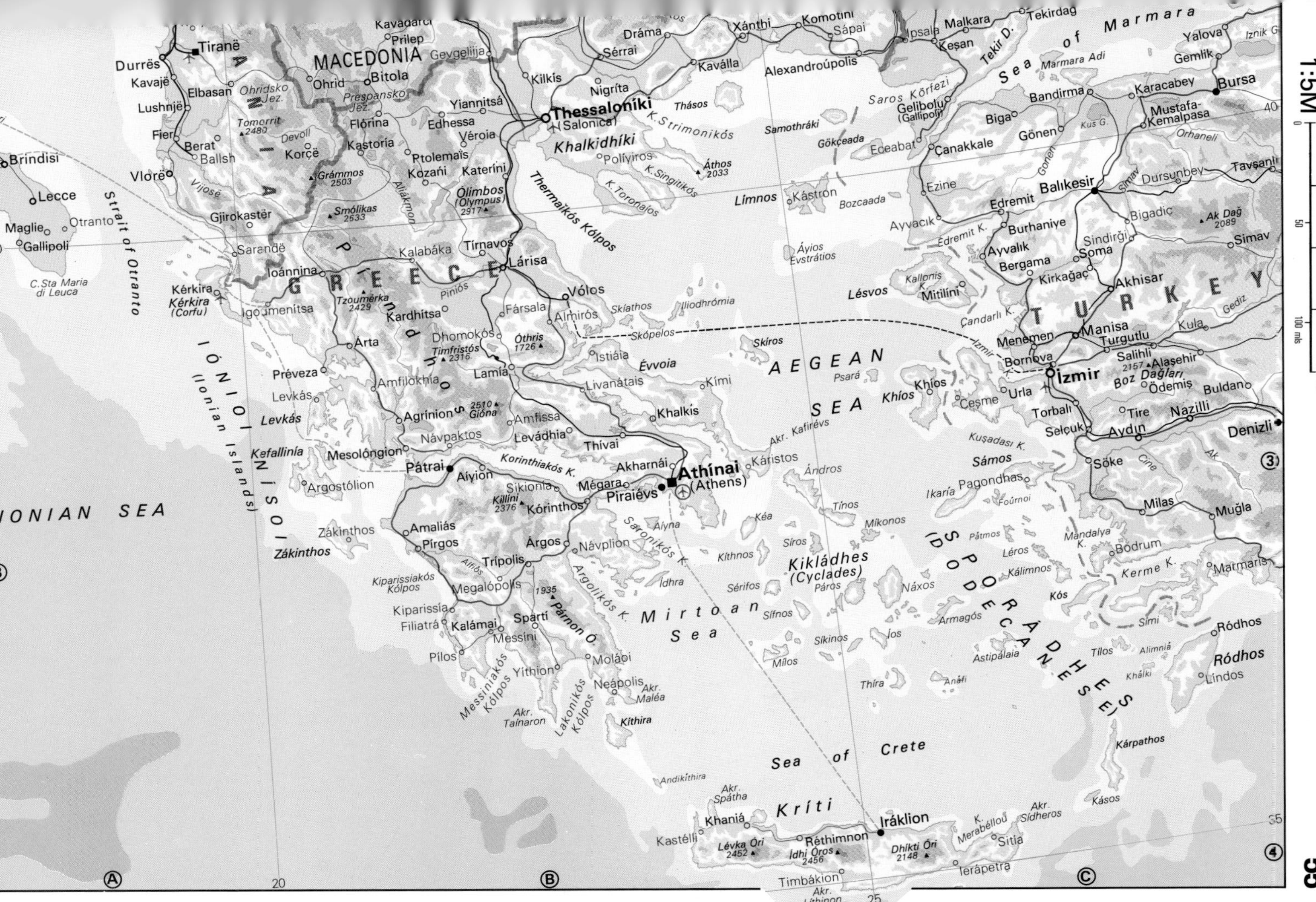
AEGEAN SEA
IONIAN SEA
IÓNIOI NÍSOI
(Ionian Islands)
Sea of Marmara
Sea of Crete
Kríti
Mirtoan Sea
Strait of Otranto
GREECE
TURKEY
ALBANIA
MACEDONIA
SPORÁDHES
DODECANESE
Kikládhes
(Cyclades)
Athínai
(Athens)
Thessaloníki
(Salonica)
İzmir
Bursa
Balıkesir
Denizli
Iráklion
Pátrai
Lárisa
Vólos
Piraiévs
Tiranë
Ioánnina
Kérkira
(Corfu)
Brindisi
Lecce
Otranto
Thermaïkós Kólpos
Khalkidhíki
Límnos
Lésvos
Khíos
Sámos
Kós
Ródhos
Kárpathos
Évvoia
Kíthira
Zákinthos
Kefallinía
Levkás
Ólimbos
(Olympus)
2917

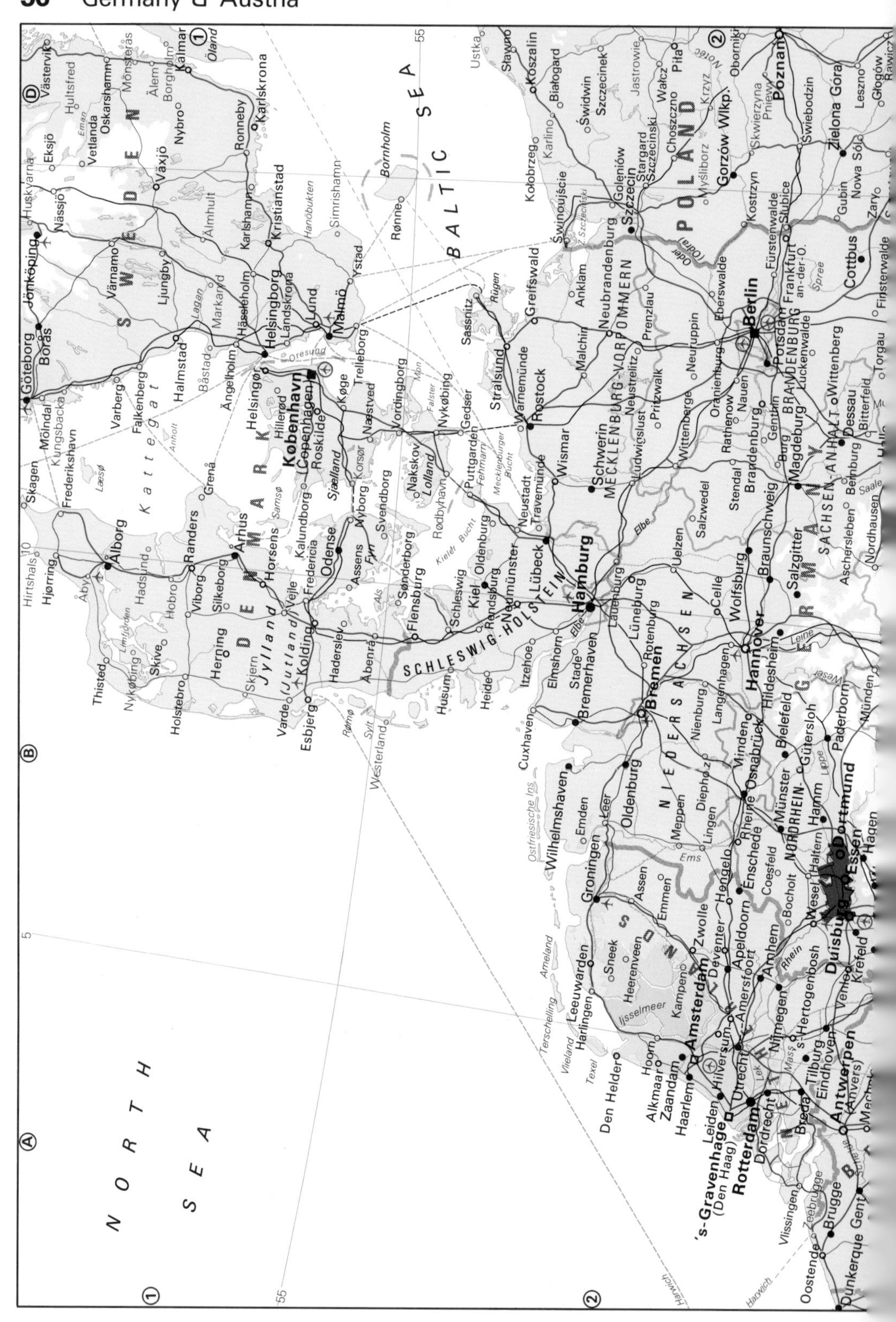
NORTH SEA
BALTIC SEA
SWEDEN
DENMARK
POLAND
SCHLESWIG-HOLSTEIN
MECKLENBURG-VORPOMMERN
NIEDERSACHSEN
BRANDENBURG
SACHSEN-ANHALT
NORDRHEIN-
Kattegat
Göteborg
Borås
Jönköping
Växjö
Kalmar
Karlskrona
Helsingborg
Malmö
Lund
Ystad
Trelleborg
Halmstad
Bornholm
Rønne
København
(Copenhagen)
Roskilde
Helsingør
Ålborg
Århus
Odense
Esbjerg
Kolding
Fredericia
Vejle
Horsens
Randers
Herning
Viborg
Frederikshavn
Skagen
Hjørring
Jylland
(Jutland)
Sjælland
Fyn
Lolland
Falster
Flensburg
Kiel
Schleswig
Rendsburg
Neumünster
Lübeck
Hamburg
Bremen
Bremerhaven
Cuxhaven
Wilhelmshaven
Oldenburg
Emden
Rostock
Wismar
Schwerin
Stralsund
Greifswald
Rügen
Sassnitz
Neubrandenburg
Szczecin
Świnoujście
Kołobrzeg
Koszalin
Gorzów Wlkp.
Poznań
Zielona Góra
Berlin
Potsdam
Frankfurt
an-der-O.
Cottbus
Brandenburg
Magdeburg
Dessau
Wittenberg
Stendal
Braunschweig
Salzgitter
Wolfsburg
Hannover
Hildesheim
Celle
Lüneburg
Uelzen
Osnabrück
Bielefeld
Gütersloh
Paderborn
Minden
Münster
Hamm
Dortmund
Essen
Duisburg
Krefeld
Hagen
Groningen
Leeuwarden
Zwolle
Enschede
Apeldoorn
Arnhem
Nijmegen
Amsterdam
Haarlem
Utrecht
Den Helder
IJsselmeer
Rotterdam
's-Gravenhage
(Den Haag)
Leiden
Dordrecht
Breda
Tilburg
Eindhoven
Antwerpen
(Anvers)
Brugge
Gent
Oostende
Vlissingen
Dunkerque
Harwich
Elbe
Weser
Ems
Oder
(Odra)
Spree
Saale
Rhein

1:5M

0 50 100 150 200 km
0 50 100 mls

CZECH REP. · Praha (Prague) · Brno · Wien (Vienna) · Bratislava · Zagreb · CROATIA · SLOVENIA · AUSTRIA · Graz · Ljubljana · Dresden · SACHSEN · Erfurt · THÜRINGEN · München (Munich) · Nürnberg · Regensburg · Salzburg · Innsbruck · ITALY · Milano (Milan) · Torino (Turin) · Frankfurt · Mainz · Stuttgart · Karlsruhe · Freiburg · Basel · Zürich · SWITZERLAND · Bern · Genève · Lyon · Grenoble · FRANCE · Strasbourg · Nancy · Metz · Dijon · Besançon · BELGIUM · LUXEMBOURG

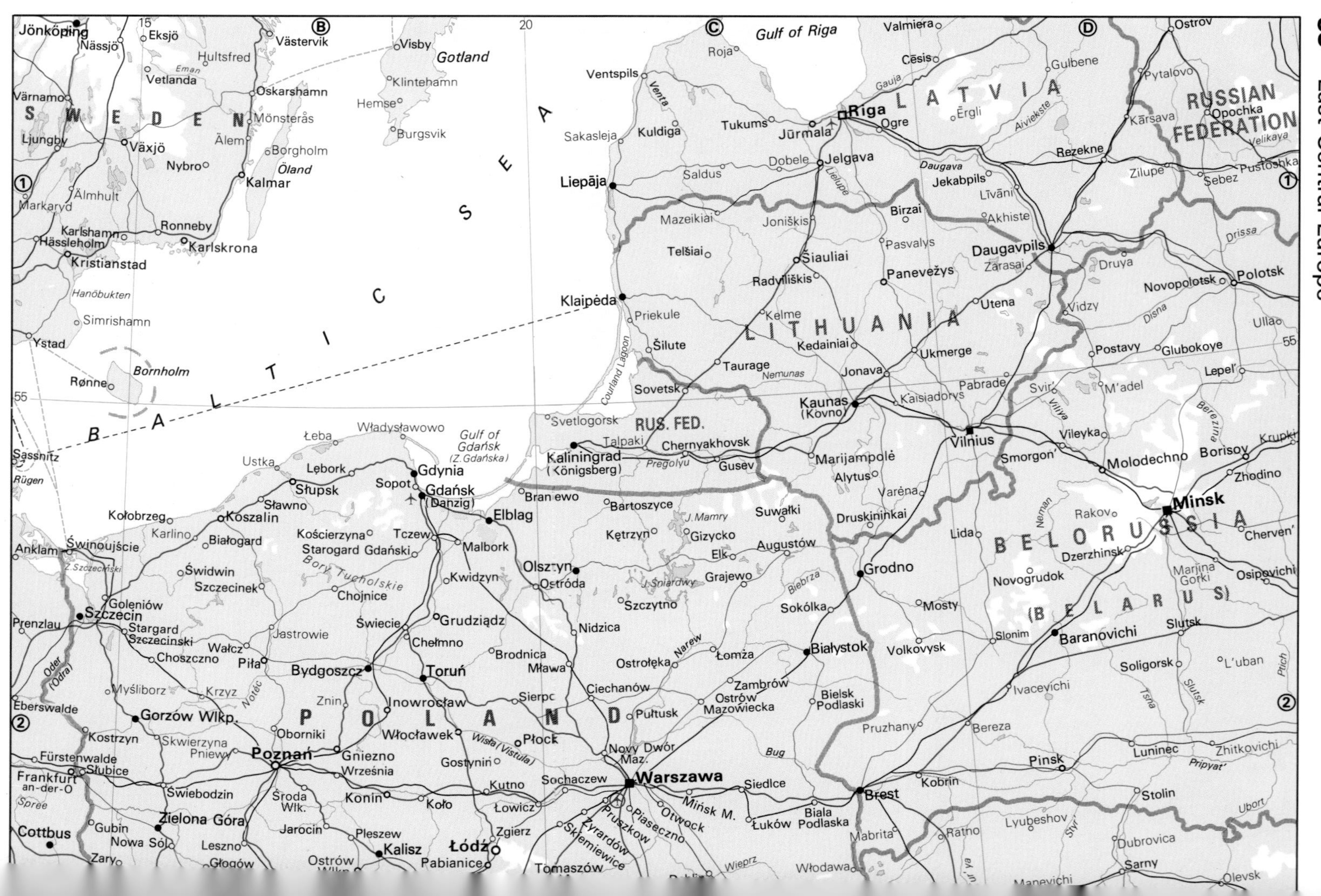
RUSSIAN FEDERATION
LATVIA
LITHUANIA
BELORUSSIA
(BELARUS)
POLAND
SWEDEN
BALTIC SEA
RUS. FED.
Gulf of Riga
Gulf of Gdańsk
(Z. Gdańska)
Gotland
Öland
Bornholm
Hanöbukten
Rügen
Courland Lagoon
Riga
Minsk
Vilnius
Warszawa
Daugavpils
Kaunas
(Kovno)
Kaliningrad
(Königsberg)
Klaipėda
Liepāja
Ventspils
Jelgava
Šiauliai
Panevežys
Grodno
Brest
Białystok
Gdańsk
(Danzig)
Gdynia
Elbląg
Olsztyn
Toruń
Bydgoszcz
Poznań
Łódź
Płock
Szczecin
Gorzów Wlkp.
Zielona Góra
Kalisz
Cottbus
Frankfurt an-der-O
Baranovichi
Pinsk
Molodechno
Polotsk
Novopolotsk
Borisov
Slutsk
Karlskrona
Kalmar
Kristianstad
Växjö
Jönköping
Visby
Rønne
Ystad
Sassnitz
Wisła (Vistula)
Oder (Odra)
Nemunas
Daugava
Neman
Berezina
Pripyat'
Bug
Narew
Noteć

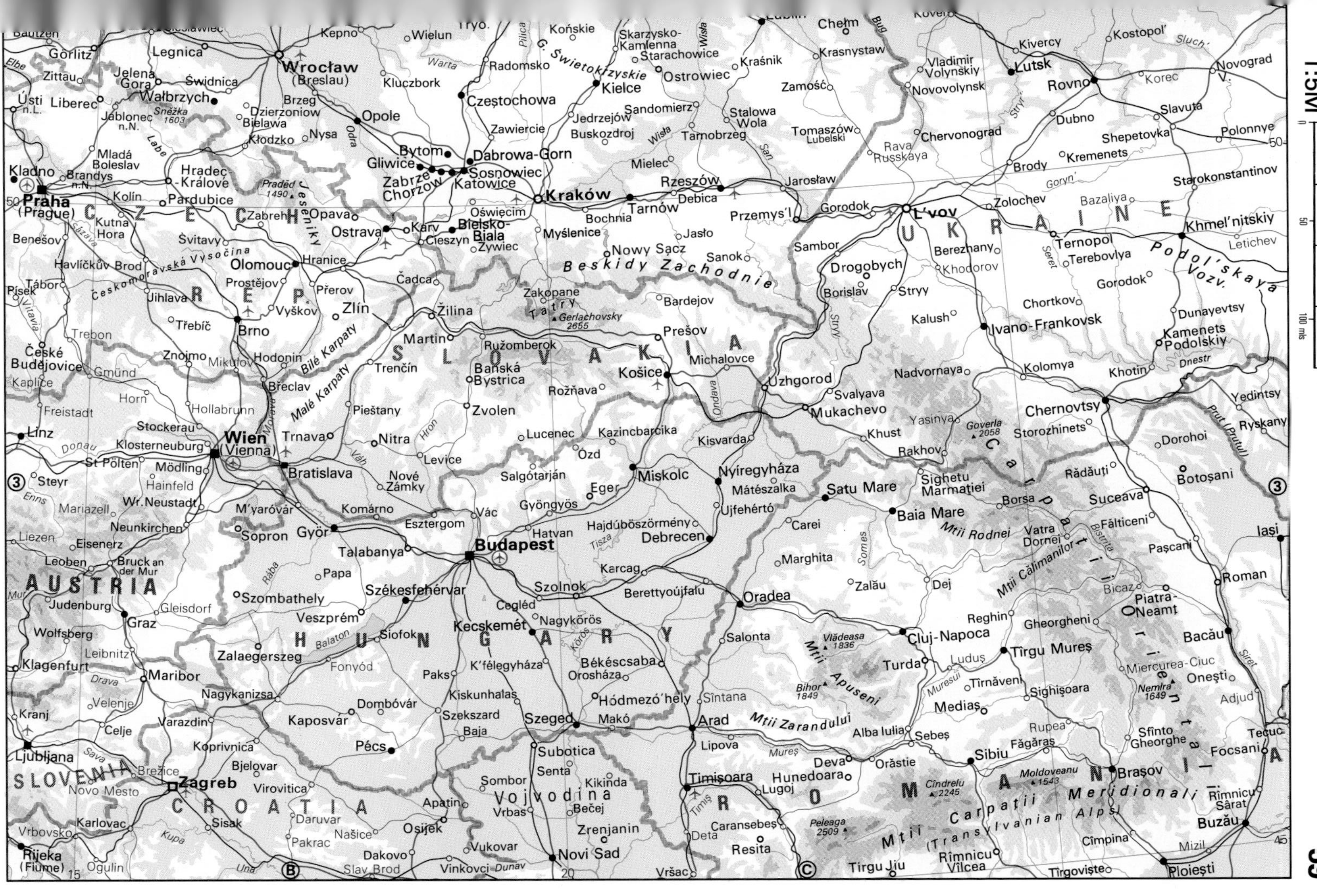
U K R A I N E
P O L A N D
C Z E C H R E P.
S L O V A K I A
H U N G A R Y
R O M A N I A
A U S T R I A
S L O V E N I A
C R O A T I A
Vojvodina
C a r p a t i i
Carpaţii Meridionali (Transylvanian Alps)
Mţii Apuseni
Mţii Zarandului
Mţii Rodnei
Mţii Călimanilor
Beskidy Zachodnie
Tatry
Gerlachovsky 2655
Goverla 2058
Moldoveanu 2543
Cindrelu 2245
Peleaga 2509
Vlădeasa 1836
Bihor 1849
Nemira 1649
Praděd 1490
Sněžka 1603
Jeseníky
Malé Karpaty
Bílé Karpaty
Českomoravská Vysočina
Podol'skaya Vozv.
Lutsk
Rovno
L'vov
Ternopol
Khmel'nitskiy
Ivano-Frankovsk
Chernovtsy
Kamenets Podolskiy
Uzhgorod
Mukachevo
Drogobych
Kraków
Katowice
Wrocław (Breslau)
Opole
Częstochowa
Kielce
Rzeszów
Tarnów
Przemys'l
Praha (Prague)
Brno
Ostrava
Olomouc
Zlín
České Budějovice
Wien (Vienna)
Linz
Graz
Bratislava
Košice
Prešov
Žilina
Banská Bystrica
Budapest
Miskolc
Debrecen
Nyíregyháza
Szeged
Pécs
Györ
Kecskemét
Székesfehérvar
Szombathely
Cluj-Napoca
Oradea
Arad
Timişoara
Sibiu
Braşov
Tîrgu Mureş
Satu Mare
Baia Mare
Suceava
Iaşi
Bacău
Buzău
Ploieşti
Zagreb
Ljubljana
Maribor
Osijek
Novi Sad
Subotica
Rijeka (Fiume)
Dunav
Donau
Tisza
Odra
Wisła
San
Bug
Dnestr
Prut (Prutul)
Siret
Mureş
Balaton
Drava
Sava

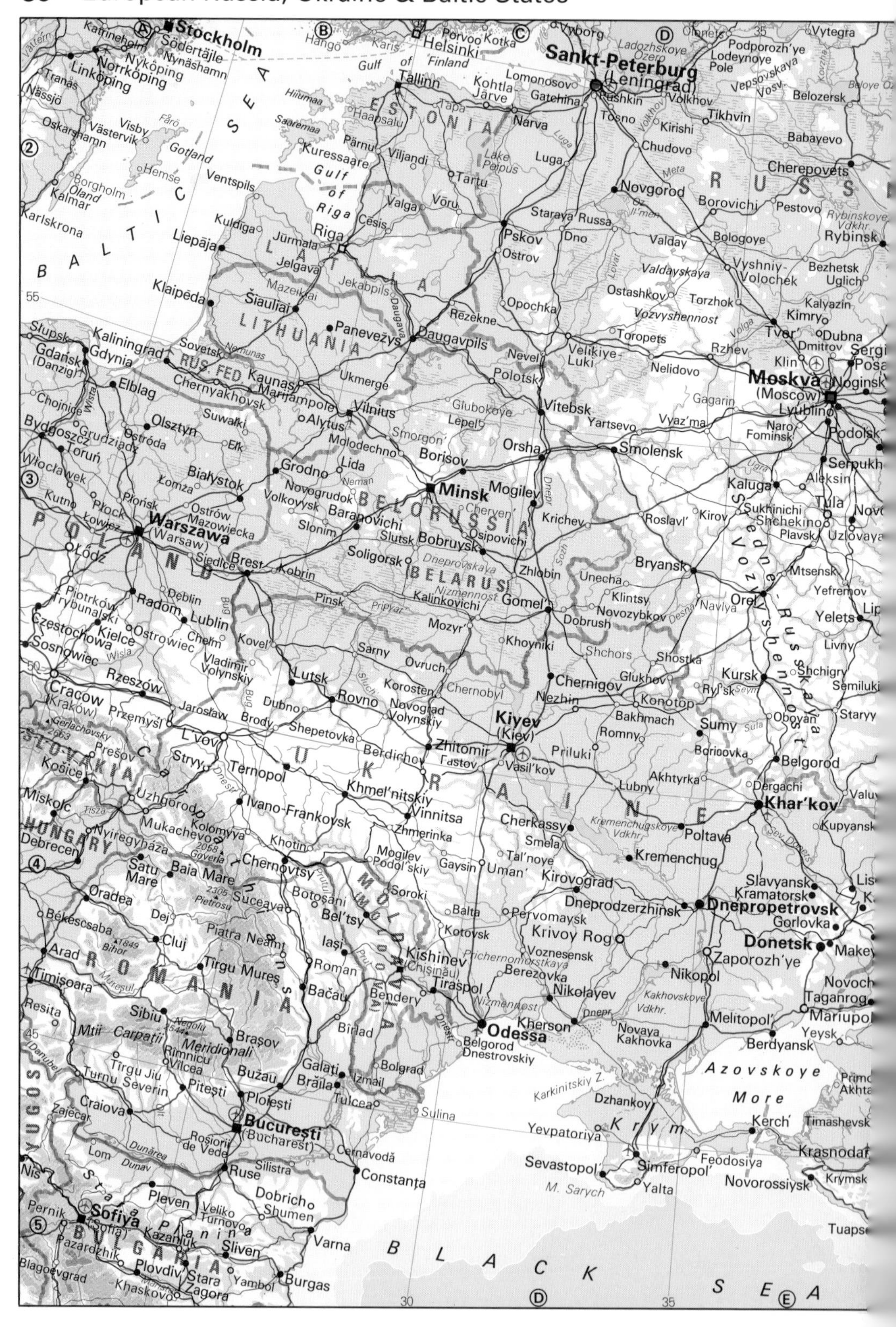
Stockholm
Södertälje
Nynäshamn
Nyköping
Norrköping
Linköping
Tranås
Nässjö
Västervik
Visby
Fårö
Gotland
Oskarshamn
Hemse
Borgholm
Öland
Kalmar
Karlskrona
B A L T I C S E A
Hangö
Karis
Porvoo
Kotka
Helsinki
Gulf of Finland
Vyborg
Sankt-Peterburg
(Leningrad)
Ladozhskoye Ozero
Olonets
Vytegra
Podporozh'ye
Lodeynoye Pole
Vepsovskaya Vosv.
Belozersk
Tallinn
Kohtla-Järve
Lomonosov
Gatchina
Pushkin
Volkhov
Tikhvin
Hiiumaa
Saaremaa
Haapsalu
Tapa
E S T O N I A
Narva
Tosno
Kirishi
Babayevo
Kuressaare
Pärnu
Viljandi
Lake Peipus
Luga
Chudovo
Cherepovets
Gulf of Riga
Tartu
Novgorod
Borovichi
Pestovo
Rybinskoye Vdkhr.
Rybinsk
Ventspils
Valga
Võru
Staraya Russa
R U S S
Kuldiga
Jūrmala
Riga
Cēsis
Pskov
Dno
Valday
Bologoye
Liepāja
Jelgava
Ostrov
Valdayskaya
Vyshniy-Volochek
Bezhetsk
Uglich
L A T V I A
Jekabpils
Daugava
Ostashkov
Torzhok
Kalyazin
Klaipėda
Mazeikiai
Šiauliai
Opochka
Vozvyshennost
Kimry
Rezekne
Tver'
Dubna
L I T H U A N I A
Panevežys
Daugavpils
Toropets
Rzhev
Dmitrov
Słupsk
Kaliningrad
Gdańsk (Danzig)
Gdynia
Sovetsk
Nemunas
RUS. FED.
Nevel'
Velikiye-Luki
Nelidovo
Klin
Sergi
Posa
Elbląg
Chernyakhovsk
Kaunas
Marijampole
Ukmerge
Polotsk
Moskva
(Moscow)
Noginsk
Chojnice
Wisła
Suwałki
Vilnius
Glubokoye
Vitebsk
Gagarin
Lyublino
Bydgoszcz
Grudziądz
Olsztyn
Ostróda
Ełk
Alytus
Smorgon'
Lepel'
Yartsevo
Vyaz'ma
Naro-Fominsk
Podolsk
Toruń
Molodechno
Borisov
Orsha
Smolensk
Włocławek
Białystok
Grodno
Lida
Neman
Serpukh
Łomża
Novogrudok
Minsk
Mogilev
Kaluga
Aleksin
Kutno
Płock
Płońsk
Ostrów Mazowiecka
Volkovysk
Baranovichi
B E L O R U S S I A
Cherven'
Dnepr
Krichev
Roslavl'
Kirov
Sukhinichi
Shchekino
Tula
Łowicz
Warszawa
(Warsaw)
Slonim
Osipovichi
Plavsk
Uzlovaya
Łódź
P O L A N D
Siedlce
Brest
Slutsk
Bobruysk
Soligorsk
Dneprovskaya
B E L A R U S
Nizmennost
Zhlobin
Sozh
Unecha
Bryansk
Mtsensk
Kobrin
Klintsy
Oryol
Yefremov
Piotrków Trybunalski
Dęblin
Radom
Lublin
Bug
Pinsk
Pripyat
Kalinkovichi
Gomel'
Novozybkov
Desna
Navlya
Yelets
Lip
Częstochowa
Kielce
Ostrowiec
Chełm
Mozyr'
Dobrush
Sosnowiec
Wisła
Kovel'
Khoyniki
Livny
Vladimir-Volynskiy
Sarny
Ovruch
Shchors
Shostka
Shchigry
Rzeszów
Lutsk
Sluch
Korosten'
Chernobyl
Chernigov
Glukhov
Kursk
Semiluki
Cracow (Kraków)
Przemyśl
Jarosław
Dubno
Rovno
Novograd-Volynskiy
Nezhin
Konotop
Ryl'sk
Seym
Gerlachovský
Brody
Shepetovka
Kiyev
(Kiev)
Bakhmach
Romny
Sumy
Sula
Oboyan'
Staryy
Prešov
L'vov
Berdichev
Zhitomir
Fastov
Priluki
Borisovka
Belgorod
S L O V A K I A
Košice
Stryy
Dnestr
Ternopol
U K R A I N E
Vasil'kov
Akhtyrka
Dergachi
Valuy
Miskolc
Tisza
Uzhgorod
Ivano-Frankovsk
Khmel'nitskiy
Vinnitsa
Lubny
Khar'kov
H U N G A R Y
Nyiregyháza
Mukachevo
Kolomyya
Zhmerinka
Cherkassy
Kremenchugskoye Vdkhr.
Poltava
Kupyansk
Debrecen
Goverla
Khotin
Mogilev-Podol'skiy
Smela
Sev. Donets
Satu Mare
Baia Mare
Chernovtsy
Gaysin
Uman'
Tal'noye
Kremenchug
Oradea
Pietrosu
Suceava
Botoşani
Soroki
Kirovograd
Slavyansk
Kramatorsk
Békéscsaba
Dej
Bel'tsy
M O L D O V A
Balta
Pervomaysk
Dneprodzerzhinsk
Dnepropetrovsk
Gorlovka
Bihor
Cluj
Piatra Neamţ
Iaşi
Kotovsk
Krivoy Rog
Donetsk
Makey
Arad
R O M A N I A
Tîrgu Mureş
Roman
Prut
Kishinev
(Chişinău)
Voznesensk
Prichernomorstkaya
Zaporozh'ye
Timişoara
Mureşul
Bacău
Berezovka
Nikopol
Novoch
Bendery
Tiraspol
Nikolayev
Kakhovskoye Vdkhr.
Taganrog
Resita
Sibiu
Negoiu
Bîrlad
Nizmennost
Dnepr
Mariupol
Mţii Carpaţii Meridionali
Braşov
Odessa
Kherson
Novaya Kakhovka
Melitopol'
Yeysk
Rimnicu Vîlcea
Belgorod Dnestrovskiy
Berdyansk
Tîrgu Jiu
Turnu Severin
Galaţi
Bolgrad
Izmail
Azovskoye More
Primo Akhta
Piteşti
Buzău
Brăila
Karkinitskiy Z.
Craiova
Ploieşti
Tulcea
Sulina
Dzhankoy
Zaječar
Bucureşti
(Bucharest)
Yevpatoriya
Krym
Kerch'
Timashevsk
Roşiorii de Vede
Lom
Dunav
Dunărea
Cernavodă
Feodosiya
Krasnodar
Niš
Ruse
Silistra
Constanţa
Sevastopol'
Simferopol'
Novorossiysk
Krymsk
Pleven
Dobrich
M. Sarych
Yalta
Veliko Turnovo
Shumen
Pernik
Sofiya
(Sofia)
Stara Planina
Tuapse
Kazanlŭk
Varna
Pazardzhik
B U L G A R I A
Sliven
B L A C K S E A
Blagoevgrad
Plovdiv
Stara Zagora
Yambol
Burgas
Khaskovo
Y U G O S L A V I A
Danube
55
50
45
30
35
A
B
C
D
E
2
3
4
5

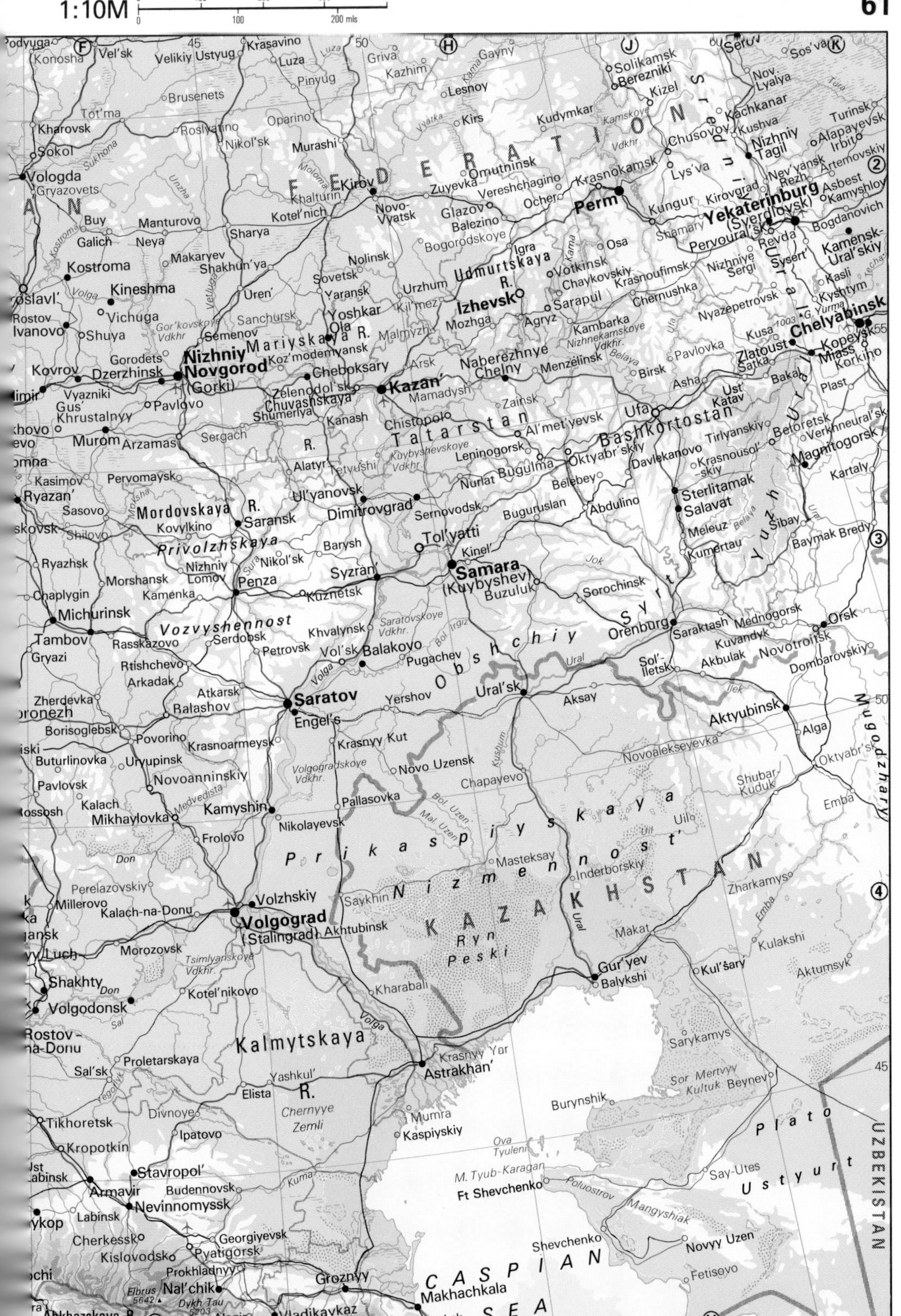

odyuga F Vel'sk Velikiy Ustyug Krasavino Luza Griva 50 Kazhim Gayny H Solikamsk Serov K
Konosha Brusenets Pinyug Lesnoy Kudymkar Berezniki Nov. Lyalya Sos'va
Kharovsk Tot'ma Rosyatino Murashi Kirs Vyatka Kachkanar Kushva Turinsk
Sokol Sukhona Nikol'sk Omutninsk Zuyevka Krasnokamsk Chusovoy Nizhniy Tagil Alapayevsk Irbito
Vologda Gryazovets Khalturin Novo-Vyatsk Glazov Ocher Perm Lys'va Nev'yansk Rezh Asbest Kamyshlov
Buy Manturovo Sharya Kirov Balezino Igra Osa Kungur Kirovgrad Yekaterinburg Sverdlovsk Bogdanovich
Kostroma Galich Neya Makaryev Shakhun'ya Nolinsk Bogorodskoye Votkinsk Pervoural'sk Revda Sysert' Kamensk-Ural'skiy
oslavl' Kineshma Uren' Yaransk Urzhum Izhevsk Chaykovskiy Krasnoufimsk Nyazepetrovsk Kasli
Rostov Vichuga Shuya Semenov Yoshkar-Ola Kil'mez' Mozhga Agryz Sarapul Chernushka Asha Kyshtym Chelyabinsk
Ivanovo Gorodets Koz'modemyansk Malmyzh Naberezhnye Chelny Kambarka Belaya Birsk Zlatoust Miass Kopeysk Korkino
Nizhniy Novgorod (Gorki) Cheboksary Arsk Mamadysh Menzelinsk Pavlovka Katav Plast
Kovrov Dzerzhinsk Zelenodol'sk Kazan Nizhnekamsk Ufa Kartaly
Vyazniki Gus-Khrustalnyy Pavlovo Shumerlya Kanash Chistopol Al'met'yevsk Bashkortostan Sterlitamak Magnitogorsk
Murom Arzamas Sergach Alatyr Tetyushi Leninogorsk Oktyabr'skiy Davlekanovo Krasnousol- skiy Salavat Verkhneural'sk
Kasimov Pervomaysk Mordovskaya Ul'yanovsk Dimitrovgrad Nurlat Bugul'ma Belebey Meleuz Sibay Baymak Bredy
Ryazan Sasovo Saransk Barysh Sernovodsk Buguruslan Abdulino Kumertau
Ryazhsk Kovylkino Nizhniy Lomov Nikol'sk Kuznetsk Kinel Sorochinsk Orenburg Saraktash Mednogorsk Orsk
Chaplygin Morshansk Kamenka Penza Syzran Tol'yatti Samara (Kuybyshev) Buzuluk Kuvandyk Novotroitsk
Michurinsk Serdobsk Khvalynsk Balakovo Pugachev Sol'- lletsk Akbulak Dombarovskiy
Tambov Rtishchevo Petrovsk Vol'sk Yershov Ural'sk Aksay Aktyubinsk Alga
Zherdevka Atkarsk Balashov Saratov Engel's Krasnyy Kut Novoalekseyevka Shubar-Kuduk Emba
Borisoglebsk Povorino Krasnoarmeysk Novo Uzensk Chapayevo Uil
Buturlinovka Uryupinsk Novoanninskiy Pallasovka Inderborskiy Zharkamys
Pavlovsk Kalach Mikhaylovka Kamyshin Nikolayevsk KAZAKHSTAN Makat Kulakshi
Perelazovskiy Millerovo Kalach-na-Donu Volzhskiy Volgograd (Stalingrad) Akhtubinsk Gur'yev Balykshi Kul'šary Aktumsyk
Shakhty Morozovsk Kotel'nikovo Kharabali Sarykamys
Volgodonsk Kalmytskaya Astrakhan' Sor Mertvyy Kultuk Beyneu
Rostov-na-Donu Proletarskaya Yashkul' Elista Krasnyy Yar Burynshik Say-Utes Ustyurt UZBEKISTAN
Tikhoretsk Divnoye Ipatovo Mumra Kaspiyskiy M. Tyub-Karagan Ft Shevchenko Mangyshlak
Armavir Stavropol Budennovsk Georgiyevsk Pyatigorsk Shevchenko Novyy Uzen
Cherkessk Kislovodsk Prokhladnyy Groznyy Makhachkala Fetisovo
Abkhazskaya Nal'chik Vladikavkaz Buynaksk CASPIAN SEA

CASPIAN SEA

North Asia - Political

1:45M 0 600 1200 1800 km 0 300 600 900 mls

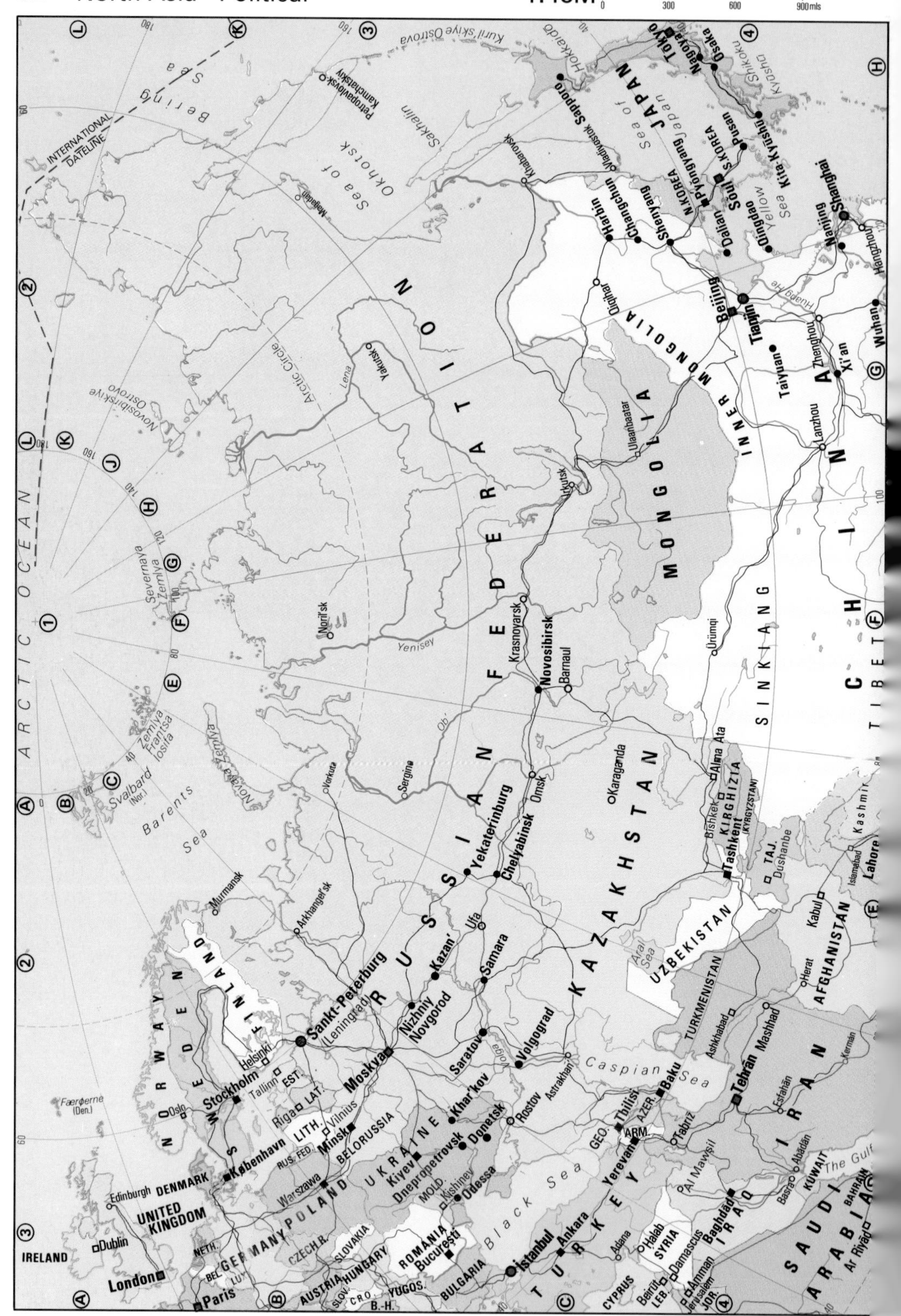

1:20M

| | 200 | 400 | 600 | 800 km |
| 0 | | 200 | | 400 mls |

SEA OF OKHOTSK

SEA OF JAPAN

YELLOW SEA

SAKHALIN

Tatarskiy Proliv

Sikhote Alin'

R U S S I A N   F E D E R A T I O N

Sredne Sibirskoye Ploskogorye

Stanovoy Khrebet

Yablonovyy Khrebet

Khrebet

M O N G O L I A

C H I N A

KOREA

Khabarovsk
Komsomol'sk
Nikolayevsk
Nakhodka
Vladivostok
Harbin
Changchun
Shenyang
Beijing
Tianjin
Dalian
P'yŏngyang
Yakutsk
Chita
Ulan-Ude
Irkutsk
Bratsk
Krasnoyarsk
Novokuznetsk
Abakan
Kemerovo
Tomsk
Achinsk
Kansk
Ulaanbaatar

Lena
Amur
Yenisey

Arctic Circle

Ozero Baykal

ALTAI

Turpan Depression

MONGOLIA

Dzungaria

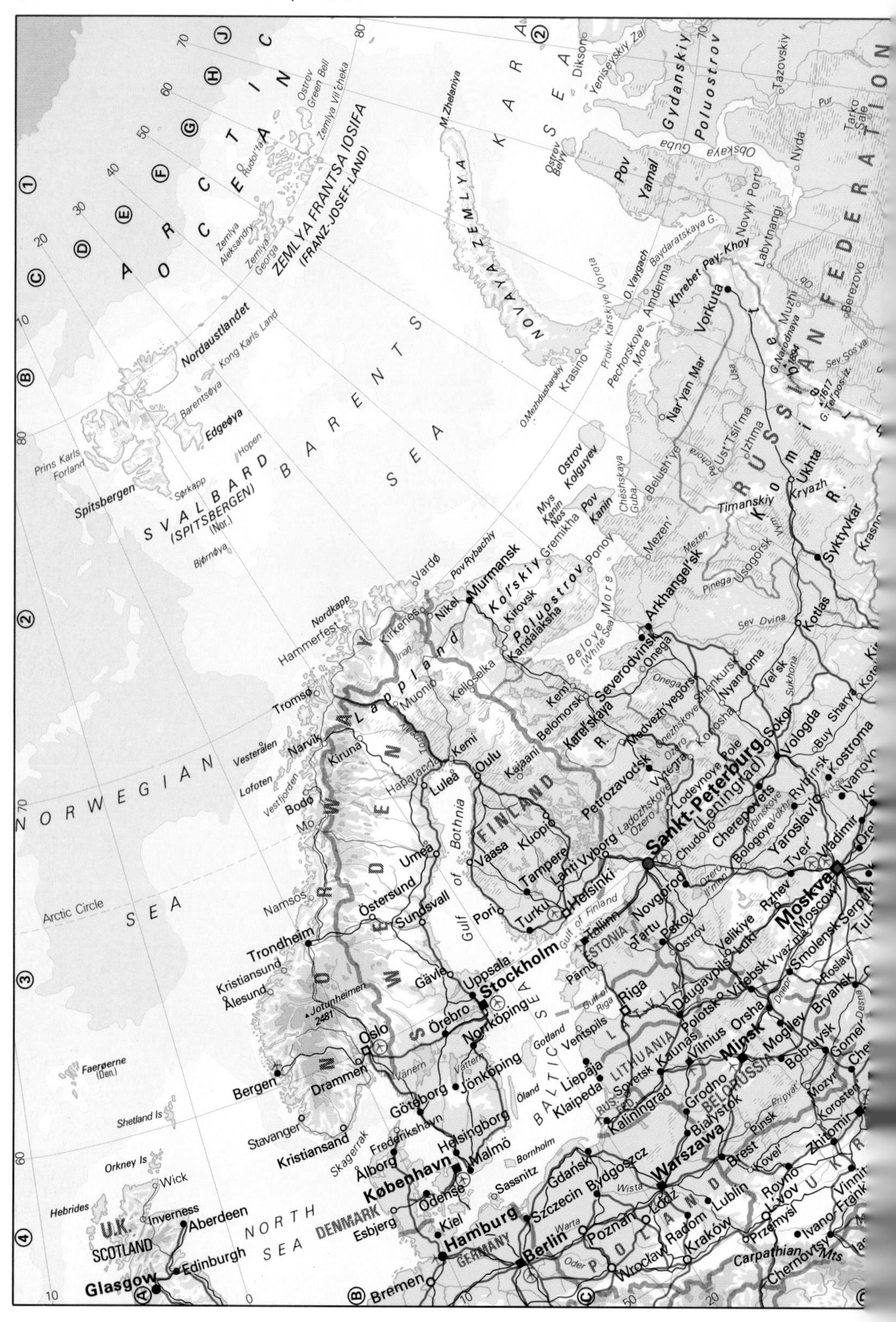

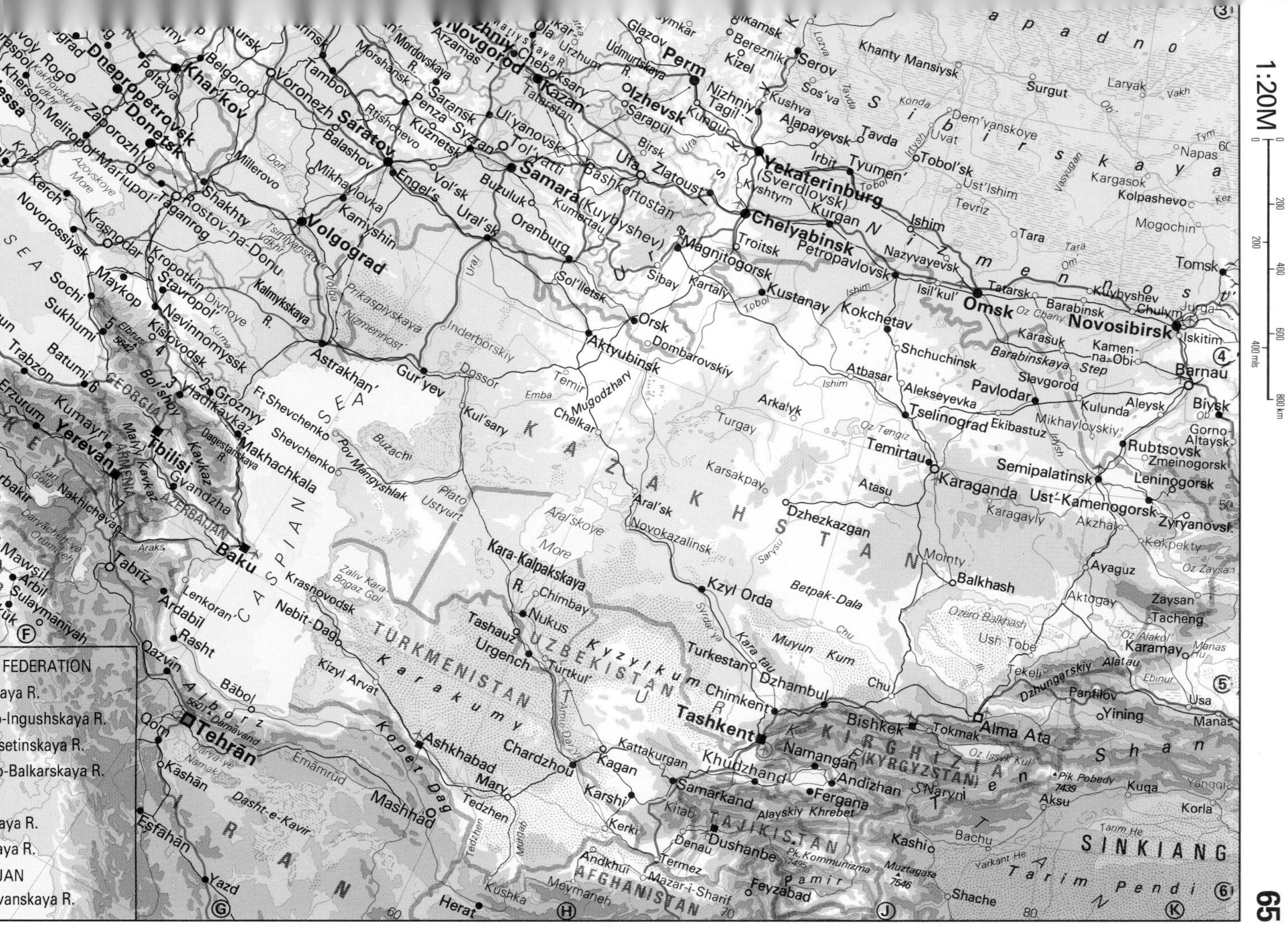

0 200 400 600 800 km
0   200   400 mls

RUSSIAN FEDERATION
1 Chuvashskaya R.
2 Checheno-Ingushskaya R.
3 Severo-Osetinskaya R.
4 Kabardino-Balkarskaya R.
GEORGIA
5 Abkhazskaya R.
6 Adzharskaya R.
AZERBAIJAN
7 Nakhichevanskaya R.

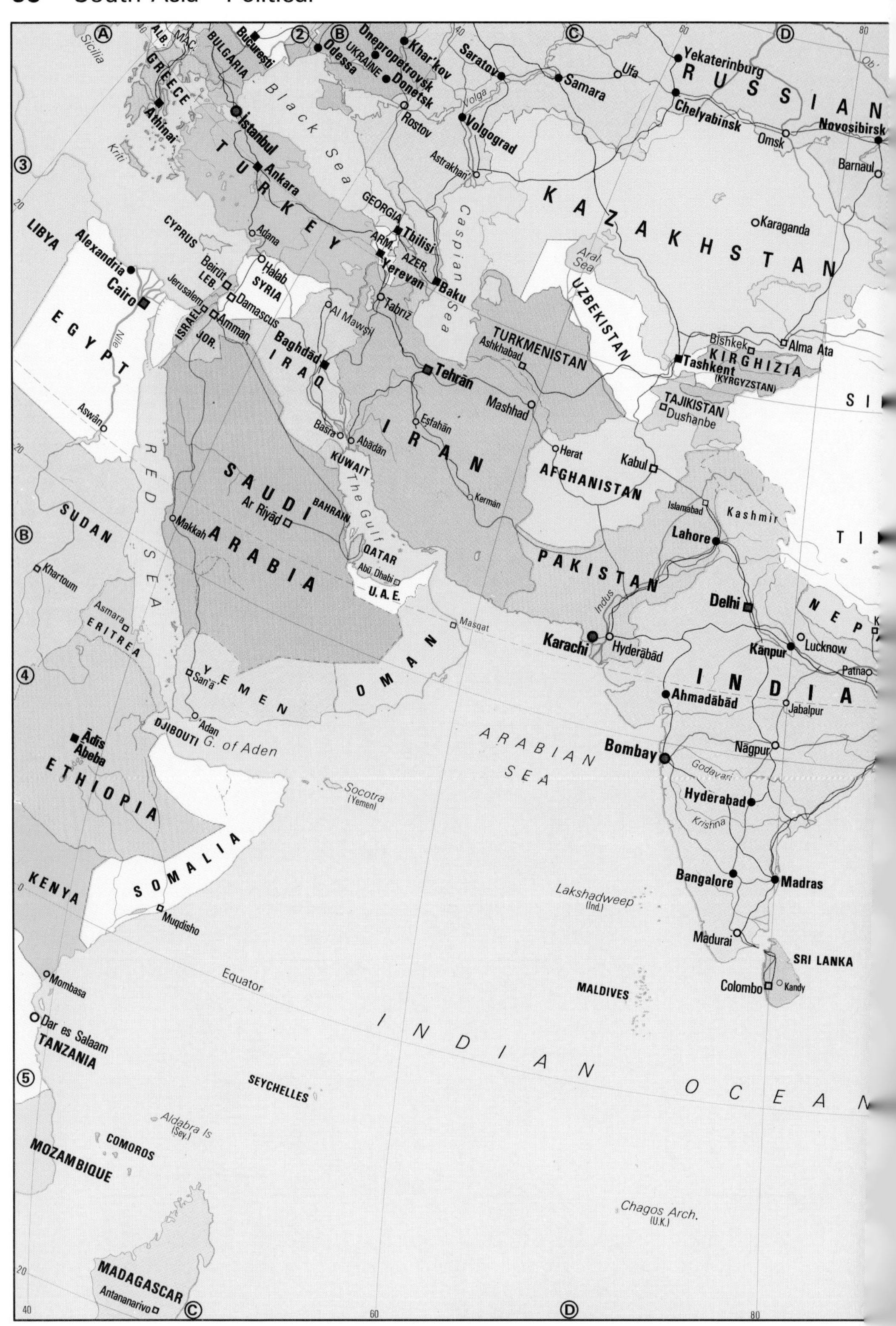
RUSSIAN
KAZAKHSTAN
TURKEY
GREECE
BULGARIA
UKRAINE
GEORGIA
ARM.
AZER.
UZBEKISTAN
TURKMENISTAN
KIRGHIZIA
(KYRGYZSTAN)
TAJIKISTAN
AFGHANISTAN
PAKISTAN
INDIA
IRAN
IRAQ
SYRIA
LEB.
ISRAEL
JOR.
CYPRUS
SAUDI ARABIA
KUWAIT
BAHRAIN
QATAR
U.A.E.
OMAN
YEMEN
EGYPT
LIBYA
SUDAN
ERITREA
DJIBOUTI
ETHIOPIA
SOMALIA
KENYA
TANZANIA
MOZAMBIQUE
COMOROS
MADAGASCAR
SEYCHELLES
MALDIVES
SRI LANKA
Black Sea
Caspian Sea
Aral Sea
RED SEA
The Gulf
G. of Aden
ARABIAN SEA
INDIAN OCEAN
Equator
Socotra (Yemen)
Lakshadweep (Ind.)
Chagos Arch. (U.K.)
Aldabra Is (Sey.)
Kashmir
Sicilia
Kriti
Nile
Volga
Indus
Godavari
Krishna
București
Odessa
Dnepropetrovsk
Khar'kov
Donetsk
Rostov
Saratov
Samara
Ufa
Yekaterinburg
Chelyabinsk
Omsk
Novosibirsk
Barnaul
Volgograd
Astrakhan'
Karaganda
Athinai
Istanbul
Ankara
Adana
Tbilisi
Yerevan
Baku
Tabrīz
Ḥalab
Beirūt
Damascus
Jerusalem
Amman
Al Mawşil
Baghdād
Tehrān
Eşfahān
Basra
Abādān
Mashhad
Herat
Kermān
Ashkhabad
Tashkent
Bishkek
Alma Ata
Dushanbe
Kabul
Islamabad
Lahore
Delhi
Karachi
Hyderābād
Lucknow
Kānpur
Patna
Ahmadābād
Jabalpur
Bombay
Nāgpur
Hyderabad
Bangalore
Madras
Madurai
Colombo
Kandy
Alexandria
Cairo
Aswân
Khartoum
Asmara
Makkah
Ar Riyāḍ
Abū Dhabi
Masqat
Şan'ā'
'Adan
Ādīs Ābeba
Muqdisho
Mombasa
Dar es Salaam
Antananarivo
S I
T I
N E P
A
B
C
D
2
3
4
5
20
40
60
80
0

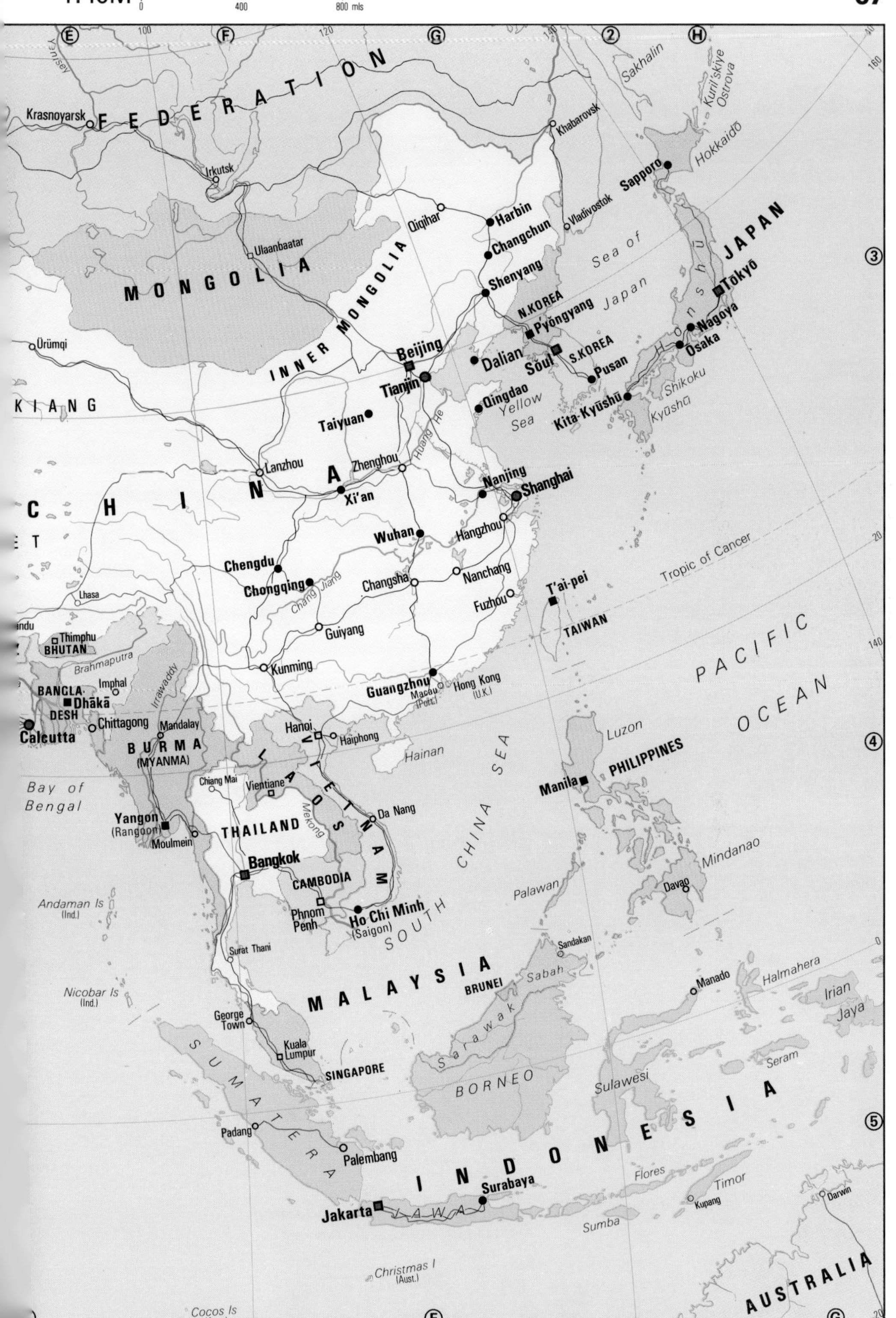

0
400   800   1200   1600 km
0   400   800 mls

FEDERATION
Krasnoyarsk
Irkutsk
Yenisey
Sakhalin
Kuril'skiye Ostrova
Khabarovsk
Hokkaidō
Sapporo
Ulaanbaatar
MONGOLIA
Qiqihar
Harbin
Changchun
Vladivostok
JAPAN
Sea of Japan
Shenyang
INNER MONGOLIA
N.KOREA
P'yŏngyang
Tōkyō
Nagoya
Honshū
Ōsaka
Ürümqi
Beijing
Tianjin
Dalian
Sŏul
S.KOREA
Pusan
Shikoku
Kita-Kyūshū
Kyūshū
XINJIANG
Qingdao
Yellow Sea
Taiyuan
Huang He
Lanzhou
Zhenghou
CHINA
Xi'an
Nanjing
Shanghai
TIBET
Hangzhou
Wuhan
Tropic of Cancer
Chengdu
Chongqing
Chang Jiang
Changsha
Nanchang
Lhasa
Fuzhou
T'ai-pei
TAIWAN
Thimphu
BHUTAN
Guiyang
Brahmaputra
Kunming
PACIFIC OCEAN
Imphal
Irrawaddy
BANGLADESH
Dhākā
Guangzhou
Macau (Port.)
Hong Kong (U.K.)
Calcutta
Chittagong
Mandalay
Hanoi
Haiphong
BURMA (MYANMA)
LAOS
VIETNAM
Hainan
Luzon
PHILIPPINES
Manila
Bay of Bengal
Chiang Mai
Vientiane
Mekong
Da Nang
Yangon (Rangoon)
Moulmein
THAILAND
Bangkok
CAMBODIA
SOUTH CHINA SEA
Palawan
Mindanao
Davao
Andaman Is (Ind.)
Phnom Penh
Ho Chi Minh (Saigon)
Surat Thani
Sandakan
MALAYSIA
BRUNEI
Sabah
Manado
Halmahera
Nicobar Is (Ind.)
Sarawak
Irian Jaya
George Town
Kuala Lumpur
SINGAPORE
Seram
BORNEO
Sulawesi
SUMATERA
INDONESIA
Padang
Palembang
Flores
Timor
Surabaya
Jakarta
JAWA
Kupang
Darwin
Sumba
Christmas I (Aust.)
AUSTRALIA
Cocos Is (Aust.)

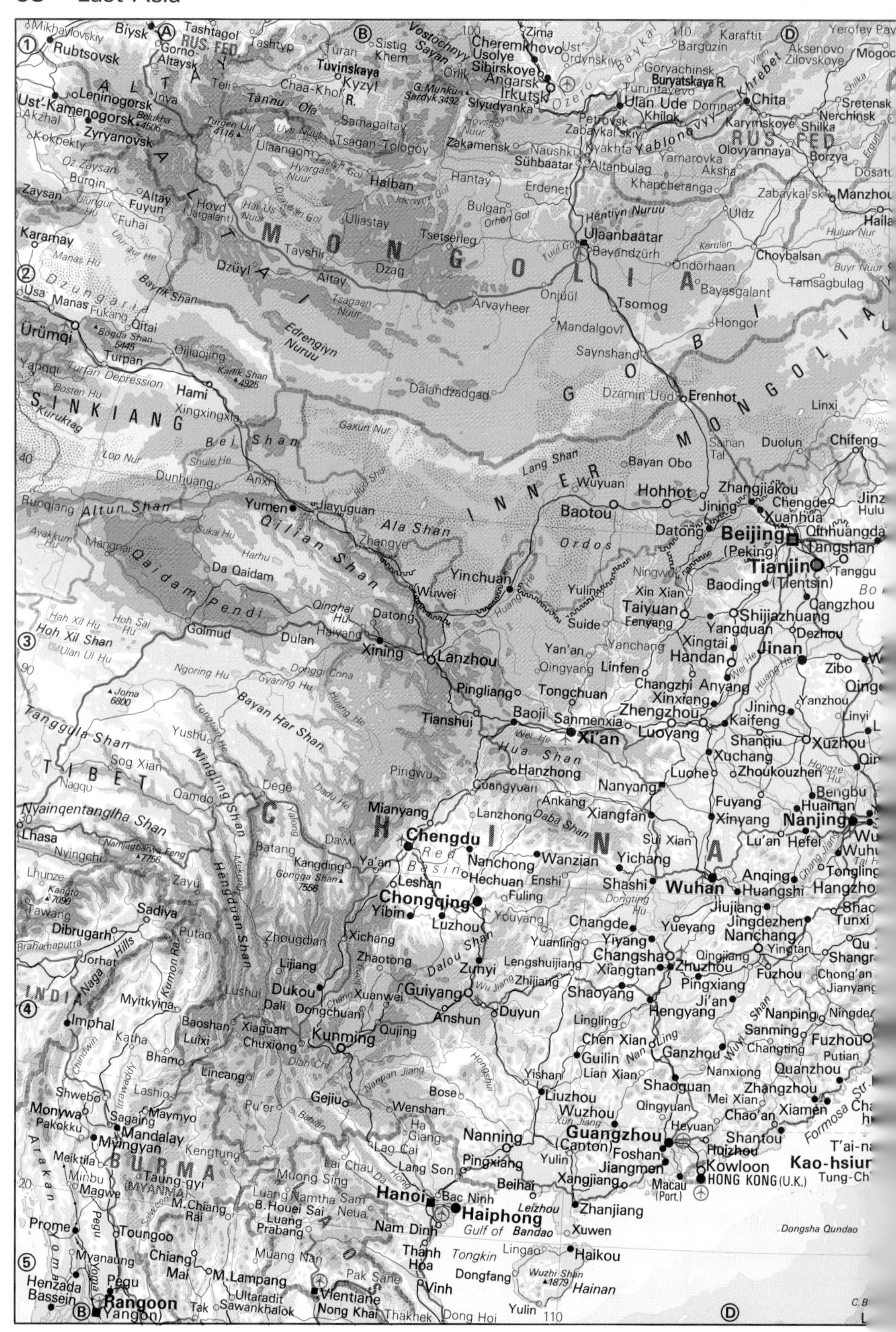
Mikhaylovskiy
Biysk
A
Tashtagol
RUS. FED.
Gorno-Altaysk
Tashtyp
Rubtsovsk
B
Turan
Sistig Khem
Vostochnyy Sayan
Zima
Cheremkhovo
Usolye Sibirskoye
Ust' Ordynskiy
Barguzin
Karaftit
D
Yerofey Pav
Aksenovo Zilovskoye
Mogoc
Tuvinskaya R.
Kyzyl
Chaa-Khol
Teli
Inya
Leninogorsk
Ust'-Kamenogorsk
Akzhal
Belukha 4506
Tannu Ola
G. Munku-Sardyk 3492
Orlik
Angarsk
Irkutsk
Slyudyanka
Goryachinsk
Buryatskaya R.
Turuntayevo
Ulan Ude
Chita
Sretensk
Nerchinsk
Shilka
Zyryanovsk
Kokpekty
Turgen Uul 4116
Uvs Nuur
Samagaltay
Tsagan-Tologoy
Hovsgol Nuur
Zakamensk
Petrovsk Zabaykal'skiy
Khilok
Domna
Yablonovyy Khrebet
Karymskoye
RUS. FED.
Olovyannaya
Borzya
Ulaangom
Naushki
Kyakhta
Yamarovka
Aksha
Dosatu
Oz. Zaysan
Burqin
Hyargas Nuur
Halban
Hantay
Sühbaatar
Altanbulag
Erdenet
Khapcheranga
Zaysan
Ulungur Hu
Altay
Fuyun
Hovd (Jargalant)
Har Us Nuur
Uliastay
Bulgan
Orhon Gol
Hentiyn Nuruu
Uldz
Zabaykal'sk
Manzhou
Haila
Hulun Nur
Karamay
Fuhai
Ulungur He
Manas Hu
MONGOLIA
Tsetserleg
Ulaanbaatar
Bayandzürh
Kerulen
Choybalsan
Tayshir
Dzag
Öndörhaan
Buyr Nuur
Dzüyl
Altay
Bayasgalant
Tamsagbulag
Dzungaria
Bayrik Shan
Arvayheer
Onjüül
Tsomog
Usa
Manas
Fukang
Qitai
Tsagaan Nuur
Hongor
Ürümqi
Bogda Shan 5445
Edrengiyn Nuruu
Mandalgovi
GOBI
Saynshand
Turpan
Qijiaojing
Karlik Shan 4925
Yanqqi
Turfan Depression
Bosten Hu
Hami
Dalandzadgad
Dzamin Uud
Erenhot
INNER MONGOLIA
Linxi
SINKIANG
Kuruktag
Xingxingxia
Gaxun Nur
Bei Shan
Saihan Tal
Duolun
Chifeng
Lop Nur
Shule He
Lang Shan
Bayan Obo
Dunhuang
Anxi
Wuyuan
Hohhot
Zhangjiakou
Chengde
Ruoqiang
Altun Shan
Yumen
Jiayuguan
Ala Shan
Baotou
Jining
Xuanhua
Datong
Beijing (Peking)
Qinhuangdao
Tangshan
Ayakkum Hu
Mangnai
Sukai Hu
Qilian Shan
Zhangye
Ordos
Tianjin (Tientsin)
Tanggu
Harhu
Qaidam Pendi
Da Qaidam
Yinchuan
Ningwu
Yulin
Baoding
Xin Xian
Wuwei
Taiyuan
Fenyang
Cangzhou
Shijiazhuang
Hah Xil Hu
Hoh Sai Hu
Qinghai Hu
Datong
Suide
Yangquan
Dezhou
Hoh Xil Shan
Ulan Ul Hu
Golmud
Dulan
Haiyang
Xining
Lanzhou
Yan'an
Yanchang
Xingtai
Handan
Jinan
Zibo
Ngoring Hu
Gyaring Hu
Donggi Cona
Qingyang
Linfen
Joma 6800
Bayan Har Shan
Huang He
Pingliang
Tongchuan
Changzhi
Anyang
Xinxiang
Yanzhou
Tianshui
Baoji
Sanmenxia
Zhengzhou
Jining
Kaifeng
Tanggula Shan
Yushu
Xi'an
Luoyang
Linyi
Wei He
Hua Shan
Shanqiu
Xuzhou
Sog Xian
Nagqu
TIBET
Ningjing Shan
Pingwu
Hanzhong
Xuchang
Luohe
Zhoukouzhen
Hongze Hu
Qamdo
Dege
Guangyuan
Nanyang
Bengbu
Huainan
Nyainqentanglha Shan
Mianyang
Ankang
Fuyang
CHINA
Lanzhong
Daba Shan
Xiangfan
Xinyang
Nanjing
Lhasa
Namjagbarwa Feng 7756
Dawu
Chengdu
Sui Xian
Lu'an
Hefei
Wuhu
Nyingchi
Batang
Red Basin
Nanchong
Wanzian
Yichang
Lhunze
Zayü
Kangding
Ya'an
Gongga Shan 7556
Hechuan
Enshi
Shashi
Wuhan
Anqing
Huangshi
Tongling
Hangzhou
Kangto 7090
Leshan
Chongqing
Fuling
Dongting Hu
Jiujiang
Tawang
Sadiya
Hengduan Shan
Yibin
Luzhou
Youyang
Changde
Yueyang
Jingdezhen
Tunxi
Dibrugarh
Putao
Zhougdian
Xichang
Yuanling
Yiyang
Nanchang
Brahamaputra
Naga Hills
Jorhat
Kumon Ra.
Lijiang
Zhaotong
Dalou Shan
Changsha
Qingjiang
Yingtan
Zunyi
Lengshuijiang
Xiangtan
Zhuzhou
Fuzhou
INDIA
Lushui
Dukou
Guiyang
Zhijiang
Pingxiang
Myitkyina
Dali
Dongchuan
Xuanwei
Shaoyang
Ji'an
Imphal
Baoshan
Xiaguan
Anshun
Duyun
Hengyang
Nanping
Luixi
Chuxiong
Kunming
Qujing
Lingling
Sanming
Fuzhou
Katha
Chen Xian
Changting
Putian
Bhamo
Guilin
Ganzhou
Wuyi Shan
Lincang
Yishan
Lian Xian
Nanxiong
Quanzhou
Lashio
Nanpan Jiang
Bose
Liuzhou
Shaoguan
Zhangzhou
Shwebo
Gejiu
Wuzhou
Mei Xian
Monywa
Pakokku
Sagaing
Maymyo
Pu'er
Wenshan
Qingyuan
Chao'an
Xiamen
Formosa Str.
Mandalay
Myingyan
Ha Giang
Nanning
Guangzhou (Canton)
Heyuan
Shantou
BURMA (MYANMA)
Kengtung
Lao Cai
Yulin
Foshan
Huizhou
Meiktila
Minbu
Taung-gyi
Muong Sing
Pingxiang
Lang Son
Jiangmen
Kowloon
HONG KONG (U.K.)
Kao-hsiung
Magwe
Luang Namtha
Sam Neua
Hanoi
Bac Ninh
Beihai
Xangjiang
Macau (Port.)
M. Chiang Rai
B. Houei Sai
Haiphong
Leizhou
Zhanjiang
Prome
Toungoo
Luang Prabang
LAOS
Nam Dinh
Gulf of Tongkin
Bandao
Xuwen
Dongsha Qundao
Myanaung
Chiang Mai
Muang Nan
Thanh Hoa
Lingao
Haikou
Henzada
Bassein
Pegu
M. Lampang
Pak Sane
Vinh
Dongfang
Wuzhi Shan 1879
Hainan
Rangoon (Yangon)
Tak
Sawankhalok
Uttaradit
Vientiane
Nong Khai
Thakhek
Dong Hoi
Yulin
110
D

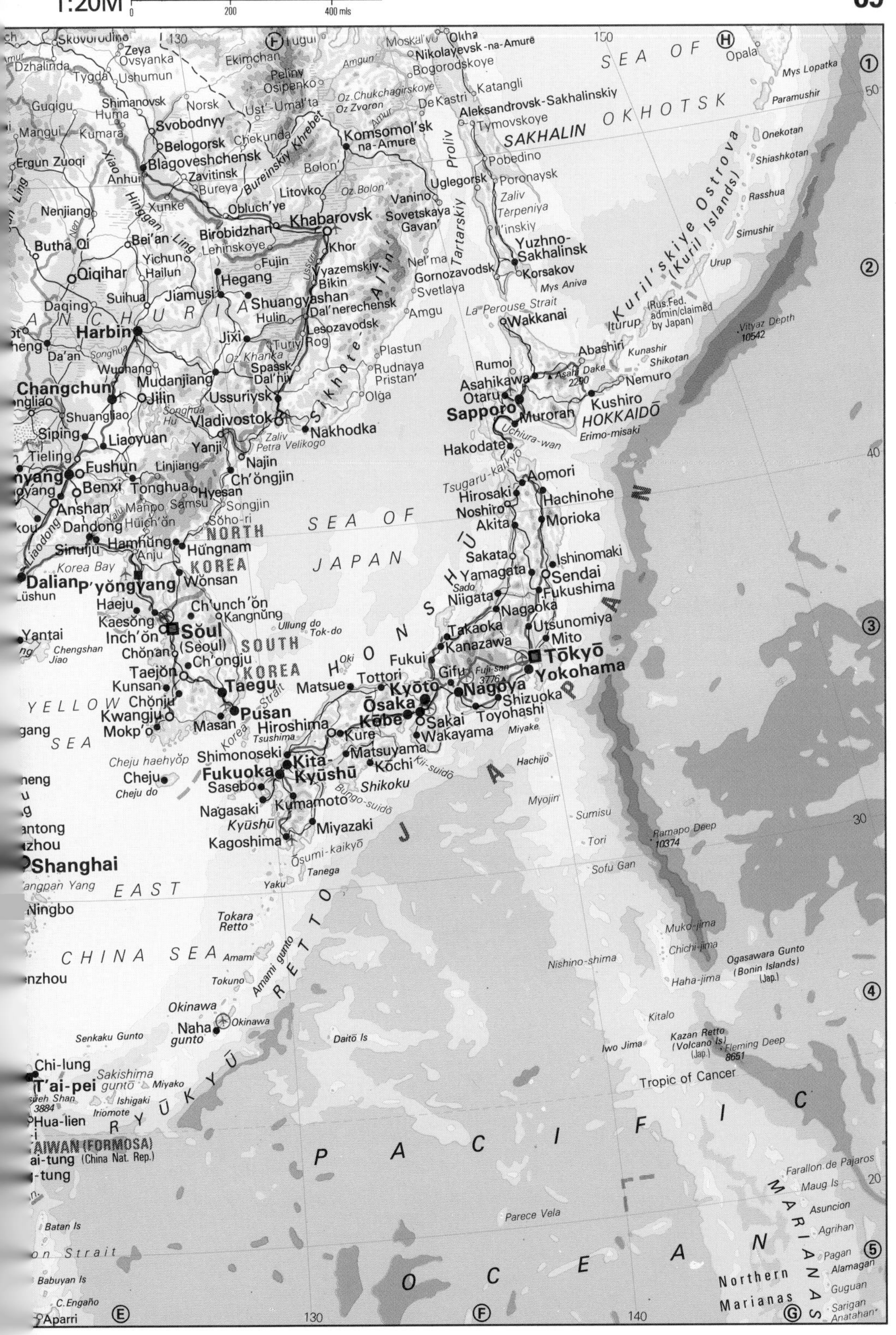

1:20M

SEA OF OKHOTSK

SAKHALIN

Kuril'skiye Ostrova (Kuril Islands)

HOKKAIDŌ

SEA OF JAPAN

H O N S H U

Tōkyō
Yokohama

YELLOW SEA

NORTH KOREA

SOUTH KOREA

Sŏul (Seoul)

SHIKOKU

KYŪSHŪ

EAST CHINA SEA

Shanghai

RYŪKYŪ RETTŌ

TAIWAN (FORMOSA)
(China Nat. Rep.)

T'ai-pei

PACIFIC OCEAN

Tropic of Cancer

Ogasawara Gunto (Bonin Islands) (Jap.)

Kazan Retto (Volcano Is.) (Jap.)

Northern Marianas

M A R I A N A S

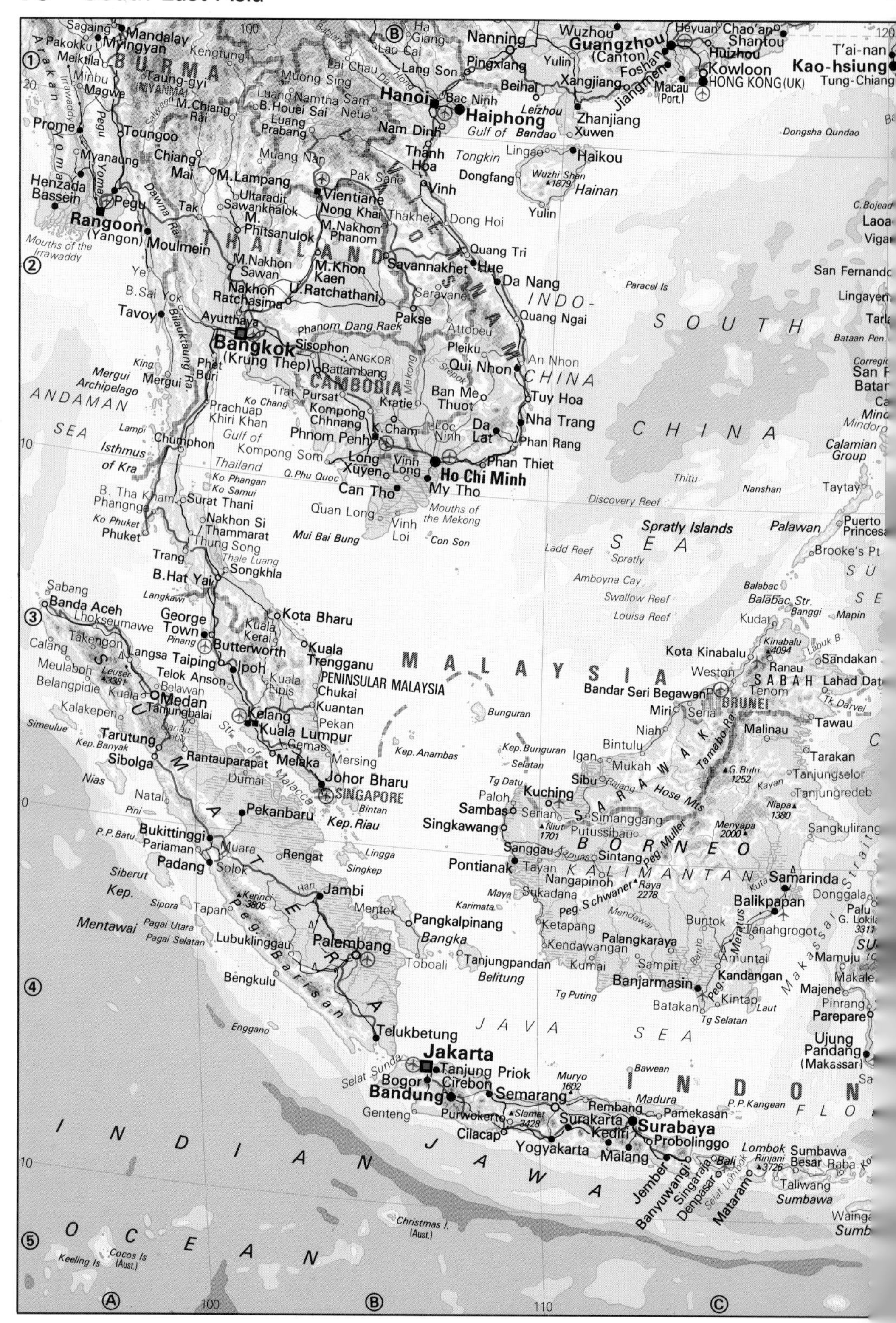
Sagaing
Mandalay
Pakokku
Myingyan
Meiktila
Kengtung
BURMA
(MYANMA)
Taung-gyi
Minbu
Magwe
Irrawaddy
Pegu
Arakan
Salween
M.Chiang Rai
Prome
Toungoo
Yoma
Chiang Mai
Myanaung
Henzada
Bassein
Pegu
Rangoon
(Yangon)
Moulmein
Mouths of the Irrawaddy
Dawna Ra.
Tak
Ye
B.Sai Yok
Tavoy
Bilauktaung Ra.
100
Babian
Lao Cai
Ha Giang
Lai Chau
Da
Hong
Muong Sing
Luang Namtha
Sam Neua
B.Houei Sai
Luang Prabang
Muang Nan
M.Lampang
Pak Sane
Vientiane
Ultaradit
Sawankhalok
M.Phitsanulok
Nong Khai
M.Nakhon Phanom
THAILAND
M.Nakhon Sawan
M.Khon Kaen
Nakhon Ratchasima
U.Ratchathani
Ayutthaya
Bangkok
(Krung Thep)
Nanning
Pingxiang
Lang Son
Hanoi
Bac Ninh
Haiphong
Nam Dinh
Thanh Hoa
Vinh
Thakhek
Dong Hoi
Savannakhet
Quang Tri
Hue
Da Nang
Saravane
Pakse
Attopeu
Quang Ngai
Phanom Dang Raek
Sisophon
ANGKOR
Battambang
CAMBODIA
Mekong
Pleiku
Srepok
Qui Nhon
An Nhon
Tuy Hoa
Ban Me Thuot
Nha Trang
Da Lat
Phan Rang
Phan Thiet
Loc Ninh
Kratie
K.Cham
Pursat
Trat
Ko Chang
Kompong Chhnang
Phnom Penh
Kompong Som
Q.Phu Quoc
Long Xuyen
Vinh Long
Ho Chi Minh
My Tho
Can Tho
Quan Long
Vinh Loi
Mouths of the Mekong
Mui Bai Bung
Con Son
Wuzhou
Guangzhou
(Canton)
Foshan
Jiangmen
Yulin
Beihai
Xangjiang
Leizhou Bandao
Zhanjiang
Xuwen
Gulf of Tongkin
Lingao
Haikou
Dongfang
Wuzhi Shan 1879
Hainan
Yulin
Heyuan
Chao'an
Shantou
Huizhou
Kowloon
HONG KONG (UK)
Macau (Port.)
T'ai-nan
Kao-hsiung
Tung-Chiang
Dongsha Qundao
120
C.Bojeador
Laoag
Vigan
San Fernando
Lingayen
Tarlac
Bataan Pen.
Corregidor
San F
Batan
Mindoro
Calamian Group
Taytay
Puerto Princesa
Palawan
Brooke's Pt
Paracel Is
INDO-CHINA
SOUTH CHINA SEA
Thitu
Nanshan
Discovery Reef
Spratly Islands
Ladd Reef
Spratly
Amboyna Cay
Swallow Reef
Louisa Reef
Balabac
Balabac Str.
Banggi
Mapin
Kudat
King
Mergui
Mergui Archipelago
Phet Buri
Prachuap Khiri Khan
ANDAMAN SEA
Lampi
Chumphon
Isthmus of Kra
Gulf of Thailand
Ko Phangan
Ko Samui
B. Tha Kham
Phangnga
Surat Thani
Ko Phuket
Phuket
Nakhon Si Thammarat
Thung Song
Thale Luang
Trang
Songkhla
B.Hat Yai
Langkawi
Sabang
Banda Aceh
Lhokseumawe
George Town
Pinang
Kota Bharu
Kuala Kerai
Takengon
Calang
Butterworth
Kuala Trengganu
Langsa
Taiping
Meulaboh
Leuser 3381
Ipoh
Telok Anson
Belawan
Kuala Lipis
Belangpidie
Kuala
Medan
PENINSULAR MALAYSIA
Chukai
MALAYSIA
Kalakepen
Tanjungbalai
Kuantan
Simeulue
Kelang
Kuala Lumpur
Pekan
Tarutung
Kep. Banyak
Str. of Malacca
Gemas
Sibolga
Rantauparapat
Melaka
Mersing
Nias
Dumai
Johor Bharu
SINGAPORE
Natal
Bintan
Pini
Pekanbaru
Kep.Riau
P.P.Batu
Bukittinggi
Pariaman
Muara
Padang
Solok
Rengat
Lingga
Singkep
Siberut
Kep. Mentawai
Hari
Jambi
Kerinci 3805
Sipora
Tapan
Mentok
Pagai Utara
Pagai Selatan
Peg. Barisan
SUMATERA
Lubuklinggau
Palembang
Pangkalpinang
Bangka
Toboali
Tanjungpandan
Belitung
Bengkulu
Enggano
Telukbetung
Selat Sunda
Jakarta
Tanjung Priok
Bogor
Cirebon
Bandung
Genteng
Semarang
Purwokerto
Slamet 3428
Cilacap
Muryo 1602
Surakarta
Yogyakarta
Kediri
Rembang
Madura
Pamekasan
Bawean
Surabaya
Probolinggo
Malang
Jember
Banyuwangi
Singaraja
Denpasar
Bali
Selat Lombok
Mataram
Lombok
Rinjani 3726
Sumbawa Besar
Raba
Taliwang
Sumbawa
P.P.Kangean
JAWA
JAVA SEA
INDONESIA
FLORES
Bunguran
Kep.Anambas
Kep.Bunguran Selatan
Tg Datu
Paloh
Sambas
Serian
Kuching
Singkawang
Niut 1701
Simanggang
Sibu
Rajang
Igan
Mukah
Bintulu
Niah
Miri
Seria
BRUNEI
Bandar Seri Begawan
Weston
Kota Kinabalu
Kinabalu 4094
Ranau
Labuk B.
Sandakan
SABAH
Lahad Datu
Tenom
Tk Darvel
Tawau
Malinau
SARAWAK
Tamabo Ra.
Hose Mts
Putussibau
G.Rulu 1252
Kayan
Tarakan
Tanjungselor
Tanjungredeb
Niapa 1380
Menyapa 2000
Sangkulirang
Pontianak
Sanggau
Kapuas
Sintang
Tayan
Peg. Muller
BORNEO
KALIMANTAN
Nangapinoh
Raya 2278
Peg. Schwaner
Maya
Sukadana
Karimata
Mendawai
Ketapang
Kendawangan
Palangkaraya
Kumai
Sampit
Barito
Buntok
Peg. Meratus
Kuta
Samarinda
Balikpapan
Tanahgrogot
Amuntai
Kandangan
Banjarmasin
Batakan
Tg Puting
Tg Selatan
Kintap
Laut
Peg.
Makassar Strait
Donggala
Palu
G. Lokila 3311
Mamuju
Majene
Makale
Pinrang
Parepare
Ujung Pandang
(Makassar)
INDIAN OCEAN
Christmas I. (Aust.)
Cocos Is (Aust.)
Keeling Is
Waingapu
Sumba
10
0
110
A
B
C
1
2
3
4
5

1:20M

200   400   600   800 km
200   400 mls

TAIWAN (FORMOSA)
(China Nat. Rep.)
Chia-i
T'ai-tung
ing-tung
Chan

P A C I F I C

Parece Vela

Farallon de Pajaros
Maug Is
Asuncion
Agrihan
Pagan
Alamagan
Guguan
Sarigan
Anatahan
Farallon
de Medinilla
Saipan
Tinian
Rota

Northern
Marianas

N O R T H E R N   M A R I A N A S

Guam
(U.S.A.)
Vero Deep
9637

O C E A N

uzon Strait
Batan Is
Babuyan Is
C. Engaño
Aparri
Tuguegarao
Ilagan
Baguio
LUZON
agupan
Baler
Cabanatuan
Quezon City
Manila
Boac
Daet Catanduanes
Naga
Legazpi
Bulan
Romblon
Catarman
Pandan
Masbate
Masbate
Samar
Oras
Panay
Catbalogan
Guiuan
Iloilo
Roxas
Leyte
Tacloban
Bacolod
Dinaget ▲10497
Cebu
Siargao ▲10265
Negros
Bohol
Siaton
Bohol Sea
Surigao
Manukan
Butuan
Ozamiz
Cagayan de Oro
L. Lanao
Marawi
Malanbang
MINDANAO
Zamboanga
Cotabato
Davao
abela
Basilan
Moro
Gulf
Digos
Jolo
Jolo
General
Santos
Sulu Arch.
Tinaca Pt.

PHILIPPINES

Polillo Is

Mansyu Deep
9818

Challenger Deep
11033

Ulithi

Yap

Ngulu

Fais

Sorol

Faraulep

Gaferut

10

Woleai
Ifalik

Fed. States of Micronesia

Lamotrek
Eauripik

Palau
Islands
(U.S.A.)
Koror

C A R O L I N E   I S L A N D S

③

L E B E S

S E A

Kepulauan
Talaud
Karakelong
Tahuna
Sangine
Kepulauan
Sangihe
Morotai
Manado
Tobelo
Buol
Kuandang
Belang
Ternate
Halmahera
Gorontalo

Sonsorol

Pulo Anna
Merir

Tobi

Helen Reef

Mapia

Equator

Ninigo Group

Wuvulu

Teluk
Weda

Waigeo

Kep. Togian
Luwuk
Kwoka
3000▲
Dampier
Selat
MOLUCCAS
Sorong
Misoöl
Cendrawasih
Peg. Arfak
2939
Manokwari
Supiori
Biak
Numfoor
Yapen
Tg d'Urville
Sarmi
Aitape
Schouten Is

Jayapura

Wewak

Karkar

PAPUA

NEW
GUINEA
④

oso
SI
Teluk
Tolo
Peleng
Taliabu Mangole
Bacan
Obi
Teluk
Cendrawasih
Dom
1340

IRIAN

Long I
Madang

Schnaft

Kep. Banggai
CERAM SEA
Piru 3019
Bula
Fakfak
Teluk Berau
Kaimana
Pegunungan Maoke
Angemuk
3741
Pk Jaya ▲
5029
JAYA
Pk Mandala▲
4702

Central Ra
Mt.
Hagen
Goroka
Kubor
4359

Lae
Menth
Wau
Salam
Morob

Namlea
Kep.
Sula
Misoöl
Bula
Kokonau
Tanahmerah
Wokam
Tk Flamingo
N E W
G U I N E A
Kikori
Kerema

Peleng
Buru
Piru
Seram
Ambon
Kep. Kai
Dobo
Kep. Banda
Kobroör
PAPUA
Mt Victoria▲
4073
Kokoda
Port
Moresby

Kendari
Wowoni
Kolaka
Butung
B A N D A   S E A
Kep.
Aru
Trangan
Fly
Murray
Gulf of
Papua

Danau
Towuti
ampone
Muna
Baubau
Kep.
Tukangbesi
Nila
Wokam
Damar
Teun
P.Kolepom
aena

Wetar
Romang
Yamdena
Kepulauan
Tanimbar
P.Kolepom
Merauke
Daru

Mulgrave I
Banks I

Flores
Lomblen
Alor
Selat Wetar
Kep. Leti
Babar
Saumlaki
Selaru
Tg Vals
Komoran
Saibai
Torres
Strait
C. York

Thursday I.
Pr.of Wales

Banks I
C O R A L

⑤

Oekusi
TIMOR
Sermata

Endeh
Atambua
Savu Sea
Kupang
Roti

A R A F U R A   S E A

Somerset
C. Grenville

Iron
Range

Great Barrier Rf.

S E A

awu

C.V. Diemen
Bathurst
Melville
Croker I.
Coburg Pen.
Dundas Str.
Gove
C. Arnhem
Pen.
Nhulunbuy

Wessel Is

Albatross B.
Weipa

Iron
Range

T I M O R ⒟   S E A
Clarence Str.
Darwin
Arnhem Land ⒠
Nhulunbuy
A U S T R A L I A
140
⒡

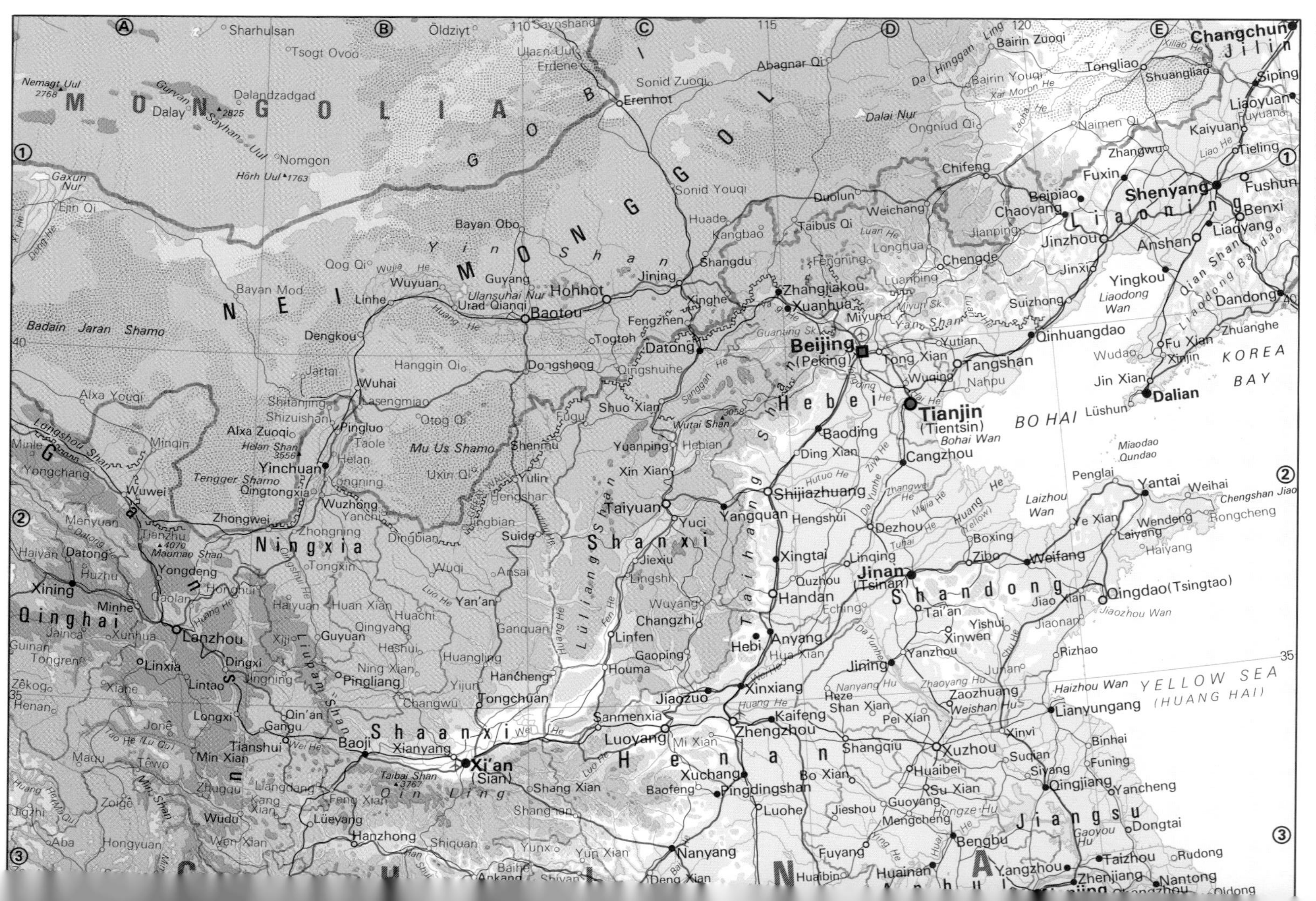
MONGOLIA
GOBI
NEI MONGGOL
Yin Shan
Sharhulsan
Tsogt Ovoo
Öldziyt
Saynshand
Ulaan Uul
Erdene
Dalandzadgad
Dalay
Nemagt Uul 2768
Gurvan Sayhan Uul 2825
Nomgon
Hörh Uul 1763
Gaxun Nur
Ejin Qi
Erenhot
Sonid Zuoqi
Sonid Youqi
Abagnar Qi
Da Hinggan Ling
Bairin Zuoqi
Bairin Youqi
Xar Moron He
Dalai Nur
Ongniud Qi
Changchun
Jilin
Siping
Liaoyuan
Tongliao
Shuangliao
Naimen Qi
Kaiyuan
Tieling
Zhangwu
Chifeng
Fuxin
Shenyang
Fushun
Benxi
Liaoyang
Anshan
Liaoning
Beipiao
Chaoyang
Jinzhou
Jianping
Duolun
Weichang
Taibus Qi
Huade
Kangbao
Shangdu
Bayan Obo
Qog Qi
Wuyuan
Guyang
Hohhot
Jining
Baotou
Urad Qianqi
Ulansuhai Nur
Linhe
Bayan Mod
Badain Jaran Shamo
Dengkou
Hanggin Qi
Dongsheng
Togtoh
Fengzhen
Xinghe
Zhangjiakou
Xuanhua
Datong
Qingshuihe
Beijing
(Peking)
Miyun
Chengde
Longhua
Luanping
Fengning
Yan Shan
Suizhong
Qinhuangdao
Jinxi
Yingkou
Liaodong Wan
Dandong
Liaodong Bandao
Qian Shan
Fu Xian
Zhuanghe
Wudao
Xinjin
Jin Xian
Dalian
Lüshun
KOREA BAY
BO HAI
Bohai Wan
Tianjin
(Tientsin)
Tangshan
Tong Xian
Wuqing
Nahpu
Yutian
Hebei
Baoding
Ding Xian
Cangzhou
Shijiazhuang
Hengshui
Dezhou
Xingtai
Handan
Anyang
Hebi
Taihang Shan
Wutai Shan 3058
Shuo Xian
Hebian
Yuanping
Xin Xian
Taiyuan
Yangquan
Yuci
Shanxi
Lüliang Shan
Jiexiu
Lingshi
Wuyang
Changzhi
Linfen
Gaoping
Houma
Jiaozuo
Xinxiang
Sanmenxia
Luoyang
Zhengzhou
Kaifeng
Henan
Xuchang
Pingdingshan
Baofeng
Luohe
Nanyang
Mi Xian
Shaanxi
Xi'an
(Sian)
Xianyang
Baoji
Tongchuan
Hancheng
Huangling
Yan'an
Ansai
Wuqi
Suide
Yulin
Shenmu
Fugu
Dingbian
Mu Us Shamo
Otog Qi
Uxin Qi
Wuhai
Jartai
Alxa Youqi
Alxa Zuoqi
Helan Shan 3556
Shizuishan
Pingluo
Yinchuan
Qingtongxia
Wuzhong
Tengger Shamo
Zhongwei
Ningxia
Zhongning
Tongxin
Haiyuan
Guyuan
Huan Xian
Qingyang
Pingliang
Liupan Shan
Xiji
Jingning
Dingxi
Lanzhou
Yongdeng
Tianzhu 4070
Maomao Shan
Wuwei
Minqin
Yongchang
Longshou Shan
Xining
Qinghai
Datong
Haiyan
Huzhu
Minhe
Gaolan
Linxia
Lintao
Longxi
Tianshui
Gangu
Qin'an
Min Xian
Min Shan
Tewo
Zhugqu
Wudu
Hanzhong
Lüeyang
Taibai Shan 3767
Qin Ling
Shang Xian
Shangnan
Ankang
Shiquan
Yun Xian
Yunxi
Deng Xian
Jinan
(Tsinan)
Shandong
Linqing
Liaocheng
Tai'an
Zibo
Boxing
Weifang
Yantai
Penglai
Weihai
Chengshan Jiao
Rongcheng
Wendeng
Laiyang
Haiyang
Ye Xian
Laizhou Wan
Miaodao Qundao
Qingdao (Tsingtao)
Jiaozhou Wan
Jiao Xian
Jiaonan
Rizhao
Yishui
Xinwen
Yanzhou
Jining
Heze
Shan Xian
Zaozhuang
Weishan Hu
Pei Xian
Shangqiu
Xuzhou
Huaibei
Su Xian
Guoyang
Mengcheng
Bo Xian
Jieshou
Fuyang
Huainan
Bengbu
Huaibin
Lianyungang
Haizhou Wan
YELLOW SEA
(HUANG HAI)
Binhai
Funing
Suqian
Siyang
Qingjiang
Yancheng
Jiangsu
Dongtai
Gaoyou Hu
Taizhou
Rudong
Yangzhou
Zhenjiang
Nantong
Huang He

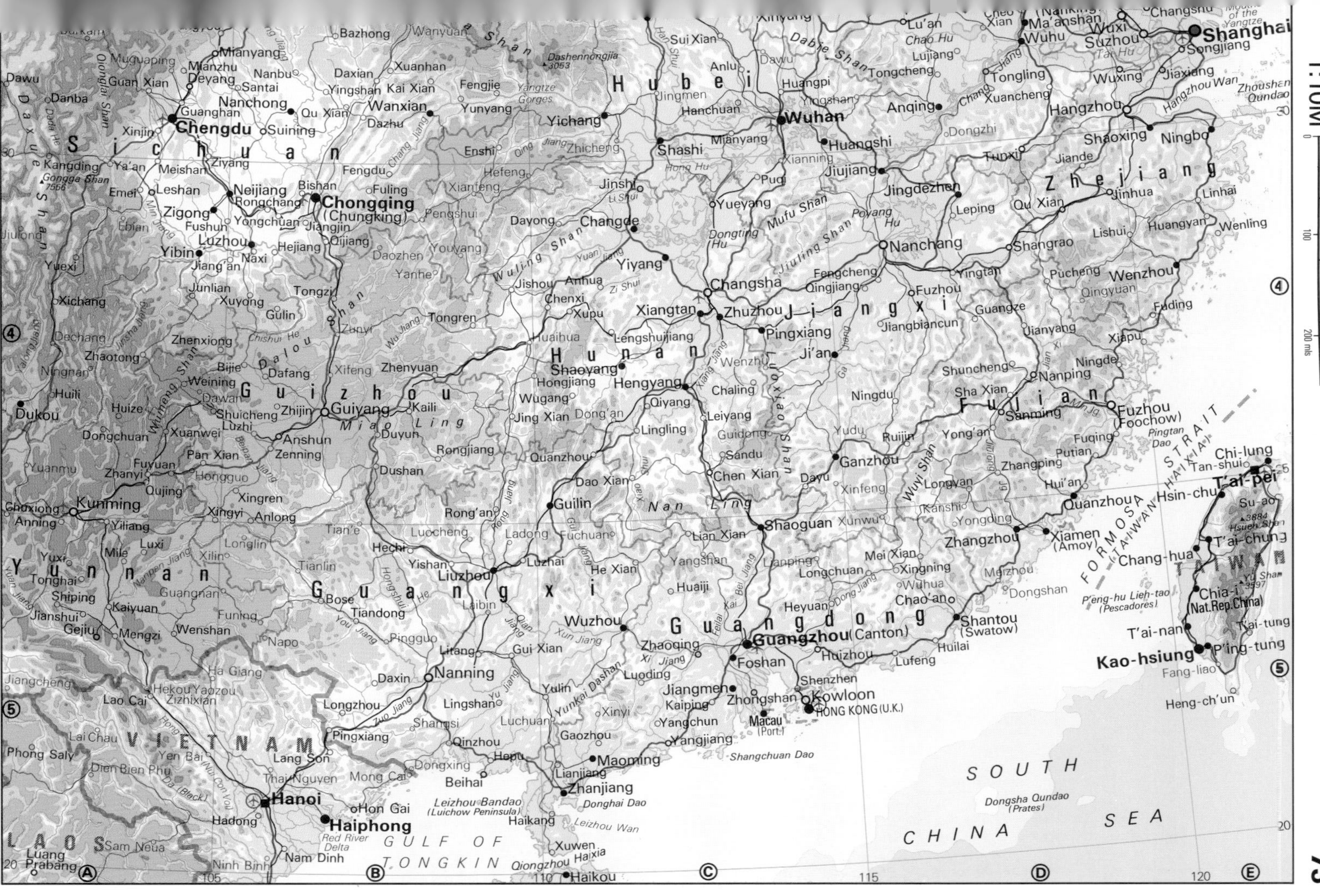

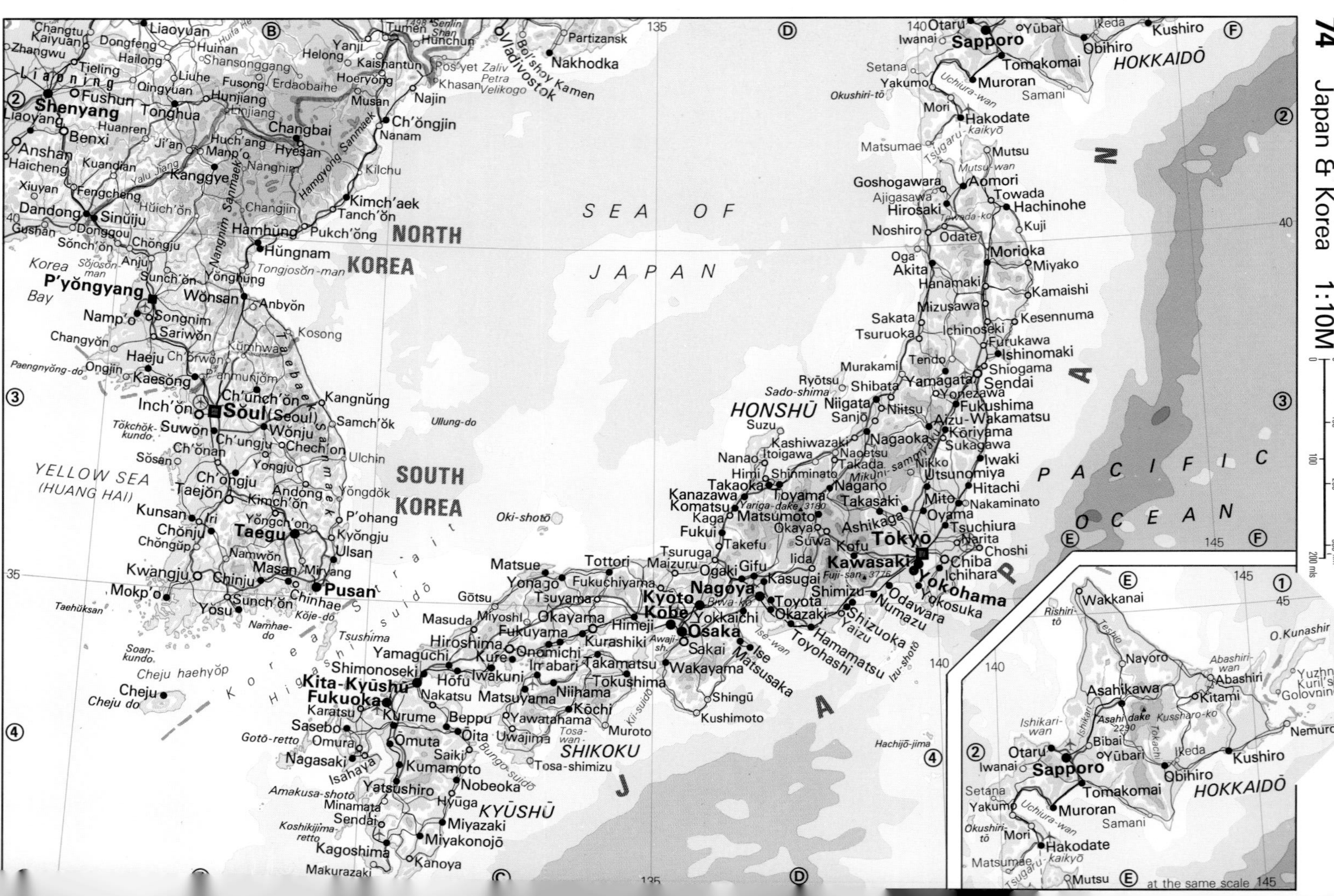

Map of Japan & Korea at scale 1:10M.

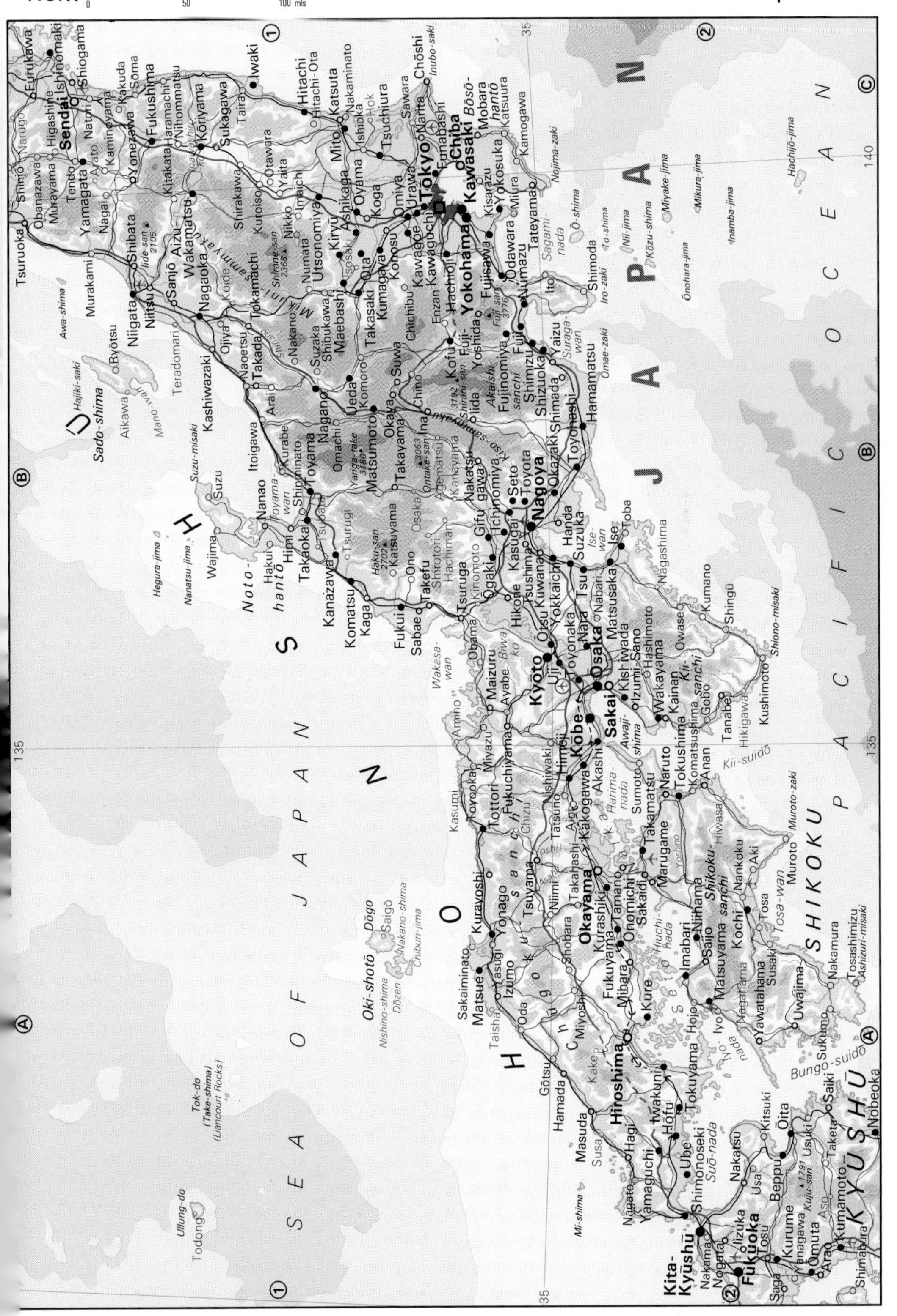
SEA OF JAPAN
PACIFIC OCEAN
JAPAN
HONSHU
SHIKOKU
KYŪSHŪ
Sado-shima
Noto-hantō
Oki-shotō
Tōkyō
Yokohama
Kawasaki
Chiba
Nagoya
Kyōto
Ōsaka
Kōbe
Sakai
Hiroshima
Okayama
Fukuoka
Kita-Kyūshū
Sendai
Niigata
Kanazawa
Toyama
Nagano
Shizuoka
Hamamatsu
Wakayama
Matsuyama
Kōchi
Takamatsu
Tokushima
Ōita
Kumamoto
Shimonoseki
Fuji-san 3776
Biwa ko
Ise-wan
Suruga-wan
Sagami-nada
Tosa-wan
Kii-suidō
Bungo-suidō
Harima-nada
Awaji-shima
Ullung-do
Tok-do (Take-shima) (Liancourt Rocks)
135
140
35

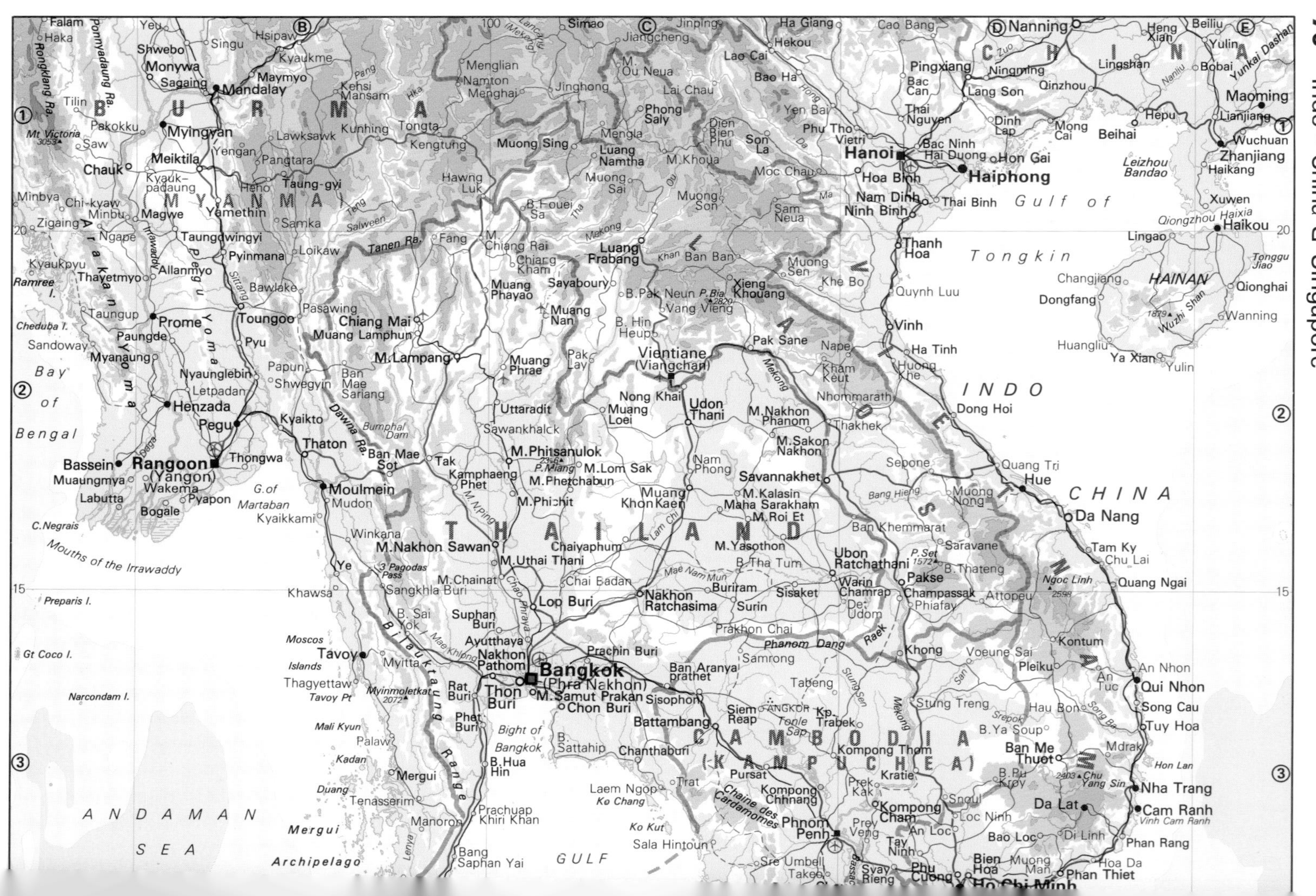
Hanoi
Haiphong
Vientiane (Viangchan)
Bangkok (Phra Nakhon)
Rangoon (Yangon)
Phnom Penh
Mandalay
Da Nang
Hue
Qui Nhon
Nha Trang
Cam Ranh
Da Lat
Phan Thiet
Haikou
Nanning
Zhanjiang
Maoming
Beihai
Luang Prabang
Chiang Mai
Moulmein
Tavoy
Mergui
Bassein
Pegu
Prome
Toungoo
Pakse
Savannakhet
Udon Thani
Nakhon Ratchasima
Battambang
Siem Reap
HAINAN
Gulf of Tongkin
INDO CHINA
THAILAND
CAMBODIA (KAMPUCHEA)
BURMA (MYANMAR)
VIETNAM
LAOS
ANDAMAN SEA
Bay of Bengal
Mouths of the Irrawaddy
G. of Martaban
Mergui Archipelago
Bight of Bangkok
Dawna Ra.
Bilauktaung Range
Arakan Yoma
Pegu Yoma
Tanen Ra.
Mekong
Irrawaddy
Salween
Chao Phraya
Chaine des Cardamomes
Tonle Sap
Mt Victoria 3053
Ponnyadaung Ra.
Rongklang Ra.
Preparis I.
Gt Coco I.
Narcondam I.
Ramree I.
Cheduba I.
C.Negrais

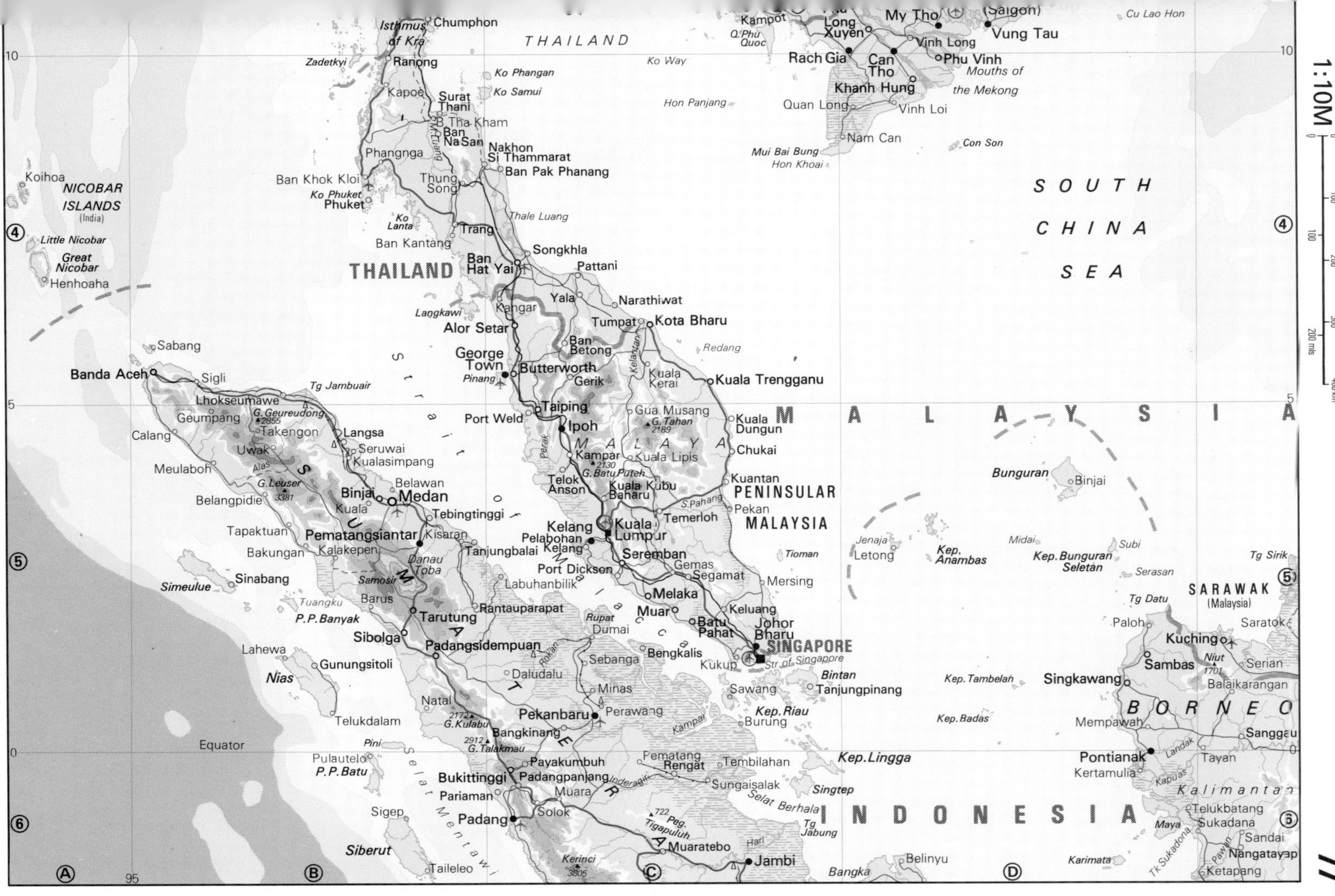

1:10M

0   100   200   300   400 km

0   100   200 mls

100 200 300 400 km
100 200 mls

Celebes Sea
Flores Sea
Makassar (Ujung Pandang)

N
D
C
B
A

MALAYSIA
SINGAPORE
BRUNEI

SARAWAK
BORNEO
KALIMANTAN
SULAWESI (CELEBES)
SABAH
INDONESIA
SUMATERA
JAVA (JAWA)
Bali
Lombok
Sumbawa
Madura

Tarakan
Tanjungselor
Tanjungredeb
Samarinda
Balikpapan
Samboja
Tenggarong
Sangkulirang
Muaratewah
Buntok
Amuntai
Barabai
Kandangan
Banjarmasin
Martapura
Pagatan
Kotabaru
Palangkaraya
Sampit
Pangkalanbuun
Sukamara
Kendawangan
Ketapang
Kotabaru
Pontianak
Sambas
Singkawang
Mempawah
Kuching
Sibu
Bintulu
Miri
Kuala Lumpur
Seremban
Melaka
Johor Bharu
Batu Pahat
Pekanbaru
Jambi
Palembang
Pangkalpinang
Belinyu
Muntok
Tanjungpandan
Manggar
Telukbetung
Tanjung Priok
Jakarta
Bogor
Bandung
Cirebon
Tegal
Pekalongan
Semarang
Kudus
Surakarta
Yogyakarta
Magelang
Madiun
Kediri
Blitar
Malang
Surabaya
Probolinggo
Jember
Banyuwangi
Denpasar
Singaraja
Mataram
Praya
Ujung Pandang (Makassar)
Pattallassang
Majene
Mamuju
Polewali
Kota Kinabalu

Selat Makassar
Selat Karimata
Selat Sunda
Java Sea
Bangka
Belitung
Kep. Lingga
Kep. Riau
Kep. Anambas
Bintan

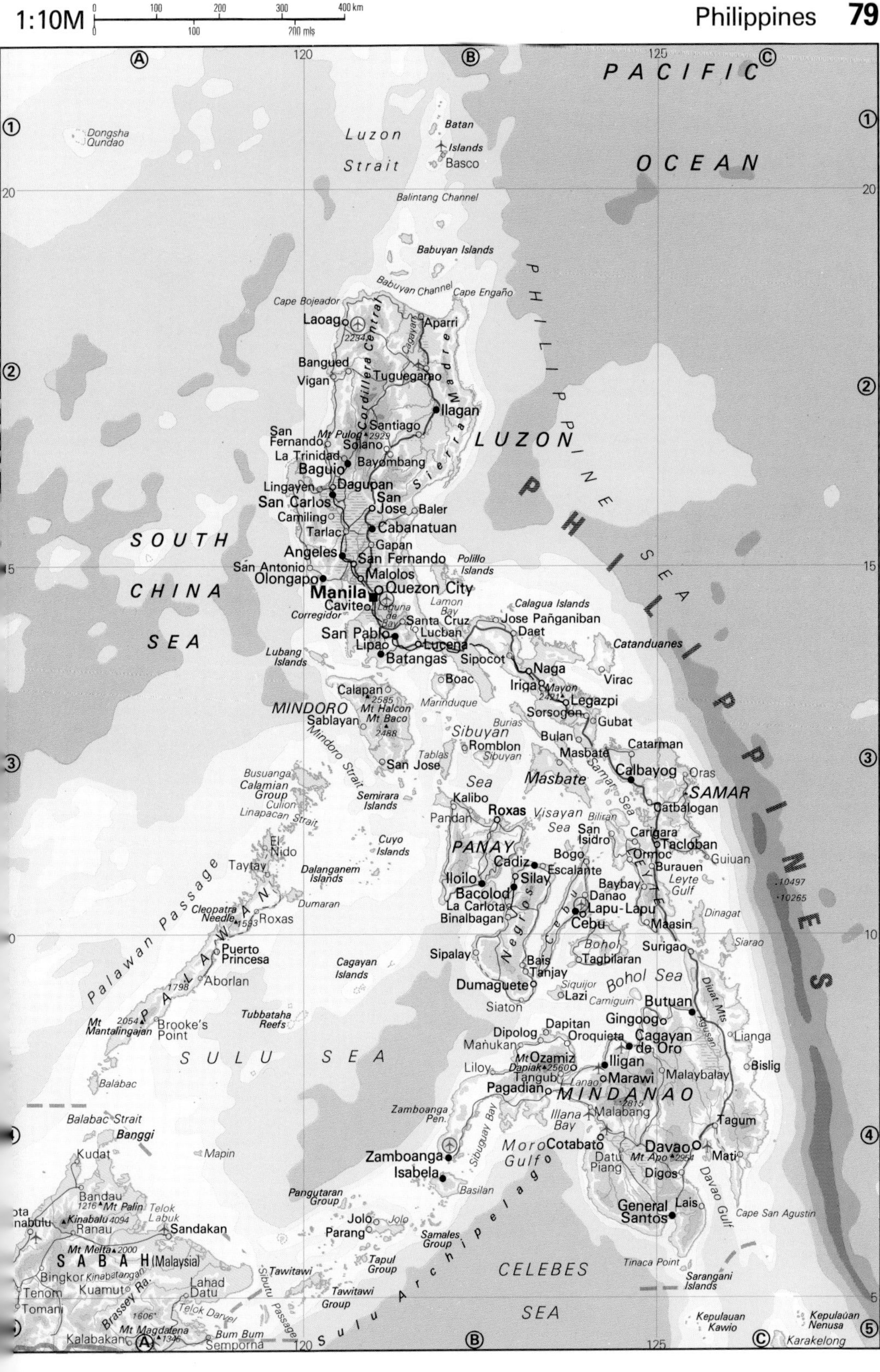

100   200   300   400 km
100   200 mls

A   120   B   125   C

① PACIFIC

Dongsha
Qundao

Luzon   Batan
Strait   ↑ Islands
                  Basco

OCEAN

20   20

Balintang Channel

Babuyan Islands

Cape Bojeador   *Babuyan Channel* Cape Engaño

Laoag   Aparri
▲2234

Bangued Tuguegarao
Vigan

② Santiago   ②
San   Mt Pulog Ilagan
Fernando ▲2929
La Trinidad Solano
Baguio   Bayombang   **LUZON**
Lingayen Dagupan
San Carlos San   Baler
Camiling Jose
Tarlac Cabanatuan
Angeles Gapan
San Antonio San Fernando Polillo
Olongapo Malolos Islands

③ SAMAR

SOUTH   Quezon City
                Manila
CHINA   Cavite Santa Cruz Jose Pañganiban
                San Pablo Lucban Daet Catanduanes
Corregidor   Lipao Lucena
SEA   Batangas Sipocot
Lubang   Boac   Naga Virac
Islands   Calapan Iriga Mayon
               ▲2585 Marinduque Legazpi
MINDORO   Mt Halcon Sorsogon Gubat
Sablayan   Mt Baco Sibuyan Bulan
               2488 Romblon Masbate Catarman

③   San Jose Tablas Sibuyan Calbayog Oras **③**
Busuanga   Sea   **Masbate** Catbalogan
Calamian   Kalibo   San
Group   Roxas Isidro Carigara
Linapacan Strait Pandan Bogo Tacloban
El   Cuyo Visayan Ormoc
Nido   Islands **PANAY** Sea Burauen
Taytay   Cadiz Guiuan
Dalanganem   Iloilo Silay Baybay Leyte
Islands   Bacolod Escalante Gulf
Dumaran   La Carlota Danao ▲10497
Roxas   Binalbagan Cebu Lapu-Lapu ▲10265
Cleopatra   Maasin
Needle ▲1593 Sipalay   Surigao Dinagat
Puerto   Bais Tagbilaran Siarao
Princesa   Tanjay Bohol
Aborlan   Cagayan Dumaguete Bohol Sea Butuan
Mt   Islands Siaton Lazi Camiguin Gingoog
Mantalingajan   Dapitan Cagayan
Brooke's   Dipolog Oroquieta de Oro Lianga
Point   Mañukan Ozamiz Iligan Bislig
Tubbataha   Liloy ▲2560 Marawi Malaybalay
Reefs   Tangub Pagadian **MINDANAO**
Balabac   Zamboanga Illana Malabang
Strait   Pen. Bay Tagum
Banggi   Sibuguey Bay Cotabato Davao
Kudat   Mapin   Zamboanga *Moro* Mati
Bandau   Isabela *Gulf* Piang Digos
Mt Palin   Basilan General Lais
Telok   Santos Cape San Agustin
Labuk
Sandakan   Jolo Jolo
SABAH Parang Samales
(Malaysia)   Group Tinaca Point
Lahad Tawitawi **CELEBES**
Datu   Group *Sulu Archipelago* Kepulauan
               Kawio Kepulauan
SEA   Nenusa
125   Karakelong

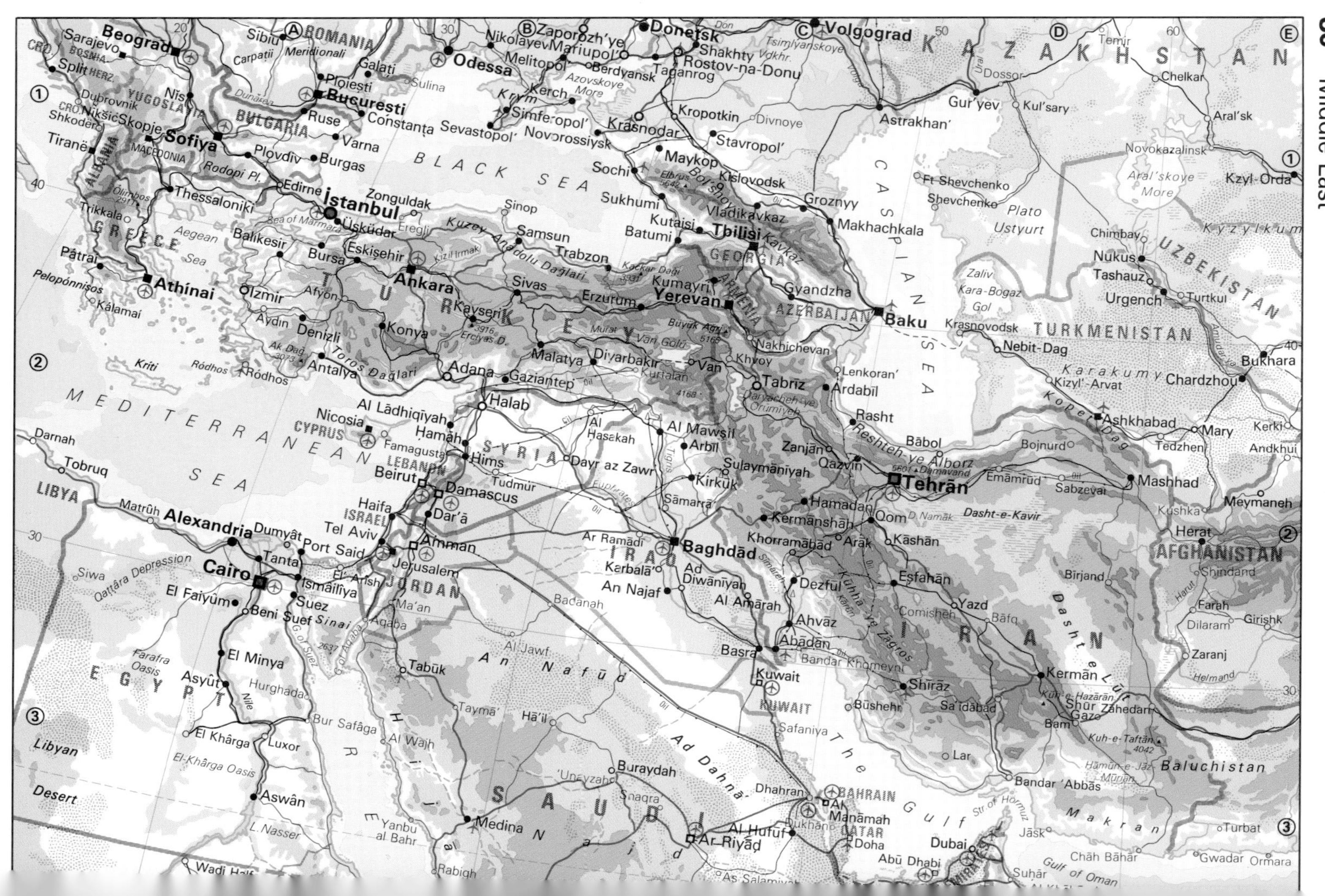
KAZAKHSTAN
UZBEKISTAN
TURKMENISTAN
AFGHANISTAN
IRAN
IRAQ
SYRIA
TURKEY
SAUDI ARABIA
EGYPT
LIBYA
JORDAN
KUWAIT
BAHRAIN
QATAR
ISRAEL
LEBANON
CYPRUS
GREECE
BULGARIA
ROMANIA
YUGOSLAVIA
MACEDONIA
GEORGIA
ARMENIA
AZERBAIJAN
CASPIAN SEA
BLACK SEA
MEDITERRANEAN SEA
The Gulf
Gulf of Oman
Aral'skoye More
Dasht-e Lut
Dasht-e-Kavir
Makran
Baluchistan
An Nafud
Ad Dahna
Hijaz
Najd
Libyan Desert
Qattara Depression
Volgograd
Astrakhan'
Gur'yev
Donetsk
Rostov-na-Donu
Odessa
Bucuresti
Beograd
Sofiya
Istanbul
Athinai
Ankara
Tbilisi
Yerevan
Baku
Tehran
Mashhad
Herat
Bukhara
Ashkhabad
Nukus
Tabriz
Esfahan
Shiraz
Kerman
Baghdad
Basra
Kuwait
Damascus
Beirut
Amman
Jerusalem
Nicosia
Alexandria
Cairo
Tel Aviv
Port Said
Suez
Aswan
Luxor
Medina
Ar Riyad
Dubai
Abu Dhabi
Doha
Manamah
Dhahran

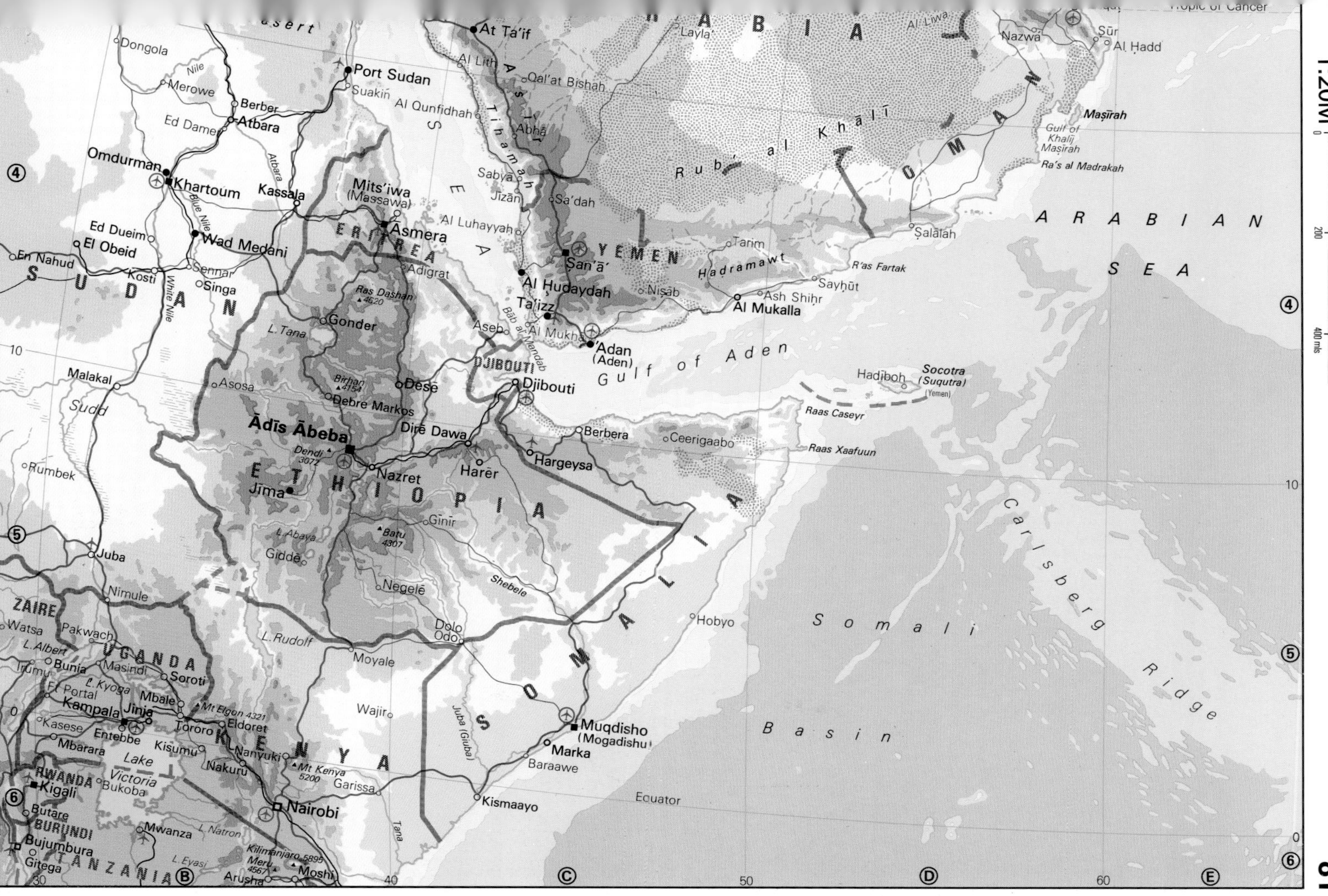

1:20M

200   400   600   800 km

200   400 mls

Tropic of Cancer

ARABIAN SEA

Carlsberg Ridge

Şūr
Al Hadd
Nizwá
Maşīrah
Gulf of
Khalij
Maşīrah
Ra's al Madrakah

O   M   A   N

Şalālah

Socotra
(Suqutra)
(Yemen)
Hadībōh
Raas Caseyr

Al Liwā'

Somali   Basin

Layla

Ras Fartak
Sayḥūt
Ash Shiḥr
Al Mukalla
Ḥaḍramawt

Raas Xaafuun

Rub' al Khālī

Dar'at Bishah

Abhā

Ḥajjah
Şa'dah
Najrān
Nişāb
Tanm
Ḥodeyta

YEMEN
Şan'ā'
Adan
(Aden)
Gulf of Aden

Cerígaabo

°Hobyo

Ecuator

At Ṭā'if
Al Lith
Al Qunfidhah
Jizān
Sabyā
Al Luḥayyah
Al Ḥudaydah
Ta'izz
Al Mukhā
Bāb al Mandab

Berbera

Shebele

MUQDISHO
(Mogadishu)
Marka
Baraawe

Tihamah

Aseb

Djibouti
Hargeysa

Juba (Giuba)

Kismaayo

Port Sudan
Suakiñ
Mitsiwa
(Massawa)
Asmera
Adigrat
Adwa
Ras Dashan
4620
ERITREA
Gonder
L. Tana

DJIBOUTI
Dirē Dawa
Harēr
Nazret
Ginir
Dēsē
Debre Markos
Birhan
Debre Markos
ĀDIS ĀBEBA
Dendi
3007

Dolo

Tana

Berber
Atbara
Atbara
Kassala

Blue Nile
Wad Medani
Singa
Sennar

White Nile

Negēlē
Moyale
L. Rudolf
Wajiro

Juba

Garissa

ETHIOPIA
Jima
Giddē
L. Ābaya

Mt Kenya
5200
Nairobi
Moshi

Khartoum
Omdurman

Merowe
Ed Damer
Atbara

Dongola

Ed Dueim
El Obeid
Kosti

Er Nahud

S   U   D   A   N

Malakal
Sobat

Rumbek

Nimule
Juba

ZAIRE

Nile

K   E   N   Y   A

Mt Elgon 4321
Eldoret
Tororo
Nakuru
Naivasha
L. Natron
Kilimanjaro 5895
Mt Meru
4567
Arusha

UGANDA
Mbale
Jinja
Kampala
Entebbe
Lake
Victoria
Bukoba
Mwanza

L. Kyoga
Masindi
Bunia
L. Albert
Portal
Kasese
Mbarara
Kigali
RWANDA
BURUNDI
Bujumbura
Gitega

TANZANIA

Butare

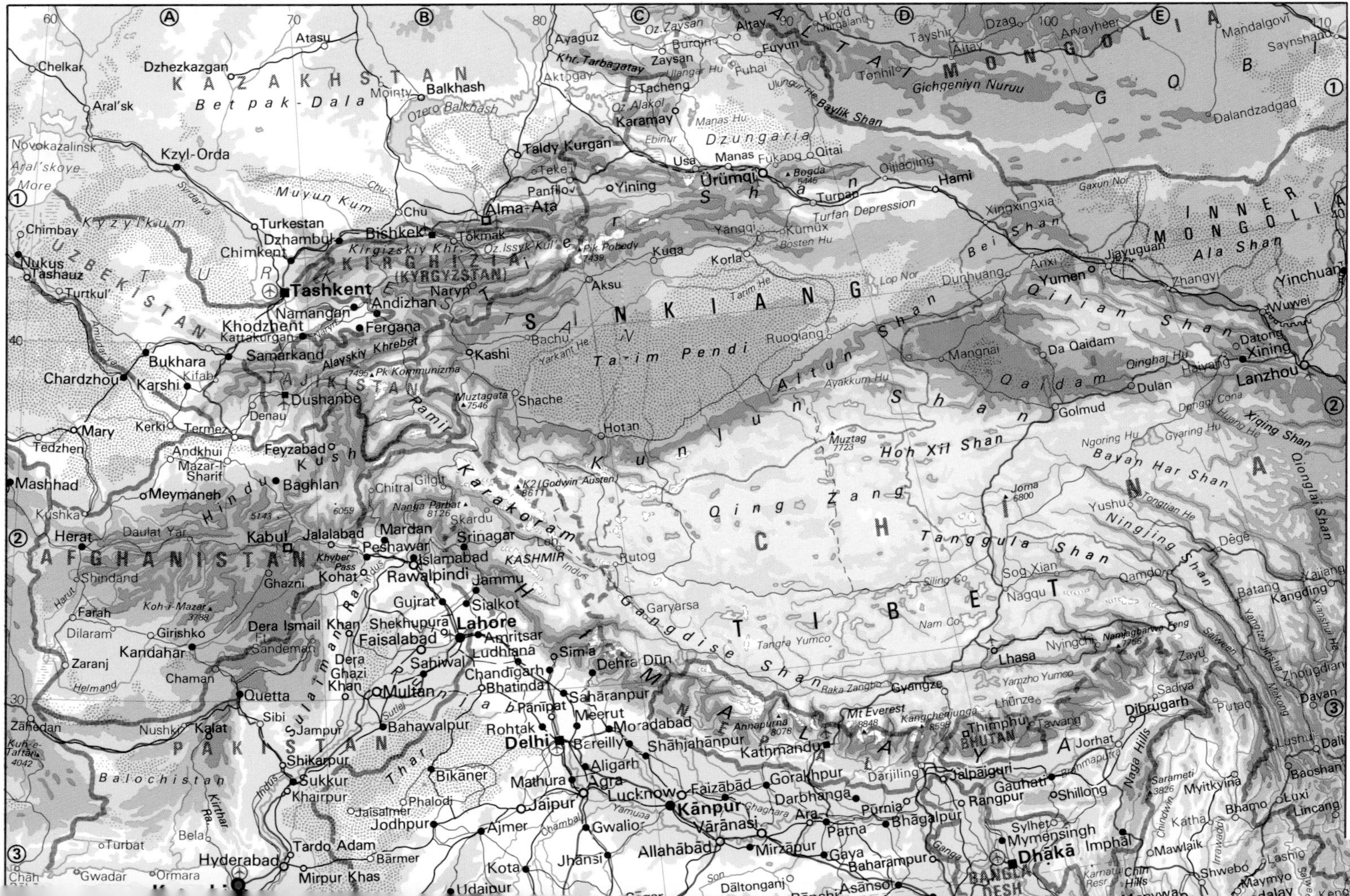
KAZAKHSTAN
MONGOLIA
GOBI
INNER MONGOLIA
SINKIANG
KIRGHIZIA (KYRGYZSTAN)
TAJIKISTAN
UZBEKISTAN
TURKMENISTAN
AFGHANISTAN
PAKISTAN
INDIA
NEPAL
BHUTAN
BANGLADESH
TIBET
CHINA
KASHMIR
Bet pak-Dala
Kyzylkum
Muyun Kum
Dzungaria
Turfan Depression
Tarim Pendi
Qaidam
Qing Zang
Tian Shan
Altai
Gichgeniyn Nuruu
Baylik Shan
Bei Shan
Qilian Shan
Altun Shan
Kunlun Shan
Hoh Xil Shan
Bayan Har Shan
Tanggula Shan
Ningjing Shan
Gangdise Shan
Himalaya
Karakoram
Hindu Kush
Pamir
Alayskiy Khrebet
Kirgizskiy Khr.
Khr. Tarbagatay
Ala Shan
Xiqing Shan
Qionglai Shan
Sulaiman Ra.
Kirthar Ra.
Balochistan
Thar
Punjab
Naga Hills
Chin Hills
Pik Pobedy 7439
Pk Kommunizma 7495
Muztagata 7546
K2 (Godwin Austen) 8611
Nanga Parbat 8126
Mt Everest 8848
Kangchenjunga 8598
Annapurna 8078
Namjagbarwa Feng 7756
Muztag 7723
Joma 6800
Bogda 5445
Koh-i-Mazar 3788
Saramati 3826
Kuh-e-Taftan 4042
Aral'skoye More
Ozero Balkhash
Oz. Zaysan
Oz. Alakol
Oz. Issyk-Kul'
Lop Nor
Bosten Hu
Qinghai Hu
Gyaring Hu
Ngoring Hu
Gaxun Nur
Nam Co
Siling Co
Tangra Yumco
Yamzho Yumco
Syrdar'ya
Amudar'ya
Chu
Indus
Sutlej
Ganga
Yamuna
Chambal
Son
Ghaghara
Brahmaputra
Tarim He
Yarkant He
Huang He
Yangtze
Jinsha
Mekong
Salween
Irrawaddy
Chindwin
Helmand
Harut
Tongtian He
Ayakkum Hu
Raka Zangbo
Chelkar
Dzhezkazgan
Atasu
Aral'sk
Novokazalinsk
Kzyl-Orda
Chimbay
Nukus
Tashauz
Turtkul'
Turkestan
Dzhambul
Chimkent
Tashkent
Khodzhent
Namangan
Andizhan
Fergana
Kattakurgan
Samarkand
Bukhara
Kifab
Karshi
Chardzhou
Dushanbe
Denau
Termez
Kerki
Mary
Tedzhen
Mashhad
Kushka
Andkhui
Mazar-i-Sharif
Feyzabad
Baghlan
Meymaneh
Herat
Shindand
Farah
Dilaram
Zaranj
Kandahar
Girishko
Chaman
Kabul
Ghazni
Jalalabad
Khyber Pass
Peshawar
Mardan
Chitral
Gilgit
Skardu
Srinagar
Islamabad
Rawalpindi
Kohat
Jammu
Gujrat
Sialkot
Lahore
Amritsar
Shekhupura
Faisalabad
Sahiwal
Dera Ismail Khan
Dera Ghazi Khan
Multan
Fort Sandeman
Quetta
Sibi
Kalat
Nushki
Zahedan
Jampur
Bahawalpur
Shikarpur
Sukkur
Khairpur
Hyderabad
Tardo Adam
Mirpur Khas
Karachi
Bela
Turbat
Gwadar
Ormara
Chah Bahar
Barmer
Jaisalmer
Phalodi
Jodhpur
Bikaner
Udaipur
Ajmer
Kota
Jaipur
Jhansi
Gwalior
Agra
Mathura
Aligarh
Delhi
Rohtak
Panipat
Bhatinda
Ludhiana
Chandigarh
Simla
Dehra Dun
Saharanpur
Meerut
Moradabad
Bareilly
Shahjahanpur
Lucknow
Kanpur
Allahabad
Varanasi
Mirzapur
Faizabad
Gorakhpur
Darbhanga
Ara
Patna
Gaya
Purnia
Bhagalpur
Baharampur
Asansol
Ranchi
Daltonganj
Kathmandu
Darjiling
Jalpaiguri
Thimphu
Tawang
Rangpur
Gauhati
Shillong
Sylhet
Mymensingh
Dhaka
Imphal
Jorhat
Dibrugarh
Sadiya
Putao
Myitkyina
Bhamo
Katha
Mawlaik
Shwebo
Monywa
Maymyo
Mandalay
Sagaing
Lashio
Kengtung
Lincang
Luxi
Baoshan
Dali
Lushui
Dayan
Zhongdian
Zayu
Nyingchi
Lhasa
Lhunze
Gyangze
Nagqu
Sog Xian
Qamdo
Batang
Yajiang
Kangding
Dege
Yushu
Golmud
Dulan
Da Qaidam
Mangnai
Ruoqiang
Dunhuang
Anxi
Yumen
Jiayuguan
Zhangye
Wuwei
Yinchuan
Lanzhou
Xining
Datong
Haiyang
Hami
Turpan
Qijiaojing
Urumqi
Fukang
Qitai
Manas
Usa
Karamay
Tacheng
Yining
Kuqa
Korla
Yanqi
Kumux
Aksu
Kashi
Bachu
Shache
Hotan
Rutog
Garyarsa
Naryn
Tokmak
Bishkek
Alma-Ata
Chu
Taldy Kurgan
Tekeli
Panfilov
Balkhash
Mointy
Aktogay
Ayaguz
Zaysan
Burqin
Altay
Fuyun
Fuhai
Hovd
Dargalant
Tayshir
Altay
Dzag
Arvayheer
Mandalgovi
Saynshand
Dalandzadgad
Tonhil

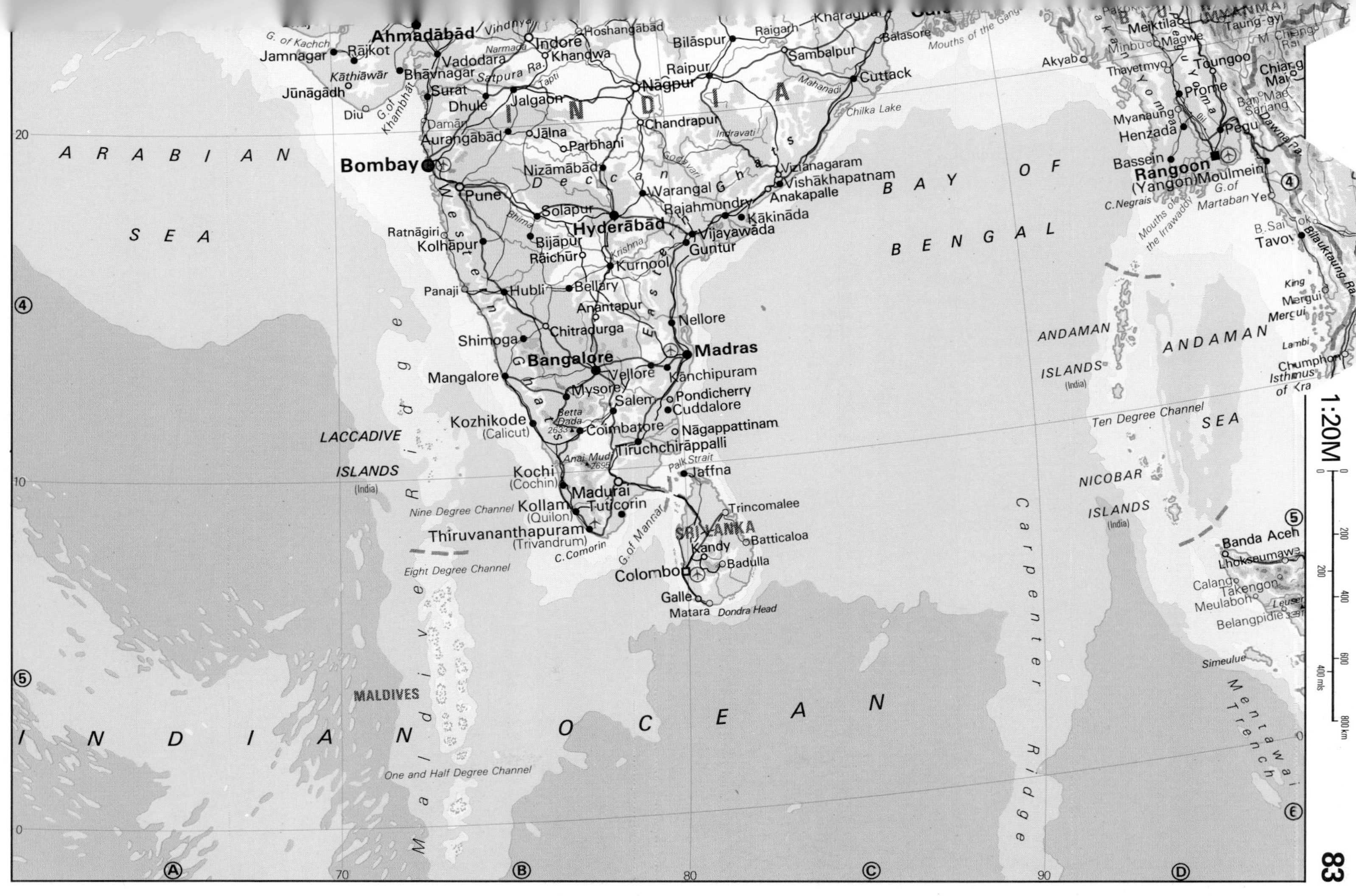

1:20M

0   200   400   600   800 km
0   200   400 mls

BURMA (MYANMAR)

Chiang Mai

Bilauktaung Ra.

Dawna Ra.

Chumphon
Isthmus
of Kra

Tavoy
B. Sal
Mergui
Lampi

Pegu
Moulmein
Rangoon
(Yangon)
G. of
Martaban Ye

Bassein

Thaton

Henzada

Myanaung

Prome

Thayetmyo

Magwe

Akyab

Mandalay

Meiktila

MENTAWAI
TRENCH

Banda Aceh
Lhoksumawe

⑤

Calang
Meulaboh
Tangse
Kenggo
Belangpidie
Simeulue

SEA

ANDAMAN

Ten Degree Channel

NICOBAR

ISLANDS
(India)

ANDAMAN

ISLANDS
(India)

Carpenter   Ridge

90

B   A   Y   O   F

B   E   N   G   A   L

Mouths of
the Irrawaddy

C. Negrais

Mouths of the Ganges

Kharagpur

Balasore

Cuttack

Sambalpur

Raigarh

Bilaspur

Raipur

Chandrapur

Nagpur

Bhandara

Roshanabad

Indore

Khandwa

Jalgaon

Bhusawal

Jalna

Aurangabad

Patbhani

Nizamabad

Hyderabad

Solapur

Bijapur

Raichur

Kurnool

Bellary

Anantapur

Chitradurga

Shimoga

Bangalore

Mysore

Mangalore

Chikla Lake

Vizianagaram

Vishakhapatnam

Anakapalle

Rajahmundry

Kakinada

Vijayawada

Guntur

Warangal

Nellore

Madras

Kanchipuram

Vellore

Pondicherry

Cuddalore

Nagappattinam

Salem

Coimbatore

Tiruchirappalli

Madurai

Tuticorin

Kochi
(Cochin)

Kollam
(Quilon)

Thiruvananthapuram
(Trivandrum)

C. Comorin

Kozhikode
(Calicut)

Panaji

Ratnagiri

Kolhapur

Pune

Bombay

Ahmadabad

Vadodara

Surat

Bhavnagar

Rajkot

Kathiawar

Jamnagar

Junagadh

Diu

Jabalpur

Chandrapun

Dhule

Damapur

G. or
Khambhat

G. or Kachch

I   N   D   I   A

Godavari

Krishna

Tungabhadra

Penner

Kaveri

Godavari

Narmada

Tapti

Vindhya Ra.

Satpura Ra.

Western   Ghats

Eastern   Ghats

Dec can

Bhima

Palk   Strait

Jaffna

Trincomalee

Batticaloa

Kandy

Badulla

SRI LANKA

Colombo

Galle

Matara   Dondra Head

G. of Mannar

Adam's   Bridge

Nine Degree Channel

Eight Degree Channel

One and Half Degree Channel

LACCADIVE

ISLANDS
(India)

MALDIVES

I   N   D   I   A   N

O   C   E   A   N

A   R   A   B   I   A   N

S   E   A

E

C

B

A

D

20

④

⑩

⑤

70

80

90

④

⑤

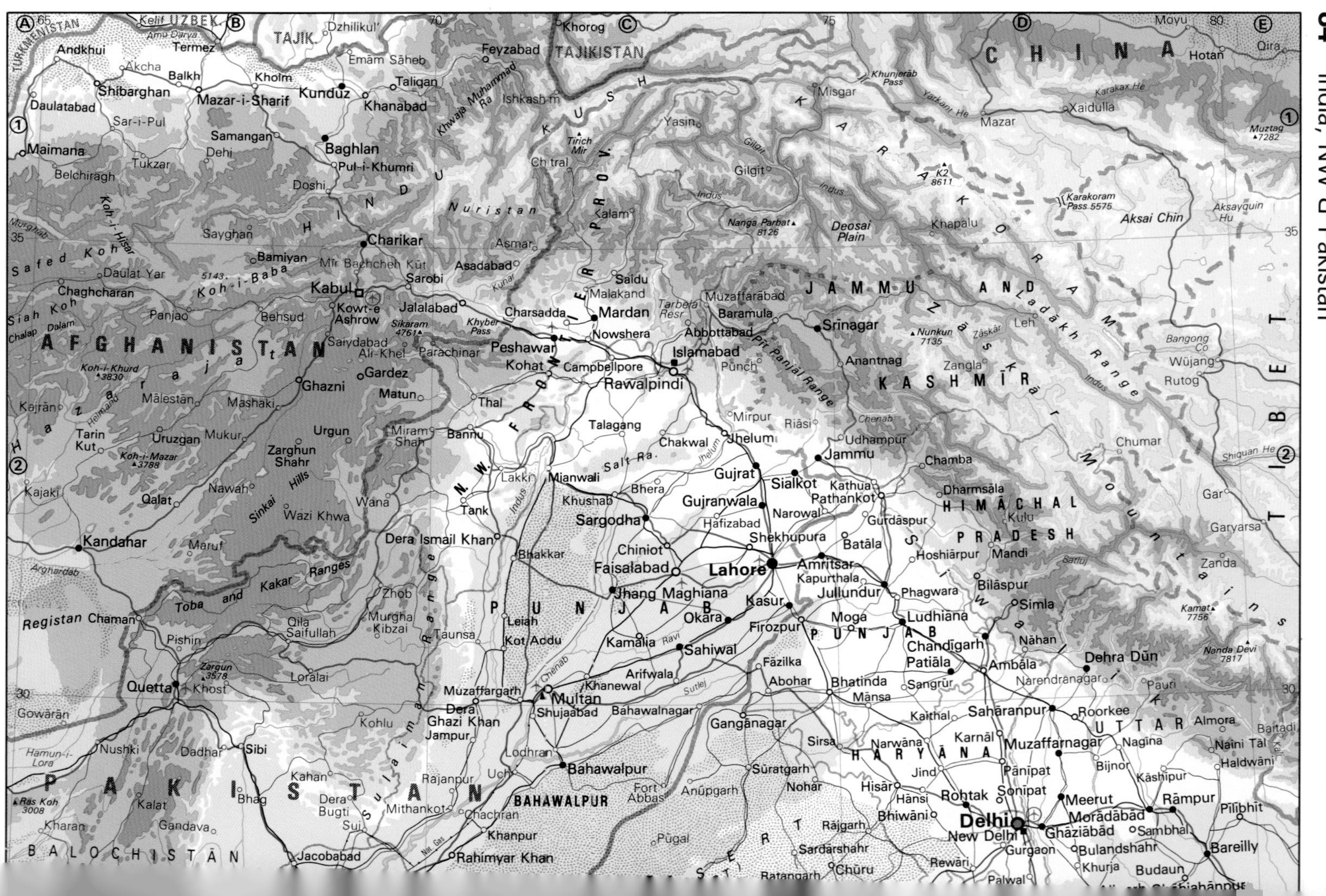

CHINA
TAJIKISTAN
TAJIK.
UZBEK.
TURKMENISTAN
AFGHANISTAN
PAKISTAN
TIBET
JAMMU AND KASHMIR
HIMACHAL PRADESH
PUNJAB
HARYANA
UTTAR
N.W. FRONTIER PROV.
BALOCHISTAN
BAHAWALPUR
KARAKORAM
HINDU KUSH
Ladakh Range
Pir Panjal Range
Zaskar Ra.
Siwalik
Salt Ra.
Sulaiman Range
Toba and Kakar Ranges
Hazarajat
Aksai Chin
Deosai Plain
Registan
Safed Koh
Siah Koh
Koh-i-Baba
Koh-i-Hisar
Khwaja Muhammad Ra
Nuristan
Sinkai Hills
Khunjerab Pass
Karakoram Pass 5575
Khyber Pass
K2 8611
Nanga Parbat 8126
Nunkun 7135
Tirich Mir
Muztag 7282
Nanda Devi 7817
Kamet 7756
Sikaram 4761
Koh-i-Khurd 3830
Koh-i-Mazar 3788
Zargun 3578
Ras Koh 3008
Tarbela Resr
Indus
Chenab
Jhelum
Ravi
Sutlej
Gilgit
Kunar
Helmand
Arghandab
Murghab
Amu Darya
Yarkant He
Karakax He
Shiquan He
Hamun-i-Lora
Hotan
Qira
Moyu
Xaidulla
Mazar
Aksayquin Hu
Rutog
Wüjang
Bangong Co
Chumar
Gar
Garyarsa
Zanda
Leh
Zangla
Khapalu
Srinagar
Anantnag
Baramula
Muzaffarabad
Gilgit
Misgar
Yasin
Jammu
Udhampur
Riasi
Chamba
Dharmsala
Kulu
Mandi
Simla
Bilaspur
Hoshiarpur
Gurdaspur
Pathankot
Kathua
Batala
Amritsar
Kapurthala
Jullundur
Phagwara
Ludhiana
Moga
Firozpur
Fazilka
Abohar
Bhatinda
Mansa
Sangrur
Patiala
Chandigarh
Ambala
Nahan
Dehra Dun
Pauri
Narendranagar
Roorkee
Saharanpur
Muzaffarnagar
Meerut
Ghaziabad
Delhi
New Delhi
Gurgaon
Rewari
Palwal
Rohtak
Sonipat
Panipat
Karnal
Kaithal
Jind
Narwana
Hisar
Hansi
Bhiwani
Sirsa
Nohar
Rajgarh
Churu
Sardarshahr
Ratangarh
Suratgarh
Ganganagar
Anupgarh
Pugal
Moradabad
Rampur
Bareilly
Pilibhit
Haldwani
Naini Tal
Almora
Nagina
Bijnor
Kashipur
Sambhal
Budaun
Bulandshahr
Khurja
Lahore
Kasur
Sheikhupura
Narowal
Sialkot
Gujranwala
Hafizabad
Gujrat
Jhelum
Mirpur
Punch
Abbottabad
Islamabad
Rawalpindi
Chakwal
Talagang
Campbellpore
Nowshera
Mardan
Peshawar
Charsadda
Kohat
Malakand
Saidu
Chitral
Kalam
Bannu
Lakki
Thal
Parachinar
Miram Shah
Wana
Tank
Dera Ismail Khan
Mianwali
Khushab
Sargodha
Bhera
Chiniot
Faisalabad
Jhang Maghiana
Okara
Sahiwal
Kamalia
Arifwala
Khanewal
Multan
Shujaabad
Bahawalpur
Bahawalnagar
Lodhran
Uch
Fort Abbas
Khanpur
Rahimyar Khan
Chachran
Mithankot
Bhakkar
Leiah
Kot Addu
Muzaffargarh
Dera Ghazi Khan
Jampur
Rajanpur
Taunsa
Zhob
Murgha Kibzai
Loralai
Qila Saifullah
Kohlu
Dera Bugti
Sui
Kahan
Sibi
Dadhar
Bhag
Jacobabad
Quetta
Pishin
Khost
Chaman
Nushki
Kalat
Gandava
Kharan
Gowaran
Kabul
Jalalabad
Asadabad
Asmar
Sarobi
Charikar
Mir Bachcheh Kut
Kowt-e Ashrow
Saiydabad
Ali-Khel
Gardez
Ghazni
Matun
Urgun
Zarghun Shahr
Wazi Khwa
Nawah
Qalat
Kandahar
Maruf
Tarin Kut
Uruzgan
Mukur
Mashaki
Malestan
Kajran
Kajaki
Bamiyan
Behsud
Panjao
Daulat Yar
Chaghcharan
Chalap Dalam
Kunduz
Khanabad
Taliqan
Feyzabad
Ishkashim
Baghlan
Pul-i-Khumri
Doshi
Saygan
Samangan
Dehi
Kholm
Mazar-i-Sharif
Balkh
Termez
Kelif
Shibarghan
Akcha
Sar-i-Pul
Tukzar
Maimana
Andkhui
Daulatabad
Belchiragh
Khorog
Dzhilikul'
Emam Saheb

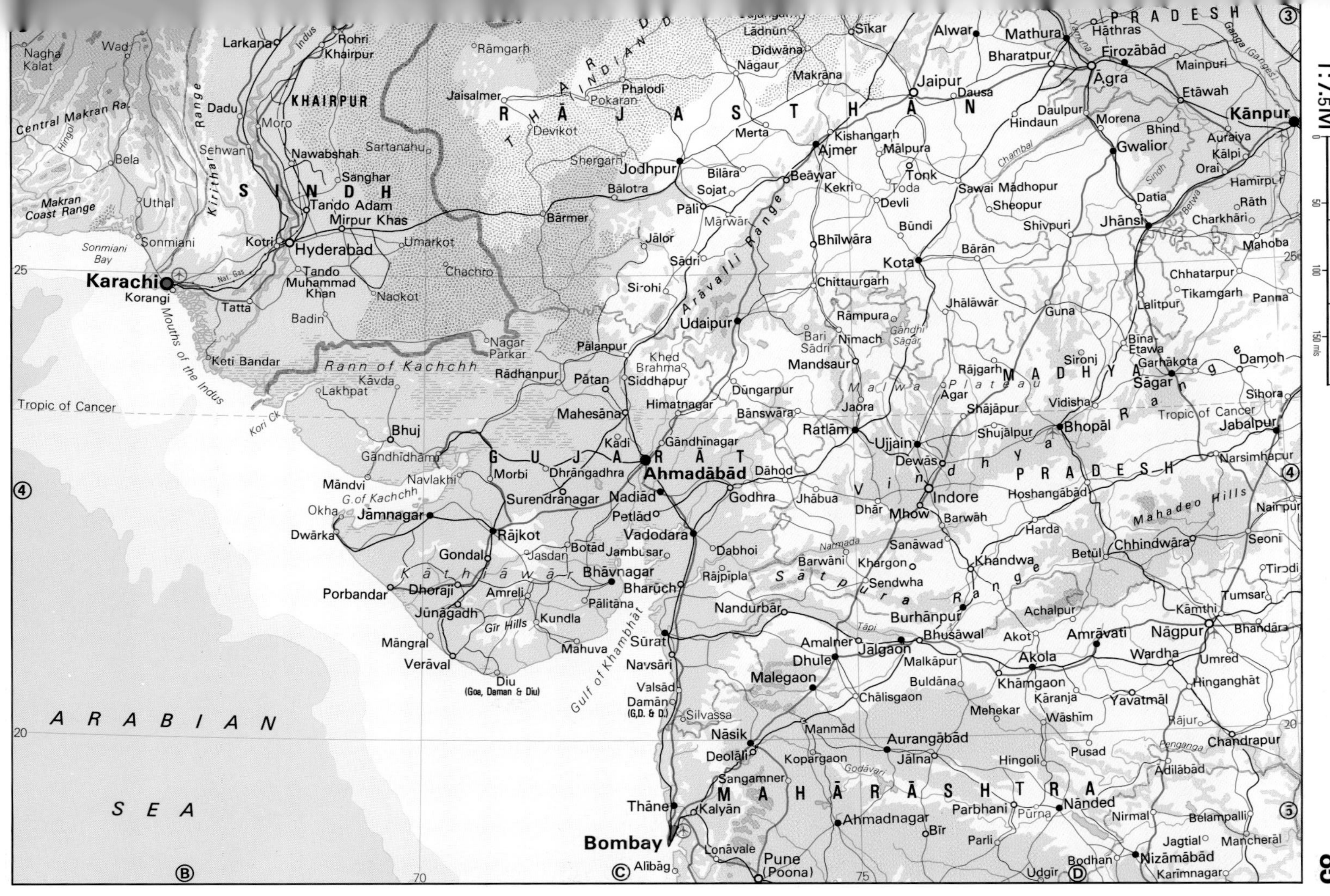
ARABIAN SEA
Karachi
Korangi
Mouths of the Indus
Sonmiani
Sonmiani Bay
Uthal
Bela
Wad
Nagha Kalat
Central Makran Ra.
Makran Coast Range
Hingol
Kirthar Range
Sehwan
Dadu
Larkana
Indus
Moro
Nawabshah
Rohri
Khairpur
KHAIRPUR
SINDH
Sanghar
Tando Adam
Mirpur Khas
Hyderabad
Tando Muhammad Khan
Kotri
Nat. Gas
Tatta
Keti Bandar
Badin
Umarkot
Naokot
Sartanahu
Chachro
Nagar Parkar
Rann of Kachchh
Kori Ck
Lakhpat
Kavda
Bhuj
Gandhidham
Mandvi
G. of Kachchh
Okha
Dwarka
Jamnagar
Navlakhi
Morbi
Porbandar
Gondal
Dhoraji
Junagadh
Mangral
Veraval
Diu
(Goa, Daman & Diu)
Kathiawar
Rajkot
Amreli
Gir Hills
Kundla
Mahuva
Jasdan
Botad
Surendranagar
Dhrangadhra
Radhanpur
Patan
Mahesana
Kadi
Palanpur
Siddhapur
Khed Brahma
Himatnagar
Gandhinagar
GUJARAT
Ahmadabad
Nadiad
Petlad
Vadodara
Jambusar
Bhavnagar
Palitana
Bharuch
Gulf of Khambhat
Surat
Navsari
Valsad
Daman (G.D. & D.)
Silvassa
Thane
Bombay
Alibag
Kalyan
Lonavale
Pune (Poona)
Nasik
Deolali
Sangamner
Kopargaon
Manmad
Malegaon
Dhule
Amalner
Jalgaon
Nandurbar
Rajpipla
Dabhoi
Godhra
Dahod
Jhabua
Ratlam
Mandsaur
Jaora
Nimach
Bari Sadri
Rampura
Gandhi Sagar
Chittaurgarh
Bhilwara
Kota
Bundi
Baran
Udaipur
Dungarpur
Banswara
Sirohi
Jalor
Sadri
Pali
Marwar
Sojat
Bilara
Jodhpur
Balotra
Barmer
Shergarh
Pokaran
Phalodi
Devikot
Jaisalmer
Ramgarh
RAJASTHAN
THAR (INDIAN DESERT)
Nagaur
Didwana
Ladnun
Makrana
Merta
Beawar
Aravalli Range
Ajmer
Kishangarh
Kekri
Devli
Malpura
Tonk
Toda
Jaipur
Sikar
Alwar
Dausa
Sawai Madhopur
Sheopur
Shivpuri
Bharatpur
Mathura
Agra
Firozabad
Hathras
Yamuna
Mainpuri
Etawah
Kanpur
Ganga (Ganges)
Kalpi
Auraiya
Orai
Hamirpur
Rath
Mahoba
Charkhari
Panna
Jhansi
Betwa
Datia
Sindh
Gwalior
Bhind
Morena
Daulpur
Hindaun
Chambal
Guna
Jhalawar
Lalitpur
Tikamgarh
Chhatarpur
Damoh
Sagar
Garhakota
Bina Etawa
Sironj
Vidisha
Bhopal
Rajgarh
Malwa Plateau
Shajapur
Shujalpur
Agar
Ujjain
Dewas
Indore
Mhow
Dhar
Barwah
Sanawad
Narmada
Khargon
Sendwha
Barwani
Satpura Range
Khandwa
Burhanpur
Bhusawal
Tapi
Harda
Hoshangabad
Vindhya Range
MADHYA PRADESH
Betul
Chhindwara
Mahadeo Hills
Jabalpur
Narsimhapur
Sihora
Seoni
Nainpur
Tirodi
Tumsar
Bhandara
Nagpur
Kamthi
Umred
Hinganghat
Wardha
Amravati
Achalpur
Yavatmal
Chandrapur
Rajur
Penganga
Adilabad
Bellampalli
Mancheral
Jagtial
Karimnagar
Nizamabad
Nirmal
Bodhan
Nanded
Pusad
Washim
Karanja
Akola
Akot
Khamgaon
Mehekar
Buldana
Malkapur
Chalisgaon
Aurangabad
Jalna
Godavari
Ahmadnagar
Bir
Parbhani
Purna
Hingoli
Parli
Udgir
MAHARASHTRA
PRADESH
Tropic of Cancer
25
20
70
75

0 50 100 150 200 300 km
50 100 150 mls

BANGLADESH · BHUTAN · CHINA · TIBET · BURMA (MYANMAR)

ASSAM · MEGHALAYA · TRIPURA · MIZORAM · MANIPUR · NAGALAND · ARUNACHAL Pradesh · SIKKIM

B I H A R · WEST BENGAL · ORISSA · MADHYA PRADESH · UTTAR PRADESH

Dhākā (Dacca) · Calcutta · Kanpur · Lucknow · Kathmandu · Lhasa · Chittagong · Cuttack · Raipur

BAY OF BENGAL

Mt Everest (Qomolangma Feng) 8848

Mouths of the Ganga (Ganges)

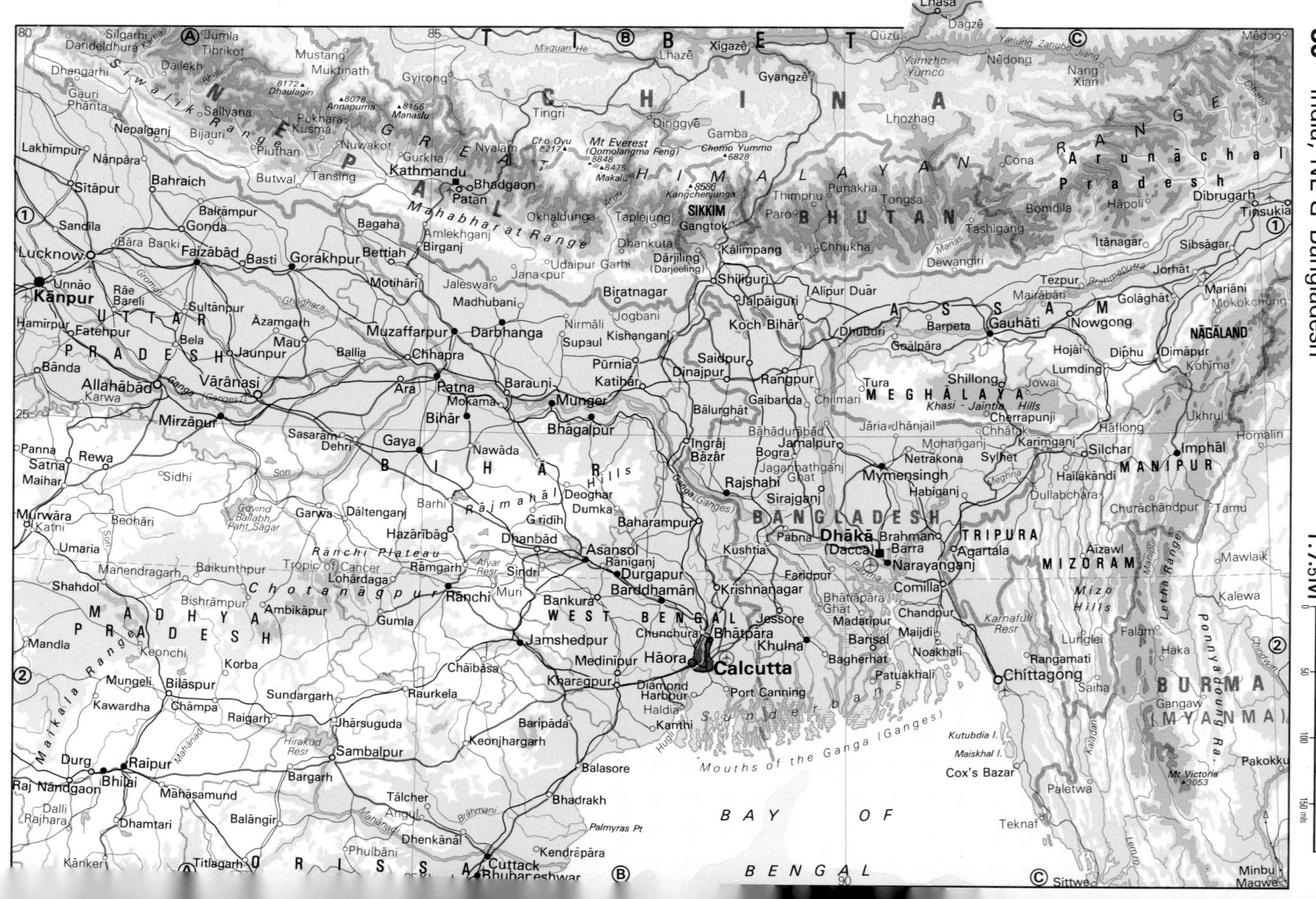

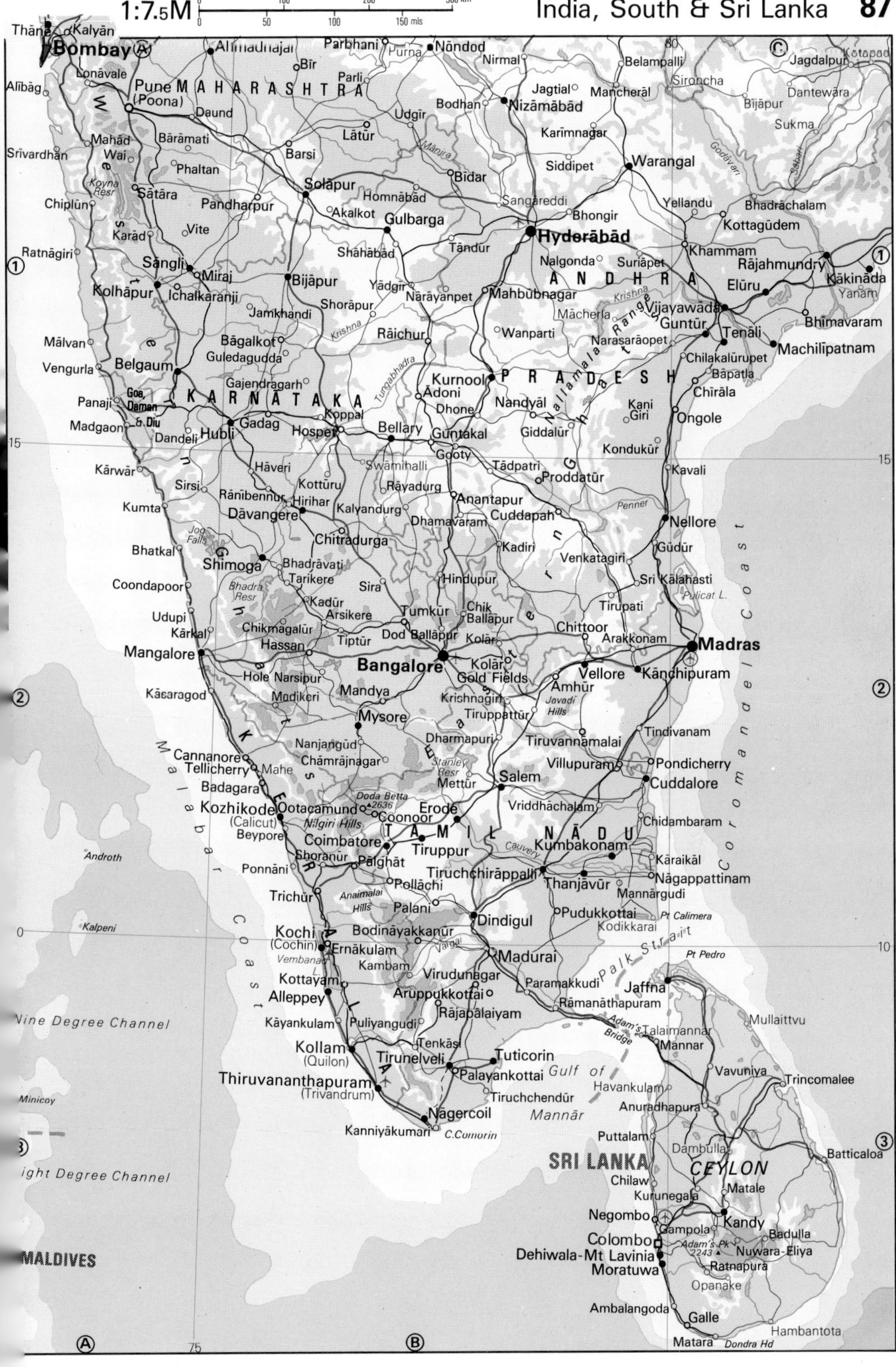

1:7.5M

100   200   300 km
0   50   100   150 mils

Bombay (A)   Thāne Kalyān
Alībāg   Lonāvale   Pune MAHARASHTRA   Parbhani   Nāndod   Nirmal
Srīvardhan   (Poona)   Ahmadnagar   Bīr   Purna   Belampalli   Jagdalpur   Kotapad
Mahād   Bārāmati   Parli   Jagtial   Mancherāl   Sironcha   Dantewāra
Chiplūn   Wai   Daund   Udgīr   Bodhan   Nizāmābād   Karīmnagar   Bijāpur   Sukma
Ratnāgiri   Phaltan   Latūr   Siddipet   Warangal   Yellandu   Bhadrāchalam
Karād   Sātāra   Barsi   Bīdar   Sangareddi   Bhongir   Khammam   Kottagūdem
Sāngli   Pandharpur   Homnābad   Shāhābād   Tāndūr   Nalgonda   Suriāpet   Rājahmundry
Kolhāpur   Miraj   Solapur   Akalkot   Gulbarga   Hyderābād   ANDHRA   Elūru   Kākināda   Yanam
Mālvan   Ichalkaranji   Bijāpur   Yādgir   Mahbūbnagar   Mācherla   Vijayawāda   Bhīmavaram
Vengurla   Jamkhandi   Narāyanpet   Wanparti   Guntūr   Tenāli   Machilipatnam
Belgaum   Bāgalkot   Shorāpur   Narasarāopet   Chilakalūrupet   Bāpatla
Panaji   Goa   Guledagudda   Raichur   KARNATAKA   PRADESH   Chīrāla
Madgaon   Daman   Gajendragarh   Kurnool   Kani   Ongole
Kārwār   Dandeli   Gadag   Koppal   Bellary   Adoni   Dhone   Nandyāl   Giddalur   Kondukür   Giri   Kavali
Sirsi   Haveri   Kottūru   Gooty   Tādpatri   Proddatūr   Nellore
Kumta   Rānibennur   Hirihar   Kalyandurg   Rāyadurg   Anantapur   Penner   Gūdūr
Bhatkal   Dāvangere   Chitrādurga   Dharmavaram   Cuddapah   Kadiri   Sri Kālahasti   Pulicat L.
Coondapoor   Shimoga   Bhadrāvati   Tarikere   Sira   Hindupur   Venkatagiri   Tirupati
Udupi   Kārkal   Chikmagalūr   Kadūr   Tumkūr   Chik   Chittoor   Arakkonam   Madras
Mangalore   Hassan   Arsikere   Dod Ballāpur   Ballāpur   Kolār   Vellore   Kānchipuram
Kāsaragod   Hole Narsipur   Tiptur   Bangalore   Kolār   Āmbūr   Nanjangūd   Mandya   Gold Fields   Krishnagiri   Javadi
Cannanore   Madikeri   Mysore   Dharmapuri   Tiruppattūr   Hills   Tindivanam
Tellicherry   Mahe   Chāmrājnagar   Tiruvannāmalai   Pondicherry
Badagara   Nanjangūd   Mettūr   Salem   Villupuram   Cuddalore
Kozhikode   Ootacamund   Coonoor   Erode   Vriddhāchalam   Chidambaram
(Calicut)   Nīlgiri Hills   Doda Betta   TAMIL NĀDU   Kumbakonam
Beypore   Coimbatore   Tiruppur   Tiruchchirāppalli   Kāraikāl
Ponnāni   Shoranur   Pālghāt   Thanjāvūr   Nāgappattinam
Trichūr   Pollāchi   Mannārgudi
Kochi   Palani   Pudukkottai   Pt Calimere
(Cochin)   Bodināyakkanūr   Dindigul   Kodikkarai
Ernākulam   Kambam   Madúrai   Jaffna
Kottayam   Virudunagar   Paramakkudi   Pt Pedro
Alleppey   Aruppukkottai   Rāmanāthapuram   Mullaittvu
Kāyankulam   Puliyangudi   Rājapālaiyam   Adam's   Talaimannar
Kollam   Tenkāsi   Tuticorin   Bridge   Mannar   Vavuniya   Trincomalee
(Quilon)   Tirunelveli
Thiruvananthapuram   Palayankottai   Gulf of   Havankulam
(Trivandrum)   Tiruchchendūr   Mannār   Anuradhapura
Nāgercoil   Puttalam
Kanniyākumari   C.Comorin   SRI LANKA   Dambulla   Batticaloa
Chilaw   CEYLON
Negombo   Kurunegala   Matale   Kandy
Colombo   Gampola   Badulla
Dehiwala-Mt Lavinia   Nuwara-Eliya
Moratuwa   Ratnapura
Ambalangoda   Opanake
Galle   Hambantota
Matara   Dondra Hd

MALDIVES

Nine Degree Channel   Androth   Kalpeni
Minicoy
Eight Degree Channel

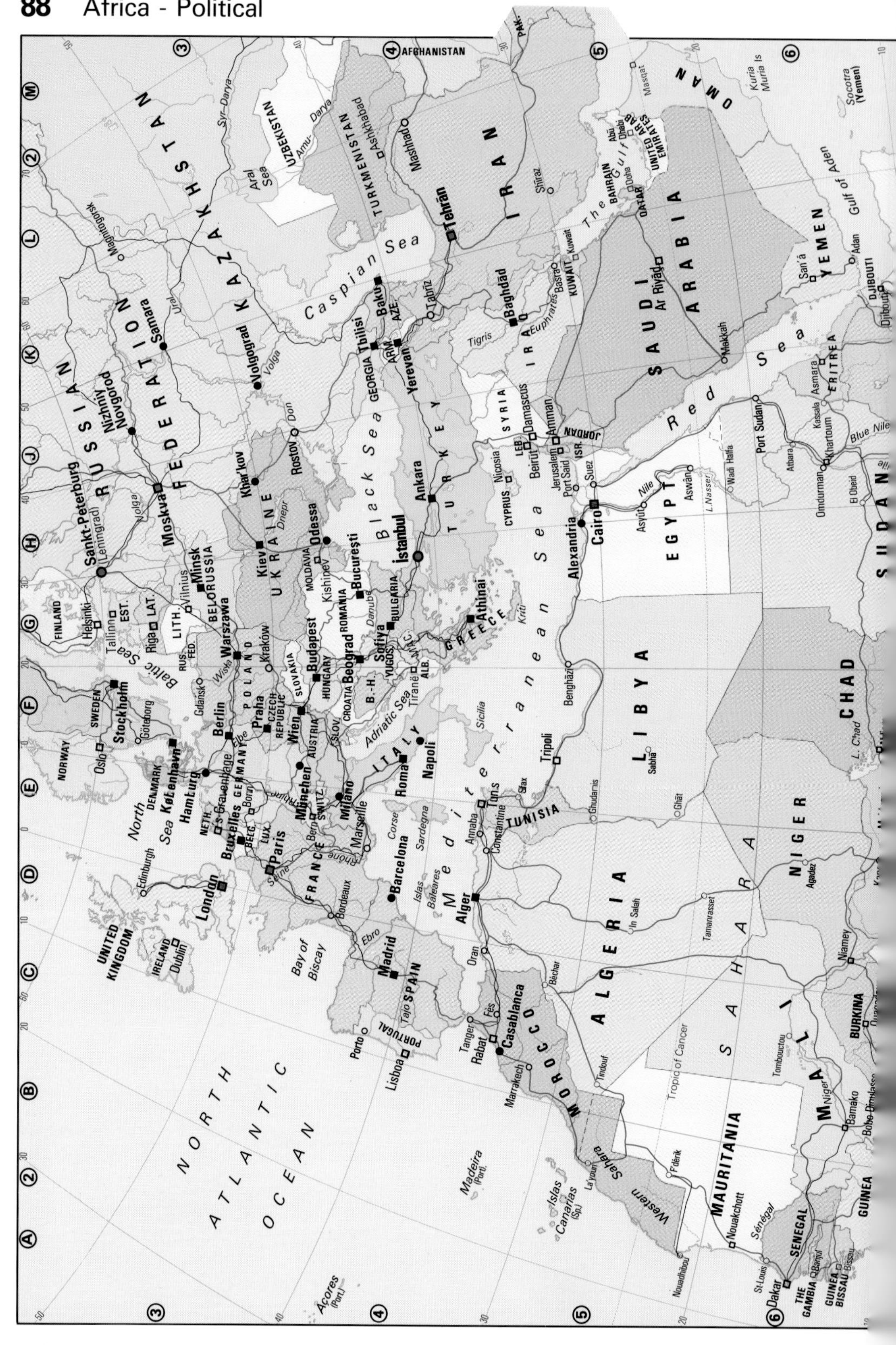
NORTH ATLANTIC OCEAN
UNITED KINGDOM
IRELAND
Dublin
London
Edinburgh
NORWAY
Oslo
SWEDEN
Stockholm
Göteborg
FINLAND
Helsinki
Tallinn
EST.
LAT.
Riga
LITH.
Vilnius
DENMARK
København
North Sea
Baltic Sea
NETH.
BELG.
Bruxelles
LUX.
Paris
FRANCE
Bordeaux
Marseille
GERMANY
Hamburg
Berlin
Bonn
München
POLAND
Warszawa
Kraków
Gdańsk
CZECH REPUBLIC
Praha
SLOVAKIA
AUSTRIA
Wien
HUNGARY
Budapest
SWITZ.
Bern
ITALY
Milano
Roma
Napoli
Corse
Sardegna
Sicilia
SLOV.
CROATIA
B.-H.
YUGOS.
Beograd
ALB.
Tiranë
MAC.
GREECE
Athinai
Kriti
BULGARIA
Sofiya
ROMANIA
Bucureşti
MOLDAVIA
Kishinev
UKRAINE
Kiev
Odessa
Khar'kov
BELORUSSIA
Minsk
RUSSIAN FEDERATION
Sankt-Peterburg (Leningrad)
Moskva
Nizhniy Novgorod
Samara
Volgograd
Rostov
KAZAKHSTAN
Magnitogorsk
UZBEKISTAN
Aral Sea
TURKMENISTAN
Ashkhabad
AFGHANISTAN
PAK.
Caspian Sea
Black Sea
GEORGIA
Tbilisi
ARM.
Yerevan
AZE.
Baku
TURKEY
İstanbul
Ankara
CYPRUS
Nicosia
SYRIA
Damascus
LEB.
Beirut
ISR.
Jerusalem
JORDAN
Amman
IRAQ
Baghdād
IRAN
Tehrān
Mashhad
Tabrīz
Shīrāz
KUWAIT
Kuwait
Basra
BAHRAIN
QATAR
Doha
UNITED ARAB EMIRATES
Abū Dhabi
Masqat
OMAN
SAUDI ARABIA
Ar Riyād
Mekkah
YEMEN
San'ā
Adan
Gulf of Aden
DJIBOUTI
Djibouti
ERITREA
Asmara
Kuria Muria Is
Socotra (Yemen)
Red Sea
Mediterranean Sea
Adriatic Sea
Bay of Biscay
SPAIN
Madrid
Barcelona
Islas Baleares
PORTUGAL
Lisboa
Porto
MOROCCO
Rabat
Casablanca
Tanger
Fès
Marrakech
ALGERIA
Alger
Oran
Constantine
Annaba
TUNISIA
Tunis
Sfax
LIBYA
Tripoli
Benghāzi
Sabhā
EGYPT
Cairo
Alexandria
Port Said
Suez
Asyūt
Aswān
L. Nasser
SUDAN
Port Sudan
Khartoum
Omdurman
Wadi Halfa
Kassala
Atbara
El Obeid
Blue Nile
CHAD
L. Chad
NIGER
Niamey
Agadez
MALI
Bamako
Tombouctou
BURKINA
MAURITANIA
Nouakchott
Nouadhibou
F'dérik
Western Sahara
La'youn
SENEGAL
Dakar
St-Louis
THE GAMBIA
Banjul
GUINEA-BISSAU
Bissau
GUINEA
SAHARA
Tropic of Cancer
Islas Canarias (Sp.)
Madeira (Port.)
Açores (Port.)
Tindouf
Béchar
In Salah
Tamanrasset
Ghāt
Ghudamis
Niger
Sénégal
Nile
Danube
Dnepr
Volga
Don
Ural
Tigris
Euphrates
Ebro
Tajo
Seine
Elbe
Wisła
Rhône
Syr-Darya
Amu-Darya
The Gulf

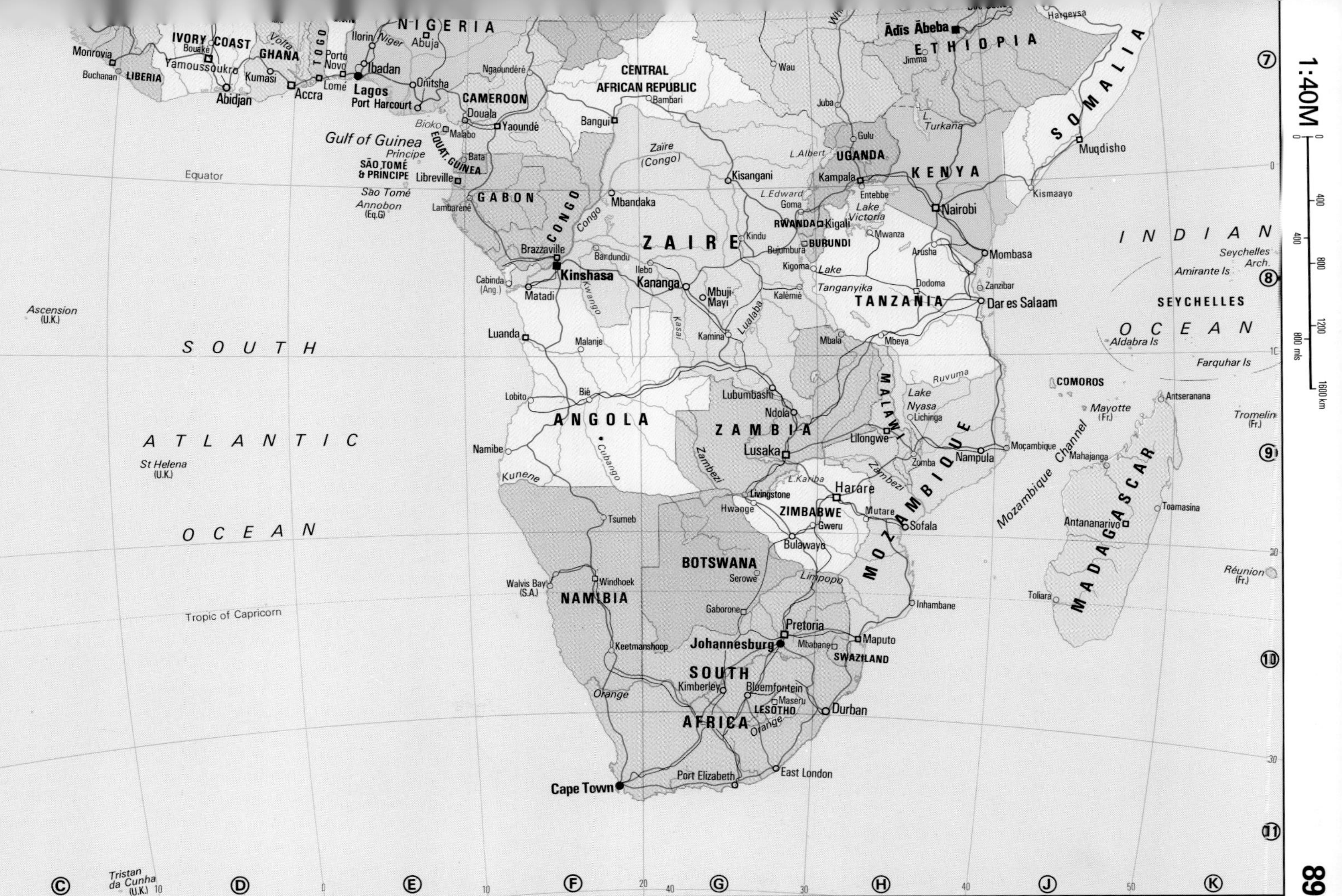

1:40M

K

J

H

G

F

E

D

C

INDIAN OCEAN

SEYCHELLES

Seychelles Arch.

Amirante Is.

Farquhar Is.

Tromelin (Fr.)

Réunion (Fr.)

Mauritius

Aldabra Is.

Mayotte (Fr.)

MADAGASCAR

Antananarivo

Antseranana

Toamasina

Toliara

Mahajanga

COMOROS

Moçambique

Mozambique Channel

SOMALIA

Hargeysa

Muqdisho

ETHIOPIA

Ādīs Ābeba

Jimma

Juba

Wau

Turkana

Gulu

KENYA

Nairobi

Mombasa

UGANDA

Kampala

Entebbe

Kisangani

L. Albert

L. Edward

Lake Victoria

Mwanza

Arusha

Dodoma

TANZANIA

Dar es Salaam

Zanzibar

Lake Tanganyika

RWANDA

Kigali

BURUNDI

Bujumbura

Kigoma

Mbeya

Mbala

Lake Nyasa (L. Malawi)

Ruvuma

Lichinga

MALAWI

Lilongwe

Blantyre

Zomba

MOZAMBIQUE

Nampula

Sofala

Moçambique

CENTRAL AFRICAN REPUBLIC

Bambari

Bangui

CAMEROON

Yaoundé

Ngaoundéré

Douala

Maiduguri

NIGERIA

Abuja

Onitsha

Ibadan

Lagos

Port Harcourt

Ilorin

Niger

Porto Novo

Lomé

Accra

Kumasi

GHANA

Volta

IVORY COAST

Bouaké

Yamoussoukro

Abidjan

LIBERIA

Buchanan

Monrovia

Bioko

EQUAT. GUINEA

Bata

Libreville

Principe

São Tomé

SÃO TOMÉ & PRINCIPE

Annobon (Eq.G.)

Gulf of Guinea

GABON

Lambaréné

CONGO

Brazzaville

Kinshasa

Matadi

Cabinda (Ang.)

Luanda

Malanje

Loge

Bie

ANGOLA

Namibe

Cubango

Cuando

Kunene

Lobito

ZAIRE

Mbandaka

Bandundu

Ilebo

Kananga

Mbuji Mayi

Kasai

Kwango

Kwilu

Congo (Zaire)

Kindu

Kalemie

Kamina

Lualaba

Lubumbashi

Ndola

ZAMBIA

Lusaka

Kabwe

Zambezi

Hwange

Livingstone

ZIMBABWE

Harare

Bulawayo

Gweru

Mutare

L. Kariba

Limpopo

BOTSWANA

Serowe

Gaborone

NAMIBIA

Windhoek

Tsumeb

Keetmanshoop

Walvis Bay (S.A.)

Orange

SOUTH AFRICA

Kimberley

Johannesburg

Pretoria

SWAZILAND

Mbabane

Maputo

LESOTHO

Maseru

Bloemfontein

Durban

East London

Port Elizabeth

Cape Town

ATLANTIC OCEAN

SOUTH

OCEAN

St Helena (UK)

Ascension (UK)

Tristan da Cunha (UK)

Equator

Tropic of Capricorn

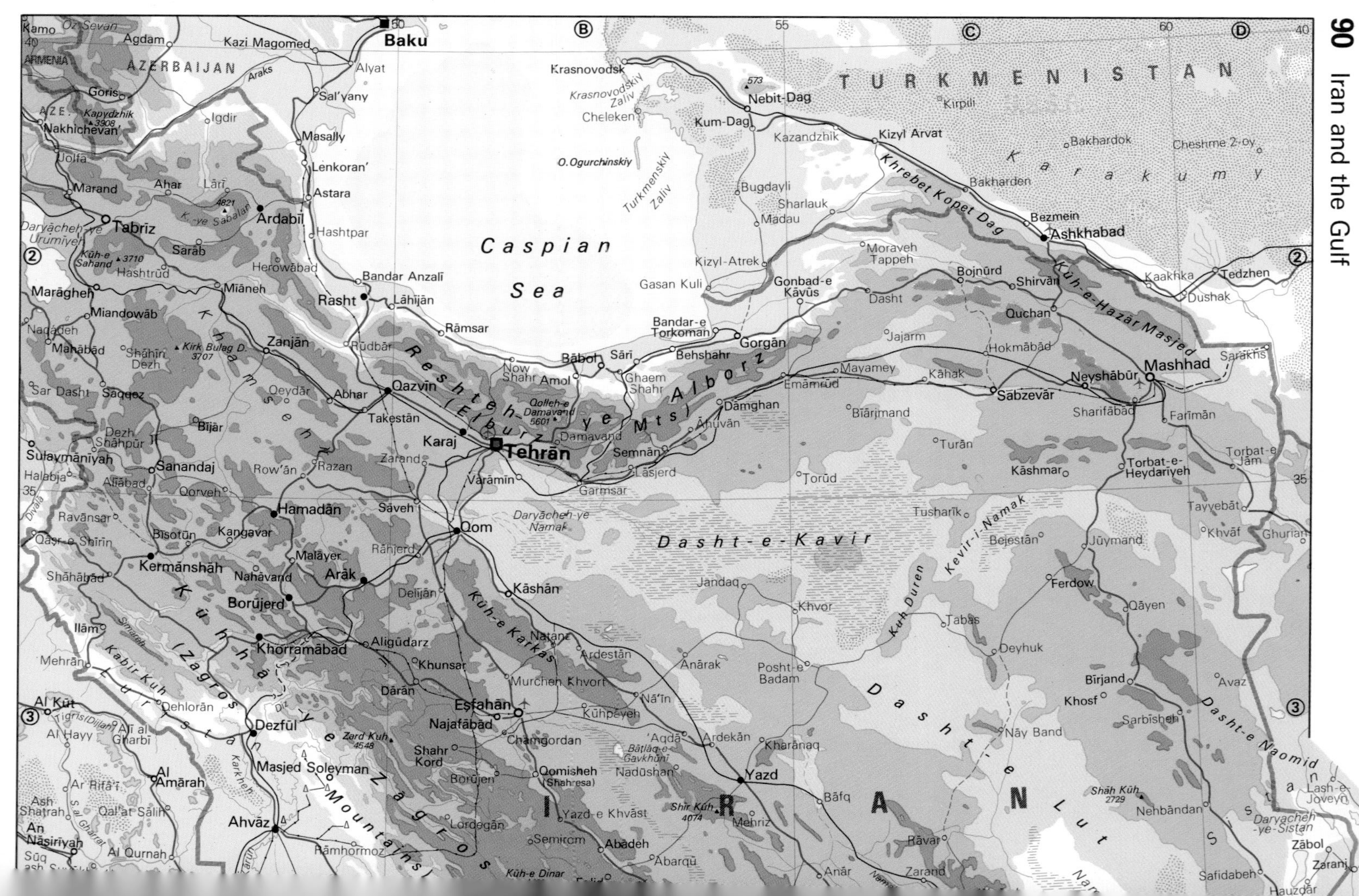
T U R K M E N I S T A N
K a r a k u m y
A Z E R B A I J A N
ARMENIA
I R A N
Caspian Sea
Dasht-e-Kavir
Dasht-e Lut
Dasht-e Naomid
Reshteh-ye Alborz (Elburz Mts)
Kūh-e Zagros (Zagros Mountains)
Khrebet Kopet Dag
Kūh-e Hazār Masjed
Kūh-e Karkas
Kevīr-i Namak
Kuh Duren
Daryācheh-ye Namak
Daryācheh-ye Urūmīyeh
Krasnovodskiy Zaliv
Turkmenskiy Zaliv
O. Ogurchinskiy
Baku
Tehrān
Tabrīz
Mashhad
Esfahān
Yazd
Qom
Kāshān
Rasht
Qazvīn
Karaj
Hamadān
Kermānshāh
Ahvāz
Dezfūl
Khorramābād
Borūjerd
Arāk
Ashkhabad
Krasnovodsk
Nebit-Dag
Kum-Dag
Kizyl Arvat
Gorgān
Semnān
Dāmghan
Sabzevār
Neyshābūr
Bīrjand
Zābol
Ardabīl
Zanjān
Sanandaj
Al Kūt
Al 'Amārah
Masjed Soleyman
Najafābād
Sulaymānīyah
Qolleh-ye Damāvand 5601
Shīr Kūh 4074
Zard Kūh 4548
Kūh-e Sahand 3710
Kūh-e Sabalān 4821
Shāh Kūh 2729
Kirk Bulag D. 3707
Kapydzhik 3908

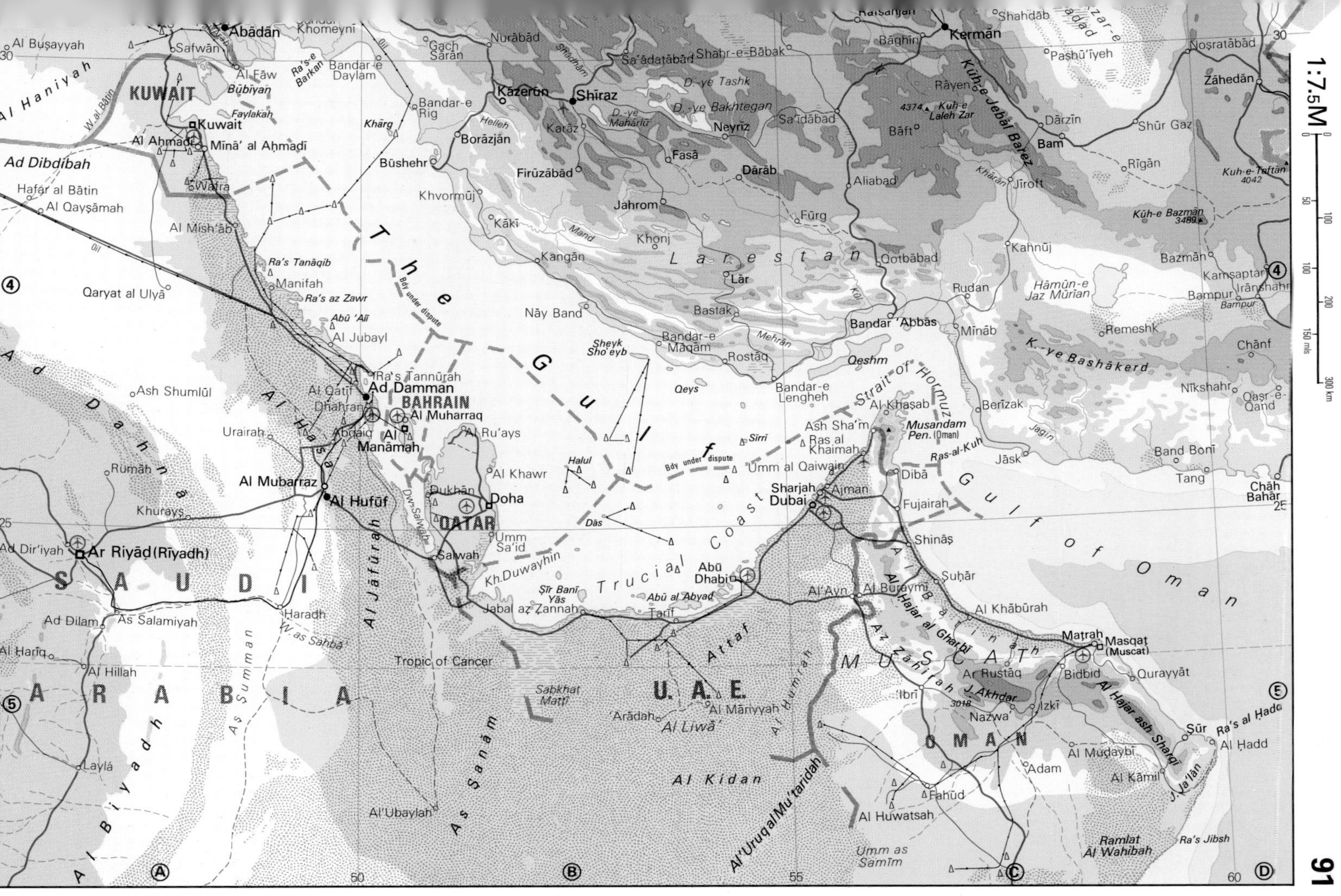

100
200
300 km
50
100
150 mls

30

Nosratābād
Zāhedān
Kūh-e Taftān
4042
Chānt

Qaṣr-e
Qārid
Chāh
Bahār
E

60
D

Kermān
Bāghīn
Māhān
Shāhdād
zar-e adād
Pashū'īyeh
Shūr Gaz
Rāyen
Kūh-e Jebāl Barez
Kūh-e Bazmān 3490
Rīgān
Dārzīn
Bam
Bazmān
Nīkshahr
Bampūr
Īrānshahr
Remeshk
Band Bonī
Tang
Ra's al Hadd
Sūr
Ra's Jibsh

Matrah Masqaṭ (Muscat)
Al Hajar ash Sharqī
Quṣayyāt
Ramlat
Al Wahībah
C

Kazerūn
Shīrāz
Qīr
Fasā
Dārāb
Nūrābād
Kūhenjān
Fīrūzābād
Borāzjān
Khonj
Kāngān
Lār
Bastak
Bandar-e Maqām
Qeys
Nāy Band
Bandar-e Lengheh
Bandar Abbās
Qeshm
Mīnāb
Jāsk
Ra's-al-Kūh
Strait of Hormuz
Musandam Pen. (Oman)
Dibā
Khasab
Fujairah
Shināṣ
Suḥār
Al Khāburah
Al Buraymī
Ibrī
Adam
Nazwā
Izkī
Bidbid
Al Mudayrib
Al Kāmil
Al Huwatsah
Umm as Samīm

OMAN

M U S C A T

Ra's al Khaimah
Umm al Qaiwain
Ajmān
Sharjah
Dubai
Abū Dhabi
U.A.E.
Al Liwā
Al Kidan
As Sanam

The Gulf
Coast
Trucial
Būshehr
Kharg
Khvormūj
Ra's az Zawr
Abū 'Alī
Al Jubayl
Ad Dammām
Al Muḥarraq
BAHRAIN
Al Manāmah
QATAR
Doha
Dukhān
Umm Sa'īd
Al Khawr
Ru'ays

KUWAIT
Kuwait
Al Aḥmadī
Mīnā' al Aḥmadī
Abādān
Khomeynī
Al Faw
Būbīyan
Safwān

Tropic of Cancer

S A U D I   A R A B I A

Ar Riyāḍ (Riyadh)
Ad Dilam
Al Hillah
Layla
Al Hufūf
Al Mubarraz
Ad Dibdibah
Qaryat al Ulyā
Ash Shumlūl
Al Hanīyah

5
A

25

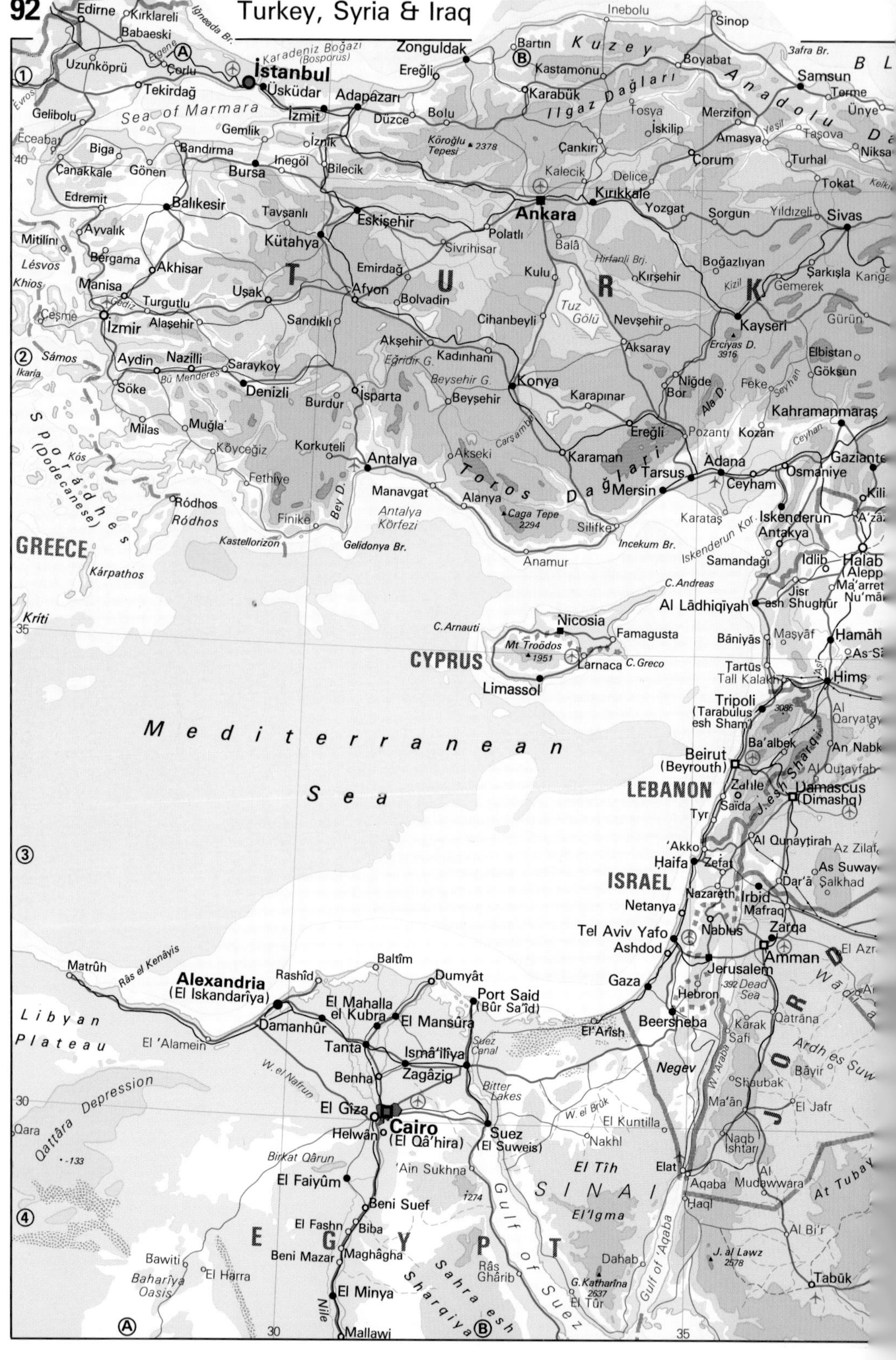

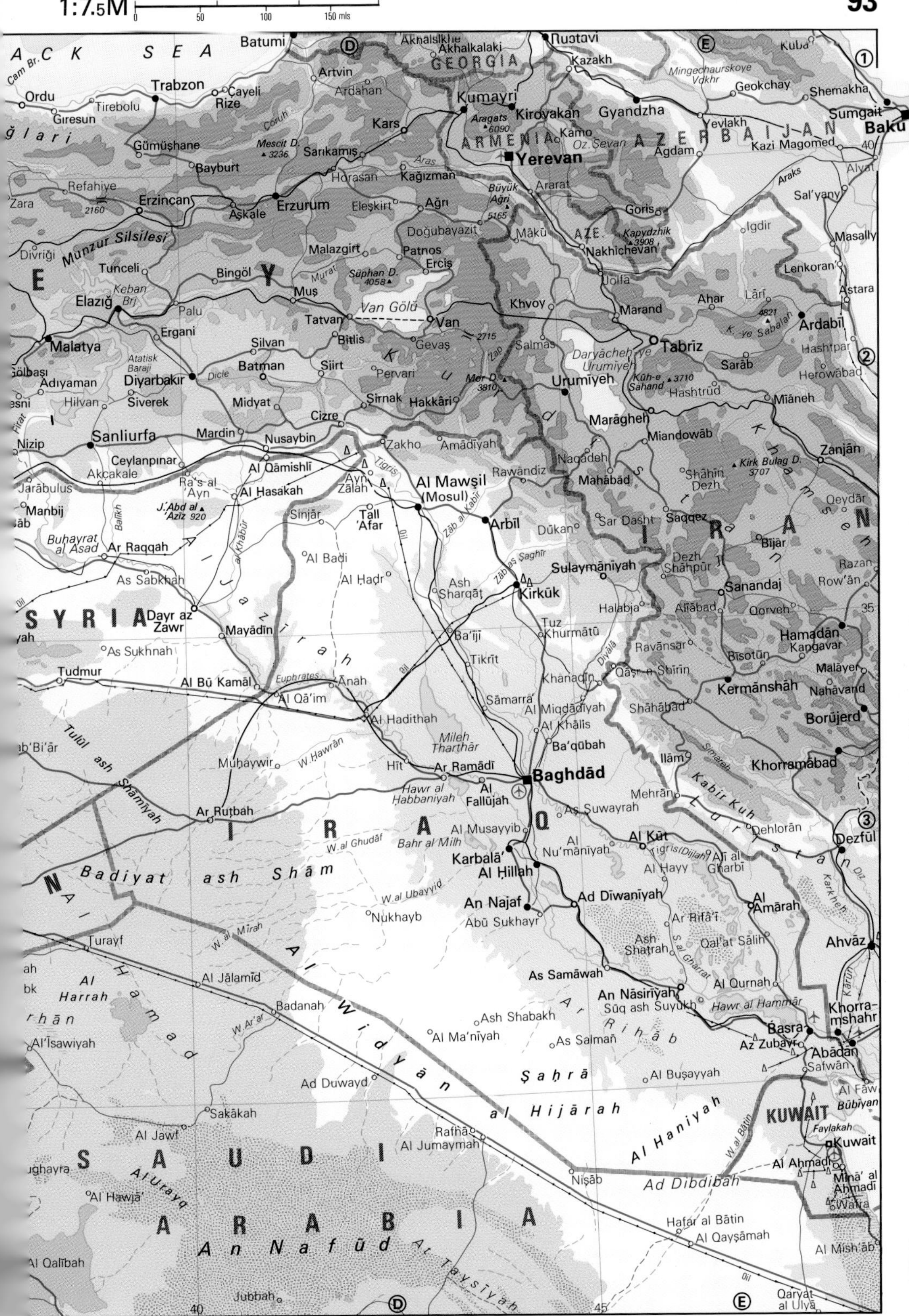

1:7.5M

0 100 200 300 km
0 50 100 150 mls

B L A C K   S E A

Cam Br.
Ğ l a r i
Ordu
Giresun
Tirebolu
Trabzon
Rize
Çayeli
Batumi
Artvin
Ardahan
Akhalisikhe
Akhalkalaki
Ruştavi
Kazakh
Mingechaurskoye Vdkhr.
Geokchay
Shemakha
Sumgait
Baku
Kazi Magomed
Sal'yany
Alyat
40

Gümüşhane
Bayburt
Kars
Sarıkamış
Horasan
Kağızman
Aragats 6050
Kirovakan
Kumayri
Kamo
Oz. Sevan
Yerevan
Agdam
Gyandzha
Yevlakh
ARMENIA
AZERBAIJAN

Refahiye
Zara
Erzincan
2160
Aşkale
Erzurum
Eleşkirt
Ağrı
Doğubayazit
Büyük Ağrı 5165
Ararat
Patnos
Iğdır
Goris
Kapydzhik 3908
Nakhichevan
AZE.
Sal'yany
Masally

Divriği
Tunceli
Bingöl
Malazgirt
Süphan D. 4058
Ercis
Mākū
Khvoy
Marand
Ahar
Lārī
k-ye Sabalān 4821
Ardabil
Hashtpar
Astara
Lenkoran

Elazığ
Keban Brj.
Palu
Ergani
Muş
Murat
Tatvan
Bitlis
Van Gölü
Van
2715
Zab
Salmas
Gevaş
Mer D. 3910
Daryācheh-ye Urumiyeh
Tabrīz
Sarāb
Herowābad
Mīāneh

Malatya
Gölbaşı
Adıyaman
Hilvan
Diyarbakir
Atatisk Baraji
Silvan
Siverek
Dicle
Batman
Siirt
Pervari
Midyat
Sirnak
Hakkāri
Sirnak
Urumiyeh
Kūh-e Sahand 3710
Hashtrūd
Marāgheh
Miandowāb
Zanjān

Nizip
Sanliurfa
Mardin
Ceylanpınar
Akcakale
Nusaybin
Zakho
Amādīyah
Ra's al
Ayn
J. Abd al
Aziz 920
Al Qāmishlī
Ayn Zālah
Rawāndiz
Naqādeh
Mahābād
Kirk Bulag D. 3707
Oeydār
IRAN

Jarābulus
Manbij
āb
Buhayrat al Asad
Ar Raqqah
Balikh
As Sabkhah
Sinjār
Al Badi
Al Hasakah
Tall 'Afar
Al Mawşil (Mosul)
Zāb al Kabīr
Arbīl
Dūkān
Sar Dasht
Saqqez
Dezh Shāhpūr
Alīābad
Shāhīn Dezh
Bijār
Razan
Row'ān
35

S Y R I A
Dayr az Zawr
Mayādin
Al Hadr
Ash Sharqāt
Kirkūk
Zāb aş Şaghīr
Sulaymāniyah
Halabja
Qorveh
Sanandaj
Hamadān
Kangavar
Bisotūn
Ravānsar
Tuz Khurmātū

As Sukhnah
Tudmur
Al Bū Kamāl
Al Qā'im
'Ānah
Euphrates
Al Haditha
Sāmarrā'
Ba'jī
Tikrīt
Khānaqīn
Qaşr-e Shīrīn
Diyālā
Shāhābād
Ilām
Smērān
Kermānshāh
Nahāvand
Malāyer
Borūjerd

Tulūl ash Shāmiyah
ba'Bi'ār
Muhaywir
W. Hawrān
Hīt
Ar Ramādī
Mileh Tharthār
Hawr al Habbaniyah
Al Fallūjah
Baghdād
Al Khāliş
Al Miqdādiyah
Ba'qūbah
Mehrān
Khorramābad

Ar Ruṭbah
W. al Ghudāf
Bahr al Milh
Al Musayyib
Karbalā'
Al Hillah
As Suwayrah
Al Nu'māniyah
Al Kūt
Tigris (Dijlah)
Al Hayy
'Alī al Gharbī
Dehlorān
Dezfūl

I R A Q
An Najaf
Nukhayb
Abū Sukhayr
Ad Dīwānīyah
Ar Rifā'ī
Ash Shatrah
Qal'at Sālih
Al 'Amārah
Ahvāz
Kārūn
Karkheh

NAJD
Badiyat ash Shām
Turayf
W. al Mīrah
Al Jālamīd
Badanah
As Samāwah
As Salmān
Al Ma'nīyah
An Nāsirīyah
Sūq ash Suyūkh
Al Qurnah
Hawr al Hammār
Az Zubayr
Basra
Abādān
Khorramshahr

Al Hamad
Al Harrah
'rhān
Al 'Īsawiyah
Sakākah
Ad Duwayd
Al Jawf
W. Ar'ar
Rafhā
Al Jumaymah
Nişāb
Ash Shabakh
Ar Rihāb
Şahrā
al Hijārah
Al Buşayyah
Al Haniyah
Ad Dibdibah
Safwān
Al Fāw
Būbiyān
KUWAIT

ghayra
'Al Hawja'
AtUraya
Qalībah
Jubbah
A n   N a f ū d
Al Taysīyah
Hafar al Bāţin
Al Qayşamah
S A U D I   A R A B I A
Al Mish'āb
Mīnā' al Ahmadi
Faylakah
Kuwait
Al Ahmadī
Al Wafra
Qaryat al Ulyā

40   45

1:2.5M

0   25   50   75   100 km
0   25   50 mls

CYPRUS

Paleokhorio Larnaca Larnaca
Lefkara Bay
Zyyi C.Kiti
Limassol C.Greco
Akrotiri Bay
C.Gata

Tartûs Arwad Dunayish Kafrûn Bashûr
An Nasirah Tall Bîsah
Safîtâ Qal'at al Hisn
(KRAK-DES CHEVALIERS) Hims
Hamîdîya Tall Kalakh (Homs)
Kleia Qoubayat Shinshar
El Mîna Halba Al Qusayr
Tripoli El Hermel Ûsîyah
(Tarâbulus esh Shâm) Hisyah
Zghorta Quriet es
Batroun Amioune Saouda Jabal
Jubail Kartaba 3086 Halimah
BYBLOS Deir el Dayr 'Atîyah 12464
LEBANON Ahmar 2659 An Nabk
Rhazîr Ba'albek Yabrûd
Jounié Bikfaya 2628 Jayrûd
Baie de St Georges Rayak Qutayfah
Beirut Ba'abda Zahle Az 1910 Dûma 'Adhrâ
(Beyrouth) Aley Zabdâni
Damour Ayn al Fîjah Duma 'Adhrâ
Beit ed Dîne Machghârab At Barada
Saïda Jezzine Rachaya Tall **Damascus**
(Sidon) (Dimâshq)
Hâsbaiya Jash Shaykh A'waj Al Hijânah
Litâni (Mt Hermon) Qatana Dayr 'Ali
Tyr Q.Shemona Marjayoun Al Kiswah
(Tyre, Sour) Jouai'ya Baniyas **SYRIA**
Enn Nâqoûra Mas'adah CEASE FIRE Ghabâghib Burâq
Bennt 1208 Al Qunaytirah LINES 1974
Jbail Har Meron Yesud Mismîyah
Nahariya Hama'ala Sanamayn Khabab
Ma'alot Khushnîya Al Lajâh 863 Shaqqâ
'Akko Tarshîha Zefat Nawâ Izra' Shahbâ
(Acre) Rama (Safad) Tiberias
B.of Haifa Q. Yam (Sea of Galilee) Shaykh Jabal al
Haifa Shefar'am Fîq Miskîn 'Arab 1735
(Hefa) Q. Ata Ma'agan Tasîl As Suwaydâ
'Atlit Tiberias Yarmûk Dar'a
Mt Oshon Nazareth Deir Abu Irbid Ramtha
Zikhron Ya'aqov Carmel Afula Sa'id Husn Salkhad
MEGIDDO Beyt Ajlûn 1247 Es Samrâ Tisfyah
CAESAREA ARMAGEDDON Shean Mafraq Sabhâ
Pardes Hanna Jenin Tubas Zarqa Er Rummân
Hadera Qabatiya Husn Qa
Netanya Tulkarm Salt Suweilih Zarqa Khanna
Sabastiya Karama Marka **Amman**
ISRAEL Kefar Sava Nablus Wadi es Sîr Sahab
Herzliyya Bat Petah Tiqwa Ba'al Hazor Kaur
Ramat Gan Yam 1016 Ramallah Jiza
Tel Aviv Holon Jericho Qasr el Kharana
Yafo (Jaffa) (Arîha) Mâdabâ Dab'a Mudeisisat
Rishon le Zion Ramla **Jerusalem** (El Quds)
Rehovot Latrun (Yerushalayim) Dhîbân Khan ez Zabîb
Ashdod Beit Jala
Bethlehem Madâbâ
Ashqelon Qiryat (Bayt Lahm)
Gat Bet Hebron Mazra
Gaza Guvrin (El Khalil) Rabba Qatrâna
Gaza Strip Sederot Dûra En Gedi
Khan Yunis Yatta Karak Qâ'el Haflra
Rafah Edh 1253 Manzil
Ofaqim Dhahiriya T.el Meise Mazâr
Râs Burûn Beersheba MEZADA El Lisân
Sabkhet (Be'er Sheva) Nevatim 'Arad Sedom
el Bardawîl Zeelim MAMSHIT Safi **JORDAN**
El 'Arîsh Be'er Dimona J.Ed Dabab Hâsâ
Revivim Yeroham 1305
Bîr Lahfân HALUZA Sede Oron Tafila Qâ'el Jinz
Qeziot SHIVTA Boqer
NIZANA AVEDAT Hazeva J.Dasred Deir Hâsâ
G.Libni Negev El Quseima Rashâdîya 1356
735 463 Danâ Jurf ed Darâwîsh
G.Maghâra 892 Mizpe 1641 Jebel
Ramon Ein J.el Atâ'ita Ithrîya
Bîr Gifgâfa Bîr Hasana G.Halâl Yahav 1082
Har Ramon Nijil Uneisa
1305 1615 Jum Suwwâna
Har Saggi Har Hakippa
1006 467

MEDITERRANEAN SEA

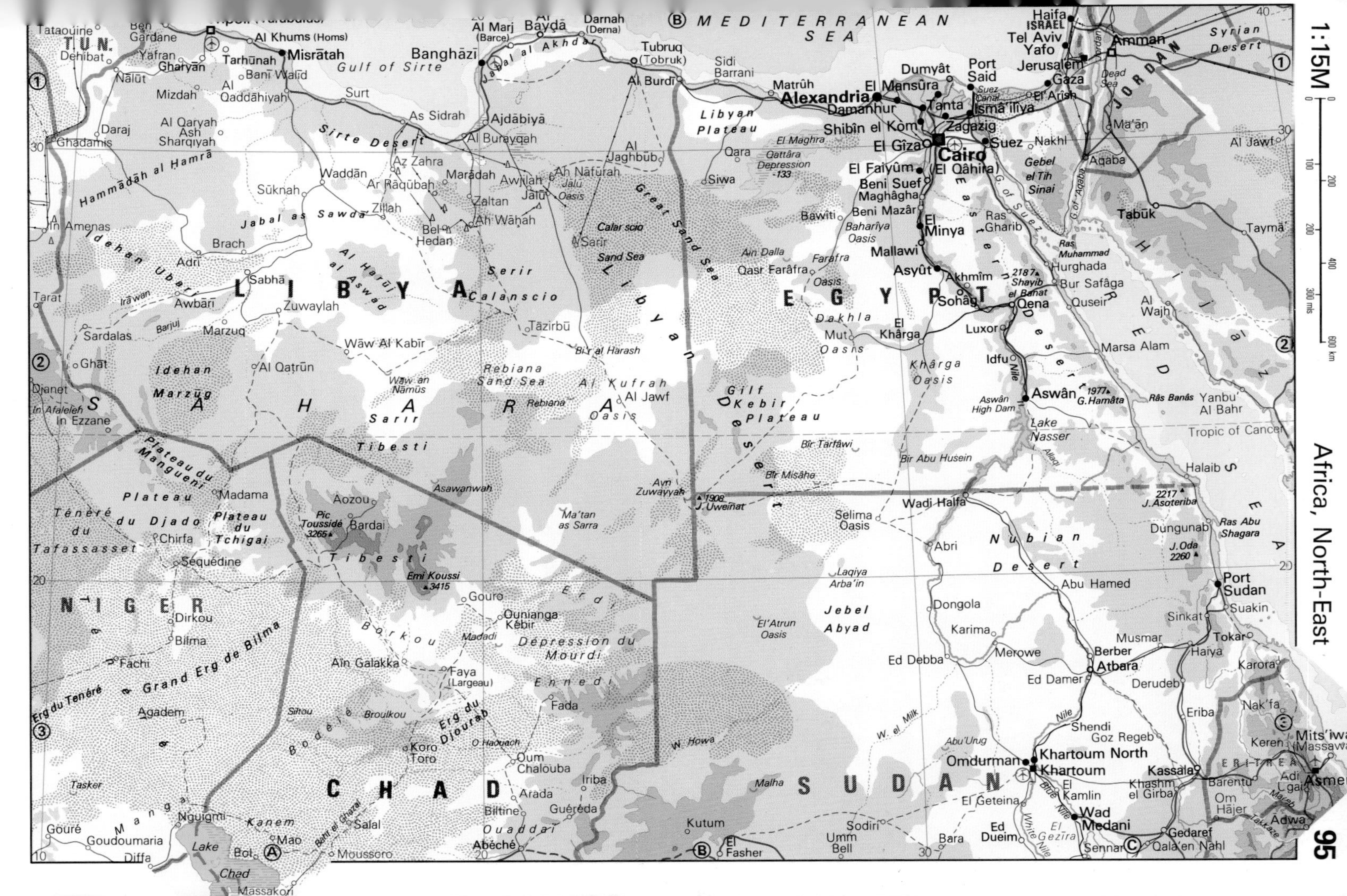
MEDITERRANEAN SEA
EGYPT
LIBYA
SUDAN
CHAD
NIGER
ERITREA
JORDAN
ISRAEL
TUN.
SAHARA
Libyan Desert
Nubian Desert
Eastern Desert
Great Sand Sea
Calanscio Sand Sea
Serir Calanscio
Rebiana Sand Sea
Libyan Plateau
Gilf Kebir Plateau
Jebel Abyad
Tibesti
Hejaz
Red Sea
Syrian Desert
Gulf of Sirte
Sirte Desert
G. of Suez
G. of Aqaba
Tropic of Cancer
Lake Nasser
Aswân High Dam
Lake Chad
Dépression du Mourdi
Ennedi
Borkou
Ouaddaï
Kanem
Ténéré du Tafassasset
Plateau du Djado
Plateau du Manguéni
Plateau du Tchigai
Grand Erg de Bilma
Idehan Ubari
Idehan Marzuq
Hammādah al Hamrā
Jabal as Sawdā
Al Harūj al Aswad
Qattâra Depression -133
Cairo (El Qâhira)
Alexandria
El Gîza
Port Said
Suez
Aswân
Luxor
Asyût
Khartoum
Khartoum North
Omdurman
Port Sudan
Wadi Halfa
Atbara
Kassala
Wad Medani
El Fasher
Banghāzī
Tubruq (Tobruk)
Misrātah
Sabhā
Marzuq
Ghāt
Al Jawf
Faya (Largeau)
Abéché
Bardai
Aozou
Emi Koussi 3415
Pic Toussidé 3265
J. 'Uweinat 1908
Amman
Jerusalem
Tel Aviv Yafo
Gaza
Haifa
Tabūk
Asmera
Mits'iwa (Massawa)

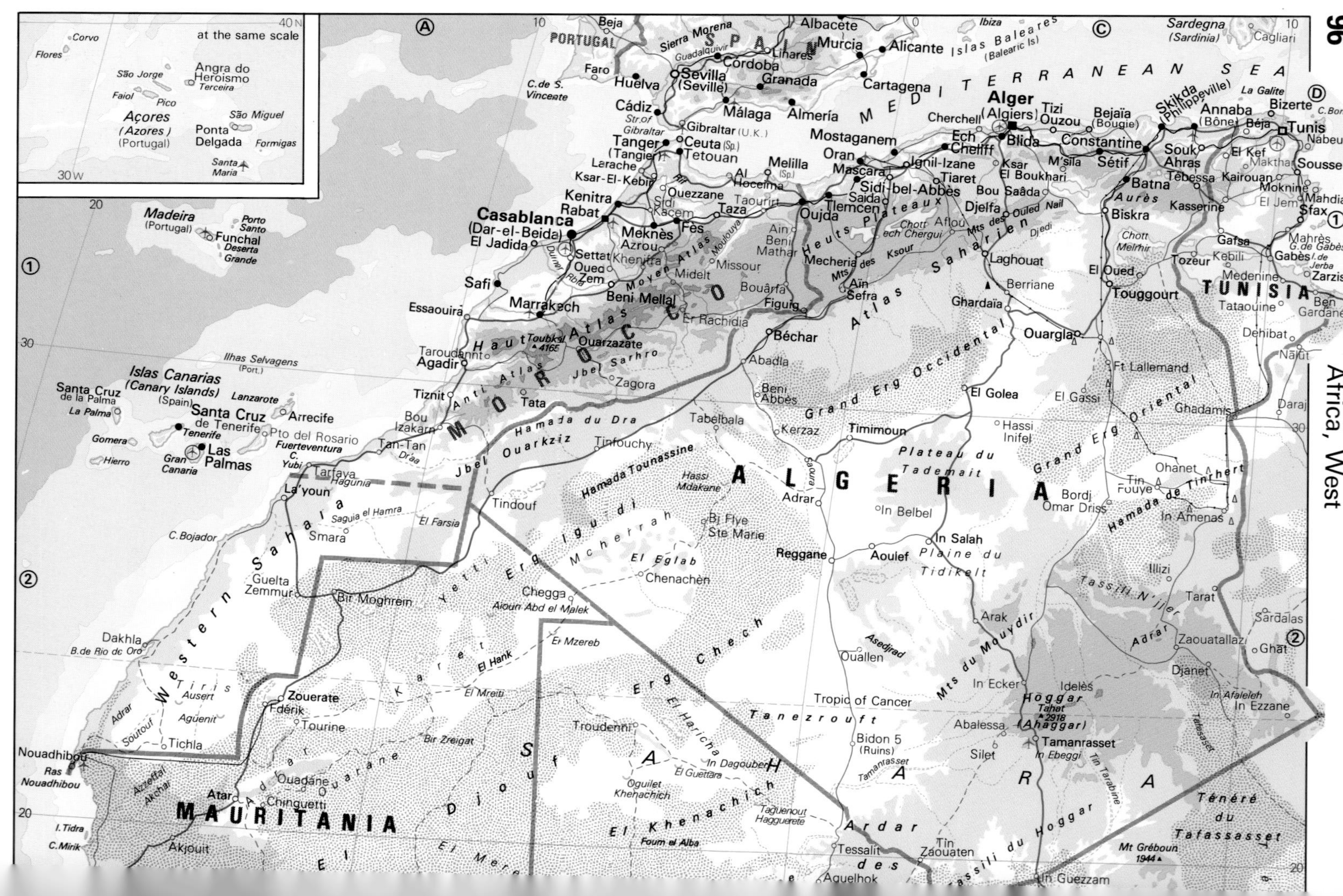

MEDITERRANEAN SEA
SPAIN
PORTUGAL
MOROCCO
ALGERIA
TUNISIA
MAURITANIA
Western Sahara
Madeira (Portugal)
Islas Canarias (Canary Islands) (Spain)
Açores (Azores) (Portugal)
at the same scale
Casablanca (Dar-el-Beida)
Rabat
Marrakech
Fès
Meknès
Tanger (Tangier)
Alger (Algiers)
Oran
Constantine
Tunis
Sfax
Sousse
Bizerte
Annaba (Bône)
Ouargla
In Salah
Tamanrasset
Tindouf
Agadir
La'youn
Dakhla
Nouadhibou
Atar
Zouerate
Las Palmas
Santa Cruz de Tenerife
Funchal
Sevilla (Seville)
Granada
Málaga
Cádiz
Gibraltar (U.K.)
Ceuta (Sp.)
Melilla (Sp.)
Grand Erg Occidental
Grand Erg Oriental
Hoggar (Ahaggar)
Tropic of Cancer

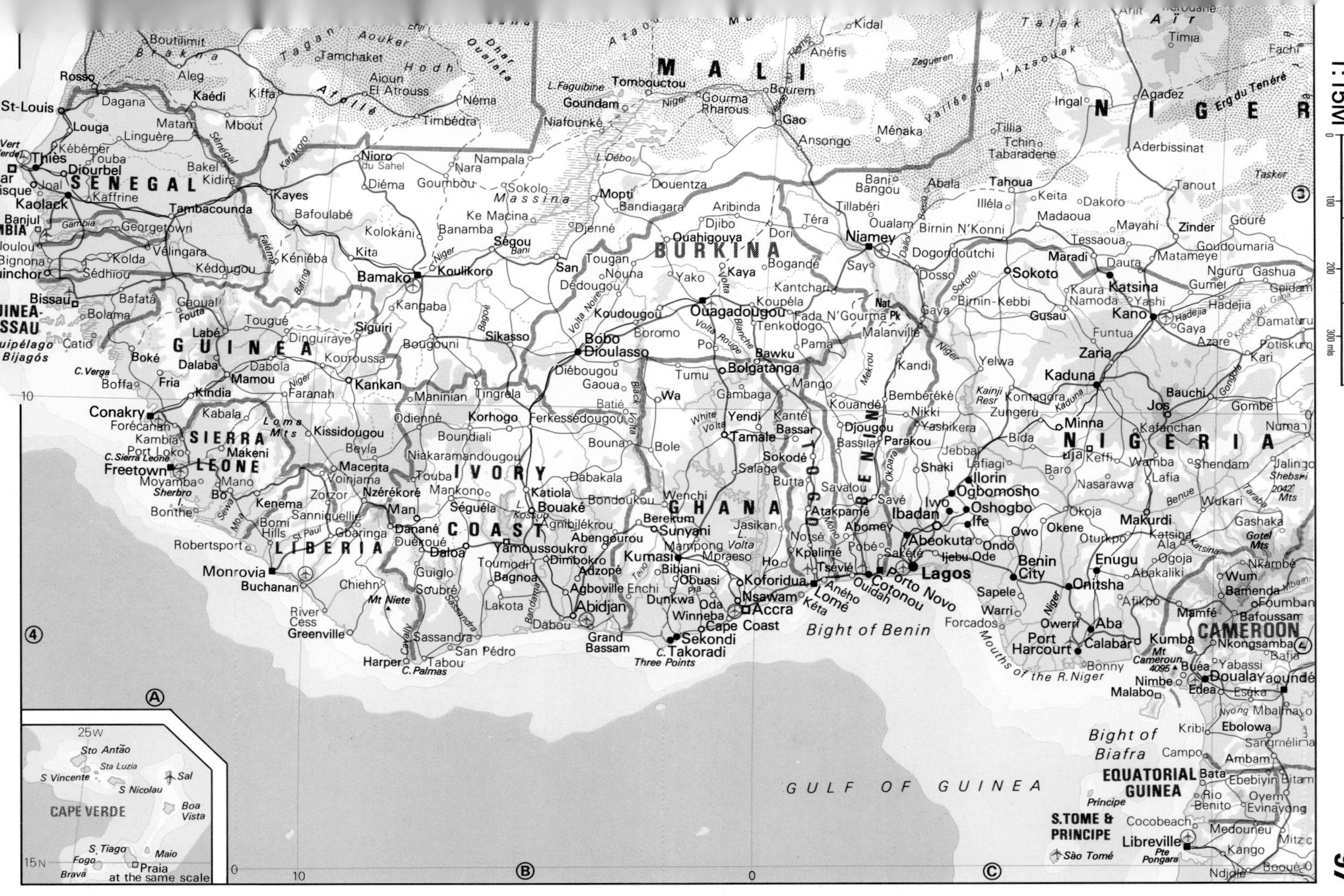
MALI
NIGER
NIGERIA
BURKINA
GHANA
TOGO
BENIN
IVORY COAST
LIBERIA
SIERRA LEONE
GUINEA
GUINEA-BISSAU
SENEGAL
THE GAMBIA
CAMEROON
EQUATORIAL GUINEA
S.TOME & PRINCIPE
CAPE VERDE
GULF OF GUINEA
Bight of Benin
Bight of Biafra
Mouths of the R. Niger
Dakar
Bamako
Niamey
Ouagadougou
Lagos
Porto Novo
Accra
Lomé
Abidjan
Monrovia
Freetown
Conakry
Bissau
Banjul
Kano
Kaduna
Ibadan
Kumasi
Tombouctou
Libreville
Yaoundé
Douala
Praia
at the same scale

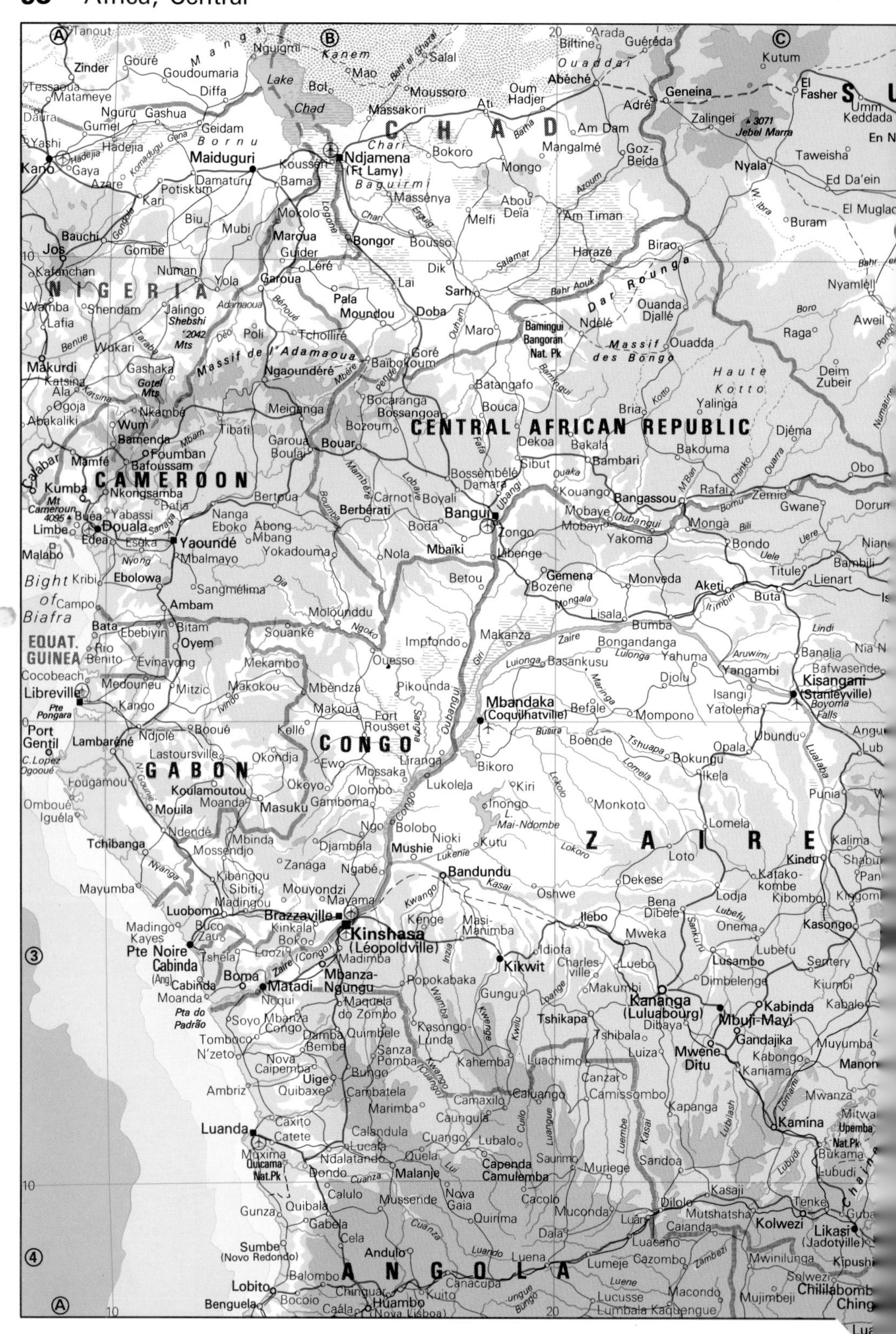
CHAD
NIGERIA
CAMEROON
CENTRAL AFRICAN REPUBLIC
EQUAT. GUINEA
GABON
CONGO
ZAIRE
ANGOLA
Lake Chad
Ndjamena (Ft Lamy)
Maiduguri
Kano
Jos
Bangui
Yaoundé
Douala
Libreville
Brazzaville
Kinshasa (Léopoldville)
Mbandaka (Coquilhatville)
Kisangani (Stanleyville)
Kananga (Luluabourg)
Mbuji-Mayi
Luanda
Lobito
Huambo (Nova Lisboa)
Likasi (Jadotville)
Bight of Biafra

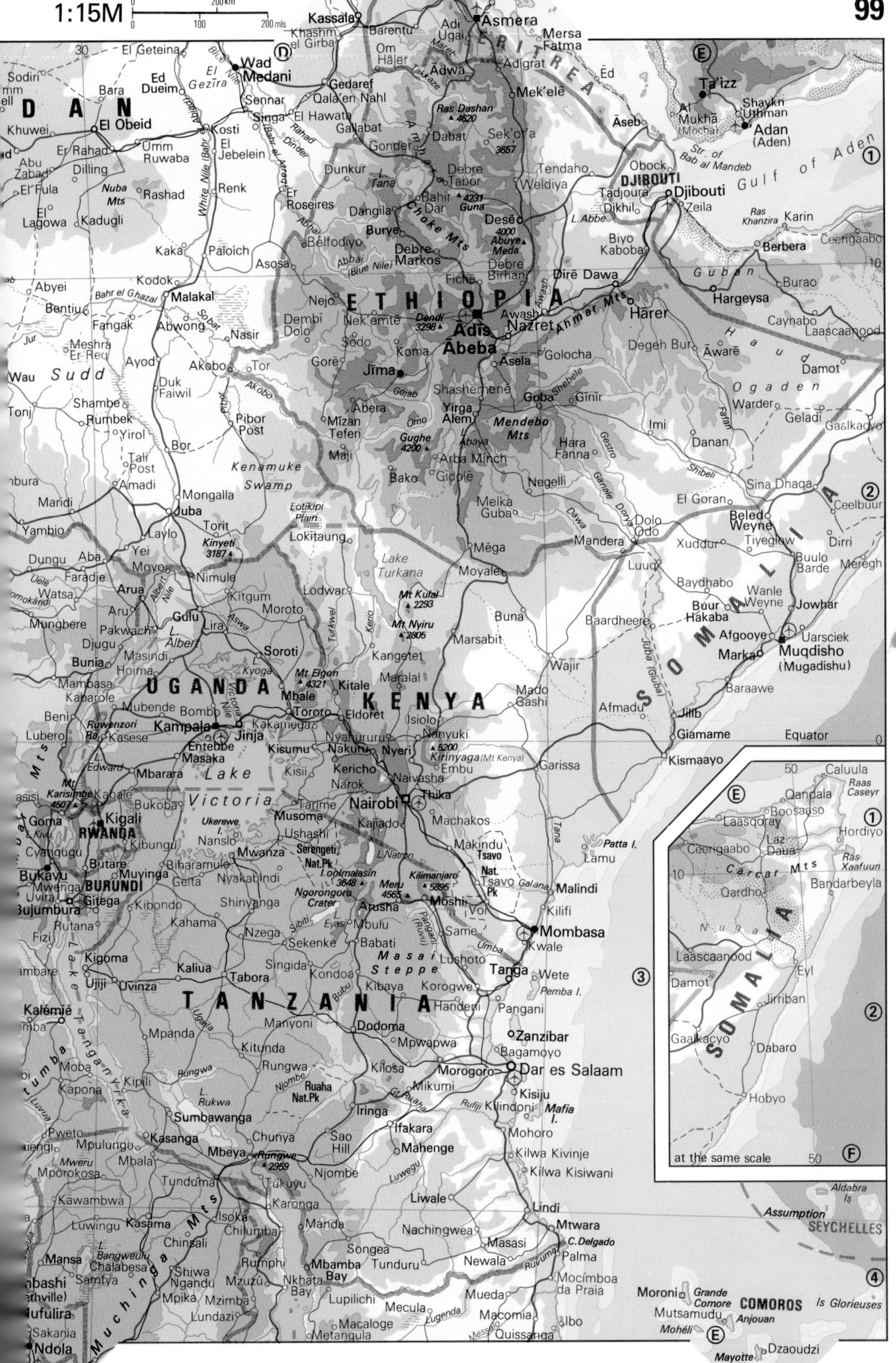

1:15M

200km
100
200 mls

30

SUDAN

Keren · Mts'iwa40 · Massawa
Kassala · Barentu · Adi Ugai · Asmera · Mersa Fatma
Khashm el Girba · Om Hājer · Adi · ERITREA
Adwa · Adigrat · Ēd · Āseb
El Geteina · Ed Dueim · Wad Medani · Gedaref · Qala'en Nahl · Mek'elē
Ta'izz · Al Mukhā (Mocha)
Shaykh 'Uthmān · Adan (Aden)
Sodiri · Bara · Sennar · Singa · El Hawata · Ras Dashan 4620 · Sek'ot'a 3657 · Dabat

El Obeid · Kosti · El Jebelein · Er Roseires · Dunkur · Debre Tabor · Tendaho · Weldiya · Obock · Gulf of Aden
Khuwei · El Rahad · Umm Ruwaba · Renk · Dangila · Bahir Dar · L. Tana · Guna 4231 · Deseõ · Weldiya · DJIBOUTI · Djibouti · Zeila
Abu Zabad · Dilling · Rashad · Asosa · Belfodiyo · Debre Markos · Fiche · Abuye Meda 4000 · Biyo Kaboba · Berbera
El Fula · Nuba Mts · Kodok · Kaka · Paloich · Abbai (Blue Nile) · Debre Birhan · Dirē Dawa · Harer · Guban
El Lagowa · Kadugli · Bentiu · Fangak · Nejo · Nek'emte · Dembi Dolo · Dendi 3298 · Adis Ābeba · Nazret · Hargeysa · Caynabo · Laascaanood
Abyei · Bahr el Ghazal · Malakal · Sodo · Gorē · Koma · Asela · Golocha · Degeh Bur · Āware · Haud · Damot

ETHIOPIA

Wau · Sudd · Er Reqi · Nasir · Akobo · Jima · Shashemenē · Goba · Ginir · Imi · Ogaden · Geladi
Tonj · Shambe · Rumbek · Yirol · Duk Faiwil · Abera · Yirga Alem · Mendebo Mts · Hara Fanna · Danan · Sina Dhaqa
Maridi · Amadi · Mongalla · Mizan Teferi · Gughe 4200 · Arba Minch · Negelli · El Goran · Beled Weyne · Ceelbuur
Yambio · Aba · Juba · Torit · Maji · Bako · Gidole · Meika Guba · Dolo Odo · Mandera · Xuddur · Dirri · Meregh

UGANDA

Dungu · Faradje · Yei · Moyo · Nimule · Lokichar · Mēga · Moyale · Luuq · Baydhabo · Wanle Weyne · Buulo Barde
Arua · Aru · Kitgum · Moroto · Lake Turkana · Mt Kulal 2293 · Buna · Baardheere · Buur Hakaba · Jowhar
Mungbere · Pakwach · Lira · Soroti · Mt Nyiru 2805 · Marsabit · Wajir · Afgooye · Markaa · Uarsciek · Muqdisho (Mugadishu)
Bunia · Masindi · Hoima · Gulu · Mt Elgon 4321 · Kitale · Meralal · Mado Gashi · Afmadu · Jilb · Giamame · Baraawe

KENYA

Beni · Mubende · Bombo · Tororo · Eldoret · Isiolo · Nanyuki · Kismaayo · Equator
Lubero · Kampala · Jinja · Kakamega · Nakuru · Nyeri · Kirinyaga (Mt Kenya) · Garissa
Kasese · Entebbe · Masaka · Kisumu · Kericho · Naivasha · Embu · Lamu · Patta I.
Goma · Kigali · Butare · Bukoba · Tarime · Narok · Nairobi · Thika · Machakos · Tana
RWANDA · Cyangugu · Lake Victoria · Musoma · Kisii · Kajiado · Makindu · Tsavo · Malindi
Bukavu · BURUNDI · Gitega · Ushashi · Ukerewe · Nansio · Loolmalasin 3648 · Menu 4565 · Tsavo Nat. Pk · Kilifi
Bujumbura · Muyinga · Biharamulo · Mwanza · Ngorongoro Crater · Kilimanjaro 5895 · Moshi · Voi · Mombasa
Fizi · Kigoma · Kaliua · Shinyanga · Arusha · Same · Kwale · Tanga · Wete · Pemba I.
Kalémié · Uvinza · Tabora · Nzega · Sekenke · Singida · Kondoa · Korogwe · Pangani · Zanzibar
Moba · Mpanda · Manyoni · Dodoma · Mpwapwa · Bagamoyo · Dar es Salaam

TANZANIA

Kipili · Rungwa · Kitunda · Rungwa Nat. Pk · Kilosa · Morogoro · Kisiju · Mafia I.
Kapona · Sumbawanga · Kasanga · Chunya · Sao Hill · Iringa · Mikumi · Kilwa Kivinje
Mpulungu · Mbala · Mbeya · 2969 · Njombe · Mahenge · Mohoro · Kilwa Kisiwani
Tunduma · Tukuyu · Isoka · Karonga · Liwale · Lindi
Kawambwa · Kasama · Chilumba · Nachingwea · Masasi · Mtwara
Mansa · Chinsali · Rumphi · Songea · Newala · C. Delgado · Palma
Bangweulu · Shiwa Ngandu · Mbamba Bay · Tunduru · Mocímboa da Praia
Mpika · Mzuzu · Mzimba · Nkhata Bay · Lupilichi · Mecula · Macomia
Lundazi · Muchinga Mts · Mzimba · Macaloge · Metangula · Quissanga
Ndola · Kushi · Metangula · Ibo

SEYCHELLES
Aldabra Is · Assumption

COMOROS · Moroni · Grande Comore · Mutsamudu · Anjouan · Is Glorieuses
Mohéli · Mayotte (Fr.) · Dzaoudzi

Inset (at the same scale):

SOMALIA

Caluula · Raas Caseyr · Qandala · Boosaaso · Laasqoray · Ceerigaabo · Bandarbeyla
Hordiyo · Laz Daua · Ras Xaafuun · Cärcar Mts · Qardho
Laascaanood · Eyl · Jiriiban · Nugaal · Damot · Gaalkacyo · Dabaro · Hobyo

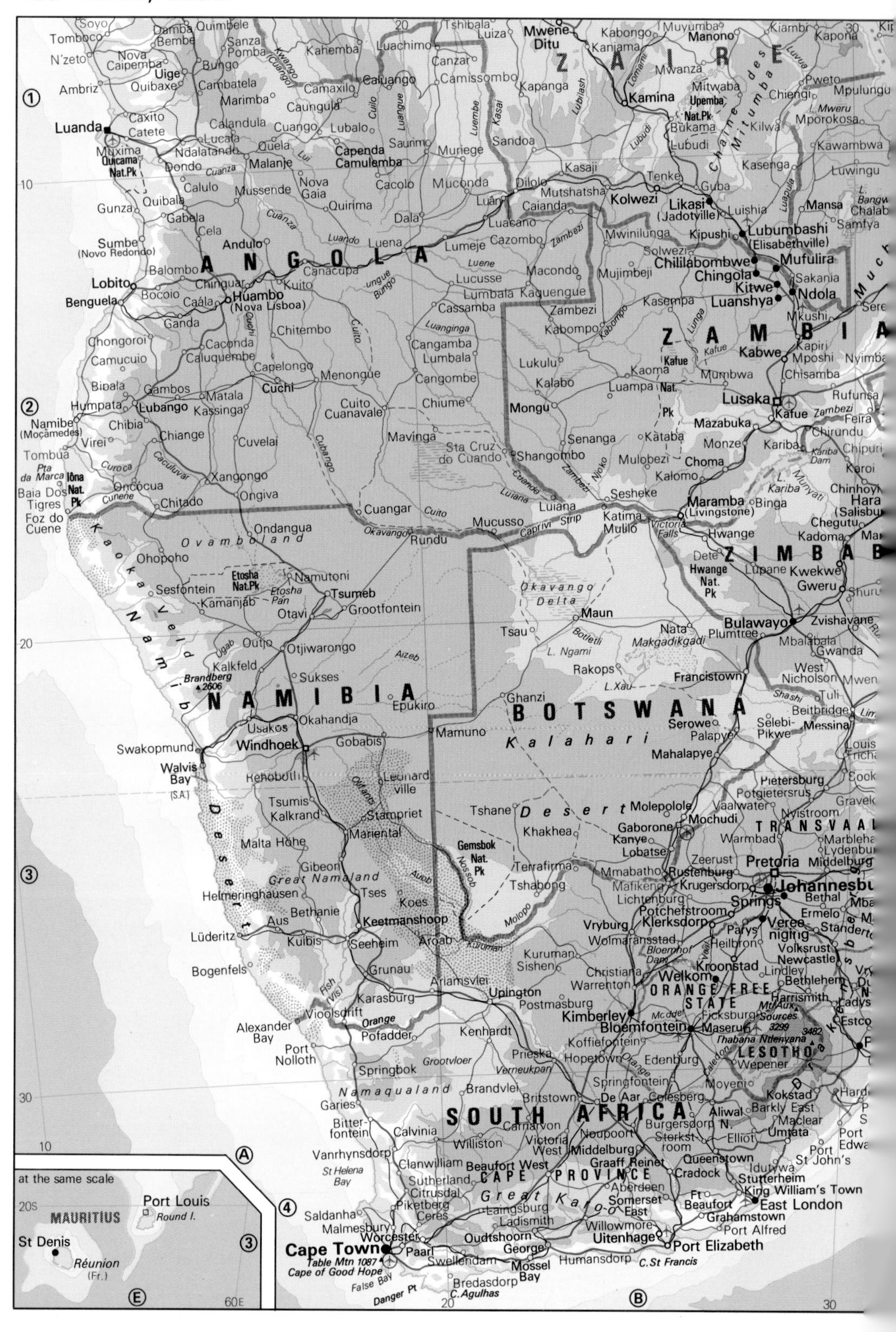
ANGOLA
ZAIRE
ZAMBIA
ZIMBABWE
NAMIBIA
BOTSWANA
SOUTH AFRICA
LESOTHO
TRANSVAAL
ORANGE FREE STATE
CAPE PROVINCE
Luanda
Lobito
Benguela
Huambo
(Nova Lisboa)
Namibe
(Moçâmedes)
Lubango
Menongue
Cuito Cuanavale
Ongiva
Kolwezi
Likasi
(Jadotville)
Lubumbashi
(Elisabethville)
Kamina
Chililabombwe
Chingola
Kitwe
Mufulira
Ndola
Luanshya
Kabwe
Lusaka
Kafue
Mongu
Maramba
(Livingstone)
Hwange
Bulawayo
Gweru
Kwekwe
Francistown
Maun
Ghanzi
Gaborone
Mochudi
Serowe
Windhoek
Swakopmund
Walvis Bay
(S.A.)
Tsumeb
Grootfontein
Otjiwarongo
Okahandja
Gobabis
Rehoboth
Mariental
Keetmanshoop
Lüderitz
Rundu
Etosha Nat.Pk
Brandberg
2606
Kaokoveld
Namib
Desert
Kalahari
Desert
Okavango Delta
Makgadikgadi
Gemsbok Nat. Pk
Caprivi Strip
Victoria Falls
Pretoria
Johannesburg
Springs
Vereeniging
Krugersdorp
Rustenburg
Potchefstroom
Klerksdorp
Pietersburg
Kroonstad
Welkom
Kimberley
Bloemfontein
Maseru
Upington
Springbok
Alexander Bay
Port Nolloth
De Aar
Beaufort West
Graaff Reinet
Queenstown
Cradock
East London
King William's Town
Grahamstown
Port Elizabeth
Uitenhage
George
Mossel Bay
Oudtshoorn
Worcester
Paarl
Cape Town
Table Mtn 1087
Cape of Good Hope
False Bay
Danger Pt
C. Agulhas
C. St Francis
Great Karoo
Namaqualand
Great Namaland
Orange
Zambezi
Okavango
Cunene
Cuanza
Cubango
Molopo
Vaal
Thabana Ntlenyana
3482
Mt Aux Sources
3299
at the same scale
MAURITIUS
Port Louis
Round I.
St Denis
Réunion
(Fr.)
20S
60E
10
20
30

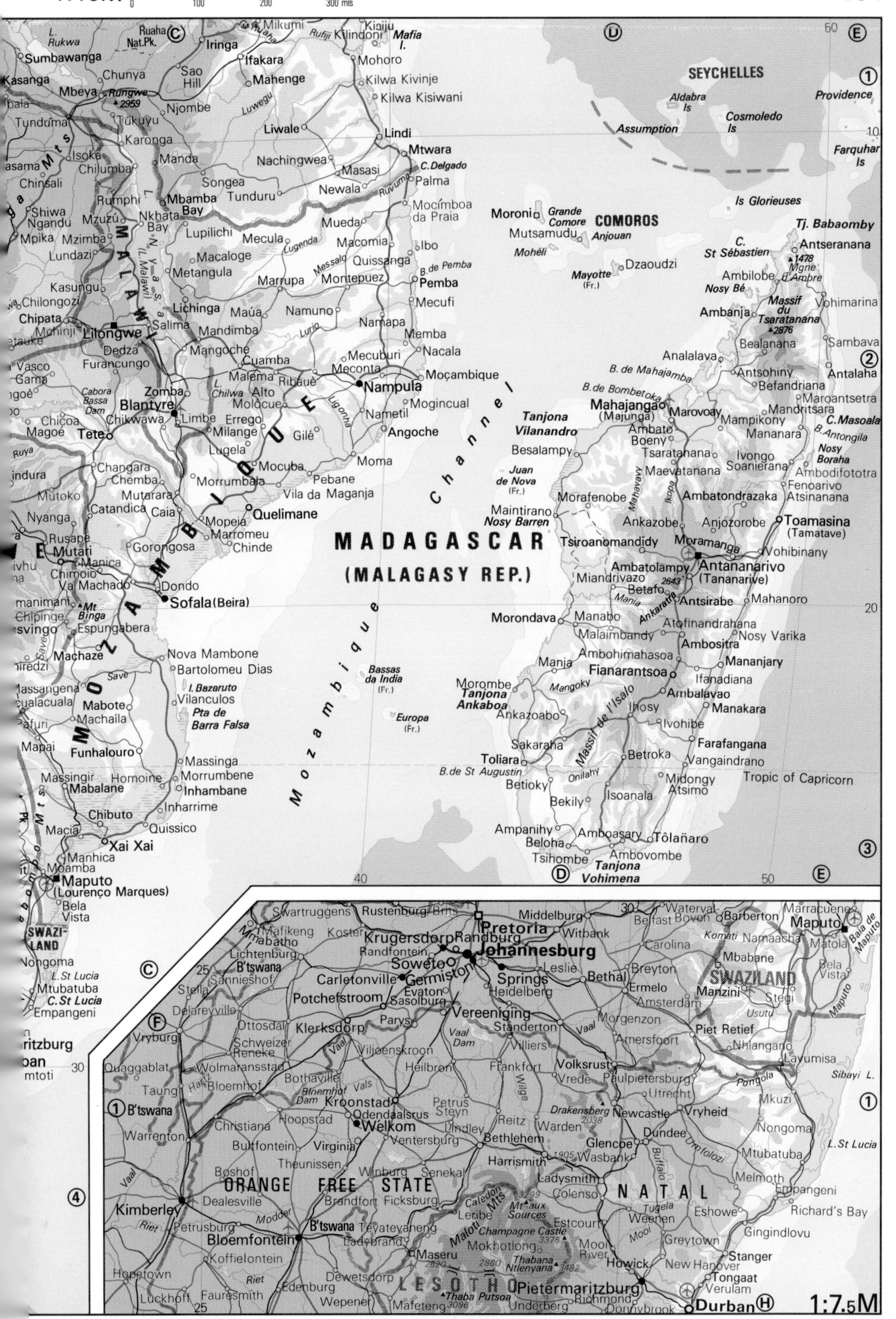

MADAGASCAR
(MALAGASY REP.)

SEYCHELLES

COMOROS

MOZAMBIQUE

Mozambique Channel

B. de Mahajamba

B. de Bombetoka

Massif de l'Isalo

Tropic of Capricorn

ORANGE FREE STATE

NATAL

SWAZILAND

LESOTHO

1:7.5M

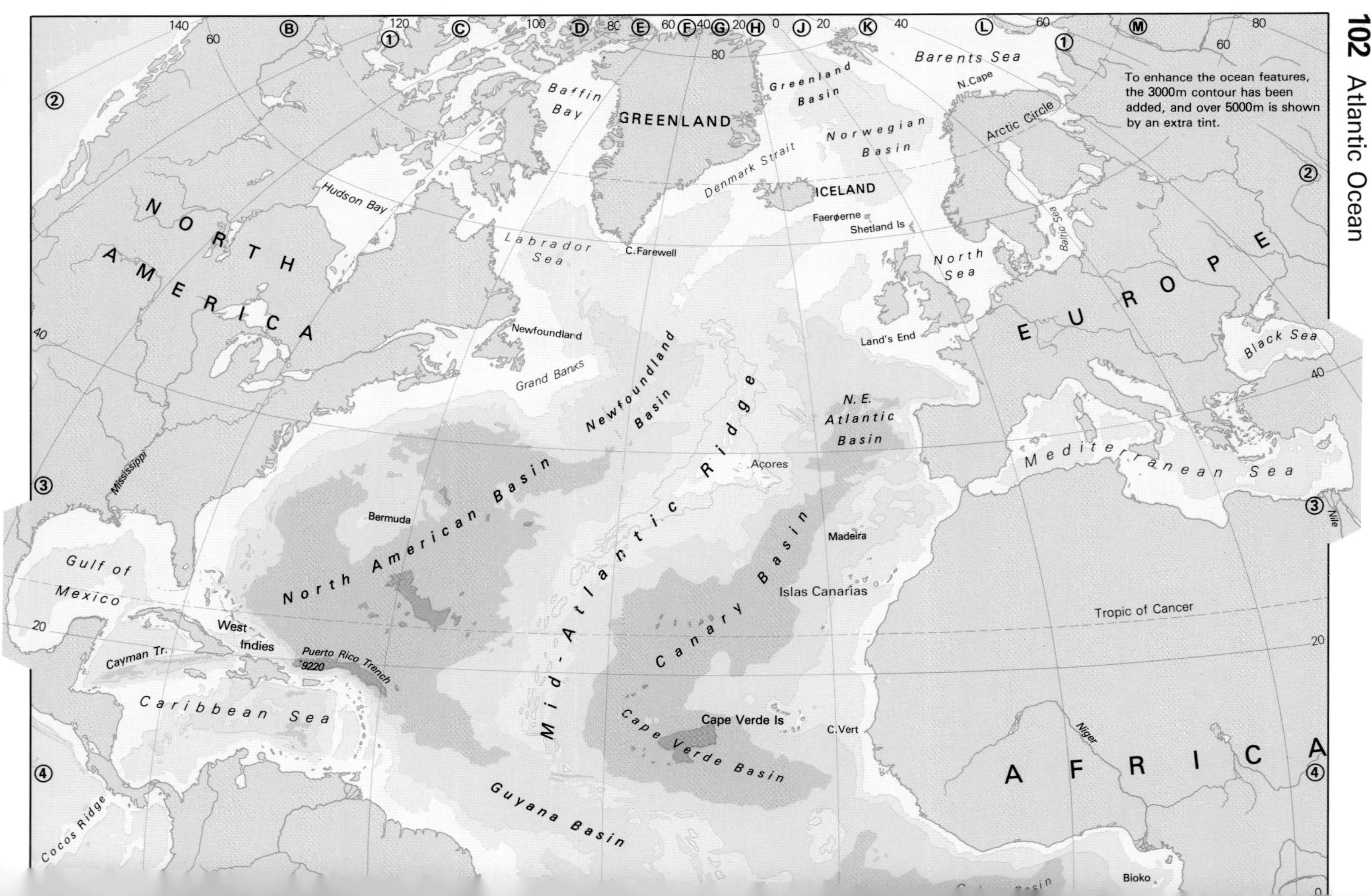
To enhance the ocean features, the 3000m contour has been added, and over 5000m is shown by an extra tint.
NORTH AMERICA
EUROPE
AFRICA
GREENLAND
ICELAND
Barents Sea
N.Cape
Arctic Circle
Baltic Sea
North Sea
Greenland Basin
Norwegian Basin
Denmark Strait
Faerøerne
Shetland Is
Land's End
Black Sea
Mediterranean Sea
Nile
Tropic of Cancer
Niger
Bioko
Baffin Bay
Hudson Bay
Labrador Sea
C.Farewell
Newfoundland
Grand Banks
Newfoundland Basin
N.E. Atlantic Basin
Açores
Mid-Atlantic Ridge
Madeira
Islas Canarias
Canary Basin
Cape Verde Is
C.Vert
Cape Verde Basin
North American Basin
Bermuda
Mississippi
Gulf of Mexico
West Indies
Puerto Rico Trench
9220
Cayman Tr.
Caribbean Sea
Guyana Basin
Cocos Ridge

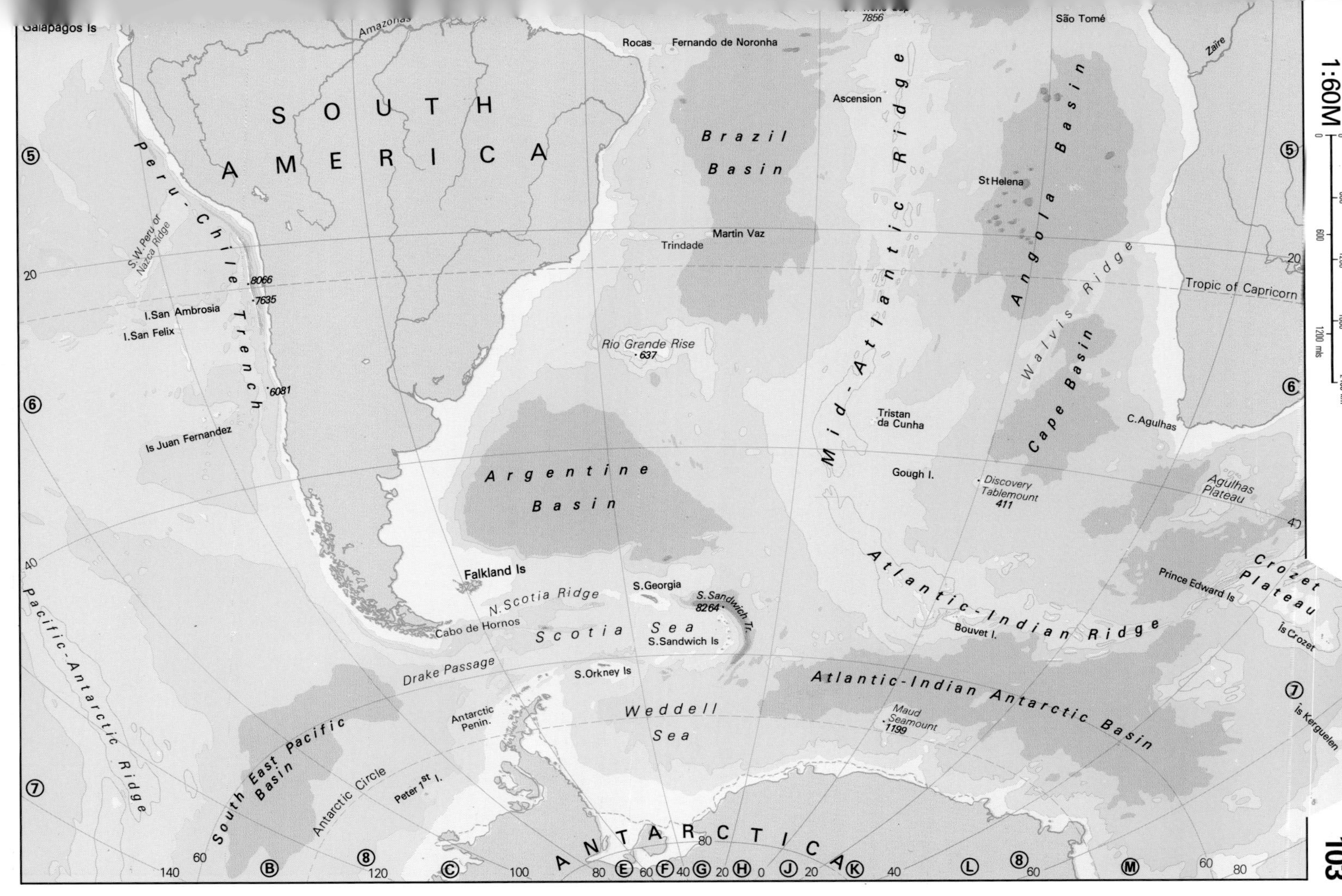

1:60M

0   600   1200   1800   2400 km
0   600   1200 mls

São Tomé

Zaïre

Amazonas

Galápagos Is

Rocas

Fernando de Noronha

Ascension
7856

St Helena

A n g o l a   B a s i n

Tropic of Capricorn

C.Agulhas

Agulhas
Plateau

W a l v i s   R i d g e

C a p e   B a s i n

Discovery
Tablemount
411

*C r o z e t
P l a t e a u*

Is Crozet

Is Kerguelen

Prince Edward Is

A t l a n t i c - I n d i a n   R i d g e

Bouvet I.

Maud
Seamount
1750

A t l a n t i c - I n d i a n   A n t a r c t i c   B a s i n

Tristan
da Cunha

Gough I.

M i d - A t l a n t i c   R i d g e

*B r a z i l
B a s i n*

Trindade

Martin Vaz

Rio Grande Rise
637

*A r g e n t i n e
B a s i n*

S O U T H

A M E R I C A

I.San Ambrosiä
8066
7635

I.San Felix

Is Juan Fernandez

*S.W. Peru or
Nazca Ridge*

P e r u - C h i l e   T r e n c h
6081

Falkland Is

Cabo de Hornos

N. Scotia Ridge

S.Georgia

S. Sandwich Tr.
8264

S.Sandwich Is

*S c o t i a
S e a*

S.Orkney Is

Drake Passage

Antarctic
Penin.

*W e d d e l l
S e a*

Peter I. I.

*S o u t h   E a s t   P a c i f i c
B a s i n*

Antarctic Circle

P a c i f i c - A n t a r c t i c   R i d g e

A N T A R C T I C A

⑤   ⑥   ④   ⑦

Ⓜ   ⑧   Ⓛ   Ⓚ   Ⓙ   Ⓗ   Ⓖ   Ⓕ   Ⓔ   Ⓒ   ⑧   Ⓑ

80   60   40   20   0   80   60   100   120   140

20   20   40

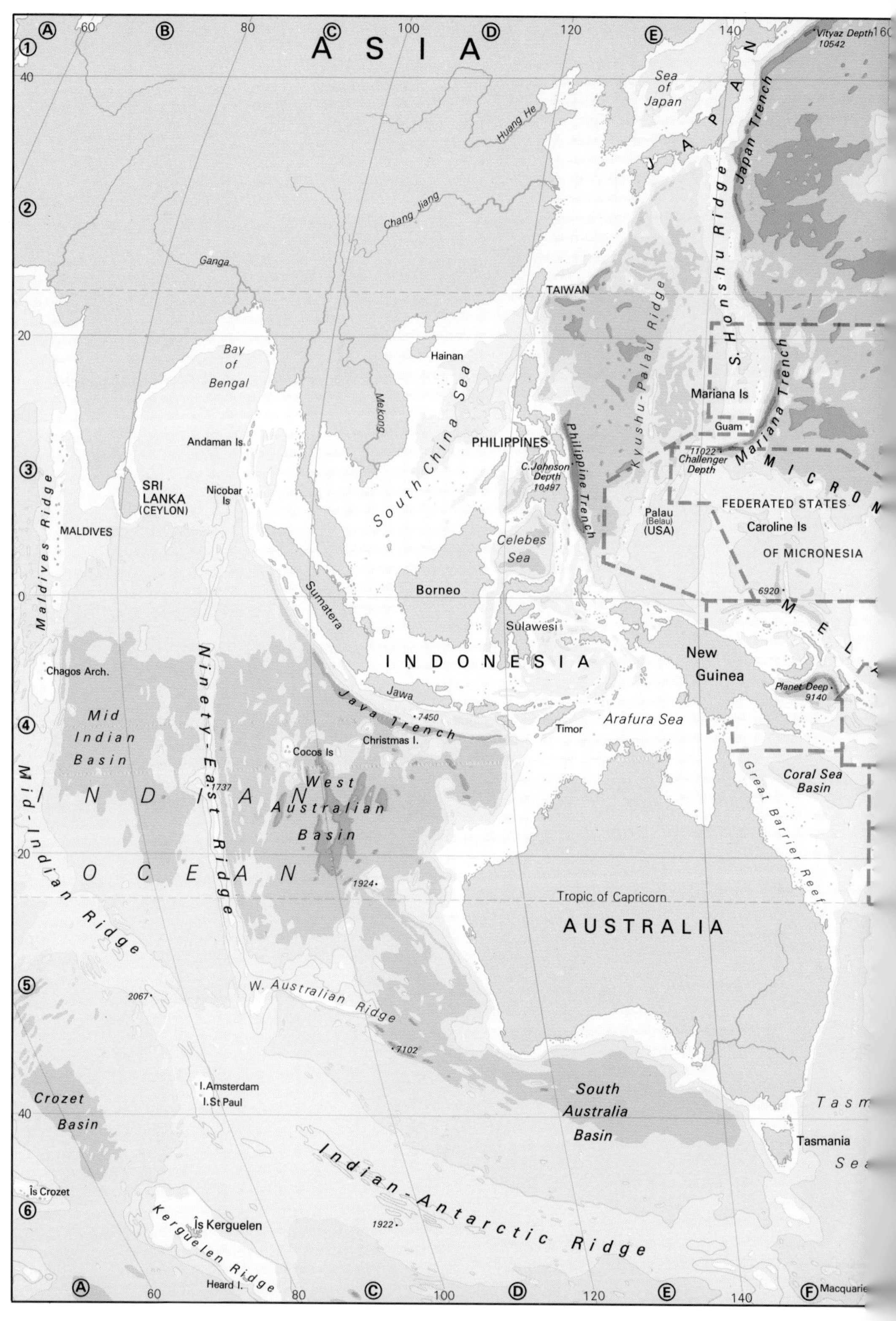

ASIA

Ⓐ 60 Ⓑ 80 Ⓒ 100 Ⓓ 120 Ⓔ 140

① 40

Sea of Japan

Vityaz Depth 10542

② Huang He

Chang Jiang

Ganga

J A P A N

S. Honshu Ridge

Japan Trench

20 TAIWAN

Bay of Bengal

Hainan

Kyushu-Palau Ridge

Mariana Is

Guam

Mariana Trench

M I C R O N

Andaman Is.

③ Maldives Ridge

SRI LANKA (CEYLON)

Nicobar Is

PHILIPPINES

C. Johnson Depth 10497

Challenger Depth 11022

Palau (Belau) (USA)

FEDERATED STATES

Caroline Is

OF MICRONESIA

6920

MALDIVES

South China Sea

Celebes Sea

Philippine Trench

M E L

Chagos Arch.

Sumatera

Borneo

Sulawesi

INDONESIA

New Guinea

Planet Deep 9140

0

Ninety-East Ridge

Mid Indian Basin

Jawa

Java Trench

7450

Christmas I.

Timor

Arafura Sea

④ Mid-Indian Ridge

I N D I A N

Cocos Is

1737

West Australian Basin

Coral Sea Basin

O C E A N

1924

20 Tropic of Capricorn

Great Barrier Reef

AUSTRALIA

⑤ 2067

W. Australian Ridge

7102

Crozet Basin

I. Amsterdam I. St Paul

South Australia Basin

Tas m

Tasmania

Sea

40

Îs Crozet

⑥ Îs Kerguelen

Kerguelen Ridge

Indian-Antarctic Ridge

1922

Heard I.

Ⓐ 60 80 Ⓒ 100 Ⓓ 120 Ⓔ 140 Ⓕ Macquarie

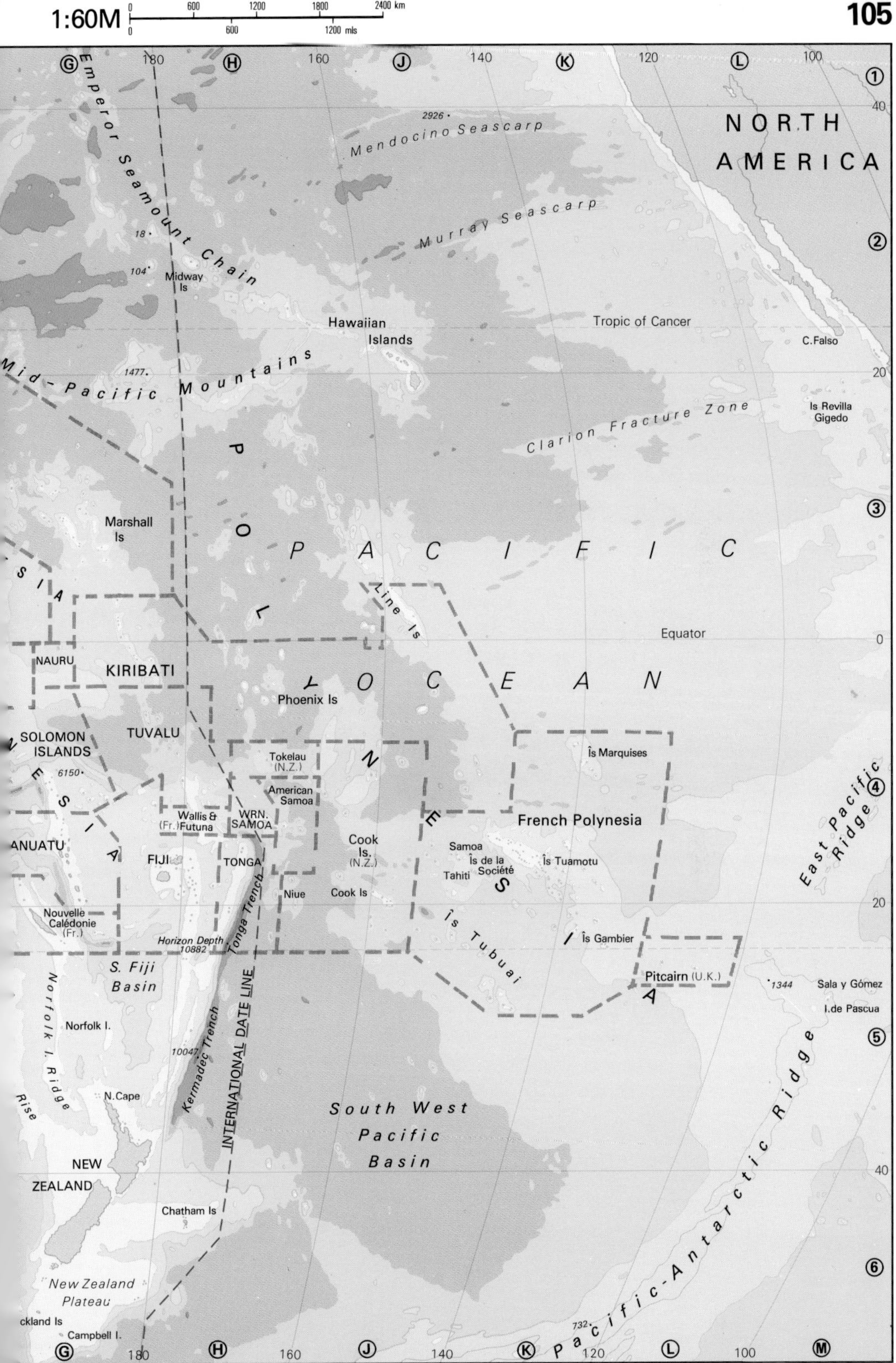

40 ①

Emperor Seamount Chain

Mendocino Seascarp

2926

180   H   160   J   140   K   120   L   100

N O R T H
A M E R I C A

②

Murray Seascarp

18

104

Midway
Is

Hawaiian
Islands

Tropic of Cancer

C. Falso

20

Mid-Pacific Mountains

1477

Clarion Fracture Zone

Is Revilla
Gigedo

③

Marshall
Is

P

O

L

Y

N

E

S

I

A

P A C I F I C C

Line Is

Equator   0

NAURU

KIRIBATI

Phoenix Is

O C E A N

TUVALU

SOLOMON
ISLANDS

6150

M E L A N E S I A

Tokelau
(N.Z.)

American
Samoa

Îs Marquises

French Polynesia

④

East Pacific Ridge

Wallis &
(Fr.) Futuna

WRN.
SAMOA

ANUATU

FIJI

TONGA

Cook
Is.
(N.Z.)

Samoa
Îs de la
Société

Tahiti

Îs Tuamotu

20

Nouvelle
Calédonie
(Fr.)

Niue

Cook Is

Îs Tubuai

Îs Gambier

Horizon Depth
10882

S. Fiji
Basin

Pitcairn (U.K.)

1344   Sala y Gómez

I. de Pascua

⑤

Norfolk I.

10047

Norfolk I. Ridge

Norfolk I.

Tonga Trench

INTERNATIONAL DATE LINE

Kermadec Trench

South West
Pacific
Basin

40

Pacific-Antarctic Ridge

N. Cape

NEW

Rise

ZEALAND

Chatham Is

⑥

New Zealand
Plateau

ckland Is

Campbell I.

G   180   H   160   J   140   K   120   L   100   M

732

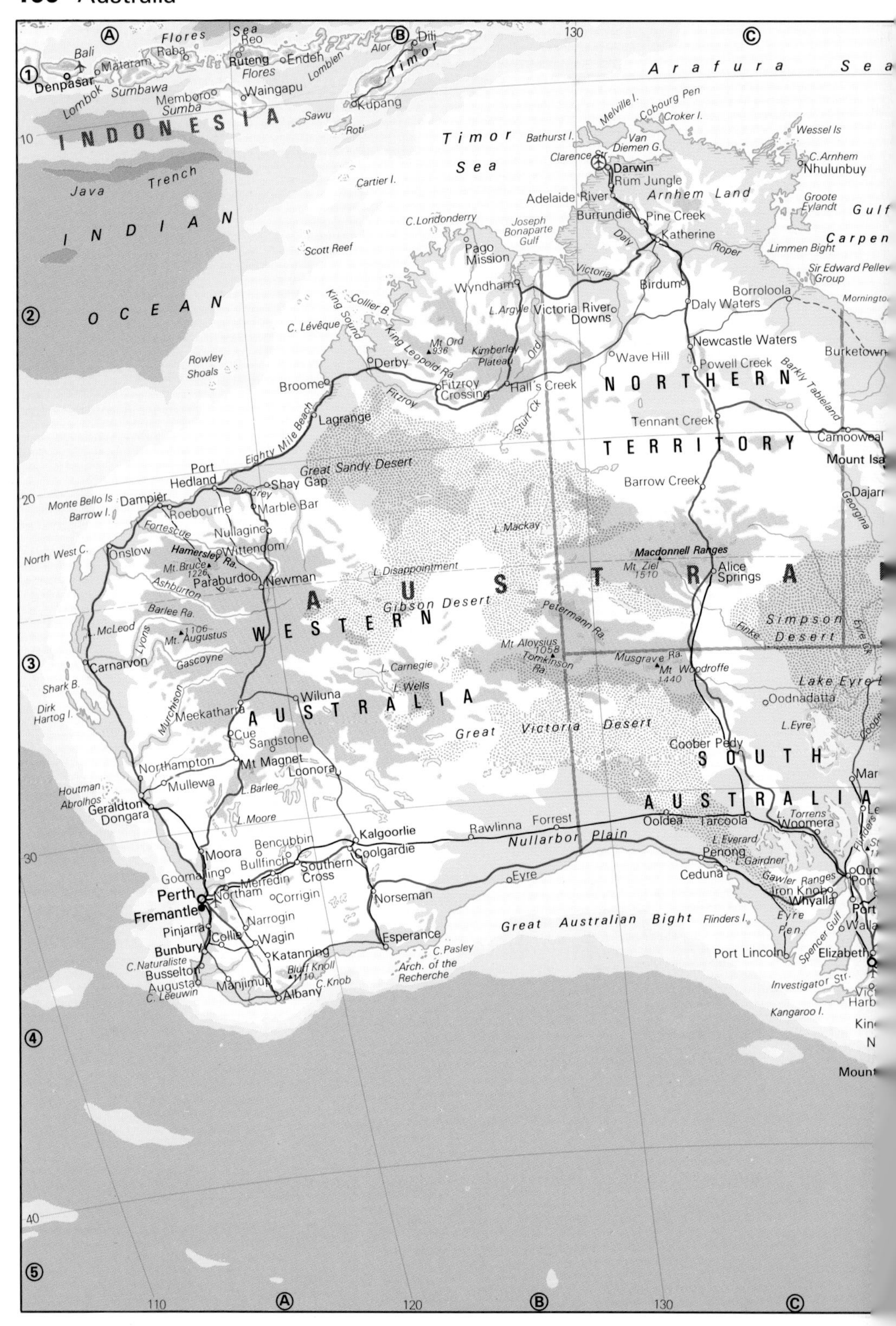
INDONESIA
INDIAN OCEAN
Java Trench
Timor Sea
Arafura Sea
Flores Sea
Darwin
Katherine
Alice Springs
Perth
Fremantle
Kalgoorlie
Port Hedland
Broome
Derby
Carnarvon
Geraldton
Albany
Esperance
Tennant Creek
Ceduna
Port Lincoln
Whyalla
Woomera
Coober Pedy
Great Sandy Desert
Gibson Desert
Great Victoria Desert
Simpson Desert
Nullarbor Plain
Great Australian Bight
Arnhem Land
Macdonnell Ranges
WESTERN AUSTRALIA
NORTHERN TERRITORY
SOUTH AUSTRALIA
AUSTRALIA

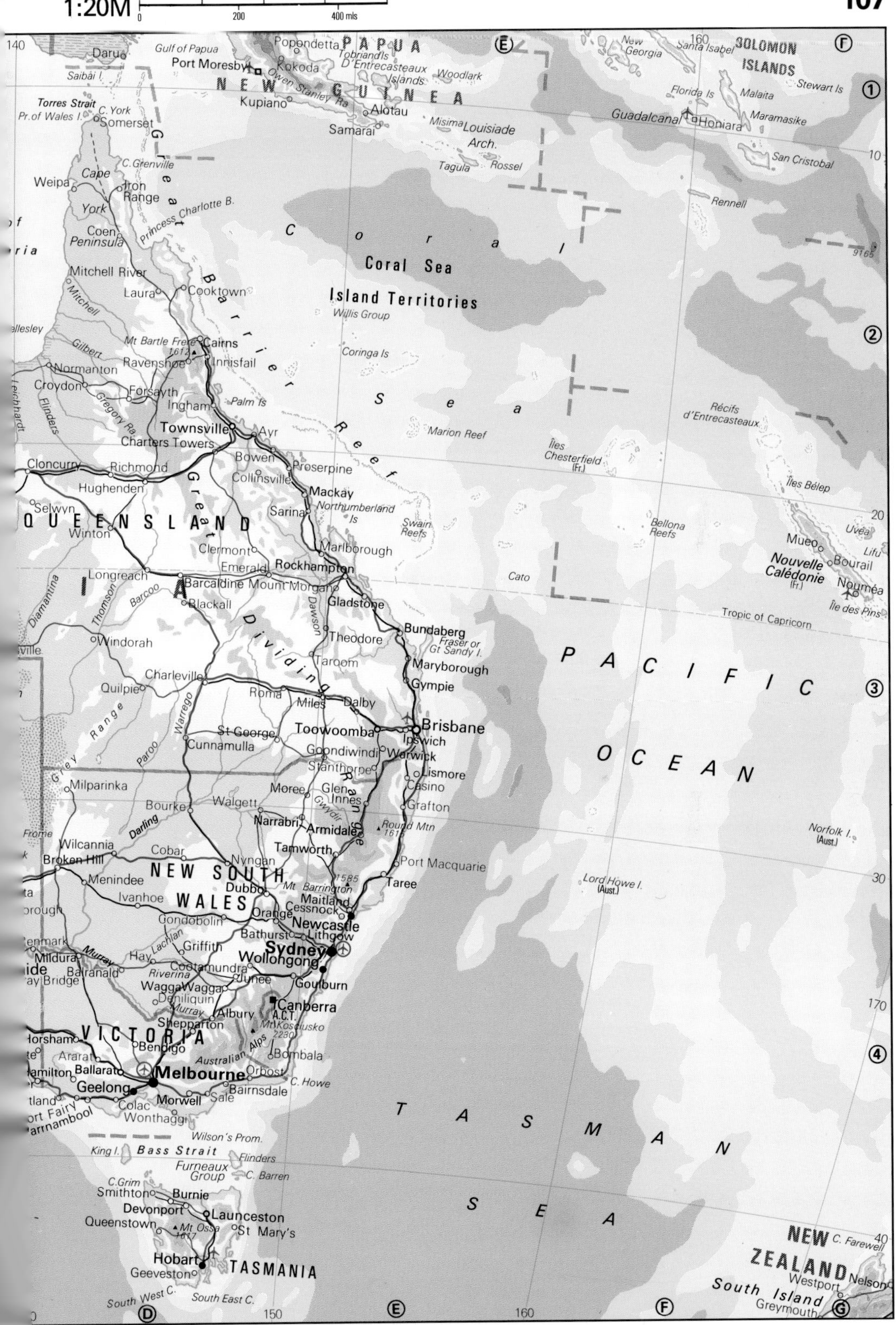

1:20M

800 km
400 mils

0 200 400 600 800 km
0 200 400 mls
PAPUA NEW GUINEA
Gulf of Papua
Daru
Saibai I.
Port Moresby
Popondetta
Kokoda
Owen Stanley Ra.
Tobriand Is
D'Entrecasteaux Islands
Woodlark
Kupiano
Alotau
Samarai
Misima
Louisiade Arch.
Tagula
Rossel
Torres Strait
Pr. of Wales I.
C. York
Somerset
C. Grenville
Weipa
Cape York Peninsula
Iron Range
Coen
Princess Charlotte B.
Great Barrier Reef
Coral Sea
Coral Sea Island Territories
Willis Group
Coringa Is
Marion Reef
Mitchell River
Mitchell
Laura
Cooktown
Mt Bartle Frere 1612
Cairns
Innisfail
Gilbert
Normanton
Ravenshoe
Croydon
Forsayth
Gregory Ra.
Flinders
Ingham
Palm Is
Townsville
Ayr
Charters Towers
Bowen
Proserpine
Collinsville
Cloncurry
Richmond
Hughenden
Mackay
Northumberland Is
Sarina
Selwyn
QUEENSLAND
Winton
Great Dividing Range
Clermont
Marlborough
Swain Reefs
Emerald
Rockhampton
Longreach
Barcaldine
Mount Morgan
Gladstone
Diamantina
Thomson
Barcoo
Blackall
Dawson
Windorah
Theodore
Bundaberg
Fraser or Gt Sandy I.
Taroom
Maryborough
Charleville
Gympie
Quilpie
Roma
Miles
Dalby
Warrego
Grey Range
St George
Toowoomba
Brisbane
Ipswich
Cunnamulla
Goondiwindi
Warwick
Paroo
Stanthorpe
Lismore
Casino
Milparinka
Moree
Glen Innes
Bourke
Walgett
Gwydir
Grafton
Darling
Narrabri
Armidale
Round Mtn 1615
Frome
Wilcannia
Cobar
Tamworth
Broken Hill
Nyngan
Port Macquarie
Menindee
NEW SOUTH WALES
Mt Barrington 1585
Taree
Dubbo
Ivanhoe
Maitland
Cessnock
Orange
Newcastle
Gondobolin
Bathurst
Lithgow
Lachlan
Griffith
Sydney
Murray
Mildura
Hay
Wollongong
Balranald
Riverina
Cootamundra
Junee
Goulburn
Wagga Wagga
Deniliquin
Canberra
A.C.T.
Albury
Shepparton
Mt Kosciusko 2230
VICTORIA
Horsham
Bendigo
Australian Alps
Ararat
Bombala
Ballarat
Melbourne
Orbost
Hamilton
C. Howe
Geelong
Bairnsdale
Morwell
Sale
Colac
Warrnambool
Wonthaggi
Wilson's Prom.
King I.
Bass Strait
Flinders
Furneaux Group
C. Barren
C. Grim
Smithton
Burnie
Devonport
Launceston
Queenstown
Mt Ossa 1617
St Mary's
Hobart
Geeveston
TASMANIA
South West C.
South East C.
New Georgia
Santa Isabel
SOLOMON ISLANDS
Florida Is
Malaita
Stewart Is
Guadalcanal
Honiara
Maramasike
San Cristobal
Rennell
9165
Récifs d'Entrecasteaux
Îles Chesterfield (Fr.)
Îles Bélep
Bellona Reefs
Uvea
Mueo
Bourail
Lifu
Nouvelle Calédonie (Fr.)
Nouméa
Île des Pins
Cato
Tropic of Capricorn
PACIFIC OCEAN
Norfolk I. (Aust.)
Lord Howe I. (Aust.)
TASMAN SEA
NEW ZEALAND
C. Farewell
Nelson
Westport
South Island
Greymouth
140
150
160
170
10
30
D
E
F
G
3

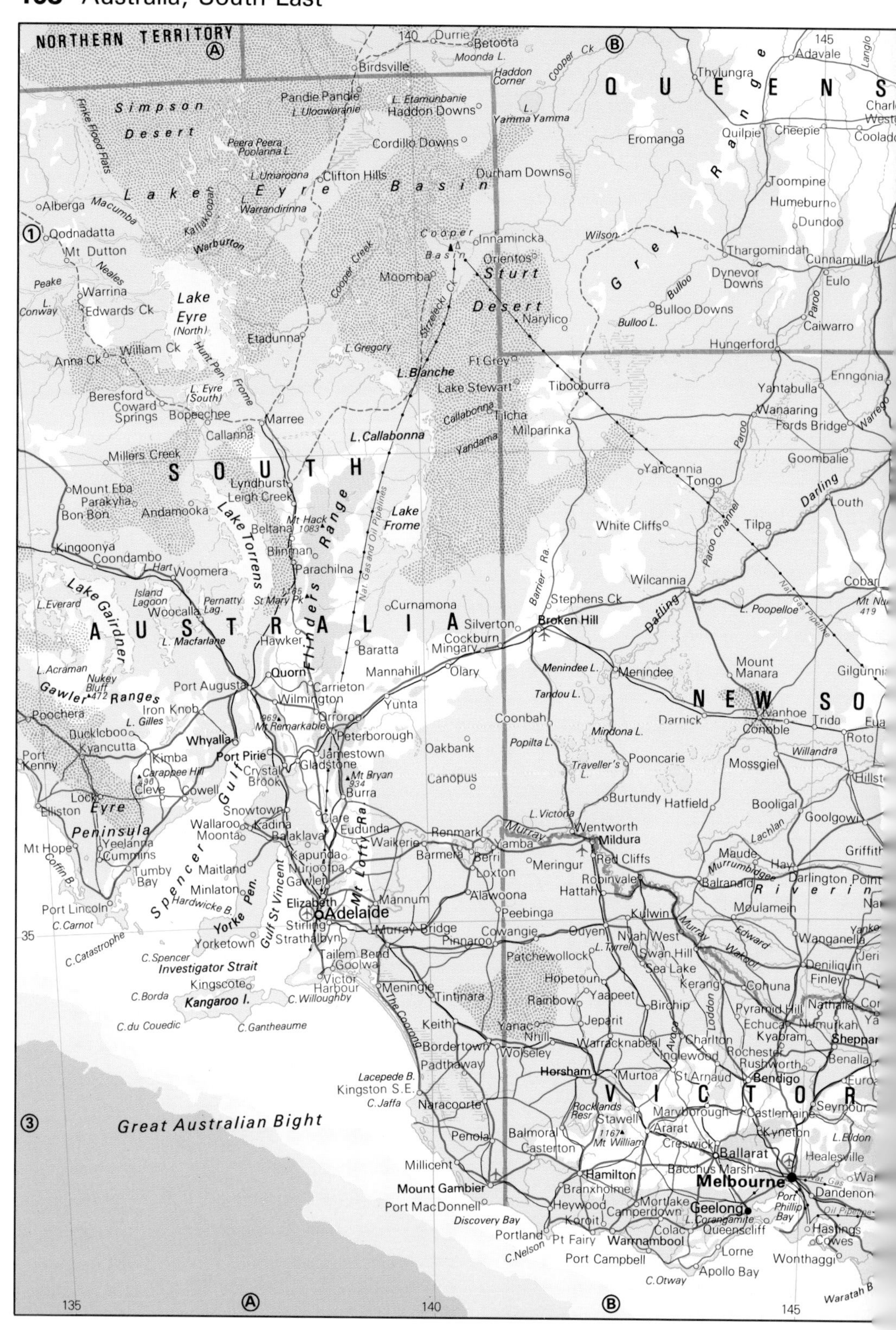
NORTHERN TERRITORY
QUEENSLAND
SOUTH AUSTRALIA
NEW SOUTH WALES
VICTORIA
Simpson Desert
Lake Eyre Basin
Sturt Desert
Grey Range
Flinders Range
Mt Lofty Ra.
Barrier Ra.
Gawler Ranges
Eyre Peninsula
Yorke Pen.
Spencer Gulf
Gulf St Vincent
Investigator Strait
Kangaroo I.
Great Australian Bight
Lake Eyre (North)
L. Eyre (South)
Lake Torrens
Lake Gairdner
Lake Frome
L. Blanche
L. Callabonna
L. Gregory
Cooper Creek
Cooper Ck
Warburton
Macumba
Neales
Finke Flood Flats
Darling
Murray
Murrumbidgee
Lachlan
Paroo
Bulloo
Warrego
Riverina
Birdsville
Betoota
Haddon Corner
Moomba
Innamincka
Marree
Oodnadatta
Port Augusta
Whyalla
Port Pirie
Port Lincoln
Adelaide
Elizabeth
Murray Bridge
Broken Hill
Mildura
Wilcannia
Tibooburra
Quilpie
Cunnamulla
Thargomindah
Eromanga
Renmark
Berri
Swan Hill
Echuca
Bendigo
Ballarat
Melbourne
Geelong
Horsham
Hamilton
Warrnambool
Portland
Mount Gambier
Naracoorte
Kingston S.E.
Penola
Millicent
Port MacDonnell
Discovery Bay
Port Phillip Bay
Seymour
Shepparton
Benalla
Wonthaggi
Apollo Bay
C. Otway
C. Nelson
Hay
Griffith
Deniliquin
Ivanhoe
Menindee
Nat. Gas and Oil Pipelines
Nat. Gas Pipeline
135
140
145
35
A
B
1
3

100   200   300 km
50   100   150 mls

Queensland labels:

Augathella   Taroom   Mundubbera   Biggenden   **Maryborough**
Ward   Dawson   Gayndah   Double Island Pt
914 Mt Hutton   Injune   Wandoan   Goomeri   Murgon   **Gympie**
Morven   Eurombah   Wondai   Tewantin
Mitchell   Guluguba   Kingaroy   Brooloo   Cooroy
Mungallala   Roma   Wallumbilla   Miles   Chinchilla   Jandowae   Nanango   Yarraman   Nambour   Maroochydore
Muckadilla   Jackson   Kilcoy   Caloundra
Angellala Ck   Condamine   Tara   Toogoolawah   Caboolture
Wyandra   Surat   Dalby   Crows Nest   Moreton I.
Glenmorgan   Meandarra   Oakey   Gatton   Redcliffe
St George   Moonie   Pittsworth   Toowoomba   Ipswich   **Brisbane**
Bollon   Millmerran   Clifton   N. Stradbroke I.
Mt Domville 642   Allora   Boonah   Beenleigh
Dirranbandi   Inglewood   Warwick   Beaudesert   **Gold Coast**
Thallon   Talwood   Killarney   Tweed Heads
Goodooga   Mungindi   Boggabilla   Goondiwindi   Stanthorpe   Murwillumbah   Mullumbimby
Hebel   Texas   Kyogle   C. Byron

P A C I F I C   O C E A N

30

New South Wales labels:

Weilmoringle   New Angledool   Yetman   Tenterfield   Casino   Ballina
Lightning Ridge   Ashley   Croppa Ck   Ashford   Deepwater   Lismore   Woodburn
Collarenebri   Garah   Moree   Warialda   Glen Innes   Grafton   Yamba   Maclean
Rokataroo   Gravesend   Inverell   Deepwater
Narran L.   Rowena   Bellata   Bingara   Guyra   Glenreagh
Burren Jc   Wee Waa   Bundarra   1508 Kaputar   Dorrigo   Coff's Harbour
Gwabegar   Narrabri   Barraba   Round Mtn 1615   Bellingen
Boggabri   Manilla   Uralla   Armidale   Nambucca Heads
Baradine   Gunnedah   Walcha   Macksville   Smoky C.
Coonabarabran   Mullaley   Kempsey
Gulargambone   Werris Creek   Black Sugarloaf 1494   Tamworth   Wauchope   Port Macquarie
Coonamble   Quirindi   Kendall
Nyngan   Gilgandra   Coolah   Murrurundi   Wingham
Nevertire   Warren   Dunedoo   Scone   Gloucester   Taree
Nymagee   Narromine   Merriwa   Gulgong   Muswellbrook   Forster   C. Hawke
Yellow Mtn 573   Dubbo   Wellington   Mudgee   Singleton   Dungog   Sugarloaf Pt
Trundle   Peak Hill   Mt Canobolas 1274   Kandos   Kurri Kurri   Maitland   Port Stephens
Condobolin   Molong   Cessnock   Raymond Terrace
Parkes   Orange   Morisset   **Newcastle**
Cargelligo   Forbes   Portland   Lithgow   Wyong   L. Macquarie
Burcher   L. Cowal   Blayney   Richmond   Tuggerah L.
Rankins Springs   Grenfell   Cowra   Bathurst   Windsor
West Wyalong   Canowindra   Karoomba   Port Jackson
Ardlethan   Young   L. Burragorang   **Parramatta**   **Sydney**
Leeton   Temora   Boorowa   Camden   Picton
Coolamon   Cootamundra   Murrumburrah   Crookwell   Campbelltown   **Wollongong**
Junee   Burrinjuck Res.   Goulburn   Bowral   Port Kembla
Wagga Wagga   The Rock   Gundagai   Yass   L. George   Shellharbour
Culcairn   Tumut   **Canberra**   Nowra   Shoalhaven R.
Walla   Holbrook   A.C.T.   Queanbeyan   Jervis B.
Albury   Tumbarumba   Ulladulla
Wodonga   Corryong   L. Eucumbene   Cooma   Batemans Bay
Beechworth   Mt Kosciusko 2230   Cobargo   Moruya
Bright   Mt Bogong 1986   Nimmitabel   Bega
Mt Buller 1804   Bombala   Merimbula
Delegate   Eden
Orbost   Genoa   C. Howe
Bairnsdale   Cann River   Pt Hicks
Sale   Lakes Entrance
Traralgon   Ninety Mile Beach
Morwell
Gippsland
Wilson's Promontory

Great Dividing Ra.   New England Ra.   Nandewar Ra.   Liverpool Ra.   Blue Mts   Snowy Mts   Australian Alps

Darling   Downs

150   155   155

Inset: TASMANIA (at the same scale)

145E   Wilson's Promontory   C. Wickham
B   C. Frankland   C
B a s s   S t r a i t
King I.   Naracoopa   **Furneaux**   Flinders I.
Currie   Grassy   Whitemark   Lady Barron   **Group**
Stokes Pt   Cape Barren I.   40S
Hunter Is.   **Banks Strait**
C. Grim   Stanley   Gladstone   Eddystone Pt
Smithton   Wynyard   George Town   C. Portland
Marrawah   Burnie   Ulverstone   Bridport   Scottsdale
Devonport   Latrobe   **Launceston**   St Helens
Waratah   Deloraine   1573   St Marys
Rosebery   Longford   Great L.   Freycinet Peninsula
Queenstown   Mt Ossa 1617   Oatlands   Oyster Bay
Strahan   Derwent Br.   Tarraleah   Maria I.
Macquarie Har.   Frenchmans Cap 1444
TASMANIA   New Norfolk   Sorell   Tasman Pen.
Maydena   **Hobart**   C. Pillar
Port Davy   Huonville   Geeveston   Storm Bay
S.W. Cape   Bruny I.
S.E. Cape

at the same scale

① ② ④

NORTH

ISLAND

N

T A S M A N

S E A

North
Cape

Three Kings Is

C. Maria
van Diemen

Rangaunu B.

Doubtless B.

Ninety Mile Beach

Ahipara B.

Tauroa Pt.

Kaitaia

Kaikohe

Hokianga Har.

Bay of Islands

Russell

C. Brett

Hikurangi

Kawakawa

Whangarei

Bream B.

Hen & Chickens Is

Dargaville

Kaipara Har.

Wellsford

Little Barrier I.

Kaukapakapa

Great Barrier I.

C. Colville

Mercury Is

Mercury Bay

Coromandel
Peninsula

Coromandel Ra.

C. Runaway

Hicks
Bay

East C.

Tokomaru
Bay

Tolaga Bay

Poverty Bay

Gisborne

Mahia
Peninsula

Portland I.

Raukumara Ra.

Bay of
Plenty

White I.

Mayor I.

Matakana I.

Tauranga Har.

Tauranga

Whakatane

Te Puke

Matata

Ohope

Opotiki

Urewera Ra.

Wairoa

H u i a r a u   R a.

Hawke
Bay

Wairoa

Napier

Havelock North

Hastings

C. Kidnappers

Eskdale

Taradale

Waipukurau

Waipawa

C. Turnagain

Herbertville

Dannevirke

Woodville

Eketahuna

Pahiatua

C. Tarakena

Haurangi

Palmerston North

Foxton

Levin

Otaki

Feilding

Wanganui

Wanganui

Marton

Taihape

Raetihi

Ohakune

Mt Ruapehu

Mt Ngauruhoe

Mt Tongariro

Taumarunui

Ohura

Taranaki
Bight

N. Taranaki Bight

New Plymouth

Waitara

Inglewood

Mt Egmont

Stratford

Eltham

Opunake

Hawera

Patea

S. Taranaki Bight

C. Egmont

Waikato

Hamilton

Cambridge

Morrinsville

Te Aroha

Paeroa

Waihi

Thames

Auckland

Manukau

Papakura

Pukekohe

Waiuku

Papatoetoe

Takapuna

Manukau
Har.

Waitemata Har.

Hauraki
Gulf

Huntly

Ngaruawahia

Te Awamutu

Glen Afton

Kawhia

Otorohanga

Te Kuiti

Waitomo

Mokau

Taupo

Rotorua

Te Aroha

Murupara

Kaweka Ra.

Ruahine Ra.

 C o o k

S t r a i t

C. Stephens

Stephens I.

Separation Pt.

Golden
Bay

Farewell Spit

C. Farewell

Collingwood

Ruby B.

NORTH ISLAND

1

A

B

C

1

A

35

40

35

40

170

175

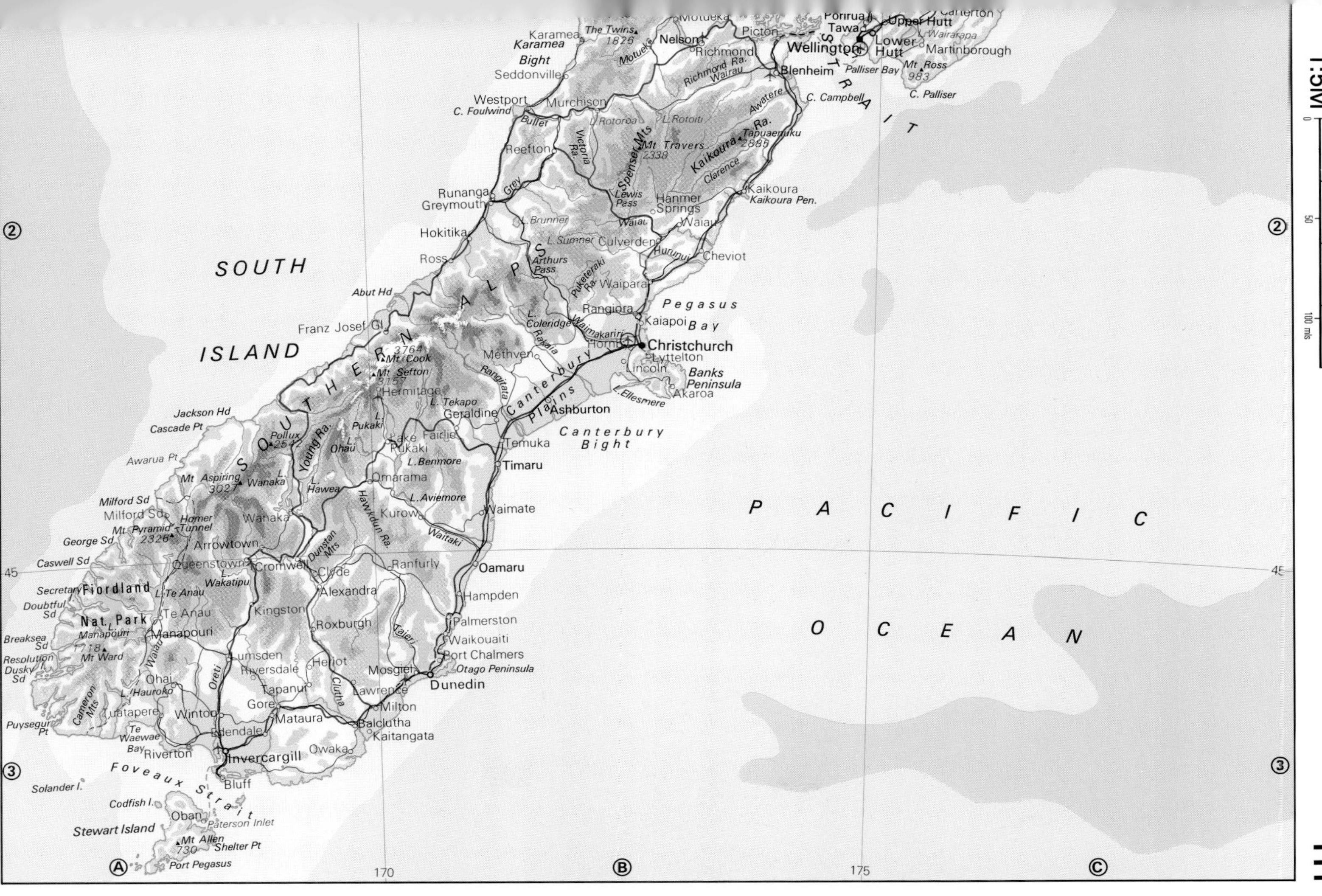

1:5M

0 50 100 150 200 km
0   50   100 mls

② ③ ©

P A C I F I C   O C E A N

B

175

170

45

SOUTH   ISLAND

S O U T H E R N   A L P S

Wellington
Lower Hutt
Upper Hutt
Porirua
Tawa
Petone
Johnsonville

Picton
Blenheim
Nelson
Richmond
Motueka
C. Campbell
C. Palliser
Palliser Bay
Martinborough
Masterton
Mt. Ross 983

Wanganui

Karamea
Karamea Bight
Seddonville
Westport
C. Foulwind
Reefton
Greymouth
Runanga
Hokitika
Ross

The Twins 1826
Murchison
Victoria Ra.
Buller
Brunner

Hanmer Springs
Lewis Pass
Cheviot
Kaikoura
Kaikoura Pen.
L. Sumner
Culverden
Waiau
Waipara
Rangiora
Kaiapoi
Christchurch
Lyttelton
Lincoln
Ellesmere
Banks Peninsula
Akaroa
Pegasus Bay

Mt. Travers 2338
Spenser Mts.
Kaikoura Ra.
Tapuaenuku 2885
Inland Kaikoura Ra.
Waiau

Arthurs Pass
Methven
Ashburton
Rakaia
Geraldine
Temuka
Timaru

Mt. Cook 3764
Mt. Sefton
Hermitage
L. Tekapo
Fairlie
Pukaki
Waimate
Oamaru
Hampden
Palmerston
Waikouaiti
Port Chalmers
Dunedin
Otago Peninsula
Mosgiel

Franz Josef Glacier
Abut Hd
Jackson Hd
Cascade Pt
Awarua Pt
Milford Sd.
George Sd.
Caswell Sd.
Secretary I.
Doubtful Sd.
Breaksea Sd.
Dusky Sd.
Resolution I.
Puysegur Pt
Solander I.

Mt. Aspiring 3027
Pollux
Young Ra.
Wanaka
L. Wanaka
L. Hawea
Ohau
L. Ohau
L. Pukaki
L. Benmore
Omarama
L. Aviemore
Kurow
L. Waitaki
Ranfurly

Fiordland Nat. Park
Homer Tunnel
Pyramid
Te Anau
L. Te Anau
Manapouri
L. Manapouri
Mt Ward
Cameron Mts.
Mt Allen 730
Shelter Pt
Port Pegasus

Queenstown
Arrowtown
Cromwell
Alexandra
Roxburgh
Heriot
Milton
Balclutha
Kaitangata
Clutha
Mataura
Ovakag

Wakatipu
L. Wakatipu
Lumsden
Riversdale
Gore
Clinton
Winton
Wintop

Waiau
Otautau
Waihopai Bay
Riverton
Invercargill
Bluff
Foveaux Strait
Oban
Codfish I.
Stewart Island
Paterson Inlet

S T R A I T

1:40M

| 0 | 400 | 800 | 1200 | 1600 km |
| 0 | 400 | | 800 mls | |

INDIAN OCEAN

Heard I. (Aust.)

ATLANTIC OCEAN

PACIFIC OCEAN

Mirny (Former USSR)

Shackleton Ice Shelf

Knox Coast

C. Poinsett

Casey (Aust.)

C. Darnley

Amery Ice Shelf

Zhongshan (China)

Davis (Aust.)

Queen Mary Land

Mawson (Aust.)

Pt. Charles

Mac. Robertson Land Mts

•3355

American Highland

Enderby Land

Molodezhnaya (Former USSR)

Syowa (Jap.)

Mizuho (Jap.)

Lambert Gl.

Wilkes Land

S. Magnetic Pole (1990)

Dumont d'Urville (Fr.)

Terre Adélie

George V Land

Ballenys Is

Sturge I.

Oates Land

Leningradskaya (Former USSR)

Vostok (Former USSR)

GREATER ANTARCTICA

Dronning Maud Land

Maitri (India)

Georg Forster (Germany)

Novolazarevskaya (Former USSR)

Prinsesse Astrid Kyst

Prinsesse Ragnhild Kyst

Sanae (S.A.)

Antarctic Circle

C. Norvegia

Coats Land

Pensacola Mts

Halley (U.K.)

Grl Belgrano (Arg.)

Berkner I.

Ronne Ice Shelf

Weddell Sea

South Pole

Amundsen-Scott (U.S.)

Q. Maud Mts

Mt Kirkpatrick 4528

Mt Markham 4351

Victoria Land

Transantarctic Mts

Scott (N.Z.)

McMurdo (U.S.)

C. Adare

C. Colbeck

Ross Ice Shelf

Roosevelt I.

Ross Sea

Scott I.

Average minimum extent of sea ice

LESSER ANTARCTICA

Mt Seelig •3022

Ellsworth Land

Vinson Massif 5140

Marie Byrd Land

Mt Sidley 4181

Walgreen Coast

Mt Kosciusko

Siple I.

Siple (U.S.)

Palmer Land

Alexander I.

Charcot I.

Antarctic Peninsula

Graham Land

Palmer Arch.

S. Shetland Is (U.K.)

Orcadas (Arg.)

S. Orkney Is (U.K.)

Signy (U.K.)

Scotia Sea

Drake Passage

Falkland Is (U.K.)

Tierra del Fuego

ARGENTINA

CHILE

Bellingshausen Sea

Amundsen Sea

Thurston I.

Peter I Øy (Nor.)

Antarctic Research Stations
1 Artigas (Uruguay)
2 Teniente Rodolfo Marsh Martin (Chile)
3 Bellingshausen (Former USSR)
4 Great Wall (China)
5 Comandante Ferraz (Brazil)
6 Henryk Arctowski (Poland)
7 Teniente Jubany (Arg.)
8 King Sejong (Korea)
9 Capitan Arturo Prat (Chile)
10 General Bernardo O'Higgins (Chile)
11 Esperanza (Arg.)
12 Vicecomodoro Marambio (Arg.)
13 Palmer (USA)
14 Faraday (UK)
15 Rothera (UK)
16 General San Martin (Arg.)

Index

In the index, the first number refers to the page, and the following letter and number to the section of the map in which the index entry can be found. For example, 48C2 **Paris** means that Paris can be found on page 48 where column C and row 2 meet.

Abbreviations used in the index

Afghan	Afghanistan	Hung	Hungary	Pol	Poland	Arch	Archipelago
Alb	Albania	Ind	Indonesia	Port	Portugal	B	Bay
Alg	Algeria	Irish Rep	Ireland	Rom	Romania	C	Cape
Ant	Antarctica	Leb	Lebanon	Russian Fed	Russian Federation	Chan	Channel
Arg	Argentina	Lib	Liberia			Gl	Glacier
Aust	Australia	Liech	Liechtenstein	S Arabia	Saudi Arabia	I(s)	Island(s)
Bang	Bangladesh	Lux	Luxembourg	Scot	Scotland	Lg	Lagoon
Belg	Belgium	Madag	Madagascar	Sen	Senegal	L	Lake
Bol	Bolivia	Malay	Malaysia	S Africa	South Africa	Mt(s)	Mountain(s)
Bulg	Bulgaria	Maur	Mauritania	Switz	Switzerland	O	Ocean
Burk	Burkina	Mor	Morocco	Tanz	Tanzania	P	Pass
Camb	Cambodia	Mozam	Mozambique	Thai	Thailand	Pen	Peninsula
Can	Canada	Neth	Netherlands	Turk	Turkey	Plat	Plateau
CAR	Central African Republic	NZ	New Zealand	USA	United States of America	Pt	Point
Den	Denmark	Nic	Nicaragaua			Res	Reservoir
Dom Rep	Dominican Republic	N Ire	Northern Ireland	Urug	Uruguay	R	River
El Sal	El Salvador	Nig	Nigeria	Ven	Venezuela	S	Sea
Eng	England	Nor	Norway	Viet	Vietnam	Sd	Sound
Eq Guinea	Equatorial Guinea	Pak	Pakistan	Yugos	Yugoslavia	Str	Strait
Eth	Ethiopia	PNG	Papua New Guinea	Zim	Zimbabwe	V	Valley
Fin	Finland	Par	Paraguay				
Germ	Germany	Phil	Philippines				

A

57B2 **Aachen** Germany
46C1 **Aalst** Belg
38K6 **Äänekoski** Fin
47C1 **Aarau** Switz
47B1 **Aare** *R* Switz
72A3 **Aba** China
97C4 **Aba** Nig
99D2 **Aba** Zaïre
91A3 **Abādān** Iran
90B3 **Abādeh** Iran
96B1 **Abadla** Alg
35B1 **Abaeté** Brazil
35B1 **Abaeté** *R* Brazil
31B2 **Abaetetuba** Brazil
72D1 **Abagnar Qi** China
97C4 **Abakaliki** Nig
63B2 **Abakan** Russian Fed
97C3 **Abala** Niger
96C2 **Abalessa** Alg
32C6 **Abancay** Peru
90B3 **Abarqū** Iran
74E2 **Abashiri** Japan
74E2 **Abashiri-wan** *B* Japan
71F4 **Abau** PNG
99D2 **Abaya** *L* Eth
99D1 **Abbai** *R* Eth
99E1 **Abbe** *L* Eth
48C1 **Abbeville** France
19B4 **Abbeville** Louisiana, USA
17B1 **Abbeville** S Carolina, USA
45B2 **Abbeyfeale** Irish Rep
47C2 **Abbiategrasso** Italy
20B1 **Abbotsford** Can
84C2 **Abbottabad** Pak
61H3 **Abdulino** Russian Fed
98C1 **Abéché** Chad
39F7 **Åbenrå** Den
97C4 **Abeokuta** Nig
99D2 **Abera** Eth
43B3 **Aberaeron** Wales
15C3 **Aberdeen** Maryland, USA
100B4 **Aberdeen** S Africa
44C3 **Aberdeen** Scot
8D2 **Aberdeen** S Dakota, USA
8A2 **Aberdeen** Washington, USA
4J3 **Aberdeen L** Can
44C3 **Aberfeldy** Scot
43C4 **Abergavenny** Wales
43B3 **Aberystwyth** Wales
81C4 **Abhā** S Arabia
90A2 **Abhar** Iran
97B4 **Abidjan** Ivory Coast
18A2 **Abilene** Kansas, USA
9D3 **Abilene** Texas, USA
43D4 **Abingdon** Eng
7B4 **Abitibi** *R* Can
7C5 **Abitibi,L** Can
61F5 **Abkhazskaya Respublika**, Georgia
84C2 **Abohar** India
97C4 **Abomey** Benin
98B2 **Abong Mbang** Cam
79A4 **Aborlan** Phil
98B1 **Abou Deïa** Chad
91A4 **Abqaiq** S Arabia
50A2 **Abrantes** Port
95C2 **Abri** Sudan
106A3 **Abrolhos** *Is* Aust
8B2 **Absaroka Range** *Mts* USA
91B5 **Abū al Abyad** *I* UAE
91A4 **Abū 'Ali** *I* S Arabia
91B5 **Abū Dhabi** UAE
95C3 **Abu Hamed** Sudan
97C4 **Abuja** Nig
33D5 **Abunã** Brazil
32D6 **Abunã** *R* Bol
93D3 **Abú Sukhayr** Iraq
111B2 **Abut Head** *C* NZ
95C3 **Abu 'Urug** *Well* Sudan
99D1 **Abuye Meda** *Mt* Eth
99C1 **Abu Zabad** Sudan
99D2 **Abwong** Sudan
56B1 **Åby** Den
94B3 **Aby 'Aweigîla** *Well* Egypt
99C2 **Abyei** Sudan
24B2 **Acambaro** Mexico
24B2 **Acaponeta** Mexico
24B3 **Acapulco** Mexico
31D2 **Acaraú** Brazil
32D2 **Acarigua** Ven
24C3 **Acatlán** Mexico
23B2 **Acatzingo** Mexico
97B4 **Accra** Ghana
85D4 **Achalpur** India
29B4 **Achao** Chile
47D1 **Achensee** *L* Austria
46E2 **Achern** Germany
41A3 **Achill** *I* Irish Rep
63B2 **Achinsk** Russian Fed
53C3 **Acireale** Italy
26C2 **Acklins** *I* Caribbean S
32C6 **Acobamba** Peru
29B2 **Aconcagua** *Mt* Chile
31D3 **Acopiara** Brazil
88B4 **Açores** *Is* Atlantic O
A Coruña = La Coruña
47C2 **Acqui** Italy
108A2 **Acraman,L** Aust
Acre = 'Akko
32C5 **Acre** State, Brazil
22C3 **Acton** USA
23B1 **Actopan** Mexico
19A3 **Ada** USA
50B1 **Adaja** *R* Spain
91C5 **Adam** Oman
35A2 **Adamantina** Brazil
98B2 **Adamaoua** Region, Nig/Cam
47D1 **Adamello** *Mt* Italy
16C1 **Adams** USA
87B3 **Adam's Bridge** India/Sri Lanka
13D2 **Adams L** Can
8A2 **Adams,Mt** USA
87C3 **Adam's Peak** *Mt* Sri Lanka
81C4 **'Adan** Yemen
92C2 **Adana** Turk
60D5 **Adapazari** Turk
112B7 **Adare,C** Ant
108B1 **Adavale** Aust
47C2 **Adda** *R* Italy
91A4 **Ad Dahna'** Region, S Arabia
96A2 **Ad Dakhla** Mor
81C4 **Ad Dālī'** Yemen
91B4 **Ad Damman** S Arabia
91A4 **Ad Dibdibah** Region, S Arabia
91A5 **Ad Dilam** S Arabia
91A5 **Ad Dir'iyah** S Arabia
93D3 **Ad Dīwanīyah** Iraq
93D3 **Ad Duwayd** S Arabia
106C4 **Adelaide** Aust
4J3 **Adelaide Pen** Can
22D3 **Adelanto** USA
Aden = 'Adan
81C4 **Aden,G of** Yemen/Somalia
97C3 **Aderbissinat** Niger
94C2 **Adhra** Syria
71E4 **Adi** *I* Indon
52B1 **Adige** *R* Italy
99D1 **Adigrat** Eth
85D5 **Adilābād** India
20B2 **Adin** USA
15D2 **Adirondack Mts** USA
99D2 **Adīs Abeba** Eth
95C3 **Adi Ugai** Eritrea
93C2 **Adıyaman** Turk
54C1 **Adjud** Rom
4E4 **Admiralty I** USA
6B2 **Admiralty Inlet** *B* Can
87B1 **Ādoni** India
48B3 **Adour** *R* France
96A2 **Adrar** Region, Maur
96C2 **Adrar** *Mts* Alg
96A2 **Adrar Soutouf** Region, Mor
98C1 **Adré** Chad
95A2 **Adri** Libya
47E2 **Adria** Italy

14B2 **Adrian** Michigan, USA
52B2 **Adriatic S** S Europe
99D1 **Ādwa** Eth
97B4 **Adzopé** Ivory Coast
55B3 **Aegean** *S* Greece
80E2 **Afghanistan** Republic, Asia
99E2 **Afgooye** Somalia
97C4 **Afikpo** Nig
38G6 **Åfjord** Nor
96C1 **Aflou** Alg
99E2 **Afmadu** Somalia
97A3 **Afollé** Region, Maur
94B2 **Afula** Israel
92B2 **Afyon** Turk
95A3 **Agadem** Niger
97C3 **Agadez** Niger
96B1 **Agadir** Mor
85D4 **Agar** India
86C2 **Agartala** India
20B1 **Agassiz** Can
97B4 **Agboville** Ivory Coast
93E1 **Agdam** Azerbaijan
75B1 **Agematsu** Japan
48C3 **Agen** France
90A3 **Agha Jārī** Iran
96A2 **Aghwinit** *Well* Mor
47D2 **Agno** *R* Italy
47E1 **Agordo** Italy
48C3 **Agout** *R* France
85D3 **Āgra** India
93D2 **Ağri** Turk
53C2 **Agri** *R* Italy
53B3 **Agrigento** Italy
55B3 **Agrínion** Greece
34A3 **Agrio** *R* Chile
53B2 **Agropoli** Italy
61H2 **Agryz** Russian Fed
6E3 **Agto** Greenland
27D3 **Aguadilla** Puerto Rico
24B1 **Agua Prieta** Mexico
24B2 **Aguascalientes** Mexico
23A1 **Aguascalientes** State, Mexico
35C1 **Aguas Formosas** Brazil
50A1 **Agueda** Port
96C3 **Aguelhok** Mali
50B2 **Aguilas** Spain
23A2 **Aguililla** Mexico
100B4 **Agulhas,C** S Africa
79C4 **Agusan** *R* Phil
Ahaggar = Hoggar
93C2 **Ahar** Iran
110B1 **Ahipara B** NZ
85C4 **Ahmadābād** India
87A1 **Ahmadnagar** India
99E2 **Ahmar** *Mts* Eth
46D1 **Ahr** *R* Germany
46D1 **Ahrgebirge** Region, Germany
23A1 **Ahuacatlán** Mexico
23A1 **Ahualulco** Mexico
39G7 **Åhus** Sweden
90B2 **Ahuvān** Iran
90A3 **Ahvāz** Iran
26A4 **Aiajuela** Costa Rica
47B1 **Aigle** Switz
47B2 **Aiguille d'Arves** *Mt* France
47B2 **Aiguille de la Grand Sassière** *Mt* France
75B1 **Aikawa** Japan
17B1 **Aiken** USA
73A5 **Ailao Shan** *Upland* China
35C1 **Aimorés** Brazil
96B1 **Ain Beni Mathar** Mor
95B2 **Ain Dalla** *Well* Egypt
51C2 **Aïn el Hadjel** Alg
95A3 **Aïn Galakka** Chad
96B1 **Aïn Sefra** Alg
92B4 **'Ain Sukhna** Egypt
75A2 **Aioi** Japan
96B2 **Aioun Abd el Malek** *Well* Maur
97B3 **Aïoun El Atrouss** Maur
30C2 **Aiquile** Bol
97C3 **Aïr** *Desert Region* Niger
13E2 **Airdrie** Can
46B1 **Aire** France
42D3 **Aire** *R* Eng
46C2 **Aire** *R* France
6C3 **Airforce I** Can
47C1 **Airolo** Switz
4E3 **Aishihik** Can
12G2 **Aishihik L** Can
46B2 **Aisne** Department, France
49C2 **Aisne** *R* France
71F4 **Aitape** PNG
58D1 **Aiviekste** *R* Latvia
72B2 **Aixa Zuogi** China
49D3 **Aix-en-Provence** France
47A2 **Aix-les-Bains** France
86B2 **Aiyar Res** India
55B3 **Aíyion** Greece
55B3 **Aíyna** *I* Greece
86C2 **Aīzawl** India
100A3 **Aizeb** *R* Namibia
74E3 **Aizu-Wakamatsu** Japan
52A2 **Ajaccio** Corse
23B2 **Ajalpan** Mexico
95B1 **Ajdābiyā** Libya
74E2 **Ajigasawa** Japan
94B2 **Ajlūn** Jordan
91C4 **Ajman** UAE
85C3 **Ajmer** India
9B3 **Ajo** USA
23A2 **Ajuchitan** Mexico
55C3 **Ak** *R* Turk
75B1 **Akaishi-sanchi** *Mts* Japan
87B1 **Akalkot** India
111B2 **Akaroa** NZ
75A2 **Akashi** Japan
61J3 **Akbulak** Russian Fed
93C2 **Akçakale** Turk
96A2 **Akchar** *Watercourse* Maur
55C3 **Akdağ** *Mt* Turk
98C2 **Aketi** Zaïre
93D1 **Akhalkalaki** Georgia
93D1 **Akhalsikhe** Georgia
55B3 **Akharnái** Greece
12D3 **Akhiok** USA
92A2 **Akhisar** Turk
58D1 **Akhiste** Latvia
95C2 **Akhmîm** Egypt
61G4 **Akhtubinsk** Russian Fed
60D4 **Akhtyrka** Ukraine
75A2 **Aki** Japan
7B4 **Akimiski I** Can
74E3 **Akita** Japan
96A3 **Akjoujt** Maur
94B2 **'Akko** Israel
4E3 **Aklavik** USA
97B3 **Aklé Aouana** *Desert Region* Maur
99D2 **Akobo** Sudan
99D2 **Akobo** *R* Sudan
84B1 **Akoha** Afghan
85D4 **Akola** India
85D4 **Akot** India
6D3 **Akpatok I** Can
55B3 **Ákra Kafirévs** *C* Greece
55B3 **Ákra Maléa** *C* Greece
38A2 **Akranes** Iceland
55C3 **Ákra Sídheros** *C* Greece
55B3 **Ákra Spátha** *C* Greece
55B3 **Ákra Taínaron** *C* Greece
10B2 **Akron** USA
94A1 **Akrotiri B** Cyprus
84D1 **Aksai Chin** *Mts* China
92B2 **Aksaray** Turk
61H3 **Aksay** Kazakhstan
84D1 **Aksayquin Hu** *L* China
92B2 **Akşehir** Turk
92B2 **Akseki** Turk
63D2 **Aksenovo Zilovskoye** Russian Fed
68D1 **Aksha** Russian Fed
82C1 **Aksu** China
61H5 **Aktau** Kazakhstan
65J5 **Aktogay** Kazakhstan
61J4 **Aktumsyk** Kazakhstan
65G4 **Aktyubinsk** Kazakhstan
38B1 **Akureyri** Iceland
Akyab = Sittwe
65K5 **Akzhal** Kazakhstan
11B3 **Alabama** State, USA
11B3 **Alabama** *R* USA
17A1 **Alabaster** USA
92C2 **Ala Dağlari** *Mts* Turk
61F5 **Alagir** Russian Fed
47B2 **Alagna** Italy
31D3 **Alagoas** State, Brazil
31D4 **Alagoinhas** Brazil
51B1 **Alagón** Spain
93E4 **Al Ahmadi** Kuwait
25D3 **Alajuela** Costa Rica
12B2 **Alakanuk** USA
38L5 **Alakurtti** Russian Fed
93E3 **Al Amārah** Iraq
21A2 **Alameda** USA
23B1 **Alamo** Mexico
9C3 **Alamogordo** USA
9C3 **Alamosa** USA
39H6 **Åland** *I* Fin
92B2 **Alanya** Turk
17B1 **Alapaha** *R* USA
65H4 **Alapayevsk** Russian Fed
92A2 **Alaşehir** Turk
68C3 **Ala Shan** *Mts* China
4C3 **Alaska** State, USA
4D4 **Alaska,G of** USA
12C3 **Alaska Pen** USA
4C3 **Alaska Range** *Mts* USA
52A2 **Alassio** Italy
12D1 **Alatna** *R* USA
61G3 **Alatyr** Russian Fed
108B2 **Alawoona** Aust
91C5 **Al'Ayn** UAE
82B2 **Alayskiy Khrebet** *Mts* Tajikistan
49D3 **Alba** Italy
92C2 **Al Bāb** Syria
51B2 **Albacete** Spain
50A1 **Alba de Tormes** Spain
93D2 **Al Badi** Iraq
54B1 **Alba Iulia** Rom
54A2 **Albania** Republic, Europe
106A4 **Albany** Aust
17B1 **Albany** Georgia, USA
15D2 **Albany** New York, USA
8A2 **Albany** Oregon, USA
7B4 **Albany** *R* Can
34B2 **Albardón** Arg
91C5 **Al Batinah** Region, Oman
71F5 **Albatross B** Aust
95B1 **Al Baydā** Libya
11C3 **Albemarle Sd** USA
50B1 **Alberche** *R* Spain
108A1 **Alberga** Aust
46B1 **Albert** France
5G4 **Alberta** Province, Can
99D2 **Albert,L** Uganda/Zaïre
10A2 **Albert Lea** USA
99D2 **Albert Nile** *R* Uganda
49D2 **Albertville** France
48C3 **Albi** France
18B1 **Albia** USA
33G2 **Albina** Suriname
14B2 **Albion** Michigan, USA
15C2 **Albion** New York, USA
92C4 **Al Bi'r** S Arabia
91A5 **Al Biyadh** Region, S Arabia
50B2 **Alborán** *I* Spain
39G7 **Ålborg** Den
93D3 **Al Bū Kamāl** Syria
47C1 **Albula** *R* Switz
9C3 **Albuquerque** USA
91C5 **Al Buraymi** Oman
95A1 **Al Burayqah** Libya
95B1 **Al Burdī** Libya
107D4 **Albury** Aust
93E3 **Al Buşayyah** Iraq
50B1 **Alcalá de Henares** Spain
53B3 **Alcamo** Italy
51B1 **Alcaniz** Spain
31C2 **Alcântara** Brazil
50B2 **Alcaraz** Spain
50B2 **Alcázar de San Juan** Spain
51B2 **Alcira** Spain
35D1 **Alcobaça** Brazil
50B1 **Alcolea de Pinar** Spain
51B2 **Alcoy** Spain
51C2 **Alcudia** Spain
89J8 **Aldabra** *Is* Indian O
63E2 **Aldan** Russian Fed
63E2 **Aldanskoye Nagor'ye** *Upland* Russian Fed
43E3 **Aldeburgh** Eng
48B2 **Alderney** *I* UK
43D4 **Aldershot** Eng
97A3 **Aleg** Maur
30E4 **Alegrete** Brazil
34C2 **Alejandro Roca** Arg
30H6 **Alejandro Selkirk** *I* Chile
63G2 **Aleksandrovsk Sakhalinskiy** Russian Fed
65J4 **Alekseyevka** Kazakhstan
60E3 **Aleksin** Russian Fed
58B1 **Älem** Sweden
35C2 **Além Paraíba** Brazil
49C2 **Alençon** France
21C4 **Alenuihaha Chan** Hawaiian Is
Aleppo = Ḩalab
6D1 **Alert** Can
49C3 **Alès** France
52A2 **Alessandria** Italy
64B3 **Ålesund** Nor
12C3 **Aleutian Range** *Mts* USA
4E4 **Alexander Arch** USA
100A3 **Alexander Bay** S Africa
17A1 **Alexander City** USA
112C3 **Alexander I** Ant
111A3 **Alexandra** NZ
29G8 **Alexandra,C** South Georgia
6C2 **Alexandra Fjord** Can
95B1 **Alexandria** Egypt
11A3 **Alexandria** Louisiana, USA
10A2 **Alexandria** Minnesota, USA
10C3 **Alexandria** Virginia, USA
55C2 **Alexandroúpolis** Greece
13C2 **Alexis Creek** Can
94B2 **Aley** Leb
65K4 **Aleysk** Russian Fed
93D3 **Al Fallūjah** Iraq
51B1 **Alfaro** Spain
54C2 **Alfatar** Bulg
93E3 **Al Fāw** Iraq
35B2 **Alfensas** Brazil
55B3 **Alfiós** *R* Greece
47D2 **Alfonsine** Italy
35C2 **Alfonzo Cláudio** Brazil
35C2 **Alfredo Chaves** Brazil
61J4 **Alga** Kazakhstan
34B3 **Algarrobo del Águila** Arg
50A2 **Algeciras** Spain
96C1 **Alger** Alg
96B2 **Algeria** Republic, Africa
53A2 **Alghero** Sardegna
Algiers = Alger
15C1 **Algonquin Park** Can
91C5 **Al Hadd** Oman
93D3 **Al Hadithah** Iraq
92C3 **Al Hadithah** S Arabia
93D2 **Al Haḑr** Iraq

91C5 **Al Hajar al Gharbī** *Mts* Oman
91C5 **Al Hajar ash Sharqī** *Mts* Oman
93C3 **Al Hamad** *Desert Region* Jordan/ S Arabia
93E4 **Al Haniyah** *Desert Region* Iraq
91A5 **Al Harīq** S Arabia
93C3 **Al Harrah** *Desert Region* S Arabia
95A2 **Al Harūj al Aswad** *Upland* Libya
91A4 **Al Hasa** Region, S Arabia
93D2 **Al Hasakah** Syria
93C4 **Al Hawjā'** S Arabia
93E3 **Al Hayy** Iraq
94C2 **Al Hījānah** Syria
93D3 **Al Hillah** Iraq
91A5 **Al Hillah** S Arabia
96B1 **Al Hoceima** Mor
91A4 **Al Hufūf** S Arabia
91B5 **Al Humrah** Region, UAE
91C5 **Al Huwatsah** Oman
90A2 **Alīābad** Iran
91C4 **Aliabad** Iran
55B2 **Aliákmon** *R* Greece
93E3 **Alī al Gharbī** Iraq
87A1 **Alībāg** India
51B2 **Alicante** Spain
9D4 **Alice** USA
106C3 **Alice Springs** Aust
53B3 **Alicudi** *I* Italy
84D3 **Aligarh** India
90A3 **Aligūdarz** Iran
84B2 **Ali-Khel** Afghan
55C3 **Alimniá** *I* Greece
86B1 **Alīpur Duār** India
14B2 **Aliquippa** USA
22B2 **Alişal** USA
93C3 **Al' Īsawiyah** S Arabia
100B4 **Aliwal North** S Africa
95B2 **Al Jaghbūb** Libya
93D3 **Al Jālamīd** S Arabia
95B2 **Al Jawf** Libya
93C4 **Al Jawf** S Arabia
93D2 **Al Jazīrah** *Desert Region* Syria/Iraq
50A2 **Aljezur** Port
91A4 **Al Jubayl** S Arabia
91C5 **Al Kāmil** Oman
93D2 **Al Khābūr** *R* Syria
91C5 **Al Khābūrah** Oman
93D3 **Al Khālis** Iraq
91C4 **Al Khasab** Oman
91B4 **Al Khawr** Qatar
95A1 **Al Khums** Libya
91B5 **Al Kidan** Region, S Arabia
94C2 **Al Kiswah** Syria
56A2 **Alkmaar** Neth
95B2 **Al Kufrah Oasis** Libya
93E3 **Al Kūt** Iraq
92C2 **Al Lādhiqīyah** Syria
86A1 **Allahābād** India
94C2 **Al Lajāh** *Mt* Syria
12D1 **Allakaket** USA
76B2 **Allanmyo** Burma
95C2 **'Allaqi** *Watercourse* Egypt
17B1 **Allatoona L** USA
15C2 **Allegheny** *R* USA
10C3 **Allegheny Mts** USA
17B1 **Allendale** USA
111A3 **Allen,Mt** NZ
15C2 **Allentown** USA
87B3 **Alleppey** India
49C2 **Aller** *R* France
47D1 **Allgäu** *Mts* Germany
8C2 **Alliance** USA
81C3 **Al Līth** S Arabia
91B5 **Al Liwā** Region, UAE
109D1 **Allora** Aust
14B2 **Alma** Michigan, USA
82B1 **Alma Ata** Kazakhstan
50A2 **Almada** Port
Al Madinah = Medina
71F2 **Almagan** *I* Pacific O
91B4 **Al Manāmah** Bahrain
93D3 **Al Ma'nīyah** Iraq
21A1 **Almanor,L** USA
51B2 **Almansa** Spain
13B1 **Alma Peak** *Mt* Can
91B5 **Al Māriyyah** UAE
95B1 **Al Marj** Libya
Almaty = Alma Ata
93D2 **Al Mawşil** Iraq
50B1 **Almazán** Spain
35C1 **Almenara** Brazil
50B2 **Almeria** Spain
61H3 **Al'met'yevsk** Russian Fed
56C1 **Älmhult** Sweden
93E3 **Al Miqdādīyah** Iraq
112C3 **Almirante Brown** *Base* Ant
34A1 **Almirante Latorre** Chile
55B3 **Almirós** Greece
91A4 **Al Mish'āb** S Arabia
50A2 **Almodôvar** Port
84D3 **Almora** India
91A4 **Al Mubarraz** S Arabia
92C4 **Al Mudawwara** Jordan
91C5 **Al Mudaybi** Oman
91B4 **Al Muharraq** Bahrain
81C4 **Al Mukallā** Yemen
81C4 **Al Mukhā** Yemen
93D3 **Al Musayyib** Iraq
44B3 **Alness** Scot
93E3 **Al Nu'mānīyah** Iraq
42D2 **Alnwick** Eng
71D4 **Alor** *I* Indon
77C4 **Alor Setar** Malay
Alost = Aalst
107E2 **Alotau** PNG
106B3 **Aloysius,Mt** Aust
34C3 **Alpachiri** Arg
14B1 **Alpena** USA
47B2 **Alpes du Valais** *Mts* Switz
52B1 **Alpi Dolomitiche** *Mts* Italy
47B2 **Alpi Graie** *Mts* Italy
9C3 **Alpine** Texas, USA
47C1 **Alpi Orobie** *Mts* Italy
47B2 **Alpi Pennine** *Mts* Italy
47C1 **Alpi Retiche** *Mts* Switz
47D1 **Alpi Venoste** *Mts* Italy
52A1 **Alps** *Mts* Europe
95A1 **Al Qaddāhiyah** Libya
94C1 **Al Qadmūs** Syria
93D3 **Al Qā'im** Iraq
93C4 **Al Qalībah** S Arabia
93D2 **Al Qāmishlī** Syria
95A1 **Al Qaryah Ash Sharqiyah** Libya
92C3 **Al Qaryatayn** Syria
91A4 **Al Qātif** S Arabia
95A2 **Al Qatrūn** Libya
91A4 **Al Qayşāmah** S Arabia
94C2 **Al Quatayfah** Syria
50A2 **Alqueva** *R* Port
92C3 **Al Qunayţirah** Syria
81C4 **Al Qunfidhah** S Arabia
93E3 **Al Qurnah** Iraq
94C1 **Al Quşayr** Syria
92C3 **Al Qutayfah** Syria
56B1 **Als** *I* Den
49D2 **Alsace** Region, France
57B2 **Alsfeld** Germany
42C2 **Alston** Eng
38J5 **Alta** Nor
29D2 **Alta Gracia** Arg
27D5 **Altagracia de Orituco** Ven
68A2 **Altai** *Mts* Mongolia
17B1 **Altamaha** *R* USA
33G4 **Altamira** Brazil
23B1 **Altamira** Mexico
53C2 **Altamura** Italy
68C1 **Altanbulag** Mongolia
71F4 **Altape** PNG
24B2 **Altata** Mexico
63A3 **Altay** China
63B3 **Altay** Mongolia
63A2 **Altay** *Mts* Russian Fed
47C1 **Altdorf** Switz
46D1 **Altenkirchen** Germany
34B3 **Altiplanicie del Payún** *Plat* Arg
47B1 **Altkirch** France
101C2 **Alto Molócue** Mozam
10A3 **Alton** USA
15C2 **Altoona** USA
34B2 **Alto Pencoso** *Mts* Arg
35A1 **Alto Sucuriú** Brazil
23B2 **Altotonga** Mexico
23A2 **Altoyac de Alvarez** Mexico
82C2 **Altun Shan** *Mts* China
20B2 **Alturas** USA
9D3 **Altus** USA
91B5 **Al'Ubaylah** S Arabia
93C4 **Al Urayq** *Desert Region* S Arabia
91B5 **Al'Uruq al Mu'taridah** Region, S Arabia
9D2 **Alva** USA
23B2 **Alvarado** Mexico
19A3 **Alvarado** USA
39G6 **Älvdalen** Sweden
19A4 **Alvin** USA
38J5 **Alvsbyn** Sweden
80B3 **Al Wajh** S Arabia
85D3 **Alwar** India
93D3 **Al Widyān** *Desert Region* Iraq/S Arabia
72A2 **Alxa Yougi** China
93E2 **Alyat** Azerbaijan
39J8 **Alytus** Lithuania
46E2 **Alzey** Germany
23B2 **Amacuzac** *R* Mexico
99D2 **Amadi** Sudan
93D2 **Amādīyah** Iraq
6C3 **Amadjuak L** Can
74B4 **Amakusa-shotō** *I* Japan
39G7 **Åmål** Sweden
63D2 **Amalat** *R* Russian Fed
55B3 **Amaliás** Greece
85D4 **Amalner** India
69E4 **Amami** *I* Japan
69E4 **Amami gunto** *Arch* Japan
100C4 **Amanzimtoti** S Africa
33G3 **Amapá** Brazil
33G3 **Amapá** State, Brazil
9C3 **Amarillo** USA
60E5 **Amasya** Turk
23A1 **Amatitan** Mexico
Amazonas = Solimões
32D4 **Amazonas** State, Brazil
28C3 **Amazonas** *R* Brazil
84D2 **Ambāla** India
87C3 **Ambalangoda** Sri Lanka
101D3 **Ambalavao** Madag
98B2 **Ambam** Cam
101D2 **Ambanja** Madag
1C7 **Ambarchik** Russian Fed
32B4 **Ambato** Ecuador
101D2 **Ambato-Boeny** Madag
101D2 **Ambatolampy** Madag
101D2 **Ambatondrazaka** Madag
57C3 **Amberg** Germany
25D3 **Ambergris Cay** *I* Belize
86A2 **Ambikāpur** India
101D2 **Ambilobe** Madag
101D3 **Amboasary** Madag
101D2 **Ambodifototra** Madag
101D3 **Ambohimahasoa** Madag
71D4 **Ambon** Indon
101D3 **Ambositra** Madag
101D3 **Ambovombe** Madag
98B3 **Ambriz** Angola
98C1 **Am Dam** Chad
64H3 **Amderma** Russian Fed
24B2 **Ameca** Mexico
23B2 **Amecacameca** Mexico
34C2 **Ameghino** Arg
56B2 **Ameland** *I* Neth
16C2 **Amenia** USA
112B10 **American Highland** *Upland* Ant
105H4 **American Samoa** *Is* Pacific O
17B1 **Americus** USA
101G1 **Amersfoort** S Africa
112C10 **Amery Ice Shelf** Ant
55B3 **Amfilokhía** Greece
55B3 **Amfissa** Greece
63F1 **Amga** Russian Fed
63F1 **Amgal** *R* Russian Fed
69F2 **Amgu** Russian Fed
69F1 **Amgun'** *R* Russian Fed
99D1 **Amhara** *Region* Eth
7D5 **Amherst** Can
16C1 **Amherst** Massachusetts, USA
Amherst = Kyaikkami
87B2 **Amhūr** India
48C2 **Amiens** France
75B1 **Amino** Japan
94B1 **Amioune** Leb
89K8 **Amirante Is** Indian O
86B1 **Amlekhgan** Nepal
92C3 **Amman** Jordan
38K6 **Ämmänsaario** Fin
56B2 **Ammersfoort** Neth
90B2 **Amol** Iran
55C3 **Amorgós** *I* Greece
7C5 **Amos** Can
Amoy = Xiamen
101D3 **Ampanihy** Madag
35B2 **Amparo** Brazil
51C1 **Amposta** Spain
85D4 **Amrāvati** India
85C4 **Amreli** India
84C2 **Amritsar** India
56A2 **Amsterdam** Neth
101H1 **Amsterdam** S Africa
15D2 **Amsterdam** USA
98C1 **Am Timan** Chad
88L3 **Amu Darya** *R* Uzbekistan
6A2 **Amund Ringes I** Can
4F2 **Amundsen G** Can
112B4 **Amundsen S** Ant
80E **Amundsen-Scott** *Base* Ant
78D3 **Amuntai** Indon
63E2 **Amur** *R* Russian Fed
33E2 **Anaco** Ven
8B2 **Anaconda** USA
20B1 **Anacortes** USA
55C3 **Anáfi** *I* Greece
93D3 **'Ānah** Iraq
21B3 **Anaheim** USA
87B2 **Anaimalai Hills** India
83C4 **Anakapalle** India
12E1 **Anaktuvuk P** USA
101D2 **Analalaya** Madag
92B2 **Anamur** Turk
75A2 **Anan** Japan
87B2 **Anantapur** India
84D2 **Anantnag** India
31B5 **Anápolis** Brazil
90C3 **Anār** Iran
90B3 **Anārak** Iran
71F2 **Anatahan** *I* Pacific O
30D4 **Añatuya** Arg
74B3 **Anbyŏn** N Korea
22C4 **Ancapa Is** USA
4D3 **Anchorage** USA
30C2 **Ancohuma** *Mt* Bol
32B6 **Ancón** Peru
52B2 **Ancona** Italy
16C1 **Ancram** USA
29B4 **Ancud** Chile
34A3 **Andacollo** Arg
108A1 **Andado** Aust
32C6 **Andahuaylas** Peru
38F6 **Andalsnes** Nor
50A2 **Andalucia** Region, Spain
17A1 **Andalusia** USA

33F6 **Arinos** *R* Brazil
23A2 **Ario de Rosales** Mexico
27L1 **Aripo,Mt** Trinidad
33E5 **Aripuana** Brazil
33E5 **Aripuaná** *R* Brazil
44B3 **Arisaig** Scot
87B2 **Ariskere** India
13B2 **Aristazabal I** Can
34B3 **Arizona** Arg
9B3 **Arizona** State, USA
39G7 **Årjäng** Sweden
61F3 **Arkadak** Russian Fed
19B3 **Arkadelphia** USA
65H4 **Arkaly** Kazakhstan
11A3 **Arkansas** State, USA
11A3 **Arkansas** *R* USA
18A2 **Arkansas City** USA
64F3 **Arkhangel'sk** Russian Fed
41B3 **Arklow** Irish Rep
47D1 **Arlberg P** Austria
49C3 **Arles** France
19A3 **Arlington** Texas, USA
15C3 **Arlington** Virginia, USA
20B1 **Arlington** Washington, USA
97C3 **Arlit** Niger
57B3 **Arlon** Belg
Armageddon = Megiddo
45C1 **Armagh** County, N Ire
45C1 **Armagh** N Ire
61F5 **Armavir** Russian Fed
23A2 **Armena** Mexico
32B3 **Armenia** Colombia
65F5 **Armenia** Republic, Europe
107E4 **Armidale** Aust
13D2 **Armstrong** Can
7C3 **Arnaud** *R* Can
92B2 **Arnauti** *C* Cyprus
56B2 **Arnhem** Neth
106C2 **Arnhem,C** Aust
106C2 **Arnhem Land** Aust
22B1 **Arnold** USA
15C1 **Arnprior** Can
46E1 **Arnsberg** Germany
100A3 **Aroab** Namibia
47C2 **Arona** Italy
12B2 **Aropuk L** USA
52A1 **Arosa** Switz
97A3 **Arquipélago dos Bijagós** *Arch* Guinea-Bissau
93D3 **Ar Ramādī** Iraq
42B2 **Arran** *I* Scot
93C2 **Ar Raqqah** Syria
95A2 **Ar Rāqūbah** Libya
49C1 **Arras** France
96A2 **Arrecife** Canary Is
34C2 **Arrecifes** Arg
23A1 **Arriaga** Mexico
93E3 **Ar Rifā't** Iraq
93E3 **Ar Rihāb** *Desert Region* Iraq
91A5 **Ar Riyāḍ** S Arabia
44B3 **Arrochar** Scot
111A2 **Arrowtown** NZ
23B1 **Arroyo Seco** Mexico
91B4 **Ar Ru'ays** Qatar
91C5 **Ar Rustaq** Oman
93D3 **Ar Rutbah** Iraq
47D2 **Arsiero** Italy
49D2 **Arsizio** Italy
61G2 **Arsk** Russian Fed
55B3 **Árta** Greece
23A2 **Arteaga** Mexico
63B2 **Artemovsk** Russian Fed
63D2 **Artemovskiy** Russian Fed
9C3 **Artesia** USA
111B2 **Arthurs P** NZ
112C2 **Artigas** *Base* Ant
29E2 **Artigas** Urug
4H3 **Artillery L** Can
48C1 **Artois** Region, France
112C2 **Arturo Prat** *Base* Ant
93D1 **Artvin** Turk
99D2 **Aru** Zaïre
33G6 **Aruanã** Brazil
27C4 **Aruba** *I* Caribbean S
86B1 **Arun** *R* Nepal
86C1 **Arunāchal Pradesh** Union Territory, India
87B3 **Aruppukkottai** India
99D3 **Arusha** Tanz
98C2 **Aruwimi** *R* Zaïre
68C2 **Arvayheer** Mongolia
47B2 **Arve** *R* France
7C5 **Arvida** Can
38H5 **Arvidsjaur** Sweden
39G7 **Arvika** Sweden
21B2 **Arvin** USA
94B1 **Arwad** *I* Syria
61F2 **Arzamas** Russian Fed
84C2 **Asadabad** Afghan
75A2 **Asahi** *R* Japan
74E2 **Asahi dake** *Mt* Japan
74E2 **Asahikawa** Japan
86B2 **Asansol** India
95A2 **Asawanwah** *Well* Libya
61K2 **Asbest** Russian Fed
15D2 **Asbury Park** USA
103H5 **Ascension** *I* Atlantic O
57B3 **Aschaffenburg** Germany
56C2 **Aschersleben** Germany
52B2 **Ascoli Piceno** Italy
47C1 **Ascona** Switz
99E1 **Aseb** Eritrea
96C2 **Asedjirad** *Upland* Alg
99D2 **Asela** Eth
38H6 **Åsele** Sweden
54B2 **Asenovgrad** Bulg
46C2 **Asfeld** France
61J2 **Asha** Russian Fed
17B1 **Ashburn** USA
111B2 **Ashburton** NZ
106A3 **Ashburton** *R* Aust
92B3 **Ashdod** Israel
19B3 **Ashdown** USA
11B3 **Asheville** USA
109D1 **Ashford** Aust
43E4 **Ashford** Eng
Ashgabat = Ashkhabad
74D3 **Ashikaga** Japan
75A2 **Ashizuri-misaki** *Pt* Japan
65G6 **Ashkhabad** Turkmenistan
10B3 **Ashland** Kentucky, USA
18A1 **Ashland** Nebraska, USA
14B2 **Ashland** Ohio, USA
8A2 **Ashland** Oregon, USA
109C1 **Ashley** Aust
16B2 **Ashokan Res** USA
94B3 **Ashqelon** Israel
93D3 **Ash Shabakh** Iraq
91C4 **Ash Sha'm** UAE
93D2 **Ash Sharqāt** Iraq
93E3 **Ash Shatrah** Iraq
81C4 **Ash Shihr** Yemen
91A4 **Ash Shumlul** S Arabia
14B2 **Ashtabula** USA
7D4 **Ashuanipi L** Can
92C3 **'Aṣī** *R* Syria
47D2 **Asiago** Italy
53A2 **Asinara** *I* Medit S
65K4 **Asino** Russian Fed
93D2 **Aşkale** Turk
39G7 **Askersund** Sweden
84C1 **Asmar** Afghan
95C3 **Asmera** Eritrea
75A2 **Aso** Japan
99D1 **Asosa** Eth
111A2 **Aspiring,Mt** NZ
93C2 **As Sabkhah** Syria
91A5 **As Salamiyah** S Arabia
92C2 **As Salamīyah** Syria
93D3 **As Salmān** Iraq
86C1 **Assam** State, India
93E3 **As Samāwah** Iraq
91B5 **As Ṣanām** Region, S Arabia
94C2 **As Sanamayn** Syria
56B2 **Assen** Neth
56B1 **Assens** Den
95A1 **As Sidrah** Libya
5H5 **Assiniboia** Can
5G4 **Assiniboine,Mt** Can
30F3 **Assis** Brazil
93C3 **As Sukhnah** Syria
93E2 **As Sulaymānīyah** Iraq
91A5 **As Summan** Region, S Arabia
99E3 **Assumption** *I* Seychelles
92C3 **As Suwaydā'** Syria
93D3 **As Suwayrah** Iraq
93E2 **Astara** Azerbaijan
52A2 **Asti** Italy
55C3 **Astipálaia** *I* Greece
50A1 **Astorga** Spain
8A2 **Astoria** USA
61G4 **Astrakhan'** Russian Fed
50A1 **Asturias** Region, Spain
30E4 **Asunción** Par
99D2 **Aswa** *R* Uganda
80B3 **Aswân** Egypt
95C2 **Aswân High Dam** Egypt
95C2 **Asyût** Egypt
92C3 **As Zilaf** Syria
97C4 **Atakpamé** Togo
71D4 **Atambua** Indon
6E3 **Atangmik** Greenland
96A2 **Atar** Maur
65J5 **Atasu** Kazakhstan
95C3 **Atatisk Baraji** *Res* Turkmenistan
95C3 **Atbara** Sudan
65H4 **Atbasar** Kazakhstan
11A4 **Atchafalaya B** USA
10A3 **Atchison** USA
16B3 **Atco** USA
23A1 **Atenguillo** Mexico
52B2 **Atessa** Italy
46B1 **Ath** Belg
13E2 **Athabasca** Can
5G4 **Athabasca** *R* Can
5H4 **Athabasca L** Can
45B2 **Athenry** Irish Rep
Athens = Athínai
11B3 **Athens** Georgia, USA
14B3 **Athens** Ohio, USA
19A3 **Athens** Texas, USA
55B3 **Athínai** Greece
41B3 **Athlone** Irish Rep
16C1 **Athol** USA
55B2 **Áthos** *Mt* Greece
45C2 **Athy** Irish Rep
98B1 **Ati** Chad
7A5 **Atikoken** Can
61F3 **Atkarsk** Russian Fed
18B2 **Atkins** USA
23B2 **Atlacomulco** Mexico
11B3 **Atlanta** Georgia, USA
14B2 **Atlanta** Michigan, USA
18A1 **Atlantic** USA
10C3 **Atlantic City** USA
16B2 **Atlantic Highlands** USA
103H8 **Atlantic Indian Basin** Atlantic O
103H7 **Atlantic Indian Ridge** Atlantic O
96C1 **Atlas Saharien** *Mts* Alg
4E4 **Atlin** Can
4E4 **Atlin L** Can
94B2 **'Atlit** Israel
23B2 **Atlixco** Mexico
11B3 **Atmore** USA
101D3 **Atofinandrahana** Madag
12D3 **Atognak I** USA
19A3 **Atoka** USA
23A1 **Atotonilco** Mexico
23B2 **Atoyac** *R* Mexico
32B2 **Atrato** *R* Colombia
91B5 **Attaf** Region, UAE
81C3 **At Tā'if** S Arabia
94C2 **At Tall** Syria
17A1 **Attalla** USA
7B4 **Attauapiskat** Can
7B4 **Attauapiskat** *R* Can
93D3 **At Taysīyah** *Desert Region* S Arabia
14A2 **Attica** Indiana, USA
46C2 **Attigny** France
15D2 **Attleboro** Massachusetts, USA
76D3 **Attopeu** Laos
92C4 **At Tubayq** *Upland* S Arabia
34B3 **Atuel** *R* Arg
39H7 **Atvidaberg** Sweden
22B2 **Atwater** USA
49D3 **Aubagne** France
46C2 **Aube** Department, France
49C3 **Aubenas** France
17A1 **Auburn** Alabama, USA
21A2 **Auburn** California, USA
14A2 **Auburn** Indiana, USA
18A1 **Auburn** Nebraska, USA
15C2 **Auburn** New York, USA
20B1 **Auburn** Washington, USA
48C3 **Auch** France
110B1 **Auckland** NZ
105G6 **Auckland Is** NZ
48C3 **Aude** *R* France
7B4 **Auden** Can
47B1 **Audincourt** France
109C1 **Augathella** Aust
57C3 **Augsburg** Germany
106A4 **Augusta** Aust
11B3 **Augusta** Georgia, USA
18A2 **Augusta** Kansas, USA
10D2 **Augusta** Maine, USA
12D3 **Augustine I** USA
58C2 **Augustów** Pol
106A3 **Augustus,Mt** Aust
46A2 **Aumale** France
85D3 **Auraiya** India
85D5 **Aurangābād** India
96C1 **Aurès** *Mts* Alg
48C3 **Aurillac** France
8C3 **Aurora** Colorado, USA
10B2 **Aurora** Illinois, USA
14B3 **Aurora** Indiana, USA
18B2 **Aurora** Mississippi, USA
100A3 **Aus** Namibia
14B2 **Au Sable** USA
10A2 **Austin** Minnesota, USA
21B2 **Austin** Nevada, USA
9D3 **Austin** Texas, USA
106C3 **Australia** Fed. State/ Monarchy
107D4 **Australian Alps** *Mts* Aust
37E4 **Austria** Federal Republic, Europe
46A1 **Authie** *R* France
24B3 **Autlán** Mexico
49C2 **Autun** France
49C2 **Auvergne** Region, France
49C2 **Auxerre** France
46B1 **Auxi-le-Château** France
49C2 **Avallon** France
22C4 **Avalon** USA
7E5 **Avalon Pen** Can
35B2 **Avaré** Brazil
90D3 **Avaz** Iran
94B3 **Avedat** *Hist Site* Israel
33F4 **Aveíro** Brazil
50A1 **Aveiro** Port
29E2 **Avellaneda** Arg
53B2 **Avellino** Italy
46B1 **Avesnes-sur-Helpe** France

92B3 **Baltīm** Egypt	97B3 **Bani** *R* Mali	33E1 **Barcelona** Ven	31D3 **Barreiros** Brazil
45B3 **Baltimore** Irish Rep	97C3 **Bani Bangou** Niger	107D3 **Barcoo** *R* Aust	107D5 **Barren,C** Aust
10C3 **Baltimore** USA	95A1 **Bani Walid** Libya	34B3 **Barda del Medio** Arg	12D3 **Barren Is** USA
86B1 **Bālurghāt** India	92C2 **Bāniyās** Syria	95A2 **Bardai** Chad	31B6 **Barretos** Brazil
61H4 **Balykshi** Kazakhstan	94B2 **Baniyas** Syria	29C3 **Bardas Blancas** Arg	13E2 **Barrhead** Can
91C4 **Bam** Iran	52C2 **Banja Luka** Bosnia-Herzegovina	86B2 **Barddhamān** India	14C2 **Barrie** Can
98B1 **Bama** Nig		59C3 **Bardejov** Slovakia	13C2 **Barrière** Can
97B3 **Bamako** Mali	78C3 **Banjarmasin** Indon	47C2 **Bardi** Italy	108B2 **Barrier Range** *Mts* Aust
98C2 **Bambari** CAR	97A3 **Banjul** The Gambia	47B2 **Bardonecchia** Italy	107E4 **Barrington,Mt** Aust
17B1 **Bamberg** USA	77B4 **Ban Kantang** Thai	43B3 **Bardsey** *I* Wales	27N2 **Barrouaillie** St Vincent and the Grenadines
57C3 **Bamberg** Germany	76D2 **Ban Khemmarat** Laos	84D3 **Bareilly** India	
98C2 **Bambili** Zaïre		64D2 **Barentsøya** *I* Barents S	4C2 **Barrow** USA
35B2 **Bambui** Brazil	77B4 **Ban Khok Kloi** Thai	64E2 **Barents S** Russian Fed	45C2 **Barrow** *R* Irish Rep
98B2 **Bamenda** Cam	71F5 **Banks I** Aust	95C3 **Barentu** Eritrea	106C3 **Barrow Creek** Aust
13C3 **Bamfield** Can	5E4 **Banks I** British Columbia, Can	86A2 **Bargarh** India	106A3 **Barrow I** Aust
98B2 **Bamingui** *R* CAR	4F2 **Banks I** Northwest Territories, Can	47B2 **Barge** Italy	42C2 **Barrow-in-Furness** Eng
98B2 **Bamingui Bangoran** National Park CAR	20C1 **Banks L** USA	63D2 **Barguzin** Russian Fed	4C2 **Barrow,Pt** USA
84B2 **Bamiyan** Afghan	111B2 **Banks Pen** NZ	63D2 **Barguzin** *R* Russian Fed	6A2 **Barrow Str** Can
91D4 **Bampur** Iran	109C4 **Banks Str** Aust	86B2 **Barhi** India	15C1 **Barry's Bay** Can
91D4 **Bampur** *R* Iran	86B2 **Bankura** India	53C2 **Bari** Italy	87B1 **Barsi** India
98C2 **Banalia** Zaïre	76B2 **Ban Mae Sariang** Thai	51D2 **Barika** Alg	9B3 **Barstow** USA
97B3 **Banamba** Mali	76B2 **Ban Mae Sot** Thai	32C2 **Barinas** Ven	49C2 **Bar-sur-Aube** France
76C3 **Ban Aranyaprathet** Thai	76D3 **Ban Me Thuot** Viet	86B2 **Baripāda** India	33F2 **Bartica** Guyana
76C2 **Ban Ban** Laos	45C1 **Bann** *R* N Ire	85C4 **Bari Sādri** India	92B1 **Bartın** Turk
77C4 **Ban Betong** Thai	77B4 **Ban Na San** Thai	86C2 **Barisal** Bang	107D2 **Bartle Frere,Mt** Aust
45C1 **Banbridge** N Ire	84C2 **Bannu** Pak	78C3 **Barito** *R* Indon	9D3 **Bartlesville** USA
43D1 **Banbury** Eng	34A3 **Baños Maule** Chile	95A2 **Barjuj** *Watercourse* Libya	101C3 **Bartolomeu Dias** Mozam
44C3 **Banchory** Scot	76C2 **Ban Pak Neun** Laos	73A3 **Barkam** China	58C2 **Bartoszyce** Pol
25D3 **Banco Chinchorro** *Is* Mexico	77C4 **Ban Pak Phanang** Thai	18C2 **Barkley,L** USA	78C4 **Barung** *I* Indon
15C1 **Bancroft** Can	76D3 **Ban Ru Kroy** Camb	13B3 **Barkley Sd** Can	85D4 **Barwāh** India
86A1 **Bānda** India	76B3 **Ban Sai Yok** Thai	100B4 **Barkly East** S Africa	85C4 **Barwāni** India
70A3 **Banda Aceh** Indon	76C3 **Ban Sattahip** Thai	106C2 **Barkly Tableland** *Mts* Aust	109C1 **Barwon** *R* Aust
97B4 **Bandama** *R* Ivory Coast	59B3 **Banská Bystrica** Slovakia	46C2 **Bar-le-Duc** France	61G3 **Barysh** Russian Fed
91C4 **Bandar Abbās** Iran	85C4 **Bānswāra** India	106A3 **Barlee,L** Aust	98B2 **Basankusu** Zaïre
90A2 **Bandar Anzalī** Iran	77B4 **Ban Tha Kham** Thai	106A3 **Barlee Range** *Mts* Aust	34D2 **Basavilbas** Arg
99F2 **Bandarbeyla** Somalia	76D2 **Ban Thateng** Laos	53C2 **Barletta** Italy	79B1 **Basco** Phil
91B4 **Bandar-e Daylam** Iran	76C2 **Ban Tha Tum** Thai	85C3 **Barmer** India	52A1 **Basel** Switz
91B4 **Bandar-e Lengheh** Iran	41B3 **Bantry** Irish Rep	108B2 **Barmera** Aust	53C2 **Basento** *R* Italy
91B4 **Bandar-e Māqām** Iran	41A3 **Bantry** *B* Irish Rep	43B3 **Barmouth** Wales	13E2 **Bashaw** Can
91D4 **Bandar-e Rig** Iran	76D3 **Ban Ya Soup** Viet	42D2 **Barnard Castle** Eng	79B1 **Bashi Chan** Phil
90B2 **Bandar-e Torkoman** Iran	78C4 **Banyuwangi** Indon	65K4 **Barnaul** Russian Fed	61H3 **Bashkortostan** Russian Fed
91A3 **Bandar Khomeynī** Iran	72C3 **Baofeng** China	16B3 **Barnegat** USA	79B4 **Basilan** *I* Phil
78C2 **Bandar Seri Begawan** Brunei	76C1 **Bao Ha** Viet	16B3 **Barnegat B** USA	43E4 **Basildon** Eng
71D4 **Banda S** Indon	72B3 **Baoji** China	6C2 **Barnes Icecap** Can	43D4 **Basingstoke** Eng
91C4 **Band Bonī** Iran	76D3 **Bao Loc** Viet	17B1 **Barnesville** Georgia, USA	8B2 **Basin Region** USA
35C2 **Bandeira** *Mt* Brazil	68B4 **Baoshan** China	14B3 **Barnesville** Ohio, USA	93E3 **Basra** Iraq
97B3 **Bandiagara** Mali	72C1 **Baotou** China	42D3 **Barnsley** Eng	46D2 **Bas-Rhin** Department, France
60C5 **Bandirma** Turk	87C1 **Bāpatla** India	43B4 **Barnstaple** Eng	76D3 **Bassac** *R* Camb
45B3 **Bandon** Irish Rep	46B1 **Bapaume** France	97C4 **Baro** Nig	13E2 **Bassano** Can
98B3 **Bandundu** Zaïre	93D3 **Ba'Qūbah** Iraq	86C1 **Barpeta** India	52B1 **Bassano** Italy
78B4 **Bandung** Indon	32J7 **Baquerizo Morena** Ecuador	32D1 **Barquisimeto** Ven	47D2 **Bassano del Grappa** Italy
25E2 **Banes** Cuba	54A2 **Bar** Montenegro, Yugos	31C4 **Barra** Brazil	97C4 **Bassari** Togo
13D2 **Banff** Can	99D1 **Bara** Sudan	44A3 **Barra** *I* Scot	101C3 **Bassas da India** *I* Mozam Chan
44C3 **Banff** Scot	99E2 **Baraawe** Somalia	109D2 **Barraba** Aust	76A2 **Bassein** Burma
5G4 **Banff** *R* Can	78D3 **Barabai** Indon	23A2 **Barra de Navidad** Mexico	27E3 **Basse Terre** Guadeloupe
13D2 **Banff Nat Pk** Can	86A1 **Bāra Banki** India	35C2 **Barra de Piraí** Brazil	97C4 **Bassila** Benin
87B2 **Bangalore** India	65J4 **Barabinsk** Russian Fed	35A1 **Barragem de São Simão** *Res* Brazil	22C2 **Bass Lake** USA
98C2 **Bangassou** CAR	65J4 **Barabinskaya Step** *Steppe* Kazakhstan/Russian Fed	35A1 **Barra do Garças** Brazil	107D4 **Bass Str** Aust
70C3 **Banggi** *I* Malay	50B1 **Baracaldo** Spain	35B1 **Barragem Agua Vermelha** *Res* Brazil	39G7 **Båstad** Sweden
95B1 **Banghāzī** Libya	26C2 **Baracoa** Cuba	50A2 **Barragem do Castelo do Bode** *Res* Port	91B4 **Bastak** Iran
76D2 **Bang Hieng** *R* Laos	94C2 **Baradá** *R* Syria	50A2 **Barragem do Maranhão** *Res* Port	86A1 **Basti** India
78B3 **Bangka** *I* Indon	109C2 **Baradine** Aust	35A2 **Barragem Três Irmãos** *Res* Brazil	52A2 **Bastia** Corse
78A3 **Bangko** Indon	87A1 **Bārāmati** India	44A3 **Barra Head** *Pt* Scot	57B3 **Bastogne** Belg
76C3 **Bangkok** Thai	84C2 **Baramula** Pak	31C6 **Barra Mansa** Brazil	19B3 **Bastrop** Louisiana, USA
82C3 **Bangladesh** Republic, Asia	85D3 **Bārān** India	32B6 **Barranca** Peru	19A3 **Bastrop** Texas, USA
84D2 **Bangong Co** *L* China	79B3 **Barangas** Phil	32C2 **Barrancabermeja** Colombia	98A2 **Bata** Eq Guinea
10D2 **Bangor** Maine, USA	4E4 **Baranof I** USA	33E2 **Barrancas** Ven	78C3 **Batakan** Indon
45D1 **Bangor** N Ire	60C3 **Baranovichi** Belorussia	30E4 **Barranqueras** Arg	84D2 **Batala** India
16B2 **Bangor** Pennsylvania, USA	108A2 **Baratta** Aust	32C1 **Barranquilla** Colombia	68B3 **Batang** China
42B3 **Bangor** Wales	86B1 **Barauni** India	44A3 **Barra,Sound of** *Chan* Scot	98B2 **Batangafo** CAR
78D3 **Bangsalsembera** Indon	31C6 **Barbacena** Brazil	16C1 **Barre** USA	79B1 **Batan Is** Phil
76B3 **Bang Saphan Yai** Thai	27F4 **Barbados** *I* Caribbean S	34B2 **Barreal** Arg	35B2 **Batatais** Brazil
79B2 **Bangued** Phil	51C1 **Barbastro** Spain	31C4 **Barreiras** Brazil	15C2 **Batavia** USA
98B2 **Bangui** CAR	101H1 **Barberton** S Africa	50A2 **Barreiro** Port	109D3 **Batemans Bay** Aust
100C2 **Bangweulu** *L* Zambia	48B2 **Barbezieux** France		17B1 **Batesburg** USA
77C4 **Ban Hat Yai** Thai	32C2 **Barbōsa** Colombia		18B2 **Batesville** Arkansas, USA
76C2 **Ban Hin Heup** Laos	27E3 **Barbuda** *I* Caribbean S		19C3 **Batesville** Mississippi, USA
76C1 **Ban Houei Sai** Laos	107D3 **Barcaldine** Aust		43C4 **Bath** Eng
76B3 **Ban Hua Hin** Thai	**Barce = Al Marj**		15C2 **Bath** New York, USA
	53C3 **Barcellona** Italy		98B1 **Batha** *R* Chad
	51C1 **Barcelona** Spain		107D4 **Bathurst** Aust
			7D5 **Bathurst** Can

101G1 **Bloemfontein** S Africa
101G1 **Bloemhof** S Africa
101G1 **Bloemhof Dam** *Res* S Africa
33F3 **Blommesteinmeer** *L* Surinam
38A1 **Blonduós** Iceland
45B1 **Bloody Foreland** *C* Irish Rep
14A3 **Bloomfield** Indiana, USA
18B1 **Bloomfield** Iowa, USA
10B2 **Bloomington** Illinois, USA
14A3 **Bloomington** Indiana, USA
16A2 **Bloomsburg** USA
78C4 **Blora** Indon
6H3 **Blosseville Kyst** *Mts* Greenland
57B3 **Bludenz** Austria
11B3 **Bluefield** USA
32A1 **Bluefields** Nic
26B3 **Blue Mountain Peak** *Mt* Jamaica
16A2 **Blue Mt** USA
109D2 **Blue Mts** Aust
27J1 **Blue Mts** Jamaica
8A2 **Blue Mts** USA
Blue Nile = Bahr el Azraq
99D1 **Blue Nile** *R* Sudan
4G3 **Bluenose L** Can
11B3 **Blue Ridge Mts** USA
13D2 **Blue River** Can
45B1 **Blue Stack** *Mt* Irish Rep
111A3 **Bluff** NZ
106A4 **Bluff Knoll** *Mt* Aust
30G4 **Blumenau** Brazil
49D2 **Blundez** Austria
20B2 **Bly** USA
12E3 **Blying Sd** USA
42D2 **Blyth** Eng
9B3 **Blythe** USA
11B3 **Blytheville** USA
97A4 **Bo** Sierra Leone
79B3 **Boac** Phil
72D2 **Boading** China
14B2 **Boardman** USA
63C3 **Boatou** China
33E3 **Boa Vista** Brazil
97A4 **Boa Vista** *I* Cape Verde
76E1 **Bobai** China
47C2 **Bóbbio** Italy
97B3 **Bobo Dioulasso** Burkina
60C3 **Bobruysk** Belorussia
17B2 **Boca Chica Key** *I* USA
32D5 **Bõca do Acre** Brazil
35C1 **Bocaiúva** Brazil
98B2 **Bocaranga** CAR
17B2 **Boca Raton** USA
59C3 **Bochnia** Pol
56B2 **Bocholt** Germany
46D1 **Bochum** Germany
100A2 **Bocoio** Angola
98B2 **Boda** CAR
63D2 **Bodaybo** Russian Fed
21A2 **Bodega Head** *Pt* USA
95A3 **Bodélé** *Region* Chad
38J5 **Boden** Sweden
47C1 **Bodensee** *L* Switz/Germany
87B1 **Bodhan** India
87B2 **Bodināyakkanūr** India
43B4 **Bodmin** Eng
43B4 **Bodmin Moor** *Upland* Eng
38G5 **Bodø** Nor
55C3 **Bodrum** Turk
98C3 **Boende** Zaïre
97A3 **Boffa** Guinea
76B2 **Bogale** Burma
19C3 **Bogalusa** USA
109C2 **Bogan** *R* Aust
97B3 **Bogandé** Burkina
6H3 **Bogarnes** Iceland
92C2 **Boğazlıyan** Turk
61K2 **Bogdanovich** Russian Fed
68A2 **Bogda Shan** *Mt* China
100A3 **Bogenfels** Namibia
109D1 **Boggabilla** Aust
109C2 **Boggabri** Aust
45B2 **Boggeragh Mts** Irish Rep
79B3 **Bogo** Phil
109C3 **Bogong,Mt** Aust
78B4 **Bogor** Indon
61H2 **Bogorodskoye** Russian Fed
32C3 **Bogotá** Colombia
63A2 **Bogotol** Russian Fed
86B2 **Bogra** Bang
72D2 **Bo Hai** *B* China
46B2 **Bohain-en-Vermandois** France
72D2 **Bohai Wan** *B* China
57C3 **Böhmer-Wald** *Upland* Germany
79B4 **Bohol** *I* Phil
79B4 **Bohol S** Phil
35A1 **Bois** *R* Brazil
14B1 **Bois Blanc I** USA
8B2 **Boise** USA
96A2 **Bojador,C** Mor
79B2 **Bojeador,C** Phil
90C2 **Bojnürd** Iran
97A3 **Boké** Guinea
109C1 **Bokhara** *R* Aust
39F7 **Boknafjord** *Inlet* Nor
98B3 **Boko** Congo
76C3 **Bokor** Camb
98C3 **Bokungu** Zaïre
98B1 **Bol** Chad
23A1 **Bolaãnos** Mexico
97A3 **Bolama** Guinea-Bissau
23A1 **Bolanos** *R* Mexico
48C2 **Bolbec** France
97B4 **Bole** Ghana
59B2 **Boleslawiec** Pol
97B3 **Bolgatanga** Ghana
60C4 **Bolgrad** Ukraine
34C3 **Bolívar** Arg
18B2 **Bolivar** Missouri, USA
18C2 **Bolivar** Tennessee, USA
30C2 **Bolivia** Republic, S America
38H6 **Bollnas** Sweden
109C1 **Bollon** Aust
32C2 **Bollvar** *Mt* Ven
52B2 **Bologna** Italy
60D2 **Bologoye** Russian Fed
69F2 **Bolon'** Russian Fed
61G3 **Bol'shoy Irgiz** *R* Russian Fed
74C2 **Bol'shoy Kamen** Russian Fed
Bol'shoy Kavkaz =Caucasus
61G4 **Bol'shoy Uzen** *R* Kazakhstan
9C4 **Bolson de Mapimi** *Desert* Mexico
43C3 **Bolton** Eng
92B1 **Bolu** Turk
38A1 **Bolungarvik** Iceland
92B2 **Bolvadin** Turk
52B1 **Bolzano** Italy
98B3 **Boma** Zaïre
107D4 **Bombala** Aust
87A1 **Bombay** India
99D2 **Bombo** Uganda
35B1 **Bom Despacho** Brazil
86C1 **Bomdila** India
97A4 **Bomi Hills** Lib
31C4 **Bom Jesus da Lapa** Brazil
63E2 **Bomnak** Russian Fed
99C2 **Bomokandi** *R* Zaïre
98C2 **Bomu** *R* CAR/Zaïre
27D4 **Bonaire** *I* Caribbean S
12F2 **Bona,Mt** USA
25D3 **Bonanza** Nic
7E5 **Bonavista** Can
108A2 **Bon Bon** Aust
98C2 **Bondo** Zaïre
97B4 **Bondoukou** Ivory Coast
Bône = 'Annaba
33E3 **Bonfim** Guyana
98C2 **Bongandanga** Zaïre
98B1 **Bongor** Chad
19A3 **Bonham** USA
53A2 **Bonifacio** Corse
52A2 **Bonifacio,Str of** *Chan* Medit S
Bonin Is = Ogasawara Gunto
17B2 **Bonita Springs** USA
57B2 **Bonn** Germany
20C1 **Bonners Ferry** USA
12H1 **Bonnet Plume** *R* Can
13E2 **Bonnyville** Can
97A4 **Bonthe** Sierra Leone
99E1 **Booaaso** Somalia
108B2 **Booligal** Aust
109D1 **Boonah** Aust
15C2 **Boonville** USA
109C2 **Boorowa** Aust
6A2 **Boothia,G of** Can
6A2 **Boothia Pen** Can
98B3 **Booué** Gabon
108A1 **Bopeechee** Aust
99D2 **Bor** Sudan
92B2 **Bor** Turk
54B2 **Bor** Serbia, Yugos
8B2 **Borah Peak** *Mt* USA
39G7 **Borås** Sweden
91B4 **Borāzjān** Iran
108A3 **Borda,C** Aust
48B3 **Bordeaux** France
4G2 **Borden I** Can
6B2 **Borden Pen** Can
16B2 **Bordentown** USA
42C2 **Borders** Region, Scot
108B3 **Bordertown** Aust
96C2 **Bordi Omar Dris** Alg
8D1 **Borens River** Can
38A2 **Borgarnes** Iceland
9C3 **Borger** USA
39H7 **Borgholm** Sweden
47C2 **Borgosia** Italy
47D1 **Borgo Valsugana** Italy
59C3 **Borislav** Ukraine
61F3 **Borisoglebsk** Russian Fed
60C3 **Borisov** Belorussia
60E3 **Borisovka** Russian Fed
95A3 **Borkou** *Region* Chad
39H6 **Borlänge** Sweden
47C2 **Bormida** Italy
47D1 **Bormio** Italy
67F5 **Borneo** *I* Malay/Indon
39H7 **Bornholm** *I* Den
55C3 **Bornova** Turk
98C2 **Boro** *R* Sudan
97B3 **Boromo** Burkina
60D2 **Borovichi** Russian Fed
106C2 **Borroloola** Aust
54B1 **Borsa** Rom
90A3 **Borūjed** Iran
90B3 **Borūjen** Iran
58B2 **Bory Tucholskie** Region, Pol
63D2 **Borzya** Russian Fed
73B5 **Bose** China
101G1 **Boshof** S Africa
54A2 **Bosna** *R* Bosnia-Herzegovina
37E4 **Bosnia-Herzegovina** Republic, Europe
75C1 **Bōsō-hantō** *B* Japan
Bosporus = Karadeniz Boğazi
51C2 **Bosquet** Alg
98B2 **Bossangoa** CAR
98B2 **Bossèmbélé** CAR
19B3 **Bossier City** USA
65K5 **Bosten Hu** *L* China
43D3 **Boston** Eng
10C2 **Boston** USA
11A3 **Boston Mts** USA
85C4 **Botād** India
54B2 **Botevgrad** Bulg
101G1 **Bothaville** S Africa
64C3 **Bothnia,G of** Sweden/Fin
100B3 **Botletli** *R* Botswana
60C4 **Botosani** Rom
100B3 **Botswana** Republic, Africa
53C3 **Botte Donato** *Mt* Italy
46D1 **Bottrop** Germany
35B2 **Botucatu** Brazil
7E5 **Botwood** Can
89D7 **Bouaké** Ivory Coast
98B2 **Bouar** CAR
96B1 **Bouârfa** Mor
98B2 **Bouca** CAR
51C2 **Boufarik** Alg
Bougie = Bejaïa
97B3 **Bougouni** Mali
46C2 **Bouillon** France
96B2 **Bou Izakarn** Mor
46D2 **Boulay-Moselle** France
8C2 **Boulder** Colorado, USA
9B3 **Boulder City** USA
22A2 **Boulder Creek** USA
48C1 **Boulogne** France
98B2 **Boumba** *R* CAR
97B4 **Bouna** Ivory Coast
8B3 **Boundary Peak** *Mt* USA
97B4 **Boundiali** Ivory Coast
107F3 **Bourail** Nouvelle Calédonie
97B3 **Bourem** Mali
49D2 **Bourg** France
49D2 **Bourg de Péage** France
48C2 **Bourges** France
48C3 **Bourg-Madame** France
49C2 **Bourgogne** Region, France
47B2 **Bourg-St-Maurice** France
108C2 **Bourke** Aust
43D4 **Bournemouth** Eng
96C1 **Bou Saâda** Alg
98B1 **Bousso** Chad
97A3 **Boutilmit** Maur
103J7 **Bouvet I** Atlantic O
34D2 **Bovril** Arg
13F2 **Bow** *R* Can
107D2 **Bowen** Aust
19A3 **Bowie** Texas, USA
13E2 **Bow Island** Can
11B3 **Bowling Green** Kentucky, USA
18B2 **Bowling Green** Missouri, USA
14B2 **Bowling Green** Ohio, USA
15C3 **Bowling Green** Virginia, USA
15C2 **Bowmanville** Can
109D2 **Bowral** Aust
13C2 **Bowron** *R* Can
72D3 **Bo Xian** China
72D2 **Boxing** China
92B1 **Boyabat** Turk
98B2 **Boyali** CAR
5J4 **Boyd** Can
16B2 **Boyertown** USA
13E2 **Boyle** Can
41B3 **Boyle** Irish Rep
45C2 **Boyne** *R* Irish Rep
17B2 **Boynoton Beach** USA
98C2 **Boyoma Falls** Zaïre
55C3 **Bozca Ada** *I* Turk
55C3 **Boz Dağlari** *Mts* Turk
8B2 **Bozeman** USA
Bozen = Bolzano
98B2 **Bozene** Zaïre
98B2 **Bozoum** CAR
47B2 **Bra** Italy
52C2 **Brač** *I* Croatia
15C1 **Bracebridge** Can
95A2 **Brach** Libya
38H6 **Bräcke** Sweden
17B2 **Bradenton** USA

42D3 **Bradford** Eng	52B1 **Brescia** Italy	20B2 **Brookings** Oregon, USA
44E1 **Brae** Scot	**Breslau = Wrocław**	8D2 **Brookings** South Dakota, USA
44C3 **Braemar** Scot	47D1 **Bressanone** Italy	
50A1 **Braga** Port	44E1 **Bressay** I Scot	16D1 **Brookline** USA
34C3 **Bragado** Arg	48B2 **Bressuire** France	16C2 **Brooklyn** Borough, New York, USA
50A1 **Bragana** Port	58C2 **Brest** Belorussia	
31B2 **Bragança** Brazil	48B2 **Brest** France	5G4 **Brooks** Can
35B2 **Bragança Paulista** Brazil	48B2 **Bretagne** Region, France	12C3 **Brooks,L** USA
		12A1 **Brooks Mt** USA
86C2 **Brahman-Baria** Bang	46B2 **Breteuil** France	4C3 **Brooks Range** Mts USA
86B2 **Brāhmani** R India	16B2 **Breton Woods** USA	
86C1 **Brahmaputra** R India	110B1 **Brett,C** NZ	17B2 **Brooksville** USA
7E5 **Braie Verte** Can	109C1 **Brewarrina** Aust	109D1 **Brooloo** Aust
60C4 **Brăila** Rom	16C2 **Brewster** New York, USA	106B2 **Broome** Aust
10A2 **Brainerd** USA		44C2 **Brora** Scot
97A3 **Brakna** Region, Maur	20C1 **Brewster** Washington, USA	20B2 **Brothers** USA
5F4 **Bralorne** Can		95A3 **Broulkou** Chad
14C2 **Brampton** Can	101G1 **Breyten** S Africa	13E3 **Browning** USA
33E3 **Branco** R Brazil	52C1 **Brežice** Slovenia	9D4 **Brownsville** USA
100A3 **Brandberg** Mt Namibia	98C2 **Bria** CAR	9D3 **Brownwood** USA
	49D3 **Briancon** France	46B1 **Bruay-en-Artois** France
56C2 **Brandenburg** Germany	49C2 **Briare** France	
	21B2 **Bridgeport** California, USA	106A3 **Bruce,Mt** Aust
56C2 **Brandenburg** State, Germany		14B1 **Bruce Pen** Can
	15D2 **Bridgeport** Connecticut, USA	59B3 **Brück an der Mur** Austria
101G1 **Brandfort** S Africa		
8D2 **Brandon** Can	19A3 **Bridgeport** Texas, USA	**Bruges = Brugge**
100B4 **Brandvlei** S Africa		99C3 **Bujumbura** Burundi
57C2 **Brandys nad Lebem** Czech Republic	22C1 **Bridgeport Res** USA	46B1 **Brugge** Belg
	16B3 **Bridgeton** USA	46D1 **Brühl** Germany
58B2 **Braniewo** Pol	27F4 **Bridgetown** Barbados	78C2 **Brunei** Sultanate, S E Asia
10B2 **Brantford** Can		
108B3 **Branxholme** Aust	7D5 **Bridgewater** Can	52B1 **Brunico** Italy
7D5 **Bras D'Or L** Can	16D2 **Bridgewater** USA	111B2 **Brunner,L** NZ
35C1 **Brasíla de Minas** Brazil	43C4 **Bridgwater** Eng	11B3 **Brunswick** Georgia, USA
	43C4 **Bridgwater B** Eng	
32D6 **Brasiléia** Brazil	42D2 **Bridlington** Eng	18B2 **Brunswick** Mississippi, USA
31B5 **Brasilia** Brazil	109C4 **Bridport** Aust	
54C1 **Brasov** Rom	47B1 **Brienzer See** L Switz	29B6 **Brunswick,Pen de** Chile
78D1 **Brassay Range** Mts Malay	46C2 **Briey** France	
	52A1 **Brig** Switz	109C4 **Bruny I** Aust
59B3 **Bratislava** Slovakia	8B2 **Brigham City** USA	61F1 **Brusenets** Russian Fed
63C2 **Bratsk** Russian Fed	109C3 **Bright** Aust	
15D2 **Brattleboro** USA	43D4 **Brighton** Eng	26A3 **Brus Laguna** Honduras
56C2 **Braunschweig** Germany	46E1 **Brilon** Germany	**Brüssel = Bruxelles**
	55A2 **Brindisi** Italy	56A2 **Bruxelles** Belg
97A4 **Brava** I Cape Verde	19B3 **Brinkley** USA	9D3 **Bryan** USA
9B3 **Brawley** USA	107E3 **Brisbane** Aust	108A2 **Bryan,Mt** Aust
45C2 **Bray** Irish Rep	15D2 **Bristol** Connecticut, USA	60D3 **Bryansk** Russian Fed
6C3 **Bray I** Can		
13D2 **Brazeau** R Can	43C4 **Bristol** Eng	19B3 **Bryant** USA
13D2 **Brazeau,Mt** Can	15D2 **Bristol** Pennsylvania, USA	59B2 **Brzeg** Pol
28D4 **Brazil** Republic, S America		93E4 **Būbiyan** I Kuwait/Iraq
	16D2 **Bristol** Rhode Island, USA	
103G5 **Brazil Basin** Atlantic O		99D3 **Bubu** R Tanz
	11B3 **Bristol** Tennessee, USA	32C2 **Bucaramanga** Colombia
9D3 **Brazos** R USA	12B3 **Bristol B** USA	
98B3 **Brazzaville** Congo	43B4 **Bristol Chan** Eng/Wales	44D3 **Buchan** Oilfield N Sea
57C3 **Brdy** Upland Czech Republic		97A4 **Buchanan** Lib
	4D3 **British** Mts USA	44D3 **Buchan Deep** N Sea
111A3 **Breaksea** Sd NZ	5F4 **British Columbia** Province, Can	6C2 **Buchan G** Can
110B1 **Bream B** USA		40C2 **Buchan Ness** Pen Scot
78B4 **Brebes** Indon	6B1 **British Empire Range** Mts Can	
44C3 **Brechin** Scot		7E5 **Buchans** Can
46C1 **Brecht** Belg	101G1 **Brits** S Africa	34C2 **Buchardo** Arg
59B3 **Břeclav** Czech Republic	100B4 **Britstown** S Africa	**Bucharest = București**
	48C2 **Brive** France	47C1 **Buchs** Switz
43C4 **Brecon** Wales	59B3 **Brno** Czech Republic	43D3 **Buckingham** Eng
43C4 **Brecon Beacons** Mts Wales	17B1 **Broad** R USA	12B1 **Buckland** USA
	7C4 **Broadback** R Can	12B1 **Buckland** R USA
43B3 **Brecon Beacons Nat Pk** Wales	44A2 **Broad Bay** Inlet Scot	108A2 **Buckleboo** Aust
	44B3 **Broadford** Scot	98B3 **Buco Zau** Congo
56A2 **Breda** Neth	5H4 **Brochet** Can	54C2 **București** Rom
100B4 **Bredasdorp** S Africa	4G2 **Brock I** Can	59B3 **Budapest** Hung
38H6 **Bredbyn** Sweden	15C2 **Brockport** USA	84D3 **Budaun** India
61J3 **Bredy** Russian Fed	16D1 **Brockton** USA	43B4 **Bude** Eng
15C2 **Breezewood** USA	15C2 **Brockville** Can	19B3 **Bude** USA
47C1 **Bregenz** Austria	6B2 **Brodeur Pen** Can	61F5 **Budennovsk** Russian Fed
47C1 **Bregenzer Ache** R Austria	42B2 **Brodick** Scot	
	58B2 **Brodnica** Pol	54A2 **Budva** Montenegro, Yugos
38A1 **Breiðafjörður** B Iceland	60C3 **Brody** Ukraine	
	19B3 **Broken Bow** Oklahoma, USA	98A2 **Buéa** Cam
47C2 **Brembo** R Italy		22B3 **Buellton** USA
17A1 **Bremen** USA	19B3 **Broken Bow L** USA	34B2 **Buena Esperanza** Arg
56B2 **Bremen** Germany	107D4 **Broken Hill** Aust	32B3 **Buenaventura** Colombia
56B2 **Bremerhaven** Germany	47C2 **Broni** Italy	
	38G5 **Brønnøysund** Nor	23A2 **Buenavista** Mexico
20B1 **Bremerton** USA	16C2 **Bronx** Borough, New York, USA	29E2 **Buenos Aires** Arg
19A3 **Brenham** USA		29D3 **Buenos Aires** State, Arg
57C3 **Brenner** P Austria/Italy	79A4 **Brooke's Point** Phil	
	18B2 **Brookfield** Missouri, USA	18B2 **Buffalo** Mississippi, USA
47D2 **Breno** Italy		
47D2 **Brenta** R Italy	11A3 **Brookhaven** USA	
22B2 **Brentwood** USA		

10C2 **Duffalo** New York, USA	
8C2 **Buffalo** South Dakota, USA	
19A3 **Buffalo** Texas, USA	
8C2 **Buffalo** Wyoming, USA	
101H1 **Buffalo** R S Africa	
13E2 **Buffalo L** Alberta, Can	
5G3 **Buffalo L** Northwest Territories, Can	
5H4 **Buffalo Narrows** Can	
17B1 **Buford** USA	
54C2 **Buftea** Rom	
59C2 **Bug** R Pol/Ukraine	
32B3 **Buga** Colombia	
90B2 **Bugdayli** Turkmenistan	
61H3 **Bugulma** Russian Fed	
61H3 **Buguruslan** Russian Fed	
93C2 **Buhayrat al Asad** Res Syria	
41C3 **Builth Wells** Wales	
34A2 **Buin** Chile	
99C3 **Bujumbura** Burundi	
98C3 **Bukama** Zaïre	
99C3 **Bukavu** Zaïre	
80E2 **Bukhara** Uzbekistan	
78C2 **Bukit Batubrok** Mt Indon	
70B4 **Bukittinggi** Indon	
99D3 **Bukoba** Tanz	
78D3 **Buku Gandadiwata** Mt Indon	
71E4 **Bula** Indon	
79B3 **Bulan** Phil	
84D3 **Bulandshahr** India	
100B3 **Bulawayo** Zim	
55C3 **Buldan** Turk	
85D4 **Buldāna** India	
68C2 **Bulgan** Mongolia	
54B2 **Bulgaria** Republic, Europe	
47B1 **Bulle** Switz	
111B2 **Buller** R NZ	
109C3 **Buller,Mt** Aust	
106A4 **Bullfinch** Aust	
108B1 **Bulloo** R Aust	
108B1 **Bulloo Downs** Aust	
108B1 **Bulloo L** Aust	
18B2 **Bull Shoals Res** USA	
34A3 **Bulnes** Chile	
71F4 **Bulolo** PNG	
101G1 **Bultfontein** S Africa	
98C2 **Bumba** Zaïre	
76B2 **Bumphal Dam** Thai	
99D2 **Buna** Kenya	
106A4 **Bunbury** Aust	
45C1 **Buncrana** Irish Rep	
107E3 **Bundaberg** Aust	
109D2 **Bundarra** Aust	
85D3 **Būndi** India	
45B1 **Bundoran** Irish Rep	
109C1 **Bungil** R Aust	
98B3 **Bungo** Angola	
75A2 **Bungo-suidō** Str Japan	
70B3 **Bunguran** I Ind	
99D2 **Bunia** Zaïre	
18B2 **Bunker** USA	
19B3 **Bunkie** USA	
17B2 **Bunnell** USA	
78C3 **Buntok** Indon	
71D3 **Buol** Indon	
94C2 **Burāg** Syria	
98C1 **Buram** Sudan	
99E2 **Burao** Somalia	
79B3 **Burauen** Phil	
80C3 **Buraydah** S Arabia	
21B3 **Burbank** USA	
109C2 **Burcher** Aust	
92B2 **Burdur** Turk	
63F3 **Bureinskiy Khrebet** Mts Russian Fed	
56C2 **Burg** Germany	
54C2 **Burgas** Bulg	
17C1 **Burgaw** USA	
47B1 **Burgdorf** Switz	
100B4 **Burgersdorp** S Africa	
50B1 **Burgos** Spain	
58B1 **Burgsvik** Sweden	

19A3	**Cameron** Texas, USA
4H2	**Cameron I** Can
111A3	**Cameron Mts** NZ
98A2	**Cameroon** Federal Republic, Africa
98A2	**Cameroun** *Mt* Cam
31B2	**Cametá** Brazil
79B4	**Camiguin** *I* Phil
79B2	**Camiling** Phil
17B1	**Camilla** USA
22B1	**Camino** USA
30D3	**Camiri** Bol
31C2	**Camocim** Brazil
98C3	**Camissombo** Angola
106C2	**Camooweal** Aust
34D2	**Campana** Arg
29A5	**Campana** *I* Chile
13B2	**Campania I** Can
111B2	**Campbell,C** NZ
13B2	**Campbell I** Can
105G6	**Campbell I** NZ
4E3	**Campbell,Mt** Can
84C2	**Campbellpore** Pak
5F5	**Campbell River** Can
7D5	**Campbellton** Can
109D2	**Campbelltown** Aust
42B2	**Campbeltown** Scot
25C3	**Campeche** Mexico
108B3	**Camperdown** Aust
31D3	**Campina Grande** Brazil
31B6	**Campinas** Brazil
35B1	**Campina Verde** Brazil
98A2	**Campo** Cam
53B2	**Campobasso** Italy
35B2	**Campo Belo** Brazil
35B1	**Campo Florido** Brazil
30D4	**Campo Gallo** Arg
30F3	**Campo Grande** Brazil
31C2	**Campo Maior** Brazil
30F3	**Campo Mourão** Brazil
35C2	**Campos** Brazil
35B1	**Campos Altos** Brazil
47D1	**Compo Tures** Italy
76D3	**Cam Ranh** Viet
5G4	**Camrose** Can
100A2	**Camucuio** Angola
27K1	**Canaan** Tobago
16C1	**Canaan** USA
100A2	**Canacupa** Angola
2F3	**Canada** Dominion, N America
29D2	**Cañada de Gomez** Arg
9C3	**Canadian** *R* USA
60C5	**Canakkale** Turk
34B3	**Canalejas** Arg
13D2	**Canal Flats** Can
24A1	**Cananea** Mexico
102G3	**Canary Basin** Atlantic O
	Canary Is = Islas Canarias
23A2	**Canas** Mexico
24B2	**Canatlán** Mexico
11B4	**Canaveral,C** USA
31D5	**Canavieiras** Brazil
107D4	**Canberra** Aust
20B2	**Canby** California, USA
55C3	**Çandarli Körfezi** *B* Turk
16C2	**Candlewood,L** USA
29E2	**Canelones** Urug
18A2	**Caney** USA
100A2	**Cangamba** Angola
100B2	**Cangombe** Angola
72D2	**Cangzhou** China
7D4	**Caniapiscau** *R* Can
53B3	**Canicatti** Italy
31D2	**Canindé** Brazil
92B1	**Çankırı** Turk
13D2	**Canmore** Can
44A3	**Canna** *I* Scot
87B2	**Cannanore** India
49D3	**Cannes** France
109C3	**Cann River** Aust
30F4	**Canoas** Brazil
13F1	**Canoe L** Can
9C3	**Canon City** USA
108B2	**Canopus** Aust
5H4	**Canora** Can
109C2	**Canowindra** Aust
45C2	**Cansore Pt** Irish Rep
43E4	**Canterbury** Eng
111B2	**Canterbury Bight** *B* NZ
111B2	**Canterbury Plains** NZ
77D4	**Can Tho** Viet
	Canton = Guangzhou
19C3	**Canton** Mississippi, USA
18B1	**Canton** Missouri, USA
10B2	**Canton** Ohio, USA
12E2	**Cantwell** USA
20C2	**Canyon City** USA
12J2	**Canyon Range** *Mts* Can
20B2	**Canyonville** USA
98C3	**Canzar** Angola
76D1	**Cao Bang** Viet
31B2	**Capanema** Brazil
35B2	**Capão Bonito** Brazil
48B3	**Capbreton** France
24B2	**Cap Corrientes** *C* Mexico
52A2	**Cap Corse** *C* Corse
48B2	**Cap de la Hague** *C* France
15D1	**Cap-de-la-Madeleine** Can
6C3	**Cap de Nouvelle-France** *C* Can
51C2	**Capdepera** Spain
23A2	**Cap de Tancitiario** *C* Mexico
109C4	**Cape Barren I** Aust
103J6	**Cape Basin** Atlantic O
7E5	**Cape Breton I** Can
97B4	**Cape Coast** Ghana
15D2	**Cape Cod B** USA
6C3	**Cape Dorset** Can
17C1	**Cape Fear** *R* USA
18C2	**Cape Girardeau** USA
6B3	**Cape Henrietta Maria** Can
	Cape Horn = Cabo de Hornos
104E3	**Cape Johnston Depth** Pacific O
35C1	**Capelinha** Brazil
4B3	**Cape Lisburne** USA
100A2	**Capelongo** Angola
15D3	**Cape May** USA
5F5	**Cape Mendocino** USA
98B3	**Capenda Camulemba** Angola
4F2	**Cape Perry** Can
100B4	**Cape Province** S Africa
7A4	**Cape Tatnam** Can
100A4	**Cape Town** S Africa
102G4	**Cape Verde** *Is* Atlantic O
102G4	**Cape Verde Basin** Atlantic O
12F3	**Cape Yakataga** USA
107D2	**Cape York Pen** Aust
46A1	**Cap Gris Nez** *C* France
26C3	**Cap-Haitien** Haiti
31B2	**Capim** *R* Brazil
112C2	**Capitán Arturo Prat** *Base* Ant
27P2	**Cap Moule à Chique** *C* St Lucia
53C3	**Capo Isola de Correnti** *C* Italy
53C3	**Capo Rizzuto** *C* Italy
55A3	**Capo Santa Maria di Leuca** *C* Italy
53B3	**Capo San Vito** Italy
53C3	**Capo Spartivento** *C* Italy
27P2	**Cap Pt** St Lucia
53B2	**Capri** *I* Italy
100B2	**Caprivi Strip** Region, Namibia
52A2	**Cap Rosso** *C* Corse
102H4	**Cap Vert** *C* Sen
32C4	**Caquetá** *R* Colombia
54B2	**Caracal** Rom
33E3	**Caracaraí** Brazil
32D1	**Caracas** Ven
35B2	**Caraguatatuba** Brazil
29B3	**Carahue** Chile
35C1	**Caraí** Brazil
35C2	**Carandaí** Brazil
31C6	**Carangola** Brazil
54B1	**Caransebeş** Rom
108A2	**Carappee Hill** *Mt* Aust
26A3	**Caratasca** Honduras
35C1	**Caratinga** Brazil
51B2	**Caravaca** Spain
35D1	**Caravelas** Brazil
18C2	**Carbondale** Illinois, USA
53A3	**Carbonia** Sardegna
7E5	**Carborear** Can
5G4	**Carcaion** Can
99E1	**Carcar Mts** Somalia
48C3	**Carcassonne** France
4E3	**Carcross** Can
23B2	**Cardel** Mexico
25D2	**Cardenas** Cuba
23B1	**Cárdenas** Mexico
43C4	**Cardiff** Wales
43B3	**Cardigan** Wales
43B3	**Cardigan B** Wales
13E2	**Cardston** Can
54B1	**Carei** Rom
33F4	**Careiro** Brazil
34A2	**Carén** Chile
14B2	**Carey** USA
48B2	**Carhaix-Plouguer** France
29D3	**Carhué** Arg
31C6	**Cariacica** Brazil
5J4	**Caribou** Can
5G4	**Caribou Mts** Alberta, Can
5F4	**Caribou Mts** British Columbia, Can
79B3	**Carigara** Phil
46C2	**Carignan** France
33E1	**Caripito** Ven
15C1	**Carleton Place** Can
101G1	**Carletonville** S Africa
18C2	**Carlinville** USA
42C2	**Carlisle** Eng
15C2	**Carlisle** USA
34C3	**Carlos** Arg
35C1	**Carlos Chagas** Brazil
45C2	**Carlow County** Irish Rep
45C2	**Carlow** Irish Rep
21B3	**Carlsbad** California, USA
9C3	**Carlsbad** New Mexico, USA
5H5	**Carlyle** Can
12G2	**Carmacks** Can
47B2	**Carmagnola** Italy
43B4	**Carmarthen** Wales
43B4	**Carmarthen B** Wales
22B2	**Carmel** California, USA
16C2	**Carmel** New York, USA
94B2	**Carmel,Mt** Israel
34D2	**Carmelo** Urug
22B2	**Carmel Valley** USA
9B4	**Carmen** *I* Mexico
29D4	**Carmen de Patagones** Arg
18C2	**Carmi** USA
21A2	**Carmichael** USA
35B1	**Carmo do Paranaiba** Brazil
50A2	**Carmona** Spain
106A3	**Carnarvon** Aust
100B4	**Carnarvon** S Africa
35D1	**Carncacá** Brazil
45C1	**Carndonagh** Irish Rep
106B3	**Carnegi,L** Aust
98B2	**Carnot** CAR
108A2	**Carnot,C** Aust
17B2	**Carol City** USA
31B3	**Carolina** Brazil
101H1	**Carolina** S Africa
17C1	**Carolina Beach** USA
104F3	**Caroline Is** Pacific O
60B4	**Carpathians** *Mts* E Europe
59D3	**Carpatii Orientali** *Mts* Rom
106C2	**Carpentaria,G of** Aust
83C5	**Carpenter Ridge** Indian O
49D3	**Carpentras** France
52B2	**Carpi** Italy
22C3	**Carpinteria** USA
17B2	**Carrabelle** USA
52B2	**Carrara** Italy
41B3	**Carrauntoohill** *Mt* Irish Rep
45C2	**Carrickmacross** Irish Rep
45B2	**Carrick on Shannon** Irish Rep
45C2	**Carrick-on-Suir** Irish Rep
108A2	**Carrieton** Aust
8D2	**Carrington** USA
50B1	**Carrión** *R* Spain
10A2	**Carroll** USA
17A1	**Carrollton** Georgia, USA
14A3	**Carrollton** Kentucky, USA
18B2	**Carrollton** Missouri, USA
18C2	**Carruthersville** USA
60E5	**Carsamba** Turk
92B2	**Carsamba** *R* Turk
8B3	**Carson City** USA
14B2	**Carsonville** USA
26B4	**Cartagena** Colombia
51B2	**Cartagena** Spain
32B3	**Cartago** Colombia
25D4	**Cartago** Costa Rica
111C2	**Carterton** NZ
18B2	**Carthage** Missouri, USA
15C2	**Carthage** New York, USA
19B3	**Carthage** Texas, USA
106B2	**Cartier I** Timor S
7E4	**Cartwright** Can
31D3	**Caruaru** Brazil
33E1	**Carúpano** Ven
46B1	**Carvin** France
34A2	**Casablanca** Chile
96B1	**Casablanca** Mor
35B2	**Casa Branca** Brazil
9B3	**Casa Grande** USA
52A1	**Casale Monferrato** Italy
47D2	**Casalmaggiore** Italy
34C3	**Casares** Arg
13C3	**Cascade Mts** Can/USA
111A2	**Cascade Pt** NZ
8A2	**Cascade Range** *Mts* USA
30F3	**Cascavel** Brazil
53B2	**Caserta** Italy
112C9	**Casey** *Base* Ant
45C2	**Cashel** Irish Rep
34C2	**Casilda** Arg
107E3	**Casino** Aust
32B5	**Casma** Peru
51B1	**Caspe** Spain
8C2	**Casper** USA
61G4	**Caspian Depression** Region Kazakhstan
65G6	**Caspian S** Asia/Europe
14C3	**Cass** USA
100B2	**Cassamba** Angola
46B1	**Cassel** France
12J3	**Cassiar** Can
4E3	**Cassiar Mts** Can
35A1	**Cassilândia** Brazil
53B2	**Cassino** Italy
22C3	**Castaic** USA
34B2	**Castaño** *R* Arg
47D2	**Castelfranco** Italy
49D3	**Castellane** France
34D3	**Castelli** Arg
51B2	**Castellon de la Plana** Spain
31C3	**Castelo** Brazil
50A2	**Castelo Branco** Port
48C3	**Castelsarrasin** France
53B3	**Castelvetrano** Italy
108B3	**Casterton** Aust

46D2	**Château-Salins** France
49C2	**Château-Thierry** France
46C1	**Châtelet** Belg
48C2	**Châtellerault** France
43E4	**Chatham** Eng
7D5	**Chatham** New Brunswick, Can
16C1	**Chatham** New York, USA
14B2	**Chatham** Ontario, Can
13A2	**Chatham Sd** Can
12H3	**Chatham Str** USA
49C2	**Châtillon** France
47B2	**Châtillon** Italy
16B3	**Chatsworth** USA
17B1	**Chattahoochee** USA
17A1	**Chattahoochee** *R* USA
11B3	**Chattanooga** USA
76A1	**Chauk** Burma
49D2	**Chaumont** France
46B2	**Chauny** France
77D3	**Chau Phu** Viet
50A1	**Chaves** Port
61H2	**Chaykovskiy** Russian Fed
50B2	**Chazaouet** Alg
34C2	**Chazón** Arg
32C2	**Chcontá** Colombia
57C2	**Cheb** Czech Republic
65F4	**Cheboksary** Russian Fed
10B2	**Cheboygan** USA
74B3	**Chech'on** S Korea
85C3	**Chechro** Pak
18A2	**Checotah** USA
76A2	**Cheduba** *I* Burma
108B1	**Cheepie** Aust
96B2	**Chegga** Maur
100C2	**Chegutu** Zim
20B1	**Chehalis** USA
74B4	**Cheju** S Korea
74B4	**Cheju do** *I* S Korea
74B4	**Cheju-haehyöp** *Str* S Korea
63F2	**Chekunda** Russian Fed
20B1	**Chelan,L** USA
90B2	**Cheleken** Turkmenistan
34B3	**Chelforo** Arg
80D1	**Chelkar** Kazakhstan
59C2	**Chelm** Pol
58B2	**Chelmno** Pol
43E4	**Chelmsford** Eng
43C4	**Cheltenham** Eng
65H4	**Chelyabinsk** Russian Fed
101C2	**Chemba** Mozam
57C2	**Chemnitz** Germany
84D2	**Chenab** *R* India/Pak
96B2	**Chenachane** Alg
20C1	**Cheney** USA
18A2	**Cheney Res** USA
72D1	**Chengda** China
73A3	**Chengdu** China
72E2	**Chengshan Jiao** *Pt* China
73C4	**Chenxi** China
73C4	**Chen Xian** China
73D3	**Cheo Xian** China
32B5	**Chepén** Peru
34B2	**Chepes** Arg
48C2	**Cher** *R* France
23A2	**Cheran** Mexico
17C1	**Cheraw** USA
48B2	**Cherbourg** France
96C1	**Cherchell** Alg
63C2	**Cheremkhovo** Russian Fed
60E2	**Cherepovets** Russian Fed
60D4	**Cherkassy** Ukraine
61F5	**Cherkessk** Russian Fed
60D3	**Chernigov** Ukraine
60D2	**Chernobyl** Ukraine
60C4	**Chernovtsy** Ukraine
61J2	**Chernushka** Russian Fed

60B3	**Chernyakhovsk** Russian Fed
61G4	**Chernyye Zemli** Region, Russian Fed
18A2	**Cherokees,L** o'the USA
34A3	**Cherquenco** Chile
86C1	**Cherrapunji** India
60C3	**Cherven'** Belorussia
59C2	**Chervonograd** Ukraine
10C3	**Chesapeake** *B* USA
42C3	**Cheshire** County, Eng
16C1	**Cheshire** USA
64F3	**Chëshskaya Guba** *B* Russian Fed
21A1	**Chester** California, USA
42C3	**Chester** Eng
18C2	**Chester** Illinois, USA
16C1	**Chester** Massachusets, USA
15C3	**Chester** Pennsylvania, USA
17B1	**Chester** S Carolina, USA
16A3	**Chester** *R* USA
42D3	**Chesterfield** Eng
6A3	**Chesterfield Inlet** Can
16A3	**Chestertown** USA
25D3	**Chetumal** Mexico
13C1	**Chetwynd** Can
12A2	**Chevak** USA
111B2	**Cheviot** NZ
40C2	**Cheviots** *Hills* Eng/ Scot
13D3	**Chewelah** USA
8C2	**Cheyenne** USA
86A1	**Chhapra** India
86C1	**Chhātak** Bang
85D4	**Chhatarpur** India
85D4	**Chhindwāra** India
86B1	**Chhuka** Bhutan
73E5	**Chia'i** Taiwan
100A2	**Chiange** Angola
76C2	**Chiang Kham** Thai
76B2	**Chiang Mai** Thai
47C1	**Chiavenna** Italy
74E3	**Chiba** Japan
86B2	**Chibāsa** India
100A2	**Chibia** Angola
7C4	**Chibougamau** Can
75A1	**Chiburi-jima** *I* Japan
101C3	**Chibuto** Mozam
10B2	**Chicago** USA
14A2	**Chicago Heights** USA
12G3	**Chichagof I** USA
43D4	**Chichester** Eng
75B1	**Chichibu** Japan
69G4	**Chichi-jima** *I* Japan
11B3	**Chickamauga L** USA
19C3	**Chickasawhay** *R* USA
9D3	**Chickasha** USA
12F2	**Chicken** USA
32A5	**Chiclayo** Peru
8A3	**Chico** USA
29C4	**Chico** *R* Arg
101C2	**Chicoa** Mozam
15D2	**Chicopee** USA
7C5	**Chicoutimi** Can
101C3	**Chicualacuala** Mozam
87B2	**Chidambaram** India
6D3	**Chidley,C** Can
17B2	**Chiefland** USA
99C3	**Chiengi** Zambia
47B2	**Chieri** Italy
46C2	**Chiers** *R* France
47C1	**Chiesa** Italy
47D2	**Chiese** *R* Italy
52B2	**Chieti** Italy
72D1	**Chifeng** China
12C3	**Chiginigak,Mt** USA
4C3	**Chigmit Mts** USA
23B2	**Chignahuapán** Mexico
12C3	**Chignik** USA
24B2	**Chihuahua** Mexico
87B2	**Chik Ballāpur** India
87B2	**Chikmagalūr** India
12C2	**Chikuminuk L** USA

101C2	**Chikwawa** Malawi
76A1	**Chi-kyaw** Burma
87C1	**Chilakalūrupet** India
23B2	**Chilapa** Mexico
87B3	**Chilaw** Sri Lanka
28B6	**Chile** Republic
34B2	**Chilecito** Mendoza, Arg
100B2	**Chililabombwe** Zambia
86B2	**Chilka** *L* India
13C2	**Chilko** *R* Can
5F4	**Chilko L** Can
13C2	**Chilkotin** *R* Can
34A3	**Chillán** Chile
34D3	**Chillar** Arg
18B2	**Chillicothe** Missouri, USA
14B3	**Chillicothe** Ohio, USA
13C3	**Chilliwack** Can
86B1	**Chilmari** India
101C2	**Chilongozi** Zambia
20B2	**Chiloquin** USA
24C3	**Chilpancingo** Mexico
43D4	**Chiltern Hills** *Upland* Eng
14A2	**Chilton** USA
101C2	**Chilumba** Malawi
69E4	**Chi-lung** Taiwan
101C2	**Chilwa** *L* Malawi
100C2	**Chimanimani** Zim
46C1	**Chimay** Belg
65G5	**Chimbay** Uzbekistan
32B4	**Chimborazo** *Mt* Ecuador
32B5	**Chimbote** Peru
65H5	**Chimkent** Kazakhstan
101C2	**Chimoio** Mozam
67E3	**China** Republic, Asia
	China National **Republic = Taiwan**
25D3	**Chinandega** Nic
32B6	**Chincha Alta** Peru
109D1	**Chinchilla** Aust
101C2	**Chinde** Mozam
86C2	**Chindwin** *R* Burma
100B2	**Chingola** Zambia
100A2	**Chinguar** Angola
96A2	**Chinguetti** Maur
74B3	**Chinhae** S Korea
100C2	**Chinhoyi** Zim
12D3	**Chiniak,C** USA
84C2	**Chiniot** Pak
74B3	**Chinju** S Korea
98C2	**Chinko** *R* CAR
75B1	**Chino** Japan
101C2	**Chinsali** Zambia
52B1	**Chioggia** Italy
101C2	**Chipata** Zambia
101C3	**Chipinge** Zim
87A1	**Chiplūn** India
43C4	**Chippenham** Eng
10A2	**Chippewa Falls** USA
32A4	**Chira** *R* Peru
87C1	**Chirāla** India
101C3	**Chiredzi** Zim
95A2	**Chirfa** Niger
32A2	**Chiriquí** *Mt* Panama
54C2	**Chirpan** Bulg
32A2	**Chirripo Grande** *Mt* Costa Rica
100B2	**Chirundu** Zim
100B2	**Chisamba** Zambia
7C4	**Chisasibi** Can
73B4	**Chishui He** *R* China
	Chişinău = Kishinev
47B2	**Chisone** *R* Italy
61H2	**Chistopol** Russian Fed
68D1	**Chita** Russian Fed
100A2	**Chitado** Angola
100A2	**Chitembo** Angola
12F2	**Chitina** USA
12F2	**Chitina** *R* USA
87B2	**Chitradurga** India
84C1	**Chitral** Pak
32A2	**Chitré** Panama
86C2	**Chittagong** Bang
85C4	**Chittaurgarh** India
87B2	**Chittoor** India
100B2	**Chiume** Angola
47D1	**Chiusa** Italy

47B2	**Chivasso** Italy
100C2	**Chivhu** *Zim*
29D2	**Chivilcoy** Arg
100C2	**Chivu** Zim
75A1	**Chizu** Japan
29C3	**Choele Choel** Arg
34C3	**Choique** Arg
24B2	**Choix** Mexico
58B2	**Chojnice** Pol
99D1	**Choke** *Mts* Eth
48B2	**Cholet** France
23B2	**Cholula** Mexico
100B2	**Choma** Zambia
86B1	**Chomo Yummo** *Mt* China/India
57C2	**Chomutov** Czech Republic
63C1	**Chona** *R* Russian Fed
74B3	**Ch'ŏnan** S Korea
76C3	**Chon Buri** Thai
32A4	**Chone** Ecuador
74B2	**Ch'öngjin** N Korea
74B3	**Chongju** N Korea
74B3	**Ch'ŏngju** S Korea
100A2	**Chongoroi** Angola
73B4	**Chongqing** China
74B3	**Chŏngŭp** S Korea
74B3	**Chŏnju** S Korea
86B1	**Chooyu** *Mt* China/Nepal
59D3	**Chortkov** Ukraine
74B3	**Ch'örwön** N Korea
59B2	**Chorzow** Pol
74E3	**Choshi** Japan
34A3	**Chos-Malal** Arg
58B2	**Choszczno** Pol
86A2	**Chotanāgpur** Region, India
96C1	**Chott Melrhir** Alg
22B2	**Chowchilla** USA
63D3	**Choybalsan** Mongolia
6A3	**Chrantrey Inlet** *B* Can
111B2	**Christchurch** NZ
101G1	**Christiana** S Africa
6D2	**Christian,C** Can
12H3	**Christian Sd** USA
6E3	**Christianshab** Greenland
104D4	**Christmas I** Indian O
65J5	**Chu** Kazakhstan
65J5	**Chu** *R* Kazakhstan
29C4	**Chubut** State, Arg
29C4	**Chubut** *R* Arg
60D2	**Chudovo** Russian Fed
	Chudskoye Ozero = Peipus, Lake
4D3	**Chugach Mts** USA
12E2	**Chugiak** USA
75A1	**Chūgoku-sanchi** *Mts* Japan
29F2	**Chuí** Brazil
29B3	**Chuillán** Chile
77C5	**Chukai** Malay
76D2	**Chu Lai** Viet
21B3	**Chula Vista** USA
12E2	**Chulitna** USA
63E2	**Chulman** Russian Fed
32A5	**Chulucanas** Peru
30C2	**Chulumani** Bol
65K4	**Chulym** Russian Fed
63A2	**Chulym** *R* Russian Fed
63B2	**Chuma** *R* Russian Fed
84D2	**Chumar** India
63F2	**Chumikan** Russian Fed
77B3	**Chumphon** Thai
74B3	**Ch'unch'ŏn** S Korea
86B2	**Chunchura** India
74B3	**Ch'ungju** S Korea
	Chungking = Chongqing
99D3	**Chunya** Tanz
63C1	**Chunya** *R* Russian Fed
27L1	**Chupara Pt** Trinidad
30C3	**Chuquicamata** Chile
52A1	**Chur** Switz

86C2 **Churāchāndpur** India
7A4 **Churchill** Can
7D4 **Churchill** *R* Labrador, Can
7A4 **Churchill** *R* Manitoba, Can
7A4 **Churchill,C** Can
7D4 **Churchill Falls** Can
5H4 **Churchill L** Can
84C3 **Chūru** India
23A2 **Churumuco** Mexico
61J2 **Chusovoy** Russian Fed
61G2 **Chuvashskaya Respublika,** Russian Fed
68B4 **Chuxiong** China
76D3 **Chu Yang Sin** *Mt* Viet
78B4 **Cianjur** Indon
47D2 **Ciano d'Enza** Italy
35A2 **Cianorte** Brazil
58C2 **Ciechanów** Pol
25E2 **Ciego de Avila** Cuba
32C1 **Ciénaga** Colombia
25D2 **Cienfuegos** Cuba
59B3 **Cieszyn** Pol
51B2 **Cieza** Spain
92B2 **Cihanbeyli** Turk
23A2 **Cihuatlán** Mexico
78B4 **Cijulang** Indon
78B4 **Cilacap** Indon
54C1 **Cîmpina** Rom
51C1 **Çinca** *R* Spain
52C2 **Činčer** *Mt* Bosnia-Herzegovina
10B3 **Cincinnati** USA
54B1 **Cindrelu** *Mt* Rom
55C3 **Cine** *R* Turk
46C1 **Ciney** Belg
34B3 **Cipolletti** Arg
4D3 **Circle** Alaska, USA
14B3 **Circleville** USA
78B4 **Cirebon** Indon
43D4 **Cirencester** Eng
47D2 **Citadella** Italy
24C3 **Citlaltepetl** *Mt* Mexico
100A4 **Citrusdal** S Africa
52B2 **Citta del Vaticano** Italy
52B2 **Città di Castello** Italy
24B2 **Ciudad Acuña** Mexico
23A2 **Ciudad Altamirano** Mexico
33E2 **Ciudad Bolivar** Ven
24B2 **Ciudad Camargo** Mexico
25C3 **Ciudad del Carmen** Mexico
23B1 **Ciudad del Maiz** Mexico
51C1 **Ciudadela** Spain
33E2 **Ciudad Guayana** Ven
24B3 **Ciudad Guzman** Mexico
23A2 **Ciudad Hidalgo** Mexico
24B1 **Ciudad Juárez** Mexico
9C4 **Ciudad Lerdo** Mexico
24C2 **Ciudad Madero** Mexico
23B2 **Ciudad Mendoza** Mexico
24B2 **Ciudad Obregon** Mexico
27C4 **Ciudad Ojeda** Ven
33E2 **Ciudad Piar** Ven
50B2 **Ciudad Real** Spain
50A1 **Ciudad Rodrigo** Spain
24C2 **Ciudad Valles** Mexico
24C2 **Ciudad Victoria** Mexico
52B2 **Civitavecchia** Italy
93D2 **Cizre** Turk
43E4 **Clacton-on-Sea** Eng
5G4 **Claire,L** Can
14C2 **Clairton** USA
47A1 **Clairvaux** France
17A1 **Clanton** USA
100A4 **Clanwilliam** S Africa
45C2 **Clara** Irish Rep
34D3 **Claraz** Arg
45B2 **Clare** County, Irish Rep
14B2 **Clare** USA
45A2 **Clare** *I* Irish Rep
15D2 **Claremont** USA
18A2 **Claremore** USA
45B2 **Claremorris** Irish Rep
109D1 **Clarence** *R* Aust
111B2 **Clarence** *R* NZ
106C2 **Clarence Str** Aust
12H3 **Clarence Str** USA
19B3 **Clarendon** USA
7E5 **Clarenville** Can
5G4 **Claresholm** Can
18A1 **Clarinda** USA
15C2 **Clarion** Pennsylvania, USA
24A3 **Clarión** *I* Mexico
15C2 **Clarion** *R* USA
105J3 **Clarion Fracture Zone** Pacific O
11B3 **Clark Hill Res** USA
14B2 **Clark,Pt** Can
14B3 **Clarksburg** USA
11A3 **Clarksdale** USA
12C3 **Clarks Point** USA
20C1 **Clarkston** USA
18B2 **Clarksville** Arkansas, USA
35A1 **Claro** *R* Brazil
29D3 **Claromecó** Arg
18A2 **Clay Center** USA
44D2 **Claymore** *Oilfield* N Sea
13B3 **Clayoquot Sd** Can
9C3 **Clayton** New Mexico, USA
15C2 **Clayton** New York, USA
41B3 **Clear** *C* Irish Rep
12E3 **Cleare,C** USA
13D1 **Clear Hills** *Mts* Can
21A2 **Clear L** USA
20B2 **Clear Lake Res** USA
13D2 **Clearwater** Can
11B4 **Clearwater** USA
13E1 **Clearwater** *R* Can
13C2 **Clearwater L** Can
9D3 **Cleburne** USA
42E2 **Cleeton** *Oilfield* North Sea
22B1 **Clements** USA
79A3 **Cleopatra Needle** *Mt* Phil
107D3 **Clermont** Aust
46B2 **Clermont** France
46C2 **Clermont-en-Argonne** France
49C2 **Clermont-Ferrand** France
46D1 **Clervaux** Germany
47D1 **Cles** Italy
108A2 **Cleve** Aust
42D2 **Cleveland** County, Eng
19B3 **Cleveland** Mississippi, USA
10B2 **Cleveland** Ohio, USA
11B3 **Cleveland** Tennessee, USA
19A3 **Cleveland** Texas, USA
41B3 **Clew** *B* Irish Rep
45A2 **Clifden** Irish Rep
109D1 **Clifton** Aust
16B2 **Clifton** New Jersey, USA
108A1 **Clifton Hills** Aust
13F3 **Climax** Can
18B2 **Clinton** Arkansas, USA
5F4 **Clinton** Can
16C2 **Clinton** Connecticut, USA
16D1 **Clinton** Massachusetts, USA
19B3 **Clinton** Mississippi, USA
18B2 **Clinton** Missouri, USA
16B2 **Clinton** New Jersey, USA
4H3 **Clinton-Colden L** Can
24B3 **Clipperton I** Pacific O
30C2 **Cliza** Bol
45B3 **Clonakilty** Irish Rep
107D3 **Cloncurry** Aust
45C1 **Clones** Irish Rep
45C2 **Clonmel** Irish Rep
10A2 **Cloquet** USA
12C2 **Cloudy Mt** USA
22C2 **Clovis** California, USA
9C3 **Clovis** New Mexico, USA
60B4 **Cluj** Rom
54B1 **Cluj-Napoca** Rom
47B1 **Cluses** France
47C2 **Clusone** Italy
111A3 **Clutha** *R* NZ
43C3 **Clwyd** County, Wales
6D2 **Clyde** Can
111A3 **Clyde** NZ
42B2 **Clyde** *R* Scot
23A2 **Coahuayana** Mexico
23A2 **Coalcomán** Mexico
13E2 **Coaldale** Can
21B2 **Coaldale** USA
21A2 **Coalinga** USA
33E5 **Coari** *R* Brazil
17A1 **Coastal Plain** USA
4E4 **Coast Mts** Can
8A2 **Coast Ranges** *Mts* USA
42B2 **Coatbridge** Scot
23B2 **Coatepec** Mexico
16B3 **Coatesville** USA
15D1 **Coaticook** Can
6B3 **Coats I** Can
112B1 **Coats Land** Region, Ant
25C3 **Coatzacoalcos** Mexico
7C5 **Cobalt** Can
25C3 **Cobán** Guatemala
107D4 **Cobar** Aust
109C3 **Cobargo** Aust
45B3 **Cobh** Irish Rep
32D6 **Cobija** Bol
16B1 **Cobleskill** USA
51B2 **Cobo de Palos** *C* Spain
7C5 **Cobourg** Can
106C2 **Cobourg Pen** Aust
57C2 **Coburg** Germany
32B4 **Coca** Ecuador
17B2 **Coca** USA
30C2 **Cochabamba** Bol
46D1 **Cochem** Germany
87B3 **Cochin** India
13E2 **Cochrane** Alberta, Can
7B5 **Cochrane** Ontario, Can
108B2 **Cockburn** Aust
16A3 **Cockeysville** USA
27H1 **Cockpit Country,The** Jamaica
25D3 **Coco** *R* Honduras/Nic
98A2 **Cocobeach** Gabon
27L1 **Cocos B** Trinidad
104C4 **Cocos Is** Indian O
23A1 **Cocula** Mexico
10C2 **Cod,C** USA
111A3 **Codfish I** NZ
7D4 **Cod I** Can
47E2 **Codigoro** Italy
31C2 **Codó** Brazil
47C2 **Codogno** Italy
8C2 **Cody** USA
56B2 **Coesfeld** Germany
8B2 **Coeur d'Alene** USA
9D3 **Coffeyville** USA
108A2 **Coffin B** Aust
109D2 **Coff's Harbour** Aust
23B2 **Cofre de Perote** *Mt* Mexico
48B2 **Cognac** France
15D2 **Cohoes** USA
108B3 **Cohuna** Aust
29B5 **Coihaique** Chile
87B2 **Coimbatore** India
50A1 **Coimbra** Port
32A3 **Cojimies** Ecuador
107D4 **Colac** Aust
31C5 **Colatina** Brazil
112B6 **Colbeck,C** Ant
43E4 **Colchester** Eng
16C2 **Colchester** USA
47B1 **Col de la Faucille** France
13E2 **Cold L** Can
52A1 **Col du Grand St Bernard** *P* Italy/Switz
47B2 **Col du Lautaret** *P* France
52A1 **Col du Mont Cenis** *P* France/Italy
14B2 **Coldwater** USA
12F1 **Coleen** *R* USA
14B2 **Coleman** Michigan, USA
101G1 **Colenso** S Africa
45C1 **Coleraine** N Ire
111B2 **Coleridge,L** NZ
100B4 **Colesberg** S Africa
22C1 **Coleville** USA
21A2 **Colfax** California, USA
19B3 **Colfax** Louisiana, USA
20C1 **Colfax** Washington, USA
24B3 **Colima** Mexico
23A2 **Colima** State, Mexico
34A2 **Colina** Chile
44A3 **Coll** *I* Scot
109C1 **Collarenebri** Aust
52A2 **Colle de Tende** *P* France/Italy
12E2 **College** USA
17B1 **College Park** Georgia, USA
16A3 **College Park** Washington, USA
19A3 **College Station** USA
106A4 **Collie** Aust
106B2 **Collier B** Aust
46A1 **Collines de L'Artois** *Mts* France
46B2 **Collines De Thiérache** France
14B2 **Collingwood** Can
110B2 **Collingwood** NZ
19C3 **Collins** Mississippi, USA
4H2 **Collinson Pen** Can
107D3 **Collinsville** Aust
18C2 **Collinsville** Illinois, USA
18A2 **Collinsville** Oklahoma, USA
34A3 **Collipulli** Chile
49D2 **Colmar** France
Cologne = Köln
35B2 **Colômbia** Brazil
32B3 **Colombia** Republic, S America
15C3 **Colombia** USA
87B3 **Colombo** Sri Lanka
25D2 **Colon** Cuba
32B2 **Colón** Panama
29E2 **Colonia** Urug
34D2 **Colonia del Sacramento** Urug
34B3 **Colonia 25 de Mayo** Arg
29C5 **Colonia Las Heras** Arg
44A3 **Colonsay** *I* Scot
23A1 **Colontlán** Mexico
27E5 **Coloradito** Ven
8C3 **Colorado** State, USA
9B3 **Colorado** *R* Arizona, USA
29D3 **Colorado** *R* Buenos Aires, Arg
9D3 **Colorado** *R* Texas, USA
9B3 **Colorado Plat** USA
8C3 **Colorado Springs** USA
22D3 **Colton** USA
16A3 **Columbia** Maryland, USA

19C3 **Columbia** Mississippi, USA
10A3 **Columbia** Missouri, USA
15C2 **Columbia** Pennsylvania, USA
11B3 **Columbia** S Carolina, USA
11B3 **Columbia** Tennessee, USA
13D2 **Columbia** *R* Can
8A2 **Columbia** *R* USA
5G4 **Columbia,Mt** Can
20C1 **Columbia Plat** USA
11B3 **Columbus** Georgia, USA
14A3 **Columbus** Indiana, USA
11B3 **Columbus** Mississippi, USA
8D2 **Columbus** Nebraska, USA
10B2 **Columbus** Ohio, USA
19A4 **Columbus** Texas, USA
20C1 **Colville** USA
4C3 **Colville** *R* USA
110C1 **Colville,C** NZ
4F3 **Colville L** Can
42C3 **Colwyn Bay** Wales
47E2 **Comacchio** Italy
22B1 **Comanche Res** USA
112C2 **Comandante Ferraz** *Base* Ant
25D3 **Comayagua** Honduras
34A2 **Combarbalá** Chile
45C2 **Comeragh** *Mts* Irish Rep
86C2 **Comilla** Bang
25C3 **Comitán** Mexico
46C2 **Commercy** France
6B3 **Committees B** Can
52A1 **Como** Italy
29C5 **Comodoro Rivadavia** Arg
23A1 **Comonfort** Mexico
87B3 **Comorin,C** India
101D2 **Comoros** *Is* Indian O
49C2 **Compiègne** France
23A1 **Compostela** Mexico
34B2 **Comte Salas** Arg
86C1 **Cona** China
97A4 **Conakry** Guinea
34B2 **Concarán** Arg
48B2 **Concarneau** France
35D1 **Conceiçao da Barra** Brazil
31B3 **Conceição do Araguaia** Brazil
35C1 **Conceiçao do Mato Dentro** Brazil
29B3 **Concepción** Chile
30E3 **Concepción** Par
29E2 **Concepción** *R* Arg
24B2 **Concepcion del Oro** Mexico
34D2 **Concepcion del Uruguay** Arg
9A3 **Conception,Pt** USA
35B2 **Conchas** Brazil
9C4 **Conchos** *R* Mexico
21A2 **Concord** California, USA
10C2 **Concord** New Hampshire, USA
29E2 **Concordia** Arg
8D3 **Concordia** USA
20B1 **Concrete** USA
109D1 **Condamine** Aust
107D4 **Condobolin** Aust
20B1 **Condon** USA
46C1 **Condroz** *Mts* Belg
17A1 **Conecuh** *R* USA
47E2 **Conegliano** Italy
89F8 **Congo** Republic, Africa
89F8 **Congo** *R* Congo
Congo,R = Zaïre
14B1 **Coniston** Can
45B2 **Connaught** Region, Irish Rep
14B2 **Conneaut** USA
10C2 **Connecticut** State, USA
15D2 **Connecticut** *R* USA
15C2 **Connellsville** USA
45B2 **Connemara,Mts of** Irish Rep
14A3 **Connersville** USA
108B2 **Conoble** Aust
19A3 **Conroe** USA
35C2 **Conselheiro Lafaiete** Brazil
77D4 **Con Son** *Is* Viet
Constance,L = Bodensee
60C5 **Constanta** Rom
96C1 **Constantine** Alg
12C3 **Constantine,C** USA
29B3 **Constitución** Chile
13F3 **Consul** Can
47E2 **Contarina** Italy
31C4 **Contas** *R* Brazil
23B2 **Contreras** Mexico
4H3 **Contuoyto L** Can
11A3 **Conway** Arkansas, USA
15D2 **Conway** New Hampshire, USA
17C1 **Conway** South Carolina, USA
108A1 **Conway,L** Aust
42C3 **Conwy** Wales
106C3 **Coober Pedy** Aust
110B2 **Cook** *Str* NZ
13B2 **Cook,C** Can
4C3 **Cook Inlet** *B* USA
105H4 **Cook Is** Pacific O
111B2 **Cook,Mt** NZ
107D2 **Cooktown** Aust
109C2 **Coolabah** Aust
108C1 **Cooladdi** Aust
109C2 **Coolah** Aust
109C2 **Coolamon** Aust
106B4 **Coolgardie** Aust
109C3 **Cooma** Aust
109C2 **Coonabarabran** Aust
109C2 **Coonambie** Aust
108B2 **Coonbah** Aust
108A2 **Coondambo** Aust
108C1 **Coongoola** Aust
87B2 **Coonoor** India
108B1 **Cooper Basin** Aust
106C3 **Cooper Creek** Aust
108B1 **Cooper Creek** *R* Aust
108A3 **Coorong,The** Aust
109D1 **Cooroy** Aust
20B2 **Coos B** USA
20B2 **Coos Bay** USA
107D4 **Cootamundra** Aust
45C1 **Cootehill** Irish Rep
23B2 **Copala** Mexico
23B2 **Copalillo** Mexico
Copenhagen = København
30B4 **Copiapó** Chile
47D2 **Copparo** Italy
12F2 **Copper** *R* USA
4D3 **Copper Centre** USA
14B1 **Copper Cliff** Can
Coppermine = Qurlurtuuk
4G3 **Coppermine** *R* Can
Coquilhatville = Mbandaka
30B4 **Coquimbo** Chile
54B2 **Corabia** Rom
17B2 **Coral Gables** USA
6B3 **Coral Harbour** Can
107D2 **Coral S** Aust/PNG
104F4 **Coral Sea Basin** Pacific O
107E2 **Coral Sea Island Territories** Aust
108B3 **Corangamite,L** Aust
33F3 **Corantijn** *R* Surinam/Guyana
46B2 **Corbeil-Essonnes** France
50A1 **Corcubíon** Spain
11B3 **Cordele** USA
50A1 **Cordillera Cantabrica** *Mts* Spain
26C3 **Cordillera Central** *Mts* Dom Rep
79B2 **Cordillera Central** *Mts* Phil
34B2 **Cordillera de Ansita** *Mts* Arg
32B5 **Cordillera de los Andes** *Mts* Peru
30C4 **Cordillera del Toro** *Mt* Arg
32C2 **Cordillera de Mérida** Ven
34A3 **Cordillera de Viento** *Mts* Arg
25D3 **Cordillera Isabelia** *Mts* Nic
32B3 **Cordillera Occidental** *Mts* Colombia
32B3 **Cordillera Oriental** *Mts* Colombia
108B1 **Cordillo Downs** Aust
29D2 **Córdoba** Arg
24C3 **Córdoba** Mexico
50B2 **Córdoba** Spain
29D2 **Córdoba** State, Arg
4D3 **Cordova** USA
Corfu = Kérkira
109D2 **Coricudgy,Mt** Aust
53C3 **Corigliano Calabro** Italy
11B3 **Corinth** Mississippi, USA
31C5 **Corinto** Brazil
45B2 **Cork** County, Irish Rep
41B3 **Cork** Irish Rep
92A1 **Çorlu** Turk
31C5 **Cornel Fabriciano** Brazil
35A2 **Cornelio Procópio** Brazil
7E5 **Corner Brook** Can
109C3 **Corner Inlet** *B* Aust
15C2 **Corning** USA
7C5 **Cornwall** Can
43B4 **Cornwall** County, Eng
43B4 **Cornwall,C** Eng
4H2 **Cornwall I** Can
6A2 **Cornwallis I** Can
32D1 **Coro** Ven
31C2 **Coroatá** Brazil
30C2 **Coroico** Bol
35B1 **Coromandel** Brazil
87C2 **Coromandel Coast** India
110C1 **Coromandel Pen** NZ
110C1 **Coromandel Range** *Mts* NZ
22D4 **Corona** California, USA
13E2 **Coronation** Can
4G3 **Coronation G** Can
34C2 **Coronda** Arg
29B3 **Coronel** Chile
34D3 **Coronel Brandsen** Arg
34C3 **Coronel Dorrego** Arg
35C1 **Coronel Fabriciano** Brazil
30E4 **Coronel Oviedo** Par
29D3 **Coronel Pringles** Arg
34C3 **Coronel Suárez** Arg
34D3 **Coronel Vidal** Arg
30B2 **Coropuna** *Mt* Peru
109C3 **Corowa** Aust
49D3 **Corps** France
9D4 **Corpus Christi** USA
9D4 **Corpus Christi,L** USA
79B3 **Corregidor** *I* Phil
35A1 **Corrente** *R* Mato Grosso, Brazil
30E4 **Corrientes** Arg
30E4 **Corrientes** State, Arg
19B3 **Corrigan** USA
106A4 **Corrigin** Aust
107E2 **Corringe Is** Aust
109C3 **Corryong** Aust
52A2 **Corse** *I* Medit S
42B2 **Corsewall** *Pt* Scot
Corsica = Corse
9D3 **Corsicana** USA
52A2 **Corte** Corse
9C3 **Cortez** USA
52B1 **Cortina d'Ampezzo** Italy
15C2 **Cortland** USA
23A2 **Coruca de Catalan** Mexico
93D1 **Çoruh** *R* Turk
60E5 **Čorum** Turk
30E2 **Corumbá** Brazil
35B1 **Corumba** *R* Brazil
35B1 **Corumbaiba** Brazil
20B2 **Corvallis** USA
96A1 **Corvo** *I* Açores
43C3 **Corwen** Wales
23B2 **Coscomatopec** Mexico
53C3 **Cosenza** Italy
101D1 **Cosmoledo** *Is* Seychelles
34C2 **Cosquín** Arg
51B2 **Costa Blanca** Region, Spain
51C1 **Costa Brava** Region, Spain
50B2 **Costa de la Luz** Region, Spain
50B2 **Costa del Sol** Region, Spain
22D4 **Costa Mesa** USA
25D3 **Costa Rica** Republic, Cent America
79B4 **Cotabato** Phil
30C3 **Cotagaita** Bol
49D3 **Côte d'Azur** Region, France
46C2 **Côtes de Meuse** *Mts* France
97C4 **Cotonou** Benin
32B4 **Cotopaxi** *Mt* Ecuador
43C4 **Cotswold Hills** *Upland* Eng
20B2 **Cottage Grove** USA
56C2 **Cottbus** Germany
108A3 **Couedic,C du** Aust
20C1 **Couer d'Alene L** USA
46B2 **Coulommiers** France
15C1 **Coulonge** *R* Can
22B2 **Coulterville** USA
4B3 **Council** USA
8D2 **Council Bluffs** USA
58C1 **Courland Lagoon** *Lg* Lithuania/Russian Fed
47B2 **Courmayeur** Italy
13B3 **Courtenay** Can
Courtrai = Kortrijk
48B2 **Coutances** France
43D3 **Coventry** Eng
50A1 **Covilhã** Spain
17B1 **Covington** Georgia, USA
19B3 **Covington** Louisiana, USA
109C2 **Cowal,L** Aust
108B3 **Cowangie** Aust
15D1 **Cowansville** Can
108A1 **Coward Springs** Aust
108A2 **Cowell** Aust
108C3 **Cowes** Aust
20B1 **Cowichan L** Can
20B1 **Cowiltz** *R* USA
109C2 **Cowra** Aust
30F2 **Coxim** Brazil
16C1 **Coxsackie** USA
86C2 **Cox's Bazar** Bang
22B2 **Coyote** USA
23A2 **Coyuca de Benitez** Mexico
59B2 **Cracow** Pol
100B4 **Cradock** S Africa
8C2 **Craig** USA
57C3 **Crailsheim** Germany
54B2 **Craiova** Rom
15D2 **Cranberry L** USA
5G5 **Cranbrook** Can
20C2 **Crane** Oregon, USA
16D2 **Cranston** USA
20B2 **Crater L** USA
20B2 **Crater Lake Nat Pk** USA
31C3 **Crateus** Brazil
31D3 **Crato** Brazil
14A2 **Crawfordsville** USA
17B1 **Crawfordville** USA
43D4 **Crawley** Eng
5H4 **Cree L** Can
46B2 **Creil** France

42D2 **Durham** Eng
11C3 **Durham** N Carolina, USA
16D1 **Durham** New Hampshire, USA
108B1 **Durham Downs** Aust
54A2 **Durmitor** *Mt* Montenegro, Yugos
44B2 **Durness** Scot
55A2 **Durrës** Alb
108B1 **Durrie** Aust
45A3 **Dursey** *I* Irish Rep
55C3 **Dursunbey** Turk
110B2 **D'Urville I** NZ
90D2 **Dushak** Turkmenistan
73B4 **Dushan** China
82A2 **Dushanbe** Tajikistan
111A3 **Dusky Sd** NZ
56B2 **Düsseldorf** Germany
73B4 **Duyun** China
92B1 **Düzce** Turk
60C2 **Dvina** *R* Latvia
85B4 **Dwārka** India
6D3 **Dyer,C** Can
11B3 **Dyersburg** USA
43B3 **Dyfed** County, Wales
61F5 **Dykh Tau** *Mt* Russian Fed
108B1 **Dynevor Downs** Aust
68B2 **Dzag** Mongolia
63C3 **Dzamin Uüd** Mongolia
101D2 **Dzaoudzi** Mayotte
68C2 **Dzarnïn Uüd** Mongolia
68B2 **Dzavhan Gol** *R* Mongolia
80E1 **Dzehezkazgan** Kazakhstan
61F2 **Dzerzhinsk** Russian Fed
63E2 **Dzhalinda** Russian Fed
65J5 **Dzhambul** Kazakhstan
60D4 **Dzhankoy** Ukraine
Dzharkent = Panfilov
65H4 **Dzhezkazgan** Kazakhstan
84B1 **Dzhilikul'** Tajikistan
65J5 **Dzhungarskiy Alatau** *Mts* Kazakhstan
59B2 **Dzierzoniow** Pol
63B3 **Dzüyl** Mongolia
82C1 **Dzungaria** Basin, China

E

7B4 **Eabamet L** Can
12F2 **Eagle** Alaska, USA
20B2 **Eagle L** California, USA
19A3 **Eagle Mountain L** USA
9C4 **Eagle Pass** USA
4E3 **Eagle Plain** Can
12E2 **Eagle River** USA
21B2 **Earlimart** USA
17B1 **Easley** USA
15C2 **East Aurora** USA
43E4 **Eastbourne** Eng
14A2 **East Chicago** USA
69E3 **East China Sea** China/Japan
83B4 **Eastern Ghats** *Mts* India
29E6 **East Falkland** *I* Falkland Is
12E1 **East Fork** *R* USA
21B2 **Eastgate** USA
16C1 **Easthampton** USA
16C2 **East Hampton** USA
14A2 **East Lake** USA
14B2 **East Liverpool** USA
100B4 **East London** S Africa
7C4 **Eastmain** Can
7C4 **Eastmain** *R* Can
17B1 **Eastman** USA
15C3 **Easton** Maryland, USA
15C2 **Easton** Pennsylvania, USA
16B2 **East Orange** USA
105L4 **East Pacific Ridge** Pacific O
17B1 **East Point** USA
42D3 **East Retford** Eng
11A3 **East St Louis** USA
1B7 **East Siberian S** Russian Fed
43E4 **East Sussex** County, Eng
17B1 **Eatonton** USA
10A2 **Eau Claire** USA
71F3 **Eauripik** *I* Pacific O
23B1 **Ebano** Mexico
98B2 **Ebebiyin** Eq Guinea
56C2 **Eberswalde** Germany
73A4 **Ebian** China
65K5 **Ebinur** *L* China
53C2 **Eboli** Italy
98B2 **Ebolowa** Cam
51B1 **Ebro** *R* Spain
92A1 **Eceabat** Turk
96C1 **Ech Cheliff** Alg
72D2 **Eching** China
20C1 **Echo** USA
4G3 **Echo Bay** Can
46D2 **Echternach** Lux
108B3 **Echuca** Aust
50A2 **Ecija** Spain
6B2 **Eclipse Sd** Can
32B4 **Ecuador** Republic, S America
99E1 **Ed** Eritrea
44C2 **Eday** *I* Scot
98C1 **Ed Da'ein** Sudan
95C3 **Ed Damer** Sudan
95C3 **Ed Debba** Sudan
44B2 **Eddrachillis** *B* Scot
99D1 **Ed Dueim** Sudan
109C4 **Eddystone Pt** Aust
98A2 **Edea** Cam
109C3 **Eden** Aust
42C2 **Eden** *R* Eng
101G1 **Edenburg** S Africa
111A3 **Edendale** NZ
46E2 **Edenkoben** Germany
46E1 **Eder** *R* Germany
6D3 **Edgell I** Can
64D2 **Edgeøya** *I* Barents S
16A3 **Edgewood** USA
94B3 **Edh Dhahiriya** Israel
55B2 **Edhessa** Greece
44C3 **Edinburgh** Scot
60C5 **Edirne** Turk
17B1 **Edisto** *R* USA
13D2 **Edith Cavell,Mt** Can
20B1 **Edmonds** USA
5G4 **Edmonton** Can
7D5 **Edmundston** Can
19A4 **Edna** USA
12H3 **Edna Bay** USA
52B1 **Edolo** Italy
94B3 **Edom** Region, Jordan
92A2 **Edremit** Turk
55C3 **Edremit Körfezi** *B* Turk
68B2 **Edrengiyn Nuruu** *Mts* Mongolia
5G4 **Edson** Can
34C3 **Eduardo Castex** Arg
12J2 **Eduni,Mt** Can
108B3 **Edward** *R* Aust
99C3 **Edward,L** Uganda/Zaïre
108A1 **Edwards Creek** Aust
9C3 **Edwards Plat** USA
18C2 **Edwardsville** USA
12H3 **Edziza,Mt** Can
12B2 **Eek** USA
46B1 **Eeklo** Belg
10B3 **Effingham** USA
6E3 **Egedesminde** Greenland
12C3 **Egegik** USA
59C3 **Eger** Hung
39F7 **Egersund** Nor
16B3 **Egg Harbor City** USA
4G2 **Eglinton I** Can
110B1 **Egmont,C** NZ
110B1 **Egmont,Mt** NZ
92B2 **Eğridir Gölü** *L* Turk
95B2 **Egypt** Republic, Africa
50B1 **Eibar** Spain
49C2 **Eibeuf** France
46D1 **Eifel** Region, Germany
44A3 **Eigg** *I* Scot
83B5 **Eight Degree Chan** Indian O
106B2 **Eighty Mile Beach** Aust
108C3 **Eildon,L** Aust
56B2 **Eindhoven** Neth
47C1 **Einsiedeln** Switz
94B3 **Ein Yahav** Israel
57C2 **Eisenach** Germany
57C3 **Eisenerz** Austria
46D1 **Eitorf** Germany
72A1 **Ejin qi** China
23B2 **Ejutla** Mexico
110C2 **Eketahuna** NZ
65J4 **Ekibastuz** Kazakhstan
63F2 **Ekimchan** Russian Fed
92B3 **Ek Mahalla el Kubra** Egypt
39H7 **Eksjo** Sweden
10B1 **Ekwen** *R* Can
92A3 **El'Alamein** Egypt
92B3 **El'Arîsh** Egypt
92B4 **Elat** Israel
95B3 **El'Atrun Oasis** Sudan
93C2 **Elazig** Turk
92C3 **El Azraq** Jordan
52B2 **Elba** *I* Italy
95C2 **El Balyana** Egypt
32C2 **El Banco** Colombia
55B2 **Elbasan** Alb
27D5 **El Baúl** Ven
57C2 **Elbe** *R* Germany
94C1 **El Bega'a** *R* Leb
14A2 **Elberta** USA
8C3 **Elbert,Mt** USA
17B1 **Elberton** USA
92C2 **Elbistan** Turk
58B2 **Elblag** Pol
29B4 **El Bolson** Arg
61F5 **Elbrus** *Mt* Russian Fed
Elburz Mts = Reshteh-ye Alborz
21B3 **El Cajon** USA
19A4 **El Campo** USA
51B2 **Elche** Spain
51B2 **Elda** Spain
32B3 **El Diviso** Colombia
96B2 **El Djouf** *Desert Region* Maur
18B2 **Eldon** USA
11A3 **El Dorado** Arkansas, USA
35B2 **Eldorado** Brazil
9D3 **El Dorado** Kansas, USA
24B2 **El Dorado** Mexico
33E2 **El Dorado** Ven
99D2 **Eldoret** Kenya
22C1 **Eleanor,L** USA
96B2 **El Eglab** Region, Alg
50B1 **El Escorial** Spain
93D2 **Eleşkirt** Turk
11C4 **Eleuthera** *I* The Bahamas
92B4 **El Faiyûm** Egypt
96B2 **El Farsia** *Well* Mor
98C1 **El Fasher** Sudan
92B4 **El Fashn** Egypt
50A1 **El Ferrol del Caudillo** Spain
99C1 **El Fula** Sudan
96C1 **El Gassi** Alg
99D1 **El Geteina** Sudan
99D1 **El Gezīra** Region, Sudan
94B3 **El Ghor** *V* Israel/Jordan
10B2 **Elgin** Illinois, USA
44C3 **Elgin** Scot
92B3 **El Gîza** Egypt
96C1 **El Golea** Alg
99D2 **Elgon,Mt** Uganda/Kenya
99E2 **El Goran** Eth
23A2 **El Grullo** Mexico
96B2 **El Guettara** *Well* Mali
96B2 **El Haricha** *Desert Region* Mali
92A4 **El Harra** Egypt
51C2 **El Harrach** Alg
99D1 **El Hawata** Sudan
23B1 **El Higo** Mexico
34A3 **El Huecu** Arg
92B4 **El'Igma** *Desert Region* Egypt
12B2 **Elim** USA
4H2 **Elira,C** Can
Elisabethville = Lubumbashi
39K6 **Elisenvaara** Fin
El Iskandarîya = Alexandria
61F4 **Elista** Russian Fed
106C4 **Elizabeth** Aust
15D2 **Elizabeth** USA
11C3 **Elizabeth City** USA
17C1 **Elizabethtown** N Carolina, USA
16A2 **Elizabethtown** Pennsylvania, USA
96B1 **El Jadida** Mor
92C3 **El Jafr** Jordan
99D1 **El Jebelein** Sudan
96D1 **El Jem** Tunisia
58C2 **Elk** Pol
16B3 **Elk** *R* Maryland, USA
14B3 **Elk** *R* W Virginia, USA
95C3 **El Kamlin** Sudan
22B1 **Elk Grove** USA
El Khalil = Hebron
80B3 **El Khârga** Egypt
80B3 **El-Khârga Oasis** Egypt
14A2 **Elkhart** USA
96B2 **El Khenachich** *Desert Region* Mali
54C2 **Elkhovo** Bulg
14C3 **Elkins** USA
8B2 **Elko** USA
16B3 **Elkton** USA
92B3 **El Kuntilla** Egypt
99C1 **El Lagowa** Sudan
4H2 **Ellef Ringnes I** Can
8A2 **Ellensburg** USA
16B2 **Ellenville** USA
6B2 **Ellesmere I** Can
111B2 **Ellesmere,L** NZ
16A3 **Ellicott City** USA
100B4 **Elliot** S Africa
7B5 **Elliot Lake** Can
94B3 **El Lisan** *Pen* Jordan
112B3 **Ellsworth Land** *Region* Ant
95B1 **El Maghra** *L* Egypt
92B3 **El Mansûra** Egypt
16B3 **Elmer** USA
96B3 **El Merelé** *Desert Region* Maur
34B2 **El Milagro** Arg
94B1 **El Mīna** Leb
92B4 **El Minya** Egypt
22B1 **Elmira** California, USA
10C2 **Elmira** New York, USA
96B2 **El Mreitl** *Well* Maur
56B2 **Elmshorn** Germany
98C1 **El Muglad** Sudan
96B2 **El Mzereb** *Well* Mali
79A3 **El Nido** Phil
99D1 **El Obeid** Sudan
23A2 **El Oro** Mexico
96C1 **El Oued** Alg
9C3 **El Paso** USA
21A2 **El Porta** USA
22C2 **El Portal** USA
50A2 **El Puerto del Sta Maria** Spain
El Qâhira = Cairo
El Quds = Jerusalem
94B3 **El Quseima** Egypt
9D3 **El Reno** USA
4E3 **Elsa** Can
25D3 **El Salvador** Republic, Cent America
22D4 **Elsinore L** USA
34B3 **El Sosneade** Arg

Elsterwerde

F

5G4 **Fort Mackay** Can
5G5 **Fort Macleod** Can
5G4 **Fort McMurray** Can
4E3 **Fort McPherson** Can
18B2 **Fort Madison** USA
8C2 **Fort Morgan** USA
11B4 **Fort Myers** USA
5F4 **Fort Nelson** Can
4F3 **Fort Norman** Can
17A1 **Fort Payne** USA
8C2 **Fort Peck Res** USA
11B4 **Fort Pierce** USA
4G3 **Fort Providence** Can
5G3 **Fort Resolution** Can
98B3 **Fort Rousset** Congo
5F4 **Fort St James** Can
13C1 **Fort St John** Can
13E2 **Fort Saskatchewan** Can
18B2 **Fort Scott** USA
4E3 **Fort Selkirk** Can
7B4 **Fort Severn** Can
61H5 **Fort Shevchenko** Kazakhstan
4F3 **Fort Simpson** Can
5G3 **Fort Smith** Can
4G3 **Fort Smith** Region, Can
11A3 **Fort Smith** USA
9C3 **Fort Stockton** USA
20B2 **Fortuna** California, USA
5G4 **Fort Vermillion** Can
17A1 **Fort Walton Beach** USA
10B2 **Fort Wayne** USA
44B3 **Fort William** Scot
9D3 **Fort Worth** USA
12F2 **Fortymile** *R* USA
12E1 **Fort Yukon** USA
73C5 **Foshan** China
47B2 **Fossano** Italy
12G3 **Foster,Mt** USA
98B3 **Fougamou** Gabon
48B2 **Fougères** France
44D1 **Foula** *I* Scot
43E4 **Foulness I** Eng
111B2 **Foulwind,C** NZ
98B2 **Foumban** Cam
49C1 **Fourmies** France
55C3 **Foúrnoi** *I* Greece
97A3 **Fouta Djallon** *Mts* Guinea
111B3 **Foveaux** *Str* NZ
43B4 **Fowey** Eng
13D2 **Fox Creek** Can
6B3 **Foxe Basin** *G* Can
6B3 **Foxe Chan** Can
6C3 **Foxe Pen** Can
110C2 **Foxton** NZ
13F2 **Fox Valley** Can
45B2 **Foynes** Irish Rep
100A2 **Foz do Cuene** Angola
30F4 **Foz do Iquaçu** Brazil
16A2 **Frackville** USA
34B2 **Fraga** Arg
16D1 **Framingham** USA
31B6 **Franca** Brazil
49C2 **France** Republic, Europe
10A2 **Frances** Can
12J2 **Frances** *R* Can
49D2 **Franche Comté** Region, France
100B3 **Francistown** Botswana
13B2 **Francois L** Can
14A2 **Frankfort** Indiana, USA
11B3 **Frankfort** Kentucky, USA
101G1 **Frankfort** S Africa
57B2 **Frankfurt** Germany
46E1 **Frankfurt am Main** Germany
56C2 **Frankfurt-an-der-Oder** Germany
57C3 **Fränkischer Alb** *Upland* Germany
14A3 **Franklin** Indiana, USA
19B4 **Franklin** Louisiana, USA
16D1 **Franklin** Massachusetts, USA
16B2 **Franklin** New Jersey, USA
14C2 **Franklin** Pennsylvania, USA
4F2 **Franklin B** Can
20C1 **Franklin D Roosevelt** *L* USA
4F3 **Franklin Mts** Can
4J2 **Franklin Str** Can
111B2 **Franz Josef Glacier** NZ
Franz-Joseph-Land = Zemlya Frantsa Iosifa
5F5 **Fraser** *R* Can
44C3 **Fraserburgh** Scot
107E3 **Fraser I** Aust
13B2 **Fraser L** Can
47B1 **Frasne** France
47C1 **Frauenfield** Switz
34D2 **Fray Bentos** Urug
40C2 **Frazerburgh** Scot
16B3 **Frederica** USA
56B1 **Fredericia** Den
15C3 **Frederick** Maryland, USA
15C3 **Fredericksburg** Virginia, USA
12H3 **Frederick Sd** USA
18B2 **Fredericktown** USA
7D5 **Fredericton** Can
6E3 **Frederikshab** Greenland
39G7 **Frederikshavn** Den
15C2 **Fredonia** USA
39G7 **Fredrikstad** Nor
16B2 **Freehold** USA
26B1 **Freeport** The Bahamas
19A4 **Freeport** Texas, USA
97A4 **Freetown** Sierra Leone
57B3 **Freiburg** Germany
57C3 **Freistadt** Austria
106A4 **Fremantle** Aust
22B2 **Fremont** California, USA
18A1 **Fremont** Nebraska, USA
14B2 **Fremont** Ohio, USA
33G3 **French Guiana** Dependency, S America
109C4 **Frenchmans Cap** *Mt* Aust
105J4 **French Polynesia** *Is* Pacific O
24B2 **Fresnillo** Mexico
8B3 **Fresno** USA
22C2 **Fresno** *R* USA
47A1 **Fretigney** France
46B1 **Frévent** France
109C4 **Freycinet Pen** Aust
97A3 **Fria** Guinea
22C2 **Friant** USA
22C2 **Friant Dam** USA
52A1 **Fribourg** Switz
57B3 **Friedrichshafen** Germany
6D3 **Frobisher B** Can
6D3 **Frobisher Bay** Can
5H4 **Frobisher L** Can
61F4 **Frolovo** Russian Fed
43C4 **Frome** Eng
108A1 **Frome** *R* Aust
43C4 **Frome** *R* Eng
106C4 **Frome,L** Aust
25C3 **Frontera** Mexico
15C3 **Front Royal** USA
53B2 **Frosinone** Italy
73C5 **Fuchuan** China
73E4 **Fuding** China
24B2 **Fuerte** *R* Mexico
30E3 **Fuerte Olimpo** Par
96A2 **Fuerteventura** *I* Canary Is
72C2 **Fugu** China
68A2 **Fuhai** China
91C4 **Fujairah** UAE
75B1 **Fuji** Japan
73D4 **Fujian** Province, China
69F2 **Fujin** China
75B1 **Fujinomiya** Japan
74D3 **Fuji-san** *Mt* Japan
75B1 **Fujisawa** Japan
75B1 **Fuji-Yoshida** Japan
63A3 **Fukang** China
74C3 **Fukuchiyima** Japan
74D3 **Fukui** Japan
74C4 **Fukuoka** Japan
74E3 **Fukushima** Japan
74C4 **Fukuyama** Japan
57B2 **Fulda** Germany
57B2 **Fulda** *R* Germany
73B4 **Fuling** China
27L1 **Fullarton** Trinidad
22D4 **Fullerton** USA
18C2 **Fulton** Kentucky, USA
15C2 **Fulton** New York, USA
46C1 **Fumay** France
75C1 **Funabashi** Japan
96A1 **Funchal** Medeira
35C1 **Fundão** Brazil
7D5 **Fundy,B of** Can
101C3 **Funhalouro** Mozam
72D3 **Funing** China
73B5 **Funing** China
97C3 **Funtua** Nig
73D4 **Fuqing** China
101C2 **Furancungo** Mozam
91C4 **Fūrg** Iran
47C1 **Furka** *P* Switz
107D5 **Furneaux Group** *Is* Aust
56C2 **Fürstenwalde** Germany
57C3 **Fürth** Germany
74D3 **Furukawa** Japan
6B3 **Fury and Hecla St** Can
74A2 **Fushun** Liaoning, China
73A4 **Fushun** Sichuan, China
74B2 **Fusong** China
57C3 **Füssen** Germany
72E2 **Fu Xian** China
72E1 **Fuxin** China
72D3 **Fuyang** China
72E1 **Fuyuan** Liaoning, China
73A4 **Fuyuan** Yunnan, China
68A2 **Fuyun** China
73D4 **Fuzhou** China
56C1 **Fyn** *I* Den

G

99E2 **Gaalkacyo** Somalia
21B2 **Gabbs** USA
100A2 **Gabela** Angola
96D1 **Gabe's** Tunisia
22B2 **Gabilan Range** *Mts* USA
98B3 **Gabon** Republic, Africa
100B3 **Gaborone** Botswana
54C2 **Gabrovo** Bulg
91B3 **Gach Sārān** Iran
17A1 **Gadsden** Alabama, USA
10A1 **Gads L** Can
53B2 **Gaeta** Italy
71F3 **Gaferut** *I* Pacific O
96C1 **Gafsa** Tunisia
60D2 **Gagarin** Russian Fed
97B4 **Gagnoa** Ivory Coast
7D4 **Gagnon** Can
61F5 **Gagra** Georgia
86B1 **Gaibanda** India
29C4 **Gaimán** Arg
17B2 **Gainesville** Florida, USA
17B1 **Gainesville** Georgia, USA
19A3 **Gainesville** Texas, USA
42D3 **Gainsborough** Eng
108A2 **Gairdner,L** Aust
44B3 **Gairloch** Scot
16A3 **Gaithersburg** USA
87B1 **Gajendragarh** India
73D4 **Ga Jiang** *R* China
99D3 **Galana** *R* Kenya
103D5 **Galapagos Is** Pacific O
42C2 **Galashiels** Scot
54C1 **Galaţi** Rom
4C3 **Galena** Alaska, USA
18B2 **Galena** Kansas, USA
27L1 **Galeota Pt** Trinidad
27L1 **Galera Pt** Trinidad
10A2 **Galesburg** USA
15C2 **Galeton** USA
61F2 **Galich** Russian Fed
50A1 **Galicia** Region, Spain
Galilee,S of = Tiberias,L
27J1 **Galina Pt** Jamaica
99D1 **Gallabat** Sudan
47C2 **Gallarate** Italy
87C3 **Galle** Sri Lanka
51B1 **Gállego** *R* Spain
Gallipoli = Gelibolu
55A2 **Gallipoli** Italy
38J5 **Gällivare** Sweden
42B2 **Galloway** District
42B2 **Galloway,Mull of** *C* Scot
8C3 **Gallup** USA
22B1 **Galt** USA
96A2 **Galtat Zemmour** Mor
25C2 **Galveston** USA
11A4 **Galveston B** USA
34C2 **Galvez** Arg
49D3 **Galvi** Corse
45B2 **Galway** County, Irish Rep
41B3 **Galway** Irish Rep
41B3 **Galway** *B* Irish Rep
86B1 **Gamba** China
97B3 **Gambaga** Ghana
4A3 **Gambell** USA
97A3 **Gambia** *R* The Gambia/Sen
97A3 **Gambia,The** Republic, Africa
98B3 **Gamboma** Congo
100A2 **Gambos** Angola
87C3 **Gampola** Sri Lanka
99E2 **Ganale Dorya** *R* Eth
15C2 **Gananoque** Can
Gand = Gent
100A2 **Ganda** Angola
98C3 **Gandajika** Zaïre
84B3 **Gandava** Pak
7E5 **Gander** Can
85C4 **Gāndhīdhām** India
85C4 **Gāndhīnagar** India
85D4 **Gāndhi Sāgar** *L* India
51B2 **Gandia** Spain
86B2 **Ganga** *R* India
85C3 **Ganganar** India
86C2 **Gangaw** Burma
72A2 **Gangca** China
82C2 **Gangdise Shan** *Mts* China
Ganges = Ganga
86B1 **Gangtok** India
72B3 **Gangu** China
8C2 **Gannett Peak** *Mt* USA
72B2 **Ganquan** China
108A3 **Gantheaume** *C* Aust
39K8 **Gantsevichi** Belorussia
73D4 **Ganzhou** China
97C3 **Gao** Mali
72A2 **Gaolan** China
72C2 **Gaoping** China
97B3 **Gaoua** Burkina
97A3 **Gaoual** Guinea
72D3 **Gaoyou Hu** *L* China
73C5 **Gaozhou** China
49D3 **Gap** France
79B2 **Gapan** Phil
84D2 **Gar** China
109C1 **Garah** Aust
31D3 **Garanhuns** Brazil
21A1 **Garberville** USA
35B2 **Garça** Brazil
35A2 **Garcias** Brazil
47D2 **Garda** Italy
9C3 **Garden City** USA
14A1 **Garden Pen** USA
34D3 **Gardey** Arg
84B2 **Gardez** Afghan

16C2 **Gardiners I** USA	
16D1 **Gardner** USA	
47D2 **Gardone** Italy	
47D2 **Gargano** Italy	
85D4 **Garhäkota** India	
61K2 **Gari** Russian Fed	
100A4 **Garies** S Africa	
99D3 **Garissa** Kenya	
19A3 **Garland** USA	
57C3 **Garmisch-Partenkirchen** Germany	
90B2 **Garmsar** Iran	
18A2 **Garnett** USA	
8B2 **Garnett Peak** *Mt* USA	
48C3 **Garonne** *R* France	
44B3 **Garry** *R* Scot	
78B4 **Garut** Indon	
86A2 **Garwa** India	
14A2 **Gary** USA	
82C2 **Garyarsa** China	
4H3 **Gary L** Can	
19A3 **Garza-Little Elm** *Res* USA	
90B2 **Gasan Kuli** Turkmenistan	
48B3 **Gascogne** Region, France	
18B2 **Gasconade** *R* USA	
106A3 **Gascoyne** *R* Aust	
98B2 **Gashaka** Nig	
97D3 **Gashua** Nig	
10D2 **Gaspé** Can	
10D2 **Gaspé,C. de** Can	
94A1 **Gata,C** Cyprus	
60C2 **Gatchina** Russian Fed	
42D2 **Gateshead** Eng	
19A3 **Gatesville** USA	
15C1 **Gatineau** Can	
15C1 **Gatineau** *R* Can	
109D1 **Gatton** Aust	
86C1 **Gauháti** India	
58C1 **Gauja** *R* Latvia	
86A1 **Gauri Phanta** India	
22B3 **Gaviota** USA	
39H6 **Gävle** Sweden	
108A2 **Gawler Ranges** *Mts* Aust	
72A1 **Gaxun Nur** *L* China	
86A2 **Gaya** India	
97C3 **Gaya** Niger	
14B1 **Gaylord** USA	
109D1 **Gayndah** Aust	
61H1 **Gayny** Russian Fed	
60C4 **Gaysin** Ukraine	
92B3 **Gaza** Israel	
92C2 **Gaziantep** Turk	
97B4 **Gbaringa** Lib	
58B2 **Gdańsk** Pol	
58B2 **Gdańsk,G of** Pol	
39K7 **Gdov** Russian Fed	
58B2 **Gdynia** Pol	
94A3 **Gebel Halâl** *Mt* Egypt	
95C2 **Gebel Hamata** *Mt* Egypt	
92B4 **Gebel Katherina** *Mt* Egypt	
94A3 **Gebel Libni** *Mt* Egypt	
94A3 **Gebel Maghâra** *Mt* Egypt	
99D1 **Gedaref** Sudan	
55C3 **Gediz** *R* Turk	
56C2 **Gedser** Den	
46C1 **Geel** Belg	
108B3 **Geelong** Aust	
109C4 **Geeveston** Aust	
97D3 **Geidam** Nig	
46D1 **Geilenkirchen** Germany	
99D3 **Geita** Tanz	
73A5 **Gejiu** China	
53B3 **Gela** Italy	
99E2 **Geladi** Eth	
46D1 **Geldern** Germany	
55C2 **Gelibolu** Turk	
92B2 **Gelidonya Burun** Turk	
46D1 **Gelsenkirchen** Germany	
39F8 **Gelting** Germany	

77C5 **Gemas** Malay	
46C1 **Gembloux** Belg	
98B2 **Gemena** Zaïre	
92C2 **Gemerek** Turk	
92A1 **Gemlik** Turk	
52B1 **Gemona** Italy	
100B3 **Gemsbok** *Nat Pk* Botswana	
98C1 **Geneina** Sudan	
34C3 **General Acha** Arg	
34C3 **General Alvear** Buenos Aires, Arg	
34B2 **General Alvear** Mendoza, Arg	
34C2 **General Arenales** Arg	
34D3 **General Belgrano** Arg	
112B2 **General Belgrano** *Base* Ant	
112C2 **General Bernardo O'Higgins** *Base* Ant	
34D3 **General Conesa** Buenos Aires, Arg	
30D3 **General Eugenio A Garay** Par	
34D3 **General Guido** Arg	
34C3 **General La Madrid** Arg	
34C2 **General Levalle** Arg	
30C4 **General Manuel Belgrano** *Mt* Arg	
34D3 **General Paz** Buenos Aires, Arg	
34C3 **General Pico** Arg	
34C2 **General Pinto** Arg	
34D3 **General Pirán** Arg	
29C3 **General Roca** Arg	
112C3 **General San Martin** *Base* Ant	
79C4 **General Santos** Phil	
34C3 **General Viamonte** Arg	
34C3 **General Villegas** Arg	
15C2 **Genesee** *R* USA	
15C2 **Geneseo** USA	
Geneva = Genève	
18A1 **Geneva** Nebraska, USA	
15C2 **Geneva** New York, USA	
Geneva,L of = LacLéman	
52A1 **Genève** Switz	
50B2 **Genil** *R* Spain	
Genoa = Genova	
109C3 **Genoa** Aust	
52A2 **Genova** Italy	
32J7 **Genovesa** *I* Ecuador	
46B1 **Gent** Belg	
78B4 **Genteng** Indon	
56C2 **Genthin** Germany	
93E1 **Geokchay** Azerbaijan	
100B4 **George** S Africa	
7D4 **George** *R* Can	
109C2 **George,L** Aust	
17B2 **George,L** Florida, USA	
15D2 **George,L** New York, USA	
111A2 **George Sd** NZ	
109C4 **George Town** Aust	
15C3 **Georgetown** Delaware, USA	
33F2 **Georgetown** Guyana	
14B3 **Georgetown** Kentucky, USA	
77C4 **George Town** Malay	
27N2 **Georgetown** St Vincent and the Grenadines	
17C1 **Georgetown** S Carolina, USA	
19A3 **Georgetown** Texas, USA	
97A3 **Georgetown** The Gambia	
112C8 **George V Land** Region, Ant	
65F5 **Georgia** Republic, Europe	
112C12 **Georg Forster** *Base* Ant	
17B1 **Georgia** State, USA	

14B1 **Georgian B** Can	
13C3 **Georgia,Str of** Can	
106C3 **Georgina** *R* Aust	
61F5 **Georgiyevsk** Russian Fed	
57C2 **Gera** Germany	
46B1 **Geraardsbergen** Belg	
111B2 **Geraldine** NZ	
106A3 **Geraldton** Aust	
10B2 **Geraldton** Can	
94B3 **Gerar** *R* Israel	
4C3 **Gerdine,Mt** USA	
12E2 **Gerdova Peak** *Mt* USA	
77C4 **Gerik** Malay	
60B4 **Gerlachovsky** *Mt* Pol	
13C1 **Germanson Lodge** Can	
56C2 **Germany** Republic, Europe	
101G1 **Germiston** S Africa	
46D1 **Gerolstein** Germany	
51C1 **Gerona** Spain	
46E1 **Geseke** Germany	
99E2 **Gestro** *R* Eth	
50B1 **Getafe** Spain	
16A3 **Gettysburg** Pennsylvania, USA	
93D2 **Gevaş** Turk	
55B2 **Gevgelija** Macedonia	
47B1 **Gex** France	
94C2 **Ghabāghib** Syria	
96C1 **Ghadamis** Libya	
90B2 **Ghaem Shahr** Iran	
86A1 **Ghāghara** *R* India	
97B4 **Ghana** Republic, Africa	
100B3 **Ghanzi** Botswana	
96C1 **Ghardaïa** Alg	
95A1 **Gharyan** Libya	
95A2 **Ghāt** Libya	
84D3 **Ghāziābād** India	
84C3 **Ghazi Khan** Pak	
84B2 **Ghazni** Afghan	
54C1 **Gheorgheni** Rom	
88E4 **Ghudamis** Alg	
90D3 **Ghurian** Afghan	
95B2 **Gialo** Libya	
99E2 **Giamame** Somalia	
53C3 **Giarre** Italy	
100A3 **Gibeon** Namibia	
50A2 **Gibraltar** Colony, SW Europe	
50A2 **Gibraltar,Str of** Spain/Africa	
106B3 **Gibson Desert** Aust	
20B1 **Gibsons** Can	
87B1 **Giddalür** India	
99D2 **Gidolē** Eth	
57B2 **Giessen** Germany	
17B2 **Gifford** USA	
74D3 **Gifu** Japan	
42B2 **Gigha** *I* Scot	
52B2 **Giglio** *I* Italy	
50A1 **Gijón** Spain	
107D2 **Gilbert** *R* Aust	
13C2 **Gilbert,Mt** Can	
101C2 **Gilé** Mozam	
94B2 **Gilead** Region, Jordan	
95B2 **Gilf Kebir Plat** Egypt	
109C2 **Gilgandra** Aust	
84C1 **Gilgit** Pak	
84C1 **Gilgit** *R* Pak	
108C2 **Gilgunnia** Aust	
7A4 **Gillam** Can	
108A2 **Gilles** *L* Aust	
13B2 **Gill I** Can	
14A1 **Gills Rock** USA	
14A2 **Gilman** USA	
22B2 **Gilroy** USA	
8D1 **Gimli** Can	
101H1 **Gingindlovu** S Africa	
79C4 **Gingoog** Phil	
99E2 **Ginir** Eth	
55B3 **Gióna** *Mt* Greece	
109C3 **Gippsland** *Mts* Aust	
14B2 **Girard** USA	
32C3 **Girardot** Colombia	
44C3 **Girdle Ness** *Pen* Scot	
93C1 **Giresun** Turk	
85C4 **Gir Hills** India	
98B2 **Giri** *R* Zaïre	

86B2 **Giridíh** India	
Girona = Gerona	
48B2 **Gironde** *R* France	
42B2 **Girvan** Scot	
111C2 **Gisborne** NZ	
46A2 **Gisors** France	
99C3 **Gitega** Burundi	
Giuba,R = Juba,R	
54C2 **Giurgiu** Rom	
46C1 **Givet** Belg	
58C2 **Gizycko** Pol	
55B2 **Gjirokastër** Alb	
4J3 **Gjoatlaven** Can	
39G6 **Gjøvik** Nor	
7D5 **Glace Bay** Can	
12G3 **Glacier Bay Nat Mon** USA	
13E3 **Glacier Nat Pk** USA/Can	
20B1 **Glacier Peak** *Mt* USA	
6B2 **Glacier Str** Can	
107E3 **Gladstone** Queensland, Aust	
108A2 **Gladstone** S Aust, Aust	
109C4 **Gladstone** Tasmania, Aust	
14A1 **Gladstone** USA	
38A1 **Glama** *Mt* Iceland	
39G6 **Glåma** *R* Nor	
46D2 **Glan** *R* Germany	
47C1 **Glarner** *Mts* Switz	
47C1 **Glarus** Switz	
18A2 **Glasco** USA	
8C2 **Glasgow** Montana, USA	
42B2 **Glasgow** Scot	
16B3 **Glassboro** USA	
43C4 **Glastonbury** Eng	
61H2 **Glazov** Russian Fed	
59B3 **Gleisdorf** Austria	
110C1 **Glen Afton** NZ	
16A3 **Glen Burnie** USA	
101H1 **Glencoe** S Africa	
9B3 **Glendale** Arizona, USA	
22C3 **Glendale** California, USA	
12E2 **Glenhallen** USA	
109D1 **Glen Innes** Aust	
109C1 **Glenmorgan** Aust	
109D2 **Glenreagh** Aust	
16A3 **Glen Rock** USA	
19A3 **Glen Rose** USA	
44C3 **Glenrothes** UK	
15D2 **Glens Falls** USA	
45B1 **Glenties** Irish Rep	
19B3 **Glenwood** Arkansas, USA	
8C3 **Glenwood Springs** USA	
39F6 **Glittertind** *Mt* Nor	
59B2 **Gliwice** Pol	
9B3 **Globe** USA	
58B2 **Głogów** Pol	
38G5 **Glomfjord** Nor	
109D2 **Gloucester** Aust	
43C4 **Gloucester** Eng	
16D1 **Gloucester** USA	
58D1 **Glubokoye** Belorussia	
60D3 **Glukhov** Russian Fed	
59B3 **Gmünd** Austria	
57C3 **Gmunden** Austria	
58B2 **Gniezno** Pol	
100A3 **Goabeg** Namibia	
87A1 **Goa, Daman and Diu** Union Territory, India	
86C1 **Goālpāra** India	
99D2 **Goba** Eth	
100A3 **Gobabis** Namibia	
34C2 **Gobernador Crespo** Arg	
34B3 **Gobernador Duval** Arg	
72B1 **Gobi** *Desert* China/Mongolia	
75B2 **Gobo** Japan	
87B1 **Godag** India	
87C1 **Godāvari** *R* India	
14B2 **Goderich** Can	
6E3 **Godhavn** Greenland	
85C4 **Godhra** India	
34B2 **Godoy Cruz** Arg	

Gods L

106B4 **Great Australian Bight** *G* Aust
16B3 **Great B** New Jersey, USA
25E2 **Great Bahama Bank** The Bahamas
110C1 **Great Barrier I** NZ
107D2 **Great Barrier Reef** *Is* Aust
16C1 **Great Barrington** USA
4F3 **Great Bear L** Can
9D2 **Great Bend** USA
107D3 **Great Dividing Range** *Mts* Aust
42D2 **Great Driffield** Eng
16B3 **Great Egg Harbor** *B* USA
112B10 **Greater Antarctic Region,** Ant
26B2 **Greater Antilles** *Is* Caribbean S
43D4 **Greater London Metropolitan County,** Eng
43C3 **Greater Manchester County,** Eng
25E2 **Great Exuma** *I* The Bahamas
8B2 **Great Falls** USA
44B3 **Great Glen** *V* Scot
86B1 **Great Himalayan Range** *Mts* Asia
11C4 **Great Inagua** *I* The Bahamas
100B4 **Great Karroo** *Mts* S Africa
109C4 **Great L** Aust
100A3 **Great Namaland Region,** Namibia
42C3 **Great Ormes Head** *C* Wales
11C4 **Great Ragged** *I* The Bahamas
99D3 **Great Ruaha** *R* Tanz
15D2 **Great Sacandaga L** USA
8B2 **Great Salt L** USA
95B2 **Great Sand Sea** Libya/Egypt
106B3 **Great Sandy Desert** Aust
8A2 **Great Sandy Desert** USA
Great Sandy I = Fraser I
4G3 **Great Slave L** Can
16C2 **Great South B** USA
106B3 **Great Victoria Desert** Aust
112C2 **Great Wall** *Base* Ant
72B2 **Great Wall** China
43E3 **Great Yarmouth** Eng
94B1 **Greco,C** Cyprus
55B3 **Greece Republic,** Europe
15C2 **Greece** USA
8C2 **Greeley** USA
6B1 **Greely Fjord** Can
14A1 **Green B** USA
14A2 **Green Bay** USA
14A3 **Greencastle** Indiana, USA
16C1 **Greenfield Massachusetts,** USA
14A2 **Greenfield Wisconsin,** USA
13F2 **Green Lake** Can
6F2 **Greenland Dependency,** N Atlantic O
102H1 **Greenland Basin** Greenland S
1B1 **Greenland S** Greenland
42B2 **Greenock** Scot
16C2 **Greenport** USA
16B3 **Greensboro Maryland,** USA
11C3 **Greensboro N Carolina,** USA
15C2 **Greensburg Pennsylvania,** USA
44B3 **Greenstone** *Pt* Scot

18C2 **Greenup** USA
17A1 **Greenville** Alabama, USA
97B4 **Greenville** Lib
19B3 **Greenville Mississippi,** USA
16D1 **Greenville N Hampshire,** USA
14B2 **Greenville** Ohio, USA
17B1 **Greenville S Carolina,** USA
19A3 **Greenville** Texas, USA
43E4 **Greenwich** Eng
16C2 **Greenwich** USA
16B3 **Greenwood Delaware,** USA
19B3 **Greenwood Mississippi,** USA
17B1 **Greenwood S Carolina,** USA
18B2 **Greers Ferry L** USA
108A1 **Gregory,L** Aust
107D2 **Gregory Range** *Mts* Aust
56C2 **Greifswald** Germany
64F3 **Gremikha** Russian Fed
56C1 **Grenå** Den
19C3 **Grenada** USA
27E4 **Grenada** *I* Caribbean S
109C2 **Grenfell** Aust
49D2 **Grenoble** France
27M2 **Grenville** Grenada
107D2 **Grenville,C** Aust
20B1 **Gresham** USA
78C4 **Gresik** Jawa, Indon
78A3 **Gresik** Sumatera, Indon
19B4 **Gretna** USA
111B2 **Grey** *R* NZ
12G2 **Grey Hunter Pk** *Mt* Can
7E4 **Grey Is** Can
16C1 **Greylock,Mt** USA
111B2 **Greymouth** NZ
107D3 **Grey Range** *Mts* Aust
45C2 **Greystones** Irish Rep
101H1 **Greytown** S Africa
101F1 **Griekwastad** S Africa
17B1 **Griffin** USA
108C2 **Griffith** Aust
107D5 **Grim,C** Aust
15C2 **Grimsby** Can
42D3 **Grimsby** Eng
38B1 **Grimsey** *I* Iceland
13D1 **Grimshaw** Can
39F7 **Grimstad** Nor
47C1 **Grindelwald** Switz
6A2 **Grinnell Pen** Can
6B2 **Grise Fjord** Can
61H1 **Griva** Russian Fed
39J7 **Grobina** Latvia
58C2 **Grodno** Belorussia
86A1 **Gromati** *R* India
56B2 **Groningen** Neth
106C2 **Groote Eylandt** *I* Aust
100A2 **Grootfontein** Namibia
100B3 **Grootvloer** *Salt L* S Africa
27P2 **Gros Islet** St Lucia
46E1 **Grosser Feldberg** *Mt* Germany
52B2 **Grosseto** Italy
46E2 **Gross-Gerau** Germany
57C3 **Grossglockner** *Mt* Austria
47E1 **Gross Venediger** *Mt* Austria
12C3 **Grosvenor,L** USA
22B2 **Groveland** USA
21A2 **Grover City** USA
15D2 **Groveton** USA
61G5 **Groznyy** Russian Fed
58B2 **Grudziadz** Pol
100A3 **Grünau** Namibia
44E2 **Grutness** Scot
61F3 **Gryazi** Russian Fed

61E2 **Gryazovets** Russian Fed
29G8 **Grytviken** South Georgia
45A2 **Gt Blasket** *I* Irish Rep
35C2 **Guaçuí** Brazil
23A1 **Guadalajara** Mexico
50B1 **Guadalajara** Spain
107E1 **Guadalcanal** *I* Solomon Is
50B2 **Guadalimar** *R* Spain
51B1 **Guadalope** *R* Spain
50B2 **Guadalqivir** *R* Spain
24B2 **Guadalupe** Mexico
3G6 **Guadalupe** *I* Mexico
27E3 **Guadeloupe** *I* Caribbean S
50B2 **Guadian** *R* Spain
50A2 **Guadiana** *R* Port
50B2 **Guadix** Spain
32D6 **Guajará Mirim** Brazil
32C1 **Guajira,Pen de** Colombia
32B4 **Gualaceo** Ecuador
34D2 **Gualeguay** Arg
34D2 **Gualeguaychú** Arg
71F2 **Guam** *I* Pacific O
34C3 **Guamini** Arg
77C5 **Gua Musang** Malay
23A1 **Guanajuato** Mexico
23A1 **Guanajuato State,** Mexico
32D2 **Guanare** Ven
25D2 **Guane** Cuba
73C5 **Guangdong Province,** China
73A3 **Guanghan** China
72C3 **Guanghua** China
73A4 **Guangmao Shan** *Mt* China
73B5 **Guangnan** China
72B3 **Guangyuan** China
73D4 **Guangze** China
67F3 **Guangzhou** China
35C1 **Guanhães** Brazil
32D3 **Guania** *R* Colombia
27E5 **Guanipa** *R* Ven
26B2 **Guantánamo** Cuba
72D1 **Guanting Shuiku** *Res* China
73B5 **Guanxi Province,** China
73A3 **Guan Xian** China
32B2 **Guapa** Colombia
33E6 **Guaporé** *R* Brazil/Bol
30C2 **Guaquí** Bol
32B4 **Guaranda** Ecuador
30F4 **Guarapuava** Brazil
35B2 **Guaratinguetá** Brazil
50A1 **Guarda** Port
35B1 **Guarda Mor** Brazil
9C4 **Guasave** Mexico
47D2 **Guastalla** Italy
25C3 **Guatemala** Guatemala
25C3 **Guatemala Republic,** Cent America
34C3 **Guatraché** Arg
32C3 **Guavrare** *R* Colombia
35B2 **Guaxupé** Brazil
27L1 **Guayaguayare** Trinidad
32A4 **Guayaquil** Ecuador
24A2 **Guaymas** Mexico
34D2 **Guayquiraro** *R* Arg
100B2 **Guba** Zaïre
99E2 **Guban Region** Somalia
79B3 **Gubat** Phil
56C2 **Gubin** Pol
87B2 **Güdür** India
14B2 **Guelpho** Can
26A2 **Guenabacoa** Cuba
98C1 **Guéréda** Chad
48C2 **Guéret** France
48B2 **Guernsey** *I* UK
23A2 **Guerrero State,** Mexico
99D2 **Gughe** *Mt* Eth
63E2 **Gugigu** China
71F2 **Guguan** *I* Pacific O
109C2 **Guiargambone** Aust

73C4 **Guidong** China
97B4 **Guiglo** Ivory Coast
73C5 **Gui Jiang** *R* China
43D4 **Guildford** Eng
73C4 **Guilin** China
47B2 **Guillestre** France
72A2 **Guinan** China
97A3 **Guinea Republic,** Africa
102H4 **Guinea Basin** Atlantic O
97A3 **Guinea-Bissau Republic,** Africa
97C4 **Guinea,G of** W Africa
26A2 **Güines** Cuba
97B3 **Guir** *Well* Mali
84C2 **Guiranwala** Pak
33E1 **Güiria** Ven
46B2 **Guise** France
79C3 **Guiuan** Phil
73B5 **Gui Xian** China
73B4 **Guiyang** China
73B4 **Guizhou Province,** China
85C4 **Gujarāt** State, India
84C2 **Gujrat** Pak
87B1 **Gulbarga** India
58D1 **Gulbene** Latvia
87B1 **Guledagudda** India
80D3 **Gulf,The** S W Asia
109C2 **Gulgong** Aust
73B4 **Gulin** China
12E2 **Gulkana** USA
12E2 **Gulkana** *R* USA
13E2 **Gull L** Can
13F2 **Gull Lake** Can
55C3 **Güllük Körfezi** *B* Turk
99D2 **Gulu** Uganda
109C1 **Guluguba** Aust
97C3 **Gumel** Nig
46D1 **Gummersbach** Germany
86A2 **Gumpla** India
93C1 **Gümüşhane** Turk
85D4 **Guna** India
99D1 **Guna** *Mt* Eth
109C3 **Gundagai** Aust
98B3 **Gungu** Zaïre
6H3 **Gunnbjørn Fjeld** *Mt* Greenland
109D2 **Gunnedah** Aust
87B1 **Guntakal** India
17A1 **Guntersville** USA
17A1 **Guntersville L** USA
87C1 **Guntür** India
77C5 **Gunung Batu Putch** *Mt* Malay
78D3 **Gunung Besar** *Mt* Indon
78D2 **Gunung Bulu** *Mt* Indon
78A3 **Gunung Gedang** *Mt* Indon
78C2 **Gunung Lawit** *Mt* Malay
78C4 **Gunung Lawu** *Mt* Indon
78D2 **Gunung Menyapa** *Mt* Indon
78D2 **Gunung Niapa** *Mt* Indon
78A3 **Gunung Patah** *Mt* Indon
78C4 **Gunung Raung** *Mt* Indon
78A3 **Gunung Resag** *Mt* Indon
78D3 **Gunung Sarempaka** *Mt* Indon
78C4 **Gunung Sumbing** *Mt* Indon
77C5 **Gunung Tahan** *Mt* Malay
78A2 **Gunung Talakmau** *Mt* Indon
100A2 **Gunza** Angola
72D3 **Guoyang** China
84D2 **Gurdäspur** India
84D3 **Gurgaon** India
86A1 **Gurkha** Nepal
92C2 **Gürün** Turk
31B2 **Gurupi** *R* Brazil

Guruve

100C2	**Guruve** Zim
72A1	**Gurvan Sayhan Uul** *Upland* Mongolia
61H4	**Gur'yev** Kazakhstan
97C3	**Gusau** Nig
58C2	**Gusev** Russian Fed
74A3	**Gushan** China
61F2	**Gus'khrustalnyy** Russian Fed
12G3	**Gustavus** USA
22B2	**Gustine** USA
11B3	**Guston** USA
56B2	**Gütersloh** Germany
18C2	**Guthrie** Kentucky, USA
18A2	**Guthrie** Oklahoma, USA
23B1	**Gutiérrez Zamora** Mexico
33F3	**Guyana** Republic, S America
102F4	**Guyana Basin** Atlantic O
72C1	**Guyang** China
48B3	**Guyenne** Region, France
9C3	**Guymon** USA
109D2	**Guyra** Aust
72B2	**Guyuan** China
109C2	**Gwabegar** Aust
85D3	**Gwalior** India
100B3	**Gwanda** Zim
98C2	**Gwane** Zaïre
82A3	**Gwardar** Pak
45B1	**Gweebarra B** Irish Rep
89G9	**Gwelo** Zim
43C4	**Gwent** County, Wales
100B2	**Gweru** Zim
109C1	**Gwydir** *R* Aust
43C3	**Gwynedd** Wales
65F5	**Gyandzha** Azerbaijan
86B1	**Gyangzê** China
68B3	**Gyaring Hu** *L* China
64J2	**Gydanskiy Poluostrov** *Pen* Russian Fed
86B1	**Gyirong** China
6F3	**Gyldenløues** Greenland
109D1	**Gympie** Aust
59B3	**Gyöngyös** Hung
59B3	**Györ** Hung

H

38K6	**Haapajärvi** Fin
60B2	**Haapsalu** Estonia
56A2	**Haarlem** Neth
46D1	**Haarstrang** Region, Germany
25D2	**Habana** Cuba
86C2	**Habiganj** Bang
74D4	**Hachijō-jima** *I* Japan
75B1	**Hachiman** Japan
74E2	**Hachinohe** Japan
75B1	**Hachioji** Japan
16B2	**Hackettstown** USA
108A2	**Hack,Mt** *Mt* Aust
42C2	**Haddington** Scot
108B1	**Haddon Corner** Aust
108B1	**Haddon Downs** Aust
97D3	**Hadejia** Nig
97C3	**Hadejia** *R* Nig
94B2	**Hadera** Israel
56B1	**Haderslev** Den
81D4	**Hadiboh** Socotra
4H2	**Hadley B** Can
73B5	**Hadong** Vietnam
81C4	**Hadramawt** Region, Yemen
56C1	**Hadsund** Den
74B3	**Haeju** N Korea
91A4	**Hafar al Bātin** S Arabia
6D2	**Haffners Bjerg** *Mt* Greenland
84C2	**Hafizabad** Pak
86C1	**Haflong** India
38A2	**Hafnafjörður** Iceland
12B3	**Hagemeister** *I* USA
56B2	**Hagen** Germany
15C3	**Hagerstown** USA
75A2	**Hagi** Japan

73A5	**Ha Giang** Vietnam
46D2	**Hagondange** France
45B2	**Hags Hd** *C* Irish Rep
46D2	**Haguenan** France
96A2	**Hagunia** *Well* Mor
69G4	**Haha-jima** *I* Japan
68B3	**Hah Xil Hu** *L* China
74A2	**Haicheng** China
76D1	**Hai Duong** Viet
94B2	**Haifa** Israel
94B2	**Haifa,B of** Israel
72D2	**Hai He** *R* China
73C5	**Haikang** China
76E1	**Haikou** China
80C3	**Ha'il** S Arabia
86C2	**Hailākāndi** India
63D3	**Hailar** China
74B2	**Hailong** China
69E2	**Hailun** China
38J5	**Hailuoto** *I* Fin
76D2	**Hainan** *I* China
12G3	**Haines** USA
12G2	**Haines Junction** Can
59B3	**Hainfeld** Austria
73B5	**Haiphong** Vietnam
26C3	**Haiti** Republic, Caribbean S
95C3	**Haiya** Sudan
72A2	**Haiyan** China
72B2	**Haiyuan** China
72D3	**Haizhou Wan** *B* China
59C3	**Hajdúböszörmény** Hung
75B1	**Hajiki-saki** *Pt* Japan
86C2	**Haka** Burma
21C4	**Hakalau** Hawaiian Is
93D2	**Hakkâri** Turk
74E2	**Hakodate** Japan
	Hakwa = Haka
75B1	**Haku** Japan
75B1	**Haku-san** *Mt* Japan
92C2	**Halab** Syria
93E3	**Halabja** Iraq
95C2	**Halaib** Sudan
94C1	**Halba** Leb
68B2	**Halban** Mongolia
56C2	**Halberstadt** Germany
79B3	**Halcon,Mt** Phil
39G7	**Halden** Nor
86B2	**Haldia** India
84D3	**Haldwāni** India
13C1	**Halfway** *R* Can
7D5	**Halifax** Can
42D3	**Halifax** Eng
6D1	**Hall Basin** *Sd* Can
6B3	**Hall Beach** Can
46C1	**Halle** Belg
56C2	**Halle** Germany
112B1	**Halley** *Base* Ant
39F6	**Hallingdal** *R* Nor
6D3	**Hall Pen** Can
106B2	**Hall's Creek** Aust
71D3	**Halmahera** *I* Indon
39G7	**Halmstad** Sweden
56B2	**Haltern** Germany
38J5	**Halti** *Mt* Nor
42C2	**Haltwhistle** Eng
91B4	**Halul** *I* Qatar
94B3	**Haluza** *Hist Site* Israel
75A2	**Hamada** Japan
96C2	**Hamada de Tinrhert** *Desert Region* Alg
96B2	**Hamada du Dra** *Upland* Alg
90A3	**Hamadān** Iran
96B2	**Hamada Tounassine** Region, Alg
92C2	**Hamāh** Syria
75B2	**Hamamatsu** Japan
39G6	**Hamar** Nor
87C3	**Hambantota** Sri Lanka
19B3	**Hamburg** Arkansas, USA
18A1	**Hamburg** Iowa, USA
16B2	**Hamburg** Pennsylvania, USA
56B2	**Hamburg** Germany
16C2	**Hamden** USA
39J6	**Hämeeninna** Fin

106A3	**Hamersley Range** *Mts* Aust
74B2	**Hamgyong Sanmaek** *Mts* N Korea
74B2	**Hamhŭng** N Korea
68B2	**Hami** China
94B1	**Hamidīyah** Syria
108B3	**Hamilton** Aust
14C2	**Hamilton** Can
110C1	**Hamilton** NZ
14B3	**Hamilton** Ohio, USA
42B2	**Hamilton** Scot
22B2	**Hamilton,Mt** USA
38K6	**Hamina** Fin
86A1	**Hamirpur** India
56B2	**Hamm** Germany
95A2	**Hammādāh al Hamra** *Upland* Libya
38H6	**Hammerdal** Sweden
38J4	**Hammerfest** Nor
14A2	**Hammond** Illinois, USA
19B3	**Hammond** Louisiana, USA
16B3	**Hammonton** USA
111B3	**Hampden** NZ
43D4	**Hampshire** County, Eng
19B3	**Hampton** Arkansas, USA
91C4	**Hāmūn-e Jaz Mūrian** *L* Iran
84B3	**Hamun-i-Lora** *Salt L* Pak
21C4	**Hana** Hawaiian Is
21C4	**Hanalei** Hawaiian Is
74E3	**Hanamaki** Japan
72C2	**Hancheng** China
73C3	**Hanchuan** China
15C3	**Hancock** Maryland, USA
10B2	**Hancock** Michigan, USA
75B2	**Handa** Japan
72C2	**Handan** China
99D3	**Handeni** Tanz
72B2	**Hanggin Qi** China
39J7	**Hangö** Fin
73E3	**Hangzhou** China
73E3	**Hangzhou Wan** *B* China
111B2	**Hanmer Springs** NZ
13E2	**Hanna** Can
18B2	**Hannibal** USA
56B2	**Hannover** Germany
39G7	**Hanöbukten** *B* Sweden
76D1	**Hanoi** Viet
16A3	**Hanover** USA
29B6	**Hanover** *I* Chile
72B3	**Han Shui** China
73C3	**Han Shui** *R* China
85D3	**Hänsi** India
68C2	**Hantay** Mongolia
72B3	**Hanzhong** China
86B2	**Hāora** India
38J5	**Haparanda** Sweden
86C1	**Hāpoli** India
92C4	**Haql** S Arabia
91A5	**Haradh** S Arabia
99E2	**Hara Fanna** Eth
75C1	**Haramachi** Japan
101C2	**Harare** Zim
98C1	**Harazé** Chad
14B2	**Harbor Beach** USA
85D4	**Harda** India
39F6	**Hardangerfjord** *Inlet* Nor
46D2	**Hardt** Region, Germany
108A2	**Hardwicke B** Aust
18B2	**Hardy** USA
99E2	**Harēr** Eth
99E2	**Hargeysa** Somalia
94B3	**Har Hakippa** *Mt* Israel
68B3	**Harhu** *L* China
78A3	**Hari** *R* Indon
75A2	**Harima-nada** *B* Japan
56B2	**Harlingen** Neth
9D4	**Harlingen** USA
43E4	**Harlow** Eng
94B2	**Har Meron** *Mt* Israel

20C2	**Harney Basin** USA
20C2	**Harney L** USA
38H6	**Härnösand** Sweden
63B3	**Har Nuur** *L* Mongolia
97B4	**Harper** Lib
12F2	**Harper,Mt** USA
15C3	**Harpers Ferry** USA
94B3	**Har Ramon** *Mt* Israel
7C4	**Harricanaw** *R* Can
16B3	**Harrington** USA
7E4	**Harrington Harbour** Can
44A3	**Harris** *District* Scot
18C2	**Harrisburg** Illinois, USA
16A2	**Harrisburg** Pennsylvania, USA
101G1	**Harrismith** S Africa
18B2	**Harrison** USA
15C3	**Harrisonburg** USA
7E4	**Harrison,C** Can
13C3	**Harrison L** Can
18B2	**Harrisonville** USA
44A3	**Harris,Sound of** *Chan* Scot
14B2	**Harrisville** USA
42D3	**Harrogate** Eng
94B3	**Har Saggi** *Mt* Israel
38H5	**Harstad** Nor
12G2	**Hart** *R* Can
39F6	**Hårteigen** *Mt* Nor
16C2	**Hartford** Connecticut, USA
14A2	**Hartford** Michigan, USA
38G6	**Hartkjølen** *Mt* Nor
108A2	**Hart,L** Aust
43B4	**Hartland Pt** Eng
42D2	**Hartlepool** Eng
19A3	**Hartshorne** USA
17B1	**Hartwell Res** USA
101F1	**Hartz** *R* S Africa
68B2	**Har Us Nuur** *L* Mongolia
43E4	**Harwich** Eng
84D3	**Haryāna** State, India
94B3	**Hāsā** Jordan
94B2	**Hāsbaiya** Leb
43D4	**Haselmere** Eng
75B2	**Hashimoto** Japan
90A2	**Hashtpar** Iran
90A2	**Hashtrüd** Iran
87B2	**Hassan** India
56B2	**Hasselt** Belg
96C2	**Hassi Inifel** Alg
96B2	**Hassi Mdakane** *Well* Alg
96C1	**Hassi Messaoud** Alg
108C3	**Hastings** Aust
43E4	**Hastings** Eng
8D2	**Hastings** Nebraska, USA
110C1	**Hastings** NZ
108B2	**Hatfield** Aust
12B1	**Hatham Inlet** USA
85D3	**Hāthras** India
76D2	**Ha Tinh** Viet
108B2	**Hattah** Aust
11C3	**Hatteras,C** USA
19C3	**Hattiesburg** USA
59B3	**Hatvan** Hung
76D3	**Hau Bon** Viet
99E2	**Haud** Region, Eth
39F7	**Haugesund** Nor
110C1	**Hauhungaroa Range** *Mts* NZ
13F1	**Haultain** *R* Can
110B1	**Hauraki G** NZ
111A3	**Hauroko,L** NZ
47C1	**Hausstock** *Mt* Switz
96B1	**Haut Atlas** *Mts* Mor
98C2	**Haute Kotto** Region, CAR
46C1	**Hautes Fagnes** *Mts* Belg
46B1	**Hautmont** Belg
96B1	**Hauts Plateaux** *Mts* Alg
90D3	**Hauzdar** Iran
18B1	**Havana** USA
	Havana = Habana
87B3	**Havankulam** Sri Lanka

Homerville

17B2 **Homestead** USA
17A1 **Homewood** USA
87B1 **Homnābād** India
101C3 **Homoine** Mozam
25D3 **Hondo** *R* Mexico
25D3 **Honduras** Republic, Cent America
25D3 **Honduras,G of** Honduras
39G6 **Hønefoss** Nor
15C2 **Honesdale** USA
21A1 **Honey L** USA
76C1 **Hong** *R* Viet
76D1 **Hon Gai** Viet
73A4 **Hongguo** China
73C4 **Hong Hu** *L* China
72B2 **Honghui** China
73C4 **Hongjiang** China
73C5 **Hong Kong** Colony, S E Asia
68D2 **Hongor** Mongolia
73B5 **Hongshui He** *R* China
72A3 **Hongyuan** China
72D3 **Hongze Hu** *L* China
107E1 **Honiara** Solomon Is
77C4 **Hon Khoai** *I* Camb
76D3 **Hon Lan** *I* Viet
38K4 **Honnigsvåg** Nor
21C4 **Honolulu** Hawaiian Is
77C4 **Hon Panjang** *I* Viet
74D3 **Honshu** *I* Japan
20B1 **Hood,Mt** USA
20B1 **Hood River** USA
45C2 **Hook Head** *C* Irish Rep
12G3 **Hoonah** USA
12A2 **Hooper Bay** USA
101G1 **Hoopstad** S Africa
56A2 **Hoorn** Neth
9B3 **Hoover Dam** USA
12E2 **Hope** Alaska, USA
19B3 **Hope** Arkansas, USA
13C3 **Hope** Can
7D4 **Hopedale** Can
64D2 **Hopen** *I* Barents S
6D3 **Hopes Advance,C** Can
108B3 **Hopetoun** Aust
100B3 **Hopetown** S Africa
18C2 **Hopkinsville** USA
20B1 **Hoquiam** USA
93D1 **Horasan** Turk
99F1 **Hordiyo** Somalia
47C1 **Horgen** Switz
105H5 **Horizon Depth** Pacific O
91C4 **Hormuz,Str of** Oman/ Iran
59B3 **Horn** Austria
6H3 **Horn** *C* Iceland
38H5 **Hornavan** *L* Sweden
19B3 **Hornbeck** USA
20B2 **Hornbrook** USA
111B2 **Hornby** NZ
7B5 **Hornepayne** Can
4F3 **Horn Mts** Can
42D3 **Hornsea** Eng
72B1 **Horn Uul** *Mt* Mongolia
30E3 **Horqueta** Par
15C2 **Horseheads** USA
56C1 **Horsens** Den
20B1 **Horseshoe Bay** Can
108B3 **Horsham** Aust
43D4 **Horsham** Eng
39G7 **Horten** Nor
4F3 **Horton** *R* Can
78C2 **Hose Mts** Malay
85D4 **Hoshangābād** India
84D2 **Hoshiārpur** India
87B1 **Hospet** India
29C7 **Hoste** *I* Chile
82B2 **Hotan** China
19B3 **Hot Springs** Arkansas, USA
8C2 **Hot Springs** S. Dakota, USA
4G3 **Hottah** Can
46A2 **Houdan** France
72C2 **Houma** China
19B4 **Houma** USA
16C2 **Housatonic** *R* USA
13B2 **Houston** Can
19C3 **Houston** Mississippi, USA
19A4 **Houston** Texas, USA
106A3 **Houtman** *Is* Aust
68B2 **Hovd** Mongolia
68C1 **Hövsgol Nuur** *L* Mongolia
14A2 **Howard City** USA
12C1 **Howard P** USA
109C3 **Howe,C** Aust
101H1 **Howick** S Africa
44C2 **Hoy** *I* Scot
39F6 **Høyanger** Nor
59B2 **Hradeç-Králové** Czech Republic
59B3 **Hranice** Czech Republic
59B3 **Hron** *R* Slovakia
73E5 **Hsin-chu** Taiwan
73E5 **Hsüeh Shan** *Mt* Taiwan
72B2 **Huachi** China
32B6 **Huacho** Peru
72C1 **Huade** China
72D3 **Huaibei** China
72D3 **Huaibin** China
72D3 **Huai He** *R* China
73C4 **Huaihua** China
73C5 **Huaiji** China
72D3 **Huainan** China
69E4 **Hua-lien** Taiwan
32B5 **Huallaga** *R* Peru
32B5 **Huallanca** Peru
32B5 **Huamachuco** Peru
100A2 **Huambo** Angola
30C2 **Huanay** Bol
32B5 **Huancabamba** Peru
32B6 **Huancavelica** Peru
32B6 **Huancayo** Peru
73D3 **Huangchuan** China
Huang Hai = Yellow S
72D2 **Huang He** *R* China
72B2 **Huangling** China
76D2 **Huangliu** China
73C3 **Huangpi** China
73D4 **Huangshan** China
73D3 **Huangshi** China
34C3 **Huanguelén** Arg
73E4 **Huangyan** China
74B2 **Huanren** China
32B5 **Huānuco** Peru
30C2 **Huanuni** Bol
72B2 **Huan Xian** China
32B5 **Huaráz** Peru
32B6 **Huarmey** Peru
32B5 **Huascarán** *Mt* Peru
30B4 **Huasco** Chile
23B2 **Huatusco** Mexico
23B1 **Huauchinango** Mexico
23B2 **Huautla** Mexico
72C2 **Hua Xian** China
24B2 **Huayapan** *R* Mexico
73C3 **Hubei** Province, China
87B1 **Hubli** India
34C3 **Hucal** Arg
74B2 **Huch'ang** N Korea
42D3 **Huddersfield** Eng
39H6 **Hudiksvall** Sweden
17B2 **Hudson** Florida, USA
14B2 **Hudson** Michigan, USA
16C1 **Hudson** New York, USA
16C1 **Hudson** *R* USA
7B4 **Hudson B** Can
5H4 **Hudson Bay** Can
13C1 **Hudson's Hope** Can
6C3 **Hudson Str** Can
76D2 **Hue** Viet
23B1 **Huejutla** Mexico
50A2 **Huelva** Spain
23A2 **Hueramo** Mexico
51B2 **Húercal Overa** Spain
51B1 **Huesca** Spain
23B2 **Huexotla** *Hist Site* Mexico
107D3 **Hughenden** Aust
12D1 **Hughes** USA
86B2 **Hugli** *R* India
19A3 **Hugo** USA
73D4 **Hui'an** China
110C1 **Huiarau Range** *Mts* NZ
74B2 **Huich'ŏn** N Korea
74B2 **Huifa He** *R* China
32B3 **Huila** *Mt* Colombia
73D5 **Huilai** China
73A4 **Huili** China
74B2 **Huinan** China
34C2 **Huinca Renancó** Arg
25C3 **Huixtla** Mexico
73A4 **Huize** China
73C5 **Huizhou** China
23B2 **Hujuápan de Léon** Mexico
69F2 **Hulin** China
15C1 **Hull** Can
42D3 **Hull** Eng
58B1 **Hultsfred** Sweden
63D3 **Hulun Nur** *L* China
69E1 **Huma** China
33E5 **Humaita** Brazil
100B4 **Humansdorp** S Africa
42D3 **Humber** *R* Eng
42D3 **Humberside** County, Eng
5H4 **Humboldt** Can
20C2 **Humboldt** *R* USA
20B2 **Humboldt B** USA
6D2 **Humboldt Gletscher** *Gl* Greenland
21B2 **Humboldt L** USA
108C1 **Humeburn** Aust
109C3 **Hume,L** Aust
100A2 **Humpata** Angola
22C2 **Humphreys** USA
38A1 **Húnaflóri** *B* Iceland
73C4 **Hunan** Province, China
74C2 **Hunchun** China
13C2 **Hundred Mile House** Can
54B1 **Hunedoara** Rom
59B3 **Hungary** Republic, Europe
108B1 **Hungerford** Aust
74B3 **Hŭngnam** N Korea
74B2 **Hunjiang** China
46D2 **Hunsrück** Mts, Germany
109D2 **Hunter** *R* Aust
13D2 **Hunter I** Can
109C4 **Hunter Is** Aust
12D2 **Hunter,Mt** USA
14A3 **Huntingburg** USA
43D3 **Huntingdon** Eng
14A2 **Huntingdon** Indiana, USA
14B3 **Huntington** W Virginia, USA
22C4 **Huntington Beach** USA
22C2 **Huntington L** USA
110C1 **Huntly** NZ
44C3 **Huntly** Scot
12J2 **Hunt,Mt** Can
108A1 **Hunt Pen** Aust
17A1 **Huntsville** Alabama, USA
15C1 **Huntsville** Can
19A3 **Huntsville** Texas, USA
76D2 **Huong Khe** Viet
71F4 **Huon Peninsula** *Pen* PNG
109C4 **Huonville** Anst
14B1 **Hurd,C** Can
80B3 **Hurghada** Egypt
8D2 **Huron** S. Dakota, USA
14B1 **Huron,L** Can/USA
34A2 **Hurtado** Chile
111B2 **Hurunui** *R* NZ
38B1 **Husavik** Iceland
54C1 **Huşi** Rom
39G7 **Huskvarna** Sweden
12C1 **Huslia** USA
94B2 **Husn** Jordan
56B2 **Husum** Germany
109C1 **Hutton,Mt** Aust
72D2 **Hutuo He** *R* China
46C1 **Huy** Belg
72A2 **Huzhu** China
52C2 **Hvar** *I* Croatia
100B2 **Hwange** Zim
100B2 **Hwange Nat Pk** Zim
15D2 **Hyannis** USA
68B2 **Hyaryas Nuur** *L* Mongolia
5E4 **Hydaburg** Can
16C2 **Hyde Park** USA
87B1 **Hyderābād** India
85B3 **Hyderabad** Pak
49D3 **Hyères** France
12J2 **Hyland** *R* Can
8B2 **Hyndman Peak** *Mt* USA
38K6 **Hyrynsalmi** Fin
13D1 **Hythe** Can
74C4 **Hyūga** Japan
39J6 **Hyvikää** Fin

I

31C4 **Iaçu** Brazil
54C2 **Ialomiţa** *R* Rom
54C1 **Iaşi** Rom
97C4 **Ibadan** Nig
32B3 **Ibagué** Colombia
54B2 **Ibar** *R* Montenegro/ Serbia, Yugos
32B3 **Ibarra** Ecuador
35B1 **Ibiá** Brazil
30E4 **Ibicui** *R* Brazil
34D2 **Ibicuy** Arg
51C2 **Ibiza** Spain
51C2 **Ibiza** *I* Spain
101D2 **Ibo** Mozam
31C4 **Ibotirama** Brazil
91C5 **'Ibrī** Oman
32B6 **Ica** Peru
32D4 **Icá** *R* Brazil
32D3 **Icana** Brazil
38A1 **Iceland** Republic, N Atlantic O
13C2 **Ice Mt** Can
87A1 **Ichalkaranji** India
74E3 **Ichihara** Japan
75B1 **Ichinomiya** Japan
74E3 **Ichinoseki** Japan
12F3 **Icy B** USA
4B2 **Icy C** USA
19B3 **Idabell** USA
8B2 **Idaho Falls** USA
20B2 **Idanha** USA
46D2 **Idar Oberstein** Germany
95A2 **Idehan Marzūg** *Desert* Libya
95A2 **Idehan Ubari** *Desert* Libya
96C2 **Idelés** Alg
68B2 **Iderlym Gol** *R* Mongolia
95C2 **Idfu** Egypt
55B3 **Ídhi Óros** *Mt* Greece
55B3 **Ídhra** *I* Greece
98B3 **Idiofa** Zaïre
12C2 **Iditarod** *R* USA
92C2 **Idlib** Syria
39K7 **Idritsa** Russian Fed
100B4 **Idutywa** S Africa
55C3 **Ierápetra** Greece
46B1 **Ieper** Belg
63D2 **Iet Oktyobr'ya** Russian Fed
99D3 **Ifakara** Tanz
71F3 **Ifalik** *I* Pacific O
101D3 **Ifanadiana** Madag
97C4 **Ife** Nig
97C3 **Iférouane** Niger
78C2 **Igan** Malay
35B2 **Igaranava** Brazil
93E2 **Igdir** Iran
39H6 **Iggesund** Sweden
34B2 **Iglesia** Arg
53A3 **Iglesias** Sardegna
6B3 **Igloolik** Can
10A2 **Ignace** Can
55B3 **Igoumenítsa** Greece
61H2 **Igra** Russian Fed
23B2 **Iguala** Mexico
35B2 **Iguape** Brazil
35B2 **Iguatama** Brazil
31D3 **Iguatu** Brazil
98A3 **Iguéla** Gabon
101D3 **Ihosy** Madag
74D3 **Iida** Japan
75B1 **Iide-san** *Mt* Japan
38K6 **Iisalmi** Fin

Islas de Margarita

78C4 **Jember** Indon
57C2 **Jena** Germany
78B2 **Jenaja** *I* Indon
47D1 **Jenbach** Austria
94B2 **Jenin** Israel
19B3 **Jennings** USA
59B2 **Jeseniky** *Upland* Czech Republic
6F3 **Jensen Nunatakker** *Mt* Greenland
6B3 **Jens Munk** *I* Can
108B3 **Jeparit** Aust
31D4 **Jequié** Brazil
35C1 **Jequital** *R* Brazil
35C1 **Jequitinhonha** Brazil
31C5 **Jequitinhonha** *R* Brazil
50A2 **Jerez de la Frontera** Spain
50A2 **Jerez de los Caballeros** Spain
94B3 **Jericho** Israel
108C3 **Jerilderie** Aust
48B2 **Jersey** *I* UK
10C2 **Jersey City** USA
15C2 **Jersey Shore** USA
18B2 **Jerseyville** USA
92C3 **Jerusalem** Israel
109D3 **Jervis B** Aust
13C2 **Jervis Inlet** *Sd* Can
52B1 **Jesenice** Slovenia
86B2 **Jessore** Bang
11B3 **Jesup** USA
34C2 **Jesus Maria** Arg
16D2 **Jewett City** USA
54A2 **Jezerce** *Mt* Alb
58C2 **Jezioro Mamry** *L* Pol
58C2 **Jezioro Sniardwy** *L* Pol
94B2 **Jezzine** Leb
85C4 **Jhabua** India
85D4 **Jhalawar** India
84C2 **Jhang Maghiana** Pak
85D3 **Jhansi** India
86A2 **Jharsuguda** India
84C2 **Jhelum** Pak
84C2 **Jhelum** *R* Pak
11C3 **J H Kerr L** USA
84D3 **Jhunjhunun** India
69F2 **Jiamusi** China
73C4 **Ji'an** Jiangxi, China
74B2 **Ji'an** Jilin, China
73D4 **Jiande** China
73B4 **Jiang'an** China
73D4 **Jiangbiancun** China
73A5 **Jiangcheng** China
73B3 **Jiang Jiang** *R* China
73C5 **Jiangmen** China
72D3 **Jiangsu** Province, China
73C4 **Jiangxi** Province, China
73A3 **Jiangyou** China
72D1 **Jianping** China
73A5 **Jianshui** China
73D4 **Jian Xi** *R* China
73D4 **Jianyang** China
72E2 **Jiaonan** China
72E2 **Jiao Xian** China
72E2 **Jiaozhou Wan** *B* China
72C2 **Jiaozuo** China
73E3 **Jiaxiang** China
68B3 **Jiayuguan** China
81B3 **Jiddah** S Arabia
72D3 **Jieshou** China
72C2 **Jiexiu** China
72A3 **Jigzhi** China
59B3 **Jihlava** Czech Republic
99E2 **Jilib** Somalia
69E2 **Jilin** China
51B1 **Jiloca** *R* Spain
99D2 **Jima** Eth
9C4 **Jiménez** Coahuila, Mexico
72D2 **Jinan** China
84D3 **Jind** India
72B2 **Jingbian** China
73D4 **Jingdezhen** China
76C1 **Jinghong** China
73C3 **Jingmen** China
72B2 **Jingning** China
73B4 **Jing Xiang** China

73D4 **Jinhua** China
72C1 **Jining** Nei Monggol, China
72D2 **Jining** Shandong, China
99D2 **Jinja** Uganda
76C1 **Jinping** China
73A4 **Jinsha Jiang** *R* China
73C4 **Jinshi** China
72E1 **Jinxi** China
72E2 **Jin Xian** China
72E1 **Jinzhou** China
33E5 **Jiparaná** *R* Brazil
32A4 **Jipijapa** Ecuador
23A2 **Jiquilpan** Mexico
91C4 **Jiroft** Iran
99E2 **Jirriban** Somalia
73B4 **Jishou** China
92C2 **Jisr ash Shughür** Syria
54B2 **Jiu** *R* Rom
73D4 **Jiujiang** China
73A4 **Jiulong** China
73D4 **Jiulong Jiang** *R* China
69F2 **Jixi** China
94B3 **Jiza** Jordan
81C4 **Jizan** S Arabia
97A3 **Joal** Sen
35C1 **João Monlevade** Brazil
31E3 **João Pessoa** Brazil
35B1 **João Pirheiro** Brazil
34B2 **Jocoli** Arg
85C3 **Jodhpur** India
38K6 **Joensuu** Fin
46C2 **Joeuf** France
13D2 **Joffre,Mt** Can
86B1 **Jogbani** India
87A2 **Jog Falls** India
101G1 **Johannesburg** S Africa
21B2 **Johannesburg** USA
6C2 **Johan Pen** Can
12D1 **John** *R* USA
20C2 **John Day** USA
20B1 **John Day** *R* USA
44C2 **John O'Groats** Scot
18A2 **John Redmond Res** USA
11B3 **Johnson City** Tennessee, USA
17B1 **Johnston** USA
27N2 **Johnston Pt** St Vincent and the Grenadines
15C2 **Johnstown** Pennsylvania, USA
77C5 **Johor Bharu** Malay
49C2 **Joigny** France
30G4 **Joinville** Brazil
61H3 **Jok** *R* Russian Fed
38H5 **Jokkmokk** Sweden
93E2 **Jolfa** Iran
10B2 **Joliet** USA
7C5 **Joliette** Can
79B4 **Jolo** Phil
79B4 **Jolo** *I* Phil
82D2 **Joma** *Mt* China
58C1 **Jonava** Lithuania
72A3 **Jonê** China
11A3 **Jonesboro** Arkansas, USA
19B3 **Jonesboro** Louisiana, USA
6B2 **Jones Sd** Can
58C1 **Joniškis** Lithuania
39G7 **Jönköping** Sweden
11A3 **Joplin** USA
92C3 **Jordan** Kingdom, S W Asia
94B2 **Jordan** *R* Israel
20C2 **Jordan Valley** USA
86C1 **Jorhat** India
38J5 **Jörn** Sweden
78C3 **Jorong** Indon
39F7 **Jørpeland** Nor
79B3 **Jose Pañganiban** Phil
106B2 **Joseph Bonaparte G** Aust
64B3 **Jotunheimen** *Mt* Nor
94B2 **Jouai'ya** Leb
94B2 **Jounié** Leb
86C1 **Jowal** India

99E2 **Jowhar** Somalia
12H2 **Joy,Mt** Can
5F5 **Juan de Fuca,Str of** Can/USA
101D2 **Juan de Nova** *I* Mozam Chan
34D3 **Juárez** Arg
31C3 **Juàzeiro** Brazil
31D3 **Juazeiro do Norte** Brazil
99D2 **Juba** Sudan
99E2 **Juba** *R* Somalia
94B1 **Jubail** Leb
93D3 **Jubbah** S Arabia
96A2 **Juby,C** Mor
51B2 **Jucar** *R* Spain
23B2 **Juchatengo** Mexico
23A1 **Juchipila** *R* Mexico
23A1 **Juchitlan** Mexico
57C3 **Judenburg** Austria
30B2 **Juilaca** Peru
73C4 **Juiling Shan** *Hills* China
31C6 **Juiz de Fora** Brazil
30C3 **Jujuy** State, Arg
30C2 **Juli** Peru
33F3 **Julianatop** *Mt* Surinam
6F3 **Julianehab** Greenland
46D1 **Jülich** Germany
86A1 **Jumla** Nepal
94B3 **Jum Suwwāna** *Mt* Jordan
85C4 **Jūnāgadh** India
72D2 **Junan** China
9D3 **Junction City** USA
31B6 **Jundiaí** Brazil
4E4 **Juneau** USA
107D4 **Junee** Aust
22C2 **June Lake** USA
52A1 **Jungfrau** *Mt* Switz
16A2 **Juniata** *R* USA
29D2 **Junín** Arg
73A4 **Junlian** China
31B6 **Juquiá** Brazil
99C2 **Jur** *R* Sudan
42B2 **Jura** *I* Scot
49D2 **Jura** *Mts* France
44B3 **Jura,Sound of** *Chan* Scot
94B3 **Jurf ed Darāwīsh** Jordan
65K4 **Jurga** Russian Fed
60B2 **Jūrmala** Latvia
32D4 **Juruá** *R* Brazil
33F6 **Juruena** *R* Brazil
94C1 **Jūsiyah** Syria
34B2 **Justo Daract** Arg
32D4 **Jutai** *R* Brazil
25D3 **Juticalpa** Honduras
Jutland = Jylland
90C3 **Jūymand** Iran
56B1 **Jylland** *Pen* Den
38K6 **Jyväskyla** Fin

K

82B2 **K2** *Mt* China/India
90C2 **Kaakhka** Turkmenistan
101H1 **Kaapmuiden** S Africa
71D4 **Kabaena** *I* Indon
97A4 **Kabala** Sierra Leone
99D3 **Kabale** Rwanda
98C3 **Kabalo** Zaïre
98C3 **Kabambare** Zaïre
99D2 **Kabarole** Uganda
98C3 **Kabinda** Zaïre
90A3 **Kabir Kuh** *Mts* Iran
100B2 **Kabompo** Zambia
100B2 **Kabompo** *R* Zambia
98C3 **Kabongo** Zaïre
84B2 **Kabul** Afghan
85B4 **Kachchh,G of** India
61J2 **Kachkanar** Russian Fed
63C2 **Kachug** Russian Fed
76B3 **Kadan** ·Burma
78D3 **Kadapongan** *I* Indon
85C4 **Kadi** India
108A2 **Kadina** Aust
92B2 **Kadinhanı** Turk
87B2 **Kadiri** India

60E4 **Kadiyevka** Ukraine
100B2 **Kadoma** Zlm
99C1 **Kadugli** Sudan
97C3 **Kaduna** Nig
97C3 **Kaduna** *R* Nig
87B2 **Kadür** India
97A3 **Kaédi** Maur
21C4 **Kaena Pt** Hawaiian Is
74B3 **Kaesöng** N Korea
97C4 **Kafanchan** Nig
97A3 **Kaffrine** Sen
94C1 **Kafrün Bashūr** Syria
100B2 **Kafue** Zambia
100B2 **Kafue** *R* Zambia
100B2 **Kafue Nat Pk** Zambia
74D3 **Kaga** Japan
65H6 **Kagan** Kazakhstan
93D1 **Kağizman** Turk
74C4 **Kagoshima** Japan
90C2 **Kāhak** Iran
99D3 **Kahama** Tanz
84B3 **Kahan** Pak
78C3 **Kahayan** *R* Indon
98B3 **Kahemba** Zaïre
46E1 **Kahler Asten** *Mt* Germany
91C4 **Kahnüj** Iran
18B1 **Kahoka** USA
21C4 **Kahoolawe** *I* Hawaiian Is
92C2 **Kahramanmaraş** Turk
21C4 **Kahuku Pt** Hawaiian Is
111B2 **Kaiapoi** NZ
33F2 **Kaieteur Fall** Guyana
72C3 **Kaifeng** China
110B1 **Kaikohe** NZ
111B2 **Kaikoura** NZ
111B2 **Kaikoura Pen** NZ
111B2 **Kaikoura Range** *Mts* NZ
73B4 **Kaili** China
21C4 **Kailua** Hawaiian Is
71E4 **Kaimana** Indon
75B2 **Kainan** Japan
97C3 **Kainji Res** Nig
110B1 **Kaipara Harbour** *B* NZ
73C5 **Kaiping** China
96D1 **Kairouan** Tunisia
22C2 **Kaiser Peak** *Mt* USA
57B3 **Kaiserslautern** Germany
74B2 **Kaishantun** China
58D2 **Kaisiadorys** Lithuania
110B1 **Kaitaia** NZ
111A3 **Kaitangata** NZ
84D3 **Kaithal** India
21C4 **Kaiwi Chan** Hawaiian Is
73B3 **Kai Xian** China
73A5 **Kaiyuan** Liaoning, China
74A2 **Kaiyuan** Yunnan, China
12C2 **Kaiyuh Mts** USA
38K6 **Kajaani** Fin
84B2 **Kajaki** Afghan
99D3 **Kajiado** Kenya
84B2 **Kajrän** Afghan
99D1 **Kaka** Sudan
99D2 **Kakamega** Kenya
75A2 **Kake** Japan
12H3 **Kake** USA
12D3 **Kakhonak** USA
65E5 **Kakhovskoye Vodokhranilishche** *Res* Ukraine
91B4 **Kākī** Iran
87C1 **Kākināda** India
75A2 **Kakogawa** Japan
4D2 **Kaktovik** USA
75C1 **Kakuda** Japan
Kalaallit Nunaat = Greenland
55B3 **Kalabáka** Greece
78D1 **Kalabakan** Malay
100B2 **Kalabo** Zambia
61F3 **Kalach** Russian Fed
61F4 **Kalach-na-Donu** Russian Fed
86C2 **Kaladan** *R* Burma
21C4 **Ka Lae** *C* Hawaiian Is

100B3 **Kalahari Desert** Botswana
38J6 **Kalajoki** Fin
63D2 **Kalakan** Russian Fed
70A3 **Kalakepen** Indon
84C1 **Kalam** Pak
55B3 **Kalámai** Greece
10B2 **Kalamazoo** USA
84B3 **Kalat** Pak
92B1 **Kalecik** Turk
78D3 **Kalembau** *I* Indon
99C3 **Kalémié** Zaïre
38L5 **Kalevala** Russian Fed
86C2 **Kalewa** Burma
12D2 **Kalgin I** USA
106B4 **Kalgoorlie** Aust
78B4 **Kalianda** Indon
79B3 **Kalibo** Phil
98C3 **Kalima** Zaïre
78C3 **Kalimantan** Province, Indon
55C3 **Kálimnos** *I* Greece
86B1 **Kālimpang** India
60B3 **Kaliningrad** Russian Fed
60C3 **Kalinkovichi** Belorussia
8B2 **Kalispell** USA
58B2 **Kalisz** Pol
99D3 **Kaliua** Tanz
38J5 **Kalix** *R* Sweden
100A3 **Kalkfeld** Namibia
100A3 **Kalkrand** Namibia
108A1 **Kallakoopah** *R* Aust
38K6 **Kallávesi** *L* Fin
55C3 **Kallonis Kólpos** *B* Greece
39H7 **Kalmar** Sweden
61G4 **Kalmytskaya Respublika,** Russian Fed
100B2 **Kalomo** Zambia
18B1 **Kalona** USA
13B2 **Kalone Peak** *Mt* Can
87A2 **Kalpeni** *I* India
85D3 **Kālpi** India
53A3 **Kalsat Khasba** Tunisia
12B2 **Kalskag** USA
12C2 **Kaltag** USA
60E3 **Kaluga** Russian Fed
39G7 **Kalundborg** Den
59C3 **Kalush** Ukraine
87B2 **Kalyandurg** India
60E2 **Kalyazin** Russian Fed
61H1 **Kama** *R* Russian Fed
74E3 **Kamaishi** Japan
84C2 **Kamalia** Pak
110C1 **Kamanawa Mts** NZ
100A2 **Kamanjab** Namibia
84D2 **Kamat** *Mt* India
87B3 **Kamban** India
61H2 **Kambarka** Russian Fed
97A4 **Kambia** Sierra Leone
59D3 **Kamenets Podolskiy** Ukraine
61F3 **Kamenka** Russian Fed
65K4 **Kamen-na-Obi** Russian Fed
61K2 **Kamensk-Ural'skiy** Russian Fed
5H3 **Kamilukuak L** Can
98C3 **Kamina** Zaïre
7A3 **Kaminak L** Can
75C1 **Kaminoyama** Japan
5F4 **Kamloops** Can
93E1 **Kamo** Armenia
75C1 **Kamogawa** Japan
99D2 **Kampala** Uganda
77C5 **Kampar** Malay
78A2 **Kampar** *R* Indon
56B2 **Kampen** Neth
76B2 **Kamphaeng Phet** Thai
77C3 **Kampot** Camb
91D4 **Kamsaptar** Iran
61J2 **Kamskoye Vodokhranilishche** *Res* Russian Fed
85D4 **Kāmthi** India
61G3 **Kamyshin** Russian Fed
61K2 **Kamyshlov** Russian Fed
7C4 **Kanaaupscow** *R* Can
98C3 **Kananga** Zaïre
61G2 **Kanash** Russian Fed
75B1 **Kanayama** Japan
74D3 **Kanazawa** Japan
4C3 **Kanbisha** USA
87B2 **Kānchipuram** India
84B2 **Kandahar** Afghan
64E3 **Kandalaksha** Russian Fed
38L5 **Kandalakshskaya Guba** *B* Russian Fed
97C3 **Kandi** Benin
109C2 **Kandos** Aust
87C3 **Kandy** Sri Lanka
15C2 **Kane** USA
6C1 **Kane Basin** *B* Can
98B1 **Kanem** *Desert Region* Chad
97B3 **Kangaba** Mali
92C2 **Kangal** Turk
6E3 **Kangâmiut** Greenland
91B4 **Kangān** Iran
77C4 **Kangar** Malay
106C4 **Kangaroo I** Aust
6E3 **Kangâtsiaq** Greenland
90A3 **Kangavar** Iran
72C1 **Kangbao** China
82C3 **Kangchenjunga** *Mt* Nepal
73A4 **Kangding** China
6G3 **Kangerdlugssuaq** *B* Greenland
6G3 **Kangerdlugssvatsaiq** *B* Greenland
99D2 **Kangetet** Kenya
74B2 **Kanggye** N Korea
7D4 **Kangiqsualujjuaq** Can
6C3 **Kangiqsujuaq** Can
7C3 **Kangirsuk** Can
74B3 **Kangnŭng** S Korea
98B2 **Kango** Gabon
68B4 **Kangto** *Mt* China
72B3 **Kang Xian** China
77D4 **Kanh Hung** Viet
98C3 **Kaniama** Zaïre
87B1 **Kani Giri** India
39J6 **Kankaanpää** Fin
14A2 **Kankakee** USA
14A2 **Kankakee** *R* USA
97B3 **Kankan** Guinea
86A2 **Kānker** India
87B3 **Kanniyākuman** India
97C3 **Kano** Nig
74C4 **Kanoya** Japan
86A1 **Kānpur** India
9D3 **Kansas** State, USA
18A2 **Kansas** *R* USA
10A3 **Kansas City** USA
73D5 **Kanshi** China
63B2 **Kansk** Russian Fed
97C3 **Kantchari** Burkina
86B2 **Kanthi** India
12D2 **Kantishna** USA
12D2 **Kantishna** *R* USA
100B3 **Kanye** Botswana
68D4 **Kao-hsiung** Taiwan
100A2 **Kaoka Veld** *Plain* Namibia
97A3 **Kaolack** Sen
100B2 **Kaoma** Zambia
21C4 **Kapaau** Hawaiian Is
98C3 **Kapanga** Zaïre
6F3 **Kap Cort Adelaer** *C* Greenland
6H3 **Kap Dalton** *C* Greenland
39H7 **Kapellskär** Sweden
6F3 **Kap Farvel** *C* Greenland
6G3 **Kap Gustav Holm** *C* Greenland
100B2 **Kapiri** Zambia
78C2 **Kapit** Malay
19B3 **Kaplan** USA
57C3 **Kaplice** Czech Republic
77B4 **Kapoe** Thai
99C3 **Kapona** Zaïre
52C1 **Kaposvár** Hung
6C2 **Kap Parry** *C* Can
6H3 **Kap Ravn** *C* Greenland
78B3 **Kapuas** *R* Indon
108A2 **Kapunda** Aust
84D2 **Kapurthala** India
7B5 **Kapuskasing** Can
109D2 **Kaputar** *Mt* Aust
93E2 **Kapydzhik** *Mt* Armenia
6D2 **Kap York** *C* Greenland
92B1 **Karabük** Turk
55C2 **Karacabey** Turk
85B4 **Karachi** Pak
87A1 **Karād** India
60E5 **Kara Daglari** *Mt* Turk
54C5 **Karadeniz Boğazi** *Sd* Turk
68D1 **Karaftit** Russian Fed
65J5 **Karaganda** Kazakhstan
65J5 **Karagayly** Kazakhstan
87B2 **Kāraikāl** India
90B2 **Karaj** Iran
92C3 **Karak** Jordan
65G5 **Kara Kalpakskaya Respublika,** Uzbekistan
84D1 **Karakax He** *R* China
71D3 **Karakelong** *I* Indon
84D1 **Karakoram** *Mts* India
84D1 **Karakoram** *P* India/China
97A3 **Karakoro** *R* Maur/Sen
65G6 **Karakumy** *Desert* Russian Fed
94B3 **Karama** Jordan
92B2 **Karaman** Turk
65K5 **Karamay** China
111B2 **Karamea** NZ
111B2 **Karamea Bight** *B* NZ
85D4 **Kāranja** India
92B2 **Karapınar** Turk
64H2 **Kara S** Russian Fed
100A3 **Karasburg** Namibia
38K5 **Karasjok** Nor
65J4 **Karasuk** Russian Fed
92C2 **Karataş** Turk
65H5 **Kara Tau** *Mts* Kazakhstan
76B3 **Karathuri** Burma
74B4 **Karatsu** Japan
91B4 **Karāz** Iran
93D3 **Karbalā'** Iraq
59C3 **Karcag** Hung
55B3 **Kardhítsa** Greece
64E3 **Karel'skaya Respublika,** Russian Fed
38J5 **Karesvando** Sweden
96B2 **Karet** *Desert Region* Maur
65K4 **Kargasok** Russian Fed
97D3 **Kari** Nig
100B2 **Kariba** Zim
100B2 **Kariba** *L* Zim/Zambia
100B2 **Kariba Dam** Zim/Zambia
95C3 **Karima** Sudan
78B3 **Karimata** *I* Indon
86C2 **Karimganj** Bang
87B1 **Karīmnagar** India
99E1 **Karin** Somalia
39J6 **Karis** Fin
99C3 **Karishimbe** *Mt* Zaïre
55B3 **Káristos** Greece
87A2 **Kārkal** India
71F4 **Karkar** *I* PNG
90A3 **Karkheh** *R* Iran
60D4 **Karkinitskiy Zaliv** *B* Ukraine
63B3 **Karlik Shan** *Mt* China
58B2 **Karlino** Pol
52C2 **Karlobag** Croatia
52C1 **Karlovac** Croatia
54B2 **Karlovo** Bulg
57C2 **Karlovy Vary** Czech Republic
39G7 **Karlshamn** Sweden
39G7 **Karlskoga** Sweden
39H7 **Karlskrona** Sweden
57B3 **Karlsruhe** Germany
39G7 **Karlstad** Sweden
12D3 **Karluk** USA
86C2 **Karnafuli Res** Bang
84D3 **Karnal** India
87A1 **Karnataka** State, India
54C2 **Karnobat** Bulg
100B2 **Karoi** Zim
99D3 **Karonga** Malawi
95C3 **Karora** Sudan
78D3 **Karossa** Indon
55C3 **Kárpathos** *I* Greece
6E2 **Karrats Fjord** Greenland
93D1 **Kars** Turk
65H4 **Karsakpay** Kazakhstan
58D1 **Kārsava** Latvia
80E2 **Karshi** Uzbekistan
38J6 **Karstula** Fin
94B1 **Kartaba** Leb
54C2 **Kartal** Turk
61K3 **Kartaly** Russian Fed
90A3 **Kārūn** *R* Iran
86A1 **Karwa** India
87A2 **Kārwār** India
68D1 **Karymskoye** Russian Fed
98B3 **Kasai** *R* Zaïre
100B2 **Kasaji** Zaïre
101C2 **Kasama** Zambia
99D3 **Kasanga** Tanz
87A2 **Kāsaragod** India
5H3 **Kasba L** Can
100B2 **Kasempa** Zambia
100B2 **Kasenga** Zaïre
99D2 **Kasese** Uganda
90B3 **Kāshān** Iran
12C2 **Kashegelok** USA
82B2 **Kashi** China
84D3 **Kāshipur** India
74D3 **Kashiwazaki** Japan
90C2 **Kashmar** Iran
66D3 **Kashmir** State, India
61F3 **Kasimov** Russian Fed
18C2 **Kaskaskia** *R* USA
38J6 **Kaskinen** Fin
61K2 **Kasli** Russian Fed
5G5 **Kaslo** Can
98C3 **Kasonga** Zaïre
98B3 **Kasongo-Lunda** Zaïre
55C3 **Kásos** *I* Greece
Kaspiyskiy = Lagan'
95C3 **Kassala** Sudan
56B2 **Kassel** Germany
96C1 **Kasserine** Tunisia
100A2 **Kassinga** Angola
92B1 **Kastamonou** Turk
55B3 **Kastélli** Greece
92A2 **Kastellorizon** *I* Greece
55B2 **Kastoría** Greece
55C3 **Kástron** Greece
74D3 **Kasugai** Japan
75A1 **Kasumi** Japan
101C2 **Kasungu** Malawi
84C2 **Kasur** Pak
100B2 **Kataba** Zambia
98C3 **Katako-kombe** Zaïre
4D3 **Katalla** USA
63G2 **Katangli** Russian Fed
106A4 **Katanning** Aust
55B2 **Kateríni** Greece
5E4 **Kates Needle** *Mt* Can/USA
82D3 **Katha** Burma
106C2 **Katherine** Aust
85C4 **Kāthiāwār** *Pen* India
86B1 **Kathmandu** Nepal
84D2 **Kathua** India
86B1 **Katihār** India
100B2 **Katima Mulilo** Namibia
4C4 **Katmai,Mt** USA
12D3 **Katmai Nat Mon** USA
86A2 **Katni** India
109D2 **Katoomba** Aust
59B2 **Katowice** Pol
39H7 **Katrineholm** Sweden

97C3 **Katsina** Nig	4F2 **Kellet,C** Can	78A2 **Kepulauan Riau** *Arch* Indon	94CJ **Khan ez Zabib** Jordan
97C4 **Katsina Ala** Nig	20C1 **Kellogg** USA	78D4 **Kepulauan Sabalana** *Arch* Indon	77D4 **Khanh Hung** Viet
75C1 **Katsuta** Japan	64D3 **Kelloselka** Fin	71D3 **Kepulauan Sangihe** *Arch* Indon	55B3 **Khaniá** Greece
75C1 **Katsuura** Japan	45C2 **Kells** Irish Rep	71D4 **Kepulauan Sula** *I* Indon	84C3 **Khanpur** Pak
75B1 **Katsuy** Japan	42B2 **Kells Range** *Hills* Scot	71D3 **Kepulauan Talaud** *Arch* Indon	65H3 **Khanty-Mansiysk** Russian Fed
65H6 **Kattakurgan** Uzbekistan	58C1 **Kelme** Lithuania	78B2 **Kepulauan Tambelan** *Is* Indon	94B3 **Khan Yunis** Egypt
39G7 **Kattegat** *Str* Den/Sweden	5G5 **Kelowna** Can	71E4 **Kepulauan Tanimbar** *I* Indon	84D1 **Khapalu** India
21C4 **Kauai** *I* Hawaiian Is	5F4 **Kelsey Bay** Can	71D4 **Kepulauan Togian** *I* Indon	68C2 **Khapcheranga** Russian Fed
21C4 **Kauai Chan** Hawaiian Is	42C2 **Kelso** Scot	71D4 **Kepulauan Tukambesi** *Is* Indon	61G4 **Kharabali** Russian Fed
21C4 **Kaulakahi Chan** Hawaiian Is	20B1 **Kelso** USA	87B2 **Kerala** State, India	86B2 **Kharagpur** India
21C4 **Kaunakaki** Hawaiian Is	64E3 **Kem'** Russian Fed	108B3 **Kerang** Aust	91C4 **Khāran** Iran
60B3 **Kaunas** Lithuania	38L6 **Kem'** *R* Russian Fed	39K6 **Kerava** Fin	84B3 **Kharan** Pak
97C3 **Kaura Namoda** Nig	97B3 **Ke Macina** Mali	60E4 **Kerch'** Ukraine	90B3 **Kharānaq** Iran
38J5 **Kautokeino** Nor	13B2 **Kemano** Can	71F4 **Kerema** PNG	91B4 **Khārg** *Is* Iran
55B2 **Kavadarci** Macedonia	65K4 **Kemerovo** Russian Fed	20C1 **Keremeps** Can	95C2 **Khārga Oasis** Egypt
55A2 **Kavajë** Alb	38J5 **Kemi** Fin	95C3 **Keren** Eritrea	85D4 **Khargon** India
87B2 **Kavali** India	38K5 **Kemi** *R* Fin	104B6 **Kerguelen Ridge** Indian O	60E4 **Khar'kov** Ukraine
55B2 **Kaválla** Greece	38K5 **Kemijärvi** Fin	99D3 **Kericho** Kenya	54C2 **Kharmanli** Bulg
85B4 **Kävda** India	46C1 **Kempen** Region, Belg	70B4 **Kerinci** *Mt* Indon	61F2 **Kharovsk** Russian Fed
75B1 **Kawagoe** Japan	26B2 **Kemps Bay** The Bahamas	99D2 **Kerio** *R* Kenya	95C3 **Khartoum** Sudan
75B1 **Kawaguchi** Japan	109D2 **Kempsey** Aust	80E2 **Kerki** Turkmenistan	95C3 **Khartoum North** Sudan
110B1 **Kawakawa** NZ	57C3 **Kempten** Germany	55A3 **Kérkira** Greece	74C2 **Khasan** Russian Fed
99C3 **Kawambwa** Zambia	12D2 **Kenai** USA	55A3 **Kérkira** *I* Greece	95C3 **Khashm el Girba** Sudan
86A2 **Kawardha** India	12D3 **Kenai Mts** USA	91C3 **Kerman** Iran	86C1 **Khasi-Jaīntia Hills** India
15C2 **Kawartha Lakes** Can	12D2 **Kenai Pen** USA	22B2 **Kerman** USA	54C2 **Khaskovo** Bulg
74D3 **Kawasaki** Japan	99D2 **Kenamuke Swamp** Sudan	90A3 **Kermānshāh** Iran	1B9 **Khatanga** Russian Fed
110C1 **Kawerau** NZ	42C2 **Kendal** Eng	21B2 **Kern** *R* USA	76B3 **Khawsa** Burma
110B1 **Kawhia** NZ	109D2 **Kendall** Aust	13F2 **Kerrobert** Can	76C2 **Khe Bo** Viet
97B3 **Kaya** Burkina	71D4 **Kendari** Indon	45B2 **Kerry** County, Irish Rep	85C4 **Khed Brahma** India
12F3 **Kayak I** USA	78C3 **Kendawangan** Indon	17B1 **Kershaw** USA	51C2 **Khemis** Alg
78D2 **Kayan** *R* Indon	86B2 **Kendrāpāra** India	78B3 **Kertamulia** Indon	96B1 **Khenifra** Mor
87B3 **Kayankulam** India	20C1 **Kendrick** USA	63D3 **Kerulen** *R* Mongolia	51D2 **Kherrata** Alg
97A3 **Kayes** Mali	97A4 **Kenema** Sierra Leone	96B2 **Kerzaz** Alg	60D4 **Kherson** Ukraine
92C2 **Kayseri** Turk	98B3 **Kenge** Zaire	55C2 **Keşan** Turk	63D2 **Khilok** Russian Fed
1B8 **Kazach'ye** Russian Fed	76B1 **Kengtung** Burma	74E3 **Kesennuma** Japan	55C3 **Khíos** Greece
93E1 **Kazakh** Azerbaijan	100B3 **Kenhardt** S Africa	38L5 **Kesten 'ga** Russian Fed	55C3 **Khíos** *I* Greece
65G5 **Kazakhstan** Republic, Asia	97A3 **Kéniéba** Mali	42C2 **Keswick** Eng	60C4 **Khmel'nitskiy** Ukraine
61G2 **Kazan'** Russian Fed	96B1 **Kenitra** Mor	65K4 **Ket** *R* Russian Fed	59C3 **Khodorov** Ukraine
54C2 **Kazanlŭk** Bulg	45B3 **Kenmare** Irish Rep	97C4 **Kéta** Ghana	84B1 **Kholm** Afghan
69G4 **Kazan Retto** *Is* Japan	45B3 **Kenmare** *R* Irish Rep	78C3 **Ketapang** Indon	76D3 **Khong** Laos
91B4 **Käzerün** Iran	19B4 **Kenner** USA	5E4 **Ketchikan** USA	91B4 **Khonj** Iran
61H1 **Kazhim** Russian Fed	18C2 **Kennett** USA	97C3 **Ketia** Niger	69F2 **Khor** Russian Fed
93E1 **Kazi Magomed** Azerbaijan	16B3 **Kennett Square** USA	85B4 **Keti Bandar** Pak	91A3 **Khoramshahr** Iran
59C3 **Kazincbarcika** Hung	20C1 **Kennewick** USA	58C2 **Ketrzyn** Pol	91B5 **Khōr Duwayhin** *B* UAE
55B3 **Kéa** *I* Greece	5F4 **Kenny Dam** Can	43D3 **Kettering** Eng	84C1 **Khorog** Tajikistan
21C4 **Kealaikahiki Chan** Hawaiian Is	7A5 **Kenora** Can	14B3 **Kettering** USA	90A3 **Khorramābad** Iran
8D2 **Kearney** USA	10B2 **Kenosha** USA	20C1 **Kettle** *R* Can	90C3 **Khosf** Iran
93C2 **Keban Baraji** *Res* Turk	43E4 **Kent** County, Eng	20C1 **Kettle River Range** *Mts* USA	84B2 **Khost** Pak
97A3 **Kébémer** Sen	20B1 **Kent** Washington, USA	7C3 **Kettlestone B** Can	60C4 **Khotin** Ukraine
96C1 **Kebili** Tunisia	14A2 **Kentland** USA	90C3 **Kevir-i Namak** *Salt Flat* Iran	12C2 **Khotol** *Mt* USA
94C1 **Kebîr** *R* Leb/Syria	14B2 **Kenton** USA	14A2 **Kewaunee** USA	60C3 **Khoyniki** Belorussia
38H5 **Kebrekaise** *Mt* Sweden	4H3 **Kent Pen** Can	14B1 **Key Harbour** Can	63F2 **Khrebet Dzhugdzhur** *Mts* Russian Fed
59B3 **Kecskemét** Hung	11B3 **Kentucky** State, USA	17B2 **Key Largo** USA	90C2 **Khrebet Kopet Dag** *Mts* Turkmenistan
58C1 **Kedainiai** Lithuania	11B3 **Kentucky L** USA	11B4 **Key West** USA	64H3 **Khrebet Pay-khoy** *Mts* Russian Fed
97A3 **Kédougou** Sen	19B3 **Kentwood** Louisiana, USA	63C2 **Kezhma** Russian Fed	82C1 **Khrebet Tarbagatay** *Mts* Kazakhstan
12J2 **Keele** *R* Can	14A2 **Kentwood** Michigan, USA	54A1 **K'feleghāza** Hung	63E2 **Khrebet Tukuringra** *Mts* Russian Fed
12H2 **Keele Pk** *Mt* Can	99D2 **Kenya** Republic, Africa	12B2 **Kgun L** USA	82A1 **Khudzhand** Tajikistan
21B2 **Keeler** USA	**Kenya,Mt = Kirinyaga**	94C2 **Khabab** Syria	86B2 **Khulna** Bang
15D2 **Keene** New Hampshire, USA	18B1 **Keokuk** USA	62H3 **Khabarovsk** Russian Fed	84D1 **Khunjerab** *P* China/India
100A3 **Keetmanshoop** Namibia	86A2 **Keonchi** India	85B3 **Khairpur** Pak	90B3 **Khunsar** Iran
18C1 **Keewanee** USA	86B2 **Keonjhargarh** India	85B3 **Khairpur** Region, Pak	91A4 **Khurays** S Arabia
6A3 **Keewatin** *Region* Can	71E4 **Kepaluan Tanimbar** *Arch* Indon	100B3 **Khakhea** Botswana	86B2 **Khurda** India
55B3 **Kefallinía** *I* Greece	6H3 **Keplavik** Iceland	55C3 **Khálki** *I* Greece	84D3 **Khurja** India
94B2 **Kefar Sava** Israel	59B2 **Kepno** Pol	55B2 **Khalkidhíki** *Pen* Greece	84C2 **Khushab** Pak
97C4 **Keffi** Nig	78B2 **Kepulauan Anambas** *Arch* Indon	55B3 **Khalkis** Greece	94B2 **Khushnīyah** Syria
38A2 **Keflavik** Iceland	71E4 **Kepulauan Aru** *Arch* Indon	61G2 **Khalturin** Russian Fed	59C3 **Khust** Ukraine
5G4 **Keg River** Can	78B2 **Kepulauan Badas** *Is* Indon	85C4 **Khambhāt,G of** India	99C1 **Khuwei** Sudan
76B1 **Kehsi Mansam** Burma	71E4 **Kepulauan Banda** *Arch* Indon	85D4 **Khāmgaon** India	85B3 **Khuzdar** Pak
108B3 **Keith** Aust	71D4 **Kepulauan Banggai** *I* Indon	76C2 **Kham Keut** Laos	90D3 **Khvāf** Iran
44C3 **Keith** Scot	78B2 **Kepulauan Bunguran Seletan** *Arch* Indon	87C1 **Khammam** India	61G3 **Khvalynsk** Russian Fed
4F3 **Keith Arm** *B* Can	71E4 **Kepulauan Kai** *Arch* Indon	90A2 **Khamseh** *Mts* Iran	90C3 **Khvor** Iran
6D3 **Kekertuk** Can	71D4 **Kepulauan Leti** *I* Indon	76C2 **Khan** *R* Laos	91B4 **Khvormūj** Iran
85D3 **Kekri** India	78A3 **Kepulauan Lingga** *Is* Indon	84B1 **Khanabad** Afghan	93D2 **Khvoy** Iran
77C5 **Kelang** Malay	70A4 **Kepulauan Mentawi** *Arch* Indon	93E3 **Khānaqin** Iraq	84C1 **Khwaja Muhammad** *Mts* Afghan
77C4 **Kelantan** *R* Malay		85D4 **Khandwa** India	
84B1 **Kelif** Turkmenistan		84C2 **Khanewal** Pak	84C2 **Khyber P** Afghan/Pak
92C1 **Kelkit** *R* Turk			
98B3 **Kellé** Congo			

75A2 **Komatsushima** Japan
64G3 **Komi Respublika,** Russian Fed
70C4 **Komodo** *I* Indon
71E4 **Komoran** *I* Indon
75B1 **Komoro** Japan
55C2 **Komotiní** Greece
76D3 **Kompong Cham** Camb
76C3 **Kompong Chhnang** *Mts* Camb
77C3 **Kompong Som** Camb
76C3 **Kompong Thom** Camb
76D3 **Kompong Trabek** Camb
63F2 **Komsomol'sk na Amure** Russian Fed
65H4 **Konda** *R* Russian Fed
99D3 **Kondoa** Tanz
87B1 **Kondukūr** India
6G3 **Kong Christian IX Land** *Region* Greenland
6F3 **Kong Frederik VI Kyst** *Mts* Greenland
64C2 **Kong Karls Land** *Is* Barents S
78D2 **Kongkemul** *Mt* Indon
98C3 **Kongolo** Zaïre
39F7 **Kongsberg** Den
39G6 **Kongsvinger** Nor
Königsberg = Kaliningrad
58B2 **Konin** Pol
54A2 **Konjic** Bosnia-Herzegovina
61F1 **Konosha** Russian Fed
75B1 **Konosu** Japan
60D3 **Konotop** Ukraine
59C2 **Końskie** Pol
49D2 **Konstanz** Germany
97C3 **Kontagora** Nig
76D3 **Kontum** Viet
92B2 **Konya** Turk
13D3 **Kootenay** *R* Can
85C5 **Kopargaon** India
6J3 **Kópasker** Iceland
38A2 **Kópavogur** Iceland
52B1 **Koper** Slovenia
80D2 **Kopet Dag** *Mts* Iran/Turkmenistan
61K2 **Kopeysk** Russian Fed
77C4 **Ko Phangan** *I* Thai
77B4 **Ko Phuket** *I* Thai
39H7 **Köping** Sweden
87B1 **Koppal** India
52C1 **Koprivnica** Croatia
85B4 **Korangi** Pak
87C1 **Koraput** India
86A2 **Korba** India
57B2 **Korbach** Germany
4B3 **Korbuk** *R* USA
55B2 **Korçë** Alb
52C2 **Korčula** *I* Croatia
72E2 **Korea B** China/Korea
74B4 **Korea Str** S Korea/Japan
59D2 **Korec** Ukraine
92B1 **Körğlu Tepesi** *Mt* Turk
97B4 **Korhogo** Ivory Coast
85B4 **Kori Creek** India
55B3 **Korinthiakós Kólpos** *G* Greece
55B3 **Kórinthos** Greece
74E3 **Kōriyama** Japan
61K3 **Korkino** Russian Fed
92B2 **Korkuteli** Turk
82C1 **Korla** China
52C2 **Kornat** *I* Croatia
60D5 **Köroğlu Tepesi** *Mt* Turk
99D3 **Korogwe** Tanz
108B3 **Koroit** Aust
71E3 **Koror** Palau Is, Pacific O
59C3 **Körös** *R* Hung
60C3 **Korosten** Ukraine
95A3 **Koro Toro** Chad
12B3 **Korovin** *I* USA
69G2 **Korsakov** Russian Fed
39G7 **Korsør** Den
46B1 **Kortrijk** Belg
55C3 **Kós** *I* Greece
77C4 **Ko Samui** *I* Thai
58B2 **Koscierzyna** Pol
107D4 **Kosciusko** *Mt* Aust
12H3 **Kosciusko I** USA
74B4 **Koshikijima-retto** *I* Japan
59C3 **Košice** Slovakia
74B3 **Kosong** N Korea
54B2 **Kosovo** Aut Republic, Serbia, Yugos
97B4 **Kossou** *L* Ivory Coast
101G1 **Koster** S Africa
99D1 **Kosti** Sudan
59D2 **Kostopol'** Ukraine
61F2 **Kostroma** Russian Fed
56C2 **Kostrzyn** Pol
39H8 **Koszalin** Pol
85D3 **Kota** India
78A4 **Kotaagung** Indon
78C3 **Kotabaharu** Indon
78D3 **Kotabaru** Indon
77C4 **Kota Bharu** Malay
78A3 **Kotabum** Indon
84C2 **Kot Addu** Pak
78D1 **Kota Kinabulu** Malay
87C1 **Kotapad** India
61G2 **Kotel'nich** Russian Fed
61F4 **Kotel'nikovo** Russian Fed
39K6 **Kotka** Fin
64F3 **Kotlas** Russian Fed
12B2 **Kotlik** USA
54A2 **Kotor** Montenegro, Yugos
60C4 **Kotovsk** Ukraine
85B3 **Kotri** Pak
87C1 **Kottagūdem** India
87B3 **Kottayam** India
98C2 **Kotto** *R* CAR
87B2 **Kottūru** India
12B1 **Kotzebue** USA
4B3 **Kotzebue Sd** USA
97C3 **Kouande** Benin
98C2 **Kouango** CAR
97B3 **Koudougou** Burkina
98B3 **Koulamoutou** Gabon
97B3 **Koulikoro** Mali
97B3 **Koupéla** Burkina
33G2 **Kourou** French Guiana
97B3 **Kouroussa** Guinea
98B1 **Kousséri** Cam
39K6 **Kouvola** Fin
38L5 **Kovdor** Russian Fed
60B3 **Kovel'** Ukraine
Kovno = Kaunas
61F2 **Kovrov** Russian Fed
61F3 **Kovylkino** Russian Fed
60E1 **Kovzha** *R* Russian Fed
77C4 **Ko Way** *I* Thai
73C5 **Kowloon** Hong Kong
84B2 **Kowt-e-Ashrow** Afghan
92A2 **Köyceğiz** Turk
38L5 **Koydor** Russian Fed
87A1 **Koyna Res** India
12B2 **Koyuk** USA
12B1 **Koyuk** *R* USA
12C2 **Koyukuk** USA
12C1 **Koyukuk** *R* USA
92C2 **Kozan** Turk
55B2 **Kozańi** Greece
Kozhikode = Calicut
61G2 **Koz'modemyansk** Russian Fed
75B2 **Kōzu-shima** *I* Japan
39F7 **Kragerø** Nor
54B2 **Kragujevac** Serbia, Yugos
77B3 **Kra,Isthmus of** Burma/Malay
Krakatau = Rakata
94C1 **Krak des Chevaliers** *Hist Site* Syria
Kraków = Cracow
54B2 **Kraljevo** Serbia, Yugos
60E4 **Kramatorsk** Ukraine
38H6 **Kramfors** Sweden
52B1 **Kranj** Slovenia
61G1 **Krasavino** Russian Fed
64G2 **Krasino** Russian Fed
59C2 **Kraśnik** Pol
61G3 **Krasnoarmeysk** Russian Fed
60E5 **Krasnodar** Russian Fed
61J2 **Krasnokamsk** Russian Fed
61K2 **Krasnotur'insk** Russian Fed
61J2 **Krasnoufimsk** Russian Fed
61J3 **Krasnousol'-skiy** Russian Fed
65G3 **Krasnovishersk** Russian Fed
65G5 **Krasnovodsk** Turkmenistan
63B2 **Krasnoyarsk** Russian Fed
59C2 **Krasnystaw** Pol
61G3 **Krasnyy Kut** Russian Fed
60E4 **Krasnyy Luch** Ukraine
61G4 **Krasnyy Yar** Russian Fed
76D3 **Kratie** Camb
6E2 **Kraulshavn** Greenland
56B2 **Krefeld** Germany
60D4 **Kremenchug** Ukraine
60D4 **Kremenchugskoye Vodokhranilische** *Res* Ukraine
59D2 **Kremenets** Ukraine
98A2 **Kribi** Cam
60D3 **Krichev** Belorussia
47E1 **Krimml** Austria
87B1 **Krishna** *R* India
87B2 **Krishnagiri** India
86B2 **Krishnangar** India
39F7 **Kristiansand** Nor
39G7 **Kristianstad** Sweden
64B3 **Kristiansund** Nor
39G7 **Kristinehamn** Sweden
38J6 **Kristiinankaupunki** Fin
55B3 **Kríti** *I* Greece
60D4 **Krivoy Rog** Ukraine
52B1 **Krk** *I* Croatia
6G3 **Kronpris Frederik Bjerge** *Mts* Greenland
39K7 **Kronshtadt** Russian Fed
101G1 **Kroonstad** S Africa
65F5 **Kropotkin** Russian Fed
101G1 **Krugersdorp** S Africa
78A4 **Krui** Indon
55A2 **Kruje** Alb
58D2 **Krupki** Belorussia
12B1 **Krusenstern,C** USA
54B2 **Kruševac** Serbia, Yugos
39K7 **Krustpils** Latvia
12G3 **Kruzof I** USA
65E5 **Krym** *Pen* Ukraine
60E5 **Krymsk** Russian Fed
58B2 **Krzyz** Pol
96C1 **Ksar El Boukhari** Alg
96B1 **Ksar el Kebir** Mor
70A3 **Kuala** Indon
77C5 **Kuala Dungun** Malay
77C4 **Kuala Kerai** Malay
77C5 **Kuala Kubu Baharu** Malay
77C5 **Kuala Lipis** Malay
77C5 **Kuala Lumpur** Malay
77C4 **Kuala Trengganu** Malay
78D1 **Kuamut** Malay
74A2 **Kuandian** China
77C5 **Kuantan** Malay
93E1 **Kuba** Azerbaijan
71F4 **Kubar** PNG
78C2 **Kuching** Malay
70C3 **Kudat** Malay
78C4 **Kudus** Indon
61H2 **Kudymkar** Russian Fed
57C3 **Kufstein** Austria
90C3 **Kuh Duren** *Upland* Iran
91C4 **Kūh e Bazmān** *Mt* Iran
90B3 **Kūh-e Dinar** *Mt* Iran
90C2 **Kūh-e-Hazār Masjed** *Mts* Iran
91C4 **Kūh-e Jebāl Barez** *Mts* Iran
90B3 **Kūh-e Karkas** *Mts* Iran
91C4 **Kuh-e Laleh Zar** *Mt* Iran
90A2 **Kūh-e Sahand** *Mt* Iran
91D4 **Kuh e Taftān** *Mt* Iran
90A2 **Kūhhaye Sabalan** *Mts* Iran
90A3 **Kūhhā-ye Zāgros** *Mts* Iran
38K6 **Kuhmo** Fin
90B3 **Kūhpāyeh** Iran
90C3 **Kūhpāyeh** *Mt* Iran
91C4 **Kūh ye Bashākerd** *Mts* Iran
90A2 **Kūh ye Sabalan** *Mt* Iran
100A3 **Kuibis** Namibia
4B4 **Kuigillingok** USA
100A2 **Kuito** Angola
12H3 **Kuiu I** USA
74E2 **Kuji** Japan
75A2 **Kuju-san** *Mt* Japan
12C3 **Kukaklek L** USA
54B2 **Kukës** Alb
77C5 **Kukup** Malay
91C4 **Kūl** *R* Iran
55C3 **Kula** Turk
61J4 **Kulakshi** Kazakhstan
99D2 **Kulal,Mt** Kenya
55B2 **Kulata** Bulg
60B2 **Kuldīga** Latvia
61H4 **Kul'sary** Kazakhstan
84D2 **Kulu** India
92B2 **Kulu** Turk
65J4 **Kulunda** Russian Fed
108B2 **Kulwin** Aust
61G5 **Kuma** *R* Russian Fed
75B1 **Kumagaya** Japan
78C3 **Kumai** Indon
74C4 **Kumamoto** Japan
75B2 **Kumano** Japan
54B2 **Kumanovo** Macedonia
63E2 **Kumara** China
97B4 **Kumasi** Ghana
65F5 **Kumayri** Armenia
98A2 **Kumba** Cam
87B2 **Kumbakonam** India
61J3 **Kumertau** Russian Fed
74B3 **Kŭmhwa** S Korea
39H7 **Kumla** Sweden
87A2 **Kumta** India
82C1 **Kümüx** China
84C2 **Kunar** *R* Afghan
39K7 **Kunda** Estonia
87A2 **Kundāpura** India
85C4 **Kundla** India
84B1 **Kunduz** Afghan
89F9 **Kunene** *R* Angola
39G7 **Kungsbacka** Sweden
61J2 **Kungur** Russian Fed
76B1 **Kunhing** Burma
82B2 **Kunlun Shan** *Mts* China
73A4 **Kunming** China
74B3 **Kunsan** S Korea
38K6 **Kuopio** Fin
52C1 **Kupa** *R* Croatia/Bosnia-Herzegovina
106B2 **Kupang** Indon
107D2 **Kupiano** PNG
12H3 **Kupreanof I** USA

Kupyansk

17B1 **Lake City** Florida, USA
17C1 **Lake City** S Carolina, USA
42C2 **Lake District** Region, Eng
22D4 **Lake Elsinore** USA
106C3 **Lake Eyre Basin** Aust
15C2 **Lakefield** Can
6D3 **Lake Harbour** Can
22C3 **Lake Hughes** USA
16B2 **Lakehurst** USA
19A4 **Lake Jackson** USA
13E2 **Lake la Biche** Can
17B2 **Lakeland** USA
7A5 **Lake of the Woods** Can
20B1 **Lake Oswego** USA
21A2 **Lakeport** USA
19B3 **Lake Providence** USA
111B2 **Lake Pukaki** NZ
109C3 **Lakes Entrance** Aust
22C2 **Lakeshore** USA
108B1 **Lake Stewart** Aust
15C1 **Lake Traverse** Can
8A2 **Lakeview** USA
20B1 **Lakeview Mt** Can
19B3 **Lake Village** USA
17B2 **Lake Wales** USA
22C4 **Lakewood** California, USA
16B2 **Lakewood** New Jersey, USA
14B2 **Lakewood** Ohio, USA
17B2 **Lake Worth** USA
86A1 **Lakhimpur** India
85B4 **Lakhpat** India
84C2 **Lakki** Pak
55B3 **Lakonikós Kólpos** G Greece
97B4 **Lakota** Ivory Coast
38K4 **Laksefjord** *Inlet* Nor
38K4 **Lakselv** Nor
34C2 **La Laguna** Arg
32A4 **La Libertad** Ecuador
34A2 **La Ligua** Chile
50A2 **La Linea** Spain
85D4 **Lalitpur** India
5H4 **La Loche** Can
13F1 **la Loche,L** Can
46C1 **La Louviète** Belg
26A4 **La Luz** Nic
7C5 **La Malbaie** Can
23B2 **La Malinche** *Mt* Mexico
50B2 **La Mancha** Region, Spain
9C3 **Lamar** Colorado, USA
18B2 **Lamar** Missouri, USA
19A4 **La Marque** USA
98B3 **Lambaréné** Gabon
32A5 **Lambayeque** Peru
112B10 **Lambert Gl** Ant
16B2 **Lambertville** USA
4F2 **Lamblon,C** Can
47C2 **Lambro** *R* Italy
76C2 **Lam Chi** *R* Thai
50A1 **Lamego** Port
47B2 **La Meije** *Mt* France
32B6 **La Merced** Peru
21B3 **La Mesa** USA
55B3 **Lamía** Greece
42C2 **Lammermuir Hills** Scot
39G7 **Lammhult** Sweden
79B3 **Lamon B** Phil
18B1 **Lamoni** USA
71F3 **Lamotrek** *I* Pacific O
43B3 **Lampeter** Wales
99E3 **Lamu** Kenya
47D1 **Lana** Italy
21C4 **Lanai** *I* Hawaiian Is
21C4 **Lanai City** Hawaiian Is
42C2 **Lanark** Scot
76B3 **Lanbi** *I* Burma
76C1 **Lancang** *R* China
42C3 **Lancashire** County, Eng
21B3 **Lancaster** California, USA

42C2 **Lancaster** Eng
18B1 **Lancaster** Mississippi, USA
15D2 **Lancaster** New Hampshire, USA
14B3 **Lancaster** Ohio, USA
10C3 **Lancaster** Pennsylvania, USA
17B1 **Lancaster** S Carolina, USA
6B2 **Lancaster Sd** Can
78B3 **Landak** *R* Indon
46E2 **Landan** Germany
57C3 **Landeck** Austria
8C2 **Lander** USA
34C2 **Landeta** Arg
57C3 **Landsberg** Germany
4F2 **Lands End** *C* Can
43B4 **Land's End** *Pt* Eng
57C3 **Landshut** Germany
39G7 **Làndskrona** Sweden
17A1 **Lanett** USA
56B2 **Langenhagen** Germany
47B1 **Langenthal** Switz
42C2 **Langholm** Scot
38A2 **Langjökull** *Mts* Iceland
77B4 **Langkawi** *I* Malay
13C3 **Langley** Can
108C1 **Langlo** *R* Aust
47B1 **Langnau** Switz
49D2 **Langres** France
70A3 **langsa** Indon
68C2 **Lang Shan** *Mts* China
76D1 **Lang Son** Viet
48C3 **Languedoc** Region, France
29B3 **Lanin** *Mt* Arg
79B4 **Lanoa,L** *L* Phil
16B2 **Lansdale** USA
7B4 **Lansdowne House** Can
16B2 **Lansford** USA
10B2 **Lansing** USA
47B2 **Lanslebourg** France
96A2 **Lanzarote** *I* Canary Is
72A2 **Lanzhou** China
47B2 **Lanzo Torinese** Italy
79B2 **Laoag** Phil
76C1 **Lao Cai** Viet
72D1 **Laoha He** *R* China
45C2 **Laois** County, Irish Rep
46B2 **Laon** France
32B6 **La Oroya** Peru
76C2 **Laos** Republic, S E Asia
49C2 **Lapalisse** France
32B2 **La Palma** Panama
96A2 **La Palma** *I* Canary Is
34B3 **La Pampa** State, Arg
33E2 **La Paragua** Ven
29E2 **La Paz** Arg
34B2 **La Paz** Arg
30C2 **La Paz** Bol
24A2 **La Paz** Mexico
69G2 **La Perouse Str** Japan/Russian Fed
23A1 **La Piedad** Mexico
20B2 **La Pine** USA
19B3 **Laplace** USA
23A2 **la Placita** Mexico
29E2 **La Plata** Arg
13F1 **La Plonge,L** Can
14A2 **La Porte** USA
39K6 **Lappeenranta** Fin
38H5 **Lappland** *Region* Sweden/Fin
34C3 **Laprida** Arg
1B8 **Laptev S** Russian Fed
38J6 **Lapua** Fin
79B3 **Lapu-Lapu** Phil
9B4 **La Purisma** Mexico
95B2 **Laqiya Arba'in** *Well* Sudan
30C3 **La Quiaca** Arg
52B2 **L'Aquila** Italy
91B4 **Lãr** Iran
96B1 **Larache** Mor
8C2 **Laramie** USA

8C2 **Laramie Range** *Mts* USA
50B2 **Larca** Spain
9D4 **Laredo** USA
91B4 **Larestan** Region, Iran
Largeau = Faya
47B2 **L'Argentière** France
17B2 **Largo** USA
42B2 **Largs** Scot
90A2 **Lãri** Iran
30C4 **La Rioja** Arg
30C4 **La Rioja** State, Arg
55B3 **Lárisa** Greece
85B3 **Larkana** Pak
92B3 **Larnaca** Cyprus
94A1 **Larnaca B** Cyprus
45D1 **Larne** N Ire
50A1 **La Robla** Spain
46C1 **La Roche-en-Ardenne** Belg
48B2 **La Rochelle** France
47B1 **La Roche-sur-Foron** France
48B2 **La Roche-sur-Yon** France
51B2 **La Roda** Spain
27D3 **La Romana** Dom Rep
5H4 **La Ronge** Can
5H4 **La Ronge,L** Can
39F7 **Larvik** Nor
65J3 **Laryak** Russian Fed
50B2 **La Sagra** *Mt* Spain
15D1 **La Salle** Can
18C1 **La Salle** USA
7C5 **La Sarre** Can
34C1 **Las Avispas** Arg
34A2 **Las Cabras** Chile
5G4 **Lascombe** Can
9C3 **Las Cruces** USA
26C3 **La Selle** *Mt* Haiti
72B2 **Lasengmia** China
30B4 **La Serena** Chile
29E3 **Las Flores** Arg
76B1 **Lashio** Burma
53C3 **La Sila** *Mts* Italy
90B2 **Lãsjerd** Iran
34A3 **Las Lajas** Chile
50A2 **Las Marismas** *Marshland* Spain
96A2 **Las Palmas de Gran Canaria** Canary Is
52A2 **La Spezia** Italy
29C4 **Las Plumas** Arg
34C2 **Las Rosas** Arg
20B2 **Lassen Peak** *Mt* USA
20B2 **Lassen Volcanic Nat Pk** USA
23B2 **las Tinai** Mexico
98B3 **Lastoursville** Gabon
52C2 **Lastovo** *I* Croatia
24B2 **Las Tres Marias** *Is* Mexico
34C2 **Las Varillas** Arg
9C3 **Las Vegas** USA
Latakia = Al Lãdhiqîyah
53B2 **Latina** Italy
34B2 **La Toma** Arg
32D1 **La Tortuga** *I* Ven
79B2 **La Trinidad** Phil
109C4 **Latrobe** Aust
94B3 **Latrun** Israel
7C5 **La Tuque** Can
87B1 **Lãtũr** India
60B2 **Latvia** Republic, Europe
107D5 **Launceston** Aust
43B4 **Launceston** Eng
29B4 **La Unión** Chile
25D3 **La Unión** El Salvador
23A2 **La Unión** Mexico
32B5 **La Unión** Peru
107D2 **Laura** Aust
15C3 **Laurel** Delaware, USA
16A3 **Laurel** Maryland, USA
11B3 **Laurel** Mississippi, USA
17B1 **Laurens** USA
17C1 **Laurinburg** USA
52A1 **Lausanne** Switz
78D3 **Laut** *I* Indon
29B5 **Lautaro** *Mt* Chile

46D2 **Lautorocken** Germany
15D1 **Laval** Can
48B2 **Laval** France
22B2 **Laveaga Peak** *Mt* USA
47C2 **Laveno** Italy
31B6 **Lavras** Brazil
4A3 **Lavrentiya** Russian Fed
101H1 **Lavumisa** Swaziland
78D1 **Lawas** Malay
76B1 **Lawksawk** Burma
18A2 **Lawrence** Kansas, USA
15D2 **Lawrence** Massachusetts, USA
111A3 **Lawrence** NZ
14A3 **Lawrenceville** Illinois, USA
9D3 **Lawton** USA
91A5 **Layla** S Arabia
99D2 **Laylo** Sudan
23A2 **Lázaro Cárdenas** Mexico
99E1 **Laz Daua** Somalia
79B4 **Lazi** Phil
8C2 **Lead** USA
13F2 **Leader** Can
18A2 **Leavenworth** USA
58B2 **Leba** Pol
18B2 **Lebanon** Missouri, USA
20B2 **Lebanon** Oregon, USA
15C2 **Lebanon** Pennsylvania, USA
92C3 **Lebanon** Republic, S W Asia
101C3 **Lebombo** *Mts* Mozam/S Africa/Swaziland
58B2 **Lebork** Pol
47A2 **Le Bourg-d'Oisans** France
47B1 **Le Brassus** Switz
29B3 **Lebu** Chile
47B1 **Le Buet** *Mt* France
46B1 **Le Cateau** France
55A2 **Lecce** Italy
52A1 **Lecco** Italy
47D1 **Lech** *R* Austria
47D1 **Lechtaler Alpen** *Mts* Austria
49C2 **Le Creusot** France
43C3 **Ledbury** Eng
13E2 **Leduc** Can
16C1 **Lee** USA
45B3 **Lee** *R* Irish Rep
41C3 **Leeds** Eng
43C3 **Leek** Eng
56B2 **Leer** Germany
17B2 **Leesburg** Florida, USA
16A3 **Leesburg** Virginia, USA
19B3 **Leesville** USA
109C2 **Leeton** Aust
56B2 **Leeuwarden** Neth
106A4 **Leeuwin,C** Aust
22C2 **Lee Vining** USA
27E3 **Leeward Is** Caribbean S
94A1 **Lefkara** Cyprus
79B3 **Legazpi** Phil
47D2 **Legnago** Italy
59B2 **Legnica** Pol
33F2 **Leguan Inlet** Guyana
32C4 **Leguizamo** Colombia
84D2 **Leh** India
48C2 **Le Havre** France
16B2 **Lehigh** *R* USA
16B2 **Lehighton** USA
84C2 **Leiah** Pak
59B3 **Leibnitz** Austria
43D3 **Leicester** County, Eng
43D3 **Leicester** Eng
107C2 **Leichhardt** *R* Aust
56A2 **Leiden** Neth
46B1 **Leie** *R* Belg
106C4 **Leigh Creek** Aust
43D4 **Leighton Buzzard** Eng

4E2 **Liverpool B** Can
42C3 **Liverpool B** Eng
6C2 **Liverpool,C** Can
109D2 **Liverpool Range** *Mts* Aust
8B2 **Livingston** Montana, USA
19B3 **Livingston** Texas, USA
44C4 **Livingston** UK
Livingstone = **Maramba**
19A3 **Livingston,L** USA
52C2 **Livno** Bosnia-Herzegovina
60E3 **Livny** Russian Fed
14B2 **Livonia** USA
52B2 **Livorno** Italy
99D3 **Liwale** Tanz
52B1 **Ljubljana** Slovenia
38G6 **Ljungan** *R* Sweden
39G7 **Ljungby** Sweden
39H6 **Ljusdal** Sweden
38H6 **Ljusnan** *R* Sweden
43C4 **Llandeilo** Wales
43C4 **Llandovery** Wales
43C3 **Llandrindod Wells** Wales
42C3 **Llandudno** Wales
43B4 **Llanelli** Wales
43C3 **Llangollen** Wales
9C3 **Llano Estacado** *Plat* USA
32C2 **Llanos** Region, Colombia/Ven
30D2 **Llanos de Chiquitos** Region, Bol
Lleida = Lérida
50A2 **Llerena** Spain
43B3 **Lleyn** *Pen* Wales
89E7 **Llorin** Nig
5H4 **Lloydminster** Can
30C3 **Llullaillaco** *Mt* Arg/Chile
30C3 **Loa** *R* Chile
49C2 **Loan** France
98B3 **Loange** *R* Zaïre
100B3 **Lobatse** Botswana
98B2 **Lobaye** *R* CAR
34D3 **Loberia** Arg
100A2 **Lobito** Angola
34D3 **Lobos** Arg
47B2 **Locano** Italy
47C1 **Locarno** Switz
44B3 **Loch Awe** *L* Scot
44A3 **Lochboisdale** Scot
44A3 **Loch Bracadale** *Inlet* Scot
44B3 **Loch Broom** *Estuary* Scot
42B2 **Loch Doon** *L* Scot
44B3 **Loch Earn** *L* Scot
44B2 **Loch Eriboll** *Inlet* Scot
44B3 **Loch Ericht** *L* Scot
48C2 **Loches** France
44B3 **Loch Etive** *Inlet* Scot
44B3 **Loch Ewe** *Inlet* Scot
44B3 **Loch Fyne** *Inlet* Scot
44B3 **Loch Hourn** *Inlet* Scot
44B2 **Lochinver** Scot
44B3 **Loch Katrine** *L* Scot
44C3 **Loch Leven** *L* Scot
44B3 **Loch Linnhe** *Inlet* Scot
44B3 **Loch Lochy** *L* Scot
44B3 **Loch Lomond** *L* Scot
44B3 **Loch Long** *Inlet* Scot
44A3 **Lochmaddy** Scot
44B3 **Loch Maree** *L* Scot
44B3 **Loch Morar** *L* Scot
44C3 **Lochnagar** *Mt* Scot
44B3 **Loch Ness** *L* Scot
44B3 **Loch Rannoch** *L* Scot
44A2 **Loch Roag** *Inlet* Scot
44B3 **Loch Sheil** *L* Scot
44B2 **Loch Shin** *L* Scot
44A3 **Loch Snizort** *Inlet* Scot
44B3 **Loch Sunart** *Inlet* Scot
44B3 **Loch Tay** *L* Scot

44B3 **Loch Torridon** *Inlet* Scot
108A2 **Lock** Aust
42C2 **Lockerbie** Scot
15C2 **Lock Haven** USA
15C2 **Lockport** USA
76D3 **Loc Ninh** Viet
53C3 **Locri** Italy
94B3 **Lod** Israel
108B3 **Loddon** *R* Aust
60D1 **Lodeynoye Pole** Russian Fed
84C3 **Lodhran** Pak
52A1 **Lodi** Italy
21A2 **Lodi** USA
98C3 **Lodja** Zaïre
47B1 **Lods** France
99D2 **Lodwar** Kenya
58B2 **Łódź** Pol
38G5 **Lofoten** *Is* Nor
8B2 **Logan** Utah, USA
4D3 **Logan,Mt** Can
14A2 **Logansport** Indiana, USA
19B3 **Logansport** Louisiana, USA
50B1 **Logroño** Spain
86A2 **Lohärdaga** India
39J6 **Lohja** Fin
76B2 **Loikaw** Burma
39J6 **Loimaa** Fin
48C2 **Loir** *R* France
49C2 **Loire** *R* France
32B4 **Loja** Ecuador
50B2 **Loja** Spain
38K5 **Lokan Tekojärvi** *Res* Fin
46B1 **Lokeren** Belg
99D2 **Lokitaung** Kenya
58D1 **Loknya** Russian Fed
98C3 **Lokolo** *R* Zaïre
98C3 **Lokoro** *R* Zaïre
6D3 **Loks Land** *I* Can
56C2 **Lolland** *I* Den
54B2 **Lom** Bulg
98C3 **Lomami** *R* Zaïre
97A4 **Loma Mts** Sierra Leone/Guinea
47C2 **Lombardia** Region, Italy
71D4 **Lomblen** *I* Indon
78D4 **Lombok** *I* Indon
97C4 **Lomé** Togo
98C3 **Lomela** Zaïre
98C3 **Lomela** *R* Zaïre
60C2 **Lomonosov** Russian Fed
47B1 **Lomont** Region, France
21A3 **Lompoc** USA
58C2 **Łomza** Pol
87A1 **Lonāvale** India
29B3 **Loncoche** Chile
7B5 **London** Can
43D4 **London** Eng
45C1 **Londonderry** County, N Ire
45C1 **Londonderry** N Ire
29B7 **Londonderry** *I* Chile
106B2 **Londonderry,C** Aust
30C4 **Londres** Arg
30F3 **Londrina** Brazil
21B2 **Lone Pine** USA
11C4 **Long** *I* The Bahamas
71F4 **Long** *I* PNG
78C2 **Long Akah** Malay
47E1 **Longarone** Italy
34A3 **Longavi** *Mt* Chile
27H2 **Long B** Jamaica
17C1 **Long B** USA
9B3 **Long Beach** California, USA
15D2 **Long Beach** New York, USA
15D2 **Long Branch** USA
73D5 **Longchuan** China
20C2 **Long Creek** USA
109C4 **Longford** Aust
45C2 **Longford** County, Irish Rep
45C2 **Longford** Irish Rep
44D3 **Long Forties** *Region* N Sea
72D1 **Longhua** China

7C4 **Long I** Can
10C2 **Long I** USA
16C2 **Long Island Sd** USA
7B4 **Longlac** Can
73B5 **Longlin** China
8C2 **Longmont** USA
78D2 **Longnawan** Indon
29B3 **Longquimay** Chile
107D3 **Longreach** Aust
72A2 **Longshou Shan** *Upland* China
42C2 **Longtown** Eng
15D1 **Longueuil** Can
34A3 **Longuimay** Chile
46C2 **Longuyon** France
11A3 **Longview** Texas, USA
8A2 **Longview** Washington, USA
46C2 **Longwy** France
72A3 **Longxi** China
77D3 **Long Xuyen** Viet
73D4 **Longyan** China
73B5 **Longzhou** China
47D2 **Lonigo** Italy
49D2 **Lons-le-Saunier** France
11C3 **Lookout,C** USA
99D3 **Loolmalasin** *Mt* Tanz
13D1 **Loon** *R* Can
45B2 **Loop Hd** *C* Irish Rep
76C3 **Lop Buri** Thai
98A3 **Lopez** *C* Gabon
68B2 **Lop Nur** *L* China
50A2 **Lora del Rio** Spain
10B2 **Lorain** USA
84B2 **Loralai** Pak
90B3 **Lordegān** Iran
107E4 **Lord Howe** *I* Aust
105G5 **Lord Howe Rise** Pacific O
6A3 **Lord Mayor B** Can
9C3 **Lordsburg** USA
35B2 **Lorena** Brazil
47E2 **Loreo** Italy
23A1 **Loreto** Mexico
48B2 **Lorient** France
108B3 **Lorne** Aust
57B3 **Lörrach** Germany
49D2 **Lorraine** *Region* France
9C3 **Los Alamos** USA
34A2 **Los Andes** Chile
29B3 **Los Angeles** Chile
9B3 **Los Angeles** USA
21A2 **Los Banos** USA
34B2 **Los Cerrillos** Arg
21A2 **Los Gatos** USA
52B2 **Lošinj** *I* Croatia
29B3 **Los Lagos** Chile
24B2 **Los Mochis** Mexico
22B3 **Los Olivos** USA
34A3 **Los Sauces** Chile
44C3 **Lossiemouth** Scot
27E4 **Los Testigos** *Is* Ven
29B2 **Los Vilos** Chile
48C3 **Lot** *R* France
34A3 **Lota** Chile
42C2 **Lothian** Region, Scot
99D2 **Lotikipi Plain** Sudan/Kenya
98C3 **Loto** Zaïre
47B1 **Lötschberg Tunnel** Switz
38K5 **Lotta** *R* Fin/Russian Fed
48B2 **Loudéac** France
97A3 **Louga** Sen
41B3 **Lough Allen** *L* Irish Rep
45C2 **Lough Boderg** *L* Irish Rep
43D3 **Loughborough** Eng
45C2 **Lough Bowna** *L* Irish Rep
45C1 **Lough Carlingford** *L* N Ire
41B3 **Lough Conn** *L* Irish Rep
41B3 **Lough Corrib** *L* Irish Rep
41B3 **Lough Derg** *L* Irish Rep

46C2 **Lough Derravaragh** *L* Irish Rep
4H2 **Loughead I** Can
45C2 **Lough Ennell** *L* Irish Rep
41B3 **Lough Erne** *L* N Ire
40B2 **Lough Foyle** *Estuary* N Ire/Irish Rep
40B3 **Lough Neagh** *L* N Ire
45C1 **Lough Oughter** *L* Irish Rep
45B2 **Loughrea** Irish Rep
45C2 **Lough Ree** *L* Irish Rep
45C2 **Lough Sheelin** *L* Irish Rep
42B2 **Lough Strangford** *L* Irish Rep
45C1 **Lough Swilly** *Estuary* Irish Rep
14B3 **Louisa** USA
70C3 **Louisa Reef** *I* S E Asia
12E2 **Louise,L** USA
107E2 **Louisiade Arch** Solomon Is
11A3 **Louisiana** State, USA
17B1 **Louisville** Georgia, USA
11B3 **Louisville** Kentucky, USA
38L5 **Loukhi** Russian Fed
48B3 **Lourdes** France
108C2 **Louth** Aust
45C2 **Louth** County, Irish Rep
42D3 **Louth** Eng
Louvain = Leuven
48C2 **Louviers** France
60D2 **Lovat** *R* Russian Fed
54B2 **Lovech** Bulg
21B1 **Lovelock** USA
52B1 **Lóvere** Italy
9C3 **Lovington** USA
38L5 **Lovozero** Russian Fed
6B3 **Low,C** Can
10C2 **Lowell** Massachusetts, USA
20B2 **Lowell** Oregon, USA
16D1 **Lowell** USA
111B2 **Lower Hutt** NZ
43E3 **Lowestoft** Eng
58B2 **Łowicz** Pol
108B2 **Loxton** Aust
5F4 **Loyd George,Mt** Can
54A2 **Loznica** Serbia, Yugos
23A2 **Loz Reyes** Mexico
65H3 **Lozva** *R* Russian Fed
100B2 **Luacano** Angola
98C3 **Luachimo** Angola
98C3 **Lualaba** *R* Zaïre
100B2 **Luampa** Zambia
100B2 **Luân** Angola
73D3 **Lu'an** China
98B3 **Luanda** Angola
100A2 **Luando** *R* Angola
100B2 **Luanginga** *R* Angola
76C1 **Luang Namtha** Laos
76C2 **Luang Prabang** Laos
98B3 **Luangue** *R* Angola
100C2 **Luangwa** *R* Zambia
72D1 **Luan He** *R* China
72D1 **Luanping** China
100B2 **Luanshya** Zambia
100B2 **Luapula** *R* Zaïre
50A1 **Luarca** Spain
98B3 **Lubalo** Angola
58D2 **L'uban** Belorussia
79B3 **Lubang Is** Phil
100A2 **Lubango** Angola
9C3 **Lubbock** USA
56C2 **Lübeck** Germany
98C3 **Lubefu** Zaïre
98C3 **Lubefu** *R* Zaïre
99C3 **Lubero** Zaïre
98C3 **Lubilash** *R* Zaïre
59C2 **Lublin** Pol
60D3 **Lubny** Ukraine
78C2 **Lubok Antu** Malay
98C3 **Lubudi** Zaïre
98C3 **Lubudi** *R* Zaïre

78A3 **Lubuklinggau** Indon
100B2 **Lubumbashi** Zaïre
98C3 **Lubutu** Zaïre
79B3 **Lucban** Phil
52B2 **Lucca** Italy
42B2 **Luce** *B* Scot
19C3 **Lucedale** USA
79B3 **Lucena** Phil
59B3 **Lucenec** Slovakia
Lucerne = Luzern
73C5 **Luchuan** China
56C2 **Luckenwalde** Germany
101F1 **Luckhoff** S Africa
86A1 **Lucknow** India
100B2 **Lucusse** Angola
46D1 **Lüdenscheid** Germany
100A3 **Lüderitz** Namibia
84D2 **Ludhiana** India
14A2 **Ludington** USA
43C3 **Ludlow** Eng
54C2 **Ludogorie** *Upland* Bulg
17B1 **Ludowici** USA
54B1 **Luduş** Rom
39H6 **Ludvika** Sweden
57B3 **Ludwigsburg** Germany
57B3 **Ludwigshafen** Germany
56C2 **Ludwigslust** Germany
98C3 **Luebo** Zaïre
98C3 **Luema** *R* Zaïre
98C3 **Luembe** *R* Angola
100A2 **Luena** Angola
100B2 **Luene** *R* Angola
72B3 **Lüeyang** China
73D5 **Lufeng** China
11A3 **Lufkin** USA
60C2 **Luga** Russian Fed
60C2 **Luga** *R* Russian Fed
52A1 **Lugano** Switz
60E4 **Lugansk** Ukraine
101C2 **Lugela** Mozam
101C2 **Lugenda** *R* Mozam
50A1 **Lugo** Spain
54B1 **Lugoj** Rom
72A3 **Luhuo** China
98B3 **Lui** *R* Angola
100B2 **Luiana** Angola
100B2 **Luiana** *R* Angola
Luichow Peninsula = Leizhou Bandao
47C2 **Luino** Italy
98B2 **Luionga** *R* Zaïre
72B2 **Luipan Shan** *Upland* China
100B2 **Luishia** Zaïre
68B4 **Luixi** China
98C3 **Luiza** Zaïre
34B2 **Luján** Arg
34D2 **Luján** Arg
73D3 **Lujiang** China
98B3 **Lukenie** *R* Zaïre
64E4 **Luki** Russian Fed
98B3 **Lukolela** Zaïre
58C2 **Łuków** Pol
98C3 **Lukuga** *R* Zaïre
100B2 **Lukulu** Zambia
38J5 **Lule** *R* Sweden
38J5 **Luleå** Sweden
54C2 **Lüleburgaz** Turk
72C2 **Lüliang Shan** *Mts* China
19A4 **Luling** USA
98C2 **Lulonga** *R* Zaïre
Luluabourg = Kananga
100B2 **Lumbala Kaquengue** Angola
11C3 **Lumberton** USA
78D1 **Lumbis** Indon
86C1 **Lumding** India
100B2 **Lumeje** Angola
111A3 **Lumsden** NZ
39G7 **Lund** Sweden
101C2 **Lundazi** Zambia
43B4 **Lundy** *I* Eng
56C2 **Lüneburg** Germany
46D2 **Lunéville** France
100B2 **Lunga** *R* Zambia
86C2 **Lunglei** India
100A2 **Lungue Bungo** *R* Angola
58D2 **Luninec** Belorussia
98B3 **Luobomo** Congo
73B5 **Luocheng** China
73C5 **Luoding** China
72C3 **Luohe** China
72C3 **Luo He** *R* Henan, China
72B2 **Luo He** *R* Shaanxi, China
73C4 **Luoxiao Shan** *Hills* China
72C3 **Luoyang** China
98B3 **Luozi** Zaïre
100B2 **Lupane** Zim
101C2 **Lupilichi** Mozam
Lu Qu = Tao He
30E4 **Luque** Par
45C1 **Lurgan** N Ire
101C2 **Lurio** *R* Mozam
90A3 **Luristan** Region, Iran
100B2 **Lusaka** Zambia
98C3 **Lusambo** Zaïre
55A2 **Lushnjë** Alb
99D3 **Lushoto** Tanz
68B4 **Lushui** China
72E2 **Lüshun** China
43D4 **Luton** Eng
60C3 **Lutsk** Ukraine
99E2 **Luuq** Somalia
99C3 **Luvua** *R* Zaïre
99D3 **Luwegu** *R* Tanz
100C2 **Luwingu** Zambia
71D4 **Luwuk** Indon
46D2 **Luxembourg** Grand Duchy, N W Europe
49D2 **Luxembourg** Lux
73A5 **Luxi** China
95C2 **Luxor** Egypt
61G1 **Luza** Russian Fed
61G1 **Luza** *R* Russian Fed
52A1 **Luzern** Switz
73B5 **Luzhai** China
73B4 **Luzhi** China
73B4 **Luzhou** China
35B1 **Luziânia** Brazil
79B2 **Luzon** *I* Phil
79B1 **Luzon Str** Phil
59C3 **L'vov** Ukraine
44C2 **Lybster** Scot
38H6 **Lycksele** Sweden
100B3 **Lydenburg** S Africa
8B3 **Lyell,Mt** USA
16A2 **Lykens** USA
43C4 **Lyme B** Eng
43C4 **Lyme Regis** Eng
11C3 **Lynchburg** USA
108A2 **Lyndhurst** Aust
15D2 **Lynn** USA
12G3 **Lynn Canal** *Sd* USA
17A1 **Lynn Haven** USA
5H4 **Lynn Lake** Can
5H3 **Lynx L** Can
49C2 **Lyon** France
12G3 **Lyon Canal** *Sd* USA
17B1 **Lyons** Georgia, USA
106A3 **Lyons** *R* Aust
47B2 **Lys** *R* Italy
61J2 **Lys'va** Russian Fed
111B2 **Lyttelton** NZ
13C2 **Lytton** Can
22A1 **Lytton** USA
58D2 **Lyubeshov** Ukraine
60E2 **Lyublino** Russian Fed

M

76C1 **Ma** *R* Viet
94B2 **Ma'agan** Jordan
94B2 **Ma'alot Tarshīha** Israel
92C3 **Ma'an** Jordan
73D3 **Ma'anshan** China
92C2 **Ma'arrat an Nu'mān** Syria
46C1 **Maas** *R* Neth
46C1 **Maaseik** Belg
79B3 **Maasin** Phil
57B2 **Maastricht** Neth
101C3 **Mabalane** Mozam
33F2 **Mabaruma** Guyana
42E3 **Mablethorpe** Eng
101C3 **Mabote** Mozam
58C2 **Mabrita** Belorussia
58D2 **M'adel** Belorussia
35C2 **Macaé** Brazil
9D3 **McAlester** USA
9D4 **McAllen** USA
101C2 **Macaloge** Mozam
33G3 **Macapá** Brazil
35C1 **Macarani** Brazil
32B4 **Macas** Ecuador
31D3 **Macaú** Brazil
73C5 **Macau** Dependency, China
98C2 **M'Bari** *R* CAR
13C2 **McBride** Can
12F2 **McCarthy** USA
13A2 **McCauley I** Can
42C3 **Macclesfield** Eng
6B1 **McClintock B** Can
4H2 **McClintock Chan** Can
16A2 **McClure** USA
22B2 **McClure,L** USA
4G2 **McClure Str** Can
19B3 **McComb** USA
8C2 **McCook** USA
6C2 **Macculloch,C** Can
13C1 **McCusker,Mt** Can
4F4 **McDame** Can
20C2 **McDermitt** USA
13E2 **Macdonald** *R* Can
106C3 **Macdonnell Ranges** *Mts* Aust
50A1 **Macedo de Cavaleiros** Port
55B2 **Macedonia** Republic, Europe
31D3 **Maceió** Brazil
97B4 **Macenta** Guinea
52B2 **Macerata** Italy
108A2 **Macfarlane,L** Aust
19B3 **McGehee** USA
45B3 **MacGillycuddys Reeks** *Mts* Irish Rep
4C3 **McGrath** USA
35B2 **Machado** Brazil
101C3 **Machaíla** Mozam
99D3 **Machakos** Kenya
32B4 **Machala** Ecuador
101C3 **Machaze** Mozam
87B1 **Mācherla** India
94B2 **Machgharab** Leb
87C1 **Machilīpatnam** India
32C1 **Machiques** Ven
32C6 **Machu-Picchu** *Hist Site* Peru
101C3 **Macia** Mozam
109C1 **MacIntyre** *R* Aust
107D3 **Mackay** Aust
106B3 **Mackay,L** Aust
14C2 **McKeesport** USA
13C1 **Mackenzie** Can
4F3 **Mackenzie** *R* Can
4E3 **Mackenzie B** Can
4G2 **Mackenzie King I** Can
4E3 **Mackenzie Mts** Can
14B1 **Mackinac,Str of** USA
14B1 **Mackinaw City** USA
12D2 **McKinley,Mt** USA
19A3 **McKinney** USA
6C2 **Mackinson Inlet** *B* Can
109D2 **Macksville** Aust
20B2 **Mclaoughlin,Mt** USA
109D1 **Maclean** Aust
100B4 **Maclear** S Africa
5G4 **McLennan** Can
13D2 **McLeod** *R* Can
4G3 **McLeod B** Can
106A3 **McLeod,L** Aust
13C1 **McLeod Lake** Can
4E3 **Macmillan** *R* Can
12H2 **Macmillan P** Can
20B1 **McMinnville** Oregon, USA
112B7 **McMurdo** *Base* Ant
13D2 **McNaughton L** Can
18B1 **Macomb** USA
53A2 **Macomer** Sardegna
101C2 **Macomia** Mozam
49C2 **Mâcon** France
11B3 **Macon** Georgia, USA
18B2 **Macon** Missouri, USA
100B2 **Macondo** Angola
18A2 **McPherson** USA
104F6 **Macquarie** *Is* Aust
109C2 **Macquarie** *R* Aust
109C4 **Macquarie Harbour** *B* Aust
109D2 **Macquarie,L** Aust
17B1 **McRae** USA
112B11 **Mac. Robertson Land** Region, Ant
45B3 **Macroom** Irish Rep
96C1 **M'Sila** Alg
4G3 **McTavish Arm** *B* Can
108A1 **Macumba** *R* Aust
47C2 **Macunaga** Italy
4F3 **McVicar Arm** *B* Can
59B3 **M'yaróvár** Hung
94B3 **Mādabā** Jordan
95A3 **Madadi** *Well* Chad
89J10 **Madagascar** *I* Indian O
95A2 **Madama** Niger
71F4 **Madang** PNG
97C3 **Madaoua** Niger
86C2 **Madaripur** Bang
90B2 **Madau** Turkmenistan
15C1 **Madawaska** *R* Can
96A1 **Madeira** *I* Atlantic O
33E5 **Madeira** *R* Brazil
7D5 **Madeleine, Îsle de la** Can
24B2 **Madera** Mexico
21A2 **Madera** USA
87A1 **Madgaon** India
86B1 **Madhubani** India
86A2 **Madhya Pradesh** State, India
87B2 **Madikeri** India
98B3 **Madimba** Zaïre
98B3 **Madingo Kayes** Congo
98B3 **Madingou** Congo
10B3 **Madison** Indiana, USA
10B2 **Madison** Wisconsin, USA
18C2 **Madisonville** Kentucky, USA
19A3 **Madisonville** Texas, USA
78C4 **Madiun** Indon
99D2 **Mado Gashi** Kenya
47D1 **Madonna Di Campiglio** Italy
87C2 **Madras** India
20B2 **Madras** USA
29A6 **Madre de Dios** *I* Chile
32D6 **Madre de Dios** *R* Bol
50B1 **Madrid** Spain
50B2 **Madridejos** Spain
78C4 **Madura** *I* Indon
87B3 **Madurai** India
75B1 **Maebashi** Japan
76B3 **Mae Khlong** *R* Thai
77B4 **Mae Nam Lunang** *R* Thai
76C2 **Mae Nam Mun** *R* Thai
76B2 **Mae Nam Ping** *R* Thai
101D2 **Maevatanana** Madag
101G1 **Mafeteng** Lesotho
109C3 **Maffra** Aust
99D3 **Mafia** *I* Tanz
101G1 **Mafikeng** S Africa
30G4 **Mafra** Brazil
92C3 **Mafraq** Jordan
32C2 **Magangué** Colombia
34D3 **Magdalena** Arg
24A1 **Magdalena** Mexico
26C4 **Magdalena** *R* Colombia
78D1 **Magdalena,Mt** Malay
56C2 **Magdeburg** Germany
31C6 **Magé** Brazil
78C4 **Magelang** Indon
47C1 **Maggia** *R* Switz
92B4 **Maghâgha** Egypt
45C1 **Magherafelt** N Ire
55A2 **Maglie** Italy
61J3 **Magnitogorsk** Russian Fed
19B3 **Magnolia** USA
101C2 **Magoé** Mozam

15D1	**Magog** Can
23B1	**Magosal** Mexico
13E2	**Magrath** Can
7A3	**Maguse River** Can
76B1	**Magwe** Burma
90A2	**Mahābād** Iran
86B1	**Mahabharat Range** Mts Nepal
87A1	**Mahād** India
85D4	**Mahadeo Hills** India
101D2	**Mahajanga** Madag
100B3	**Mahalapye** Botswana
86A2	**Mahānadi** R India
101D2	**Mahanoro** Madag
16A2	**Mahanoy City** USA
87A1	**Maharashtra** State, India
86A2	**Māhāsamund** India
76C2	**Maha Sarakham** Thai
101D2	**Mahavavy** R Madag
87B1	**Mahbūbnagar** India
96D1	**Mahdia** Tunisia
87B2	**Mahe** India
85D4	**Mahekar** India
101D2	**Mahéli** / Comoros
86A2	**Mahendragarh** India
99D3	**Mahenge** Tanz
85C4	**Mahesāna** India
110C1	**Mahia Pen** NZ
85D3	**Mahoba** India
51C2	**Mahón** Spain
12J1	**Mahony L** Can
96D1	**Mahrés** Tunisia
85C4	**Mahuva** India
32C1	**Maicao** Colombia
47B1	**Maiche** France
43E4	**Maidstone** Eng
98B1	**Maiduguri** Nig
86A2	**Maihar** India
86C2	**Maijdi** Bang
76B3	**Mail Kyun** / Burma
84A1	**Maimana** Afghan
14B1	**Main Chan** Can
98B3	**Mai-Ndombe** L Zaïre
10D2	**Maine** State, USA
48B2	**Maine** Region France
44C2	**Mainland** / Scot
85D3	**Mainpuri** India
46A2	**Maintenon** France
101D2	**Maintirano** Madag
57B2	**Mainz** Germany
97A4	**Maio** / Cape Verde
29C2	**Maipó** Mt Arg/Chile
34D3	**Maipú** Arg
32D1	**Maiquetía** Ven
47B2	**Maira** R Italy
86C1	**Mairābāri** India
86C2	**Maiskhal I** Bang
107E4	**Maitland** New South Wales, Aust
108A2	**Maitland** S Australia, Aust
112C12	**Maitri** Base Ant
74D3	**Maizuru** Japan
70C4	**Majene** Indon
30B2	**Majes** R Peru
99D2	**Maji** Eth
72D2	**Majia He** R China
	Majunga = Mahajanga
70C4	**Makale** Indon
86B1	**Makalu** Mt China/ Nepal
98B2	**Makanza** Zaïre
52C2	**Makarska** Croatia
61F2	**Makaryev** Russian Fed
	Makassar = Ujung Pandang
78D3	**Makassar Str** Indon
61H4	**Makat** Kazakhstan
97A4	**Makeni** Sierra Leone
60E4	**Makeyevka** Ukraine
100B3	**Makgadikgadi** Salt Pan Botswana
61G5	**Makhachkala** Russian Fed
99D3	**Makindu** Kenya
88H5	**Makkah** S Arabia
7E4	**Makkovik** Can
59C3	**Makó** Hung
98B2	**Makokou** Gabon
110C1	**Makorako,Mt** NZ
98B2	**Makoua** Congo
85C3	**Makrāna** India
85A3	**Makran Coast Range** Mts Pak
96C1	**Makthar** Tunisia
93D2	**Mākū** Iran
98C3	**Makumbi** Zaïre
74C4	**Makurazaki** Japan
97C4	**Makurdi** Nig
79B4	**Malabang** Phil
87A2	**Malabar Coast** India
89E7	**Malabo** Bioko
77C5	**Malacca,Str of** S E Asia
32C2	**Málaga** Colombia
50B2	**Malaga** Spain
101D3	**Malaimbandy** Madag
107F1	**Malaita** / Solomon Is
99D2	**Malakal** Sudan
84C2	**Malakand** Pak
78C4	**Malang** Indon
98B3	**Malange** Angola
97C3	**Malanville** Benin
39H7	**Mälaren** L Sweden
34B3	**Malargüe** Arg
12F3	**Malaspina Gl** USA
93C2	**Malatya** Turk
101C2	**Malawi** Republic, Africa
	Malawi,L = Nyasa,L
79C4	**Malaybalay** Phil
90A3	**Maläyer** Iran
70B3	**Malaysia** Federation, S E Asia
93D2	**Malazgirt** Turk
58B2	**Malbork** Pol
56C2	**Malchin** Germany
18C2	**Malden** USA
83B5	**Maldives Is** Indian O
104B4	**Maldives Ridge** Indian O
29F2	**Maldonado** Urug
47D1	**Male** Italy
85C4	**Malegaon** India
59B3	**Malé Karpaty** Upland Slovakia
101C2	**Malema** Mozam
84B2	**Mālestān** Afghan
38H5	**Malgomaj** L Sweden
95B3	**Malha** Well Sudan
20C2	**Malheur L** USA
97B3	**Mali** Republic, Africa
78D1	**Malinau** Indon
99E3	**Malindi** Kenya
	Malines = Mechelen
40B2	**Malin Head** Pt Irish Rep
86A2	**Malkala Range** Mts India
85D4	**Malkāpur** India
55C2	**Malkara** Turk
54C2	**Malko Tŭrnovo** Bulg
44B3	**Mallaig** Scot
95C2	**Mallawi** Egypt
47D1	**Málles Venosta** Italy
51C2	**Mallorca** / Spain
45B2	**Mallow** Irish Rep
38G6	**Malm** Nor
38J5	**Malmberget** Sweden
46D1	**Malmédy** Germany
43C4	**Malmesbury** Eng
100A4	**Malmesbury** S Africa
39G7	**Malmö** Sweden
61G2	**Malmyzh** Russian Fed
79B3	**Malolos** Phil
15D2	**Malone** USA
101G1	**Maloti Mts** Lesotho
38F6	**Mäloy** Nor
28A2	**Malpelo** / Colombia
34A2	**Malpo** R Chile
85D3	**Mālpura** India
8C2	**Malta** Montana, USA
53B3	**Malta Chan** Malta/ Italy
53B3	**Malta** / Medit S
100A3	**Maltahöhe** Namibia
42D2	**Malton** Eng
39G6	**Malung** Sweden
87A1	**Mālvan** India
19B3	**Malvern** USA
85D4	**Malwa Plat** India
61G4	**Malyy Uzen'** R Kazakhstan
63D2	**Mama** Russian Fed
61H2	**Mamadysh** Russian Fed
99C2	**Mambasa** Zaïre
71E4	**Mamberamo** R Indon
98B2	**Mambéré** R CAR
98A2	**Mamfé** Cam
33D6	**Mamoré** R Bol
97A3	**Mamou** Guinea
101D2	**Mampikony** Madag
97B4	**Mampong** Ghana
94B3	**Mamshit** Hist Site Israel
100B3	**Mamuno** Botswana
97B4	**Man** Ivory Coast
21C4	**Mana** Hawaiian Is
101D3	**Manabo** Madag
33E4	**Manacapuru** Brazil
51C2	**Manacor** Spain
71D3	**Manado** Indon
25D3	**Managua** Nic
101D3	**Manakara** Madag
101D2	**Mananara** Madag
101D3	**Mananjary** Madag
111A3	**Manapouri** NZ
111A3	**Manapouri,L** NZ
86C1	**Manas** Bhutan
82C1	**Manas** China
65K5	**Manas Hu** L China
86A1	**Manaslu** Mt Nepal
16B2	**Manasquan** USA
33F4	**Manaus** Brazil
92B2	**Manavgat** Turk
93C2	**Manbij** Syria
42B2	**Man,Calf of** / Eng
87B1	**Mancheral** India
15D2	**Manchester** Connecticut, USA
42C3	**Manchester** Eng
10C2	**Manchester** New Hampshire, USA
16A2	**Manchester** Pennsylvania, USA
69E2	**Manchuria** Hist Region, China
91B4	**Mand** R Iran
101C2	**Manda** Tanz
35A2	**Mandaguari** Brazil
39F7	**Mandal** Nor
76B1	**Mandalay** Burma
68C2	**Mandalgovī** Mongolia
8C2	**Mandan** USA
14A2	**Mandelona** USA
99E2	**Mandera** Eth
26B3	**Mandeville** Jamaica
101C2	**Mandimba** Mozam
86A2	**Mandla** India
101D2	**Mandritsara** Madag
85D4	**Mandsaur** India
53C2	**Manduria** Italy
85B4	**Māndvi** India
87B2	**Mandya** India
58D2	**Manevichi** Ukraine
42D3	**Manfield** Eng
53C2	**Manfredonia** Italy
98B1	**Manga** Desert Region Niger
110C1	**Mangakino** NZ
54C2	**Mangalia** Rom
98B1	**Mangalmé** Chad
87A2	**Mangalore** India
78B3	**Manggar** Indon
68B3	**Mangnia** China
101C2	**Mangoche** Malawi
101D3	**Mangoky** R Madag
71D4	**Mangole** / Indon
85B4	**Mängral** India
63E2	**Mangui** China
8D3	**Manhattan** USA
31C6	**Manhuacu** Brazil
101D2	**Mania** R Madag
101C2	**Manica** Mozam
7D5	**Manicouagan** R Can
91A4	**Manifah** S Arabia
79B3	**Manila** Phil
109D2	**Manilla** Aust
97B3	**Maninian** Ivory Coast
86C2	**Manipur** State, India
86C2	**Manipur** R Burma
92A2	**Manisa** Turk
41C3	**Man,Isle of** Irish S
14A2	**Manistee** USA
14A2	**Manistee** R USA
14A1	**Manistique** USA
5H4	**Manitoba** Province, Can
5J4	**Manitoba,L** Can
13F2	**Manito L** Can
14A1	**Manitou Is** USA
7B5	**Manitoulin** / Can
14A2	**Manitowoc** USA
15C1	**Maniwaki** Can
32B2	**Manizales** Colombia
101D3	**Manja** Madag
106A4	**Manjimup** Aust
87B1	**Mānjra** R India
10A2	**Mankato** USA
97B4	**Mankono** Ivory Coast
12D2	**Manley Hot Springs** USA
110B1	**Manly** USA
85C4	**Manmād** India
78A3	**Manna** Indon
108A2	**Mannahill** Aust
87B3	**Mannar** Sri Lanka
87B3	**Mannār,G of** India
87B2	**Mannārgudi** India
57B3	**Mannheim** Germany
13D1	**Manning** Can
17B1	**Manning** USA
108A2	**Mannum** Aust
97A4	**Mano** Sierra Leone
71E4	**Manokwari** Indon
98C3	**Manono** Zaïre
76B3	**Manoron** Burma
75B1	**Mano-wan** B Japan
74B2	**Manp'o** N Korea
84D3	**Mānsa** India
100B2	**Mansa** Zambia
6B3	**Mansel I** Can
19B2	**Mansfield** Arkansas, USA
108C3	**Mansfield** Aust
19B3	**Mansfield** Louisiana, USA
16D1	**Mansfield** Massachusetts, USA
10B2	**Mansfield** Ohio, USA
15C2	**Mansfield** Pennsylvania, USA
71E2	**Mansyu Deep** Pacific O
32A4	**Manta** Ecuador
79A4	**Mantalingajan,Mt** Phil
32B6	**Mantaro** R Peru
22B2	**Manteca** USA
48C2	**Mantes** France
52B1	**Mantova** Italy
38J6	**Mantta** Fin
61F2	**Manturovo** Russian Fed
35A2	**Manuel Ribas** Brazil
79B4	**Manukan** Phil
110B1	**Manukau** NZ
71F4	**Manus** / Pacific O
50B2	**Manzanares** Spain
25E2	**Manzanillo** Cuba
24B3	**Manzanillo** Mexico
63D3	**Manzhouli** China
94C3	**Manzil** Jordan
101C3	**Manzini** Swaziland
98B1	**Mao** Chad
72A2	**Maomao Shan** Mt China
73C5	**Maoming** China
101C3	**Mapai** Mozam
71E3	**Mapia** Is Pacific O
79A4	**Mapin** / Phil
5H5	**Maple Creek** Can
101H1	**Maputo** Mozam
101H1	**Maputo** R Mozam
	Ma Qu = Huange He
72A3	**Maqu** China
86B1	**Maquan He** R China
98B3	**Maquela do Zombo** Angola
29C4	**Maquinchao** Arg
31B3	**Marabá** Brazil
32C1	**Maracaibo** Ven
32D1	**Maracay** Ven
95A2	**Marādah** Libya
97C3	**Maradi** Niger
90A2	**Marāgheh** Iran

99D2 **Maralal** Kenya
107F1 **Maramasike** /
    Solomon Is
100B2 **Maramba** Zambia
90A2 **Marand** Iran
31B2 **Maranhöa** State,
    Brazil
109C1 **Maranoa** R Aust
32B4 **Marañón** R Peru
7B5 **Marathon** Can
17B2 **Marathon** Florida,
    USA
78D2 **Maratua** / Indon
23A2 **Maravatio** Mexico
79B4 **Marawi** Phil
34B2 **Marayes** Arg
50B2 **Marbella** Spain
106A3 **Marble Bar** Aust
100B3 **Marblehall** S Africa
16D1 **Marblehead** USA
57B2 **Marburg** Germany
57B2 **Marche** Belg
50A2 **Marchean** Spain
46C1 **Marche-en-Famenne**
    Belg
32J7 **Marchena** / Ecuador
17B2 **Marco** USA
34C2 **Marcos Juárez** Arg
12E2 **Marcus Baker,Mt**
    USA
15D2 **Marcy,Mt** USA
84C2 **Mardan** Pak
29E3 **Mar del Plata** Arg
93D2 **Mardin** Turk
99D1 **Mareb** R Eritrea/Eth
16B1 **Margaretville** USA
43E4 **Margate** Eng
54B1 **Marghita** Rom
109C4 **Maria I** Aust
104F3 **Mariana** Is Pacific O
13E1 **Mariana Lake** Can
104F3 **Marianas Trench**
    Pacific O
86C1 **Mariäni** India
19B3 **Marianna** Arkansas,
    USA
17A1 **Marianna** Florida,
    USA
7G4 **Maria Van Diemen,C**
    NZ
59B3 **Mariazell** Austria
52C1 **Maribor** Slovenia
99C2 **Maridi** Sudan
112B5 **Marie Byrd Land**
    Region, Ant
27F3 **Marie Galante** /
    Caribbean S
39H6 **Mariehamn** Fin
46C1 **Mariembourg** Belg
33G2 **Marienburg** Surinam
100A3 **Mariental** Namibia
39G7 **Mariestad** Sweden
17B1 **Marietta** Georgia,
    USA
14B3 **Marietta** Ohio, USA
19A3 **Marietta** Oklahoma,
    USA
27Q2 **Marigot** Dominica
60B3 **Marijampole**
    Lithuania
31B6 **Marilia** Brazil
98B3 **Marimba** Angola
79B3 **Marinduque** / Phil
10B2 **Marinette** USA
30F3 **Maringá** Brazil
98C2 **Maringa** R Zaïre
18B2 **Marion** Arkansas,
    USA
18C2 **Marion** Illinois, USA
10B2 **Marion** Indiana, USA
10B2 **Marion** Ohio, USA
17C1 **Marion** S Carolina,
    USA
11B3 **Marion,L** USA
107E2 **Marion Reef** Aust
21B2 **Mariposa** USA
22B2 **Mariposa** R USA
22B2 **Mariposa Res** USA
60C5 **Marista** R Bulg
60E4 **Mariupol'** Ukraine
61G2 **Mariyskaya**
    Respublika,
    Russian Fed
94B2 **Marjayoun** Leb

58D2 **Marjina Gorki**
    Belorussia
94B3 **Marka** Jordan
99E2 **Marka** Somalia
56C1 **Markaryd** Sweden
43C3 **Market Drayton** Eng
43D3 **Market Harborough**
    Eng
112A **Markham,Mt** Ant
22C1 **Markleeville** USA
16D1 **Marlboro**
    Massachusetts, USA
107D3 **Marlborough** Aust
46B2 **Marle** France
19A3 **Marlin** USA
48C3 **Marmande** France
55C2 **Marmara Adi** / Turk
92A1 **Marmara,S of** Turk
55C3 **Marmaris** Turk
14B3 **Marmet** USA
52B1 **Marmolada** Mt Italy
12D3 **Marmot B** USA
47A1 **Marnay** France
46B2 **Marne** Department,
    France
46B2 **Marne** R France
98B2 **Maro** Chad
101D2 **Maroantsetra** Madag
101C2 **Marondera** Zim
33G3 **Maroni** R French
    Guiana
109D1 **Maroochydore** Aust
98B1 **Maroua** Cam
101D2 **Marovoay** Madag
11B4 **Marquesas Keys** Is
    USA
10B2 **Marquette** USA
46A1 **Marquise** France
109C2 **Marra** R Aust
101H1 **Marracuene** Mozam
96B1 **Marrakech** Mor
106C3 **Marree** Aust
19B4 **Marrero** USA
101C2 **Marromeu** Mozam
101C2 **Marrupa** Mozam
95C2 **Marsa Alam** Egypt
99D2 **Marsabit** Kenya
53B3 **Marsala** Italy
49D3 **Marseille** France
12B2 **Marshall** Alaska, USA
14A3 **Marshall** Illinois, USA
14B2 **Marshall** Michigan,
    USA
18B2 **Marshall** Missouri,
    USA
11A3 **Marshall** Texas, USA
105G3 **Marshall Is** Pacific O
18B2 **Marshfield** Missouri,
    USA
26B1 **Marsh Harbour**
    The Bahamas
19B4 **Marsh I** USA
12H2 **Marsh L** Can
76B2 **Martaban,G of**
    Burma
78A3 **Martapura** Indon
78C3 **Martapura** Indon
15D2 **Martha's Vineyard** /
    USA
49D2 **Martigny** Switz
59B3 **Martin** Slovakia
111C2 **Martinborough** NZ
34B3 **Martín de Loyola** Arg
23B1 **Martínez de la Torre**
    Mexico
27E4 **Martinique** /
    Caribbean S
17A1 **Martin,L** USA
15C3 **Martinsburg** USA
14B2 **Martins Ferry** USA
103G6 **Martin Vaz** /
    Atlantic O
49D3 **Martiques** France
110C2 **Marton** NZ
50B2 **Martos** Spain
78D1 **Marudi** Malay
84B2 **Maruf** Afghan
75A2 **Marugame** Japan
85C3 **Märwär** India
65H6 **Mary** Turkmenistan
107E3 **Maryborough**
    Queensland, Aust
108B3 **Maryborough**
    Victoria, Aust

5F4 **Mary Henry,Mt** Can
10C3 **Maryland** State, USA
42C2 **Maryport** Eng
21A2 **Marysville** California,
    USA
18A2 **Marysville** Kansas,
    USA
20B1 **Marysville**
    Washington, USA
10A2 **Maryville** Iowa, USA
18B1 **Maryville** Missouri,
    USA
95A2 **Marzuq** Libya
    Masada = Mezada
94B2 **Mas'adah** Syria
99D3 **Masai Steppe** Tanz
    Upland Tanz
99D3 **Masaka** Uganda
93E2 **Masally** Azerbaijan
74B3 **Masan** S Korea
101C2 **Masasi** Tanz
25D3 **Masaya** Nic
79B3 **Masbate** Phil
79B3 **Masbate** / Phil
96C1 **Mascara** Alg
23A1 **Mascota** Mexico
35D1 **Mascote** Brazil
101G1 **Maseru** Lesotho
66C3 **Mashad** Iran
84B2 **Mashaki** Afghan
90C2 **Mashhad** Iran
98B3 **Masi-Manimba** Zaïre
99D2 **Masindi** Uganda
99C3 **Masisi** Zaïre
90A3 **Masjed Soleyman**
    Iran
101E2 **Masoala** C Madag
10A2 **Mason City** USA
91C5 **Masqat** Oman
52B2 **Massa** Italy
10C2 **Massachusetts** State,
    USA
15D2 **Massachusetts B**
    USA
98B1 **Massakori** Chad
101C3 **Massangena** Mozam
    Massawa = Mits'iwa
15D2 **Massena** USA
98B1 **Massénya** Chad
14B1 **Massey** Can
49C2 **Massif Central** Mts
    France
98B2 **Massif de**
    l'Adamaoua Mts
    Cam
26C3 **Massif de la Hotte**
    Mts Haiti
101D3 **Massif de l'Isalo**
    Upland Madag
98C2 **Massif des Bongo**
    Upland CAR
49D2 **Massif du Pelvoux**
    Mts France
101D2 **Massif du**
    Tsaratanana Mt
    Madag
14B2 **Massillon** USA
97B3 **Massina** Region, Mali
101C3 **Massinga** Mozam
101C3 **Massingir** Mozam
61H4 **Masteksay**
    Kazakhstan
111C2 **Masterton** NZ
74C4 **Masuda** Japan
98B3 **Masuku** Gabon
100C3 **Masvingo** Zim
92C2 **Maşyāf** Syria
98B3 **Matadi** Zaïre
25D3 **Matagalpa** Nic
7C4 **Matagami** Can
9D4 **Matagorda B** USA
110C1 **Matakana** I NZ
100A2 **Matala** Angola
87C3 **Matale** Sri Lanka
97A3 **Matam** Sen
97C3 **Matameye** Niger
24C2 **Matamoros** Mexico
95B2 **Ma'tan as Sarra** Well
    Libya
7D5 **Matane** Can
25D2 **Matanzas** Cuba
34A2 **Mataquito** R Chile
87C3 **Matara** Sri Lanka
106A1 **Mataram** Indon

30B2 **Matarani** Peru
51C1 **Mataró** Spain
111A3 **Mataura** NZ
24B2 **Matehuala** Mexico
27L1 **Matelot** Trinidad
53C2 **Matera** Italy
59C3 **Mátészalka** Hung
85D3 **Mathura** India
79C4 **Mati** Phil
78D3 **Matisiri** / Indon
43D3 **Matlock** Eng
33F6 **Mato Grosso** Brazil
33F6 **Mato Grosso** State,
    Brazil
30E2 **Mato Grosso do Sul**
    State, Brazil
101H1 **Matola** Mozam
91C5 **Matrah** Oman
92A3 **Matrûh** Egypt
74C3 **Matsue** Japan
74E2 **Matsumae** Japan
74D3 **Matsumoto** Japan
74D4 **Matsusaka** Japan
74C4 **Matsuyama** Japan
7B5 **Mattagami** R Can
15C1 **Mattawa** Can
52A1 **Matterhorn** Mt Italy/
    Switz
26C2 **Matthew Town**
    The Bahamas
16C2 **Mattituck** USA
18C2 **Mattoon** USA
84B2 **Matun** Afghan
27L1 **Matura B** Trinidad
33E2 **Maturin** Ven
86A1 **Mau** India
101C2 **Maúa** Mozam
49C1 **Maubeuge** France
108B2 **Maude** Aust
103J8 **Maud Seamount**
    Atlantic O
21C4 **Maui** / Hawaiian Is
34A3 **Maule** R Chile
14B2 **Maumee** USA
14B2 **Maumee** R USA
100B2 **Maun** Botswana
21C4 **Mauna Kea** Mt
    Hawaiian Is
21C4 **Mauna Loa** Mt
    Hawaiian Is
4F3 **Maunoir** L Can
4F3 **Maunoir,L** Can
48C2 **Mauriac** France
96A2 **Mauritania** Republic,
    Africa
100E3 **Mauritius** / Indian O
100B2 **Mavinga** Angola
86C2 **Mawlaik** Burma
    Mawlamyine =
    Moulmein
112C10 **Mawson** Base Ant
78B3 **Maya** / Indon
63F2 **Maya** R Russian Fed
93D2 **Mayädïn** Syria
11C4 **Mayaguana** /
    The Bahamas
27D3 **Mayagüez** Puerto
    Rico
97C3 **Mayahi** Niger
98B3 **Mayama** Congo
90C2 **Mayamey** Iran
42B2 **Maybole** Scot
10C3 **May,C** USA
109C4 **Maydena** Aust
46D1 **Mayen** Germany
48B2 **Mayenne** France
13D2 **Mayerthorpe** Can
18C2 **Mayfield** USA
61E5 **Maykop** Russian Fed
65H6 **Maymaneh** Afghan
76B1 **Maymyo** Burma
4E3 **Mayo** Can
45B2 **Mayo** County,
    Irish Rep
16A3 **Mayo** USA
45B1 **Mayo,Mts of**
    Irish Rep
79B3 **Mayon** Mt Phil
51C2 **Mayor** Mt Spain
34C3 **Mayor Buratovich**
    Arg
110C1 **Mayor I** NZ
30D2 **Mayor P Lagerenza**
    Par

101D2 **Mayotte** *I* Indian O
27H2 **May Pen** Jamaica
16B3 **May Point,C** USA
47D1 **Mayrhofen** Austria
16B3 **Mays Landing** USA
14B3 **Maysville** USA
98B3 **Mayumba** Gabon
100B2 **Mazabuka** Zambia
84D1 **Mazar** China
94B3 **Mazār** Jordan
53B3 **Mazara del Vallo** Italy
84B1 **Mazar-i-Sharif** Afghan
24B2 **Mazatlán** Mexico
60B2 **Mazeikiai** Lithuania
94B3 **Mazra** Jordan
101C3 **Mbabane** Swaziland
98B2 **Mbaïki** CAR
99D3 **Mbala** Zambia
100B3 **Mbalabala** Zim
99D2 **Mbale** Uganda
98B2 **Mbalmayo** Cam
98B2 **Mbam** *R* Cam
101C2 **Mbamba Bay** Tanz
98B2 **Mbandaka** Zaïre
98B3 **Mbanza Congo** Angola
98B3 **Mbanza-Ngungu** Zaïre
99D3 **Mbarara** Uganda
98B2 **Mbènza** Congo
98B2 **Mbére** *R* Cam
99D3 **Mbeya** Tanz
98B3 **Mbinda** Congo
97A3 **Mbout** Maur
98C3 **Mbuji-Mayi** Zaïre
99D3 **Mbulu** Tanz
96B2 **Mcherrah** Region, Alg
101C2 **Mchinji** Malawi
76D3 **Mdrak** Viet
9B3 **Mead,L** USA
5H4 **Meadow Lake** Can
14B2 **Meadville** USA
7E4 **Mealy Mts** Can
109C1 **Meandarra** Aust
5G4 **Meander River** Can
45C2 **Meath** County, Irish Rep
49C2 **Meaux** France
16C1 **Mechanicville** USA
56A2 **Mechelen** Belg
96B1 **Mecheria** Alg
56C2 **Mecklenburg-Vorpommern** *State* Germany
56C2 **Mecklenburger Bucht** *B* Germany
101C2 **Meconta** Mozam
101C2 **Mecuburi** Mozam
101D2 **Mecufi** Mozam
101C2 **Mecula** Mozam
70A3 **Medan** Indon
34C3 **Medanos** Arg
34D2 **Médanos** Arg
13E2 **Medecine Hat** Can
32B2 **Medellin** Colombia
96D1 **Medenine** Tunisia
8A2 **Medford** USA
54C2 **Medgidia** Rom
34B2 **Media Agua** Arg
54B1 **Mediaş** Rom
20C1 **Medical Lake** USA
5G5 **Medicine Hat** Can
35C1 **Medina** Brazil
80B3 **Medina** S Arabia
50B1 **Medinaceli** Spain
50B1 **Medina del Campo** Spain
50A1 **Medina de Rio Seco** Spain
86B2 **Medinīpur** India
88E4 **Mediterranean S** Europe
13F2 **Medley** Can
61J3 **Mednogorsk** Russian Fed
86D1 **Mêdog** China
98B2 **Medouneu** Gabon
61F3 **Medvedista** *R* Russian Fed
64E3 **Medvezh'yegorsk** Russian Fed
106A3 **Meekatharra** Aust
84D3 **Meerut** India
99D2 **Mēga** Eth
55B3 **Megalópolis** Greece
55B3 **Mégara** Greece
86C1 **Meghālaya** State, India
86C2 **Meghna** *R* Bang
94B2 **Megiddo** *Hist Site* Israel
91B4 **Mehran** *R* Iran
90B3 **Mehriz** Iran
35B1 **Meia Ponte** *R* Brazil
98B2 **Meiganga** Cam
76B1 **Meiktila** Burma
47C1 **Meiringen** Switz
73A4 **Meishan** China
57C2 **Meissen** Germany
73D5 **Mei Xian** China
73D5 **Meizhou** China
30B3 **Mejillones** Chile
98B2 **Mekambo** Gabon
99D1 **Mek'elē** Eth
96B1 **Meknès** Mor
76D3 **Mekong** *R* Camb
97C3 **Mekrou** *R* Benin
77C5 **Melaka** Malay
104F4 **Melanesia** *Region* Pacific O
78C3 **Melawi** *R* Indon
107D4 **Melbourne** Aust
11B4 **Melbourne** USA
9C4 **Melchor Muźguiz** Mexico
61J3 **Meleuz** Russian Fed
98B1 **Melfi** Chad
5H4 **Melfort** Can
96B1 **Melilla** N W Africa
29B4 **Melimoyu** *Mt* Chile
34C2 **Melincué** Arg
34A2 **Melipilla** Chile
60E4 **Melitopol'** Ukraine
6D2 **Meliville Bugt** *B* Greenland
99D2 **Melka Guba** Eth
101H1 **Melmoth** S Africa
34C2 **Melo** Arg
29F2 **Melo** Urug
22B2 **Melones Res** USA
12D1 **Melozitna** *R* USA
47C1 **Mels** Switz
43D3 **Melton Mowbry** Eng
49C2 **Melun** France
5H4 **Melville** Can
27Q2 **Melville,C** Dominica
4F3 **Melville Hills** *Mts* Can
106C2 **Melville I** Aust
4G2 **Melville I** Can
7E4 **Melville,L** Can
6B3 **Melville Pen** Can
45B1 **Melvin,L** Irish Rep
101D2 **Memba** Mozam
106A1 **Memboro** Indon
57C3 **Memmingen** Germany
78B2 **Mempawan** Indon
11B3 **Memphis** Tennessee, USA
19B3 **Mena** USA
43B3 **Menai Str** Wales
97C3 **Ménaka** Mali
14A2 **Menasha** USA
78C3 **Mendawai** *R* Indon
49C3 **Mende** France
99D2 **Mendebo** *Mts* Eth
43C4 **Mendip Hills** *Upland* Eng
20B2 **Mendocino,C** USA
105J2 **Mendocino Seascarp** Pacific O
22B2 **Mendota** California, USA
29C2 **Mendoza** Arg
29C3 **Mendoza** State, Arg
55C3 **Menemen** Turk
46B1 **Menen** Belg
72D3 **Mengcheng** China
78B3 **Menggala** Indon
76B1 **Menghai** China
73A5 **Mengla** China
76B1 **Menglian** China
73A5 **Mengzi** China
107D4 **Menindee** Aust
108B2 **Menindee L** Aust
108A3 **Meningie** Aust
14A1 **Menominee** USA
14A2 **Menomonee Falls** USA
100A2 **Menongue** Angola
51C1 **Menorca** *I* Spain
12F2 **Mentasta Mts** USA
78B3 **Mentok** Indon
14B2 **Mentor** USA
46B2 **Ménu** France
72A2 **Menyuan** China
61H2 **Menzelinsk** Russian Fed
56B2 **Meppen** Germany
78D2 **Merah** Indon
18B2 **Meramec** *R* USA
52B1 **Merano** Italy
71F4 **Merauke** Indon
8A3 **Merced** USA
22B2 **Merced** *R* USA
29B2 **Mercedario** *Mt* Chile
29C2 **Mercedes** Arg
29E2 **Mercedes** Buenos Aires, Arg
30E4 **Mercedes** Corrientes, Arg
29E2 **Mercedes** Urug
110C1 **Mercury B** NZ
110C1 **Mercury Is** NZ
4F2 **Mercy B** Can
6D3 **Mercy,C** Can
99E2 **Meregh** Somalia
76B3 **Mergui** Burma
76B3 **Mergui Arch** Burma
25D2 **Mérida** Mexico
50A2 **Mérida** Spain
32C2 **Mérida** Ven
11B3 **Meridian** USA
109C3 **Merimbula** Aust
108B2 **Meringur** Aust
95C3 **Merowe** Sudan
106A4 **Merredin** Aust
42B2 **Merrick** *Mt* Scot
14A2 **Merrillville** USA
13C2 **Merritt** Can
17B2 **Merritt Island** USA
109D2 **Merriwa** Aust
99E1 **Mersa Fatma** Eritrea
51B2 **Mers el Kebir** Alg
42C3 **Mersey** *R* Eng
42C3 **Merseyside** Metropolitan County, Eng
92B2 **Mersin** Turk
77C5 **Mersing** Malay
85C3 **Merta** India
43C4 **Merthyr Tydfil** Wales
50A2 **Mertola** Port
99D3 **Meru** *Mt* Tanz
60E5 **Merzifon** Turk
46D2 **Merzig** Germany
9B3 **Mesa** USA
46E1 **Meschede** Germany
93D1 **Mescit Dağ** *Mt* Turk
12C3 **Meshik** USA
99C2 **Meshra Er Req** Sudan
47C1 **Mesocco** Switz
55B3 **Mesolóngion** Greece
19A3 **Mesquite** Texas, USA
101C2 **Messalo** *R* Mozam
53C3 **Messina** Italy
100B3 **Messina** S Africa
55B3 **Messíni** Greece
55B3 **Messiniakós Kólpos** *G* Greece
54B2 **Mesta** *R* Bulg
52B1 **Mestre** Italy
32C3 **Meta** *R* Colombia
60D2 **Meta** *R* Russian Fed
32D2 **Meta** *R* Ven
6C3 **Meta Incognito Pen** Can
19B4 **Metairie** USA
20C1 **Metaline Falls** USA
30D4 **Metán** Arg
101C2 **Metangula** Mozam
53C2 **Metaponto** Italy
44C3 **Methil** Scot
16D1 **Methuen** USA
111B2 **Methven** NZ
12H3 **Metlakatla** USA
18C2 **Metropolis** USA
87B2 **Mettūr** India
49D2 **Metz** France
70A3 **Meulaboh** Indon
46A2 **Meulan** France
46C2 **Meuse** Department, France
49D2 **Meuse** *R* France
19A3 **Mexia** USA
24A1 **Mexicali** Mexico
24B2 **Mexico** Federal Republic, Cent America
24C3 **México** Mexico
23A2 **México** State, Mexico
18B2 **Mexico** USA
24C2 **Mexico,G of** Cent America
94B3 **Mezada** *Hist Site* Israel
23B2 **Mezcala** Mexico
64F3 **Mezen'** Russian Fed
64G2 **Mezhdusharskiy, Ostrov** *I* Russian Fed
85D4 **Mhow** India
23B2 **Miahuatlán** Mexico
11B4 **Miami** Florida, USA
18B2 **Miami** Oklahoma, USA
11B4 **Miami Beach** USA
90A2 **Miandowāb** Iran
101D2 **Miandrivazo** Madag
90A2 **Mīāneh** Iran
84C2 **Mianwali** Pak
73A3 **Mianyang** China
73C3 **Mianyang** China
73A3 **Mianzhu** China
72E2 **Miaodao Qundao** *Arch* China
73B4 **Miao Ling** *Upland* China
61K3 **Miass** Russian Fed
59C3 **Michalovce** Slovakia
27D3 **Miches** Dom Rep
10B2 **Michigan** State, USA
14A2 **Michigan City** USA
10B2 **Michigan,L** USA
7B5 **Michipicoten I** Can
23A2 **Michoacan** State, Mexico
54C2 **Michurin** Bulg
61F3 **Michurinsk** Russian Fed
104F3 **Micronesia** *Region* Pacific O
78B2 **Midai** *I* Indon
102F4 **Mid Atlantic Ridge** Atlantic O
46B1 **Middelburg** Neth
20B2 **Middle Alkali L** USA
16D2 **Middleboro** USA
100B4 **Middleburg** Cape Province, S Africa
16A2 **Middleburg** Pennsylvania, USA
101G1 **Middleburg** Transvaal, S Africa
16B1 **Middleburgh** USA
15D2 **Middlebury** USA
11B3 **Middlesboro** USA
42D2 **Middlesbrough** Eng
16C2 **Middletown** Connecticut, USA
16B3 **Middletown** Delaware, USA
15D2 **Middletown** New York, USA
14B3 **Middletown** Ohio, USA
16A2 **Middletown** Pennsylvania, USA
96B1 **Midelt** Mor
43C4 **Mid Glamorgan** County, Wales
104B4 **Mid Indian Basin** Indian O
104B4 **Mid Indian Ridge** Indian O
7C5 **Midland** Can
14B2 **Midland** Michigan, USA
9C3 **Midland** Texas, USA
101D3 **Midongy Atsimo** Madag

105G2 **Mid Pacific Mts**
Pacific O
20C2 **Midvale** USA
105H2 **Midway Is** Pacific O
18A2 **Midwest City** USA
93D2 **Midyat** Turk
54B2 **Midžor** *Mt* Serbia,
Yugos
59B2 **Mielec** Pol
54C1 **Miercurea-Ciuc** Rom
50A1 **Mieres** Spain
16A2 **Mifflintown** USA
75A2 **Mihara** Japan
72D1 **Mijun Shuiku** *Res*
China
54B2 **Mikhaylovgrad** Bulg
61F3 **Mikhaylovka**
Russian Fed
65J4 **Mikhaylovskiy**
Russian Fed
38K6 **Mikkeli** Fin
55C3 **Mikonos** *I* Greece
59B3 **Mikulov**
Czech Republic
99D3 **Mikumi** Tanz
74D3 **Mikuni-sammyaku**
Mts Japan
75B2 **Mikura-jima** *I* Japan
32B4 **Milagro** Ecuador
Milan = **Milano**
51C2 **Milana** Alg
101C2 **Milange** Mozam
52A1 **Milano** Italy
92A2 **Milas** Turk
107D4 **Mildura** Aust
73A5 **Mile** China
93D3 **Mileh Tharthār** *L*
Iraq
107E3 **Miles** Aust
8C2 **Miles City** USA
16C2 **Milford** Connecticut,
USA
15C3 **Milford** Delaware,
USA
15D2 **Milford**
Massachusetts, USA
18A1 **Milford** Nebraska,
USA
16B2 **Milford**
Pennsylvania, USA
43B4 **Milford Haven** Wales
43B4 **Milford Haven** *Sd*
Wales
18A2 **Milford L** USA
111A2 **Milford Sd** NZ
13E2 **Milk River** Can
49C3 **Millau** France
16C2 **Millbrook** USA
17B1 **Milledgeville** USA
12F2 **Miller,Mt** USA
61F4 **Millerovo**
Russian Fed
16A2 **Millersburg** USA
108A1 **Millers Creek** Aust
16C1 **Millers Falls** USA
16C2 **Millerton** USA
22C2 **Millerton L** USA
108B3 **Millicent** Aust
109D1 **Millmerran** Aust
45B2 **Milltown Malbay**
Irish Rep
22A2 **Mill Valley** USA
15D3 **Millville** USA
6H2 **Milne Land** *I*
Greenland
21C4 **Milolii** Hawaiian Is
55B3 **Milos** *I* Greece
107D3 **Milparinka** Aust
16A2 **Milroy** USA
111A3 **Milton** NZ
16A2 **Milton** Pennsylvania,
USA
10B2 **Milwaukee** USA
51C2 **Mina** *R* Alg
93E4 **Mīnā' al Ahmadī**
Kuwait
91C4 **Mīnāb** Iran
74C4 **Minamata** Japan
78A2 **Minas** Indon
29E2 **Minas** Urug
31B5 **Minas Gerais** State,
Brazil
35C1 **Minas Novas** Brazil
25C3 **Minatitlan** Mexico

76A1 **Minbu** Burma
76A1 **Minbya** Burma
34A2 **Mincha** Chile
44A3 **Minch,Little** *Sd* Scot
44A2 **Minch,North** *Sd*
Scot
40B2 **Minch,The** *Sd* Scot
12D2 **Minchumina,L** USA
47D2 **Mincio** *R* Italy
79B4 **Mindanao** *I* Phil
19B3 **Minden** Louisiana,
USA
56B2 **Minden** Germany
108B2 **Mindona L** Aust
79B3 **Mindoro** *I* Phil
79B3 **Mindoro Str** Phil
45C3 **Mine Hd** *C* Irish Rep
43C4 **Minehead** Eng
30F2 **Mineiros** Brazil
19A3 **Mineola** USA
23B1 **Mineral de Monte**
Mexico
16A2 **Minersville** USA
108B2 **Mingary** Aust
72A2 **Minhe** China
87A3 **Minicoy** *I* India
73D4 **Min Jiang** *R* Fujian,
China
73A4 **Min Jiang** *R*
Sichuan, China
22C2 **Minkler** USA
108A2 **Minlaton** Aust
72A2 **Minle** China
97C4 **Minna** Nig
10A2 **Minneapolis** USA
5J4 **Minnedosa** Can
10A2 **Minnesota** State,
USA
50A1 **Miño** *R* Spain
8C2 **Minot** USA
72A2 **Minqin** China
72A3 **Min Shan** *Upland*
China
60C3 **Minsk** Belorussia
58C2 **Mińsk Mazowiecki**
Pol
12E2 **Minto** USA
4G2 **Minto Inlet** *B* Can
7C4 **Minto,L** Can
63B2 **Minusinsk**
Russian Fed
72A3 **Min Xian** China
7E5 **Miquelon** Can
22D3 **Mirage L** USA
87A1 **Miraj** India
29E3 **Miramar** Arg
84B2 **Miram Shah** Pak
50B1 **Miranda de Ebro**
Spain
47D2 **Mirandola** Italy
84B2 **Mir Bachchen Kūt**
Afghan
78D1 **Miri** Malay
96A3 **Mirik,C** Maur
63A1 **Mirnoye** Russian Fed
63D1 **Mirnyy** Russian Fed
112C9 **Mirnyy** *Base* Ant
84C2 **Mirpur** Pak
85B3 **Mirpur Khas** Pak
55B3 **Mirtoan S** Greece
74B3 **Miryang** S Korea
86A1 **Mirzāpur** India
23B2 **Misantla** Mexico
84C1 **Misgar** Pak
14A2 **Mishawaka** USA
12B1 **Misheguk Mt** USA
75A2 **Mi-shima** *I* Japan
107E2 **Misima** *I* Solomon Is
30F4 **Misiones** State, Arg
59C3 **Miskolc** Hung
94C2 **Mismīyah** Syria
71E4 **Misoöl** *I* Indon
95A1 **Misrātah** Libya
7B5 **Missinaibi** *R* Can
20B1 **Mission City** Can
15C2 **Mississauga** Can
11A3 **Mississippi** State,
USA
11A3 **Mississippi** *R* USA
19C3 **Mississippi Delta**
USA
8B2 **Missoula** USA
96B1 **Missour** Mor
11A3 **Missouri** State, USA

10A2 **Missouri** *R* USA
10C1 **Mistassini,L** Can
30B2 **Misti** *Mt* Peru
109C1 **Mitchell** Aust
8D2 **Mitchell** USA
107D2 **Mitchell** *R* Aust
11B3 **Mitchell,Mt** USA
45B2 **Mitchelstown**
Irish Rep
84C3 **Mithankot** Pak
55C3 **Mitilíni** Greece
23B2 **Mitla** Mexico
54B2 **Mitrovica** Serbia,
Yugos
95C3 **Mits'īwa** Eritrea
32C3 **Mitu** Colombia
99C3 **Mitumbar** *Mts* Zaïre
98C3 **Mitwaba** Zaïre
98B2 **Mitzic** Gabon
75B1 **Miura** Japan
72C3 **Mi Xian** China
69F3 **Miyake** *I* Japan
75B2 **Miyake-jima** *I* Japan
69E4 **Miyako** *I* Japan
74C4 **Miyakonojō** Japan
74C4 **Miyazaki** Japan
75B1 **Miyazu** Japan
74C4 **Miyoshi** Japan
72D1 **Miyun** China
99D2 **Mizan Teferi** Eth
95A1 **Mizdah** Libya
45B3 **Mizen Hd** *C*
Irish Rep
54C1 **Mizil** Rom
86C2 **Mizo Hills** India
86C2 **Mizoram** Union
Territory, India
94B3 **Mizpe Ramon** Israel
112B11 **Mizuho** *Base* Ant
74E3 **Mizusawa** Japan
39H7 **Mjolby** Sweden
100B2 **Mkushi** Zambia
101H1 **Mkuzi** S Africa
57C2 **Mladá Boleslav**
Czech Republic
58C2 **Mława** Pol
52C2 **Mljet** *I* Croatia
100B3 **Mmabatho** S Africa
84D2 **Mnadi** India
97A4 **Moa** *R* Sierra Leone
94B3 **Moab** Region,
Jordan
9C3 **Moab** USA
98B3 **Moanda** Congo
98B3 **Moanda** Gabon
99C3 **Moba** Zaïre
75C1 **Mobara** Japan
98C2 **Mobaye** CAR
98C2 **Mobayi** Zaïre
10A3 **Moberly** USA
11B3 **Mobile** USA
11B3 **Mobile B** USA
8C2 **Mobridge** USA
101D2 **Moçambique** Mozam
76C1 **Moc Chau** Viet
100B3 **Mochudi** Botswana
101D2 **Mocimboa da Praia**
Mozam
32B3 **Mocoa** Colombia
35B2 **Mococa** Brazil
34D2 **Mocoreta** *R* Arg
23B1 **Moctezuma** *R*
Mexico
101C2 **Mocuba** Mozam
47B2 **Modane** France
101G1 **Modder** *R* S Africa
52B2 **Modena** Italy
46D2 **Moder** *R* France
8A3 **Modesto** USA
22B2 **Modesto Res** USA
53B3 **Modica** Italy
59B3 **Mödling** Austria
107D4 **Moe** Aust
47C1 **Moesa** *R* Switz
42C2 **Moffat** Scot
84D2 **Moga** India
35B2 **Mogi das Cruzes**
Brazil
60C3 **Mogilev** Belorussia
60C4 **Mogilev Podolskiy**
Ukraine
35B2 **Mogi-Mirim** Brazil
101D2 **Mogincual** Mozam
47E2 **Mogliano** Italy

34B2 **Mogna** Arg
68D1 **Mogocha**
Russian Fed
65K4 **Mogochin**
Russian Fed
50A2 **Moguer** Spain
110C1 **Mohaka** *R* NZ
86C2 **Mohanganj** Bang
15D2 **Mohawk** *R* USA
99D3 **Mohoro** Tanz
65J5 **Mointy** Kazakhstan
38G5 **Mo i Rana** Nor
48C3 **Moissac** France
21B2 **Mojave** USA
22D3 **Mojave** *R* USA
9B3 **Mojave Desert** USA
78C4 **Mojokerto** Indon
86B1 **Mokama** India
110B1 **Mokau** *R* NZ
22B1 **Mokelumne**
Aqueduct USA
22B1 **Mokelumne Hill**
USA
22B1 **Mokelumne North**
Fork *R* USA
101G1 **Mokhotlong**
Lesotho
96D1 **Moknine** Tunisia
86C1 **Mokokchūng** India
98B1 **Mokolo** Cam
74B4 **Mokp'o** S Korea
61F3 **Moksha** *R*
Russian Fed
23B1 **Molango** Mexico
55B3 **Moláoi** Greece
60C4 **Moldavia** Republic,
Europe
38F6 **Molde** Nor
Moldova = **Moldavia**
54B1 **Moldoveanu** *Mt*
Rom
100B3 **Molepolole**
Botswana
53C2 **Molfetta** Italy
34A3 **Molina** Chile
30B2 **Mollendo** Peru
60C3 **Molodechno**
Belorussia
112C11 **Molodezhnaya** *Base*
Ant
21C4 **Molokai** *I* Hawaiian
Is
61G2 **Moloma** *R*
Russian Fed
109C2 **Molong** Aust
100B3 **Molopo** *R* Botswana
98B2 **Molounddu** Cam
8D1 **Molson L** Can
71D4 **Molucca** *S* Indon
71D4 **Moluccas** *Is* Indon
101C2 **Moma** Mozam
31C3 **Mombaca** Brazil
99D3 **Mombasa** Kenya
98C2 **Mompono** Zaïre
56C2 **Mon** *I* Den
44A3 **Monach** *Is* Scot
49D3 **Monaco**
Principality, Europe
44B3 **Monadhliath** *Mts*
Scot
45C1 **Monaghan** County,
Irish Rep
45C1 **Monaghan** Irish Rep
27D3 **Mona Pass**
Caribbean S
13B2 **Monarch Mt** Can
5G4 **Monashee Mts** Can
41B3 **Monastereven**
Irish Rep
47B2 **Moncalieri** Italy
31B2 **Monção** Brazil
38L5 **Monchegorsk**
Russian Fed
56B2 **Mönchen-gladbach**
Germany
24B2 **Monclova** Mexico
7D5 **Moncton** Can
9C4 **Monctova** Mexico
50A1 **Mondego** *R* Port
52A2 **Mondovi** Italy
27H1 **Moneague** Jamaica
14C2 **Monessen** USA
18B2 **Monett** USA
52B1 **Monfalcone** Italy

Mount Holly

19D3 **Nacogdoches** USA	76D1 **Nam Dinh** Viet	97B3 **Nara** Mali	85C4 **Navlakhi** India
76A3 **Nacondam** I Indian O	101C2 **Nametil** Mozam	107D4 **Naracoorte** Aust	60D3 **Navlya** Russian Fed
24B1 **Nacozari** Mexico	74B4 **Namhae-do** I S Korea	23B1 **Naranjos** Mexico	24B2 **Navojoa** Mexico
85C4 **Nadiād** India	100A2 **Namib Desert** Namibia	87C1 **Narasarãopet** India	55B3 **Návpaktos** Greece
50B2 **Nador** Mor	100A2 **Namibe** Angola	77C4 **Narathiwat** Thai	55B3 **Návplion** Greece
90B3 **Nadūshan** Iran	100A3 **Namibia** Republic, Africa	86C2 **Narayanganj** Bang	85C4 **Navsāri** India
59C3 **Nadvornaya** Ukraine	82D3 **Namjagbarwa Feng** Mt China	87B1 **Nārāyenpet** India	94C2 **Nawá** Syria
56C1 **Naestved** Den	71D4 **Namlea** Indon	49C3 **Narbonne** France	86B2 **Nawāda** India
95B2 **Nafūrah** Libya	109C2 **Namoi** R Aust	84D2 **Narendranagar** India	84B2 **Nawah** Afghan
75A2 **Nagahama** Japan	13D1 **Nampa** Can	6C2 **Nares Str** Can	85B3 **Nawrabshah** Pak
82D3 **Naga Hills** Burma	20C2 **Nampa** USA	58C2 **Narew** R Pol	73B4 **Naxi** China
75B1 **Nagai** Japan	97B3 **Nampala** Mali	75C1 **Narita** Japan	55C3 **Náxos** I Greece
86C1 **Nāgāland** State, India	76C2 **Nam Phong** Thai	85C4 **Narmada** R India	23A1 **Nayar** Mexico
74D3 **Nagano** Japan	74B3 **Namp'o** N Korea	84D3 **Nārnaul** India	90C3 **Nay Band** Iran
74D3 **Nagaoka** Japan	101C2 **Nampula** Mozam	60E2 **Naro Fominsk** Russian Fed	91B4 **Nāy Band** Iran
86C1 **Nagaon** India	38G6 **Namsos** Nor	99D3 **Narok** Kenya	74E2 **Nayoro** Japan
87B2 **Nāgappattinam** India	76B1 **Namton** Burma	84C2 **Narowal** Pak	94B2 **Nazareth** Israel
85C4 **Nagar Parkar** Pak	86D2 **Namtu** Burma	107D4 **Narrabri** Aust	48B2 **Nazay** France
74B4 **Nagasaki** Japan	13B2 **Namu** Can	109C1 **Narran** L Aust	32C6 **Nazca** Peru
75B2 **Nagashima** Japan	101C2 **Namuno** Mozam	109C1 **Narran** R Aust	92A2 **Nazilli** Turk
75A2 **Nagato** Japan	46C1 **Namur** Belg	109C2 **Narrandera** Aust	63B2 **Nazimovo** Russian Fed
85C3 **Nāgaur** India	100A2 **Namutoni** Namibia	106A4 **Narrogin** Aust	13C2 **Nazko** R Can
87B3 **Nāgercoil** India	74B3 **Namwŏn** S Korea	109C2 **Narromine** Aust	99D2 **Nazret** Eth
85B3 **Nagha Kalat** Pak	13C3 **Nanaimo** Can	85D4 **Narsimhapur** India	91C5 **Nazwa** Oman
84D3 **Nagina** India	74B2 **Nanam** N Korea	87C1 **Narsipatnam** India	65J4 **Nazyvayevsk** Russian Fed
74D3 **Nagoya** Japan	109D1 **Nanango** Aust	6F3 **Narssalik** Greenland	98B3 **Ndalatando** Angola
85D4 **Nāgpur** India	74D3 **Nanao** Japan	6F3 **Narssaq** Greenland	98C2 **Ndélé** CAR
82D2 **Nagqu** China	75B1 **Nanatsu-jima** I Japan	6F3 **Narssarssuaq** Greenland	98B3 **Ndendé** Gabon
59B3 **Nagykanizsa** Hung	73B3 **Nanbu** China	75C1 **Narugo** Japan	98B1 **Ndjamena** Chad
59B3 **Nagykörös** Hung	73D4 **Nanchang** China	75A2 **Naruto** Japan	98B3 **Ndjolé** Gabon
69E4 **Naha** Japan	73B3 **Nanchong** China	60C2 **Narva** Russian Fed	100B2 **Ndola** Zambia
8A2 **Nahaimo** Can	49D2 **Nancy** France	38H5 **Narvik** Nor	109C1 **Neabul** Aust
84D2 **Nāhan** India	87B1 **Nānded** India	84D3 **Narwāna** India	108A1 **Neales** R Aust
4F3 **Nahanni Butte** Can	109D2 **Nandewar Range** Mts Aust	64G3 **Nar'yan Mar** Russian Fed	55B3 **Neápolis** Greece
94B2 **Nahariya** Israel	85C4 **Nandurbar** India	108B1 **Narylico** Aust	43C4 **Neath** Wales
90A3 **Nahāvand** Iran	87B1 **Nandyāl** India	65J5 **Naryn** Kirghizia	109C1 **Nebine** R Aust
46D2 **Nahe** R Germany	98B2 **Nanga Eboko** Cam	97C4 **Nasarawa** Nig	65G6 **Nebit Dag** Turkmenistan
72D2 **Nahpu** China	84C1 **Nanga Parbat** Mt Pak	103D5 **Nasca Ridge** Pacific O	8C2 **Nebraska** State, USA
72E1 **Naimen Qi** China	78C3 **Nangapinoh** Indon	16D1 **Nashua** USA	18A1 **Nebraska City** USA
7D4 **Nain** Can	78C3 **Nangatayap** Indon	19B3 **Nashville** Arkansas, USA	13C2 **Nechako** R Can
90B3 **Nā'īn** Iran	74B2 **Nangnim Sanmaek** Mts N Korea	11B3 **Nashville** Tennessee, USA	19A3 **Neches** R USA
84D3 **Naini Tai** India	86C1 **Nang Xian** China	54A1 **Našice** Croatia	34D3 **Necochea** Arg
44C3 **Nairn** Scot	67F3 **Nangzhou** China	85D4 **Nāsik** India	86C1 **Nêdong** China
99D3 **Nairobi** Kenya	87B2 **Nanjangūd** India	99D2 **Nasir** Sudan	9B3 **Needles** USA
90B3 **Najafābād** Iran	72D3 **Nanjing** China	13B1 **Nass** R Can	14A2 **Neenah** USA
74C2 **Najin** N Korea	**Nanking = Nanjing**	26B1 **Nassau** The Bahamas	5J4 **Neepawa** Can
75A2 **Nakama** Japan	75A2 **Nankoku** Japan	16C1 **Nassau** USA	46C1 **Neerpelt** Belg
74E3 **Nakaminato** Japan	73C4 **Nan Ling** Region, China	95C2 **Nasser,L** Egypt	63C2 **Neftelensk** Russian Fed
75A2 **Nakamura** Japan	76D1 **Nanliu** R China	39G7 **Nässjö** Sweden	99D2 **Negelē** Eth
75B1 **Nakano** Japan	73B5 **Nanning** China	7C4 **Nastapoka Is** Can	94B3 **Negev** Desert Israel
75A1 **Nakano-shima** I Japan	6F3 **Nanortalik** Greenland	100B3 **Nata** Botswana	60B4 **Negolu** Mt Rom
74C4 **Nakatsu** Japan	73A5 **Nanpan Jiang** R China	31D3 **Natal** Brazil	87B3 **Negombo** Sri Lanka
75B1 **Nakatsu-gawa** Japan	86A1 **Nānpāra** India	70A3 **Natal** Indon	76A2 **Negrais,C** Burma
95C3 **Nak' fa** Eritrea	73D4 **Nanping** China	101H1 **Natal** Province, S Africa	32A4 **Ne_ritos** Peru
93E2 **Nakhichevan** Azerbaijan	6A1 **Nansen Sd** Can	90B3 **Natanz** Iran	33E4 **Negro** R Amazonas, Brazil
92B4 **Nakhl** Egypt	99D3 **Nansio** Tanz	7D4 **Natashquan** Can	29C4 **Negro** R Arg
74C2 **Nakhodka** Russian Fed	48B2 **Nantes** France	7D4 **Natashquan** R Can	34D2 **Negro** R Urug
76C3 **Nakhon Pathom** Thai	13E2 **Nanton** Can	19B3 **Natchez** USA	79B4 **Negros** I Phil
76C3 **Nakhon Ratchasima** Thai	72E3 **Nantong** China	19B3 **Natchitoches** USA	54C2 **Negru Voda** Rom
77C4 **Nakhon Si Thammarat** Thai	10C2 **Nantucket** I USA	108C3 **Nathalia** Aust	90D3 **Nehbandan** Iran
12H3 **Nakina** Can	35C1 **Nanuque** Brazil	6H2 **Nathorsts Land** Region Greenland	73B4 **Neijiang** China
7B4 **Nakina** Ontario, Can	72C3 **Nanyang** China	13C1 **Nation** R Can	72B1 **Nei Monggol** Autonomous Region, China
12C3 **Naknek** USA	72D2 **Nanyang Hu** L China	21B3 **National City** USA	32B3 **Neiva** Colombia
12C3 **Naknek L** USA	99D2 **Nanyuki** Kenya	75C1 **Natori** Japan	99D2 **Nejo** Eth
4C4 **Nakrek** USA	74D3 **Naoetsu** Japan	99D3 **Natron** L Tanz	99D2 **Nek'emtē** Eth
39G8 **Nakskov** Den	85B4 **Naokot** Pak	106A4 **Naturaliste,C** Aust	60D2 **Nelidovo** Russian Fed
99D3 **Nakuru** Kenya	22A1 **Napa** USA	47D1 **Nauders** Austria	87B2 **Nellore** India
13D2 **Nakusp** Can	12B2 **Napaiskak** Can	56C2 **Nauen** Germany	69F2 **Nel'ma** Russian Fed
61F5 **Nal'chik** Russian Fed	15C2 **Napanee** Can	16C2 **Naugatuck** USA	13D3 **Nelson** Can
87B1 **Nalgonda** India	65K4 **Napas** Russian Fed	57C2 **Naumburg** Germany	111B2 **Nelson** NZ
87B1 **Nallamala Range** Mts India	6E3 **Napassoq** Greenland	94B3 **Naur** Jordan	7A4 **Nelson** R Can
95A1 **Nālūt** Libya	76D2 **Nape** Laos	105G4 **Nauru** I / Pacific O	108B3 **Nelson,C** Aust
101H1 **Namaacha** Mozam	110C1 **Napier** NZ	63C2 **Naushki** Russian Fed	12B2 **Nelson I** USA
65G6 **Namak** L Iran	**Naples = Napoli**	23B1 **Nautla** Mexico	97B3 **Néma** Maur
90C3 **Namakzar-e Shadad** Salt Flat Iran	17B2 **Naples** Florida, USA	9C3 **Navajo Res** USA	72A1 **Nemagt Uul** Mt Mongolia
65J5 **Namangan** Uzbekistan	19B3 **Naples** Texas, USA	50A2 **Navalmoral de la Mata** Spain	58C1 **Neman** R Lithuania
101C2 **Namapa** Mozam	73B5 **Napo** China	29C7 **Navarino** I Chile	54C1 **Nemira** Mt Rom
100A4 **Namaqualand** Region, S Africa	32C4 **Napo** R Peru/Ecuador	51B1 **Navarra** Province, Spain	74F2 **Nemuro** Japan
109D1 **Nambour** Aust	53B2 **Napoli** Italy	34D3 **Navarro** Arg	63E3 **Nen** R China
109D2 **Nambucca Heads** Aust	90A2 **Naqadeh** Iran	19A3 **Navasota** USA	41B3 **Nenagh** Irish Rep
77D4 **Nam Can** Viet	92C4 **Naqb Ishtar** Jordan	19A3 **Navasota** R USA	12E2 **Nenana** USA
82D2 **Nam Co** L China	75B2 **Nara** Japan	50A1 **Navia** R Spain	12E2 **Nenana** R USA
		34A2 **Navidad** Chile	43D3 **Nene** R Eng
			69E2 **Nenjiang** China
			18A2 **Neodesha** USA

99D3 **Njombe** Tanz
98B2 **Nkambé** Cam
101C2 **Nkhata Bay** Malawi
98B2 **Nkongsamba** Cam
97C3 **N'Konni** Niger
86C2 **Noakhali** Bang
12B1 **Noatak** USA
12C1 **Noatak** *R* USA
74C4 **Nobeoka** Japan
47D1 **Noce** *R* Italy
23A1 **Nochistlán** Mexico
23B2 **Nochixtlán** Mexico
19A3 **Nocona** USA
24A1 **Nogales** Sonora, Mexico
9B3 **Nogales** USA
23B2 **Nogales** Veracruz, Mexico
47D2 **Nogara** Italy
75A2 **Nogata** Japan
60E2 **Noginsk** Russian Fed
34D2 **Nogoyá** Arg
34D2 **Nogoyá** *R* Arg
84C3 **Nohar** India
75B2 **Nojima-zaki** *C* Japan
98B2 **Nola** CAR
61G2 **Nolinsk** Russian Fed
16D2 **Nomans Land** *I* USA
12A2 **Nome** USA
46D2 **Nomeny** France
72B1 **Nomgon** Mongolia
5H3 **Nonachol L** Can
76C2 **Nong Khai** Thai
101H1 **Nongoma** S Africa
12B1 **Noorvik** USA
13B3 **Nootka Sd** Can
98B3 **Noqui** Angola
7C5 **Noranda** Can
46B1 **Nord** Department, France
64D2 **Nordaustlandet** *I* Barents S
13D2 **Nordegg** Can
38F6 **Nordfjord** *Inlet* Nor
39F8 **Nordfriesische** *Is* Germany
56C2 **Nordhausen** Germany
56B2 **Nordhrein Westfalen** State, Germany
38J4 **Nordkapp** *C* Nor
6E3 **Nordre** Greenland
38H5 **Nord Stronfjället** *Mt* Sweden
1B9 **Nordvik** Russian Fed
45C2 **Nore** *R* Irish Rep
43E3 **Norfolk** County, Eng
8D2 **Norfolk** Nebraska, USA
11C3 **Norfolk** Virginia, USA
107F3 **Norfolk I** Aust
18B2 **Norfolk L** USA
105G5 **Norfolk Ridge** Pacific O
1C10 **Noril'sk** Russian Fed
18C1 **Normal** USA
19A2 **Norman** USA
48B2 **Normandie** Region, France
107D2 **Normanton** Aust
12J1 **Norman Wells** Can
4B3 **Norne** USA
15C2 **Norristown** USA
39H7 **Norrköping** Sweden
39H6 **Norrsundet** Sweden
39H7 **Norrtälje** Sweden
106B4 **Norseman** Aust
63F2 **Norsk** Russian Fed
102J2 **North** *S* N W Europe
42D2 **Northallerton** Eng
106A4 **Northam** Aust
102E3 **North American Basin** Atlantic O
106A3 **Northampton** Aust
43D3 **Northampton** County, Eng
43D3 **Northampton** Eng
15D2 **Northampton** USA
4G3 **North Arm** *B* Can
17B1 **North Augusta** USA
6D4 **North Aulatsvik** *I* Can
13F2 **North Battleford** Can

7C5 **North Bay** Can
20B2 **North Bend** USA
44C3 **North Berwick** Scot
7D5 **North,C** Can
7G4 **North C** NZ
11B3 **North Carolina** State, USA
20B1 **North Cascade Nat Pk** USA
14B1 **North Chan** Can
42B2 **North Chan** Ire/Scot
8C2 **North Dakota** State, USA
43E4 **North Downs** Eng
14C2 **North East** USA
102H2 **North East Atlantic Basin** Atlantic O
4B3 **Northeast C** USA
40B3 **Northern Ireland** UK
27L1 **Northern Range** *Mts* Trinidad
106C2 **Northern Territory** Aust
44C3 **North Esk** *R* Scot
16C1 **Northfield** Massachusetts, USA
12D2 **North Fork** *R* USA
110B1 **North I** NZ
74B3 **North Korea** Republic, S E Asia
North Land = Severnaya Zemlya
19B3 **North Little Rock** USA
1B4 **North Magnetic Pole** Can
17B2 **North Miami** USA
17B2 **North Miami Beach** USA
8C2 **North Platte** USA
8C2 **North Platte** *R* USA
27R3 **North Pt** Barbados
14B1 **North Pt** USA
40B2 **North Rona** *I* Scot
44C2 **North Ronaldsay** *I* Scot
13F2 **North Saskatchewan** *R* Can
40D2 **North Sea** N W Europe
4D3 **North Slope** Region USA
109D1 **North Stradbroke** *I* Aust
110B1 **North Taranaki Bight** *B* NZ
9C3 **North Truchas Peak** *Mt* USA
44A3 **North Uist** *I* Scot
42C2 **Northumberland** County, Eng
107E3 **Northumberland Is** Aust
7D5 **Northumberland Str** Can
20B1 **North Vancouver** Can
43E3 **North Walsham** Eng
12F2 **Northway** USA
106A3 **North West C** Aust
84C2 **North West Frontier** Province, Pak
7D4 **North West River** Can
4F3 **North West Territories** Can
42D2 **North York Moors Nat Pk** Eng
12B2 **Norton B** USA
12B2 **Norton Sd** USA
112B1 **Norvegia,C** Ant
16C2 **Norwalk** Connecticut, USA
14B2 **Norwalk** Ohio, USA
39F6 **Norway** Kingdom, Europe
5J4 **Norway House** Can
6A2 **Norwegian B** Can
102H1 **Norwegian Basin** Norewegian S
64A3 **Norwegian S** N W Europe
16C2 **Norwich** Connecticut, USA

43C3 **Norwich** Eng
16D1 **Norwood** Massachusetts, USA
14B3 **Norwood** Ohio, USA
54C2 **Nos Emine** *C* Bulg
74D2 **Noshiro** Japan
54C2 **Nos Kaliakra** *C* Bulg
44E1 **Noss** *I* Scot
91D4 **Nosträbäd** Iran
101D2 **Nosy Barren** *I* Madag
101D2 **Nosy Bé** *I* Madag
101E2 **Nosy Boraha** *I* Madag
101D3 **Nosy Varika** Madag
58B2 **Notec** *R* Pol
5G4 **Notikeuin** Can
53C3 **Noto** Italy
39F7 **Notodden** Nor
75B1 **Noto-hantō** *Pen* Japan
7E5 **Notre Dams B** Can
43D3 **Nottingham** County, Eng
43D3 **Nottingham** Eng
6C3 **Nottingham I** Can
6C3 **Nottingham Island** Can
96A2 **Nouadhibou** Maur
97A3 **Nouakchott** Maur
107F3 **Nouméa** Nouvelle Calédonie
97B3 **Nouna** Burkina
107F3 **Nouvelle Calédonie** *I* S W Pacific O
98B3 **Nova Caipemba** Angola
35A2 **Nova Esperança** Brazil
35C2 **Nova Friburgo** Brazil
100A2 **Nova Gaia** Angola
35B2 **Nova Granada** Brazil
35B2 **Nova Horizonte** Brazil
35C1 **Nova Lima** Brazil
Nova Lisboa = Huambo
35A2 **Nova Londrina** Brazil
101C3 **Nova Mambone** Mozam
47C2 **Novara** Italy
7D5 **Nova Scotia** Province, Can
22A1 **Novato** USA
35C1 **Nova Venécia** Brazil
60D4 **Novaya Kakhovka** Ukraine
64G2 **Novaya Zemlya** *I* Barents S
54C2 **Nova Zagora** Bulg
31C2 **Nove Russas** Brazil
54A1 **Nové Zámky** Slovakia
60D2 **Novgorod** Russian Fed
47C2 **Novi Ligure** Italy
54C2 **Novi Pazar** Bulg
54B2 **Novi Pazar** Serbia, Yugos
54A1 **Novi Sad** Serbia, Yugos
61J3 **Novoalekseyevka** Kazakhstan
61F3 **Novoanninskiy** Russian Fed
61E4 **Novocherkassk** Russian Fed
60C3 **Novograd Volynskiy** Ukraine
58D2 **Novogrudok** Russian Fed
30F4 **Novo Hamburgo** Brazil
65H5 **Novokazalinsk** Kazakhstan
65K4 **Novokuznetsk** Russian Fed
112B12 **Novolazarevskaya** *Base* Ant
52C1 **Novo Mesto** Slovenia
60E3 **Novomoskovsk** Russian Fed

60F5 **Nnvorossiysk** Russian Fed
65K4 **Novosibirsk** Russian Fed
1B8 **Novosibirskiye Ostrova** *I*
61J3 **Novotroitsk** Russian Fed
61G3 **Novo Uzensk** Russian Fed
59C2 **Novovolynsk** Ukraine
61G2 **Novo Vyatsk** Russian Fed
60D3 **Novozybkov** Russian Fed
58C2 **Novy Dwór Mazowiecki** Pol
61K2 **Novyy Lyalya** Russian Fed
61H5 **Novyy Port** Russian Fed
61H5 **Novyy Uzen** Kazakhstan
58B2 **Nowa Sól** Pol
18A2 **Nowata** USA
Nowgong = Nagaon
12D2 **Nowitna** *R* USA
109D2 **Nowra** Aust
90B2 **Now Shahr** Iran
84C2 **Nowshera** Pak
59C3 **Nowy Sącz** Pol
12H3 **Noyes I** USA
46B2 **Noyon** France
97B4 **Nsawam** Ghana
99D1 **Nuba** *Mts* Sudan
81B3 **Nubian Desert** Sudan
34A3 **Nuble** *R* Chile
9D4 **Nueces** *R* USA
5J3 **Nueltin L** Can
26A2 **Nueva Gerona** Cuba
34A3 **Nueva Imperial** Chile
9C4 **Nueva Laredo** Mexico
34D2 **Nueva Palmira** Urug
24B2 **Nueva Rosita** Mexico
26B2 **Nuevitas** Cuba
24B1 **Nuevo Casas Grandes** Mexico
24C2 **Nuevo Laredo** Mexico
99E2 **Nugaal** Region, Somalia
6E2 **Nûgâtsiaq** Greenland
6E2 **Nugssuag** *Pen* Greenland
6E2 **Nûgussaq** *I* Greenland
108A2 **Nukey Bluff** *Mt* Aust
93D3 **Nukhayb** Iraq
65G5 **Nukus** Uzbekistan
12C2 **Nulato** USA
106B4 **Nullarbor Plain** Aust
97D4 **Numan** Nig
75B1 **Numata** Japan
98C2 **Numatinna** *R* Sudan
74D3 **Numazu** Japan
71E4 **Numfoor** *I* Indon
108C3 **Numurkah** Aust
12B2 **Nunapitchuk** USA
84D2 **Nunkun** *Mt* India
53A2 **Nuoro** Sardegna
91B3 **Nurābād** Iran
47C2 **Nure** *R* Italy
108A2 **Nuriootpa** Aust
84C1 **Nuristan** Upland Afghan
61H3 **Nurlat** Russian Fed
38K6 **Nurmes** Fin
57C3 **Nürnberg** Germany
108C2 **Nurri,Mt** Aust
93D2 **Nusaybin** Turk
12C3 **Nushagak** *R* USA
12C3 **Nushagak B** USA
12C3 **Nushagak Pen** USA
84B3 **Nushki** Pak
7D4 **Nutak** Can
12F2 **Nutzotin Mts** USA
Nuuk = Godthåb
86A1 **Nuwakot** Nepal
87C3 **Nuwara-Eliya** Sri Lanka
6C3 **Nuyukjuak** Can

Nyack

59B3 **Opava** Czech Republic
17A1 **Opelika** USA
19B3 **Opelousas** USA
12C2 **Ophir** USA
58D1 **Opochka** Russian Fed
59B2 **Opole** Pol
Oporto = Porto
110C1 **Opotiki** NZ
17A1 **Opp** USA
38F6 **Oppdal** Nor
110B1 **Opunake** NZ
54B1 **Oradea** Rom
38B2 **Oraefajökull** *Mts* Iceland
85D3 **Orai** India
96B1 **Oran** Alg
30D3 **Orán** Arg
109C2 **Orange** Aust
22D4 **Orange** California, USA
49C3 **Orange** France
19B3 **Orange** Texas, USA
100A3 **Orange** *R* S Africa
17B1 **Orangeburg** USA
101G1 **Orange Free State** Province, S Africa
17B1 **Orange Park** USA
14B2 **Orangeville** Can
56C2 **Oranienburg** Germany
79C3 **Oras** Phil
54B1 **Orăştie** Rom
54B1 **Oraviţa** Rom
52B2 **Orbetello** Italy
109C3 **Orbost** Aust
46B1 **Orchies** France
47B2 **Orco** *R* Italy
106B2 **Ord** *R* Aust
106B2 **Ord,Mt** Aust
93C1 **Ordu** Turk
39H7 **Örebro** Sweden
8A2 **Oregon** State, USA
14B2 **Oregon** USA
20B1 **Oregon City** USA
39H6 **Oregrund** Sweden
60E2 **Orekhovo Zuyevo** Russian Fed
60E3 **Orel** Russian Fed
61H3 **Orenburg** Russian Fed
34D3 **Orense** Arg
50A1 **Orense** Spain
56C1 **Oresund** *Str* Den/Sweden
111A3 **Oreti** *R* NZ
55C3 **Orhaneli** *R* Turk
68C2 **Orhon Gol** *R* Mongolia
23B2 **Oriental** Mexico
108B1 **Orientos** Aust
51B2 **Orihuela** Spain
15C2 **Orillia** Can
33E2 **Orinoco** *R* Ven
86A2 **Orissa** State, India
53A3 **Oristano** Sardegna
38K6 **Orivesi** *L* Fin
33F4 **Oriximina** Brazil
23B2 **Orizaba** Mexico
35B1 **Orizona** Brazil
44C2 **Orkney** *I* Scot
35B2 **Orlândia** Brazil
17B2 **Orlando** USA
48C2 **Orléanais** *Region* France
48C2 **Orléans** France
63B2 **Orlik** Russian Fed
82A3 **Ormara** Pak
79B3 **Ormoc** Phil
17B2 **Ormond Beach** USA
46C2 **Ornain** *R* France
47B1 **Ornans** France
48B2 **Orne** *R* France
38H6 **Ornsköldsvik** Sweden
32C3 **Orocué** Colombia
94B3 **Oron** Israel
Orontes = 'Āşī
79B4 **Oroquieta** Phil
59C3 **Orosháza** Hung
21A2 **Oroville** California, USA

20C1 **Oroville** Washington, USA
47B1 **Orsières** Switz
65G4 **Orsk** Russian Fed
38F6 **Ørsta** Nor
48B3 **Orthez** France
50A1 **Ortigueira** Spain
47D1 **Ortles** *Mts* Italy
27L1 **Ortoire** *R* Trinidad
93E2 **Orūmīyeh** Iran
30C2 **Oruro** Bol
61J2 **Osa** Russian Fed
18B2 **Osage** *R* USA
75B1 **Osaka** Japan
25D4 **Osa,Pen de** Costa Rica
18C2 **Osceola** Arkansas, USA
18B1 **Osceola** Iowa, USA
20C2 **Osgood Mts** USA
15C2 **Oshawa** Can
75B2 **Ō-shima** *I* Japan
10B2 **Oshkosh** USA
97C4 **Oshogbo** Nig
7B5 **Oshosh** USA
98B3 **Oshwe** Zaïre
54A1 **Osijek** Croatia
65K5 **Osinniki** Russian Fed
58D2 **Osipovichi** Belorussia
18B1 **Oskaloosa** USA
60A2 **Oskarshamn** Sweden
39G7 **Oslo** Nor
92C2 **Osmaniye** Turk
56B2 **Osnabrück** Germany
30F4 **Osório** Brazil
29B4 **Osorno** Chile
50B1 **Osorno** Spain
20C1 **Osoyoos** Can
13C1 **Ospika** *R* Can
107D5 **Ossa,Mt** Aust
16C2 **Ossining** USA
60D2 **Ostashkov** Russian Fed
Ostend = Oostende
38G6 **Østerdalen** *V* Nor
38G6 **Östersund** Sweden
56B2 **Ostfriesische Inseln** *Is* Germany
39H6 **Östhammär** Sweden
53B2 **Ostia** Italy
47D2 **Ostiglia** Italy
59B3 **Ostrava** Czech Republic
58B2 **Ostróda** Pol
58B2 **Ostroleka** Pol
60C2 **Ostrov** Russian Fed
64J2 **Ostrov Belyy** *I* Russian Fed
64H1 **Ostrov Greem Bell** *I* Barents S
64F3 **Ostrov Kolguyev** *I* Russian Fed
74F2 **Ostrov Kunashir** *I* Russian Fed
64F2 **Ostrov Mechdusharskiy** *I* Barents S
90B2 **Ostrov Ogurchinskiy** *I* Turkmenistan
64G1 **Ostrov Rudol'fa** *I* Barents S
64G2 **Ostrov Vaygach** *I* Russian Fed
1B7 **Ostrov Vrangelya** *I* Russian Fed
58B2 **Ostrów Wlkp.** Pol
59C2 **Ostrowiec** Pol
58C2 **Ostrów Mazowiecka** Pol
50A2 **Osuna** Spain
15C2 **Oswega** USA
15C2 **Oswego** USA
43C3 **Oswestry** Eng
59B2 **Oświęcim** Pol
75B1 **Ota** Japan
111B3 **Otago Pen** NZ
110C2 **Otaki** NZ
74E2 **Otaru** Japan
32B3 **Otavalo** Ecuador
100A2 **Otavi** Namibia
75C1 **Otawara** Japan
20C1 **Othello** USA
55B3 **Óthris** *Mt* Greece

16C1 **Otis** Massachusetts, USA
16B2 **Otisville** USA
100A3 **Otjiwarongo** Namibia
72B2 **Otog Qi** China
110C1 **Otorohanga** NZ
55A2 **Otranto** Italy
55A2 **Otranto,Str of** *Chan* Italy/Alb
14A2 **Otsego** USA
75B1 **Otsu** Japan
39F6 **Otta** Nor
39F7 **Otta** *R* Nor
15C1 **Ottawa** Can
18A2 **Ottawa** Kansas, USA
15C1 **Ottawa** *R* Can
7B4 **Ottawa Is** Can
7B4 **Otter Rapids** Can
6B1 **Otto Fjord** Can
101G1 **Ottosdal** S Africa
18B1 **Ottumwa** USA
46D2 **Ottweiler** Germany
97C4 **Oturkpo** Nig
32B5 **Otusco** Peru
108B3 **Otway,C** Aust
58C2 **Otwock** Pol
47D1 **Ötz** Austria
47D1 **Ötzal** *Mts* Austria
76C1 **Ou** *R* Laos
19B3 **Ouachita** *R* USA
19B3 **Ouachita,L** USA
19B3 **Ouachita Mts** USA
96A2 **Ouadane** Maur
98C2 **Ouadda** CAR
98C1 **Ouaddaï** *Desert Region* Chad
97B3 **Ouagadougou** Burkina
97B3 **Ouahigouya** Burkina
98C2 **Ouaka** CAR
97C3 **Oualam** Niger
96C2 **Ouallen** Alg
98C2 **Ouanda Djallé** CAR
96A2 **Ouarane** *Region,* Maur
96C1 **Ouargla** Alg
98C2 **Ouarra** *R* CAR
96B1 **Ouarzazate** Mor
51C2 **Ouassel** *R* Alg
98B2 **Oubangui** *R* Congo
46B1 **Oudenaarde** Belg
100B4 **Oudtshoorn** S Africa
51B2 **Oued Tlélat** Alg
96B1 **Oued Zem** Mor
98B2 **Ouesso** Congo
96B1 **Ouezzane** Mor
98B2 **Ouham** *R* Chad
97C4 **Ouidah** Benin
96B1 **Oujda** Mor
38J6 **Oulainen** Fin
38K6 **Oulu** *R* Fin
38K6 **Oulujärvi** *L* Fin
95B3 **Oum Chalouba** Chad
98B1 **Oum Hadjer** Chad
95B3 **Oum Haouach** *Watercourse* Chad
38K5 **Ounas** *R* Fin
95B3 **Ounianga Kébir** Chad
46D1 **Our** *R* Germany
46B2 **Ourcq** *R* France
Ourense = Orense
31C3 **Ouricurí** Brazil
35B2 **Ourinhos** Brazil
35C2 **Ouro Prêto** Brazil
46C1 **Ourthe** *R* Belg
42D2 **Ouse** *R* Eng
43E3 **Ouse** *R* Eng
40B2 **Outer Hebrides** *Is* Scot
22C4 **Outer Santa Barbara** *Chan* USA
100A3 **Outjo** Namibia
38K6 **Outokumpu** Fin
108B3 **Ouyen** Aust
47C2 **Ovada** Italy
34A2 **Ovalle** Chile
100A2 **Ovamboland** *Region,* Namibia
61H5 **Ova Tyuleni** *Is* Kazakhstan
38J5 **Övertorneå** Sweden

50A1 **Oviedo** Spain
60C3 **Ovruch** Ukraine
63E2 **Ovsyanka** Russian Fed
111A3 **Owaka** NZ
75B2 **Owase** Japan
11B3 **Owensboro** USA
21B2 **Owens L** USA
14B2 **Owen Sound** Can
107D1 **Owen Stanley Range** *Mts* PNG
97C4 **Owerri** Nig
97C4 **Owo** Nig
14B2 **Owosso** USA
20C2 **Owyhee** *R* USA
20C2 **Owyhee Mts** USA
32B6 **Oxapampa** Peru
39H7 **Oxelösund** Sweden
43D4 **Oxford** County, Eng
43D4 **Oxford** Eng
16D1 **Oxford** Massachusetts, USA
19C3 **Oxford** Mississippi, USA
45B1 **Ox Mts** Irish Rep
22C3 **Oxnard** USA
74D3 **Oyama** Japan
13E2 **Oyen** Can
98B2 **Oyem** Gabon
44B3 **Oykel** *R* Scot
39F6 **Øyre** Nor
109C4 **Oyster B** Aust
79B4 **Ozamiz** Phil
17A1 **Ozark** USA
18B2 **Ozark Plat** USA
18B2 **Ozarks,L of the** USA
59C3 **Özd** Hung
65K5 **Ozero Alakol** *L* Kazakhstan/Russian Fed
65J5 **Ozero Balkhash** *L* Kazakhstan
63C2 **Ozero Baykal** *L* Kazakhstan
65J4 **Ozero Chany** *L* Russian Fed
69F1 **Ozero Chukchagirskoye** Russian Fed
69F1 **Ozero Evoron** Russian Fed
Ozero Chudskoye = Peipus,L
60D2 **Ozero Il'men** *L* Russian Fed
38L5 **Ozero Imandra** *L* Russian Fed
82B1 **Ozero Issyk Kul'** *L* Kirghizia
69F2 **Ozero Khanka** *L* China/Russian Fed
38L5 **Ozero Kovdozero** *L* Russian Fed
38L5 **Ozero Kuyto** *L* Russian Fed
38L5 **Ozero Pyaozero** *L* Russian Fed
65H4 **Ozero Tengiz** *L* Kazakhstan
38L5 **Ozero Topozero** *L* Russian Fed
65K5 **Ozero Zaysan** *L* Kazakhstan
23B1 **Ozuluama** Mexico

P

100A4 **Paarl** S Africa
44A3 **Pabbay** *I* Scot
58B2 **Pabianice** Pol
86B2 **Pabna** Bang
58D2 **Pabrade** Lithuania
32B5 **Pacasmayo** Peru
23B1 **Pachuca** Mexico
105K6 **Pacific-Antarctic Ridge** Pacific O
22B2 **Pacific Grove** USA
78C4 **Pacitan** Indon
35C1 **Pacuí** *R* Brazil
70B4 **Padang** Indon
56B2 **Paderborn** Germany
5J3 **Padlei** Can
86C2 **Padma** *R* Bang
47D2 **Padova** Italy
9D4 **Padre I** USA

Padstow

34C3 **Quemuquemú** Arg
13C2 **Quensel L** Can
34D3 **Quequén** Arg
34D3 **Quequén** *R* Arg
23A1 **Querétaro** Mexico
23A1 **Queretaro** *State* Mexico
13C2 **Quesnel** Can
84B2 **Quetta** Pak
25C3 **Quezaltenango** Guatemala
79B3 **Quezon City** Phil
100A2 **Quibala** Angola
98B3 **Quibaxe** Angola
32B2 **Quibdó** Colombia
48B2 **Quiberon** France
98B3 **Quicama Nat Pk** Angola
73A4 **Quijing** China
34A2 **Quilima** Chile
34C2 **Quilino** Arg
32C6 **Quillabamba** Peru
30C2 **Quillacollo** Bol
48C3 **Quillan** France
5H4 **Quill L** Can
5H4 **Quill Lakes** Can
34A2 **Quillota** Chile
87B3 **Quilon** India
108B1 **Quilpie** Aust
34A2 **Quilpué** Chile
98B3 **Quimbele** Angola
48B2 **Quimper** France
48B2 **Quimperlé** France
21A2 **Quincy** California, USA
10A3 **Quincy** Illinois, USA
16D1 **Quincy** Massachusetts, USA
34B2 **Quines** Arg
12B3 **Quinhagak** USA
76D3 **Qui Nhon** Viet
50B2 **Quintanar de la Orden** Spain
34A2 **Quintero** Chile
34C2 **Quinto** *R* Arg
34A3 **Quirihue** Chile
100A2 **Quirima** Angola
109D2 **Quirindi** Aust
101D2 **Quissanga** Mozam
101C3 **Quissico** Mozam
32B4 **Quito** Ecuador
31D2 **Quixadá** Brazil
108A2 **Quorn** Aust
4G3 **Qurlurtuuk** Can
95C2 **Quseir** Egypt
6E3 **Qutdligssat** Greenland
Quthing = Moyeni
73B3 **Qu Xian** Sichuan, China
73D4 **Qu Xian** Zhejiang, China
76D2 **Quynh Luu** Viet
72C2 **Quzhou** China
86C1 **Qüzü** China

R

38J6 **Raahe** Fin
44A3 **Raasay** *I* Scot
44A3 **Raasay,Sound of Chan** Scot
99F1 **Raas Caseyr** *C* Somalia
52B2 **Rab** *I* Croatia
78D4 **Raba** Indon
59B3 **Rába** *R* Hung
96B1 **Rabat** Mor
94B3 **Rabba** Jordan
80B3 **Rabigh** S Arabia
47B2 **Racconigi** Italy
7E5 **Race,C** Can
94B2 **Rachaya** Leb
57C3 **Rachel** *Mt* Germany
76D3 **Rach Gia** Viet
14A2 **Racine** USA
59D3 **Rădăuţi** Rom
85C4 **Radhanpur** India
27L1 **Radix,Pt** Trinidad
58C2 **Radom** Pol
59B2 **Radomsko** Pol
58C1 **Radviliškis** Lithuania
4G3 **Rae** Can
86A1 **Rãe Bareli** India
6B3 **Rae Isthmus** Can

4G3 **Rae L** Can
110C1 **Raetihi** NZ
34C2 **Rafaela** Arg
94B3 **Rafah** Egypt
98C2 **Rafai** CAR
93D3 **Rafhã Al Jumaymah** S Arabia
91C3 **Rafsanjãn** Iran
98C2 **Raga** Sudan
27R3 **Ragged Pt** Barbados
53B3 **Ragusa** Italy
99D1 **Rahad** *R* Sudan
84C3 **Rahimyar Khan** Pak
90B3 **Rãhjerd** Iran
34D2 **Raíces** Arg
87B1 **Rãichur** India
86A2 **Raigarh** India
108B3 **Rainbow** Aust
17A1 **Rainbow City** USA
20B1 **Rainier** USA
20B1 **Rainier,Mt** USA
10A2 **Rainy L** Can
12D2 **Rainy P** USA
10A2 **Rainy River** Can
86A2 **Raipur** India
87C1 **Rãjahmundry** India
78C2 **Rajang** *R* Malay
84C2 **Rajanpur** Pak
87B3 **Rãjapãlaiyam** India
85C3 **Rãjasthan** State, India
84D3 **Rãjgarh** India
85D4 **Rãjgarh** State, India
85C4 **Rãjkot** India
86B2 **Rãjmahãl Hills** India
86A2 **Raj Nãndgaon** India
85C4 **Rãjpipla** India
86B2 **Rajshahi** Bang
85D4 **Rajur** India
111B2 **Rakaia** *R* NZ
78B4 **Rakata** *I* Indon
82C3 **Raka Zangbo** *R* China
59C3 **Rakhov** Ukraine
100B3 **Rakops** Botswana
58D2 **Rakov** Belorussia
11C3 **Raleigh** USA
7A5 **Ralny L** Can
94B2 **Rama** Israel
94B3 **Ramallah** Israel
87B3 **Rãmanãthapuram** India
69G3 **Ramapo Deep** Pacific O
94B2 **Ramat Gan** Israel
46A2 **Rambouillet** France
86B2 **Rãmgarh** Bihar, India
85C3 **Rãmgarh** Rajasthan, India
90A3 **Rãmhormoz** Iran
94B3 **Ramla** Israel
91C5 **Ramlat Al Wahibah** Region, Oman
21B3 **Ramona** USA
84D3 **Rãmpur** India
85D4 **Rãmpura** India
90B2 **Rãmsar** Iran
42B2 **Ramsey** Eng
16B2 **Ramsey** USA
43B4 **Ramsey I** Wales
43E4 **Ramsgate** Eng
94C2 **Ramtha** Jordan
71F4 **Ramu** *R* PNG
34A2 **Rancagua** Chile
86B2 **Rãnchi** India
86A2 **Rãnchi Plat** India
101G1 **Randburg** S Africa
39G7 **Randers** Den
101G1 **Randfontein** S Africa
15D2 **Randolph** Vermont, USA
111B3 **Ranfurly** NZ
86C2 **Rangamati** Bang
111B2 **Rangiora** NZ
110C1 **Rangitaiki** *R* NZ
111B2 **Rangitate** *R* NZ
110C1 **Rangitikei** *R* NZ
Rangoon = Yangon
86B1 **Rangpur** India
87B2 **Rãnibennur** India
8A2 **Ranier,Mt** *Mt* USA
86B2 **Rãniganj** India
109C2 **Rankins Springs** Aust
6A3 **Ranklin Inlet** Can

85B4 **Rann of Kachchh** *Flood Area* India
77B4 **Ranong** Thai
70A3 **Rantauparapat** Indon
18C1 **Rantoul** USA
49D3 **Rapallo** Italy
34A2 **Rapel** *R* Chile
6D3 **Raper,C** Can
8C2 **Rapid City** USA
14A1 **Rapid River** USA
15C3 **Rappahannock** *R* USA
47C1 **Rapperswil** Switz
16B2 **Raritan B** USA
95C2 **Ras Abu Shagara** *C* Sudan
93D2 **Ra's al 'Ayn** Syria
91C5 **Ra's al Hadd** *C* Oman
91C4 **Ras al Kaimah** UAE
91C4 **Ras-al-Kuh** *C* Iran
81D4 **Ra's al Madrakah** *C* Oman
91A4 **Ra's az Zawr** *C* S Arabia
95C2 **Rãs Bãnas** *C* Egypt
94A3 **Ras Burũn** *C* Egypt
99D1 **Ras Dashan** *Mt* Eth
90A3 **Ra's-e-Barkan** *Pt* Iran
92A3 **Rãs el Kenâyis** *Pt* Egypt
81D4 **Ra's Fartak** *C* Yemen
95C2 **Rãs Ghârib** Egypt
99D1 **Rashad** Sudan
94B3 **Rashãdïya** Jordan
92B3 **Rashid** Egypt
90A2 **Rasht** Iran
91C5 **Ra's Jibish** *C* Oman
99E1 **Ras Khanzira** *C* Somalia
84B3 **Ras Koh** *Mt* Pak
95C2 **Rãs Muhammad** *C* Egypt
96A2 **Ras Nouadhibou** *C* Maur
69H2 **Rasshua** *I* Russian Fed
61F3 **Rasskazovo** Russian Fed
91A4 **Ra's Tanãqib** *C* S Arabia
91B4 **Ra's Tannũrah** S Arabia
57B3 **Rastatt** Germany
Ras Uarc = Cabo Tres Forcas
99F1 **Ras Xaafuun** *C* Somalia
84C3 **Ratangarh** India
76B3 **Rat Buri** Thai
85D3 **Rath** India
56C2 **Rathenow** Germany
45B2 **Rathkeale** Irish Rep
45C1 **Rathlin** *I* N Ire
45B2 **Rãth Luirc** Irish Rep
85D4 **Ratlãm** India
87A1 **Ratnãgiri** India
87C3 **Ratnapura** Sri Lanka
58C2 **Ratno** Ukraine
47D1 **Rattenberg** Austria
39H6 **Rättvik** Sweden
12H3 **Ratz,Mt** Can
34D3 **Rauch** Arg
110C1 **Raukumara Range** *Mts* NZ
35C2 **Raul Soares** Brazil
39J6 **Rauma** Fin
86A2 **Raurkela** India
90A3 **Ravãnsar** Iran
90C3 **Rãvar** Iran
59C2 **Rava Russkaya** Ukraine
16C1 **Ravena** USA
52B2 **Ravenna** Italy
57B3 **Ravensburg** Germany
107D2 **Ravenshoe** Aust
42E2 **Ravenspurn** *Oilfield* N Sea
84C2 **Ravi** *R* Pak
84C2 **Rawalpindi** Pak
93D2 **Rawãndiz** Iraq
58B2 **Rawicz** Pol
106B4 **Rawlinna** Aust

8C2 **Rawlins** USA
29C4 **Rawson** Arg
78C3 **Raya** *Mt* Indon
87B2 **Rãyadurg** India
94C2 **Rayak** Leb
7E5 **Ray,C** Can
91C4 **Rãyen** Iran
22C2 **Raymond** California, USA
20B1 **Raymond** Washington, USA
109D2 **Raymond Terrace** Aust
12D1 **Ray Mts** USA
23B1 **Rayon** Mexico
90A2 **Razan** Iran
54C2 **Razgrad** Bulg
54C2 **Razim** *L* Rom
43D4 **Reading** Eng
16B2 **Reading** USA
4G3 **Read Island** Can
16C1 **Readsboro** USA
34B2 **Real de Padre** Arg
34C3 **Realicó** Arg
95B2 **Rebiana** *Well* Libya
95B2 **Rebiana Sand Sea** Libya
38L6 **Reboly** Russian Fed
106B4 **Recherche,Arch of the** *Is* Aust
31E3 **Recife** Brazil
107F2 **Récifs D'Entrecasteaux** Nouvelle Calédonie
46D1 **Recklinghausen** Germany
30E4 **Reconquista** Arg
19B3 **Red** *R* USA
77C4 **Redang** *I* Malay
16B2 **Red Bank** New Jersey, USA
21A1 **Red Bluff** USA
42D2 **Redcar** Eng
13E2 **Redcliff** Can
109D1 **Redcliffe** Aust
108B2 **Red Cliffs** Aust
13E2 **Red Deer** Can
13E2 **Red Deer** *R* Can
20B2 **Redding** USA
10A2 **Red L** USA
7A4 **Red Lake** Can
22D3 **Redlands** USA
16A3 **Red Lion** USA
20B2 **Redmond** USA
18A1 **Red Oak** USA
48B2 **Redon** France
22C4 **Redondo Beach** USA
12D2 **Redoubt V** USA
73B5 **Red River Delta** Vietnam
80B3 **Red Sea** Africa/ Arabian Pen
13E2 **Redwater** Can
22A2 **Redwood City** USA
14A2 **Reed City** USA
22C2 **Reedley** USA
20B2 **Reedsport** USA
111B2 **Reefton** NZ
93C2 **Refahiye** Turk
35D1 **Regência** Brazil
57C3 **Regensburg** Germany
96C2 **Reggane** Alg
53C3 **Reggio di Calabria** Italy
47D2 **Reggio Nell'Emilia** Italy
54B1 **Reghin** Rom
5H4 **Regina** Can
100A3 **Rehoboth** Namibia
15C3 **Rehoboth Beach** USA
94B3 **Rehovot** Israel
32D1 **Reicito** Ven
43D4 **Reigate** Eng
46C2 **Reims** France
5H4 **Reindeer** *R* Can
50B1 **Reinosa** Spain
16A3 **Reisterstown** USA
101G1 **Reitz** S Africa
4H3 **Reliance** Can
108A2 **Remarkable,Mt** Aust
78C4 **Rembang** Indon
91C4 **Remeshk** Iran

46D1 **Remscheid** Germany
18C2 **Rend,L** USA
56B2 **Rendsburg** Germany
15C1 **Renfrew** Can
78A3 **Rengat** Indon
34A2 **Rengo** Chile
59D3 **Reni** Ukraine
99D1 **Renk** Sudan
6H2 **Renland** *Pen* Greenland
108B2 **Renmark** Aust
107F2 **Rennell** *I* Solomon Is
48B2 **Rennes** France
21B2 **Reno** USA
47D2 **Reno** *R* Italy
15C2 **Renovo** USA
16C1 **Rensselaer** USA
20B1 **Renton** USA
70D4 **Reo** Indon
35B2 **Represa de Furnas** *Dam* Brazil
30E3 **Represa Ilha Grande** *Dam* Brazil
30E3 **Represa Itaipu** *Dam* Brazil
35A2 **Represa Porto Primavera** *Dam* Brazil
35B1 **Represa Três Marias** *Dam* Brazil
20C1 **Republic** USA
41B3 **Republic of Ireland** NW Europe
6B3 **Repulse Bay** Can
15C1 **Réservoir Baskatong** *Res* Can
10C1 **Réservoir de la Grande 2** *Res* Can
10C1 **Réservoir de la Grande 3** *Res* Can
7C4 **Réservoir de la Grande 4** *Res* Can
7C5 **Réservoir Cabonga** *Res* Can
7D4 **Réservoir Caniapiscau** *Res* Can
7C5 **Réservoir Gouin** *Res* Can
10D1 **Réservoir Manicouagan** *Res* Can
90B2 **Reshteh-ye Alborz** *Mts* Iran
72A2 **Reshui** China
30E4 **Resistencia** Arg
54B1 **Resita** Rom
6A2 **Resolute** Can
111A3 **Resolution I** NZ
6D3 **Resolution Island** Can
101H1 **Ressano Garcia** Mozam
34B2 **Retamito** Arg
46C2 **Rethel** France
55B3 **Réthimnon** Greece
89K10 **Reunion** *I* Indian O
51C1 **Reus** Spain
47C1 **Reuss** *R* Switz
47D1 **Reutte** Austria
61K3 **Revda** Russian Fed
13D2 **Revelstoke** Can
24A3 **Revillagigedo** *Is* Mexico
12H3 **Revillagigedo I** USA
46C2 **Revin** France
94B3 **Revivim** Israel
86A2 **Rewa** India
84D3 **Rewari** India
8B2 **Rexburg** USA
38A2 **Reykjavik** Iceland
24C2 **Reynosa** Mexico
48B2 **Rezé** France
58D1 **Rezekne** Latvia
61K2 **Rezh** Russian Fed
47C1 **Rhätikon** *Mts* Austria/Switz
94B1 **Rhazīr** Republic, Leb
56B2 **Rhein** *R* W Europe
56B2 **Rheine** Germany
47B1 **Rheinfelden** Switz
49D2 **Rheinland Pfalz** Region, Germany
47C1 **Rheinwaldhorn** *Mt* Switz
Rhine = Rhein
16C2 **Rhinebeck** USA
10B2 **Rhinelander** USA
47C2 **Rho** Italy
15D2 **Rhode Island** State, USA
16D2 **Rhode Island Sd** USA
Rhodes = Ródhos
49C3 **Rhône** *R* France
43C3 **Rhyl** Wales
31D4 **Riachão do Jacuipe** Brazil
50A1 **Ria de Arosa** *B* Spain
50A1 **Ria de Betanzos** *B* Spain
50A1 **Ria de Corcubion** *B* Spain
50A1 **Ria de Lage** *B* Spain
50A1 **Ria de Sta Marta** *B* Spain
50A1 **Ria de Vigo** *B* Spain
84C2 **Riāsi** Pak
50A1 **Ribadeo** Spain
35A2 **Ribas do Rio Pardo** Brazil
101C2 **Ribauè** Mozam
42C3 **Ribble** *R* Eng
35B2 **Ribeira** Brazil
35B2 **Ribeirão Prêto** Brazil
32D6 **Riberalta** Bol
15C2 **Rice L** Can
10A2 **Rice Lake** USA
101H1 **Richard's Bay** S Africa
19A3 **Richardson** USA
12G1 **Richardson Mts** Can
8B3 **Richfield** USA
20C1 **Richland** USA
22A2 **Richmond** California, USA
101H1 **Richmond** Natal, S Africa
109D2 **Richmond** New South Wales, Aust
111B2 **Richmond** NZ
107D3 **Richmond** Queensland, Aust
10C3 **Richmond** Virginia, USA
111B2 **Richmond Range** *Mts* NZ
15C2 **Rideau,L** Can
17B1 **Ridgeland** USA
15C2 **Ridgway** USA
27D4 **Riecito** Ven
47D1 **Rienza** *R* Italy
57C2 **Riesa** Germany
29B6 **Riesco** *I* Chile
101F1 **Riet** *R* S Africa
52B2 **Rieti** Italy
50B2 **Rif** *Mts* Mor
58C1 **Riga** Latvia
60B2 **Riga,G of** Estonia/Latvia
91C4 **Rigān** Iran
20C1 **Riggins** USA
7E4 **Rigolet** Can
39J6 **Riihimaki** Fin
52B1 **Rijeka** Croatia
13E2 **Rimbey** Can
39H7 **Rimbo** Sweden
52B2 **Rimini** Italy
54C1 **Rîmnicu Sărat** Rom
54B1 **Rîmnicu Vîlcea** Rom
10D2 **Rimouski** Can
23A1 **Rincón de Romos** Mexico
39F7 **Ringkøbing** Den
98A2 **Rio Benito** Eq Guinea
32D5 **Rio Branco** Brazil
24B1 **Rio Bravo del Norte** *R* Mexico/USA
32C1 **Riochacha** Colombia
35B2 **Rio Claro** Brazil
27L1 **Rio Claro** Trinidad
34C3 **Rio Colorado** Arg
34C2 **Rio Cuarto** Arg
31D4 **Rio de Jacuipe** Brazil
35C2 **Rio de Janeiro** Brazil
35C2 **Rio de Janeiro** State, Brazil
29E3 **Rio de la Plata** *Est* Arg/Urug
29C6 **Rio Gallegos** Arg
29C6 **Rio Grande** Arg
30F5 **Rio Grande** Brazil
26A4 **Rio Grande** Nic
25D3 **Rio Grande** *R* Nic
24B2 **Rio Grande** *R* Mexico/USA
23A1 **Rio Grande de Santiago** Mexico
31D3 **Rio Grande do Norte** State, Brazil
30F4 **Rio Grande do Sul** State, Brazil
103G6 **Rio Grande Rise** Atlantic O
26C4 **Riohacha** Colombia
49C2 **Riom** France
32B4 **Riombamba** Ecuador
30C2 **Rio Mulatos** Bol
29C3 **Río Negro** State, Arg
30F4 **Rio Pardo** Brazil
34C2 **Rio Tercero** Arg
33E6 **Rio Theodore Roosevelt** *R* Brazil
29B6 **Rio Turbio** Arg
35A1 **Rio Verde** Brazil
23A1 **Rio Verde** Mexico
14B3 **Ripley** Ohio, USA
14B3 **Ripley** West Virginia, USA
42D2 **Ripon** Eng
22B2 **Ripon** USA
94B3 **Rishon le Zion** Israel
16A3 **Rising Sun** USA
39F7 **Risør** Nor
6E2 **Ritenberk** Greenland
22C2 **Ritter,Mt** USA
20C1 **Ritzville** USA
34B2 **Rivadavia** Arg
34A1 **Rivadavia** Chile
34C3 **Rivadavia Gonzalez Moreno** Arg
47D2 **Riva de Garda** Italy
34C3 **Rivera** Arg
29E2 **Rivera** Urug
22B2 **Riverbank** USA
97B4 **River Cess** Lib
16C2 **Riverhead** USA
108B3 **Riverina** Aust
111A3 **Riversdale** NZ
22D4 **Riverside** USA
13B2 **Rivers Inlet** Can
111A3 **Riverton** NZ
8C2 **Riverton** USA
17D2 **Riviera Beach** USA
7C4 **Rivière aux Feuilles** *R* Can
7D4 **Rivière de la Baleine** *R* Can
7D4 **Rivière du Petit Mècatina** *R* Can
46C2 **Rivigny-sur-Ornain** France
93D1 **Rize** Turk
72D2 **Rizhao** China
Rizhskiy Zaliv = Riga,G of
39F7 **Rjukan** Nor
6B2 **Roanes Pen** Can
49C2 **Roanne** France
17A1 **Roanoke** Alabama, USA
11C3 **Roanoke** Virginia, USA
11C3 **Roanoke** *R* USA
45B3 **Roaringwater B** Irish Rep
38J6 **Robertsforz** Sweden
19B2 **Robert S Kerr Res** USA
97A4 **Robertsport** Lib
7C5 **Roberval** Can
30H6 **Robinson Crusoe** *I* Chile
108B2 **Robinvale** Aust
13D2 **Robson,Mt** Can
24A3 **Roca Partida** *I* Mexico
103G5 **Rocas** *I* Atlantic O
31E2 **Rocas** *I* Brazil
29F2 **Rocha** Urug
42C3 **Rochdale** Eng
48B2 **Rochefort** France
5G3 **Rocher River** Can
108B3 **Rochester** Aust
7C5 **Rochester** Can
43E4 **Rochester** Eng
10A2 **Rochester** Minnesota, USA
15D2 **Rochester** New Hampshire, USA
10C2 **Rochester** New York, USA
10B2 **Rockford** USA
11B3 **Rock Hill** USA
10A2 **Rock Island** USA
108B3 **Rocklands Res** Aust
17B2 **Rockledge** USA
8C2 **Rock Springs** Wyoming, USA
110B2 **Rocks Pt** NZ
109C3 **Rock,The** Aust
16C2 **Rockville** Connecticut, USA
14A3 **Rockville** Indiana, USA
16A3 **Rockville** Maryland, USA
14B1 **Rocky Island L** Can
13E2 **Rocky Mountain House** Can
8B1 **Rocky Mts** Can/USA
12B2 **Rocky Pt** USA
56C2 **Rødbyhavn** Den
34B2 **Rodeo** Arg
49C3 **Rodez** France
55C3 **Ródhos** Greece
55C3 **Ródhos** *I* Greece
52C2 **Rodi Garganico** Italy
54B2 **Rodopi Planina** *Mts* Bulg
106A3 **Roebourne** Aust
46C1 **Roermond** Neth
46B1 **Roeselare** Belg
6B3 **Roes Welcome Sd** Can
18B2 **Rogers** USA
14B1 **Rogers City** USA
20B2 **Rogue** *R* USA
85B3 **Rohn** Pak
84D3 **Rohtak** India
58C1 **Roja** Latvia
35A2 **Rolândia** Brazil
18B2 **Rolla** USA
109C1 **Roma** Aust
52B2 **Roma** Italy
47C2 **Romagnano** Italy
17C1 **Romain,C** USA
54C1 **Roman** Rom
103H5 **Romanche Gap** Atlantic O
71D4 **Romang** *I* Indon
60B4 **Romania** Republic, E Europe
17B2 **Romano,C** USA
49D2 **Romans sur Isère** France
79B3 **Romblon** Phil
Rome = Roma
17A1 **Rome** Georgia, USA
15C2 **Rome** New York, USA
49C2 **Romilly-sur-Seine** France
15C3 **Romney** USA
60D3 **Romny** Ukraine
56B1 **Rømø** *I* Den
47B1 **Romont** Switz
48C2 **Romorantin** France
50A2 **Ronda** Spain
33E6 **Rondônia** Brazil
24F6 **Rondônia** State, Brazil
30F2 **Rondonópolis** Brazil
73B4 **Rong'an** China
73B4 **Rongchang** China
72E2 **Rongcheng** China
73B4 **Rongjiang** China
73B4 **Rong Jiang** *R* China
76A1 **Rongklang Range** *Mts* Burma
39G7 **Rønne** Den
39H7 **Ronneby** Sweden
112B2 **Ronne Ice Shelf** Ant
46B1 **Ronse** Belg
46A1 **Ronthieu** Region, France
9C3 **Roof Butte** *Mt* USA

84D3 **Roorkee** India
46C1 **Roosendaal** Neth
112B6 **Roosevelt I** Ant
106C2 **Roper** R Aust
33E3 **Roraima** State, Brazil
33E2 **Roraime** Mt Ven
38G6 **Røros** Nor
47C1 **Rorschach** Switz
38G6 **Rørvik** Nor
27Q2 **Rosalie** Dominica
22C3 **Rosamond L** USA
34C2 **Rosario** Arg
31C2 **Rosário** Brazil
34D2 **Rosario del Tala** Arg
48B2 **Roscoff** France
45B2 **Roscommon** County, Irish Rep
41B3 **Roscommon** Irish Rep
45C2 **Roscrea** Irish Rep
27E3 **Roseau** Irish Rep
109C4 **Rosebery** Aust
20B2 **Roseburg** USA
19A4 **Rosenberg** USA
57C3 **Rosenheim** Germany
13F2 **Rosetown** Can
54B2 **Roşiori de Vede** Rom
39G7 **Roskilde** Den
60D3 **Roslavl'** Russian Fed
61E2 **Roslyatino** Russian Fed
111B2 **Ross** NZ
12H2 **Ross** R Can
40B3 **Rossan** Pt Irish Rep
53C3 **Rossano** Italy
19C3 **Ross Barnet Res** USA
15C1 **Rosseau L** L Can
107E2 **Rossel I** Solomon Is
112A **Ross Ice Shelf** Ant
20B1 **Ross L** USA
13D3 **Rossland** Can
45C2 **Rosslare** Irish Rep
111C2 **Ross,Mt** NZ
97A3 **Rosso** Maur
43C4 **Ross-on-Wye** Eng
60E4 **Rossosh** Russian Fed
4E3 **Ross River** Can
112B6 **Ross S** Ant
91B4 **Rostâq** Iran
56C2 **Rostock** Germany
Rostov = Rostov-na-Donu
61E4 **Rostov-na-Donu** Russian Fed
17B1 **Roswell** Georgia, USA
9C3 **Roswell** New Mexico, USA
71F2 **Rota** Pacific O
56B2 **Rotenburg** Niedersachsen, Germany
46E1 **Rothaar-Geb** Region Germany
112C3 **Rothera** Base Ant
42D3 **Rotherham** Eng
42B2 **Rothesay** Scot
71D5 **Roti** I Indon
108C2 **Roto** Aust
111B2 **Rotoiti,L** NZ
111B2 **Rotoroa,L** NZ
110C1 **Rotorua** NZ
110C1 **Rotorua,L** NZ
56A2 **Rotterdam** Neth
46B1 **Roubaix** France
48C2 **Rouen** France
42E3 **Rough** Oilfield N Sea
Roulers = Roeselare
101E3 **Round I** Mauritius
109D2 **Round Mt** Aust
8C2 **Roundup** USA
44C2 **Rousay I** Scot
48C3 **Roussillon** Region, France
10C2 **Rouyn** Can
38K5 **Rovaniemi** Fin
47D2 **Rovereto** Italy
47D2 **Rovigo** Italy
52B1 **Rovinj** Croatia
59D2 **Rovno** Ukraine
90A2 **Row'ān** Iran
109C1 **Rowena** Aust
6C3 **Rowley I** Can
106A2 **Rowley Shoals** Aust

79A3 **Roxas** Palawan, Phil
79B3 **Roxas** Panay, Phil
111A3 **Roxburgh** NZ
45C2 **Royal Canal** Irish Rep
43D3 **Royal Leamington Spa** Eng
14B2 **Royal Oak** USA
43E4 **Royal Tunbridge Wells** Eng
48B2 **Royan** France
46B2 **Roye** France
43D3 **Royston** Eng
59C3 **Rožňava** Slovakia
46B2 **Rozoy** France
61F3 **Rtishchevo** Russian Fed
99D3 **Ruaha Nat Pk** Tanz
110C1 **Ruahine Range** Mts NZ
110C1 **Ruapehu,Mt** NZ
65D3 **Rub al Khālī** Desert S Arabia
44A3 **Rubha Hunish** Scot
35A2 **Rubinéia** Brazil
65K4 **Rubtsovsk** Russian Fed
12C2 **Ruby** USA
91C4 **Rudan** Iran
90A2 **Rūdbār** Iran
69F2 **Rudnaya Pristan'** Russian Fed
54B2 **Rudoka Planina** Mt Macedonia
72E3 **Rudong** China
14B1 **Rudyard** USA
46A1 **Rue** France
48C2 **Ruffec** France
99D3 **Rufiji** R Tanz
34C2 **Rufino** Arg
97A3 **Rufisque** Sen
100B2 **Rufunsa** Zambia
43D3 **Rugby** Eng
39G8 **Rügen** I Germany
56B2 **Ruhr** R Germany
73D4 **Ruijin** China
54B2 **Rujen** Mt Bulg/Macedonia
99D3 **Rukwa** L Tanz
44A3 **Rum I** Scot
54A1 **Ruma** Serbia, Yugos
91A4 **Rumāh** S Arabia
98C2 **Rumbek** Sudan
26C2 **Rum Cay** I Caribbean S
47A2 **Rumilly** France
106C2 **Rum Jungle** Aust
101C2 **Rumphi** Malawi
111B2 **Runanga** NZ
110C1 **Runaway,C** NZ
100C3 **Rundi** R Zim
100A2 **Rundu** Namibia
99D3 **Rungwa** Tanz
99D3 **Rungwa** R Tanz
99D3 **Rungwe** Mt Tanz
82C2 **Ruoqiang** China
68C2 **Ruo Shui** R China
54C1 **Rupea** Rom
7C4 **Rupert** R Can
46D1 **Rur** R Germany
32D6 **Rurrenabaque** Bol
101C2 **Rusape** Zim
54C2 **Ruse** Bulg
18B1 **Rushville** Illinois, USA
108B3 **Rushworth** Aust
19A3 **Rusk** USA
17B2 **Ruskin** USA
110B1 **Russell** NZ
18B2 **Russellville** Arkansas, USA
18C2 **Russellville** Kentucky, USA
21A2 **Russian** R USA
62C3 **Russian Fed** Asia/Europe
93E1 **Rustavi** Georgia
101G1 **Rustenburg** S Africa
19B3 **Ruston** USA
99C3 **Rutana** Burundi
46E1 **Rüthen** Germany
23B2 **Rutla** Mexico
15D2 **Rutland** USA
84D2 **Rutog** China
Ruvu = Pangani

101D2 **Ruvuma** R Tanz/Mozam
99D2 **Ruwenzori Range** Mts Uganda/Zaire
101C2 **Ruya** R Zim
59B3 **Ružomberok** Slovakia
99C3 **Rwanda** Republic, Africa
60E3 **Ryazan'** Russian Fed
61F3 **Ryazhsk** Russian Fed
60E2 **Rybinsk** Russian Fed
60E2 **Rybinskoye Vodokhranilishche** Res Russian Fed
13D1 **Rycroft** Can
43D4 **Ryde** Eng
43E4 **Rye** Eng
20C2 **Rye Patch Res** USA
60D3 **Ryl'sk** Russian Fed
61G4 **Ryn Peski** Desert Kazakhstan
74D3 **Ryōtsu** Japan
59D3 **Ryskany** Moldavia
69E4 **Ryūkyū Retto** Arch Japan
59C2 **Rzeszów** Pol
60D2 **Rzhev** Russian Fed

S

91B3 **Sa'ādatābād** Iran
56C2 **Saale** R Germany
47B1 **Saanen** Switz
46D2 **Saar** R Germany
46D2 **Saarbrücken** Germany
46D2 **Saarburg** Germany
39J7 **Saaremaa** I Estonia
46D2 **Saarland** State, Germany
46D2 **Saarlouis** Germany
34C3 **Saavedra** Arg
54A2 **Šabac** Serbia, Yugos
51C1 **Sabadell** Spain
75B1 **Sabae** Japan
78D1 **Sabah** State, Malay
26C4 **Sabanalarga** Colombia
70A3 **Sabang** Indon
87C1 **Sabari** R India
94B2 **Sabastiya** Israel
30C2 **Sabaya** Bol
93C3 **Sab'Bi'ār** Syria
94C2 **Sabhā** Jordan
95A2 **Sabhā** Libya
24B2 **Sabinas** Mexico
24B2 **Sabinas Hidalgo** Mexico
19A3 **Sabine** R USA
19B4 **Sabine L** USA
91B5 **Sabkhat Maṭṭi** Salt Marsh UAE
94A3 **Sabkhet El Bardawil** Lg Egypt
79B3 **Sablayan** Phil
7D5 **Sable,C** Can
17B2 **Sable,C** USA
7D5 **Sable I** Can
90C2 **Sabzevār** Iran
20C1 **Sacajawea Peak** USA
10A1 **Sachigo** R Can
57C2 **Sachsen** State, Germany
56C2 **Sachsen-Anhalt** State, Germany
4F2 **Sachs Harbour** Can
47B1 **Säckingen** Germany
22B1 **Sacramento** USA
22B1 **Sacramento** R USA
21A1 **Sacramento** V USA
9C3 **Sacramento Mts** USA
81C4 **Sa'dah** Yemen
54B2 **Sadanski** Bulg
82D3 **Sadiya** India
50A2 **Sado** R Port
74D3 **Sado-shima** I Japan
85C3 **Sādri** India
Safad = Zefat
84A2 **Safed Koh** Mts Afghan
39G7 **Saffle** Sweden
92C3 **Safi** Jordan
96B1 **Safi** Mor

90D3 **Safidabeh** Iran
94C1 **Şāfītā** Syria
93E3 **Şafwān** Iraq
75A2 **Saga** Japan
76B1 **Sagaing** Burma
75B2 **Sagami-nada** B Japan
85D4 **Sāgar** India
16C2 **Sag Harbor** USA
14B2 **Saginaw** USA
14B2 **Saginaw B** USA
26B2 **Sagua de Tánamo** Cuba
26B2 **Sagua la Grande** Cuba
7C5 **Saguenay** R Can
51B2 **Sagunto** Spain
94C3 **Sahāb** Jordan
50A1 **Sahagún** Spain
96C2 **Sahara** Desert N Africa
84D3 **Saharanpur** India
84C2 **Sahiwal** Pak
93D3 **Şahrā al Hijārah** Desert Region Iraq
23A1 **Sahuayo** Mexico
107D1 **Saibai I** Aust
96C1 **Saïda** Alg
94B2 **Säida** Leb
91C4 **Sa'īdabad** Iran
51B2 **Saidia** Mor
86B1 **Saidpur** India
84C2 **Saidu** Pak
75A1 **Saigō** Japan
Saigon = Ho Chi Minh
86C2 **Saiha** India
68D2 **Saihan Tal** China
75A2 **Saijo** Japan
74C4 **Saiki** Japan
42C2 **St Abb's Head** Pt Scot
43D4 **St Albans** Eng
15D2 **St Albans** Vermont, USA
14B3 **St Albans** West Virginia, USA
43C4 **St Albans Head** C Eng
13E2 **St Albert** Can
46B1 **St Amand-les-Eaux** France
48C2 **St Amand-Mont Rond** France
17A2 **St Andrew B** USA
44C3 **St Andrews** Scot
17B1 **St Andrew Sd** USA
27H1 **St Ann's Bay** Jamaica
7E4 **St Anthony** Can
108B3 **St Arnaud** Aust
17B2 **St Augustine** USA
43B4 **St Austell** Eng
46D2 **St-Avold** France
42C2 **St Bees Head** Pt Eng
47B2 **St-Bonnet** France
43B4 **St Brides B** Wales
48B2 **St-Brieuc** France
15C2 **St Catharines** Can
27M2 **St Catherine,Mt** Grenada
17B1 **St Catherines I** USA
43D4 **St Catherines Pt** Eng
49C2 **St Chamond** France
18B2 **St Charles** Missouri, USA
14B2 **St Clair** USA
14B2 **St Clair,L** Can/USA
14B2 **St Clair Shores** USA
49D2 **St Claud** France
10A2 **St Cloud** USA
47B1 **Ste Croix** Switz
27E3 **St Croix** I Caribbean S
43B4 **St Davids Head** Pt Wales
46B2 **St Denis** France
101E3 **St Denis** Réunion
46C2 **St Dizier** France
12F2 **St Elias,Mt** USA
12G2 **St Elias Mts** Can
48B2 **Saintes** France
49C2 **St Étienne** France
18B2 **St Francis** R USA
100B4 **St Francis,C** S Africa

29B4 **San Carlos de Bariloche** Arg	34A3 **San Javier** Chile	25D3 **San Miguel** El Salvador	33E3 **Santa Elena** Ven
69E4 **San-chung** Taiwan	34D2 **San Javier** Sante Fe, Arg	22B3 **San Miguel** I USA	34C2 **Santa Fe** Arg
61G2 **Sanchursk** Russian Fed	74D3 **Sanjō** I Japan	23A1 **San Miguel del Allende** Mexico	34C2 **Santa Fe** State, Arg
34A3 **San Clemente** Chile	31C6 **San João del Rei** Brazil	34D3 **San Miguel del Monte** Arg	9C3 **Santa Fe** USA
22D4 **San Clemente** USA	22B2 **San Joaquin** R USA	30C4 **San Miguel de Tucumán** Arg	35A1 **Santa Helena de Goiás** Brazil
21B3 **San Clemente I** USA	22B2 **San Joaquin Valley** USA	73D4 **Sanming** China	73B3 **Santai** China
34C2 **San Cristóbal** Arg	32A1 **San José** Costa Rica	9B3 **San Nicolas** I USA	29B6 **Santa Inés** I Chile
25C3 **San Cristóbal** Mexico	25C3 **San José** Guatemala	34C2 **San Nicolás de los Arroyos** Arg	34B3 **Santa Isabel** La Pampa, Arg
32C2 **San Cristóbal** Ven	79B2 **San Jose** Luzon, Phil	101G1 **Sannieshof** S Africa	34C2 **Santa Isabel** Sante Fe, Arg
32J7 **San Cristóbal** I Ecuador	79B3 **San Jose** Mindoro, Phil	97B4 **Sanniquellie** Lib	107E1 **Santa Isabel** I Solomon Is
107F2 **San Cristobal** I Solomon Is	22B2 **San Jose** USA	59C3 **Sanok** Pol	21A2 **Santa Lucia** Ra USA
25E2 **Sancti Spíritus** Cuba	9B4 **San José** I Mexico	26B5 **San Onofore** Colombia	21A2 **Santa Lucia Range** Mts USA
78C3 **Sandai** Indon	30D2 **San José de Chiquitos** Bol	22D4 **San Onofre** USA	97A4 **Santa Luzia** I Cape Verde
70C3 **Sandakan** Malay	34D2 **San José de Feliciano** Arg	79B3 **San Pablo** Phil	9B4 **Santa Margarita** I Mexico
44C2 **Sanday** I Scot	34B2 **San José de Jachal** Arg	22A1 **San Pablo B** USA	22D4 **Santa Margarita** R USA
9C3 **Sanderson** USA	34C2 **San José de la Dormida** Arg	34D2 **San Pedro** Buenos Aires, Arg	30F4 **Santa Maria** Brazil
13F1 **Sandfly L** Can	31B6 **San José do Rio Prêto** Brazil	97B4 **San Pédro** Ivory Coast	26C4 **Santa Maria** Colombia
21B3 **San Diego** USA	24B2 **San José del Cabo** Mexico	30D3 **San Pedro** Jujuy, Arg	21A3 **Santa Maria** USA
92B2 **Sandikli** Turk	34B2 **San Juan** Arg	30E3 **San Pedro** Par	96A1 **Santa Maria** I Açores
86A1 **Sandīla** India	27D3 **San Juan** Puerto Rico	22C4 **San Pedro Chan** USA	23B1 **Santa Maria** R Queretaro, Mexico
39F7 **Sandnes** Nor	34B2 **San Juan** State, Arg	9C4 **San Pedro de los Colonias** Mexico	23A1 **Santa Maria del Rio** Mexico
38G5 **Sandnessjøen** Nor	27L1 **San Juan** Trinidad	25D3 **San Pedro Sula** Honduras	32C1 **Santa Marta** Colombia
98C3 **Sandoa** Zaïre	32D3 **San Juan** Ven	53A3 **San Pietro** I Medit S	22C3 **Santa Monica** USA
59C2 **Sandomierz** Pol	26B2 **San Juan** Mt Cuba	24A1 **San Quintin** Mexico	22C4 **Santa Monica B** USA
38D3 **Sandoy** Føroyar	8C3 **San Juan** Mts USA	34B2 **San Rafael** Arg	29E2 **Santana do Livramento** Brazil
20C1 **Sandpoint** USA	34B2 **San Juan** R Arg	22A2 **San Rafael** USA	32B3 **Santander** Colombia
49D2 **Sandrio** Italy	23B2 **San Juan** R Mexico	22C3 **San Rafael Mts** USA	50B1 **Santander** Spain
18A2 **Sand Springs** USA	25D3 **San Juan** R Nic/ Costa Rica	49D3 **San Remo** Italy	51C2 **Santañy** Spain
106A3 **Sandstone** Aust	23B2 **San Juan Bautista** Mexico	34D2 **San Salvador** Arg	22C3 **Santa Paula** USA
73C4 **Sandu** China	30E4 **San Juan Bautista** Par	26C2 **San Salvador** I Caribbean S	31C2 **Santa Quitéria** Brazil
14B2 **Sandusky** USA	22B2 **San Juan Bautista** USA	32J7 **San Salvador** I Ecuador	33G4 **Santarem** Brazil
39H6 **Sandviken** Sweden	25D3 **San Juan del Norte** Nic	30C3 **San Salvador de Jujuy** Arg	50A2 **Santarém** Port
7A4 **Sandy L** Can	27D4 **San Juan de los Cayos** Ven	51B1 **San Sebastian** Spain	22A1 **Santa Rosa** California, USA
34C2 **San Elcano** Arg	23A1 **San Juan de loz Lagoz** Mexico	53C2 **San Severo** Italy	25D3 **Santa Rosa** Honduras
9B3 **San Felipe** Baja Cal, Mexico	23A1 **San Juan del Rio** Mexico	30C2 **Santa Ana** Bol	34C3 **Santa Rosa** La Pampa, Arg
34A2 **San Felipe** Chile	25D3 **San Juan del Sur** Nic	25C3 **Santa Ana** Guatemala	34B2 **Santa Rosa** Mendoza, Arg
23A1 **San Felipe** Guanajuato, Mexico	20B1 **San Juan Is** USA	22D4 **Santa Ana** USA	34B2 **Santa Rosa** San Luis, Arg
27D4 **San Felipe** Ven	23B2 **San Juan Tepozcolula** Mexico	22D4 **Santa Ana Mts** USA	22B3 **Santa Rosa** I USA
51C1 **San Feliu de Guixols** Spain	29C5 **San Julián** Arg	34A3 **Santa Bárbara** Chile	24A2 **Santa Rosalía** Mexico
28A5 **San Felix** I Pacific O	34C2 **San Justo** Arg	24B2 **Santa Barbara** Mexico	20C2 **Santa Rosa Range** Mts USA
34A2 **San Fernando** Chile	60D2 **Sankt-Peterburg** Russian Fed	22C3 **Santa Barbara** USA	31D3 **Santa Talhada** Brazil
79B2 **San Fernando** Phil	98C3 **Sankuru** R Zaïre	22C4 **Santa Barbara** I USA	35C1 **Santa Teresa** Brazil
79B2 **San Fernando** Phil	22A2 **San Leandro** USA	22B3 **Santa Barbara Chan** USA	53A2 **Santa Teresa di Gallura** Sardegna
50A2 **San Fernando** Spain	93C2 **Şanlıurfa** Turk	22C3 **Santa Barbara Res** USA	22B3 **Santa Ynez** R USA
27E4 **San Fernando** Trinidad	32B3 **San Lorenzo** Ecuador	22C4 **Santa Catalina** I USA	22B3 **Santa Ynez Mts** USA
22C3 **San Fernando** USA	34C2 **San Lorenzo** Arg	22C4 **Santa Catalina,G of** USA	17C1 **Santee** R USA
32D2 **San Fernando** Ven	22B2 **San Lucas** USA	30F4 **Santa Catarina** State, Brazil	47C2 **Santhia** Italy
17B2 **Sanford** Florida, USA	34B2 **San Luis** Arg	26B2 **Santa Clara** Cuba	34A2 **Santiago** Chile
12F2 **Sanford,Mt** USA	34B2 **San Luis** State, Arg	22B2 **Santa Clara** USA	27C3 **Santiago** Dom Rep
34C2 **San Francisco** Arg	23A1 **San Luis de la Paz** Mexico	22C3 **Santa Clara** R USA	32A2 **Santiago** Panama
27C3 **San Francisco** Dom Rep	21A2 **San Luis Obispo** USA	29C6 **Santa Cruz** Arg	79B2 **Santiago** Phil
22A2 **San Francisco** USA	23A1 **San Luis Potosi** Mexico	30D2 **Santa Cruz** Bol	32B4 **Santiago** R Peru
22A2 **San Francisco B** USA	22B2 **San Luis Res** USA	34A2 **Santa Cruz** Chile	50A1 **Santiago de Compostela** Spain
24B2 **San Francisco del Oro** Mexico	53A3 **Sanluri** Sardegna	79B3 **Santa Cruz** Phil	26B2 **Santiago de Cuba** Cuba
23A1 **San Francisco del Rincon** Mexico	33D2 **San Maigualida** Mts Ven	29B5 **Santa Cruz** State, Arg	30D4 **Santiago del Estero** Arg
22D3 **San Gabriel Mts** USA	34D3 **San Manuel** Arg	22A2 **Santa Cruz** USA	30D4 **Santiago del Estero** State, Arg
85C5 **Sangamner** India	34A2 **San Marcos** Chile	22C4 **Santa Cruz** I USA	22D4 **Santiago Peak** Mt USA
18C2 **Sangamon** R USA	23B2 **San Marcos** Mexico	35D1 **Santa Cruz Cabrália** Brazil	31C5 **Santo** State, Brazil
71F2 **Sangan** I Pacific O	52B2 **San Marino** Republic, Europe	22C3 **Santa Cruz Chan** USA	35A2 **Santo Anastácio** Brazil
87B1 **Sangāreddi** India	34B2 **San Martin** Mendoza, Arg	96A2 **Santa Cruz de la Palma** Canary Is	30F4 **Santo Angelo** Brazil
78D4 **Sangeang** I Indon	112C3 **San Martin** Base Ant	26B2 **Santa Cruz del Sur** Cuba	97A4 **Santo Antão** I Cape Verde
22C2 **Sanger** USA	47D1 **San Martino di Castroza** Italy	96A2 **Santa Cruz de Tenerife** Canary Is	35A2 **Santo Antonio da Platina** Brazil
72C2 **Sanggan He** R China	23B2 **San Martin Tuxmelucan** Mexico	100B2 **Santa Cruz do Cuando** Angola	27D3 **Santo Domingo** Dom Rep
78C2 **Sanggau** Indon	22A2 **San Mateo** USA	35B2 **Santa Cruz do Rio Pardo** Brazil	
98B2 **Sangha** R Congo	30E2 **San Matias** Bol	22A2 **Santa Cruz Mts** USA	
85B3 **Sanghar** Pak	72C3 **Sanmenxia** China	34D2 **Santa Elena** Arg	
76B2 **Sangkhla Buri** Thai			
78D2 **Sangkulirang** Indon			
87A1 **Sāngli** India			
98B2 **Sangmélima** Cam			
9B3 **San Gorgonio Mt** USA			
9C3 **Sangre de Cristo** Mts USA			
34C2 **San Gregorio** Arg			
22A2 **San Gregorio** USA			
84D2 **Sangrür** India			
30E4 **San Ignacio** Arg			
79B3 **San Isidro** Phil			
32B2 **San Jacinto** Colombia			
21B3 **San Jacinto Peak** Mt USA			

35B2	**Santos** Brazil	78C2	**Saratok** Malay
35C2	**Santos Dumont** Brazil	61G3	**Saratov** Russian Fed
30E4	**Santo Tomé** Arg	61G3	**Saratovskoye Vodokhranilishche** Res Russian Fed
29B5	**San Valentin** Mt Chile	67F4	**Sarawak** State, Malay
34A2	**San Vicente** Chile	92A2	**Saraykoy** Turk
98B3	**Sanza Pomba** Angola	90C3	**Sarbisheh** Iran
30E4	**São Borja** Brazil	47D1	**Sarca** R Italy
35B2	**São Carlos** Brazil	95A2	**Sardalas** Libya
33G5	**São Félix** Mato Grosso, Brazil	90A2	**Sar Dasht** Iran
35C2	**São Fidélis** Brazil	52A2	**Sardegna** I Medit S
35C1	**São Francisco** Brazil		**Sardinia = Sardegna**
31D3	**São Francisco** R Brazil	38H5	**Sarektjåkkå** Mt Sweden
30G4	**São Francisco do Sul** Brazil	84C2	**Sargodha** Pak
35B1	**São Gotardo** Brazil	98B2	**Sarh** Chad
99D3	**Sao Hill** Tanz	90B2	**Sārī** Iran
35C2	**São João da Barra** Brazil	94B2	**Sarida** R Isreal
35B2	**São João da Boa Vista** Brazil	93D1	**Sarikamiş** Turk
35C1	**São João da Ponte** Brazil	107D3	**Sarina** Aust
		47B1	**Sarine** R Switz
35C2	**São João del Rei** Brazil	84B1	**Sar-i-Pul** Afghan
35B2	**São Joaquim da Barra** Brazil	95B2	**Sarir** Libya
		95A2	**Sarir Tibesti** Desert Libya
96A1	**São Jorge** I Açores	74B3	**Sariwŏn** N Korea
35B2	**São José do Rio Prêto** Brazil	48B2	**Sark** I UK
35B2	**São José dos Campos** Brazil	92C2	**Sarkişla** Turk
		71E4	**Sarmi** Indon
31C2	**São Luís** Brazil	29C5	**Sarmiento** Arg
35B1	**São Marcos** R Brazil	39G6	**Särna** Sweden
35C1	**São Maria do Suaçui** Brazil	47C1	**Sarnen** Switz
35D1	**São Mateus** Brazil	14B2	**Sarnia** Can
35C1	**São Mateus** R Brazil	58D2	**Sarny** Ukraine
96A1	**São Miguel** I Açores	6E2	**Saroaq** Greenland
49C2	**Saône** R France	84B2	**Sarobi** Afghan
97A4	**São Nicolau** I Cape Verde	78A3	**Sarolangun** Indon
		55B3	**Saronikós Kólpos** G Greece
35B2	**São Paulo** Brazil	47C2	**Saronno** Italy
35A2	**São Paulo** State, Brazil	55C2	**Saros Körfezi** B Turk
31C3	**São Raimundo Nonato** Brazil	39G7	**Sarpsborg** Nor
		46D2	**Sarralbe** France
35B1	**São Romão** Brazil	46D2	**Sarrebourg** France
35B2	**São Sebastia do Paraiso** Brazil	46D2	**Sarreguemines** France
35A1	**São Simão** Goias, Brazil	46D2	**Sarre-Union** France
		51B1	**Sarrion** Spain
35B2	**São Simão** Sao Paulo, Brazil	85B3	**Sartanahu** Pak
		53A2	**Sartène** Corse
97A4	**São Tiago** I Cape Verde	48B2	**Sarthe** R France
		61H4	**Sarykamys** Kazakhstan
97C4	**São Tomé** I W Africa		
97C4	**São Tomé and Principe** Republic, W Africa	66H6	**Sŏrysu** R Kazakhstan
		86A2	**Sasarām** India
96B2	**Saoura** Watercourse Alg	74B4	**Sasebo** Japan
		5H4	**Saskatchewan** Province, Can
35B2	**São Vicente** Brazil		
97A4	**São Vincente** I Cape Verde	5H4	**Saskatchewan** R Can
55C2	**Sápai** Greece	13F2	**Saskatoon** Can
78D4	**Sape** Indon	101G1	**Sasolburg** S Africa
97C4	**Sapele** Nig	61F3	**Sasovo** Russian Fed
74E2	**Sapporo** Japan	97B4	**Sassandra** Ivory Coast
53C2	**Sapri** Italy		
18A2	**Sapulpa** USA	97B4	**Sassandra** R Ivory Coast
90A2	**Saqqez** Iran	53A2	**Sassari** Sardegna
10C2	**Saquenay** R Can	56C2	**Sassnitz** Germany
90A2	**Sarāb** Iran	47D2	**Sassuolo** Italy
54A2	**Sarajevo** Bosnia-Herzegovina	34C2	**Sastre** Arg
		87A1	**Sātāra** India
90D2	**Sarakhs** Iran	4G2	**Satellite B** Can
61J3	**Saraktash** Russian Fed	78D4	**Satengar** Is Indon
		39H6	**Säter** Sweden
63A2	**Sarala** Russian Fed	17B1	**Satilla** R USA
15D2	**Saranac L** USA	61J2	**Satka** Russian Fed
15D2	**Saranac Lake** USA	84D2	**Satluj** R India
55B3	**Sarandë** Alb	86A2	**Satna** India
79C4	**Sarangani Is** Phil	85C4	**Sātpura Range** Mts India
61G3	**Saransk** Russian Fed		
61H2	**Sarapul** Russian Fed	54B1	**Satu Mare** Rom
17B2	**Sarasota** USA	34D2	**Sauce** Arg
54C1	**Sarata** Ukraine	39F7	**Sauda** Nor
15D2	**Saratoga Springs** USA	80C3	**Saudi Arabia** Kingdom, Arabian Pen
		46D2	**Sauer** R Germany/ Lux
		46D1	**Sauerland** Region, Germany
		38B1	**Sauðárkrókur** Iceland

14A2	**Saugatuck** USA	14B3	**Scioto** R USA
16C1	**Saugerties** USA	109D2	**Scone** Aust
13B2	**Saugstad,Mt** Can	6H2	**Scoresby Sd** Greenland
7B5	**Sault Sainte Marie** Can	103F7	**Scotia Ridge** Atlantic O
14B1	**Sault Ste Marie** Can	103F7	**Scotia S** Atlantic O
14B1	**Sault Ste Marie** USA	44B3	**Scotland** Country, UK
71E4	**Saumlaki** Indon		
48B2	**Saumur** France	112B7	**Scott** Base Ant
98C3	**Saurimo** Angola	13B2	**Scott,C** Can
27M2	**Sauteurs** Grenada	9C2	**Scott City** USA
54A2	**Sava** R Serbia, Yugos	112C6	**Scott I** Ant
97C4	**Savalou** Benin	6C2	**Scott Inlet** B Can
17B1	**Savannah** Georgia, USA	20B2	**Scott,Mt** USA
17B1	**Savannah** R USA	106B2	**Scott Reef** Timor S
76C2	**Savannakhet** Laos	8C2	**Scottsbluff** USA
26B3	**Savanna la Mar** Jamaica	17A1	**Scottsboro** USA
		109C4	**Scottsdale** Aust
7A4	**Savant Lake** Can	10C2	**Scranton** USA
76D2	**Savarane** Laos	47D1	**Scuol** Switz
97C4	**Savé** Benin		**Scutari = Shkodër**
101C3	**Save** R Mozam	5J4	**Seal** R Can
90B3	**Sāveh** Iran	108B3	**Sea Lake** Aust
46D2	**Saverne** France	18B2	**Searcy** USA
47B2	**Savigliano** Italy	22B2	**Seaside** California, USA
46B2	**Savigny** France		
49D2	**Savoie** Region France	20B1	**Seaside** Oregon, USA
49D3	**Savona** Italy	16B3	**Seaside Park** USA
38K6	**Savonlinna** Fin	20B1	**Seattle** USA
4A3	**Savoonga** USA	22A1	**Sebastopol** USA
38K5	**Savukoski** Fin	58D1	**Sebez** Russian Fed
71D4	**Savu S** Indon	17B2	**Sebring** USA
76A1	**Saw** Burma	111A3	**Secretary I** NZ
85D3	**Sawai Mādhopur** India	18B2	**Sedalia** USA
		46C2	**Sedan** France
78A2	**Sawang** Indon	111B2	**Seddonville** NZ
76B2	**Sawankhalok** Thai	94B3	**Sede Boqer** Israel
75C1	**Sawara** Japan	94B3	**Sederot** Israel
12E1	**Sawtooth Mt** USA	97A3	**Sédhiou** Sen
106B2	**Sawu** I Indon	94B3	**Sedom** Israel
97C3	**Say** Niger	100A3	**Seeheim** Namibia
84B1	**Sayghan** Afghan	111B2	**Sefton,Mt** NZ
91B5	**Sayhūt** Yemen	77C5	**Segamat** Malay
61G4	**Saykhin** Kazakhstan	51B2	**Segorbe** Spain
68D2	**Saynshand** Mongolia	97B3	**Ségou** Mali
61H5	**Say-Utes** Kazakhstan		**Segovia = Coco**
16C2	**Sayville** USA	50B1	**Segovia** Spain
13B2	**Sayward** Can	51C1	**Segre** R Spain
57C3	**Sázava** R Czech Republic	97B4	**Séguéla** Ivory Coast
		96A2	**Seguia el Hamra** Watercourse Mor
51C2	**Sbisseb** R Alg	34C2	**Segundo** R Arg
42C2	**Scafell Pike** Mt Eng	78D2	**Seguntur** Indon
44E1	**Scalloway** Scot	50B2	**Segura** R Spain
44C2	**Scapa Flow** Sd Scot	85B3	**Sehwan** Pak
15C2	**Scarborough** Can	46D2	**Seille** R France
42D2	**Scarborough** Eng	38J6	**Seinäjoki** Fin
27E4	**Scarborough** Tobago	48C2	**Seine** R France
44A2	**Scarp** I Scot	46B2	**Seine-et-Marne** Department, France
45B2	**Scarriff** Irish Rep		
52A1	**Schaffhausen** Switz	99D3	**Sekenke** Tanz
57C3	**Scharding** Austria	99D1	**Sek'ot'a** Eth
46D1	**Scharteberg** Mt Germany	20B1	**Selah** USA
		71E4	**Selaru** I Indon
7D4	**Schefferville** Can	78D4	**Selat Alas** Str Indon
46B1	**Schelde** R Belg	78B3	**Selat Bangka** Str Indon
10C2	**Schenectady** USA		
47D2	**Schio** Italy	78A3	**Selat Berhala** B Indon
46D1	**Schleiden** Germany		
56B2	**Schleswig** Germany	71E4	**Selat Dampier** Str Indon
56B2	**Schleswig Holstein** State, Germany	78B3	**Selat Gaspar** Str Indon
16B1	**Schoharie** USA		
71F4	**Schouten** Is PNG	78D4	**Selat Lombok** Str Indon
7B5	**Schreiber** Can		
21B2	**Schurz** USA	78D4	**Selat Sape** Str Indon
16A2	**Schuykill Haven** USA	78B4	**Selat Sunda** Str Indon
16B2	**Schuylkill** R USA		
57B3	**Schwabische Alb** Upland Germany	71D4	**Selat Wetar** Chan Indon
57B3	**Schwarzwald** Upland Germany	12B1	**Selawik** USA
12C1	**Schwatka Mts** USA	12C1	**Selawik** R USA
47D1	**Schwaz** Austria	12B1	**Selawik L** USA
57C2	**Schweinfurt** Germany	42D3	**Selby** Eng
		55C3	**Selçuk** Turk
101G1	**Schweizer Reneke** S Africa	12D3	**Seldovia** USA
56C2	**Schwerin** Germany	100B3	**Selebi Pikwe** Botswana
47C1	**Schwyz** Switz	6H3	**Selfoss** Iceland
53B3	**Sciacca** Italy	95B2	**Selima Oasis** Sudan
		5J4	**Selkirk** Can
		42C2	**Selkirk** Scot

13D2 **Selkirk Mts** Can
22C2 **Selma** California, USA
50B2 **Selouane** Mor
12H2 **Selous,Mt** Can
78B3 **Selta Karimata** *Str* Indon
32C5 **Selvas** Region, Brazil
107D3 **Selwyn** Aust
4E3 **Selwyn Mts** Can
78C4 **Semarang** Indon
61E2 **Semenov** Russian Fed
12C3 **Semidi Is** USA
60E3 **Semiluki** Russian Fed
19A2 **Seminole** Oklahoma, USA
17B1 **Seminole,L** USA
65K4 **Semipalatinsk** Kazakhstan
79B3 **Semirara Is** Phil
90B3 **Semirom** Iran
78C2 **Semitau** Indon
90B2 **Semnān** Iran
46C2 **Semois** *R* Belg
23B2 **Sempoala** Hist Site, Mexico
32D5 **Sena Madureira** Brazil
100B2 **Senanga** Zambia
19C3 **Senatobia** USA
74E3 **Sendai** Honshū, Japan
74C4 **Sendai** Kyūshū, Japan
85D4 **Sendwha** India
15C2 **Seneca Falls** USA
97A3 **Senegal** Republic, Africa
97A3 **Sénégal** *R* Maur Sen
101G1 **Senekal** S Africa
31D4 **Senhor do Bonfim** Brazil
52B2 **Senigallia** Italy
52C2 **Senj** Croatia
69E4 **Senkaku Gunto** *Is* Japan
46B2 **Senlis** France
99D1 **Sennar** Sudan
7C5 **Senneterre** Can
49C2 **Sens** France
54A1 **Senta** Serbia, Yugos
98C3 **Sentery** Zaïre
13C2 **Sentinel Peak** *Mt* Can
85D4 **Seoni** India
Seoul = Soul
110B2 **Separation Pt** NZ
76D2 **Sepone** Laos
7D4 **Sept-Iles** Can
95A2 **Séquédine** Niger
21B2 **Sequoia** Nat Pk, USA
71D4 **Seram** *I* Indon
78B4 **Serang** Indon
78B2 **Serasan** *I* Indon
54A2 **Serbia** Republic, Yugos
61F3 **Serdobsk** Russian Fed
77C5 **Seremban** Malay
99D3 **Serengeti Nat Pk** Tanz
100C2 **Serenje** Zambia
59D3 **Seret** *R* Ukraine
61G2 **Sergach** Russian Fed
65H3 **Sergino** Russian Fed
31D4 **Sergipe** State, Brazil
60E2 **Segiyev Posad** Russian Fed
78C2 **Seria** Brunei
78C2 **Serian** Malay
55B3 **Sérifos** *I* Greece
47C2 **Serio** *R* Italy
95B2 **Serir Calanscio** *Desert* Libya
46C2 **Sermaize-les-Bains** France
71D4 **Sermata** *I* Indon
61H3 **Sernovodsk** Russian Fed
65H4 **Serov** Russian Fed
100B3 **Serowe** Botswana
50A2 **Serpa** Port

60E3 **Serpukhov** Russian Fed
35B2 **Serra da Canastra** *Mts* Brazil
50A1 **Serra da Estrela** *Mts* Port
35B2 **Serra da Mantiqueira** *Mts* Brazil
35A1 **Serra da Mombuca** Brazil
35C1 **Serra do Cabral** *Mt* Brazil
33F5 **Serra do Cachimbo** *Mts* Brazil
35A1 **Serra do Caiapó** *Mts* Brazil
35A2 **Serra do Cantu** *Mts* Brazil
35C2 **Serra do Caparaó** *Mts* Brazil
31C5 **Serra do Chifre** Brazil
35C1 **Serra do Espinhaço** *Mts* Brazil
35B2 **Serra do Mar** *Mts* Brazil
35A2 **Serra do Mirante** *Mts* Brazil
33G3 **Serra do Navio** Brazil
35B2 **Serra do Paranapiacaba** *Mts* Brazil
33F6 **Serra dos Caiabis** *Mts* Brazil
35A2 **Serra dos Dourados** *Mts* Brazil
33E6 **Serra dos Parecis** *Mts* Brazil
35B1 **Serra dos Pilões** *Mts* Brazil
35A1 **Serra Dourada** *Mts* Brazil
33F6 **Serra Formosa** *Mts* Brazil
55B2 **Sérrai** Greece
25D3 **Serrana Bank** *Is* Caribbean S
51B1 **Serrana de Cuenca** *Mts* Spain
35A1 **Serranópolis** Brazil
33E3 **Serra Pacaraima** *Mts* Brazil/Ven
33E3 **Serra Parima** *Mts* Brazil
33G3 **Serra Tumucumaque** Brazil
46B2 **Serre** *R* France
34B2 **Serrezuela** Arg
31D4 **Serrinha** Brazil
6G3 **Serrmilik** Greenland
35C1 **Serro** Brazil
35A2 **Sertanópolis** Brazil
72A3 **Sêrtar** China
78C3 **Seruyan** *R* Indon
100A2 **Sesfontein** Namibia
100B2 **Sesheke** Zambia
47B2 **Sestriere** Italy
74D2 **Setana** Japan
49C3 **Sète** France
35C1 **Sete Lagoas** Brazil
96C1 **Sétif** Alg
75B1 **Seto** Japan
75A2 **Seto Naikai** *S* Japan
96B1 **Settat** Mor
42C2 **Settle** Eng
5G4 **Settler** Can
50A2 **Sêtubal** Port
93E1 **Sevan,Oz** *L* Armenia
60D5 **Sevastopol'** Ukraine
7B4 **Severn** *R* Can
43C3 **Severn** *R* Eng
1B9 **Severnaya Zemlya** *I* Russian Fed
63C2 **Severo-Baykalskoye Nagorye** *Mts* Russian Fed
60E4 **Severo Donets** Ukraine
64E3 **Severodvinsk** Russian Fed
64H3 **Severo Sos'va** *R* Russian Fed
8B3 **Sevier** *R* USA
8B3 **Sevier L** USA
50A2 **Sevilla** Spain

Seville = Sevilla
54C2 **Sevlievo** Bulg
97A4 **Sewa** *R* Sierra Leone
12E2 **Seward** Alaska, USA
18A1 **Seward** Nebraska, USA
12A1 **Seward Pen** USA
13D1 **Sexsmith** Can
89K8 **Seychelles** *Is* Indian O
38C1 **Seyðisfjörður** Iceland
92C2 **Seyhan** Turk
60E3 **Seym** *R* Russian Fed
108C3 **Seymour** Aust
16C2 **Seymour** Connecticut, USA
14A3 **Seymour** Indiana, USA
46B2 **Sézanne** France
96D1 **Sfax** Tunisia
54C1 **Sfînto Gheorghe** Rom
56A2 **'s-Gravenhage** Neth
72B3 **Shaanxi** Province, China
98C3 **Shabunda** Zaïre
82B2 **Shache** China
112C9 **Shackleton Ice Shelf** Ant
85B3 **Shadadkot** Pak
91B3 **Shādhām** *R* Iran
43C4 **Shaftesbury** Eng
29G8 **Shag Rocks** *Is* South Georgia
90A3 **Shāhabād** Iran
94C2 **Shahbā** Syria
91C3 **Shahdap** Iran
86A2 **Shahdol** India
90A2 **Shāhin Dezh** Iran
90C3 **Shāh Kūh** Iran
91C3 **Shahr-e Bābak** Iran
Shahresa = Qomisheh
90B3 **Shahr Kord** Iran
87B1 **Shājābād** India
84D3 **Shājahānpur** India
85D4 **Shājapur** India
61F4 **Shakhty** Russian Fed
61G2 **Shakhun'ya** Russian Fed
97C4 **Shaki** Nig
12B2 **Shaktoolik** USA
61J2 **Shamary** Russian Fed
99D2 **Shambe** Sudan
16A2 **Shamokin** USA
16B1 **Shandaken** USA
72D2 **Shandong** Province, China
73C5 **Shangchuan Dao** *I* China
72C1 **Shangdu** China
73E3 **Shanghai** China
72C3 **Shangnan** China
100B2 **Shangombo** Zambia
73D4 **Shangra** China
73B5 **Shangsi** China
72C3 **Shang Xian** China
41B3 **Shannon** *R* Irish Rep
72D3 **Shanqiu** China
74B2 **Shansonggang** China
63F2 **Shantarskiye Ostrova** *I* Russian Fed
73D5 **Shantou** China
72C2 **Shanxi** Province, China
72D3 **Shan Xian** China
73C5 **Shaoguan** China
73E4 **Shaoxing** China
73C4 **Shaoyang** China
44C2 **Shapinsay** *I* Scot
94C2 **Shaqqā** Syria
72A1 **Sharhulsan** Mongolia
90C2 **Sharīfābād** Iran
91C4 **Sharjah** UAE
106A3 **Shark B** Aust
90C2 **Sharlauk** Turkmenistan
94B2 **Sharon,Plain of** Israel
61G2 **Sharya** Russian Fed
99D2 **Shashemanē** Eth
73C3 **Shashi** China
20B2 **Shasta L** USA
20B2 **Shasta,Mt** USA

93E3 **Shaṭṭ al Gharrat** *R* Iraq
94B3 **Shaubak** Jordan
13F3 **Shaunavon** Can
22C2 **Shaver L** USA
16B2 **Shawangunk Mt** USA
15D1 **Shawinigan** Can
19A2 **Shawnee** Oklahoma, USA
73D4 **Sha Xian** China
106B3 **Shay Gap** Aust
94C2 **Shaykh Miskin** Syria
99E1 **Shaykh 'Uthmān** Yemen
60E3 **Shchekino** Russian Fed
60E3 **Shchigry** Russian Fed
60D3 **Shchors** Ukraine
65J4 **Shchuchinsk** Kazakhstan
99E2 **Shebele** *R* Eth
14A2 **Sheboygan** USA
98B2 **Shebshi** *Mts* Nig
12F1 **Sheenjek** *R* USA
45C1 **Sheep Haven** *Estuary* Irish Rep
43E4 **Sheerness** Eng
94B2 **Shefar'am** Israel
42D3 **Sheffield** Eng
84C2 **Shekhupura** Pak
13B1 **Shelagyote Peak** *Mt* Can
16C1 **Shelburne Falls** USA
14A2 **Shelby** Michigan, USA
8B2 **Shelby** Montana, USA
14A3 **Shelbyville** Indiana, USA
12H2 **Sheldon,Mt** Can
12D3 **Shelikof Str** USA
109D2 **Shellharbour** Aust
111A3 **Shelter Pt** NZ
20B1 **Shelton** USA
93E1 **Shemakha** Azerbaijan
18A1 **Shenandoah** USA
15C3 **Shenandoah** *R* USA
15C3 **Shenandoah Nat Pk** USA
97C4 **Shendam** Nig
95C2 **Shendi** Sudan
72C2 **Shenmu** China
72E1 **Shenyang** China
73C5 **Shenzhen** China
85D3 **Sheopur** India
59D2 **Shepetovka** Ukraine
108C3 **Shepparton** Aust
6B2 **Sherard,C** Can
43C4 **Sherborne** Eng
97A4 **Sherbro I** Sierra Leone
15D1 **Sherbrooke** Can
85C3 **Shergarh** India
19B3 **Sheridan** Arkansas, USA
8C2 **Sheridan** Wyoming, USA
19A3 **Sherman** USA
56B2 **s-Hertogenbosh** Neth
12H3 **Sheslay** Can
40C1 **Shetland** *Is* Scot
Shevchenko = Aktau
91B4 **Sheyk Sho'eyb** *I* Iran
69H2 **Shiashkotan** *I* Russian Fed
84B1 **Shibarghan** Afghan
74D3 **Shibata** Japan
95C1 **Shibin el Kom** Egypt
75B1 **Shibukawa** Japan
72C2 **Shijiazhuang** China
84B3 **Shikarpur** Pak
67G3 **Shikoku** *I* Japan
75A2 **Shikoku-sanchi** *Mts* Japan
86B1 **Shiliguri** India
68D1 **Shilka** Russian Fed
68D1 **Shilka** *R* Russian Fed
16B2 **Shillington** USA
86C1 **Shillong** India
61F3 **Shilovo** Russian Fed
75A2 **Shimabara** Japan

75B2 **Shimada** Japan	54B1 **Sibiu** Rom	23B2 **Sierra de Zongolica**
69E1 **Shimanovsk**	70A3 **Sibolga** Indon	Mexico
Russian Fed	86C1 **Sibsāgār** India	34C2 **Sierra Grande** *Mts*
74D3 **Shimizu** Japan	78C2 **Sibu** Malay	Arg
84D2 **Shimla** India	79B4 **Sibuguay B** Phil	97A4 **Sierra Leone**
75B2 **Shimoda** Japan	98B2 **Sibut** CAR	Republic, Africa
87B2 **Shimoga** India	79B3 **Sibuyan** *I* Phil	97A4 **Sierra Leone,C** Sierra
74C4 **Shimonoseki** Japan	79B3 **Sibuyan S** Phil	Leone
75B1 **Shinano** *R* Japan	73A3 **Sichuan** Province,	79B2 **Sierra Madre** *Mts*
91C5 **Shināş** Oman	China	Phil
74D4 **Shingū** Japan	53B3 **Sicilia** *I* Medit S	23A2 **Sierra Madre del Sur**
75C1 **Shinjō** Japan	53B3 **Sicilian** *Chan* Italy/	*Mts* Mexico
74D3 **Shinminato** Japan	Tunisia	24B2 **Sierra Madre**
94C1 **Shinshār** Syria	**Sicily = Sicilia**	**Occidental** *Mts*
99D3 **Shinyanga** Tanz	32C6 **Sicuani** Peru	Mexico
74E3 **Shiogama** Japan	85C4 **Siddhapur** India	24C2 **Sierra Madre Oriental**
75B2 **Shiono-misaki** *C*	87B1 **Siddipet** India	*Mts* Mexico
Japan	86A2 **Sidhi** India	34B2 **Sierra Malanzan** *Mts*
73A5 **Shiping** China	95B1 **Sidi Barrani** Egypt	Arg
16A2 **Shippensburg** USA	96B1 **Sidi Bel Abbès** Alg	9C4 **Sierra Mojada**
72B3 **Shiquan** China	96B1 **Sidi Kacem** Mor	Mexico
75C1 **Shirakawa** Japan	44C3 **Sidlaw Hills** Scot	50A2 **Sierra Morena** *Mts*
75B1 **Shirane-san** *Mt*	112B5 **Sidley,Mt** Ant	Spain
Japan	20B1 **Sidney** Can	50B2 **Sierra Nevada** *Mts*
75B1 **Shirani-san** *Mt*	8C2 **Sidney** Nebraska,	Spain
Japan	USA	21A2 **Sierra Nevada** *Mts*
91B4 **Shiraz** Iran	15C2 **Sidney** New York,	USA
90B3 **Shir Kūh** Iran	USA	32C1 **Sierra Nevada de**
75B1 **Shirotori** Japan	14B2 **Sidney** Ohio, USA	**Santa Marta** *Mts*
90C2 **Shirvān** Iran	17B1 **Sidney Lanier,L**	Colombia
12A1 **Shishmaref** USA	USA	34B2 **Sierra Pié de Palo**
12A1 **Shishmaref Inlet**	**Sidon = Säida**	*Mts* Arg
USA	58C2 **Siedlce** Pol	47B1 **Sierre** Switz
4B3 **Shishmaret** USA	46D1 **Sieg** *R* Germany	55B3 **Sífnos** *I* Greece
72B2 **Shitanjing** China	46D1 **Siegburg** Germany	59C3 **Sighetu Marmației**
14A3 **Shively** USA	46D1 **Siegen** Germany	Rom
85D3 **Shivpuri** India	76C3 **Siem Reap** Camb	54B1 **Sighişoara** Rom
94B3 **Shivta** *Hist Site*	52B2 **Siena** Italy	38B1 **Siglufjörður** Iceland
Israel	58B2 **Sierpc** Pol	50B1 **Sigüenza** Spain
101C2 **Shiwa Ngandu**	23B2 **Sierra Andrés Tuxtla**	97B3 **Siguiri** Guinea
Zambia	Mexico	**Sihanoukville =**
72C3 **Shiyan** China	34B3 **Sierra Auca Mahuida**	**Kompong Som**
72B2 **Shizuishan** China	*Mts* Arg	85E4 **Sihora** India
75B1 **Shizuoka** Japan	9C3 **Sierra Blanca** USA	93D2 **Siirt** Turk
54A2 **Shkodër** Alb	51B1 **Sierra de Albarracin**	68B3 **Sikai Hu** *L* China
109D2 **Shoalhaven** *R* Aust	*Mts* Spain	85D3 **Sīkar** India
75A2 **Shobara** Japan	50B2 **Sierra de Alcaraz** *Mts*	84B2 **Sikaram** *Mt* Afghan
87B2 **Shoranūr** India	Spain	97B3 **Sikasso** Mali
87B1 **Shorāpur** India	34B2 **Sierra de Cordoba**	18C2 **Sikeston** USA
21B2 **Shoshone Mts** USA	*Mts* Arg	55C3 **Sikinos** *I* Greece
60D3 **Shostka** Ukraine	50A1 **Sierra de Gredos** *Mts*	55B3 **Sikionía** Greece
19B3 **Shreveport** USA	Spain	86B1 **Sikkim** State, India
43C3 **Shrewsbury** Eng	50A2 **Sierra de Guadalupe**	50A1 **Sil** *R* Spain
43C3 **Shropshire** County,	*Mts* Spain	47D1 **Silandro** Italy
Eng	50B1 **Sierra de**	23A1 **Silao** Mexico
72E1 **Shuanglia** China	**Guadarrama** *Mts*	79B3 **Silay** Phil
69F2 **Shuangyashan**	Spain	86C2 **Silchar** India
China	51B1 **Sierra de Guara** *Mts*	96C2 **Silet** Alg
61J4 **Shubar-Kuduk**	Spain	86A1 **Silgarhi** Nepal
Kazakhstan	51B1 **Sierra de Gudar** *Mts*	92B2 **Silifke** Turk
72D2 **Shu He** *R* China	Spain	82C2 **Siling Co** *L* China
73A4 **Shuicheng** China	23B2 **Sierra de Juárez**	54C2 **Silistra** Bulg
84C3 **Shujaabad** Pak	Mexico	39F7 **Silkeborg** Den
85D4 **Shujālpur** India	34C3 **Sierra de la Ventana**	47E1 **Sillian** Austria
68B2 **Shule He** China	*Mts* Arg	18B2 **Siloam Springs** USA
54C2 **Shumen** Bulg	51C1 **Sierra del Codi** *Mts*	19B3 **Silsbee** USA
61G2 **Shumerlya**	Spain	95A3 **Şiltou** *Well* Chad
Russian Fed	34B2 **Sierra del Morro** *Mt*	58C1 **Silute** Lithuania
73D4 **Shuncheng** China	Arg	93D2 **Silvan** Turk
12C1 **Shungnak** USA	34B3 **Sierra del Nevado**	35B1 **Silvania** Brazil
72C2 **Shuo Xian** China	*Mts* Arg	85C4 **Silvassa** India
91C4 **Shūr Gaz** Iran	24B2 **Sierra de los**	21B2 **Silver City** Nevada,
100B2 **Shurugwi** Zim	**Alamitos** *Mts*	USA
13D2 **Shuswap L** Can	Mexico	9C3 **Silver City** New
61F2 **Shuya** Russian Fed	50B2 **Sierra de los Filabres**	Mexico, USA
12D3 **Shuyak I** USA	Spain	20B2 **Silver Lake** USA
82D3 **Shwebo** Burma	23A1 **Sierra de los**	16A3 **Silver Spring** USA
76B2 **Shwegyin** Burma	**Huicholes** Mexico	13B2 **Silverthrone Mt** Can
84A2 **Siah Koh** *Mts*	23B2 **Sierra de Miahuatlán**	108B2 **Silverton** Aust
Afghan	Mexico	47C1 **Silvretta** *Mts*
84C2 **Sialkot** Pak	23A1 **Sierra de Morones**	Austria/Switz
Sian = Xi'an	*Mts* Mexico	78C2 **Simanggang** Malay
79C4 **Siarao** *I* Phil	50A2 **Sierra de Ronda** *Mts*	76C1 **Simao** China
79B4 **Siaton** Phil	Spain	90A3 **Simareh** *R* Iran
58C1 **Šiauliai** Lithuania	34B2 **Sierra de San Luis**	55C3 **Simav** Turk
65G4 **Sibay** Russian Fed	*Mts* Arg	55C3 **Simav** *R* Turk
101H1 **Sibayi L** S Africa	50B2 **Sierra de Segura** *Mts*	61G3 **Simbirsk**
52C2 **Šibenik** Croatia	Spain	Russian Fed
70A4 **Siberut** *I* Indon	50B1 **Sierra de Urbion** *Mts*	15C2 **Simcoe,L** Can
84B3 **Sibi** Pak	Spain	70A3 **Simeulue** *I* Indon
68C1 **Sibirskoye**	34B2 **Sierra de Uspallata**	60D5 **Simferopol'** Ukraine
Russian Fed	*Mts* Arg	55C3 **Simi** *I* Greece
98B3 **Sibiti** Congo	34B2 **Sierra de Valle Fértil**	46D1 **Simmern** Germany
99D3 **Sibiti** *R* Tanz	*Mts* Arg	13B2 **Simoon Sound** Can

49D2 **Simplon** *Mt* Switz
47C1 **Simplon** *P* Switz
4C2 **Simpson,C** USA
106C3 **Simpson Desert** Aust
6B3 **Simpson Pen** Can
39G7 **Simrishamn** Sweden
69H2 **Simushir** *I*
Russian Fed
99E2 **Sina Dhaqa** Somalia
92B4 **Sinai** *Pen* Egypt
32B2 **Sincelejo** Colombia
17B1 **Sinclair,L** USA
85D3 **Sind** *R* India
85B3 **Sindh** Region, Pak
55C3 **Sindirği** Turk
86B2 **Sindri** India
50A2 **Sines** Port
99D1 **Singa** Sudan
77C5 **Singapore** Republic,
S E Asia
77C5 **Singapore,Str of**
S E Asia
78D4 **Singaraja** Indon
99D3 **Singida** Tanz
78B2 **Singkawang** Indon
109D2 **Singleton** Aust
78A3 **Singtep** *I* Indon
76B1 **Singu** Burma
53A2 **Siniscola** Sardegna
93D2 **Sinjär** Iraq
84B2 **Sinkai Hills** *Mts*
Afghan
95C3 **Sinkat** Sudan
82C1 **Sinkiang**
Autonomous Region,
China
33G2 **Sinnamary** French
Guiana
92C1 **Sinop** Turk
54B1 **Sintana** Rom
78C2 **Sintang** Indon
50A2 **Sintra** Port
32B2 **Sinú** *R* Colombia
74A2 **Sinŭiju** N Korea
59B3 **Siofok** Hung
47B1 **Sion** Switz
8D2 **Sioux City** USA
8D2 **Sioux Falls** USA
10A2 **Sioux Lookout** Can
79B4 **Sipalay** Phil
27L1 **Siparia** Trinidad
69F2 **Siping** China
112B3 **Siple** *Base* Ant
112B5 **Siple I** Ant
79B3 **Sipocot** Phil
70A4 **Sipora** Indon
79B4 **Siquijor** *I* Phil
87B2 **Sira** India
53C3 **Siracusa** Italy
86B2 **Sirajganj** Bang
13C2 **Sir Alexander,Mt** Can
91B5 **Sir Banī Yās** *I* UAE
106C2 **Sir Edward Pellew**
Group *Is* Aust
54C1 **Siret** *R* Rom
12J2 **Sir James**
McBrien,Mt Can
87B2 **Sir Kālahasti** India
13D2 **Sir Laurier,Mt** Can
93D2 **Şirnak** Turk
85C4 **Sirohi** India
87B1 **Sironcha** India
85D4 **Sironj** India
55B3 **Síros** *I* Greece
91B4 **Sirri** *I* Iran
84D3 **Sirsa** India
13D2 **Sir Sandford,Mt** Can
87A2 **Sirsi** India
95A1 **Sirte Desert** Libya
95A1 **Sirte,G of** Libya
52C1 **Sisak** Croatia
76C2 **Sisaket** Thai
76C3 **Sisophon** Camb
46B2 **Sissonne** France
90D3 **Sistan** Region, Iran/
Afghan
49D3 **Sisteron** France
63B2 **Sistig Khem**
Russian Fed
86A1 **Sītapur** India
55C3 **Sitia** Greece
4E4 **Sitka** USA
12D3 **Sitkalidak I** USA
12D3 **Sitkinak** *I* USA

97A3 **Tamchaket** Maur
50A1 **Tamega** *R* Port
23B1 **Tamiahua** Mexico
87B2 **Tamil Nādu** State, India
76D2 **Tam Ky** Viet
17B2 **Tampa** USA
17B2 **Tampa B** USA
39J6 **Tampere** Fin
23B1 **Tampico** Mexico
68D2 **Tamsagbulag** Mongolia
86C2 **Tamu** Burma
23B1 **Tamuis** Mexico
109D2 **Tamworth** Aust
43D3 **Tamworth** Eng
38K4 **Tana** Nor
99D1 **Tana** *L* Eth
99E3 **Tana** *R* Kenya
38K5 **Tana** *R* Nor/Fin
75B2 **Tanabe** Japan
38K4 **Tanafjord** *Inlet* Nor
78D3 **Tanahgrogot** Indon
71E4 **Tanahmerah** Indon
12D1 **Tanana** USA
12E2 **Tanana** *R* USA
Tananarive = Antananarivo
47C2 **Tanaro** *R* Italy
74B2 **Tanch'ŏn** N Korea
34D3 **Tandil** Arg
78B2 **Tandjong Datu** *Pt* Indon
71E4 **Tandjung d'Urville** *C* Indon
78D3 **Tandjung Layar** *C* Indon
78B3 **Tandjung Lumut** *C* Indon
78D2 **Tandjung Mangkalihet** *C* Indon
78C3 **Tandjung Sambar** *C* Indon
78C2 **Tandjung Sirik** *C* Malay
71E4 **Tandjung Vals** *C* Indon
85B3 **Tando Adam** Pak
85B3 **Tando Muhammad Khan** Pak
108B2 **Tandou L** Aust
87B1 **Tāndūr** India
110C1 **Taneatua** NZ
76B2 **Tanen Range** *Mts* Burma/Thai
96B2 **Tanezrouft** *Desert Region* Alg
91C4 **Tang** Iran
99D3 **Tanga** Tanz
60E4 **Tanganrog** Russian Fed
99C3 **Tanganyika,L** Tanz/Zaïre
96B1 **Tanger** Mor
82C2 **Tanggula Shan** *Mts* China
Tangier = Tanger
78A2 **Tangjungpinang** Indon
82C2 **Tangra Yumco** *L* China
72D2 **Tangshan** China
79B4 **Tangub** Phil
63C2 **Tanguy** Russian Fed
Tanintharyi = Tenasserim
79B4 **Tanjay** Phil
101D3 **Tanjona Ankaboa** *C* Madag
101D2 **Tanjona Babaomby** *C* Madag
101D2 **Tanjona Vilanandro** *C* Madag
101D3 **Tanjona Vohimena** *C* Madag
78C4 **Tanjong Bugel** *C* Indon
78B4 **Tanjong Cangkuang** *C* Indon
78C3 **Tanjong Puting** *C* Indon
78C3 **Tanjong Selatan** *C* Indon
78D3 **Tanjung** Indon
70A3 **Tanjungbalai** Indon
78A3 **Tanjung Jabung** *Pt* Indon
78B3 **Tanjungpandan** Indon
78B4 **Tanjung Priok** Indon
78D2 **Tanjungredeb** Indon
78D2 **Tanjungselor** Indon
84C2 **Tank** Pak
68B1 **Tannu Ola** *Mts* Russian Fed
97B4 **Tano** *R* Ghana
97C3 **Tanout** Niger
23B1 **Tanquián** Mexico
73E4 **Tan-shui** Taiwan
86A1 **Tansing** Nepal
95C1 **Tanta** Egypt
96A2 **Tan-Tan** Mor
4B3 **Tanunak** USA
99D3 **Tanzania** Republic, Africa
72A3 **Tao He** *R* China
72B2 **Taole** China
96B1 **Taourirt** Mor
60C2 **Tapa** Estonia
25C3 **Tapachula** Mexico
33F4 **Tapajós** *R* Brazil
34C3 **Tapalquén** Arg
70B4 **Tapan** Indon
111A3 **Tapanui** NZ
32D5 **Tapauá** *R* Brazil
85D4 **Tapi** *R* India
86B1 **Taplejung** Nepal
111B2 **Tapuaeniku** *Mt* NZ
35B2 **Tapuaritinga** Brazil
79B4 **Tapul Group** *Is* Phil
33E4 **Tapurucuara** Brazil
109D1 **Tara** Aust
65J4 **Tara** Russian Fed
65J4 **Tara** *R* Russian Fed
54A2 **Tara** *R* Bosnia-Herzegovina/Montenegro, Yugos
97D4 **Taraba** *R* Nig
30D2 **Tarabuco** Bol
Tarābulus = Tripoli
50B1 **Taracón** Spain
110C1 **Taradale** NZ
78D2 **Tarakan** Indon
44A3 **Taransay** *I* Scot
53C2 **Taranto** Italy
32B5 **Tarapoto** Peru
49C2 **Tarare** France
110C2 **Tararua Range** *Mts* NZ
96C2 **Tarat** Alg
110C1 **Tarawera** NZ
51B1 **Tarazona** Spain
44C3 **Tarbat Ness** *Pen* Scot
84C2 **Tarbela Res** Pak
42B2 **Tarbert** Strathclyde, Scot
44A3 **Tarbert** Western Isles, Scot
48C3 **Tarbes** France
106C4 **Tarcoola** Aust
109C2 **Tarcoon** Aust
109D2 **Taree** Aust
96A2 **Tarfaya** Mor
95A1 **Tarhūnah** Libya
91B5 **Tarīf** UAE
30D3 **Tarija** Bol
87B2 **Tarikere** India
81C4 **Tarīm** Yemen
99D3 **Tarime** Tanz
82C1 **Tarim He** *R* China
82C2 **Tarim Pendi** *Basin* China
84B2 **Tarin Kut** Afghan
18A1 **Tarkio** USA
79B2 **Tarlac** Phil
32B6 **Tarma** Peru
49C3 **Tarn** *R* France
59C2 **Tarnobrzeg** Pol
59C3 **Tarnów** Pol
107D3 **Taroom** Aust
51C1 **Tarragona** Spain
109C4 **Tarraleah** Aust
51C1 **Tarrasa** Spain
16C2 **Tarrytown** USA
92B2 **Tarsus** Turk
44D2 **Tartan** *Oilfield* N Sea
47D2 **Tartaro** *R* Italy
60C2 **Tartu** Estonia
92C3 **Tartūs** Syria
35C1 **Tarumirim** Brazil
70A3 **Tarutung** Indon
52B1 **Tarvisio** Italy
80D1 **Tashauz** Turkmenistan
86C1 **Tashigang** Bhutan
82A1 **Tashkent** Uzbekistan
65K4 **Tashtagol** Russian Fed
63A2 **Tashtyp** Russian Fed
78B4 **Tasikmalaya** Indon
94B2 **Tasīl** Syria
6E2 **Tasiussaq** Greenland
95A3 **Tasker** *Well* Niger
110B2 **Tasman B** NZ
107D5 **Tasmania** *I* Aust
111B2 **Tasman Mts** NZ
109C4 **Tasman Pen** Aust
107E4 **Tasman S** NZ Aust
92C1 **Taşova** Turk
96C2 **Tassili du Hoggar** *Desert* Region, Alg
96C2 **Tassili N'jjer** *Desert* Region, Alg
96B2 **Tata** Mor
96D1 **Tataouine** Tunisia
65J4 **Tatarsk** Russian Fed
69G2 **Tatarskiy Proliv** *Str* Russian Fed
61G2 **Tatarstan** Russian Fed
75B1 **Tateyama** Japan
5G3 **Tathlina L** Can
12E2 **Tatitlek** USA
13C2 **Tatla Lake** Can
59B3 **Tatry** *Mts* Pol/Slovakia
75A2 **Tatsuno** Japan
85B4 **Tatta** Pak
35B2 **Tatuí** Brazil
93D2 **Tatvan** Turk
31C3 **Tauá** Brazil
35B2 **Taubaté** Brazil
110C1 **Taumarunui** NZ
101F1 **Taung** S Africa
76B2 **Taungdwingyi** Burma
76B1 **Taung-gyi** Burma
76A2 **Taungup** Burma
84C2 **Taunsa** Pak
43C4 **Taunton** Eng
16D2 **Taunton** USA
46E1 **Taunus** Region, Germany
110C1 **Taupo** NZ
110C1 **Taupo,L** NZ
58C1 **Taurage** Lithuania
110C1 **Tauranga** NZ
110C1 **Tauranga Harbour** *B* NZ
110B1 **Tauroa Pt** NZ
7A3 **Tavani** Can
7A3 **Tavani** Can
65H4 **Tavda** *R* Russian Fed
43B4 **Tavistock** Eng
76B3 **Tavoy** Burma
76B3 **Tavoy Pt** Burma
92A2 **Tavsanli** Turk
111B2 **Tawa** NZ
19A3 **Tawakoni,L** USA
14B2 **Tawas City** USA
70C3 **Tawau** Malay
98C1 **Taweisha** Sudan
79B4 **Tawitawi** *I* Phil
79B4 **Tawitawi Group** *Is* Phil
23B2 **Taxco** Mexico
23B2 **Taxcoco** Mexico
44C3 **Tay** *R* Scot
78C3 **Tayan** Indon
12B1 **Taylor** Alaska, USA
13C1 **Taylor** Can
14B2 **Taylor** Michigan, USA
19A3 **Taylor** Texas, USA
18C2 **Taylorville** USA
80B3 **Taymā'** S Arabia
63B1 **Taymura** *R* Russian Fed
76D3 **Tay Ninh** Viet
63B2 **Tayshet** Russian Fed
68B2 **Tayshir** Mongolia
44C3 **Tayside** Region, Scot
79A3 **Taytay** Phil
90D3 **Tayyebāt** Iran
96B1 **Taza** Mor
95B2 **Tazirbu** Libya
12E2 **Tazlina L** USA
64J3 **Tazovskiy** Russian Fed
65F5 **Tbilisi** Georgia
98B3 **Tchibanga** Gabon
95A2 **Tchigai,Plat du** Niger
97C3 **Tchin Tabaradene** Niger
98B2 **Tchollíré** Cam
58B2 **Tczew** Pol
111A3 **Te Anau** NZ
111A3 **Te Anau,L** NZ
110C1 **Te Aroha** NZ
110C1 **Te Awamutu** NZ
96C1 **Tébessa** Alg
23A2 **Teboman** Mexico
23A2 **Tecailtlān** Mexico
21B3 **Tecate** Mexico
61K2 **Techa** *R* Russian Fed
23A1 **Tecolotlán** Mexico
23A2 **Tećpan** Mexico
54C1 **Tecuci** Rom
18A1 **Tecumseh** USA
80E2 **Tedzhen** Turkmenistan
65H6 **Tedzhen** *R* Turkmenistan
42D2 **Tees** *R* Eng
33E4 **Tefé** Brazil
78B4 **Tegal** Indon
78B4 **Tegineneng** Indon
25D3 **Tegucigalpa** Honduras
21B3 **Tehachapi Mts** USA
21B2 **Tehachapi P** USA
4J3 **Tehek L** Can
90B2 **Tehrān** Iran
23B2 **Tehuacán** Mexico
23B2 **Tehuantepec** Mexico
23B2 **Tehuitzingo** Mexico
43B3 **Teifi** *R* Wales
50A2 **Tejo** *R* Port
23A2 **Tejupilco** Mexico
111B2 **Tekapo,L** NZ
82B1 **Tekeli** Kazakhstan
92A1 **Tekirdağ** Turk
55C2 **Tekir Dağlari** *Mts* Turk
86C2 **Teknaf** Bang
110C1 **Te Kuiti** NZ
25D3 **Tela** Honduras
94B2 **Tel Aviv Yafo** Israel
34B3 **Telén** Arg
21B2 **Telescope Peak** *Mt* USA
33F5 **Teles Pires** *R* Brazil
47D1 **Telfs** Austria
63A2 **Teli** Russian Fed
94B3 **Tell el Meise** *Mt* Jordan
12A1 **Teller** USA
87B2 **Tellicherry** India
77C5 **Telok Anson** Malay
78D2 **Tĕlok Darvel** Malay
71E4 **Tĕlok Flamingo** *B* Indon
78C3 **Tĕlok Kumai** *B* Indon
78B4 **Tĕlok Pelabuanratu** *B* Indon
78D4 **Tĕlok Saleh** *B* Indon
78C3 **Tĕlok Sampit** *B* Indon
78B3 **Tĕlok Sukadona** *B* Indon
23B2 **Teloloapán** Mexico
64G3 **Tel'pos-iz** *Mt* Russian Fed
58C1 **Telšiai** Lithuania
78C3 **Telukbatang** Indon
71E4 **Teluk Berau** *B* Indon
78B4 **Telukbetung** Indom
70D4 **Teluk Bone** *B* Indon
71E4 **Teluk Cendrawasih** *B* Indon
78D3 **Teluk Mandar** *B* Indon
71D4 **Teluk Tolo** *B* Indon

Tisīyah

94C2 **Tisīyah** Syria
59C3 **Tisza** *R* Hung
86A2 **Titlagarh** India
54B2 **Titov Veles**
    Macedonia
98C2 **Titule** Zaïre
17B2 **Titusville** USA
43C4 **Tiverton** Eng
52B2 **Tivoli** Italy
23B2 **Tixtla** Mexico
99E2 **Tiyeglow** Somalia
23B2 **Tizayuca** Mexico
25D2 **Tizimin** Mexico
96C1 **Tizi Ouzou** Alg
96B2 **Tiznit** Mor
23A1 **Tizpan el Alto**
    Mexico
23B2 **Tlacolula** Mexico
23B2 **Tlacotalpan** Mexico
23A2 **Tlalchana** Mexico
23B2 **Tlalnepantla** Mexico
23B2 **Tlalpan** Mexico
23A1 **Tlaltenango** Mexico
23B2 **Tlancualpicán**
    Mexico
23B2 **Tlapa** Mexico
23B2 **Tlapacoyan** Mexico
23A1 **Tlaquepaque** Mexico
23B2 **Tlaxcala** Mexico
23B2 **Tlaxcala** State,
    Mexico
23B2 **Tlaxiaco** Mexico
96B1 **Tlemcem** Alg
101D2 **Toamasina** Madag
34C3 **Toay** Arg
75B2 **Toba** Japan
84B2 **Toba and Kakar**
    Ranges *Mts* Pak
27E4 **Tobago** *I*
    Caribbean S
13C2 **Toba Inlet** *Sd* Can
71D3 **Tobelo** Indon
14B1 **Tobermory** Can
44A3 **Tobermory** Scot
71E3 **Tobi** *I* Pacific O
21B1 **Tobin,Mt** USA
65H4 **Tobol** *R* Kazakhstan
70D4 **Toboli** Indon
65H4 **Tobol'sk** Russian Fed
    Tobruk = Tubruq
31B2 **Tocantins** *R* Brazil
31B3 **Tocantins** State,
    Brazil
17B1 **Toccoa** USA
47C1 **Toce** *R* Italy
30R3 **Tocopilla** Chile
30C3 **Tocorpuri** *Mt* Chile
32D1 **Tocuyo** *R* Ven
85D3 **Toda** India
47C1 **Tödi** *Mt* Switz
75A1 **Todong** S Korea
9B4 **Todos Santos**
    Mexico
13E2 **Tofield** Can
13B3 **Tofino** Can
12B3 **Togiak** USA
12B3 **Togiak B** USA
97C4 **Togo** Republic, Africa
72C1 **Togtoh** China
12F2 **Tok** USA
74E2 **Tokachi** *R* Japan
75B1 **Tokamachi** Japan
95C3 **Tokar** Sudan
69E4 **Tokara Retto** *Arch*
    Japan
92C1 **Tokat** Turk
74B3 **Tŏkchŏk-kundo** *Arch*
    S Korea
75A1 **Tok-do** *I* S Korea
82B1 **Tokmak** Kirghizia
110C1 **Tokomaru Bay** NZ
12H3 **Toku** *R* Can/USA
78C3 **Tokung** Indon
69E4 **Tokuno** *I* Japan
74C4 **Tokushima** Japan
75A2 **Tokuyama** Japan
74D3 **Tōkyō** Japan
110C1 **Tolaga Bay** NZ
101D3 **Tôlañaro** Madag
30F3 **Toledo** Brazil
50B2 **Toledo** Spain
14B2 **Toledo** USA
19B3 **Toledo Bend Res**
    USA

101D3 **Toliara** Madag
23B1 **Toliman** Mexico
32B3 **Tolina** *Mt* Colombia
51B1 **Tolosa** Spain
29B3 **Toltén** Chile
23B2 **Toluca** Mexico
61G3 **Tol'yatti** Russian Fed
74E2 **Tomakomai** Japan
78D1 **Tomani** Malay
58C2 **Tomaszów**
    Mazowiecka Pol
11B3 **Tombigbee** *R* USA
98B3 **Tomboco** Angola
35C2 **Tombos** Brazil
97B3 **Tombouctou** Mali
100A2 **Tombua** Angola
34A3 **Tomé** Chile
50B2 **Tomelloso** Spain
50A2 **Tomer** Pol
106B3 **Tomkinson Range**
    Mts Aust
63E2 **Tommot**
    Russian Fed
55B2 **Tomorrit** *Mt* Alb
65K4 **Tomsk** Russian Fed
16B3 **Toms River** USA
25C3 **Tonalá** Mexico
20C1 **Tonasket** USA
15C2 **Tonawanda** USA
105H4 **Tonga** *Is* Pacific O
101H1 **Tongaat** S Africa
73D3 **Tongcheng** China
72B2 **Tongchuan** China
72A2 **Tongde** China
46C1 **Tongeren** Belg
76E2 **Tonggu Jiao** *I* China
73A5 **Tonghai** China
74B2 **Tonghua** China
74B3 **Tongjosŏn-man**
    N Korea
76D1 **Tongkin,G of** China/
    Viet
72E1 **Tonglia** China
73D3 **Tongling** China
108B2 **Tongo** Aust
34A2 **Tongoy** Chile
73B4 **Tongren** Guizhou,
    China
72A2 **Tongren** Qinghai,
    China
86C1 **Tongsa** Bhutan
76B1 **Tongta** Burma
68B3 **Tongtian He** *R* China
44B2 **Tongue** Scot
72D2 **Tong Xian** China
72B2 **Tongxin** China
73B4 **Tongzi** China
9C4 **Tonichi** Mexico
99C2 **Tonj** Sudan
85D3 **Tonk** India
18A2 **Tonkawa** USA
76C3 **Tonle Sap** *L* Camb
21B2 **Tonopah** USA
12E2 **Tonsina** USA
8B2 **Tooele** USA
109D1 **Toogoolawah** Aust
108B1 **Toompine** Aust
109D1 **Toowoomba** Aust
22C1 **Topaz L** USA
18A2 **Topeka** USA
9C4 **Topolobampo**
    Mexico
20B1 **Toppenish** USA
99D2 **Tor** Eth
55C3 **Torbali** Turk
90C2 **Torbat-e-Heydarīyeh**
    Iran
90D2 **Torbat-e Jām** Iran
12D2 **Torbert,Mt** USA
50A1 **Tordesillas** Spain
56C2 **Torgau** Germany
46B1 **Torhout** Belg
69G3 **Tori** *I* Japan
47B2 **Torino** Italy
99D2 **Torit** Sudan
35A1 **Torixoreu** Brazil
50A1 **Tormes** *R* Spain
13E2 **Tornado Mt** Can
38J5 **Torne** *L* Sweden
38H5 **Torneträsk** Sweden
7D4 **Torngat** *Mts* Can
38J5 **Tornio** Fin
34C3 **Tornquist** Arg
15C2 **Toronto** Can

60D2 **Toropets**
    Russian Fed
99D2 **Tororo** Uganda
92B2 **Toros Dağlari** *Mts*
    Turk
43C4 **Torquay** Eng
22C4 **Torrance** USA
50A2 **Torrão** Port
51C1 **Torreblanca** Spain
53B2 **Torre del Greco** Italy
50B1 **Torrelavega** Spain
50B2 **Torremolinos** Spain
108A2 **Torrens,L** Aust
24B2 **Torreón** Mexico
47B2 **Torre Pellice** Italy
107D2 **Torres Str** Aust
50A2 **Torres Vedras** Port
16C2 **Torrington**
    Connecticut, USA
8C2 **Torrington**
    Wyoming, USA
9C4 **Torrón** Mexico
38D3 **Tórshavn** Føroyar
47C2 **Tortona** Italy
51C1 **Tortosa** Spain
90C2 **Torüd** Iran
58B2 **Toruń** Pol
40B2 **Tory** *I* Irish Rep
60D2 **Torzhok** Russian Fed
75A2 **Tosa** Japan
74C4 **Tosa-shimizu** Japan
74C4 **Tosa-wan** *B* Japan
75B2 **To-shima** *I* Japan
    Toshkent = Tashkent
60D2 **Tosno** Russian Fed
75A2 **Tosu** Japan
92B1 **Tosya** Turk
61F1 **Tot'ma** Russian Fed
43C4 **Totnes** Eng
33F2 **Totness** Surinam
23B2 **Totolapan** Mexico
51B2 **Totona** Spain
109C2 **Tottenham** Aust
74C3 **Tottori** Japan
97B4 **Touba** Ivory Coast
97A3 **Touba** Sen
96B1 **Toubkal** *Mt* Mor
97B3 **Tougan** Burkina
96C1 **Touggourt** Alg
97A3 **Tougué** Guinea
46C2 **Toul** France
49D3 **Toulon** France
48C3 **Toulouse** France
97B4 **Toumodi** Ivory Coast
76B2 **Toungoo** Burma
46B1 **Tourcoing** France
96A2 **Tourine** Maur
46B1 **Tournai** Belg
48C2 **Tours** France
74E2 **Towada** Japan
74E2 **Towada-ko** *L* Japan
15C2 **Towanda** USA
107D2 **Townsville** Aust
16A3 **Towson** USA
43C4 **Towy** *R* Wales
74D3 **Toyama** Japan
75B1 **Toyama-wan** *B*
    Japan
75B2 **Toyohashi** Japan
75B2 **Toyonaka** Japan
75A1 **Toyooka** Japan
74D3 **Toyota** Japan
96C1 **Tozeur** Tunisia
46D2 **Traben-Trarbach**
    Germany
93C1 **Trabzon** Turk
22B2 **Tracy** California, USA
34A3 **Traiguén** Chile
13D3 **Trail** Can
41B3 **Tralee** Irish Rep
45B2 **Tralee B** Irish Rep
45C2 **Tramore** Irish Rep
39G7 **Tranås** Sweden
77B4 **Trang** Thai
71E4 **Trangan** *I* Indon
109C2 **Trangie** Aust
12E2 **Transalaskan Pipeline**
    USA
100B3 **Transvaal** Province,
    S Africa
    Transylvanian Alps =
    Munţii Carpaţii
    Meridionali
53B3 **Trapani** Italy

109C3 **Traralgon** Aust
97A3 **Trarza** Region, Maur
76C3 **Trat** Thai
108B2 **Traveller's** *L* Aust
56C2 **Travemünde**
    Germany
14A2 **Traverse City** USA
12C1 **Traverse Peak** *Mt*
    USA
111B2 **Travers,Mt** NZ
47C2 **Trebbia** *R* Italy
59B3 **Třebič**
    Czech Republic
54A2 **Trebinje** Bosnia-
    Herzegovina
57C3 **Trebon**
    Czech Republic
29F2 **Treinta y Tres** Urug
29C4 **Trelew** Arg
39G7 **Trelleborg** Sweden
43B3 **Tremadog B** Wales
15D1 **Tremblant,Mt** Can
13C2 **Trembleur L** Can
16A2 **Tremont** USA
59B3 **Trenčín** Slovakia
34C3 **Trenque Lauquén**
    Arg
43D3 **Trent** *R* Eng
47D1 **Trentino** Region, Italy
47D1 **Trento** Italy
15C2 **Trenton** Can
18B1 **Trenton** Missouri,
    USA
16B2 **Trenton** New Jersey,
    USA
7E5 **Trepassey** Can
34C3 **Tres Arroyos** Arg
35B2 **Tres Corações** Brazil
30F3 **Três Lagoas** Brazil
34C3 **Tres Lomas** Arg
22B2 **Tres Pinos** USA
35C2 **Três Rios** Brazil
47C2 **Treviglio** Italy
47E2 **Treviso** Italy
47C2 **Trezzo** Italy
87B2 **Trichür** India
108C2 **Trida** Aust
46D2 **Trier** Germany
52B1 **Trieste** Italy
45C2 **Trim** Irish Rep
87C3 **Trincomalee**
    Sri Lanka
33E6 **Trinidad** Bol
29E2 **Trinidad** Urug
9C3 **Trinidad** USA
34C3 **Trinidad** *I* Arg
27E4 **Trinidad** *I*
    Caribbean S
103G6 **Trindade** *I* Atlantic O
27E4 **Trinidad & Tobago**
    Republic, Caribbean S
19A3 **Trinity** USA
9D3 **Trinity** *R* USA
7E5 **Trinity B** Can
12D3 **Trinity Is** USA
17A1 **Trion** USA
94B1 **Tripoli** Leb
95A1 **Tripoli** Libya
55B3 **Trípolis** Greece
86C2 **Tripura** State, India
103H6 **Tristan da Cunha** *Is*
    Atlantic O
87B3 **Trivandrum** India
59B3 **Trnava** Slovakia
107E1 **Trobriand Is** PNG
15D1 **Trois-Riviéres** Can
65H4 **Troitsk** Russian Fed
39G7 **Trollhättan** Sweden
38F6 **Trollheimen** *Mt* Nor
89K9 **Tromelin** *I* Indian O
38H5 **Tromsø** Nor
38G6 **Trondheim** Nor
38G6 **Trondheimfjord** *Inlet*
    Nor
42B2 **Troon** Scot
102J3 **Tropic of Cancer**
103J6 **Tropic of Capricorn**
96B2 **Troudenni** Mali
7A4 **Trout L** Ontario, Can
17A1 **Troy** Alabama, USA
16C1 **Troy** New York, USA
14B2 **Troy** Ohio, USA
54B2 **Troyan** Bulg
49C2 **Troyes** France

Umm al Qaiwain

91B5 Trucial Coast Region, UAE
21A2 Truckee R USA
25D3 Trujillo Honduras
32B5 Trujillo Peru
50A2 Trujillo Spain
32C2 Trujillo Ven
109C2 Trundle Aust
7D5 Truro Can
43B4 Truro Eng
68B2 Tsagaan Nuur L Mongolia
68B1 Tsagan-Tologoy Russian Fed
101D2 Tsaratanana Madag
100B3 Tsau Botswana
99D3 Tsavo Kenya
99D3 Tsavo Nat Pk Kenya
65J4 Tselinograd Kazakhstan
100A3 Tses Namibia
68C2 Tsetserleg Mongolia
97C4 Tsévié Togo
100B3 Tshabong Botswana
100B3 Tshane Botswana
98B3 Tshela Zaïre
98C3 Tshibala Zaïre
98C3 Tshikapa Zaïre
98C3 Tshuapa R Zaïre
101D3 Tsihombe Madag
61F4 Tsimlyanskoye Vodokhranilishche Res Russian Fed
Tsinan = Jinan
Tsingtao = Qingdao
101D2 Tsiroanomandidy Madag
13B2 Tsitsutl Peak Mt Can
58D2 Tsna R Belorussia
72B1 Tsogt Ovoo Mongolia
68C2 Tsomog Mongolia
75B2 Tsu Japan
75B1 Tsubata Japan
74E3 Tsuchira Japan
74E2 Tsugaru-kaikyō Str Japan
100A2 Tsumeb Namibia
100A3 Tsumis Namibia
75B1 Tsunugi Japan
74D3 Tsuruga Japan
74D3 Tsuruoka Japan
75B1 Tsushima Japan
74B4 Tsushima I Japan
74C3 Tsuyama Japan
50A1 Tua R Port
45B2 Tuam Irish Rep
60E5 Tuapse Russian Fed
111A3 Tuatapere NZ
30G4 Tubarão Brazil
94B2 Tubas Israel
79A4 Tubbataha Reefs Is Phil
57B3 Tübingen Germany
95B1 Tubruq Libya
16B3 Tuckerton USA
9B3 Tucson USA
30C4 Tucumán State, Arg
34B2 Tucunuco Arg
33E2 Tucupita Ven
51B1 Tudela Spain
93C3 Tudmur Syria
101H1 Tugela R S Africa
109D2 Tuggerah L Aust
12D3 Tugidak I USA
79B2 Tuguegarao Phil
63F2 Tugur Russian Fed
72D2 Tuhai He R China
4E3 Tuktoyaktuk USA
58C1 Tukums Latvia
99D3 Tukuyu Tanz
84B1 Tukzar Afghan
60E3 Tula Russian Fed
23B1 Tulancingo Mexico
78A3 Tulangbawang R Indon
32B3 Tulcán Colombia
60C5 Tulcea Rom
100B3 Tuli India
94B2 Tulkarm Israel
48C2 Tulle France
19B3 Tullos USA
45C2 Tullow Irish Rep
18A2 Tulsa USA

93C3 Tulūl ash Shāmīyah Desert Region Syria/S Arabia
63C2 Tulun Russian Fed
78C4 Tulungagung Indon
32B3 Tumaco Colombia
109C3 Tumbarumba Aust
32A4 Tumbes Ecuador
108A2 Tumby Bay Aust
74B2 Tumen China
87B2 Tumkūr India
77C4 Tumpat Malay
85D4 Tumsar India
97B3 Tumu Ghana
109C3 Tumut Aust
109C3 Tumut R Aust
27L1 Tunapuna Trinidad
93C2 Tunceli Turk
99D3 Tunduma Zambia
101C2 Tunduru Tanz
54C2 Tundzha R Bulg
87B1 Tungabhadra R India
68D4 Tung-Chiang Taiwan
38B2 Tungnafellsjökull Mts Iceland
12J2 Tungsten Can
63B1 Tunguska R Russian Fed
87C1 Tuni India
96D1 Tunis Tunisia
88E4 Tunisia Republic, N Africa
32C2 Tunja Colombia
12B2 Tuntutuliak USA
12B2 Tununak USA
34B2 Tunuyán Arg
34B2 Tunuyán R Arg
22C2 Tuolumne Meadows USA
35A2 Tupã Brazil
35B1 Tupaciguara Brazil
19C3 Tupelo USA
30C3 Tupiza Bol
15D2 Tupper Lake USA
34B2 Tupungato Arg
29C2 Tupungato Mt Arg
86C1 Tura India
63C1 Tura Russian Fed
61K2 Tura R Russian Fed
90C2 Turān Iran
63B2 Turan Russian Fed
93C3 Turayf S Arabia
80E3 Turbat Pak
32B2 Turbo Colombia
54B1 Turda Rom
63A3 Turfan Depression China
65H4 Turgay Kazakhstan
63B3 Turgen Uul Mt Mongolia
54C2 Turgovishte Bulg
92A2 Turgutlu Turk
92C1 Turhal Turk
39K7 Türi Estonia
51B2 Turia R Spain
Turin = Torino
61K2 Turinsk Russian Fed
69F2 Turiy Rog Russian Fed
99D2 Turkana,L Kenya/Eth
80E1 Turkestan Region, C Asia
82A1 Turkestan Kazakhstan
92C2 Turkey Republic, W Asia
80D1 Turkmenistan Republic, Asia
90B2 Turkmenskiy Zaliv B Turkmenistan
27C2 Turks Is Caribbean S
39J6 Turku Fin
99D2 Turkwel R Kenya
22B2 Turlock USA
22B2 Turlock L USA
110C2 Turnagain,C NZ
25D3 Turneffe I Belize
16C1 Turners Falls USA
46C1 Turnhout Belg
13F1 Turnor L Can
54B2 Turnu Măgurele Rom
63A3 Turpan China
26B2 Turquino Mt Cuba
80E1 Turtkul' Uzbekistan

18A2 Turtle Creek Res USA
13F2 Turtle L Can
63A1 Turukhansk Russian Fed
68C1 Turuntayevo Russian Fed
35A1 Turvo R Goias, Brazil
35B2 Turvo R São Paulo, Brazil
58C2 Tur'ya R Ukraine
19C3 Tuscaloosa USA
18C2 Tuscola USA
90C3 Tusharik Iran
Tutera = Tudela
87B3 Tuticorin India
54C2 Tutrakan Bulg
57B3 Tuttlingen Germany
68C2 Tuul Gol R Mongolia
105G4 Tuvalu Is Pacific O
63B2 Tuvinskaya Respublika, Russian Fed
23A2 Tuxpan Jalisco, Mexico
24B2 Tuxpan Nayarit, Mexico
23B1 Tuxpan Veracruz, Mexico
23B2 Tuxtepec Mexico
25C3 Tuxtla Gutiérrez Mexico
50A1 Túy Spain
76D3 Tuy Hoa Viet
92B2 Tuz Gölü Salt L Turk
93D3 Tuz Khurmātū Iraq
54A2 Tuzla Bosnia-Herzegovina
60E2 Tver' Russian Fed
42C2 Tweed R Eng/Scot
109D1 Tweed Heads Aust
42C2 Tweedsmuir Hills Scot
7E5 Twillingate Can
8B2 Twin Falls USA
111B2 Twins,The Mt NZ
14A2 Two Rivers USA
63E2 Tygda Russian Fed
19A3 Tyler USA
65K3 Tym R Russian Fed
69G1 Tymovskoye Russian Fed
42D2 Tyne R Eng
42D2 Tyne and Wear Metropolitan County, Eng
42D2 Tynemouth Eng
38G6 Tynset Nor
12D3 Tyonek USA
94B2 Tyr Leb
Tyre = Tyr
45C1 Tyrone County, N Ire
108B3 Tyrrell,L Aust
53B2 Tyrrhenian S Italy
65H4 Tyumen' Russian Fed
43B3 Tywyn Wales
55B3 Tzoumérka Mt Greece

U

99E2 Uarsciek Somalia
35C2 Ubá Brazil
35C1 Ubaí Brazil
98B2 Ubangi R CAR
47B2 Ubaye R France
75A2 Ube Japan
50B2 Ubeda Spain
6E2 Ubekendt Ejland I Greenland
35B1 Uberaba Brazil
35B1 Uberlândia Brazil
76C2 Ubon Ratchathani Thai
58D2 Ubort R Belorussia
98C3 Ubundi Zaïre
32C5 Ucayali R Peru
84C3 Uch Pak
63F2 Uchar R Russian Fed
74E2 Uchiura-wan B Japan
63B2 Uda R Russian Fed
85C4 Udaipur India
86B1 Udaipur Garhi Nepal

34D3 Udaquoila Arg
39G7 Uddevalla Sweden
38H5 Uddjaur L Sweden
87B1 Udgir India
84D2 Udhampur India
61H2 Udmurtskaya Respublika, Russian Fed
76C2 Udon Thani Thai
63F2 Udskaya Guba B Russian Fed
87A2 Udupi India
75B1 Ueda Japan
99C2 Uele R Zaïre
56C2 Uelzen Germany
98C2 Uere R Zaïre
61J3 Ufa Russian Fed
61J2 Ufa R Russian Fed
100A3 Ugab R Namibia
99D3 Ugaila R Tanz
12D3 Ugak B USA
99D2 Uganda Republic, Africa
12C3 Ugashik B USA
12C3 Ugashik L USA
47B2 Ugine France
69G2 Uglegorsk Russian Fed
60E2 Uglich Russian Fed
60E3 Ugra R Russian Fed
44A3 Uig Scot
98B3 Uíge Angola
61H4 Uil Kazakhstan
8B2 Uinta Mts USA
100B4 Uitenhage S Africa
59C3 Ujfehértó Hung
75B2 Uji Japan
99C3 Ujiji Tanz
30C3 Ujina Chile
85D4 Ujjain India
70C4 Ujung Pandang Indon
99D3 Ukerewe I Tanz
86C1 Ukhrul India
21A2 Ukiah California, USA
20C1 Ukiah Oregon, USA
58C1 Ukmerge Lithuania
60C4 Ukraine Republic, Europe
68C2 Ulaanbaatar Mongolia
68B2 Ulaangom Mongolia
72C1 Ulaan Uul Mongolia
82C1 Ulangar Hu L China
68C1 Ulan Ude Russian Fed
68B3 Ulan Ul Hu L China
34B2 Ulapes Arg
74B3 Ulchin S Korea
54A2 Ulcinj Montenegro, Yugos
68D2 Uldz Mongolia
68B2 Uliastay Mongolia
58D1 Ulla Lithuania
109D3 Ulladulla Aust
44B3 Ullapool Scot
38H5 Ullsfjorden Inlet Nor
42C2 Ullswater L Eng
74C3 Ullung-do I S Korea
57C3 Ulm Germany
108A1 Uloowaranie,L Aust
74B3 Ulsan S Korea
45C1 Ulster Region, N Ire
65K5 Ulungur He R China
65K5 Ulungur Hu L China
44A3 Ulva I Scot
42C2 Ulverston Eng
109C4 Ulverstone Aust
63G2 Ulya R Russian Fed
60D4 Uman Ukraine
6E2 Umanak Greenland
86A2 Umaria India
85B3 Umarkot Pak
108A1 Umaroona,L Aust
20C1 Umatilla USA
38L5 Umba Russian Fed
99D3 Umba R Tanz
38H6 Ume R Sweden
38J6 Umea Sweden
101H1 Umfolozi R S Africa
4C3 Umiat USA
91C4 Umm al Qaiwain UAE

32D2 **Venezuela** Republic, S America
87A1 **Vengurla** India
12C3 **Veniaminof V** USA
Venice = Venezia
87B2 **Venkatagiri** India
56B2 **Venlo** Neth
58C1 **Venta** R Latvia
101G1 **Ventersburg** S Africa
58C1 **Ventspils** Latvia
32D3 **Ventuari** R Ven
22C3 **Ventura** USA
60D1 **Vepsovskaya Vozvyshennost'** *Upland* Russian Fed
30D4 **Vera** Arg
51B2 **Vera** Spain
23B2 **Veracruz** Mexico
23B1 **Veracruz** State, Mexico
85C4 **Veräval** India
47C2 **Verbania** Italy
47C2 **Vercelli** Italy
35A1 **Verde** R Goias, Brazil
23A1 **Verde** R Jalisco, Mexico
35A1 **Verde** R Mato Grosso do Sul, Brazil
23B2 **Verde** R Oaxaca, Mexico
Verde,C = Cap Vert
35C1 **Verde Grande** R Brazil
34C3 **Verde,Pen** Arg
49D3 **Verdon** R France
46C2 **Verdun** France
101G1 **Vereeniging** S Africa
61H2 **Vereshchagino** Russian Fed
97A3 **Verga,C** Guinea
34D3 **Vergara** Arg
50A1 **Verín** Spain
63D2 **Verkh Angara** R Russian Fed
61J3 **Verkhneural'sk** Russian Fed
63E1 **Verkhnevilyuysk** Russian Fed
1C8 **Verkhoyansk** Russian Fed
35A1 **Vermelho** R Brazil
13E2 **Vermilion** Can
10C2 **Vermont** State, USA
22B2 **Vernalis** USA
13D2 **Vernon** Can
46A2 **Vernon** France
9D3 **Vernon** USA
17B2 **Vero Beach** USA
54B2 **Veroia** Greece
47D2 **Verolanuova** Italy
47D2 **Verona** Italy
46B2 **Versailles** France
101H1 **Verulam** S Africa
46C1 **Verviers** Belg
46B2 **Vervins** France
46C2 **Vesle** R France
49D2 **Vesoul** France
38G5 **Vesterålen** Is Nor
38G5 **Vestfjorden** Inlet Nor
38A2 **Vestmannaeyjar** Iceland
53B2 **Vesuvio** Mt Italy
59B3 **Veszprém** Hung
39H7 **Vetlanda** Sweden
61F2 **Vetluga** R Russian Fed
46B1 **Veurne** Belg
47B1 **Vevey** Switz
46A2 **Vexin** Region, France
47A2 **Veynes** France
50A1 **Viana do Castelo** Port
Viangchan = Vientiane
49E3 **Viareggio** Italy
39F7 **Viborg** Den
53C3 **Vibo Valentia** Italy
Vic = Vich
112C2 **Vicecomodoro Marambio** Base Ant
52B1 **Vicenza** Italy
51C1 **Vich** Spain
32D3 **Vichada** R Colombia
61F2 **Vichuga** Russian Fed

49C2 **Vichy** France
19B3 **Vicksburg** USA
35C2 **Vicosa** Brazil
106C4 **Victor Harbour** Aust
34C2 **Victoria** Arg
13C3 **Victoria** Can
34A3 **Victoria** Chile
78D1 **Victoria** Malay
108B3 **Victoria** State, Aust
9D4 **Victoria** USA
106C2 **Victoria** R Aust
26B2 **Victoria de las Tunas** Cuba
100B2 **Victoria Falls** Zambia/Zim
4G2 **Victoria I** Can
108B2 **Victoria,L** Aust
99D3 **Victoria,L** C Africa
112B7 **Victoria Land** Region, Ant
86C2 **Victoria,Mt** Burma
99D2 **Victoria Nile** R Uganda
111B2 **Victoria Range** Mts NZ
106C2 **Victoria River Downs** Aust
4H3 **Victoria Str** Can
15D1 **Victoriaville** Can
100B4 **Victoria West** S Africa
34B3 **Victorica** Arg
21B3 **Victorrobile** USA
34A2 **Vicuña** Chile
34C2 **Vicuña Mackenna** Arg
17B1 **Vidalia** USA
54C2 **Videle** Rom
54B2 **Vidin** Bulg
85D4 **Vidisha** India
58D1 **Vidzy** Belorussia
29D4 **Viedma** Arg
26A4 **Viejo** Costa Rica
Vielha = Viella
51C1 **Viella** Spain
Vienna = Wien
18C2 **Vienna** Illinois, USA
14B3 **Vienna** W Virginia, USA
49C2 **Vienne** France
48C2 **Vienne** R France
76C2 **Vientiane** Laos
47C1 **Vierwaldstätter See** L Switz
48C2 **Vierzon** France
53C2 **Vieste** Italy
70B2 **Vietnam** Republic, S E Asia
76D1 **Vietri** Viet
27P2 **Vieux Fort** St Lucia
79B2 **Vigan** Phil
47C2 **Vigevano** Italy
48B3 **Vignemale** Mt France
50A1 **Vigo** Spain
87C1 **Vijayawāda** India
55A2 **Vijosë** R Alb
38B2 **Vik** Iceland
54B2 **Vikhren** Mt Bulg
13E2 **Viking** Can
38G6 **Vikna** I Nor
101C2 **Vila da Maganja** Mozam
101C2 **Vila Machado** Mozam
101C3 **Vilanculos** Mozam
Vilanova i la Geltrú = Villanueva-y-Geltrú
50A1 **Vila Real** Port
101C2 **Vila Vasco da Gama** Mozam
35C2 **Vila Velha** Brazil
58D2 **Vileyka** Belorussia
38H6 **Vilhelmina** Sweden
33E6 **Vilhena** Brazil
60C2 **Viljandi** Estonia
101G1 **Viljoenskroon** S Africa
9C3 **Villa Ahumada** Mexico
34B2 **Villa Atuel** Arg
50A1 **Villaba** Spain
23A2 **Villa Carranza** Mexico

52B1 **Villach** Austria
34B2 **Villa Colon** Arg
34C2 **Villa Constitución** Arg
34C1 **Villa de Maria** Arg
23A1 **Villa de Reyes** Mexico
34B2 **Villa Dolores** Arg
47D2 **Villafranca di Verona** Italy
34C2 **Villa General Mitre** Arg
34B2 **Villa General Roca** Arg
34D2 **Villaguay** Arg
25C3 **Villahermosa** Mexico
23A1 **Villa Hidalgo** Mexico
34C2 **Villa Huidobro** Arg
34C3 **Villa Iris** Arg
34C2 **Villa Maria** Arg
30D3 **Villa Montes** Bol
23A1 **Villaneuva** Mexico
50A1 **Villa Nova de Gaia** Port
50A2 **Villanueva de la Serena** Spain
51C1 **Villanueva-y-Geltrú** Spain
34B3 **Villa Regina** Arg
51B2 **Villarreal** Spain
29B3 **Villarrica** Chile
30E4 **Villarrica** Par
50B2 **Villarrobledo** Spain
34D2 **Villa San José** Arg
34C2 **Villa Valeria** Arg
32C3 **Villavicencio** Colombia
49C2 **Villefranche** France
7C5 **Ville-Marie** Can
51B2 **Villena** Spain
46B2 **Villeneuve-St-Georges** France
48C3 **Villeneuve-sur-Lot** France
19B3 **Ville Platte** USA
46B2 **Villers-Cotterêts** France
49C2 **Villeurbanne** France
101G1 **Villiers** S Africa
87B2 **Villupuram** India
58D2 **Vilnius** Lithuania
63D1 **Vilyuy** R Russian Fed
63E1 **Vilyuysk** Russian Fed
34A2 **Viña del Mar** Chile
51C1 **Vinaroz** Spain
14A3 **Vincennes** USA
38H5 **Vindel** R Sweden
85D4 **Vindhya Range** Mts India
16B3 **Vineland** USA
16D2 **Vineyard Haven** USA
76D2 **Vinh** Viet
76D3 **Vinh Cam Ranh** B Viet
77D4 **Vinh Loi** Viet
77D3 **Vinh Long** Viet
18A2 **Vinita** USA
54A1 **Vinkovci** Croatia
60C4 **Vinnitsa** Ukraine
112B3 **Vinson Massif** *Upland* Ant
100A3 **Vioolsdrift** S Africa
47D1 **Vipiteno** Italy
79B3 **Virac** Phil
87B2 **Virddhāchalam** India
100A2 **Virei** Angola
35C1 **Virgem da Lapa** Brazil
101G1 **Virginia** S Africa
10C3 **Virginia** State, USA
10A2 **Virginia** USA
21B2 **Virginia City** USA
27E3 **Virgin Is** Caribbean S
52C1 **Virovitica** Croatia
46C2 **Virton** Belg
87B3 **Virudunagar** India
52C2 **Vis** I Croatia
21B2 **Visalia** USA
79B3 **Visayan S** Phil
39H7 **Visby** Sweden
4H2 **Viscount Melville Sd** Can

54A2 **Višegrad** Bosnia-Herzegovina
50A1 **Viseu** Port
83C4 **Vishākhapatnam** India
47B1 **Visp** Switz
49C1 **Vissingen** Neth
21B3 **Vista** USA
Vistula = Wisla
57C3 **Vitavia** R Czech Republic
87A1 **Vite** India
60D2 **Vitebsk** Belorussia
52B2 **Viterbo** Italy
50A1 **Vitigudino** Spain
63D2 **Vitim** R Russian Fed
50B1 **Vitora** Spain
31C6 **Vitória** Brazil
31C4 **Vitória da Conquista** Brazil
48B2 **Vitré** France
46C2 **Vitry-le-Francois** France
38J5 **Vittangi** Sweden
53B3 **Vittoria** Italy
47E2 **Vittorio Veneto** Italy
69H2 **Vityaz Depth** Pacific O
50A1 **Vivero** Spain
63B1 **Vivi** R Russian Fed
34D3 **Vivorata** Arg
63C2 **Vizhne-Angarsk** Russian Fed
83C4 **Vizianagaram** India
54B1 **Vlădeasa** Mt Rom
61F5 **Vladikavkaz** Russian Fed
65F4 **Vladimir** Russian Fed
59C2 **Vladimir Volynskiy** Ukraine
74C2 **Vladivostok** Russian Fed
56A2 **Vlieland** I Neth
46B1 **Vlissingen** Neth
55A2 **Vlorë** Alb
57C3 **Vöcklabruck** Austria
76D3 **Voeune Sai** Camb
47C2 **Voghera** Italy
101D2 **Vohibinany** Madag
101E2 **Vohimarina** Madag
99D3 **Voi** Kenya
97B4 **Voinjama** Lib
49D2 **Voiron** France
54A1 **Vojvodina** Aut *Republic* Serbia, Yugos
26A5 **Volcán Baru** Mt Panama
23B2 **Volcán Citlaltepetl** Mt Mexico
30C3 **Volcáno Lullaillaco** Mt Chile
34A3 **Volcáno Copahue** Mt Chile
34A3 **Volcáno Domuyo** Mt Chile
Volcano Is = Kazan Retto
29B3 **Volcáno Lanin** Mt Arg
30C3 **Volcán Ollagüe** Mt Chile
34A3 **Volcáno Llaima** Mt Chile
34B2 **Volcáno Maipo** Mt Arg
34A3 **Volcáno Peteroa** Mt Chile
34B3 **Volcáno Tromen** V Arg
23A2 **Volcán Paracutin** Mt Mexico
32B3 **Volcán Puraće** Mt Colombia
34A2 **Volcán Tinguiririca** Mt Arg/Chile
61J2 **Volchansk** Russian Fed
61G4 **Volga** R Russian Fed
61F4 **Volgodonsk** Russian Fed

Volgograd

61F4	**Volgograd** Russian Fed
61G3	**Volgogradskoye Vodokhranilishche** Res Russian Fed
60D2	**Volkhov** Russian Fed
60D2	**Volkhov** R Russian Fed
58C2	**Volkovysk** Belorussia
101G1	**Volksrust** S Africa
61F2	**Vologda** Russian Fed
48B2	**Volognes** France
55B3	**Vólos** Greece
61G3	**Vol'sk** Russian Fed
22B2	**Volta** USA
97B3	**Volta Blanche** R Burkina
97B4	**Volta,L** Ghana
97B3	**Volta Noire** R Burkina
35C2	**Volta Redonda** Brazil
97B3	**Volta Rouge** R Burkina
61F4	**Volzhskiy** Russian Fed
12D2	**Von Frank Mt** USA
6J3	**Vopnafjörður** Iceland
47C1	**Voralberg** Province, Austria
47C1	**Vorder Rhein** R Switz
56C1	**Vordingborg** Den
64H3	**Vorkuta** Russian Fed
39G6	**Vorma** R Nor
60E3	**Voronezh** Russian Fed
38M5	**Voron'ya** R Russian Fed
39K7	**Võru** Estonia
49D2	**Vosges** Mt France
39F6	**Voss** Nor
63B2	**Vostochnyy Sayan** Mts Russian Fed
112B9	**Vostok** Base Ant
61H2	**Votkinsk** Russian Fed
46C2	**Vouziers** France
60D4	**Voznesensk** Ukraine
54B2	**Vranje** Serbia, Yugos
54B2	**Vratsa** Bulg
54A1	**Vrbas** Serbia, Yugos
52C2	**Vrbas** R Serbia, Yugos
52B1	**Vrbovsko** Bosnia-Herzegovina
101G1	**Vrede** S Africa
33F2	**Vreed en Hoop** Guyana
54B1	**Vršac** Serbia, Yugos
52C2	**Vrtoče** Bosnia-Herzegovina
100B3	**Vryburg** S Africa
101H1	**Vryheid** S Africa
54A1	**Vukovar** Croatia
13E2	**Vulcan** Can
53B3	**Vulcano** I Italy
77D3	**Vung Tau** Viet
38J5	**Vuollerim** Sweden
38L6	**Vyartsilya** Russian Fed
61H2	**Vyatka** R Russian Fed
69F2	**Vyazemskiy** Russian Fed
60D2	**Vyaz'ma** Russian Fed
61F2	**Vyazniki** Russian Fed
60C1	**Vyborg** Russian Fed
64G3	**Vym'** R Russian Fed
43C3	**Vyrnwy** R Wales
60D2	**Vyshiy Volochek** Russian Fed
59B3	**Vyškov** Czech Republic
60E1	**Vytegra** Russian Fed

W

97B3	**Wa** Ghana
13E1	**Wabasca** Can
5G4	**Wabasca** R Can
13E1	**Wabasca L** Can
14A2	**Wabash** USA
14A3	**Wabash** R USA
5J4	**Wabowden** Can
7D4	**Wabush** Can
17B2	**Waccasassa B** USA
16D1	**Wachusett Res** USA
19A3	**Waco** USA
85B3	**Wad** Pak
95A2	**Waddān** Libya
5F4	**Waddington,Mt** Can
93E4	**Wadi al Bātin** Watercourse Iraq
93D3	**Wadi al Ghudāf** Watercourse Iraq
94C2	**Wadi al Harīr** V Syria
93D3	**Wadi al Mirah** Watercourse Iraq/ S Arabia
93D3	**Wadi al Ubayyid** Watercourse Iraq
93D3	**Wadi Ar'ar** Watercourse S Arabia
91A5	**Wadi as Hsabā'** Watercourse S Arabia
92C3	**Wadi as Sirhān** V Jordan/S Arabia
94C2	**Wadi az Zaydi** V Syria
94C3	**Wadi edh Dhab'i** V Jordan
94A3	**Wadi el 'Arish** V Egypt
94C3	**Wadi el Ghadaf** V Jordan
94B3	**Wadi el Hasa** V Jordan
94C3	**Wadi el Janab** V Jordan
94B3	**Wadi el Jeib** V Israel/ Jordan
95B3	**Wadi el Milk** Watercourse Sudan
92A3	**Wadi el Natrun** Watercourse Egypt
94B3	**Wadi es Sir** Jordan
94B3	**Wadi Fidan** V Jordan
94B3	**Wadi Hareidin** V Egypt
93D3	**Wadi Hawrān** R Iraq
95B3	**Wadi Howa** Watercourse Sudan
98C1	**Wadi Ibra** Watercourse Sudan
94C2	**Wadi Luhfi** Watercourse Jordan
94B3	**Wadi Mujib** V Jordan
94B3	**Wadi Qîtaiya** V Egypt
80B3	**Wadi Sha'it** Watercourse Egypt
99D1	**Wad Medani** Sudan
93E4	**Wafra** Kuwait
6B3	**Wager B** Can
6A3	**Wager Bay** Can
109C3	**Wagga Wagga** Aust
106A4	**Wagin** Aust
95A2	**Wāha** Libya
21C4	**Wahaiwa** Hawaiian Is
18A1	**Wahoo** USA
8D2	**Wahpeton** USA
87A1	**Wai** India
111A3	**Waiau** NZ
111A3	**Waiau** R NZ
111B2	**Waiau** R NZ
71E3	**Waigeo** I Indon
110C1	**Waihi** NZ
110C1	**Waikaremoana,L** NZ
110C1	**Waikato** R NZ
108A2	**Waikerie** Aust
111B3	**Waikouaiti** NZ
21C4	**Wailuku** Hawaiian Is
111B2	**Waimakariri** R NZ
111B2	**Waimate** NZ
21C4	**Waimea** Hawaiian Is
106B1	**Waingapu** Indon
13E2	**Wainwright** Can
4B2	**Wainwright** USA
111B2	**Waipara** NZ
110C2	**Waipukurau** NZ
111C2	**Wairarapa,L** NZ
111B2	**Wairau** R NZ
110C1	**Wairoa** NZ
110C1	**Wairoa** R NZ
111B2	**Waitaki** R NZ
110B1	**Waitara** NZ
110C1	**Waitomo** NZ
110B1	**Waiuku** NZ
75B1	**Wajima** Japan
99E2	**Wajir** Kenya
75B1	**Wakasa-wan** B Japan
111A3	**Wakatipu,L** NZ
74D4	**Wakayama** Japan
42D3	**Wakefield** Eng
27H1	**Wakefield** Jamaica
16D2	**Wakefield** Rhode Island, USA
76B2	**Wakema** Burma
69G2	**Wakkanai** Japan
108B3	**Wakool** R Aust
59B2	**Walbrzych** Pol
109D2	**Walcha** Aust
58B2	**Walcz** Pol
46D1	**Waldbröl** Germany
16B2	**Walden** USA
43C3	**Wales** Country, UK
12A1	**Wales** USA
6B3	**Wales I** Can
109C2	**Walgett** Aust
112B4	**Walgreen Coast** Region, Ant
99C3	**Walikale** Zaïre
21B2	**Walker L** USA
14B2	**Walkerton** Can
8B2	**Wallace** USA
108A2	**Wallaroo** Aust
109C3	**Walla Walla** Aust
20C1	**Walla Walla** USA
16C2	**Wallingford** USA
105H4	**Wallis and Futuna** Is Pacific O
20C1	**Wallowa** USA
20C1	**Wallowa Mts** Mts USA
109C1	**Wallumbilla** Aust
18B2	**Walnut Ridge** USA
110C1	**Walouru** NZ
43D3	**Walsall** Eng
9C3	**Walsenburg** USA
9C3	**Walsenburgh** USA
17B1	**Walterboro** USA
17A1	**Walter F George Res** USA
16D1	**Waltham** USA
100A3	**Walvis Bay** S Africa
103J6	**Walvis Ridge** Atlantic O
97C4	**Wamba** Nig
98B3	**Wamba** R Zaïre
18A2	**Wamego** USA
84B2	**Wana** Pak
108B1	**Wanaaring** Aust
111A2	**Wanaka** NZ
111A2	**Wanaka,L** NZ
14B1	**Wanapitei L** Can
109C1	**Wandoan** Aust
108B3	**Wanganella** Aust
110C1	**Wanganui** NZ
110C1	**Wanganui** R NZ
109C3	**Wangaratta** Aust
99E2	**Wanle Weyne** Somalia
76E2	**Wanning** China
87B1	**Wanparti** India
73B3	**Wanxian** China
73B3	**Wanyuan** China
13D2	**Wapiti** R Can
18B2	**Wappapello,L** USA
16C2	**Wappingers Falls** USA
87B1	**Warangal** India
109C4	**Waratah** Aust
108C3	**Waratah B** Aust
108C3	**Warburton** Aust
108A1	**Warburton** R Aust
109C1	**Ward** R Aust
101G1	**Warden** S Africa
99E2	**Warder** Eth
85D4	**Wardha** India
111A3	**Ward,Mt** NZ
5F4	**Ware** Can
16C1	**Ware** USA
16D2	**Wareham** USA
109D1	**Warialda** Aust
76C2	**Warin Chamrap** Thai
100B3	**Warmbad** S Africa
16B2	**Warminster** USA
21B2	**Warm Springs** USA
56C2	**Warnemünde** Germany
20B2	**Warner Mts** USA
17B1	**Warner Robins** USA
108B3	**Warracknabeal** Aust
108A1	**Warrandirinna,L** Aust
107D3	**Warrego** R Aust
19B3	**Warren** Arkansas, USA
109C2	**Warren** Aust
16D2	**Warren** Massachusetts, USA
14B2	**Warren** Ohio, USA
15C2	**Warren** Pennsylvania, USA
45C1	**Warrenpoint** N Ire
18B2	**Warrensburg** USA
101F1	**Warrenton** S Africa
15C3	**Warrenton** USA
97C4	**Warri** Nig
108A1	**Warrina** Aust
42C3	**Warrington** Eng
108B3	**Warrnambool** Aust
	Warsaw = Warszawa
58C2	**Warszawa** Pol
59B2	**Warta** R Pol
109D1	**Warwick** Aust
43D3	**Warwick** County, Eng
43D3	**Warwick** Eng
16B2	**Warwick** New York, USA
16D2	**Warwick** Rhode Island, USA
8B3	**Wasatch Range** Mts USA
101H1	**Wasbank** S Africa
21B2	**Wasco** USA
4H2	**Washburn L** Can
85D4	**Wāshim** India
10C3	**Washington** District of Columbia, USA
17B1	**Washington** Georgia, USA
14A3	**Washington** Indiana, USA
18B2	**Washington** Missouri, USA
16B2	**Washington** New Jersey, USA
14D2	**Washington** Pennsylvania, USA
8A2	**Washington** State, USA
14B3	**Washington Court House** USA
6D1	**Washington Land** Can
15D2	**Washington,Mt** USA
43E3	**Wash,The** Eng
85A3	**Washuk** Pak
12E2	**Wasilla** USA
7C4	**Waskaganish** Can
26A4	**Waspán** Nic
70D4	**Watampone** Indon
16C2	**Waterbury** USA
45C2	**Waterford** County, Irish Rep
41B3	**Waterford** Irish Rep
45C2	**Waterford Harbour** Irish Rep
46C1	**Waterloo** Belg
10A2	**Waterloo** USA
15C2	**Watertown** New York, USA
101H1	**Waterval-Boven** S Africa
10D2	**Waterville** Maine, USA
16C1	**Watervliet** USA
5G4	**Waterways** Can
43D4	**Watford** Eng
15C2	**Watkins Glen** USA
8C1	**Watrous** Can
99C2	**Watsa** Zaïre
12J2	**Watson Lake** Can
22B2	**Watsonville** USA
71F4	**Wau** PNG
99C2	**Wau** Sudan
7B5	**Waua** Can
109D2	**Wauchope** Aust
17B2	**Wauchula** USA
14A2	**Waukegan** USA
10B2	**Wausau** USA

Winifreda

19B3 **Yazoo City** USA	13D2 **Yoho Nat Pk** Can	72C3 **Yun Xian** China	72D3 **Zaozhuang** China
76B2 **Ye** Burma	98B2 **Yokadouma** Cam	73B3 **Yunyang** China	93D2 **Zap** R Turk
59D3 **Yedintsy** Moldavia	75B2 **Yokkaichi** Japan	32B5 **Yurimaguas** Peru	39K7 **Zapadnaja Dvina** R
108A2 **Yeelanna** Aust	75B1 **Yokohama** Japan	73E5 **Yu Shan** Mt Taiwan	Russian Fed
60E3 **Yefremov**	75B1 **Yokosuka** Japan	38L6 **Yushkozero**	65H3 **Zapadno-Sibirskaya**
Russian Fed	74C3 **Yonago** Japan	Russian Fed	Nizmennost'
61F4 **Yegorlyk** R	74E3 **Yonezawa** Japan	82D2 **Yushu** Tibet, China	Lowland Russian Fed
Russian Fed	73D4 **Yong'an** China	73A5 **Yuxi** China	63B2 **Zapadnyy Sayan** Mts
99D2 **Yei** Sudan	72A2 **Yongchang** China	74F2 **Yuzhno-Kuril'sk**	Russian Fed
65H4 **Yekaterinburg**	74B3 **Yŏngch'on** S Korea	Russian Fed	34A3 **Zapala** Arg
Russian Fed	73B4 **Yongchuan** China	69G2 **Yuzhno-Sakhalinsk**	60E4 **Zaporozh'ye** Ukraine
60E3 **Yelets** Russian Fed	72A2 **Yongdeng** China	Russian Fed	93C2 **Zara** Turk
44E1 **Yell** I Scot	73D5 **Yongding** China	61J3 **Yuzh Ural** Mts	23A1 **Zaragoza** Mexico
87C1 **Yellandu** India	72D2 **Yongding He** R	Russian Fed	50B1 **Zaragoza** Spain
Yellow = Huang He	China	46A2 **Yvelines** Department,	90B2 **Zarand** Iran
8B1 **Yellowhead P** Can	74B3 **Yŏngdŏk** S Korea	France	90C3 **Zarand** Iran
4G3 **Yellowknife** Can	74B3 **Yŏnghŭng** N Korea	47B1 **Yverdon** Switz	80E2 **Zaranj** Afghan
5G4 **Yellowmead P** Can	74B3 **Yongju** S Korea		33D2 **Zarara** Ven
109C2 **Yellow Mt** Aust	72B2 **Yongning** China		58D1 **Zarasai** Lithuania
69E3 **Yellow Sea** China/	16C2 **Yonkers** USA	**Z**	34D2 **Zárate** Arg
Korea	49C2 **Yonne** R France	56A2 **Zaandam** Neth	90B3 **Zard Kuh** Mt Iran
8C2 **Yellowstone** R USA	42D3 **York** Eng	93D2 **Zāb al Babir** R Iraq	12H3 **Zarembo I** USA
8B2 **Yellowstone L** USA	18A1 **York** Nebraska, USA	93D2 **Zāb as Şaghīr** R Iraq	84B2 **Zarghun Shahr**
6B1 **Yelverton B** Can	16A3 **York** Pennsylvania,	68D2 **Zabaykal'sk**	Afghan
97C3 **Yelwa** Nig	USA	Russian Fed	84B2 **Zargun** Mt Pak
81C4 **Yemen** Republic,	107D2 **York,C** Aust	59B3 **Zabreh**	97C3 **Zaria** Nig
Arabian Pen	108A2 **Yorke Pen** Aust	Czech Republic	92C3 **Zarqa** Jordan
76C1 **Yen Bai** Viet	108A3 **Yorketown** Aust	59B2 **Zabrze** Pol	94B2 **Zarqa** R Jordan
97B4 **Yendi** Ghana	7A4 **York Factory** Can	23A2 **Zacapu** Mexico	32B4 **Zaruma** Ecuador
76B1 **Yengan** Burma	41C3 **Yorkshire Moors**	24B2 **Zacatecas** Mexico	58B2 **Zary** Pol
63B2 **Yeniseysk**	Moorland Eng	23B2 **Zacatepec** Morelos,	96D1 **Zarzis** Tunisia
Russian Fed	42D2 **Yorkshire Wolds**	Mexico	84D2 **Zāskār** Mts India
63B1 **Yeniseyskiy Kryazh**	Upland Eng	23B2 **Zacatepec** Oaxaca,	84D2 **Zāskār** R India
Ridge Russian Fed	5H4 **Yorkton** Can	Mexico	94C2 **Zatara** R Jordan
64J2 **Yeniseyskiy Zal** B	22B2 **Yosemite L** USA	23B2 **Zacatlan** Mexico	**Zatoka Gdańska =**
Russian Fed	22C1 **Yosemite Nat Pk**	23A1 **Zacoalco** Mexico	Gdańsk,G of
12D2 **Yentna** R USA	USA	23B1 **Zacualtipan** Mexico	69E1 **Zavitinsk**
43C4 **Yeo** R Eng	75A2 **Yoshii** R Japan	52C2 **Zadar** Croatia	Russian Fed
109C2 **Yeoval** Aust	75A2 **Yoshino** R Japan	76B3 **Zadetkyi** I Burma	59B2 **Zawiercie** Pol
43C4 **Yeovil** Eng	61G2 **Yoshkar Ola**	50A2 **Zafra** Spain	63C2 **Zayarsk** Russian Fed
63C1 **Yerbogachen**	Russian Fed	95C1 **Zagazig** Egypt	65K5 **Zaysan** Kazakhstan
Russian Fed	74B4 **Yŏsu** S Korea	96B1 **Zagora** Mor	82D3 **Zayü** China
65F5 **Yerevan** Armenia	41B3 **Youghal** Irish Rep	52C1 **Zagreb** Croatia	68B4 **Zayü** Mt China
21B2 **Yerington** USA	45C3 **Youghal Harb**	91D4 **Zāhedān** Iran	58B2 **Zduńska Wola** Pol
21B3 **Yermo** USA	Irish Rep	94B2 **Zahle** Leb	46B1 **Zeebrugge** Belg
69E1 **Yerofey-Pavlovich**	73B5 **You Jiang** R China	51C2 **Zahrez Chergui**	94B3 **Zeelim** Israel
Russian Fed	109C2 **Young** Aust	Marshland Alg	101G1 **Zeerust** S Africa
94B3 **Yeroham** Israel	34D2 **Young** Urug	61H2 **Zainsk** Russian Fed	94B2 **Zefat** Israel
61G3 **Yershov** Russian Fed	111A2 **Young Range** Mts	98C3 **Zaïre** Republic, Africa	97C3 **Zegueren**
Yerushalayim =	NZ	98B3 **Zaïre** R Zaïre/Congo	Watercourse Mali
Jerusalem	13E2 **Youngstown** Can	54B2 **Zajecăr** Yugos	99E1 **Zeila** Somalia
92C1 **Yeşil** R Turk	14B2 **Youngstown** Ohio,	68C1 **Zakamensk**	57C2 **Zeitz** Germany
94B2 **Yesud Hama'ala**	USA	Russian Fed	72A2 **Zekog** China
Israel	22A1 **Yountville** USA	93D2 **Zakho** Iraq	61G2 **Zelenodol'sk**
109D1 **Yetman** Aust	73B4 **Youyang** China	55B3 **Zákinthos** I Greece	Russian Fed
96B2 **Yetti** Maur	92B2 **Yozgat** Turk	59B3 **Zakopane** Pol	39K6 **Zelenogorsk**
93E1 **Yevlakh** Azerbaijan	20B2 **Yreka** USA	59B3 **Zalaegerszeg** Hung	Russian Fed
60D4 **Yevpatoriya**	39G7 **Ystad** Sweden	54B1 **Zalău** Rom	47D1 **Zell** Austria
Ukraine	43C3 **Ystwyth** R Wales	56C2 **Zalew Szczeciński** Lg	98C2 **Zemio** CAR
72E2 **Ye Xian** China	44C3 **Ythan** R Scot	Pol	64F1 **Zemlya Aleksandry** I
60E4 **Yeysk** Russian Fed	73C4 **Yuan Jiang** R	98C1 **Zalingei** Sudan	Barents S
55B2 **Yiannitsá** Greece	Hunan, China	63F2 **Zaliv Akademii** B	64F2 **Zemlya Frantsa Iosifa**
73A4 **Yibin** China	73A5 **Yuan Jiang** R	Russian Fed	Is Barents S
73C3 **Yichang** China	Yunnan, China	65G5 **Zaliv Kara-Bogaz Gol**	64F1 **Zemlya Georga** I
69E2 **Yichun** China	73A4 **Yuanmu** China	B Turkmenistan	Barents S
72B2 **Yijun** China	72C2 **Yuanping** China	74C2 **Zaliv Petra Velikogo**	64H1 **Zemlya Vil'cheka** I
54C2 **Yildiz Dağlari** Upland	21A2 **Yuba City** USA	B Russian Fed	Barents S
Turk	74E2 **Yūbari** Japan	69G2 **Zaliv Turpeniya** B	73B4 **Zenning** China
92C2 **Yıldızeli** Turk	25D3 **Yucatan** Pen Mexico	Russian Fed	47B1 **Zermatt** Switz
73A5 **Yiliang** China	25D2 **Yucatan Chan**	95A2 **Zaltan** Libya	63E2 **Zeya** Russian Fed
72B2 **Yinchuan** China	Mexico/Cuba	89H9 **Zambesi** R Mozam	63E2 **Zeya** Res
72D3 **Ying He** R China	72C2 **Yuci** China	100B2 **Zambezi** Zambia	Russian Fed
72E1 **Yingkou** China	63F2 **Yudoma** R	100B2 **Zambezi** R Zambia	50A1 **Zêzere** R Port
73D3 **Yingshan** Hubei,	Russian Fed	100B2 **Zambia** Republic,	94B1 **Zghorta** Leb
China	73D4 **Yudu** China	Africa	58B2 **Zgierz** Pol
72B3 **Yingshan** Sichuan,	73A4 **Yuexi** China	79B4 **Zamboanga** Phil	72D1 **Zhangjiakou** China
China	73C4 **Yueyang** China	79B4 **Zamboanga Pen**	73D4 **Zhangping** China
73D4 **Yingtan** China	54A2 **Yugoslavia**	Phil	72D2 **Zhangwei He** R
82C1 **Yining** China	Republic, Europe	58C2 **Zambrów** Pol	China
72B1 **Yin Shan** Upland	73B5 **Yu Jiang** R China	32B4 **Zamora** Ecuador	72E1 **Zhangwu** China
China	12C2 **Yukon** R Can/USA	23A2 **Zamora** Mexico	72A2 **Zhangye** China
99D2 **Yirga Alem** Eth	4E3 **Yukon Territory** Can	50A1 **Zamora** Spain	73D5 **Zhangzhou** China
99D2 **Yirol** Sudan	76E1 **Yulin** Guangdong,	59C2 **Zamość** Pol	73C5 **Zhanjiang** China
63D3 **Yirshi** China	China	72A3 **Zamtang** China	73A4 **Zhanyi** China
73B5 **Yishan** China	73C5 **Yulin** Guangxi, China	98B3 **Zanaga** Congo	73C5 **Zhaoqing** China
72D2 **Yishui** China	72B2 **Yulin** Shaanxi, China	50B2 **Záncara** R Spain	73A4 **Zhaotong** China
55B3 **Yithion** Greece	9B3 **Yuma** USA	84D2 **Zanda** China	72D2 **Zhaoyang Hu** L
38J6 **Yivieska** Fin	68B3 **Yumen** China	14B3 **Zanesville** USA	China
73C4 **Yiyang** China	72D2 **Yunan** China	84D2 **Zangla** India	61J4 **Zharkamys**
38K5 **Yli-Kitka** L Fin	34A3 **Yungay** Chile	90A2 **Zanjān** Iran	Russian Fed
38J5 **Ylilornio** Sweden	73C5 **Yunkai Dashan** Hills	34B2 **Zanjitas** Arg	63E1 **Zhatay** Russian Fed
19A4 **Yoakum** USA	China	34B2 **Zanjon** R Arg	73D4 **Zhejiang** Province,
23B2 **Yogope** Mexico	108A2 **Yunta** Aust	99D3 **Zanzibar** Tanz	China
78C4 **Yogyakarta** Indon	72C3 **Yunxi** China	99D3 **Zanzibar** I Tanz	
		96C2 **Zaouatallaz** Alg	67F3 **Zhengou** China

72C3 **Zhengzhou** China
72D3 **Zhenjiang** China
73A4 **Zhenxiong** China
73B4 **Zhenyuan** China
61F3 **Zherdevka**
    Russian Fed
73C3 **Zhicheng** China
68C1 **Zhigalovo**
    Russian Fed
73B4 **Zhijin** China
58D2 **Zhitkovichi**
    Belorussia
60C3 **Zhitomir** Ukraine
60D3 **Zhlobin** Belorussia
60C4 **Zhmerinka** Ukraine
84B2 **Zhob** Pak
58D2 **Zhodino** Latvia
72B2 **Zhongning** China
112C10 **Zhongshan** *Base* Ant
73C5 **Zhongshan** China
72B2 **Zhongwei** China
68B4 **Zhougdian** China
73E3 **Zhoushan Quandao**
    Arch China
72E2 **Zhuanghe** China
72A3 **Zhugqu** China
73C3 **Zhushan** China

73C4 **Zhuzhou** China
72D2 **Zibo** China
106C3 **Ziel,Mt** Aust
58B2 **Zielona Góra** Pol
76A1 **Zigaing** Burma
73A4 **Zigong** China
97A3 **Ziguinchor** Sen
23A2 **Zihuatanejo** Mexico
94B2 **Zikhron Ya'aqov**
    Israel
59B3 **Žilina** Slovakia
95A2 **Zillah** Libya
47D1 **Ziller** *R* Austria
47D1 **Zillertaler Alpen** *Mts*
    Austria
58D1 **Zilupe** Russian Fed
63C2 **Zima** Russian Fed
23B1 **Zimapan** Mexico
23B2 **Zimatlan** Mexico
100B2 **Zimbabwe** Republic,
    Africa
94B3 **Zin** *R* Israel
23B2 **Zinacatepec** Mexico
23A2 **Zinapécuaro** Mexico
97C3 **Zinder** Niger
73C4 **Zi Shui** China
23A2 **Zitácuaro** Mexico

57C2 **Zittau** Germany
72D2 **Ziya He** *R* China
72A3 **Ziyang** China
61J2 **Zlatoust**
    Russian Fed
59B3 **Zlin** Czech Republic
65K4 **Zmeinogorsk**
    Russian Fed
58B2 **Znin** Pol
59B3 **Znoimo**
    Czech Republic
100B3 **Zoekmekaar**
    S Africa
47B1 **Zofinger** Switz
72A3 **Zoigê** China
59D3 **Zolochev** Ukraine
101C2 **Zomba** Malawi
98B2 **Zongo** Zaïre
92B1 **Zonguldak** Turk
97B4 **Zorzor** Lib
96A2 **Zouerate** Maur
54B1 **Zrenjanin** Serbia,
    Yugos
47C1 **Zug** Switz
47D1 **Zugspitze** *Mt*
    Germany
50A2 **Zújar** *R* Spain

100C2 **Zumbo** Mozam
23B2 **Zumpango** Mexico
97C4 **Zungeru** Nig
73B4 **Zunyi** China
76D1 **Zuo** *R* China
73B5 **Zuo Jiang** *R* China
47C1 **Zürich** Switz
47C1 **Zürichsee** *L* Switz
95A1 **Zuwärah** Libya
95A2 **Zuwaylah** Libya
61H2 **Zuyevka**
    Russian Fed
100B4 **Zvishavane** Zim
59B3 **Zvolen** Slovakia
54A2 **Zvornik** Bosnia-
    Herzegovina
97B4 **Zwedru** Lib
46D2 **Zweibrücken**
    Germany
47B1 **Zweisimmen** Switz
57C2 **Zwickau** Germany
56B2 **Zwolle** Neth
58C2 **Zyrardów** Pol
65K5 **Zyryanovsk**
    Kazakhstan
59B3 **Żywiec** Pol
94A1 **Zyyi** Cyprus